# Guide® to Bed & Breakfasts in the Northwest

## 1st Edition

## Also available from IDG Books Worldwide:

*Beyond Disney: The Unofficial Guide to Universal, Sea World, and the Best of Central Florida,* by Bob Sehlinger and Amber Morris

*Inside Disney: The Incredible Story of Walt Disney World and the Man Behind the Mouse,* by Eve Zibart

*Mini Las Vegas: The Pocket-Sized Unofficial Guide to Las Vegas,* by Bob Sehlinger

*Mini-Mickey: The Pocket-Sized Unofficial Guide to Walt Disney World,* by Bob Sehlinger

*The Unofficial Guide to Bed & Breakfasts in New England,* by Lea Lane

*The Unofficial Guide to Branson, Missouri,* by Eve Zibart and Bob Sehlinger

*The Unofficial Guide to California with Kids,* by Colleen Dunn Bates and Susan LaTempa

*The Unofficial Guide to Chicago,* by Joe Surkiewicz and Bob Sehlinger

*The Unofficial Guide to Cruises,* by Kay Showker with Bob Sehlinger

*The Unofficial Guide to Disneyland,* by Bob Sehlinger

*The Unofficial Guide to Florida with Kids,* by Pam Brandon

*The Unofficial Guide to the Great Smoky and Blue Ridge Region,* by Bob Sehlinger and Joe Surkiewicz

*The Unofficial Guide to Las Vegas,* by Bob Sehlinger

*The Unofficial Guide to London,* by Lesley Logan

*The Unofficial Guide to Miami and the Keys,* by Bob Sehlinger and Joe Surkiewicz

*The Unofficial Guide to New Orleans,* by Bob Sehlinger and Eve Zibart

*The Unofficial Guide to New York City,* by Eve Zibart and Bob Sehlinger with Jim Leff

*The Unofficial Guide to Paris,* by David Applefield

*The Unofficial Guide to San Francisco,* by Joe Surkiewicz and Bob Sehlinger with Richard Sterling

*The Unofficial Guide to Skiing in the West,* by Lito Tejada-Flores, Peter Shelton, Seth Masia, Ed Chauner, and Bob Sehlinger

*The Unofficial Guide to Walt Disney World,* by Bob Sehlinger

*The Unofficial Guide to Walt Disney World for Grown-Ups,* by Eve Zibart

*The Unofficial Guide to Walt Disney World with Kids,* by Bob Sehlinger

*The Unofficial Guide to Washington, D.C.,* by Bob Sehlinger and Joe Surkiewicz with Eve Zibart

# U<sup>the</sup>nofficial Guide® to

# Bed & Breakfasts in the Northwest

### 1st Edition

Sally O'Neal Coates

Every effort has been made to ensure the accuracy of information throughout this book. Bear in mind, however, that prices, schedules, etc., are
constantly changing. Readers should always verify information before
making final plans.

**IDG Books Worldwide, Inc.**
An International Data Group Company
919 E. Hillsdale Blvd., Suite 400
Foster City, California 94404

Produced by Menasha Ridge Press

MACMILLAN is a registered trademark of Macmillan General Reference
USA, Inc., a wholly owned subsidiary of IDG Books Worldwide, Inc.
*UNOFFICIAL GUIDE* is a registered trademark of Macmillan General Refer-
ence USA, Inc., a wholly owned subsidiary of IDG Books Worldwide, Inc.

ISBN    0-02-863277-X
ISSN    1522-3361

Manufactured in the United States of America

10  9  8  7  6  5  4  3  2  1

To my sisters, Peggy and Donna,
who taught me to appreciate the finer things in life

—S O'C

# Contents

List of Maps    ix
About the Author and Illustrator    xi
Acknowledgments    xiii

**Introduction    1**
How Come "Unofficial"?    1
What Makes It a Bed-and-Breakfast?    2
Who Stays at Bed-and-Breakfasts?    3
You and Your Hosts    6
Planning Your Visit    6
What the Ratings Mean    9
The Profiles Clarified    11
Making the Most of Your Stay    15
Northwest Bed-and-Breakfasts    16
Ten Reasons to Get out and Go    18
A Few of My Favorite Things    20
Mini Indexes    22

**1 British Columbia    35**
Zone 1: Victoria    37
Zone 2: Vancouver    55

**2 Washington    77**
Zone 3: Washington Coast and Olympic Peninsula    78
Zone 4: Northwest Washington    111
Zone 5: Greater Seattle and Tacoma    165
Zone 6: Washington's I-5 South    210

Zone 7: Washington's Cascades   221
Zone 8: Northeast Washington   258
Zone 9: Southeast Washington   276

## 3 Oregon   297

Zone 10: Oregon Coast   298
Zone 11: Greater Portland   335
Zone 12: Willamette Valley   348
Zone 13: Southern Oregon   369
Zone 14: Mt. Hood and Columbia Gorge   388
Zone 15: Central Oregon   405
Zone 16: Eastern Oregon   420

### Appendix

Additional Bed-and-Breakfasts and
    Small Inns   439

Subject Index   449

# List of Maps

The Northwest    xiv–xv
Zone 1: Victoria    39
Zone 2: Vancouver    57
Zone 3: Washington Coast and Olympic Peninsula    80–81
Zone 4: Northwest Washington    112–113
Zone 5: Greater Seattle and Tacoma    166–167
Zone 6: Washington's I-5 South    211
Zone 7: Washington's Cascades    222–223
Zone 8: Northeast Washington    259
Zone 9: Southeast Washington    277
Zone 10: Oregon Coast    300–301
Zone 11: Greater Portland    336
Zone 12: Willamette Valley    349
Zone 13: Southern Oregon    370
Zone 14: Mt. Hood and Columbia Gorge    389
Zone 15: Central Oregon    406
Zone 16: Eastern Oregon    422

# About the Author and Illustrator

Pacific Northwest native *Sally O'Neal Coates* is a writer, musician, and outdoor enthusiast based in Richland, Washington. Her other travel books include *Hot Showers, Soft Beds, and Dayhikes in the Central Cascades; Hot Showers, Soft Beds, and Dayhikes in the North Cascades;* and *Great Bike Rides in Eastern Washington and Oregon.* She plays trombone in a Glenn Miller–style swing band, sings alto in an a cappella pop quartet, and travels to hiking trails and bed-and-breakfasts whenever possible with her husband, Doug.

Born and raised in New York City, *Giselle Simons* received her Bachelor of Fine Arts degree from Cornell University. She currently lives on Manhattan's Upper West Side, where she works as an illustrator, architectural design drafter, and graphic designer. She is caretaker to a dog, two cats, an increasing number of fish, and her husband, Jeff.

# Acknowledgments

A book like this takes the cooperation and good humor of a large number of people. First and foremost, I would like to thank the hundreds of B&B owners and operators who opened their properties (usually their homes) to me, endured my questions, smiled as I tweaked their linens, and offered me a cup of coffee or even a hot shower and a soft bed. Operating a B&B is usually a labor of love as much as a business—you are good souls!

I also appreciate those who helped me with my field work, and now realize that travel writing, while a wonderful profession, is hard work: my dear friend Katie Sanborn, my sister Peggy O'Neal, and my husband, Doug Coates.

As with everything I've ever published, and everything I write, this book would not have been written had my writing group, Marilyn Morford and Diane Molleson, not encouraged me to keep writing three books ago.

Finally, thanks to my co-workers at Washington State University, who tolerated my prolonged absences during the course of this work, and who undoubtedly realize it will happen again. Once a writer, always a writer.

Thanks, Catherine and Jane, for putting up with me.

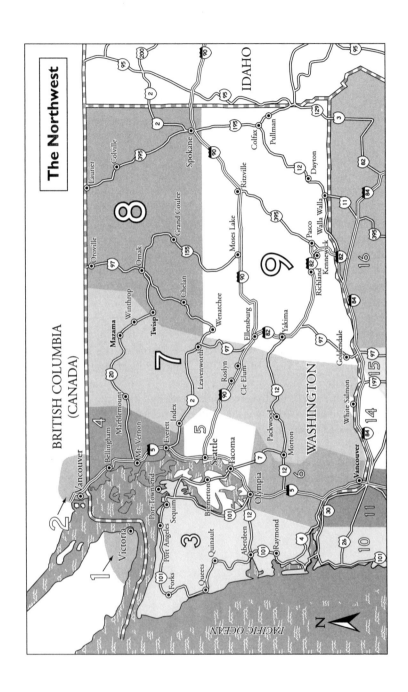

# The Northwest

BRITISH COLUMBIA (CANADA)

WASHINGTON

IDAHO

PACIFIC OCEAN

N

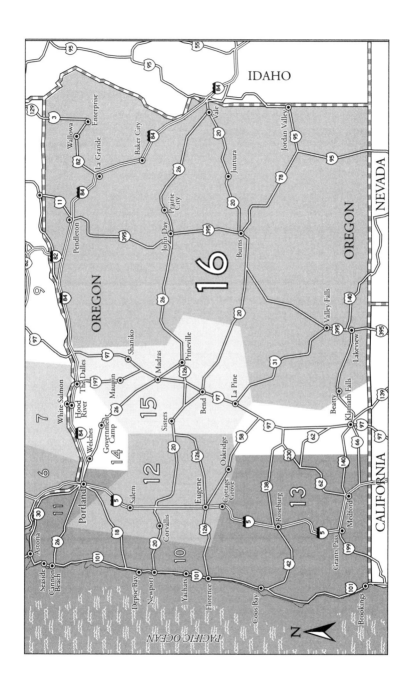

# Introduction

## How Come "Unofficial"?

The book in your hands is part of a unique travel and lifestyle guidebook series begun in 1985 with *The Unofficial Guide to Walt Disney World.* That guide, a comprehensive, behind-the-scenes, hands-on prescription for getting the most out of a complex amusement park facility, spawned a series of like titles: *The Unofficial Guide to Chicago, The Unofficial Guide to New Orleans,* and so on. Today, dozens of *Unofficial Guides* help millions of savvy readers navigate some of the world's more complex destinations and situations.

The *Unofficial Guides to Bed & Breakfasts* continue the tradition of insightful, incisive, cut-to-the-chase information, presented in an accessible, easy-to-use format. Unlike in some popular books, no property can pay to be included—those reviewed are solely our choice. And we don't simply rehash the promotional language of these establishments. We visit the good, the bad, and the quirky. We finger the linens, chat with the guests, and sample the scones. We screen hundreds of lodgings, affirming or debunking the acclaimed, discovering or rejecting the new and the obscure. In the end, we present detailed profiles of the lodgings we feel represent the best of the best, select lodgings representing a broad range of prices and styles within each geographic region.

We also include introductions for each state and zone to give you an idea of the nearby general attractions. Area maps with the properties listed by city help you pinpoint your general destination. And detailed mini indexes help you look up properties by categories and lead you to places that best fit your needs.

With *The Unofficial Guides to Bed & Breakfasts,* we strive to help you find the perfect lodging for every trip. This guide is unofficial because we answer to no one but you.

## LETTERS, COMMENTS, AND QUESTIONS FROM READERS

We expect to learn from our mistakes, as well as from the input of our readers, and to improve with each book and edition. Many of those who use the *Unofficial Guides* write to us to ask questions, make comments, or share their own discoveries and lessons learned. We appreciate all such input, both positive and critical, and encourage our readers to continue writing. Readers' comments and observations will contribute immeasurably to the improvement of revised editions of the *Unofficial Guides.*

### How to Write the Author

Sally O'Neal Coates
*The Unofficial Guide to Bed & Breakfasts in the Northwest*
P.O. Box 43673
Birmingham, AL 35243

When you write, be sure to put your return address on your letter as well as on the envelope—they may get separated. And remember, our work takes us out of the office for long periods of research, so forgive us if our response is delayed.

# What Makes It a Bed-and-Breakfast?

Comparing the stale, sterile atmosphere of most hotels and motels to the typical bed-and-breakfast experience—cozy guest room, intimate parlor, friendly hosts, fresh-baked cookies, not to mention a delicious breakfast— why stay anywhere *other than* a bed-and-breakfast? But this isn't a promotional piece for the bed-and-breakfast life. Bed-and-breakfasts are not hotels. Here are some of the differences:

A bed-and-breakfast or small inn, as we define it, is a small property (about 3 to 25 guest rooms, with a few exceptions) with hosts around, a distinct personality, individually decorated rooms, and breakfast included in the price (again, with a few exceptions). Many of these smaller properties have owners living right there; at others, the owners are nearby, a phone call away.

Recently, the bed-and-breakfast and small inn trade has taken off— with mixed results. This growth has taken place on both fronts: the low and high ends. As bed-and-breakfasts gain popularity, anyone with a spare bedroom can pop an ad in the Yellow Pages for "Billy's Bedroom B&B." These enterprises generally lack professionalism, don't keep regular hours or days of operation, are often unlicensed, and were avoided in this guide.

On the other end of the spectrum are luxury premises with more amenities than the finest hotels. Whether historic homes or lodgings built to be bed-and-breakfasts or inns, interiors are posh, baths are private and ensuite, and breakfasts are gourmet affairs. In-room whirlpool tubs and fireplaces are *de rigueur,* and extras range from in-room refrigerators (perhaps stocked with champagne) to complimentary high tea to free use of state-of-the-art recreational equipment to . . . the list goes on! (One long-time innkeeper, whose historic home was tidily and humbly maintained by hours of elbow grease and common sense, dubbed this new state of affairs "the amenities war.")

The result is an industry in which a simple homestay bed-and-breakfast with a shared bath and common rooms can be a budget experience, while a new, upscale bed-and-breakfast can be the luxury venue of a lifetime.

# Who Stays at Bed-and-Breakfasts?

American travelers are finally catching on to what Europeans have known for a long time. Maybe it's a backlash against a cookie-cutter, strip-mall landscape, or a longing for a past that maybe never was, and for an idealized, short-term interaction with others. Maybe it's a need for simple pleasures in a world over-the-top with theme parks and high-tech wonders. Who can say for sure?

The bed-and-breakfast trade has grown so large that it includes niches catering to virtually every need: some bed-and-breakfasts and small inns are equipped to help travelers conduct business, others provide turn-down service and fresh flowers by the honeymooners' canopied bed, and still others offer amenities for reunions or conferences. Whatever your needs, there is a bed-and-breakfast or small inn tailored to your expectations. The challenge, and one this guide was designed to help you meet, is sifting through the choices until you find the perfect place.

### Romantics

More and more, properties are establishing at least one room or suite with fireplace, whirlpool, canopied king, and the trappings of romance. Theme rooms can also be especially fun for fantasizing. Always check out the privacy factor. Sometimes a property that caters to families has a carriage house in the back or a top-floor room away from the others. If an inn allows children under 16, don't be surprised if it's noisy; look for ones that are for older children or adults only.

### Families

Face it, Moms and Dads: rumpled surroundings will sometimes have to be accepted where children are welcome. You may have to give up pristine decor and breakfast tea served in bone china for the relaxed, informal mood, but on the upside, you won't have to worry as much about Caitlin or Michael knocking over the Wedgwood collection on the sideboard.

When an establishment says kids are "welcome," that usually means a really kid-friendly place. Check the age restrictions. If your children are under-aged but well-behaved, let the host know; often they will make exceptions. (But be sure it's true—other guests are counting on it.) On the flip side, honeymooners or other folks who might prefer common areas free of crayons, and breakfasts without sugar-frosted confetti, may want to look elsewhere.

Generally, bed-and-breakfasts are not ideal for high-action kids. But if your children enjoy games, puzzles, books, a chance for quiet pleasures, and meeting others; if they don't need TVs; and if they can be counted on to be thoughtful and follow instructions ("whisper before 9 a.m.," "don't put your feet on the table"), you and your kids can have a wonderful experience together—and so can the rest of the guests.

## Business Travelers

For individual business travelers, bed-and-breakfasts and small inns are becoming much more savvy at anticipating your needs, but in differing degrees. While phone lines and data ports are fairly common, they vary from one bed-and-breakfast to another. Some say they offer data ports when in fact they have two phone jacks in every room but only one phone line servicing the entire property. This can be fine for a three-room inn in the off-season, but if you're trying to conduct business, look for properties with private lines and/or dedicated data ports. If in doubt, ask. Rooms are often available with desks, but these also vary, particularly in surface area and quality of lighting. If this is an important feature, ask for specifics and make sure you secure a room with a desk when you reserve.

Some establishments even offer couriers, secretarial support, and laundry/dry cleaning. And for business travelers who don't have time to take advantage of a leisurely and sumptuous breakfast, hosts often provide an early-morning alternative, sometimes continental, sometimes full.

Finally, there are intangibles to consider. After the sterile atmosphere of the trade show, meeting hall, or boardroom, a small inn with a host and a plate of cookies and a personal dinner recommendation can be nice to come home to.

The atmosphere is also a plus for business meetings or seminars: the relaxed surroundings are quite conducive to easygoing give and take. During the week when guest rooms are often available, some bed-and-breakfasts and small inns are usually eager to host business groups.

Discounts are often included and special services such as catering and equipment are offered if you rent the entire property. But forget weekends; these properties are still tourist oriented.

### Independents

If you are on your own, small lodgings are ideal. Look for a place with single rates, and even if a special rate isn't listed, you can often negotiate a small discount. If you want some interaction, just sit in the parlor, lounge, or common rooms, and talk to people before meals. Most of the time if you're friendly and interested, you'll get an invite to join someone at a table. You could talk to the innkeepers about this even before you arrive, and they might fix you up with friendly folks. (And if you are traveling with others, invite a single to join you.) As for breakfast, communal tables are perfect for singles. Note our profiles to choose properties with that in mind.

### Groups

Whether you are part of a wedding, reunion, or just a group of people who want to travel together, an inn or bed-and-breakfast is a delightful place to stay. The atmosphere is special, your needs are taken care of in a personal way, the grounds are most often spacious and lovely, and in the evening you can all retire in close proximity. It's especially fun when you take over the whole place—so you may want to choose an especially small property if that's your goal.

### Those with Special Needs

Look in our profiles for mention of disabled facilities or access. Then call for details to determine just how extensive the accessibility is. Remember also that some of these houses are quite old, and owners of a small bed-and-breakfast will not have a team of accessibility experts on retainer, so be specific with your questions. If doorways must be a certain width to accommodate a wheelchair or walker, know how many inches before you call; if stairs are difficult for Great Aunt Agnes, don't neglect to find out how many are present outside, as well as inside. And if a property that seems otherwise special doesn't seem to have facilities, perhaps you can patch things together, such as a room on the first floor. Realistically, though, some historic properties were built with many stairs and are situated on hilltops or in rural terrain, so you will have to choose very carefully.

If you suffer from allergies or aversions, talk this over when you book. A good innkeeper will make every attempt to accommodate you. As for food, if you request a special meal and give enough notice, you can often get what you like. That's one of the joys of a small, personalized property.

# You and Your Hosts

Hosts are the heart of your small inn or bed-and-breakfast experience and color all aspects of the stay. They can make or break a property, and sometimes an unassuming place will be the most memorable of all because of the care and warmth of the hosts. Typically, they are well versed in navigating the area and can be a wealth of "insider information" on restaurants, sight-seeing, and the like.

While many—most, in these guides—hosts live on the premises, they often have designed or remodeled their building so that their living quarters are separate. Guests often have their own living room, den, parlor, and sitting room; you may be sharing with other guests, but not so much with your hosts. The degree of interaction between host families and guests varies greatly; we try to give a feel for the extremes in the introduction to each profile. In most cases, hosts are accessible but not intrusive; they will swing through the common areas and chat a bit, but are sensitive to guests' need for privacy. Sometimes hosts are in another building altogether; in the other extreme, you intimately share living space with your hosts. This intimate, old-style bed-and-breakfast arrangement is called a "homestay." We try to note this.

In short, most bed-and-breakfast hosts are quite gracious in accommodating travelers' needs, and many are underpinning their unique small lodging with policies and amenities from hotel-style lodgings. But bed-and-breakfasts and small inns are not The Sheraton, and being cognizant of the differences can make your experience more pleasant.

# Planning Your Visit

## WHEN YOU CHOOSE

If you're not sure where you want to travel, browse through our listings. Maybe something in an introduction or a description of a property will spark your interest.

If you know you are going to a certain location, note the properties in that zone, and then read the entries. You can also call for brochures or take a further look at Web sites, especially to see rooms or to book directly.

We've provided a listing of some useful Web sites; sites specific to the Northwest can be found later in this chapter on page 18.

## WHEN YOU BOOK

Small properties usually require booking on your own. Some travel agents will help, but they may charge a fee, because many small properties don't

| Helpful Web Sites | |
|---|---|
| *www.virtualcities.com* | *innsnorthamerica.com* |
| *bbchannel.com* | *johansens.com* |
| *bbonline.com* | *relaischateaux.fr/[name of* |
| *bnbcity.com* | *inn]* |
| *bnbinns.com* | *travel.com/accom/bb/usa* |
| *epicurious.com* | *travelguide.com* |
| *getawayguides.com* | *trip.com* |
| *innbook.com* | *triple1.com* |
| *inns.com* | *virtualcities.com* |

give travel agents commissions. The fastest, easiest ways to book are through the Internet or a reservation service, but if you have special needs or questions, we suggest contacting properties directly to get exactly what you want.

Ask about any special needs or requirements, and make sure your requests are clear. Most of these properties are not designed for people in wheelchairs, so be sure to ask ahead of time if you need that accessibility. Specify what's important to you—privacy, king-size bed, fireplace, tub versus shower, view, first-floor access. A host won't necessarily know what you want, so make sure you decide what is important—writing it down will help you remember. Note the room you want by name, or ask for the "best" room if you're not sure. Remember to ask about parking conditions—does the property have off-street parking or will you have to find a place on the street? And if air-conditioning is a must for you, always inquire—some bed-and-breakfasts do not have it.

Verify prices, conditions, and any factors or amenities that are important to you. The best time to call is in the early afternoon, before new guests arrive for the day and when hosts have the most free time. Book as soon as possible; for weekends and holidays, preferred properties could be filled a year or more in advance.

## A Word about Negotiating Rates

Negotiating a good rate can be more straightforward at a bed-and-breakfast than at a hotel. For starters, the person on the other end of the line will probably be the owner and will have the authority to offer you a discount. Second, the bed-and-breakfast owner has a smaller number of rooms and guests to keep track of than a hotel manager and won't have to do a lot of checking to know whether something is available. Also, because the number of rooms is small, each room is more important. In a bed-and-breakfast with four rooms, the rental of each room increases the occupancy rate by 25%.

To get the best rate, just ask. If the owner expects a full house, you'll probably get a direct and honest "no deal." On the other hand, if there are rooms and you are sensitive about price, chances are you'll get a break. In either event, be polite and don't make unreasonable requests. If you are overbearing or contentious on the phone, the proprietor may suddenly discover no rooms available.

## SOME CONSIDERATIONS

Like snowflakes, no two bed-and-breakfasts are alike. Some are housed in historic homes or other buildings (churches, fraternal halls, barns, castles . . . !). Some are humble and cozy, some are grand and opulent. Some are all in one building, while others are scattered amongst individual, free-standing units. Some offer a breakfast over which you'll want to linger for hours, others . . . well, others make a darn good muffin. Bed-and-breakfasts are less predictable than hotels and motels but can be much more interesting. A few bed-and-breakfast aficionados have discovered that "interesting" sometimes comes at a price. This guide takes the "scary" out of "interesting" and presents only places that meet a certain standard of cleanliness, predictability, and amenities. However, there are certain questions and issues common to bed-and-breakfasts and small inns that first-time visitors should consider:

### Choosing Your Room

Check out your room before lugging your luggage (not having elevators is usually part of the charm). This is standard procedure at small properties and saves time and trouble should you prefer another room. When a guest room has an open door, it usually means the proud innkeeper wants you to peek. You may just find a room that you like better than the one you are assigned, and it may be available, so ask.

### Bathrooms

Americans are picky about their potties. While the traditional (sometimes referred to as "European-style") bed-and-breakfast set-up involved several bedrooms sharing a bath, this is becoming less common. Even venerable Victorians are being remodeled to include private baths. In fact, many bed-and-breakfasts offer ultra-luxurious bath facilities, including jetted tubs, dual vanities, and so forth. Our advice is not to reject shared bath facilities out of hand, as these can be excellent values. Do check the bedroom-to-bath ratio, however. Two rooms sharing a bath can be excellent; three or more can be problematic with a full house.

## Security

Many bed-and-breakfasts have property locks and room locks as sophisticated as hotels and motels. Others do not. For the most part, inns with 3½ stars or more have quality locks throughout the premises. (Many with lower rankings do as well.) Beyond locks, most bed-and-breakfasts provide an additional measure of security in that they are small properties, generally in a residential district, and typically with live-in hosts on the premises. Single female travelers might take comfort in coming "home" to a facility like this as opposed to a 150-room hotel with a cardlock system but God-knows-what lurking in the elevator.

## Privacy

At a hotel, you can take your key and hole up in solitude for the duration of your stay. It's a little harder at a bed-and-breakfast, especially if you take part in a family-style breakfast (although many inns offer the option of an early continental breakfast if you're pressed for time or feeling antisocial, and some offer ensuite breakfast service—these options are noted in the profiles). Most bed-and-breakfast hosts we've met are very sensitive to guests' needs for privacy and seem to have a knack for being as helpful or as unobtrusive as you wish. If privacy is hard to achieve at a given property, we've noted that in the profile.

## Autonomy

Most bed-and-breakfasts provide a key to the front door and/or an unlocked front door certain hours of the day. While you might be staying in a family-style atmosphere, you are seldom subject to rules such as a curfew. (A few properties request that guests be in by a specific time; these policies are noted and rare.) Some places have "quiet hours," usually from about 10 or 11 p.m. until about 7 a.m. Such policies tend to be in place when properties lack sufficient sound insulation and are noted in the profile. Generally, higher ratings tend to correspond with better sound insulation.

# What the Ratings Mean

We have organized this book so that you can get a quick idea of each property by checking out the ratings, reading the information at the beginning of each entry and then, if you're interested, reading the more detailed overview of each property. Obviously ratings are subjective, and people of good faith (and good taste) can and do differ. But you'll get a good, relative idea, and the ability to quickly compare properties.

**Overall Rating**   The overall ratings are represented by stars, which range in number from one to five and represent our opinion of the quality of the property as a whole. It corresponds something like this:

| | |
|---|---|
| ★★★★★ | The Best |
| ★★★★½ | Excellent |
| ★★★★ | Very Good |
| ★★★½ | Good |
| ★★★ | Good Enough |
| ★★½ | Fair |
| ★★ | Not So Good |
| ★½ | Barely Acceptable |
| ★ | Unacceptable |

The overall rating for the bed-and-breakfast or small inn experience takes into account all factors of the property, including guest rooms and public rooms, food, facilities, grounds, maintenance, hosts, and something we'll call "specialness," for lack of a better phrase. Many times it involves the personalities and pesonal touches of the hosts.

Some properties have fairly equal star levels for all of these things, but most have some qualities that are better than others. Also, large, ambitious properties that serve dinner would tend to have a slightly higher star rating for the same level of qualities than a smaller property (the difference, say, between a great novel and a great short story; the larger it is the harder it is to pull off, hence the greater the appreciation). Yet a small property can earn five stars with a huge dose of "specialness."

Overall ratings and room quality ratings do not always correspond. While guest rooms may be spectacular, the rest of the inn may be average, or vice versa. Generally, though, we've found through the years that a property is usually consistently good or bad throughout.

**Room Quality Rating**   The quality ratings, stated in the form of a letter grade, represent our opinion of the quality of the guest rooms and bathrooms only. For the room quality ratings we factored in view, size, closet space, bedding, seating, desks, lighting, soundproofing, comfort, style, privacy, decor, "taste," and other intangibles. A really great private bathroom with a claw-foot tub and antique table might bring up the rating of an otherwise average room. Conversely, poor maintenance or lack of good lighting will lower the rating of a spacious, well-decorated room. Sometimes a few rooms are really special while others are standard, and we have averaged these where possible. It's difficult to codify this, but all factors are weighed, and the grades seem to come up easily.

It corresponds something like this:

A = Excellent
B = Very Good
C = Good
D = Acceptable

**Value Rating**    The value ratings—A to D—are a combination of the overall and room quality ratings, divided by the cost of an average guest room. They are an indication rather than a scientific formulation—a general idea of value for money. If getting a good deal means the most to you, choose a property by looking at the value rating. Otherwise, the overall and room quality ratings are better indicators of a satisfying experience. An A value, A room quality, five-star inn or bed-and-breakfast would be ideal, but most often, you'll find a C value, and you are getting your money's worth. If a wonderful property is fairly priced, it may only get a C value rating, but you still might prefer the experience to an average property that gets an A value rating.

**Price**    Our price range is the lowest-priced room to the highest-priced room in high season. The range does not usually include specially priced times such as holidays and low season. The room rate is based on double occupancy and assumes breakfast is included. It does not assume that other meals are included in the rate. However, be sure to check the inn's Food & Drink category. Lodgings where MAP, which stands for the hotel industry's standard Modified American Plan, is applicable offer breakfast and dinner in the room rate. Unless specifically noted, prices quoted in the profiles do not include gratuities or state and local taxes, which can be fairly steep. Gratuities are optional; use your own discretion. Prices change constantly, so check before booking.

# The Profiles Clarified

The bulk of information about properties is straightforward, but much of it is in abbreviated style, so the following clarifications may help. They are arranged in the order they appear in the profile format.

Many of the properties in this book have similar names or even the same name; for example, there's the Green Gables Guesthouse in Seattle and the Green Gables Inn in Walla Walla. Town names, too, can be strikingly similar. Make sure you don't confuse properties or town names when selecting an inn.

## Location

First, check the map for location. Our directions are designed to give you a general idea of the property's location. For more complete directions, call the property or check its Web site.

## Building

This category denotes the design and architecture of the building. Many of the properties in the *Unofficial Guides* are historically and architecturally interesting. Here are a few architectural terms you may want to brush up on, in no particular order: Hip-roof, Colonial, Craftsman, Queen Anne, Blued Pine, Cape Cod, Northwest Contemporary, Foursquare, Bird's Eye Maple, Art Deco, Rumford fireplace, Georgian, Victorian, Arts and Crafts, Seattle Box, Eastlake, Greek Revival, Edwardian, claw-foot tub, and many more. The more you know the jargon, the better you can select the property you want.

## Food & Drink

For food and drink, we offer a taste of the inn or bed-and-breakfast, so to speak. Most properties go all out to fill you up at breakfast, so that you could easily skip lunch (factor that into the value). In some areas, however, the tourist board regulates that properties can only serve a continental breakfast without a hot dish. Note whether we state "full breakfast," if that experience is paramount. In most cases, a bed-and-breakfast breakfast— even a continental—tends to include more homemade items, greater selection, and greater care in presentation.

In this category, what we call "specialties" are really typical dishes, which may not always be served, but should give you a good idea of the cuisine. And a very few bed-and-breakfasts and inns do not include the breakfast in the price. However, it is almost always offered as an option.

Many inns and bed-and-breakfasts offer afternoon tea, snacks, sherry, or pre-dinner wine and cheese. Note that if an inn offers meals to the public as well as guests, the atmosphere becomes less personal. Also, if MAP is noted in this category, it means the inn offers meals other than breakfast as part of the room rate.

Some inns provide alcoholic beverages to guests, some forbid consumption of alcohol—either extreme is noted in the inn's profile. The norm is that alcohol consumption is a private matter, and guests may bring and consume their own, if they do so respectfully. Glassware is generally provided. Bed-and-breakfasts are not well suited to drunkenness and partying.

A diet and a bed-and-breakfast or small inn go together about as well as a haystack and a lighted match. Come prepared to eat. Some bed-and-breakfasts will serve dinner on request, and we included that info when it was available.

Most bed-and-breakfasts are sensitive to dietary needs and preferences but need to be warned of this in advance. When you make your reservation, be sure to explain if you are diabetic, wheat- or dairy-intolerant, vegetarian/vegan, or otherwise restricted. Many proprietors pride themselves on accommodating difficult diets.

## Recreation

We do not usually spell out whether the activities noted in the format are on-site. With some exceptions, assume that golf, tennis, fishing, canoeing, downhill skiing, and the like are not on-site (since these are small properties, not resorts). Assume that games and smaller recreational activities are on the property. But there are some exceptions, so ask.

## Amenities & Services

These blend a bit. Generally, amenities include extras such as swimming pools and games, and services cover perks such as business support and turning down beds in the evening. Business travelers should note if any services are mentioned, and if there are public rooms, group discounts, and so forth to back them up. Almost all bed-and-breakfasts and inns can provide advice regarding touring, restaurants, and local activities; many keep maps and brochures on hand.

## Deposit

Unless otherwise noted, "refund" usually means "minus a service charge," which varies from $10 or so to 50 percent or more. The more popular the property, usually the more deposit you'll have to put down, and the further ahead. When canceling after the site's noted policy, most will still refund, less a fee, if the room is rerented. Check back on this.

## Discounts

Discounts may extend to singles, long-stay guests, kids, seniors, packages, and groups. Even though discounts may not be listed in the text, it doesn't hurt to ask, as these sorts of things can be flexible in small establishments, midweek, off-season, last-minute, and when innkeepers may want to fill their rooms. This category also includes a dollar figure for additional persons sharing a room (beyond the two included in the basic rate).

## Credit Cards

For those properties that do accept credit cards (we note those that do not), we've listed credit cards accepted with the following codes:

| | | | |
|---|---|---|---|
| V | VISA | MC | MasterCard |
| AE | American Express | D | Discover |
| DC | Diner's Club International | CB | Carte Blanche |

## Check-in/Out

As small operators, most bed-and-breakfast hosts need to know approximately when you'll be arriving. Many have check-in periods (specified in the profiles) during which the hosts or staff will be available to greet you. Most can accommodate arrival beyond their stated check-in period but need to be advised so they can arrange to be home or get a key to you. Think about it—they have to buy groceries and go to the kids' soccer games and get to doctors' appointments just like you. And they have to sleep sometime. Don't show up at 11:30 p.m. and expect a smiling bellhop—the same person who lets you in is probably going to be up at 5 or 6 a.m. slicing mushrooms for your omelet!

Check-in times are often flexible, but, as with any commercial lodging, check-out times can be critical, as the innkeeper must clean and prepare your room for incoming guests. If you need to stay longer, ask and you'll often get an extension. Sometimes a host will let you leave your bags and enjoy the common areas after check-out, as long as you vacate your room.

Please take cancellation policies seriously. A "no-show" is not a cancellation! If an establishment has a seven-day, or 72-hour, or whatever, cancellation policy, you are expected to call and cancel your reservation prior to that time, or you could be liable for up to the full amount of your reserved stay. After all, a four-unit bed-and-breakfast has lost 25% of its revenue if you arbitrarily decide not to show up.

## Smoking

We've indicated in the inn's profile if smoking is banned outright or if there are designated rooms where it's allowed. Usually it's fine to smoke outside, what with the excellent ventilation, but ask your hosts before you light up. Be mindful, too, of how you dispose of the butts—when you flick them into a nearby shrub, it's likely that your hosts, not some sanitation team, will be plucking them out next week.

## Pets

We have not mentioned most of the inn-house pets in the profiles, as this situation changes even more frequently than most items. Many properties have pets on the premises. Don't assume that because an establishment does not allow guests to bring pets that pets aren't around. Dogs and cats and birds (and monkeys, pigs, goats, llamas, etc.) are often around. If you forsee a problem with this, be sure to clarify "how around," before booking. If properties allow pets, we have noted this, but most do not. And if you can't bear to leave your own beloved Fido or Miss Kitty for long periods, and want to stay in an inn that does not allow them, good innkeepers often know of reputable boarding facilities nearby.

## Open

Properties often claim they are open all year, but they can close at any time—at the last minute for personal reasons or if business is slow. Similarly, properties that close during parts of the year may open specially for groups. If you can get a bunch of family or friends together, it's a great way to stay at popular inns and bed-and-breakfasts that would be otherwise hard to book. And remember, in low-season things slow down, dinners may not be served, and even when some properties are "open," they may be half-closed.

## AN IMPORTANT NOTE

Facts and situations change constantly in the small-lodging business. Innkeepers get divorced, prices go up, puppies arrive, chefs quit in the middle of a stew, and rooms get redecorated, upgraded, and incorporated. So use this format as a means to get a good overall idea of the property, and then inquire when you book about the specific details that matter most. Changes will definitely occur, so check to be sure.

# Making the Most of Your Stay

Once you're settled in, it's a good idea to scope out the entire place, or you may not realize until too late that your favorite book was on the shelf, or that an old-fashioned swing would have swung you into the moonlight on a warm evening. If you are alone in the inn, it can feel like the property is yours (and that, in fact, is a good reason to go midweek or off-season).

Take advantage of the special charms of these lodgings: the fireplace, the piano, other guests, the gardens. What makes an inn or bed-and-breakfast experience an integral part of a trip are small moments that can become cherished memories.

Did you love it? You can perhaps duplicate in your daily life some of the touches that made the experience special, whether it was warm towels, an early weekend breakfast by candlelight, or a special recipe for stuffed French toast. Hosts usually enjoy sharing ideas and recipes.

A small inn or bed-and-breakfast, perhaps set in a village or town where at least a few blocks retain a look of history and often grace, encourages you to relax, lie back, unwind, open up, read, talk, get romantic, dream, slow down, look up at the stars and down at the grass, smell the coffee—and of course, the roses climbing on the pergola or lining the walkway. These small lodgings are stress-busters, far away from sitcoms and fast food and the media mania du jour. They are cozy places to settle into and curl up with a book, or a honey, or a dream. Or, if you must, a laptop and a cell phone.

# Northwest Bed-and-Breakfasts

The bed-and-breakfast industry has mushroomed all over the nation, and the Northwest is no exception. You need only look at towns like Ashland, Oregon, or areas like Washington's San Juan Islands to see the growth. In the early 1980s, a handful of bed-and-breakfast–style lodgings operated in Ashland and the San Juans. Today, each of these tourist destinations offers over 75 bed-and-breakfasts or inns.

This guide strives to capture the wide range of styles represented in the Northwest: a collection of cabins with in-room, self-serve breakfasts; a beachfront luxury home with ensuite whirlpool tubs; an organic farm with shared-with-host bath and homestyle dinners by arrangement. You'll find dozens of restored Victorians, from "faded ladies" (with a strong sense of history but genteel-shabby antique furnishings) to those that have been totally gutted and refurbished with shiny reproductions. You'll find a place where a guided kayak tour is included in the room rate, and one with its own windsurfing school. You can stay on a buffalo or llama ranch, in a recreated European castle, or a one-room schoolhouse.

The population of the Northwest is concentrated west of the Cascade Mountains. Consequently, you'll find a larger number of properties there, and an overall higher level of sophistication. Needs of the business traveler are more completely addressed by properties along the Interstate-5 corridor than by those in the desert plains east of the Cascades. Prices, too, tend to be higher west of the Cascades, with popular tourist areas highest of all: Victoria, the Oregon coast, the San Juan Islands. Properties within a three-hour radius of major metropolitan cities tend to be expensive, while prices in the urban areas themselves are softened a bit by competition. Far-flung areas of the Cascades, the eastern deserts, northeast Washington, and the Olympic peninsula can offer exceptional bargains.

## GATHERING INFORMATION

This is a lodging guidebook. While each zone has a brief introduction, and each profile lists a few nearby attractions, this book in no way purports to be a guidebook to the Northwest.

In addition to consulting one or more of the many useful Northwest guidebooks on the market, we suggest turning to the Internet and to your prospective bed-and-breakfast hosts as sources of information. Don't abuse your hosts, but they can (a) steer you to some good phone numbers and other resources, and (b) perhaps mail you a flyer or two about local sites and happenings with your reservation confirmation.

Some of the bed-and-breakfasts profiled in this guide have links from their Web pages to Web pages of interest in their region.

Also on-line, we find the following sources particularly useful for planning activities in the Northwest:

**For British Columbia:**

Travel and Tourism Planning Site for BC: travel.bc.ca

Victoria Tourism Mall: tourismmall.victoria.bc.ca

Victoria and Vancouver BC: www.vacationsbc.com

Tourist Information Center: www.tourismkiosk.com

**For Washington:**

Washington State Tourism: www.tourism.wa.gov

Dan Youra's Official Olympic Peninsula Guide: www.youra.com/ olympic

San Juan Islands Guide: www.sanjuanguide.com

The Methow Valley Web Page: www.methow.com

Leavenworth: www.leavenworth.org

**For Oregon:**

Official Oregon Tourism Web Site: www.traveloregon.com

Oregon, USA—Essential Links: www.el.com/To/Oregon/Links

If you'll be traveling in the Puget Sound area, to the San Juans or Whidbey Island, around the Kitsap Peninsula, to Port Townsend and Port Angeles from the Seattle/Tacoma metro area, or from the Seattle area to Victoria, BC, be sure to consult the ferry schedules at (206) 808-7977, (888) 808-7977 (Washington only), (800) 84-FERRY (Washington only, automated), or the Internet at www.wsdot.wa.gov/ferries. Note that schedules are seasonal; they change several times a year. They are also subject to weather conditions.

Speaking of weather, don't blithely assume you can traipse back and forth across the Cascade Mountains any time of the year. Some roads (such as parts of Washington's North Cascades Highway, Highway 20) are closed during the winter. Others experience periodic closures. Consult the following resources:

- Washington State Mountain Pass Road Report: traffic.wsdot.wa.gov/sno-info or (888) SNO-INFO (766-4636)
- AAA Pass Report: (425) 646-2190
- Oregon Department of Transportation: (503) 588-2941

## BED-AND-BREAKFASTS ON THE INTERNET

The World Wide Web is full of home pages for bed-and-breakfasts and small inns. It's full of booking services and tourism information sites that link you to home pages and listings for bed-and-breakfasts and small inns. Once you link up to one of the thousands of bed-and-breakfast or small inn sites within the Northwest, you can revel in detailed descriptions and click your way through colored photographs until your head spins (believe us, we know). If you see something you like, you can, in some cases, submit a reservation request on-line, or e-mail the hosts directly for a little cyberchat about your specific needs.

There's no denying that the Internet is a great resource for travelers in general, and for bed-and-breakfast/small inn seekers in particular. The problem comes in sorting the wheat from the chaff and in remembering that a great Web site does not necessarily equal a great lodging experience. (Think about it: do you want your bed-and-breakfast host spending his time whipping up omelets and cruising the local farmer's market or sitting in front of a computer til 3 a.m. in his underwear scanning photos of his backyard gazebo?)

Out-of-date information is another serious problem with Internet listings. We found one particular Northwest database that listed hundreds of inns, conveniently separated into geographic areas. What a resource, right? Upon calling the telephone numbers, we discovered that over half the listings were defunct. Many others were the scary type of bed-and-breakfast we're trying to avoid—the "let's-rent-Johnnie's-room-while-he's-at-college" type.

---

### Useful Northwest Web Sites

| | |
|---|---|
| bcbandb.com | www.innsite.com |
| www.wbbg.com | www.ohwy.com |
| www.obbg.org | www.pacificharbor.com/bbinn |
| bbcanada.com | www.travelguides.com/bandb |
| www.bbchannel.com | www.virtualcities.com |
| www.moriah.com | |

---

# Ten Reasons to Get out and Go

Does anyone need an excuse to "get out and go" in the great Northwest? We think not! Since Meriwether Lewis grabbed his old pal William Clark and struck out for the Pacific in 1804, the going has been its own excuse in this part of the world. The following pages offer three hundred more reasons: you can be a Pacific Northwest pioneer today, and let someone else do the laundry and the cooking! But just in case you need a final motivating reason to hit the trail, we offer the following great excuses to get going:

1. History. Lewis and Clark. The Oregon Trail. The Whitman Mission. Chiefs Joseph and Seattle. The Real West lives here—in the not-so-distant past. Excellent museums, exhibits, and living history presentations can be found throughout Washington, Oregon, and British Columbia. Not to mention more recent history, which can be enjoyed at places like the Boeing Museum of Flight in Seattle.

2. Music. From Woody Guthrie to Kurt Cobain, the Pacific Northwest has inspired songwriters and musicians in all genres. Grunge, jazz, ethnic, pop, folk . . . let a concert or a festival draw you out to explore.

3. Our Magnificent Mountains. Sure, everybody has his version of The Great Outdoors, but you don't find a string of pearls like Mt. Baker, Glacier Peak, Mt. Rainier, Mount St. Helens, Mt. Adams, Mt. Hood, Mt. Jefferson, the Three Sisters, and Mt. McLoughlin just anywhere.

4. The Wild West. "Toppenish, where the West still lives!" boasts a little eastern Washington town, festooned with murals and authentic Western history. The world-famous Pendleton (Oregon) Round-Up is a rodeo of epic proportions held each September. And some parts of the Northwest—such as the whole of cattle-ranching eastern Oregon—will make you feel as though you've stepped back a century and a half.

5. Native America. Pow-wows, salmon fests, traditional dancing, centuries-old crafts . . . Washington, Oregon, and British Columbia are rife with opportunities to enjoy the culture of the original Americans.

6. Animals and Vegetables. From the rhododendrons west of the Cascades to the sagebrush plains in the east, the plants of the Northwest are reason enough to get out and go. As are the birds, the whales, the deer, and the elk. Not to mention the more cultivated flora and fauna: produce stands with Walla Walla Sweet onions, Wenatchee apples, Yakima peaches; rural animal parks; and urban zoos.

7.  Recreate! Hiking, skiing, snowboarding, fishing, hunting, whitewater rafting, diving, bicycling, snowmobiling, rockhounding, hot-air ballooning, rock climbing—it's all here.

8.  Wine Country. Crisp chardonnays, spicy merlots, oaky cabernets, and soft reislings await in the Northwest's many wine valleys. And don't miss the ales, porters, and other microbrews—Washington produces three-quarters of America's hops, you know!

9.  Local Festivals. Skagit Valley tulips. Mt. Hood jazz. Columbia River hydroplanes. And, throughout Washington, Oregon, and British Columbia, arts and crafts, antiques, parades, music, and local color.

10. Be an *Unofficial* Correspondent. Look out for new or special properties not profiled in this book. If you provide us with five new lodgings that we choose to visit and write about in the next edition, we'll credit you and send a copy when the edition is published. That's reason enough to get out and explore the majesty of the Northwest.

# A Few of My Favorite Things
## PROPERTY NAMES

- Birds of a Feather (Victoria, BC)
- ThistleDown House (Vancouver, BC)
- Hasty Pudding House (Anacortes, WA)
- Domaine Madeleine (Port Angeles, WA)
- Toad Hall (Sequim, WA)
- Schnauzer Crossing (Bellingham, WA)
- Turtleback Farm Inn (Orcas Island, WA)
- Panacea (San Juan Island, WA)
- Chambered Nautilus (Seattle, WA)
- Growly Bear (Ashland, WA)
- A Stone's Throw (Index, WA)
- Oar House (Newport, OR)
- Yankee Tinker (Beaverton, OR)
- Shrew's House (Ashland, OR)
- Rags to Walkers Guest Ranch (Sisters, OR)

## SPECIAL DISHES

- Candied smoked salmon, "Barry's beans," and spicy rosemary potatoes at Wayward Navigator (Victoria, BC)
- High tea with dainty bakery treats at Prior House (Victoria, BC)
- Smoked salmon, wild mushroom, sharp Tillamook cheddar frittata at Boreas (Long Beach, WA)
- Sinful stuffed French toast (cream cheese, pecans, chocolate, raspberries!) at St. Helens Manorhouse (Morton, WA)
- Imported Italian chocolates and cheeses at Franklin Street Station (Astoria, OR)
- To-die-for cookies from the bottomless jar at Channel House (Anacortes, WA) and Sandlake Country Inn (Cloverdale, OR)
- Asian-flair vegetable frittata at Brightwood Guest House (Brightwood, OR)
- Pumpkin tarts at Old Welches Inn (Welches, OR)

## MISCELLANY

No one feels sorry for us when we talk about the rigors of researching a book like this one. But despite the fabulous food and elegant decor, endless hours on the road can become a grind without those "special moments" that touch the heart and refresh the spirit:

- Getting to hug the Samoyed dog at Kangaroo House (Orcas Island, WA), walk with the Newfoundland at Woods House (Ashland, OR), wiffle the llama at Llama Ranch (Trout Lake, WA), commune with the goat at Pine River Ranch (Leavenworth, WA), and pet the Persian kitty at BayView B&B (West Vancouver, BC), as well as interact with all the other wonderful pets.
- Rain on the roof of the turret room at Log Castle (Langley, WA)
- Improvisational harp concert in the former-church-sanctuary great room at Angels of the Sea (Vashon Island, WA)
- Hanging bed at Wellspring (Ashland, WA)
- "General Mess" mudroom with slickers, boots, kites, sand pails, and beach paraphernalia at SeaQuest (Yachats, OR)
- Super-high ceilings, pedestal whirlpool tub, and writing desk near the fireplace at Stratford Manor (Bellingham, WA)
- Formal "vest and tie" breakfast presentation at Katy's Inn (La Conner, WA)
- "For the Train" gift-wrapped earplugs at Campbell House (Eugene, OR)
- Vibrant foyer decor at Springbrook Hazelnut Farm (Newberg, OR)—it just makes you happy to walk in!

- Deer in the backyard at Squaw Creek Inn and Blue Spruce (Sisters, OR)
- Teddy bears on the bed at Cowslip's Belle (Ashland, OR)
- . . . and, most of all, each and every innkeeper who, upon seeing that look of weariness in our eyes, said, "Can I get you something? A cup of coffee or tea? Glass of water or soft drink? Would you like a scone?" Bless your hearts!

# Mini Indexes

## Top 30 Overall

### Five Stars
River Run Cottages
All Season's River Inn
Run of the River
Sea Quest B&B
Schnauzer Crossing
Dove House
The Lion and the Rose
Domaine Madeleine
Stratford Manor
The Campbell House
Thornewood Castle
Laburnum Cottage
BJ's Garden Gate
The Haterleigh B&B
Illahee Manor
La Cachette B&B
Springbrook Hazelnut Farm
St. Bernards
Brightwood Guest House
Cozy Rose Inn
Cliff House B&B
China Beach B&B Retreat
Guest House Cottages

### Four-and-a-Half Stars
A Touch of Europe B&B Inn
Eagle's Nest Inn
The Edwin K B&B
Serenity B&B
BayView B&B

Blue Heron Inn
Hunter Creek Farm Bed, Barn, & Breakfast

## Top 30 by Room Quality
River Run Cottages
All Season's River Inn
Run of the River
Sea Quest B&B
Schnauzer Crossing
Dove House
The Lion and the Rose
Domaine Madeleine
Stratford Manor
The Campbell House
Thornewood Castle
Laburnum Cottage
BJ's Garden Gate
The Haterleigh B&B
Illahee Manor
La Cachette B&B
Springbrook Hazelnut Farm
St. Bernards
Brightwood Guest House
Cozy Rose Inn
Cliff House B&B
China Beach B&B Retreat
Guest House Cottages
A Touch of Europe B&B Inn
Eagle's Nest Inn
The Edwin K B&B
Serenity B&B
BayView B&B

Blue Heron Inn
Hunter Creek Farm Bed, Barn, &
   Breakfast

**Top Values**
River Run Cottages
Laburnum Cottage
A Touch of Europe B&B Inn
Foxbridge B&B
A Stone's Throw B&B
Harrison House
Hasty Pudding House
Joan Brown's B&B
Johnson Heritage House
Wayward Navigator
The Parker House B&B
The Portico Victorian B&B
A Treehouse B&B
Casablanca
Reflections
Mountainside Manor B&B
Sage Country Inn
The Yankee Tinker
DeNonno's B&B
Georgian House B&B
Jasmer's at Mt. Rainier
Juniper Acres
Palmer Farm B&B
Baer House B&B
The Hummingbird Inn
Clear Creek Farm B&B
Marquee House
Sunnyside Inn B&B
Oslo's B&B
Grant House
Birds of a Feather B&B
Brookhaven Lodge
1900 Sears & Roebuck Home
The Beryl House
Sonshine B&B
Grandma's House B&B
Mill Inn

Craigmyle Guest House
Kingston Hotel
Stehekin Valley Ranch

**Budget Accommodations**
At least some rooms rent for less
than $75.

**British Columbia**
Birds of a Feather B&B
Braemar Manor
Claddagh House
Craigmyle Guest House
Dashwood Manor
Joan Brown's B&B
Johnson Heritage House
Kingston Hotel
Mountainside Manor
A Treehouse B&B
Wayward Navigator

**Washington**
7Cs Guest Ranch
Angels of the Sea
Autumn Pond
Benson Farmstead
Blair House
Blue Willow
Brigadoon
Brookhaven Lodge
Bush House Country Inn
Casablanca B&B
Channel House
Cooney Mansion
Country Hill B&B
The Farm
Flying L Ranch
Four Winds Guest House
The Gold House Inn
Grandma's House B&B
Greywolf Inn
Harbinger Inn
Harbor House

Haus Rohrbach
Hotel Usk
Huckleberry Lodge, Forks
Hummingbird Inn
Inn at Penn Cove
Iron Horse Inn
James House
Jasmer's at Mt. Rainier
Kangaroo House
Katy's Inn
Lizzies
Lytle House
Maple Meadows B&B
Marianna Stoltz House
Miller Tree Inn, Forks
Mt. Baker B&B
Nantucket Inn
North Garden Inn
The Olde Glencove Hotel
Olympic Lights
Oslo's B&B
Otters Pond B&B
Outlook Inn
Palmer Farm
The Portico Victorian B&B
Ravenscroft Inn
Reflections
Ridgeway Farm B&B
Rimrock Inn
Shumway Mansion
Sunnyside Inn
A Touch of Europe B&B Inn
Waverly Place B&B
Weinhard Hotel
The Whitetail Inn
Yodeler Inn B&B

**Oregon**
1900 Sears & Roebuck Home
Baer House
Barnstormer B&B
Beryl House
Bingen Haus

Blue Bucket Inn
Brier Rose Inn
Brookside B&B
C&J Lodge
Cannon Beach Hotel
Chandler's Bed, Bread & Trail
Chapman House B&B
Clear Creek Farm
Clementine's B&B
Elliott House
Frenchglen Hotel
Georgian House B&B
Grandview B&B
Grant House
Harrison House
Home Farm B&B
Hood River Hotel
Hotel Diamond
Juniper Acres
Lara House
Lyle Hotel, Lyle
Marquee House
Marsh Haven Farm
Mill Inn
Old Welches Inn
Our Place in the Country
The Parker House B&B
Riverside School House
Rosebriar Hotel
Sage Country Inn
Shaniko Historic Hotel
Sonshine B&B
Steens Mountain Inn
Steiger Haus
Strawberry Mountain Inn
Sylvia Beach Hotel
Yankee Tinker B&B

**Dinner Served**

**British Columbia**
Spinnakers Brewpub & Guest
    House

**Washington**
Birchfield Manor
Blue Heron Inn
Brookhaven Lodge
Bush House Country Inn
Cady Lake Manor
The Purple House
Rutherglen Mansion
The Shelburne Country Inn
Stehekin Valley Ranch
The Whitetail Inn
The Wild Iris

**Oregon**
C&J Lodge
Clear Creek Farm B&B
Frenchglen Hotel
Hood River Hotel
Hotel Diamond
Sylvia Beach Hotel

**Family-Oriented**
**British Columbia**
Braemar Manor
Craigmyle Guest House
Dashwood Manor
Kingston Hotel
Pendrell Suites
Spinnakers Brewpub & Guest
    House

**Washington**
7C's Guest Ranch
Alexander's Inn
Angels of the Sea B&B
Ann Starrett Mansion
Bacon Mansion
Blackbird Lodge
Bush House Inn
Cady Lake Manor
Casablanca
Chuckanut Manor B&B
Cobblestone B&B Inn
The Colonial Manor

DeNonno's B&B
Edenwild Inn
Flying L Ranch
The Gold House Inn
Grandma's House B&B
The Green Gables Guesthouse
Growly Bear B&B
Harbor House B&B
Haus Rohrbach
The Hotel Usk
The Hummingbird Inn
Iron Horse Inn
Kangaroo House
Llama Ranch B&B
Manitou Lodge
Mildred's B&B
Mt. Baker B&B
North Garden Inn
Ovenell's Heritage Inn
Redmond House B&B
Rockaway Beach Guest House
Rutherglen Mansion
Spring Bay Inn
Stehekin Valley Ranch
Sunnyside Inn B&B
Vintage Inn
Weinhard Hotel
Yodeler Inn B&B

**Oregon**
1900 Sears & Roebuck House
The Bingen House
Brier Rose Inn B&B
Brookside B&B
C&J Lodge
The Campbell House B&B
Canon Beach Hotel
Clear Creek Farm B&B
The Courtyard
Cowslip's Belle B&B
DiamondStone Guest Lodge
Floras Lake House B&B
Frenchglen Hotel

Harrison House
Hearthstone Inn
Hood River Hotel
Hunter Creek Farm Bed, Barn, &
  Breakfast
The Inn of the White Salmon
Lithia Springs Inn
Marquee House
Mill Inn
The Mosier House
Mt. Hood B&B
Oak Street Station B&B
Rags to Walkers Guest Ranch
Riverside School House
Rosebriar Hotel
Sonshine B&B
Squaw Creek B&B Inn
Steens Mountain Inn
Strawberry Mountain Inn
Winchester Country Inn
The Yankee Tinker

## Farm or Rural Setting

### British Columbia
Birds of a Feather B&B

### Washington
7C's Guest Ranch
Alexander's Inn
Benson Farmstead
Birchfield Manor
The Blue Heron Inn
Brigadoon B&B
Brookhaven Lodge
Buck Bay Farm
Cady Lake Manor
Casablanca
Cascade Mountain Inn
Chestnut Hill B&B
China Beach B&B Retreat
The Colonial Manor
Country Hill B&B
Cozy Rose Inn

DeNonno's B&B
Duffy House
Eagle's Nest Inn
The Farm, a B&B
Flying L Ranch
Foxbridge B&B
Glacier Guest Suite
Grandma's House B&B
Greywolf Inn
Growly Bear B&B
Guest House Cottages
Haus Rohrbach
Huckleberry Lodge
Illahee Manor
Island Tyme
La Chachette B&B
Llama Ranch B&B
The Log House
MacKay Harbor Inn
Manitou Lodge
Maple Meadows B&B
Miller Tree Inn
Mountain Meadows Inn
Olympic Lights
Ovenell's Heritage Inn
Palmer Farm
Pine River Ranch
Ridgway Farm B&B
Roaring River B&B
Samish Point by the Bay
South Bay B&B
Spring Bay Inn
Stehekin Valley Ranch
Stratford Manor
Trumpeter Inn
Turtleback Farm Inn
Warm Springs Inn
Wellspring
The Whitetail Inn
Wildwood Manor

### Oregon
Barnstormer B&B

The Beryl House
Brightwood Guest House
Brookside B&B
Chapman House B&B
Clear Creek Farm B&B
DiamondStone Guest Lodge
Eagle's View B&B
Frenchglen Hotel
Home Farm B&B
Hotel Diamond
Hunter Creek Farm Bed, Barn, & Breakfast
The Inn at Aurora
Juniper Acres
Lighthouse B&B
Lithia Springs Inn
Marsh Haven Farm B&B
Mattey House B&B
McKenzie View
Mt. Ashland Inn
Mt. Hood B&B
Mt. Hood Hamlet B&B
Our Place in the Country
Pine Meadow Inn B&B
Rags to Walkers Guest Ranch
Riverside School House
Sandlake Country Inn
Strawberry Mountain Inn

## Groups, Conferences, and/or Weddings Easily Accommodated

### British Columbia
Joan Brown's B&B
Laburnum Cottage
River Run Cottages

### Washington
Angelica's B&B
Ann Starrett Mansion
Bacon Mansion
Benson Farmstead
Birchfield Manor

Blackbird Lodge
Blue Heron Inn
Bradley House
The Buchanan Inn
Cady Lake Manor
Carriage House B&B
Casablanca
Cascade Mountain Inn
Chambered Nautilus
China Beach B&B Retreat
Chinaberry Hill
Cooney Mansion B&B Inn
A Cottage Creek Inn
Cozy Rose Inn
DeVoe Mansion
Domaine Madeleine
The DoveShire B&B
The Farm, a B&B
Flying L Ranch
Fotheringham House B&B
Foxbridge B&B
Haus Loreli
Huckleberry Lodge
Illahee Manor
Iron Horse Inn
La Cahchette B&B
Log Castle B&B
Love's Victorian B&B
Lytle House
MacKay Harbor Inn
Maple Meadows B&B
Maple Rose Inn
Nantucket Inn
The Olde Glencove Hotel
Ovenell's Heritage Inn
Palmer Farm B&B
The Portico Victorian B&B
Reflections
Ridgeway Farm B&B
Rutherglen Mansion
The SeaSuns B&B
Selah Inn
Shumway Mansion

Simone's Groveland Cottage B&B
   Inn
South Bay B&B
St. Helens Manorhouse
Stone Creek Inn
Sunnyside Inn B&B
Swantown Inn
Thornewood Castle
Toad Hall
A Touch of Europe B&B Inn
A Tree House B&B
Victorian Gardens 1888 B&B
Villa Heidelberg
Vintage Inn
Warm Springs Inn
Wellspring
The Wild Iris

**Oregon**
1900 Sears & Roebuck House
Baer House B&B
Barnstormer B&B
C&J Lodge
The Campbell House
Chandler's Bed, Bread, & Trail
   Inn
Chapman House B&B
Columbia Gorge Hotel
Coos Bay Manor
DiamondStone Guest Lodge
Eagle's View B&B
The Elliott House
Falcon's Crest Inn
Franklin Street Station
Gilbert Inn
Gracie's Landing
Grant House
Harrison House
Home Farm B&B
Hunter Creek Farm Bed, Barn, &
   Breakfast
Mattey House B&B

Mt. Ashland Inn
Mt. Hood B&B
Our Place in the Country
The Parker House B&B
Portland's White House
Rags to Walkers Guest Ranch
Rosebriar Hotel
Sage Country Inn
Shaniko Historic Hotel
Squaw Creek B&B Inn
St. Bernards
Stang Manor Inn
Strawberry Mountain Inn
Winchester Country Inn

**Historic**
This list includes only properties
that are 100 years old or older.

**British Columbia**
Joan Brown's B&B
O Canada House
Ryan's B&B
Spinnakers Brewpub & Guest
   House

**Washington**
Ann Starrett Mansion
Blair House
Chick-ADee Inn
Chinaberry Hill
The Farm, a B&B
Fotheringham House B&B
Growly Bear B&B
Harbour House B&B
The Inn at Penn Cove
The James House
Katy's Inn
Lizzie's
Lytle House
Mildred's B&B
North Garden Inn

The Olde Glencove Hotel
Olympic Lights
The Purple House
A Quail's Roost Inn
Redmond House B&B
The Shelburne Country Inn
Stone Creek Inn
Susan's Surrey House
Swantown Inn
A Touch of Europe B&B Inn
Turtleback Farm Inn
Victorian Gardens 1888 B&B
Weinhard Hotel
The White Swan Guest House

**Oregon**
1900 Sears & Roebuck Home
Anderson's Boarding House
Antique Rose Inn
Arden Forest Inn
Baer House B&B
The Bingen Haus
Brier Rose Inn B&B
The Campbell House
Clear Creek Farm B&B
Clementine's B&B
Country Willows B&B Inn
Franklin Street Station
General Hooker's B&B
Gilbert Inn
Grandview B&B
Grant House
The Johnson House
MacMaster House
Marsh Haven Farm B&B
Mattey House B&B
Mill Inn
Oak Street Station B&B
Old Welches Inn
Riverside School House
Sandlake Country Inn
Shaniko Historic Hotel

**Island Setting**

**British Columbia**
Abigail's Hotel
Beaconsfield Inn
Birds of a Feather B&B
Claddagh House
Craigmyle Guest House
Dashwood Manor
The Haterleigh B&B
Joan Brown's B&B
Prior House B&B Inn
Ryan's B&B
Spinnakers Brewpub & Guest
    House
Wayward Navigator

**Washington**
Angels of the Sea B&B
Artist's Studio Loft B&B
Blair House
The Buchanan Inn
Buck Bay Farm
Channel House
Chestnut Hill B&B
Duffy House
Eagle's Nest Inn
Edenwild Inn
Hasty Pudding House
The Inn at Penn Cove
Inn at Swifts Bay
Island Tyme
Kangaroo House
The MacKay Harbor Inn
Nantucket Inn
Olympic Lights
Otters Pond B&B
Panacea
Rockaway Beach Guest House
Spring Bay Inn
The Tree House B&B
Trumpeter Inn

Turtleback Farm Inn
Wharfside B&B
The White Swan Guest House
Wildwood Manor

## Mountain Setting

### British Columbia
Mountainside Manor B&B

### Washington
All Season's River Inn
Autumn Pond
Blue Heron Inn
Brookhaven Lodge
Bush House Country Inn
Cascade Mountain Inn
Country Hill B&B
The Farm, a B&B
Flying L Ranch
Glacier Guest Suite
Grandma's House B&B
Haus Rohrbach
Llama Ranch B&B
Mountain Meadows Inn
Mt. Baker B&B
The Purple House
Simone's Groveland Cottage
    B&B Inn
St. Helens Manorhouse
A Stone's Throw B&B
Stratford Manor
Wellspring
The Whitetail Inn

### Oregon
The Beryl House
Chapman House B&B
Conklin's Guest House
DiamondStone Guest Lodge
Falcon's Crest Inn
Hotel Diamond
Juniper Acres
Mt. Ashland Inn

Mt. Hood B&B
Riverside School House
Squaw Creek B&B Inn
Steens Mountain Inn
Strawberry Mountain Inn

## Pet-Friendly B&Bs and Small Inns

These lodgings indicated a willingness to accommodate pets. Restrictions may apply, such as certain types of pets, pets in a specific room only, or pets during certain times of year only. In all cases, pet accommodations should be prearranged. If a fee or deposit applies, this will be listed in the profile.

### Zone 1
Dashwood Manor
Joan Brown's Bed & Breakfast,
Ryan's Bed & Breakfast

### Zone 2
BayView B&B
Pendrell Suites
River Run Cottages

### Zone 3
Manitou Lodge
Maple Rose Inn
Miller Tree Inn
Simone's Groveland Cottage

### Zone 4
Blair House
Harbor House
Island Tyme
Maple Meadows Bed & Breakfast

### Zone 5
Angels of the Sea
Illahee Manor (cottages only)
The Olde Glencove Hotel

**Zone 7**
Brookhaven Lodge at Clark's Skagit
  River Resort (no pets in B&B,
  but many other types of lodg-
  ings on compound)
Llama Ranch B&B
Mountain Meadows Inn
Mt. Baker Bed & Breakfast
Ovenell's Heritage Inn
St. Helens Manorhouse
Yodeler Inn B&B

**Zone 8**
Cobblestone Bed & Breakfast Inn
Hotel Usk
The Log House
Love's Victorian Bed & Breakfast
The Whitetail Inn

**Zone 9**
Birchfield Manor
Outlook Inn
The Purple House
Weinhard Hotel

**Zone 10**
Coos Bay Manor

**Zone 11**
Barnstormer Bed & Breakfast

**Zone 14**
Beryl House
Brookside B&B
Columbia Gorge Hotel
Hood River Hotel
Inn of the White Salmon
Mount Hood Hamlet

**Zone 15**
Clear Creek Farm
DiamondStone Guest Lodge
Sonshine B&B
Squaw Creek B&B Inn

**Romantic**

**British Columbia**
Abigail's Hotel
Bayview B&B
Beaconsfield Inn
Dashwood Manor
English Bay Inn
The Haterleigh B&B
Joan Brown's B&B
Laburnum Cottage
O Canada House
Prior House B&B Inn
River Run Cottages
Thistledown House
A Treehouse B&B

**Washington**
A Stone's Throw B&B
Alexander's Inn
All Season's River Inn
Angelica's B&B
Ann Starrett Mansion
Artist's Studio Loft
Birchfield Manor
BJ's Garden Gate
Boreas B&B Inn
Brigadoon B&B
Chestnut Hill B&B
China Beach B&B
Chinaberry Hill
Cozy Rose Inn
DeVoe Mansion
Domaine Madeleine
Dove House
Doveshire B&B
Eagle's Nest Inn
Fotheringham House B&B
Green Gables Guest House
Green Gables Inn
Guest House Cottages
Hummingbird Inn

Illahee Manor
Inn at Swifts Bay
Katy's Inn
La Cachette B&B
Love's Victorian B&B
Lytle House
Maple Meadows B&B
Maple Rose
Mary Kay's Romantic Whaley
    Mansion Inn
Mountain Meadows Inn
Panacea
Roaring River B&B
Rockaway Beach Guest House
Run of the River
Samish Point by the Bay
Schnauzer Crossing
Seasuns B&B
Shelburne Country Inn
St. Helens Manorhouse
Stratford Manor
Thornewood Castle
Touch of Europe B&B Inn
Victorian Gardens 1888 B&B
Wellspring

**Oregon**
Antique Rose Inn
Bandon Beach House
Blue Spruce B&B
Brightwood Guest House
Campbell House
Channel House
Clear Creek Farm B&B
Cliff House B&B
Columbia Gorge Hotel
Conklin's Guest House
Country Willows B&B Inn
Cowslip's Belle B&B
Doublegate Inn
Eagle's View B&B
The Edwin K B&B
Falcon's Crest Inn

Inn of the White Salmon
The Lion and the Rose
McKenzie View
Morning Star
Mt. Hood Hamlet
Old Welches Inn
Parker House
Pine Meadow Inn B&B
Portland's White House
Rags to Walkers Guest Ranch
Sage Country Inn
Sandlake Country Inn
Sather House
Sea Quest
Secret Garden
Serenity B&B
St. Bernards
Stang Manor Inn
Woods House

**Rustic**

**Washington**
Brookhaven Lodge
The Farm, a B&B
Flying L Ranch
Glacier Guest Suite
Stehekin Valley Ranch
Wellspring

**Oregon**
Frenchglen Hotel
Marsh Haven Farm B&B

**Solo-Oriented**

**British Columbia**
Bayview B&B
English Bay Inn
The Haterleigh B&B
Laburnum Cottage
West End Guest House

**Washington**
Boreas B&B Inn
Buck Bay Farm

Cady Lake Manor
Cascade Mountain Inn
China Beach B&B Retreat
Cooney Mansion B&B Inn
Duffy House
Foxbridge B&B
Green Gables Guesthouse
Growly Bear B&B
Log Castle B&B
Lytle House
Otters Pond B&B
Panacea
A Quail's Roost Inn
Ridgeway Farm B&B
Roberta's B&B
Run of the River
Salisbury House
Schnauzer Crossing
Spring Bay Inn
St. Helens Manorhouse
Thornewood Castle
Toad Hall
Warm Springs Inn

**Oregon**
Arden Forest Inn
Bandon Beach House
The Beryl House
The Bingen House
C&J Lodge
Chapman House B&B
Clear Creek Farm B&B
Doublegate Inn B&B
The Edwin K B&B
Floras Lake House B&B
Hunter Creek Farm Bed, Barn,
    & Breakfast
The Inn of the White Salmon
Lighthouse B&B
Mt. Hood B&B
Mt. Hood Hamlet B&B
Newport Belle B&B
Old Welches Inn

Our Place in the Country
Pine Meadows Inn B&B
Rags to Walkers Guest Ranch
Sea Quest B&B
Sylvia Beach Hotel

## Smoking Allowed

These accommodations allow
smoking somewhere in the house.
Check the profiles for details.

**British Columbia**
Kingston Hotel

**Washington**
Chuckanut Manor B&B
The Hotel Usk

**Oregon**
Brookside B&B
Columbia Gorge Hotel
The Elliott House
Gracie's Landing
Hood River Hotel

## Waterside

**British Columbia**
BayView B&B
Beachside B&B
Birds of a Feather B&B
River Run Cottages
Spinnakers Brewpub & Guest
    House

**Washington**
All Season's River Inn
Autumn Pond
BJ's Garden Gate
Boreas B&B Inn
Buck Bay Farm
Cady Lake Manor
China Beach B&B Retreat
Commencement Bay B&B
A Cottage Creek Inn
Cozy Rose InnDeNonno's B&B

Domaine Madeleine
Dove House
Duffy House
Flying L Ranch
Foxbridge B&B
Gaslight Inn
Grandma's House B&B
Greywolf Inn
Growly Bear B&B
Guest House Cottages
Harbinger Inn
Harbor House B&B
Haus Lorelei
The Hotel Usk
Illahee Manor
The Inn at Penn Cove
Inn at Swifts Bay
Island Tyme
The James House
La Cachette B&B
Log Castle B&B
The Log House
MacKay Harbor Inn
Mountain Meadows Inn
The Olde Glencove Hotel
Otters Pond B&B
Pine River Ranch
Roaring River B&B
Rockaway Beach Guest House
Run of the River
Samish Point by the Bay
Schnauzer Crossing
Selah Inn
Simone's Groveland Cottage B&B
   Inn
South Bay B&B

Spring Bay Inn
Stratford Manor
Thornewood Castle
The Tree House B&B
Trumpeter Inn
Tugboat Challenger
Turtleback Farm Inn
Warm Springs Inn
Wharfside B&B
The Whitetail Inn

**Oregon**
Anderson's Boarding House
Bandon Beach House
Brightwood Guest House
C&J Lodge
Cliff House B&B
Conklin's Guest House
Eagle's View B&B
Floras Lake House B&B
Gracie's Landing
Home by the Sea B&B
Home Farm B&B
Inn at Nesika Beach
Lakecliff Estate
Lighthouse B&B
Marquee House
McKenzie View
Morning Star
Mt. Hood B&B
Oak Street Station B&B
Old Welches Inn
Riverside School House
Sea Quest B&B
Squaw Creek B&B
Sylvia Beach Hotel

# British Columbia

From the very British double-decker buses and high teas of Victoria to the wild Fraser River and the pristine Canadian Rockies; from the cosmopolitan bustle of Vancouver to the bountiful orchards of the Okanogan, British Columbia embodies the best of the Pacific Northwest. Wilderness, mountains, rivers, cities, history, and charm abound in this unspoiled province, Canada's gateway to the Pacific.

British Columbia is vast and varied; this book makes no attempt to cover all the touring regions. Rather, we concentrated on the two major cities. Tourist-savvy Victoria and Vancouver are rife with bed-and-breakfasts and are easily accessible, just north of the United States–Canada border. Should you have the time and the inclination to explore beyond these metropolitan areas, your bed-and-breakfast hosts will likely be able to recommend lodgings in the less populated areas.

Vancouver Island is the home of Victoria and also the departure point (Port Hardy) for cruises heading north along the Inside Passage to Alaska. Victoria is situated on the island's southeast corner, while Port Hardy and other seaport communities nestle on the north shore. In between, beaches and bays provide prime whale-watching sites, acres of parks and forest land offer serenity and hiking opportunities, and the fishing is phenomenal. The increasingly popular Gulf Islands, with their slow pace and water-oriented lifestyle, lie just off the coast.

Over on the mainland, all roads lead to Vancouver. Shopping, culture, urban attractions, and amenities abound in this international melting pot. Nearby, the fertile Fraser Valley offers peaceful country scenery, beautiful Whistler provides an upscale ski resort atmosphere, and the Sunshine Coast, tucked between the Coast Mountain Range and the sea, beckons as a quiet alternative getaway.

As with all of the Pacific Northwest, the comforts of the city lie within minutes of the wonders of nature. Boating, hiking, and skiing are all within easy day-trip distance of the urban bed-and-breakfasts in this section. If your goal is to come face-to-face with a mountain goat, you might have to backpack out a day or two. But if you want to experience the grandeur of the Northwest, yet prefer starting the day with a hot shower and a bountiful breakfast, Victoria and Vancouver are great places from which to start.

When entering Canada, U.S. citizens should be prepared with two pieces of identification, such as driver's license, credit card, voter registration, or passport, including birth certificates or passports for children. U.S. residents who are not citizens should also have their green card, and citizens from other countries should have a valid passport. Also note that all bed-and-breakfast pricing for British Columbia is given in Canadian dollars (CDN$), which typically exchange at about 1.5 to the U.S. dollar.

# Zone 1
# Victoria

Quintessentially British, tourist-friendly Victoria perches at the southeastern tip of Vancouver Island. In and around Victoria, you'll find red double-decker buses, verdant parks, fine museums, incredible gardens, and more bed-and-breakfasts than you can shake a teacup at.

The focal point of the tourist's Victoria is the Inner Harbor. Clean and picturesque, it is the arrival point for many visitors and is surrounded by some of the city's most notable attractions.

The first stop for many is the ivy-covered Empress Hotel, where you can shell out CDN$39 per person for high tea. Yes, you're herded in like cattle; yes, it's overpriced; yes, it's touristy. Yes, you should do it anyway. It's a celebration, a visual delight, and, hey, you gotta eat lunch anyway. Call (250) 389-2727 at least two weeks in advance during summer; secure a table in the tea lobby, where seatings are at 12:30, 2, 3:30, or 5 daily.

The Royal British Columbia Museum is another must-see just off the harbor. Its natural and human history collections are truly impressive and expertly presented. Open 9 to 5 daily.

Other Inner Harbor attractions (besides prime people-watching) include the Undersea Gardens (a glass-walled observation bubble dips below the harbor surface), Crystal Gardens (tropical plant and butterfly conservatory), Royal Theatre (performing arts venue), the requisite Wax Museum, and the Parliament buildings. Nearby, Beacon Hill Park offers acres of shady respite, with walking paths, a wading pool, a rose garden, and even a place to play cricket.

Away from the harbor, the Fort Street shopping district draws antique aficionados, while Oak Bay Village is a more relaxed, trendier retail neighborhood than downtown. Architecture and history buffs enjoy Craigdarroch Castle (now a museum of the late-18th-century "good life"), Christ Church Cathedral, and Government House (the lieutenant governor's official residence) and its 30-acre gardens.

Speaking of gardens, don't miss 50 acre Butchart Gardens, with its Sunken, Japanese, Rose, and Italian gardens, and fountains too. Open all year, it's easy day-trip distance north of town by automobile or tour bus.

Just west of town, Fort Rodd Hill is a maritime and military historic site, complete with 19th-century buildings, beach, park, and lighthouse. It sits near Esquimalt Lagoon, a migratory bird sanctuary, and Royal Roads University's Hatley Park and "castle." Here, too, is access to the Galloping Goose Trail (one of Canada's nationwide networks of multiuse trails following abandoned railway beds) and Thetis Lake, a recreation area featuring fishing, swimming, nature trails, and horseback riding.

From the United States, the most common way to get to Victoria is by ferry. For service from Seattle, call (800) 888-2535 or visit www.victoria-clipper.com. From Port Angeles, call (800) 633-1589 (in Washington), (360) 452-8088, or (360) 457-4491 or visit www.cityofpa.net/ferry or www.northolympic.com/coho. From Bellingham (May–Oct.), call (800) 443-4552 or visit www.whales.com. From Anacortes to Sidney, BC (just north of Victoria), via the San Juan Islands, call (800) 843-3779 (in Washington) or visit www.wsdot.wa.gov.ferries/. For border crossing information, see page 56 in Zone 2.

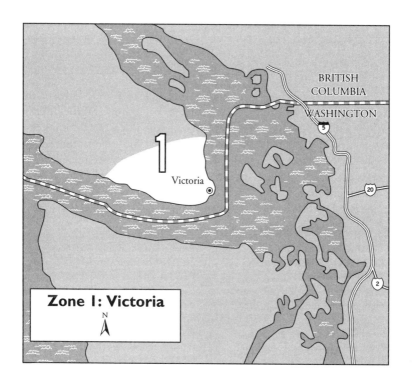

Zone 1: Victoria

N

**Victoria**
Abigail's Hotel, p. 40
Beaconsfield Inn, p. 41
Birds of a Feather B&B, p. 42
Claddagh House, p. 44
Craigmyle Guest House, p. 45
Dashwood Manor, p. 46
The Haterleigh B&B, p. 47
Joan Brown's B&B, p. 48
Prior House B&B Inn, p. 49
Ryan's B&B, p. 50
Spinnakers Brewpub & Guesthouse, p. 52
Wayward Navigator, p. 53

## ABIGAIL'S HOTEL, Victoria

Overall: ★★★★     Room Quality: A     Value: C     Price: CDN $179–$299

Abigail's strikes a nice balance between being a luxury hotel and a warm and friendly bed-and-breakfast. The number of rooms and the professional staff are more in keeping with a hotel experience, but the innkeepers, owners of the popular inn since 1996, strive for personal touches as well. The sunny open-to-the-kitchen dining room, for example, where guests can watch the chef in action, provides a welcome intimacy. Abigail's would make a nice "transition B&B" experience for those who aren't sure they'd like a bed-and-breakfast.

### SETTING & FACILITIES

**Location:** Downtown Victoria, north of Beacon Hill Park & east of the Inner Harbor
**Near:** Inner Harbor, Royal Theatre, Empress Hotel, museums, gardens, Parliament buildings, Beacon Hill Park, Christ Church Cathedral, Craigdarroch Castle, Fort Street antiquing
**Building:** 1930 apt. building
**Grounds:** Landscaped front patio

**Public Space:** Front patio, library, breakfast room
**Food & Drink:** Snacks (fruit, muffins), coffee & tea; sherry & hors d'oeuvres (afternoon); full breakfast; breakfast-in-bed option
**Recreation:** Double-decker bus touring, cricket, lawn bowling, golf, surf fishing
**Amenities & Services:** Pay phone off lobby, gift shop; concierge

### ACCOMMODATIONS

**Units:** 22 rooms & suites
**All Rooms:** Flowers, down duvet, robes, hairdryer, guest guide
**Some Rooms:** Whirlpool, fireplace, CD, mini-fridge, canopy bed, balcony
**Bed & Bath:** Mostly queens or kings, some w/ 2 doubles; private ensuite bath
**Favorites:** Any of the six "celebration suites"

**Comfort & Decor:** Soft colors, country furnishings, quality appointments; rooms are carpeted. Six newly renovated "celebration suites" include four-poster king beds, wood-burning fireplaces, Arts and Crafts–style furnishings, and marble baths with double whirlpool tubs. The library has a hardwood floor and fireplace.

## RATES, RESERVATIONS, & RESTRICTIONS

**Deposit:** 1st night; 7-day cancellation or forfeit unless rebooked
**Discounts:** Off-season, special packages
**Credit Cards:** V, MC, AE
**Check-in/Out:** 3–9/11
**Smoking:** Outside only
**Pets:** No
**Kids:** 10 & older only

**Minimum Stay:** None
**Open:** All year
**Hosts:** Daniel & Frauke Behune
906 McClure St.
Victoria, BC, V8V 3E7
(800) 561-6565 or (250) 388-5363
Fax: (250) 388-7787
innkeeper@abigailshotel.com
www.abigailshotel.com

## BEACONSFIELD INN, Victoria

Overall: ★★★★½     Room Quality: A     Value: D     Price: CDN $200–$350

You're Lord of the Manor in this stately Edwardian heritage inn. Soft strains of classical music greet you in the dark-wood-paneled entry foyer, imparting a sense of British majesty. The impressive library is designed for reading and relaxation and looks like the perfect place to unwind before, say, a fox hunt. Prices are staggering, but you are assured a certain standard of comfort (be sure to note the off-season and shoulder-season discounts, and factor in the exchange rate for the Canadian dollar if applicable). A bit less personal than some smaller establishments. Excellent location.

### SETTING & FACILITIES

**Location:** Downtown just east of Inner Harbor & just north of Beacon Hill Park
**Near:** Inner Harbor, gardens, Royal Theatre, Empress Hotel, museums, Parliament buildings, Beacon Hill Park, Christ Church Cathedral
**Building:** Edwardian manor
**Grounds:** Neat, attractive yard; lavender, roses, dwarf maples
**Public Space:** DR, sunroom, library

**Food & Drink:** In-room wine & chocolates; beverages in guest fridge; snacks, tea, & sherry (afternoon); full breakfast; cont'l option always avail.
**Recreation:** Double-decker bus touring, cricket, lawn bowling, golf, surf fishing
**Amenities & Services:** Guest fridge, ice, games, books, pay phone; fitness club nearby, concierge

### ACCOMMODATIONS

**Units:** 9 guest rooms & suites
**All Rooms:** Hairdryer, robes, English antiques, down comforters
**Some Rooms:** Whirlpool, fireplace, stained glass window(s), desk, sitting area, private patio
**Bed & Bath:** Queens; private ensuite baths

**Favorites:** Attic, Garden, Emily Carr, Gatekeeper's
**Comfort & Decor:** Exclusive men's club ambiance, with deep, rich colors and stately furnishings upholstered in leather or tapestry/brocade. The masculinity is offset by gilt-framed artwork and floral accents.

### RATES, RESERVATIONS, & RESTRICTIONS

**Deposit:** Visa or MC; 7-day cancellation, forfeit unless rebooked; $20 cancellation fee
**Discounts:** Off-season, shoulder season; CDN $65 add'l person
**Credit Cards:** V, MC
**Check-in/Out:** 3–6/11
**Smoking:** Outside only
**Pets:** No
**Kids:** No

**Minimum Stay:** 2 nights most weekends
**Open:** All year
**Hosts:** Con & Judi Sollid, owners; Janet & Dale, assistant innkeepers
998 Humboldt St.
Victoria, BC V8V 2Z8
(888) 884-4044 or (250) 384-4044
Fax: (250) 384-4052
beaconsfield@islandnet.com
www.islandnet.com/beaconsfield

## BIRDS OF A FEATHER B&B, Victoria

| Overall: ★★★ | Room Quality: C | Value: A | Price: CDN $85–$120 |
|---|---|---|---|

This waterfront in-home bed-and-breakfast has an exquisite location and warm, casual hosts. Dieter and Annette's motto, "Be more than just a tourist . . . be our guest!" is apparent in everything they do. Their attitude is one of total hospitality. Their homestay bed-and-breakfast includes shared living facilities, and they enjoy interacting with their guests (as do their well-behaved pets). Incredible location on the lagoon provides great views (lighthouse, Mt. Baker, Victoria skyline) and recreation opportunities. Plan to stay several days and enjoy the natural setting as well as the easy access to downtown, "tourist Victoria."

## SETTING & FACILITIES

**Location:** On the shore of Esquimalt Lagoon, a few miles west of Victoria proper
**Near:** Wildlife preserve, Royal Roads University and Hatley Castle, Galloping Goose Trail, lighthouse, Fort Rodd Hill, 700-acre old-growth forest; short drive to Victoria
**Building:** Private waterfront home
**Grounds:** Pretty lawn, stream, views
**Public Space:** LR, DR, decks, hot-tub atrium

**Food & Drink:** Snacks, tea, coffee (24 hours); full breakfast
**Recreation:** Casual fishing, crabbing, clamming, historic touring
**Amenities & Services:** Bikes, rowboats (w/ life jackets), campfire pit, phone, 1808 piano, sound system, books (esp. bird field guides), games, kennel, hot tub; airport pickup & similar courtesies, e-mail

## ACCOMMODATIONS

**Units:** 3 guest rooms
**All Rooms:** TV, mini-fridge
**Some Rooms:** Extra beds &/or roll-away potential
**Bed & Bath:** Double, queen, twins, or king; private baths
**Favorites:** Fancy Feathers
**Comfort & Decor:** Fresh, pale, homey, country-style decor. Rooms

have birding themes: Fancy Feathers is largest, with a queen, a daybed, and room for 2 roll-aways; Bird House is somewhat dark but very private, with a double bed; Just Nesting has a twin/king conversion bed, plus roll-away capacity. Central heat and air; no room controls.

## RATES, RESERVATIONS, & RESTRICTIONS

**Deposit:** Credit card; 10-day cancellation requested
**Discounts:** Extended stays; CDN $25 add'l person
**Credit Cards:** V, MC
**Check-in/Out:** After 2/11 (flexible)
**Smoking:** Outside only
**Pets:** Not in rooms; on-site kennel
**Kids:** OK in Fancy Feathers and Just Nesting

**Minimum Stay:** None
**Open:** All year
**Hosts:** Dieter Gerhard & Annette Moen
206 Portsmouth Dr.
Victoria, BC V9C 1R9
(250) 391-8889
frontdesk@VictoriaLodging.com
www.VictoriaLodging.com

## CLADDAGH HOUSE, Victoria

| Overall: ★★★ | Room Quality: D | Value: C | Price: CDN $95–$195 |
|---|---|---|---|

Very quiet home on periphery of downtown's bustle, with good access to both the touristy activities of downtown and the pleasant neighborhood of Oak Bay. The current hosts took over this established inn in 1998 and are working to modernize some things—witness the big-screen TV and high-tech sound system in the sunroom. The Erin Room's bed is a futon, Ardmore's is a twin/king conversion. Rostrevor is larger and has a private entrance, but a double bed. The feature suite, Tara, is 1,050 square feet and sleeps up to six with two sofa-sleepers and a king.

### SETTING & FACILITIES

**Location:** East of downtown near Oak Bay
**Near:** Oak Bay Village (shops, restaurants), Government House Gardens, University of Victoria
**Building:** 1913 character home
**Grounds:** Herb & vegetable garden, raspberries, flowers
**Public Space:** LR, DR, sunroom, balcony

**Food & Drink:** Coffee & sherry; in-room truffles; full breakfast or early cont'l option
**Recreation:** Shopping, antiquing, golf, surf fishing, theater
**Amenities & Services:** Big-screen TV, video library, ensuite phone available, sound system; guest pick-up

### ACCOMMODATIONS

**Units:** 3 guest rooms, 1 suite
**All Rooms:** Cut flowers, filtered ice water
**Some Rooms:** Tub or whirlpool, TV, private entrance, tea service
**Bed & Bath:** Queen or twin/king conversion; ensuite private baths
**Favorites:** Tara Suite

**Comfort & Decor:** Comfortable older home with an emphasis on relaxed conviviality rather than deluxe or antique decor. Raspberry and teal dining room. Eclectic mix of old and modern motifs. Beds could be improved. Rooms have individual heat controls.

### RATES, RESERVATIONS, & RESTRICTIONS

**Deposit:** Credit card; 14-day cancellation
**Discounts:** Extended stay, off-season; CDN $25 add'l person
**Credit Cards:** V, MC, AE
**Check-in/Out:** 4–6 or by arrangement/11
**Smoking:** Outside only
**Pets:** No
**Kids:** By arrangement, in suite only

**Minimum Stay:** 2 nights preferred on weekends
**Open:** All year
**Hosts:** Ken Brown & Elaine Johnston
1761 Lee Ave.
Victoria, BC V8R 4W7
(250) 370-2816
Fax: (250) 592-0228
claddagh@pinc.com
www.bc-biz.com/claddaghhouse

## CRAIGMYLE GUEST HOUSE, Victoria

| Overall: ★★½ | Room Quality: D | Value: A | Price: CDN $65–$165 |
|---|---|---|---|

This European-style guest house offers value, breakfast, experienced hosts, and good location. Operated by Jim and Cathy since 1975, Craigmyle was probably Victoria's first bed-and-breakfast. Rooms and common areas are cheerful and adequate, always spotless, refurbished as needed for wear and tear, rather than for the latest fashion. Hosts live next door; you have a key for 24-hour access. Good value. Off-season rates as low as CDN $25 per person per night, including breakfast.

### SETTING & FACILITIES

**Location:** East of harbors
**Near:** Government House Gardens, Fort Street antiquing, Inner Harbor
**Building:** 1913 guest house
**Grounds:** Pleasant rear yard looks up at Craigdarroch Castle; hillside front yard
**Public Space:** Guest lounge, back patio

**Food & Drink:** Tea & coffee (24 hours); simple full English breakfast
**Recreation:** Castle tour, double-decker bus tours, cricket, lawn bowling, golf
**Amenities & Services:** TV/VCR, guest kitchen (w/ fridge & micro), pay phone, iron

### ACCOMMODATIONS

**Units:** 17 guest rooms
**All Rooms:** Basic, clean, comfortable, but small
**Some Rooms:** Tile bath, tub, extra bed or sofa-sleeper
**Bed & Bath:** Various beds; all private baths, most ensuite
**Favorites:** #23 is best; #3 good value; come early & look around

**Comfort & Decor:** Basic to the point of Spartan, this hotel will be comfortable to those accustomed to European budget lodgings. Some sound transference; carpet helps. Furnishings and wallpapers are cheerful, mixed, and modest, tending toward threadbare. Windows open for ventilation.

### RATES, RESERVATIONS, & RESTRICTIONS

**Deposit:** $5 nonrefundable; 5-day cancellation requested
**Discounts:** Off-season; CDN $80–95 dbl.; CDN $140–165 family
**Credit Cards:** V, MC, AE
**Check-in/Out:** 2–6/10:30 (flexible—please call)
**Smoking:** Outside only
**Pets:** No
**Kids:** Welcome

**Minimum Stay:** None
**Open:** All year
**Hosts:** Jim & Catherine Pace
1037 Craigdarroch Rd.
Victoria, BC V8S 2A5
(888) 595-5411 or (250) 595-5411
Fax: (250) 370-5276
craigmyle@vicsurf.com
www.bctravel.com/craigmyle.html

## DASHWOOD MANOR, Victoria

Overall: ★★★★     Room Quality: B     Value: C     Price: CDN $75–$285

This Edwardian-style Tudor mansion offers 14 unique suites with views and self-serve ensuite breakfast. Designed and built for British Columbia Light & Power Company manager Arthur Lineham, the edifice includes solid granite foundation and lower walls and massive exposed beams. Woodwork includes slashed grain fir and white oak paneling, and hardwood flooring. The highly visible landmark, perched above the Straits of Juan de Fuca, was purchased by Derek Dashwood and family in 1978, and has been renovated to the tune of three-quarters of a million dollars. Surprisingly, children and pets are welcome.

### SETTING & FACILITIES

**Location:** At SE corner of Beacon Hill Park, corner of Dallas & Cook, facing Straits
**Near:** Inner Harbor attractions
**Building:** 1912 Tudor mansion
**Grounds:** Narrow lawn w/ border plantings
**Public Space:** Guest reception area
**Food & Drink:** Self-serve breakfast
groceries & coffee service in room
**Recreation:** Museums, double-decker bus tours, lawn bowling, golf, surf fishing, theater
**Amenities & Services:** Guest phone, laundry facilities; vacation packages (e.g., golf, romance, cruise-and-car, train)

### ACCOMMODATIONS

**Units:** 14 suites
**All Rooms:** Kitchen or kitchenette, TV
**Some Rooms:** Fireplace, whirlpool, balcony
**Bed & Bath:** Queen beds (some also have sofa-sleepers); private baths
**Favorites:** Buckingham, Somerset, Windsor, Cambridge
**Comfort & Decor:** Beamed ceilings, chandeliers, leaded glass. First-floor suites feature fireplaces and opulent Edwardian decor. Second-floor suites vary; some include whirlpools, some have exceptional ocean views. Third-floor suites include celebration units like the romantic Somerset.

### RATES, RESERVATIONS, & RESTRICTIONS

**Deposit:** 1st night; 14-day cancellation (CDN $20)
**Discounts:** Longer stays, off-season, packages; CDN $45 add'l person
**Credit Cards:** V, MC
**Check-in/Out:** 2–10/11
**Smoking:** Outside only
**Pets:** Welcome
**Kids:** Welcome
**No-Nos:** Smoking inside
**Minimum Stay:** None
**Open:** All year
**Hosts:** Derek Dashwood, family, & staff
One Cook St.
Victoria, BC, V8V 3W6
(800) 667-5517 or (250) 385-5517
Fax: (250) 383-1760
reservations@dashwoodmanor.com
www.dashwoodmanor.com

## THE HATERLEIGH B&B, Victoria

Overall: ★★★★★   Room Quality: A   Value: C   Price: CDN $187–$297

Perfect combination of professionally operated luxury and hands-on, friendly hosts. (Often, an inn this classy is swarming with staff; here, Paul and Elizabeth do everything except the behind-the-scenes house-keeping.) "Legendary" breakfasts include exotic and sculpted fresh fruit, fresh breads, and entrees such as West Coast Scones, topped with salmon, cheese, mushrooms, and Hollandaise sauce. A convivial atmos-phere prevails at these celebration meals. For a top-of-the-line Victoria experience, Haterleigh is our favorite, based on atmosphere and decor, food, hosts, and location.

### SETTING & FACILITIES

**Location:** 2 blocks south of Inner Harbor
**Near:** Undersea Gardens, museums, Inner Harbor, Parliament buildings, Empress Hotel, Crystal Garden, Bea-con Hill Park
**Building:** 6,000-sq.-ft. heritage mansion
**Grounds:** Front lawn w/ flower gar-dens; brick side drive; small back porch

**Public Space:** Guest lobby, porch/deck, guest LR
**Food & Drink:** Afternoon sherry; lemonade & iced tea in season; full breakfast (see comments)
**Recreation:** Double-decker bus touring, lawn games, golf, surf fishing, theater
**Amenities & Services:** Guest phone (in lobby), menus; surprises and delightful extras

### ACCOMMODATIONS

**Units:** 6 guest rooms
**All Rooms:** Personalized guest guides, handmade chocolates, robes, exceptional antiques, designer bedding & window treatments, down duvet, hairdryer
**Some Rooms:** Sitting/dressing area, jetted tub, English clawfoot tub, view, private deck
**Bed & Bath:** Queen or king; private ensuite baths
**Favorites:** Each is exceptional

**Comfort & Decor:** Fabulous origi-nal turn-of-the-century stained glass—some of the most impressive we've ever seen in a private home. High ceilings, coving and molding, sub-tle wallpapers, fireplaces. Each guest room is spacious and luxurious, with ironed-on-the-bed duvets and other classy touches. Rooms have individu-ally controlled thermostats and win-dows that open.

## RATES, RESERVATIONS, & RESTRICTIONS

**Deposit:** 1st night; 14-day cancellation
**Discounts:** Off-season
**Credit Cards:** V, MC
**Check-in/Out:** 4/11
**Smoking:** No
**Pets:** No
**Kids:** Over 16 only
**Minimum Stay:** 2 nights July & Aug.

**Open:** All year
**Hosts:** Paul & Elizabeth Kelly
243 Kingston St.
Victoria, BC V8V 1V5
(250) 384-9995
Fax: (250) 384-1935
paulk@haterleigh.com
www.haterleigh.com

## JOAN BROWN'S B&B, Victoria

Overall: ★★★★    Room Quality: B    Value: A    Price: CDN $80–$150

Step through the screening of a privacy hedge into another world—late 19th-century elegance. The columned entrance sits symmetrically in the middle of a wide, manicured lawn. Joan, a vivacious and gracious hostess with loads of charm, has had the bed-and-breakfast since 1989. Rooms are oversized and elegant. Guests are asked to be out of the home 10:30–4 (flexible). If you need the predictability of modern hotel amenities (TV, phone, etc.), look elsewhere, but if you want to experience the grandeur of another era, you can't top Joan Brown's. One of our favorites in Victoria.

## SETTING & FACILITIES

**Location:** East of downtown, near Government House Gardens
**Near:** Craigdarroch Castle, Fort Street, Inner Harbor activities
**Building:** 1881 Georgian-Italianate mansion
**Grounds:** Huge lawn & garden; tall hedges

**Public Space:** Guest lounge, DR, library
**Food & Drink:** Sherry; elegant full breakfast
**Recreation:** Museums, cricket, golf, surf fishing, theater, antiquing
**Amenities & Services:** Groups, dinners, & luncheons

## ACCOMMODATIONS

**Units:** 5 guest rooms (w/ overflow potential)

**All Rooms:** Spacious, ornate, gracious; robes

**Some Rooms:** Sitting room, decorative fireplace, balcony, tile bath, tub bath

**Bed & Bath:** Various beds; some private baths, some shared

**Favorites:** Yellow-and-blue room that was originally main lounge

**Comfort & Decor:** 14-foot ceilings in many areas. Original stained glass and chandelier in stunningly opulent main lounge. Ornate plasterwork and woodwork, original floors, gilt-accent ceilings.

## RATES, RESERVATIONS, & RESTRICTIONS

**Deposit:** 1st night

**Discounts:** None

**Credit Cards:** Not accepted

**Check-in/Out:** Flexible

**Smoking:** Outside only

**Pets:** OK in some rooms; by arrangement

**Kids:** OK in some rooms; by arrangement

**Minimum Stay:** None

**Open:** All year

**Host:** Joan Brown
729 Pemberton Rd.
Victoria, BC V8S 3R3
(250) 592-5929

## PRIOR HOUSE B&B INN, Victoria

Overall: ★★★★½     Room Quality: A     Value: C     Price: CDN $195–$270

If good food and lots of it is a priority for you, Prior House delivers. Between the extensive breakfast and the high tea, complete with rich, delicious homemade treats (all included in room rate), innkeeper Agnes says "guests leave more cuddly than when they arrived." Gardens are beautiful, tidy, and colorful; patio is a quiet place to relax after a bustling day of touring. Prior House offers 8,500 square feet of Edwardian elegance and easy access to all downtown attractions.

## SETTING & FACILITIES

**Location:** Just NE of downtown
**Near:** Craigdarroch Castle, gardens, Fort Street, Inner Harbor
**Building:** 1912 Edwardian Lt. Governor's Mansion
**Grounds:** Large lawn, extensive flowers, brick patio, hedges
**Public Space:** Guest parlor, DR, library, terrace, mezzanine sitting area
**Food & Drink:** Sherry anytime; full afternoon high tea; full breakfast (ensuite avail.)
**Recreation:** Museums, double-decker bus touring, lawn games, golf, surf fishing, antiquing
**Amenities & Services:** Piano, video library, guest phone, extensive toiletries/sundries basket; high tea free to guests

## ACCOMMODATIONS

**Units:** 3 guest rooms, 4 suites
**All Rooms:** TV/VCR, fridge, hairdryer, robes, down (or hypoallergenic) comforters
**Some Rooms:** View, iron, sitting area, desk, library, fireplace, whirlpool
**Bed & Bath:** Queen or king; private baths, all but 1 ensuite
**Favorites:** Lt. Governor's Suite
**Comfort & Decor:** 11 fireplaces grace the rooms and common areas. Dark wood, rich brocade, abundant antiques, fresh flowers, "English elegance." Individual room heaters and blackout draperies ensure a good night's sleep.

## RATES, RESERVATIONS, & RESTRICTIONS

**Deposit:** 1st night; 14-day cancellation; $15 fee
**Discounts:** Off-season, shoulder season; CDN $45 add'l person
**Credit Cards:** V, MC
**Check-in/Out:** 4–6 or by arrangement/noon
**Smoking:** Outside only
**Pets:** No
**Kids:** No in most rooms; OK in one suite by arrangement
**Minimum Stay:** 2 days, weekends, holidays, July & Aug.
**Open:** All year
**Hosts:** Candis & Ted Cooperrider, Agnes & Alan Campbell
620 St. Charles
Victoria, BC V8S 3N7
(250) 592-8847
Fax: (250) 592-8223
innkeeper@priorhouse.com
www.priorhouse.com

## RYAN'S B&B, Victoria

Overall: ★★★½    Room Quality: C    Value: C    Price: CDN $125–$185

Spacious Victorian with large rooms and bountiful breakfasts (e.g., "white cloud" buttermilk biscuits with homemade jams and jellies, entrees such as flans, frittatas, crepes, or stuffed French toast, plus turkey sausage and Arabian coffee). Upstairs rooms are more charming (i.e., more period furnishings and Victorian appearance), while downstairs rooms are a bit more modern (i.e., modern bath fixtures, TVs), though still with a few well-placed antiques. Ryan's has been a bed-and-breakfast since the early 1990s, and Kathy, your knowledgeable, helpful, unpretentious hostess, has been the proprietor since 1996.

## SETTING & FACILITIES

**Location:** 3 blocks south of Inner Harbor
**Near:** Undersea Gardens, museums, Inner Harbor, Parliament buildings, Empress Hotel, Crystal Garden, Beacon Hill Park
**Building:** 1892 Californian-style Victorian "bungalow" (not to be confused with "small")
**Grounds:** Double lot w/ wonderful flowers
**Public Space:** DR, main guest parlor, wraparound porch, downstairs guest parlor
**Food & Drink:** Afternoon sherry in high season; full breakfast
**Recreation:** Double-decker bus touring, antiquing, cricket, golf, surf fishing, theater
**Amenities & Services:** Games, pay phone, guidebooks; concierge services, special treats for special occasions

## ACCOMMODATIONS

**Units:** 8 guest rooms
**All Rooms:** High ceilings
**Some Rooms:** Clawfoot tub, bubble bath, four-poster bed, private entrance, sitting area, desk, view, private deck, TV
**Bed & Bath:** Queens (2 w/ extra single); private baths (7 of 8 ensuite)
**Favorites:** Room 4: premiere room; Room 8: private entrance; Room 5: small deck
**Comfort & Decor:** Beautifully restored home has exceptional woodwork, extra-high ceilings, ornate crown moldings, and many original light fixtures. Decor includes fresh, well-coordinated paint and wallpapers and many antique and period furnishings. Area rugs over carpet or hardwood floors. Steam heat; some rooms with individual controls.

## RATES, RESERVATIONS, & RESTRICTIONS

**Deposit:** Credit card; 7-day cancellation or forfeit unless rebooked
**Discounts:** Off-season; CDN $30 add'l person
**Credit Cards:** V, MC
**Check-in/Out:** Flexible, early (luggage drop-off can be really early, just ask)/11
**Smoking:** Outside only
**Pets:** By arrangement; host pets in residence
**Kids:** By arrangement
**Minimum Stay:** None
**Open:** All year
**Host:** Kathy Jensen
224 Superior St.
Victoria, BC V8V 1T3
(250) 389-0012
Fax: (250) 389-2857
ryans@bc1.com
www.bc1.com/users/ryans

## SPINNAKERS BREWPUB & GUEST HOUSE, Victoria

Overall: ★★★★½    Room Quality: A    Value: C    Price: CDN $169–$250

Spinnnakers Brewpub (opened 1984—Canada's first licensed in-house brewpub since Prohibition) is a clever, convivial place, with a *Cheers* atmosphere and a waterfront view. Owners purchased the decorous 1884 Victorian two doors down and converted it to a classy five-room guest house in 1998. At our visit, they were renovating an adjacent-to-pub apartment building into four additional rooms—roomy, modern suites with a host of luxury amenities. Hosts and pub staff work hard to ensure your satisfaction.

### SETTING & FACILITIES

**Location:** Just across the harbor from downtown
**Near:** Victoria Harbor, harbor ferry stop, Maritime Museum, Market Square, Bastion Square, Inner Harbor; 15-min. waterfront walk to downtown
**Building:** 1884 heritage guest house and stylish contemporary garden apt.
**Grounds:** Limited; English culinary herb garden
**Public Space:** Adjacent restaurant
**Food & Drink:** Coffee basket to your room in a.m.; full breakfast at Spinnaker's Restaurant
**Recreation:** Paved waterfront jogging path; downtown Victoria activities
**Amenities & Services:** Book exchange library

## ACCOMMODATIONS

**Units:** 9 guest rooms in 2 buildings
**All Rooms:** Robes, highest-quality bath amenities, phone, hairdryer, umbrella
**Some Rooms:** Outside patio or deck, whirlpool, steamer shower, kitchen or access
**Bed & Bath:** Queens; ensuite private baths
**Favorites:** Comparable—choose the 1884 guest house for antique elegance or the garden apt. building for spacious, contemporary lodgings

**Comfort & Decor:** Completely refurbished buildings include top-of-the-line bath fixtures, well-chosen antiques, quality beds, fine artwork, upscale window treatments and bedding, and comfortable, high-end furnishings. Soft, pale tones (ecru, pale peach) on walls complement the largely original wood moldings. Individual heat controls in rooms.

## RATES, RESERVATIONS, & RESTRICTIONS

**Deposit:** Credit card; 48-hour cancellation
**Discounts:** Off-season, extended stay; some rooms accommodate 4–5 people
**Credit Cards:** V, MC, AE, D
**Check-in/Out:** After 3/11 (very flexible)
**Smoking:** No
**Pets:** No

**Kids:** Welcome
**Minimum Stay:** None
**Open:** All year
**Hosts:** Paul Hadfield & Mary Jameson
308 Catherine St.
Victoria, BC V9A 3S8
(250) 384-2739
Fax: (250) 384-3246
spinnakers@spinnakers.com
www.spinnakers.com

## WAYWARD NAVIGATOR, Victoria

Overall: ★★★★      Room Quality: B      Value: A      Price: CDN $95

Wayward Navigator offers a well-executed nautical theme, with 1,200 square feet of guest lounge area, a boatload of amenities, and a five-star breakfast—one of the most ambitious in the business. (Sample menu: fresh fruit cup with molded sherbet, hearty date-nut muffins, smoked candied salmon, freshly squeezed orange juice, regular or meat-free eggs Benedict with asparagus, roasted spicy rosemary potatoes, and a side of Barry's Famous Beans.) If Nancy and Barry had a Victorian home two blocks from the Inner Harbor, it would be the most sought-after bed-and-breakfast in Victoria. They take hospitality to the extreme and are doing a fabulous job.

## SETTING & FACILITIES

**Location:** A few miles west of Victoria proper
**Near:** Galloping Goose Trail, Thetis Lake, downtown
**Building:** Private hillside residence
**Grounds:** Terraced backyard, decks, patio, outdoor fireplace, hot-tub gazebo
**Public Space:** LR/guest lounge; English pub room w/ antique bar; decks
**Food & Drink:** Beverages & snacks; amazing multicourse breakfast
**Recreation:** Jogging, bicycling, in-line skating; Victoria activities
**Amenities & Services:** Hot tub, guest phone, cable, VCR, sound system, wet bar (w/ micro., kettle, fridge, coffeemaker), extra treats for celebrations & longer stays, umbrellas, games, pinball machine; hosts' fax avail., Internet info searches, e-mail retrieval

## ACCOMMODATIONS

**Units:** 2 guest rooms (expansion to 4 units planned)
**All Rooms:** Robes, hairdryer, down comforter, dimmer switches
**Some Rooms:** Desk, bathtub
**Bed & Bath:** Queens (brass or sleigh); private bath
**Favorites:** Quite similar: White Star (ensuite bath w/ tub); Great Eastern (slightly larger, desk, shower-only bath adjacent)
**Comfort & Decor:** Mahogany, cherry, and brass decor in the White Star guest room; mahogany, walnut, and crystal in the Great Eastern. Museum-quality prints, seafaring history abounds. Spotlessly clean. Comfortable, well-ventilated rooms are carpeted and have individual thermostats.

## RATES, RESERVATIONS, & RESTRICTIONS

**Deposit:** 1st night; 48-hour cancellation or refund subject to circumstances and rebooking
**Discounts:** None
**Credit Cards:** V, MC
**Check-in/Out:** 3–6 or by arrangement/11 (flexible)
**Smoking:** Outside only
**Pets:** Call
**Kids:** OK, but no more than 2 people per room
**Minimum Stay:** None
**Open:** All year
**Hosts:** Nancy Fry & Barry Rinas
337 Damon Dr.
Victoria, BC V9B 5G5
(888) 478-6808 or (250) 478-6836
Fax: (250) 478-6850
nancy@wayward.com
www.wayward.com

# Zone 2
# Vancouver

Cosmopolitan and friendly, Vancouver sits on the southwest shore of the British Columbia mainland, across the Strait of Georgia from Victoria and Vancouver Island. From the antique shops of Gastown to the family attractions of Stanley Park, from the hiking and skiing at Grouse Mountain or nearby Whistler to the exotic sights of the West Coast's second-largest Chinatown, this bustling port city literally has something for everybody, including plenty of bed-and-breakfasts.

The downtown core is dense and bustling, with several quality bed-and-breakfasts and attractions, including Stanley Park (gardens, aquarium, petting zoo, trails, mini-golf), Robson and Denman Streets shopping areas, and English Bay and beach. Hard-core shoppers will head for Granville Island, a "Fantasy Island" for the credit card set. At the east side of downtown, Gastown is worth seeing—a restored historic district complete with cobblestone streets, gas lamps, specialty stores, and restaurants. And Vancouver's Chinatown is not to be missed. Second only to San Francisco's, it's a kaleidoscope of Asian sights, sounds, tastes, and smells.

The area north of downtown is divided between West Vancouver (north and west of downtown) and North Vancouver (farther north). West Vancouver is home to a few bed-and-breakfasts and the local shopping, restaurant, beach, and park district referred to as Ambleside. This district includes our only on-the-water Vancouver property.

North Vancouver is the woodsy residential margin of the city, where the high country meets the city. Beautiful homes, quiet parks, and outstanding bed-and-breakfasts are found here. Here, too, is the overrated Capilano Suspension Bridge and its associated Disneyesque exhibits. A far better experience (unless you're traveling with children or other hard-to-amuse entertainment junkies) is the no-fee Capilano River Regional Park, a beautiful area for strolling and getting away from it all. Hard-core hikers may want to tackle the Baden-Powell Trail or Grouse Mountain. At the far north edge of town, Grouse Mountain is also a family ski hill with 13 downhill runs and an excellent restaurant. Serious skiers head for Whistler, a full-fledged ski and golf destination resort 75 miles north of Vancouver.

The area south of downtown has much to recommend it as well. More bed-and-breakfast value for the buck, for one thing, and a number of very nice, well-established properties from which to choose. On the south shore of English Bay is the upbeat Kitsilano District, an area with ethnic restaurants and fun retail shops. Also south of downtown, the University of British Columbia campus includes the renowned Museum of Anthropology. Other attractions in the south-of-downtown districts include Queen Elizabeth Park, Bloedel Floral Conservatory, and VanDusen Botanical Garden.

Farther south, in the town of Ladner, we've profiled one really special bed-and-breakfast on the Fraser River. Nearby on Westham Island, you'll find Reifel Migratory Bird Sanctuary, with its walking trails, gift shop, and more than 200 species of birds.

Vancouver is easily accessed from the United States. Simply drive north on Interstate 5 until it becomes Canada Highway 99. Using this route, you'll pass through the picturesque and often busy Peach Arch international park and border crossing—not a great choice on a Friday evening or Sunday afternoon. Locals often take the Highway 539 (Canada Highway 13) "truck crossing" about a dozen miles east of the I-5 melee, or the Sumas crossing, another 10 miles east. From points in Canada, the Trans-Canada Highway will get you to Vancouver. Vancouver is also served by the Vancouver International Airport and offers public transportation as well as rental cars and taxi service.

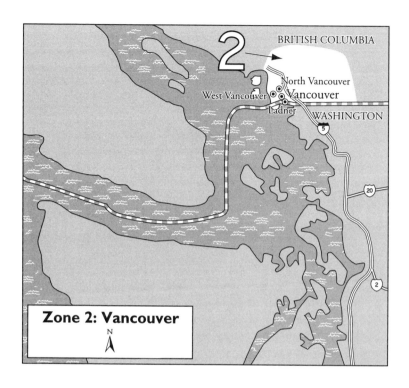

## Zone 2: Vancouver

N

**Ladner**
River Run Cottages, p. 58

**North Vancouver**
Braemar Manor, p. 59
Laburnum Cottage, p. 60
Mountainside Manor B&B, p. 61
ThistleDown House, p. 63

**Vancouver**
English Bay Inn, p. 64
Johnson Heritage House, p. 65
Kingston Hotel, p. 66
The Langtry, p. 67
O Canada House, p. 68
Pendrell Suites, p. 69
Penny Farthing Inn, p. 70
A TreeHouse B&B, p. 71
West End Guest House, p. 73

**West Vancouver**
BayView B&B, p. 74
Beachside B&B, p. 75

## RIVER RUN COTTAGES, Ladner

Overall: ★★★★★     Room Quality: A     Value: A     Price: CDN $120–$175

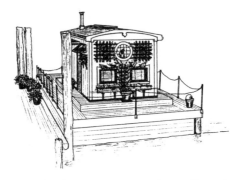

Arrive to the sound of soft music, a personal note from the innkeepers (with special information pertinent to your unit, plus a map and the next morning's breakfast menu), and a fresh-baked treat. The River Run Cottages are a collection of on-the-water units run by friendly innkeepers who are accessible but never intrusive. A thorough in-room guide provides you with everything you need to know to function independently in your cottage as well as to enjoy the surrounding region. Very upscale appointments, yet extremely relaxed atmosphere.

### SETTING & FACILITIES

**Location:** On the Fraser River in Ladner, just south of Vancouver

**Near:** Reifel Bird Sanctuary, Victoria ferries

**Building:** Riverfront home (two units), riverfront loft unit, floating cottage

**Grounds:** Docks & walkways festooned w/ colorful hanging baskets and seasonal decor; part of a community of comfortably clustered riverfront homes, floating cabins, & various boats

**Public Space:** Each unit is self-contained w/ living & sleeping quarters

**Food & Drink:** Snacks, beverages, sherry, & fresh-baked afternoon treats; full breakfast brought to your unit

**Recreation:** Kayaking, bicycling, hiking, bird-watching

**Amenities & Services:** Kayaks, bikes, complete house-produced guest guide, binoculars, games, umbrellas; small (10) retreats, seminars, workshops; celebration extras; newspaper; eco-sensitive towel option

## ACCOMMODATIONS

**Units:** 4 suites
**All Rooms:** Microwave, beverage-stocked mini-fridge, electric kettle, woodstove w/ wood, alarm clock, private over-the-river deck w/ patio furniture, hairdryers, sound system & CDs, custom beds, coffeemaker, top-quality toiletries, books, fresh flowers, phone, robes
**Some Rooms:** Jetted tub, gas grill, sofa-sleeper, wheelchair-friendly
**Bed & Bath:** Queens; private ensuite baths
**Favorites:** Each is unique: Waterlily is a cozy houseboat; Northwest Room and Keepers Quarters are two halves of one over-the-water unit and can be joined as a suite with a sleeping capacity up to 6; Netloft is a 2-level suite

**Comfort & Decor:** Deluxe contemporary decor; handsome woods, tile work, leather and richly upholstered furniture. Special furnishings in some units such as bent-willow chairs. One unit has a slate-and-glass-block shower, another a Japanese soaking tub. Designer linens and choice of down or hypoallergenic duvets. Top-quality fixtures; exclusive artistic touches.

## RATES, RESERVATIONS, & RESTRICTIONS

**Deposit:** 1st night; 10-day cancellation or forfeit unless rebooked
**Discounts:** Jan. & Feb.; 2nd & 3rd nights; CDN $20 add'l person
**Credit Cards:** V, MC
**Check-in/Out:** 3/noon
**Smoking:** Outside only
**Pets:** OK by arrangement; host pets on site
**Kids:** OK by arrangement
**No-Nos:** Unattended small children on docks
**Minimum Stay:** None

**Open:** All year
**Hosts:** Bill & Janice Harkley, Terry & Deborah Millichamp, co-owners & evening innkeepers; Sue Mills and Karen Bond, daytime innkeepers
4551 River Rd. West
Ladner, BC V4K 1R9
(604) 946-7778
Fax: (604) 940-1970
riverrun@direct.ca
www.virtualcities.com/ons/bc/l/bcl660 1.htm or
cimarron.net/canada/bc/riverrun.html

## BRAEMAR MANOR, North Vancouver

| Overall: ★★½ | Room Quality: D | Value: B | Price: CDN $95–$115 |
|---|---|---|---|

A homestay-style bed-and-breakfast in a residential neighborhood, Braemar Manor is unassuming, pleasant, and away from the hubbub of commercial areas, yet not far from downtown or the attractions of North Vancouver. With its full breakfast and friendly local advice, it's a reasonable alternative to the more commercial bed-and-breakfasts. Downstairs suite offers plenty of room to spread out.

## SETTING & FACILITIES

**Location:** Residential neighborhood in the hills above North Vancouver
**Near:** Grouse Mountain, Baden-Powell Hiking Trail, tennis, short drive to downtown
**Building:** Contemporary residence
**Grounds:** Back & side patios
**Public Space:** Hosts' LR & DR;

downstairs suite has ample living area
**Food & Drink:** Cappuccino on arrival; tea & bottled water; full breakfast
**Recreation:** Hiking, tennis
**Amenities & Services:** Local coupons

## ACCOMMODATIONS

**Units:** 1 room, 1 suite
**All Rooms:** Wall-to-wall carpet, fridge, TV, table & chairs
**Some Rooms:** Pool table, fireplace, desk
**Bed & Bath:** Queen plus single (Guest Suite) or extra queen (Garden Suite); full baths
**Favorites:** Garden Suite
**Comfort & Decor:** Upstairs room

(referred to as Guest Suite, but not as "suite-like" as downstairs room) is pale taupe with black lacquer accents. Downstairs room (referred to as Garden Suite) is large and fully self-contained. The better value of the two, it includes a kitchenette (wet bar, coffeemaker, electric kettle, micro.), fireplace, private entrance, desk, and pool table.

## RATES, RESERVATIONS, & RESTRICTIONS

**Deposit:** 1st night; 7-day cancellation
**Discounts:** Off-season, extended stay; CDN $25 add'l person
**Credit Cards:** Not accepted
**Check-in/Out:** 4 (or by arrangement)/noon
**Smoking:** No
**Pets:** No
**Kids:** Welcome

**Minimum Stay:** 2 nights
**Open:** All year
**Hosts:** Lenka & Mike
699 E. Braemar Rd.
North Vancouver, BC V7N 4G1
(604) 980-4354
Fax: (604) 980-4537
lenka@direct.ca
www.portal.ca/~lenka/

## LABURNUM COTTAGE, North Vancouver

Overall: ★★★★★    Room Quality: A    Value: A    Price: CDN $80–$225

Laburnum Cottage is nothing short of magical, inside and out. The elegant gardens include bridges, rock work, a stream, and a deck with automatic awning. Surrounded by parklands, the property feels secluded, but its location just off Capilano and the highway make downtown access easy. The stories and the personality of your hostess are reason enough to visit Laburnum Cottage, and we mean that with the greatest affection. If you need more reason, the breakfasts, prepared by Delphine's chef to her exacting standards, are elaborate and delicious, served in the sunny breakfast room with the pride of an experienced hostess who loves to entertain.

## SETTING & FACILITIES

**Location:** Just east of Capilano Rd. & just north of Hwy. I
**Near:** Capilano Suspension Bridge, regional park, Grouse Mountain, par-3 golf, restaurants
**Building:** Private home w/ cottage outbuildings
**Grounds:** Half-acre of fantastic, well-tended English-style gardens

**Public Space:** Drawing room w/ grand piano; patio & deck
**Food & Drink:** Afternoon tea or sherry; lavish full breakfast
**Recreation:** Hiking, tennis, mountain biking, par-3 golf
**Amenities & Services:** Piano, books, phone; concierge, weddings

## ACCOMMODATIONS

**Units:** 4 guest rooms, 2 cottages
**All Rooms:** Robes, toiletries, super-deluxe bedding
**Some Rooms:** Deck access, fireplace, soaker tub, TV, kitchenette, sitting area, extra bed
**Bed & Bath:** Queen or king; private ensuite bath
**Favorites:** Summerhouse Cottage,

Carriage House
**Comfort & Decor:** Delphine's decor will take your breath away—English romance is the theme throughout. Ecru, pale peach, pale pink, silver, and eggshell mix with a wide array of textures and florals. Exceptional fabrics, antique furnishings, quality fixtures.

## RATES, RESERVATIONS, & RESTRICTIONS

**Deposit:** 1st night; 7-day cancellation or forfeit; CDN $15 cancellation fee
**Discounts:** Off-season, specials
**Credit Cards:** V, MC
**Check-in/Out:** 2–6 (flexible)/11
**Smoking:** Outside only
**Pets:** No
**Kids:** By arrangement
**Minimum Stay:** 2 nights in cottages

**Open:** All year
**Hosts:** Delphine Masterton, family, & staff
1388 Terrace Ave.
North Vancouver, BC V7R 1B4
(888) 207-8901 or (604) 988-4877
Fax: (604) 988-4877
www.vancouver-bc.com/Laburnum-CottageBB

## MOUNTAINSIDE MANOR B&B, North Vancouver

Overall: ★★★★     Room Quality: C     Value: A     Price: CDN $85–$135

This distinctive, white, contemporary home is the last house on the road heading up to Grouse Mountain. It's also the halfway point on the Baden-Powell Trail and offers nice views and a sense of privacy because of its adjacency to open forest lands. Whether by car or bus, you can also access downtown and the rest of Vancouver easily from here. Enjoy modern amenities and a bright, open atmosphere.

## SETTING & FACILITIES

**Location:** At the foot of Grouse Mountain, at north end of Capilano Road/Nancy Greene Way
**Near:** Grouse Mountain (hiking trails, excellent restaurant), Capilano Lake, Capilano Suspension Bridge
**Building:** West Coast Contemporary home
**Grounds:** Rear deck, small rear yard w/ attractive gardens & hillside landscaping

**Public Space:** LR, DR, back deck
**Food & Drink:** Full breakfast, menu changes daily
**Recreation:** Skiing, hiking, mountain biking
**Amenities & Services:** Hot tub (hosts will fire it up w/ a bit of advance notice), fireplace, guest phone; on public transportation line

## ACCOMMODATIONS

**Units:** 4 guest rooms
**All Rooms:** Teddy bear, hairdryer, TV, view
**Some Rooms:** Coffeemakers, AC, ensuite whirlpool, skylight bath, dual sinks, seating area
**Bed & Bath:** King, queen, or king/twin conversion; 2 private baths, 2 share a bath

**Favorites:** Panorama Room
**Comfort & Decor:** Very bright, airy, and contemporary, with pale mint plush carpet, glass block accents, and artistic color schemes. Guest room walls are painted with geometric lines for an unusual but pleasant effect. Fresh flowers adorn rooms.

## RATES, RESERVATIONS, & RESTRICTIONS

**Deposit:** 1st night; 7-day cancellation
**Discounts:** Off-season extended stays; CDN $20 add'l person (rollaway)
**Credit Cards:** V, MC, DC
**Check-in/Out:** 4/noon
**Smoking:** Outside only
**Pets:** No
**Kids:** By arrangement
**Minimum Stay:** 2 nights in

Panorama Room
**Open:** All year
**Hosts:** Anne & Mike Murphy
5909 Nancy Greene Way
North Vancouver, BC V7R 4W6
(604) 990-9772
Fax: (604) 985-8470
mtnside@ibm.net
www.vancouver-bc.com/
MountainsideManor

## THISTLEDOWN HOUSE, North Vancouver

Overall: ★★★★½     Room Quality: A     Value: B     Price: CDN $125–$219

A distinctive lodging with fine finish work, exceptional decor, and gracious hosts. Creative breakfast menus might include asparagus-chicken-sweet-red-pepper crepe with demi-glace, medallions of pork on pastry pillows with béarnaise, or alder-smoked Pacific salmon croustadine. Assistant host Talla (the resident Scottish terrier) is a delight. Location on Capilano Road provides good access but a bit of street noise and exhaust; house is well built, so street noise doesn't seem to be a problem inside.

### SETTING & FACILITIES

**Location:** Halfway between downtown & Grouse Mountain
**Near:** Capilano Suspension Bridge, Capilano Regional Park, Murdo Fraser Park, Edgemont Village
**Building:** 1920 Craftsman-style heritage-listed home
**Grounds:** Half-acre parcel; commodious back lawn w/ gardens & deck

**Public Space:** Front porch, LR, deck
**Food & Drink:** Fruit, sherry; afternoon tea included in price; full gourmet breakfast
**Recreation:** Hiking, tennis, mountain biking, par-3 golf
**Amenities & Services:** Guest phone, piano, office for using your computer or faxing

### ACCOMMODATIONS

**Units:** 5 guest rooms
**All Rooms:** Carpet, robes, room-darkening drapes, hairdryer, choice of down or silk duvet
**Some Rooms:** Gas fireplace, jetted tub, private patio or balcony, sitting area, desk
**Bed & Bath:** Queen, king, or twins; private ensuite baths

**Favorites:** Under the Apple Tree
**Comfort & Decor:** Richly decorated in muted, tasteful colors such as sage and ecru, and accented with well-placed, eclectic antiques and artwork (Ruth's interior design experience is evident). Exceptional linens and fixtures. Living room has wood-burning fireplace and comfortable leather furniture.

## RATES, RESERVATIONS, & RESTRICTIONS

**Deposit:** 1st night; 10-day cancellation
**Discounts:** Extended stay, off-season packages
**Credit Cards:** V, MC
**Check-in/Out:** 4–6 (flexible; early luggage drop-off OK)/11
**Smoking:** Outside only
**Pets:** No; host dog
**Kids:** 12 & over only

**Minimum Stay:** None
**Open:** All year
**Hosts:** Ruth Crameri & Rex Davidson
3910 Capilano Rd.
North Vancouver, BC V7R 4J2
(888) 633-7173 or (604) 986-7173
Fax: (604) 980-2939
info@thistle-down.com
www.thistle-down.com

## ENGLISH BAY INN, Vancouver

Overall: ★★★★    Room Quality: B    Value: D    Price: CDN $170–$285

Very elegant, adult-only inn is in the best possible location for exploring Stanley Park and English Bay, each a mere block away. Charming, dedicated host takes special pride in his breakfasts, gourmet fare served at an amazing antique table in a convivial dinner-party atmosphere. Small wonder guests come back again and again. Antique aficionados will appreciate Bob's knowledge and his collection. The adjacent property, Chilco House, was added in 1996; this unit has two rooms (vibrantly decorated in mango and lemon tones) and its own pleasant, antique-furnished sitting and dining room.

### SETTING & FACILITIES

**Location:** Excellent West End location
**Near:** English Bay (beach), Stanley Park (aquarium, zoo), cruise ship terminal, Robson Street, Denman Street, Gastown, Chinatown, Granville Island, downtown
**Building:** 1930s Tudor-style plus unit across street
**Grounds:** Small, trim front lawn w/
hydrangeas; private, lush, colorful back garden
**Public Space:** LR, DR, garden
**Food & Drink:** Afternoon port & sherry; full gourmet breakfast
**Recreation:** In-line skating at Stanley Park or along English Bay; tennis, swimming, theater
**Amenities & Services:** Fireplace

### ACCOMMODATIONS

**Units:** 6 guest rooms, 1 suite
**All Rooms:** Phones, TV avail., robes, duvet
**Some Rooms:** Four-poster, sleigh, or canopy bed, skylight, private balcony, whirlpool tub, sitting room
**Bed & Bath:** Queen or king; private bath
**Favorites:** Room Five
**Comfort & Decor:** Hardwood floors with Persian rugs, French chandeliers, exquisite antique furnishings. High, coved ceilings. Color schemes include pastels, teal, salmon. Modern fixtures and quality appointments; designer linens.

## RATES, RESERVATIONS, & RESTRICTIONS

**Deposit:** 1st night; 48-hour cancellation or forfeit unless rebooked
**Discounts:** None
**Credit Cards:** V, MC, AE (cash preferred)
**Check-in/Out:** After 3/11
**Smoking:** No
**Pets:** No

**Kids:** No
**Minimum Stay:** 2 nights weekends
**Open:** All year
**Hosts:** Bob Chapin
1968 Comox St.
Vancouver, BC V6G 1R4
(604) 683-8002

## JOHNSON HERITAGE HOUSE, Vancouver

| Overall: ★★★★ | Room Quality: B | Value: A | Price: CDN $75–$145 |
|---|---|---|---|

Serving travelers since 1990, Ron and Sandy Johnson have put together a unique, cheerful, whimsical bed-and-breakfast that is both functional and fun. They obviously love acquiring unusual antiques and impressing guests with their unusual collection and amusing themes (a mermaid bathroom, a barbershop bathroom, a flamingo bathroom; a carousel room, a cobblestone sitting area complete with streetlamp). The very thorough in-room guest guides are both useful and humorous.

## SETTING & FACILITIES

**Location:** West Vancouver, between the university & Granville St.
**Near:** Beaches, airport, Anthropology Museum, botanical gardens, Queen Elizabeth Park, Univ. of B.C., Granville Island, Kitsilano district, downtown
**Building:** 1920 Craftsman home
**Grounds:** Terraced, highly landscaped lawns add to theme park feeling of

whimsical interior
**Public Space:** LR, two sitting areas, deck, DR
**Food & Drink:** Full breakfast
**Recreation:** Golf, tennis, swimming, hiking, museums
**Amenities & Services:** Reading material, guest guidebooks

## ACCOMMODATIONS

**Units:** 5 guest rooms, 1 suite
**All Rooms:** Phone, fax-modem line, hairdryer, robes, toiletries
**Some Rooms:** Fireplace, sitting area, cathedral ceiling, view, bidet, jetted tub, clawfoot tub, ceiling fan, TV
**Bed & Bath:** Queen or king (some w/ extra bed/daybed); suite & 3 rooms have private baths, 2 rooms share a bath

**Favorites:** Carousel Suite; Mountain View
**Comfort & Decor:** Known for their whimsical antique collection and award-winning decor. Large living room features antique-brick fireplace. Hardwood floors with Persian rugs. Stunning kitchen with stamped-metal ceiling, stone floor, cherry cabinets.

## RATES, RESERVATIONS, & RESTRICTIONS

**Deposit:** Credit card; 14-day cancellation
**Discounts:** Single occupancy
**Credit Cards:** Taken as deposit only; prefer cash, check, or traveler's check
**Check-in/Out:** After 3/11
**Smoking:** No
**Pets:** No
**Kids:** Over 12 only

**Minimum Stay:** 2 days on weekends; somewhat flexible
**Open:** All year
**Hosts:** Ron & Sandy Johnson
2278 West 34th Ave.
Vancouver, BC V6M 1G6
(604) 266-4175
Fax: (604) 266-4175
fun@johnsons-inn-vancouver.com
www.johnsons-inn-vancouver.com

## KINGSTON HOTEL, Vancouver

| Overall: ★★ | Room Quality: D | Value: A | Price: CDN $55–$95 |
|---|---|---|---|

Remember, this is a very basic, very "budget" accommodation. If you've stayed in cheap European hotels, you'll probably be OK with it. The private-bath rooms tend to book up well in advance. A few smoking rooms are available on the first floor, which can result in some "drift" upward. No parking—find your own. Request a room that doesn't front Richards and that isn't adjacent to a bathroom to minimize noise.

## SETTING & FACILITIES

**Location:** Mid-downtown; 5 blocks SW of Gastown
**Near:** Sky Train, Chinatown, downtown attractions
**Building:** 1910 three-level quasi-Tudor
**Grounds:** N/A (on a busy traffic corridor)
**Public Space:** Sauna, coin-op laundry, TV/breakfast room, small mezzanine sitting area; pub next door

**Food & Drink:** Toast & beverages (6:30–11 a.m.); pub next door serves microbrews & pub grub lunch & dinner
**Recreation:** Antiquing; in-line skating at Stanley Park
**Amenities & Services:** Vending machines, coin-op laundry; bulletin board with local events, front door is locked at 11 p.m. (guests have keys), front desk staffed 24 hours

## ACCOMMODATIONS

**Units:** 56 guest rooms
**All Rooms:** Phone, chair, reading lamp(s), sink
**Some Rooms:** TV, desk
**Bed & Bath:** Double(s) or twins; 8 private baths, 48 share 6 baths (2 per floor, sex-segregated)
**Favorites:** Room 201: 2 double beds & private bath

**Comfort & Decor:** Rooms are simple and inexpensively but tastefully furnished with a mix of basic motel furnishings and a few heritage or retro pieces. Wall-to-wall carpet. Well maintained and updated; tile baths are clean. Individually controlled steam heat; windows open.

## RATES, RESERVATIONS, & RESTRICTIONS

**Deposit:** 1st night; 24-hour cancellation or forfeit unless rebooked
**Discounts:** Seniors, single occupancy, off-season
**Credit Cards:** V, MC, AE
**Check-in/Out:** 11 (room may not be cleared, but luggage drop-off OK)/11
**Smoking:** OK in some first-floor rooms
**Pets:** No
**Kids:** Welcome

**No-Nos:** Checks, smoking above 1st floor
**Minimum Stay:** None
**Open:** All year
**Hosts:** Fred O'Hagan
757 Richards St.
Vancouver, BC V6B 3A6
(888) 713-3304 or (604) 684-9024
Fax: (604) 684-9917
www.vancouver-bc.com/kingstonhotel/

## THE LANGTRY, Vancouver

| Overall: ★★★★ | Room Quality: A | Value: C | Price: CDN $175 |

The Langtry is a curious (and very attractive) hybrid of self-contained condo/apartment–style accommodations and a fully hosted bed-and-breakfast. While your multiroom suite contains all the living, dining, and kitchen facilities you need for a private stay, your host also offers afternoon sherry or port and a full breakfast in his own elegantly appointed apartment. Haike (from Holland) is an excellent and knowledgeable host, whose years of hospitality-industry experience and sophisticated sense of decorating make your stay a pleasure.

## SETTING & FACILITIES

**Location:** Fashionable West End district between downtown & Stanley Park
**Near:** English Bay (beach), Robson Street, Denman Street, cruise ship terminal, Gastown, Chinatown, Granville Island
**Building:** 1939 apt. building
**Grounds:** Narrow, landscaped front

lawn w/ border plantings
**Public Space:** Breakfast served in proprietor's DR; garden patio area
**Food & Drink:** Afternoon sherry & port; full breakfast
**Recreation:** In-line skating; near tennis, swimming, theater
**Amenities & Services:** Fax machine; touring assistance

## ACCOMMODATIONS

**Units:** 4 apts.

**All Rooms:** Hairdryer iron, TV/stereo/VCR, equipped kitchen, quality mattress, fresh flowers, private phone line

**Some Rooms:** Unique decor in each (see "Comfort & Decor")

**Bed & Bath:** Queen; private ensuite baths

**Favorites:** Each includes 725 sq. ft. of living space, w/ full bath, foyer, kitchen, DR, & LR; decor varies

**Comfort & Decor:** All units feature inlaid oak floors with Persian-type rugs, ceramic tile, coved ceilings, and antique furnishings. Decor varies by period: one is Art Nouveau/Deco, one is 30s/40s, one is 20s, and one is Scottish Victorian.

## RATES, RESERVATIONS, & RESTRICTIONS

**Deposit:** 1st night; 2-week cancellation or forfeit

**Discounts:** Off-season, extended stay

**Credit Cards:** V, MC

**Check-in/Out:** Flexible/noonish

**Smoking:** Outside only

**Pets:** No

**Kids:** 8 & over only

**Minimum Stay:** None

**Open:** All year

**Hosts:** Haike Kingma
968 Nicola St.
Vancouver, BC V6G 2C8
(604) 687-7798 or
cell (604) 816-5476
Fax: (604) 687-7892
info@thelangtry.com
www.thelangtry.com

## O CANADA HOUSE, Vancouver

Overall: ★★★★½     Room Quality: A     Value: B     Price: CDN $150–$195

This extravagantly restored, decorated, and modernized Victorian could be your best downtown choice; we were extremely impressed with it. The hosts have anticipated many guest needs, and their attention to detail is excellent. The guest pantry is a very considerate feature. Professional staff on hand 24 hours. The home is said to be the house in which the national anthem, "O Canada," was composed; it is an official heritage site. Less personal than some, but very well done.

## SETTING & FACILITIES

**Location:** Fashionable West End district between downtown & Stanley Park

**Near:** Gastown, Chinatown, shopping (Robson & Denman Streets), dining, Granville Island, English Bay (beach), Stanley Park (aquarium, zoo)

**Building:** 1897 Victorian

**Grounds:** Tidy back garden w/ exuberant flowers; attractive little front yard

**Public Space:** Front porch, LR, parlor, dining area, guest pantry

**Food & Drink:** Evening sherry; 24-hour snacks & beverages; full breakfast

**Recreation:** In-line skating at Stanley Park

**Amenities & Services:** Video library, guest pantry

## ACCOMMODATIONS

**Units:** 6 suites

**All Rooms:** TV/VCR, fan, sitting area, mini-fridge, phone, closet/armoire, robes, hairdryer

**Some Rooms:** Clawfoot tub, desk, skylights, private patio

**Bed & Bath:** Queen or king; ensuite private bath

**Favorites:** The Penthouse is 750 sq. ft., the entire 3rd floor. The Cottage, while a bit dim, is a private, detached unit w/ brick patio.

**Comfort & Decor:** Elegantly decorated in a late-Victorian style, with antiques throughout, including light fixtures. High ceilings, rich woodwork, tile baths, plush carpet, designer linens, original artwork. Central (forced-air gas) heat system; auxiliary heaters available. Restored with great attention to its period of origin, but with fully modern mechanicals.

## RATES, RESERVATIONS, & RESTRICTIONS

**Deposit:** Call

**Discounts:** Off-season, extended stay, AAA

**Credit Cards:** V, MC

**Check-in/Out:** Flexible/11

**Smoking:** No

**Pets:** No

**Kids:** Over 12 only

**Minimum Stay:** 2 days on weekends

**Open:** All year

**Hosts:** Mike Browne & Jim Britten
1114 Barclay St.
Vancouver, BC V6E 1H1
(604) 688-0556
Fax: (604) 488-0556
www.vancouver-bc.com/OCanada-House

---

## PENDRELL SUITES, Vancouver

Overall: ★★★★    Room Quality: B    Value: C    Price: CDN $99–$425

Handsomely furnished, spacious units designed to function as your own upscale apartment (therefore, pets and kids are OK). Very private. Better suited for longer stays. While many hotel-style amenities (shampoo, coffee, etc.) are lacking, access to provisions is excellent. Come expecting a spacious, airy, classy, unequipped apartment, and you'll be pleased. Many celebrities have stayed here, and the hosts are quick to tell you that Scully's X-files apartment is one of their suites.

## SETTING & FACILITIES

**Location:** Fashionable West End area between downtown & Stanley Park
**Near:** Stanley Park (aquarium, zoo), English Bay (beach), Robson Street, Denman Street, cruise ship terminal, Gastown, Chinatown, Granville Island
**Building:** 1910 brick heritage building, restored
**Grounds:** Brick patio w/ garden, pond, sitting area
**Public Space:** Garden; all-suite property has ample space in each suite, including living, dining, & kitchen areas, plus den/office in some; for "room-within-a-suite" option (as available), shared space includes living, dining, & kitchen areas of that suite
**Food & Drink:** None provided—full kitchens in all units; shopping nearby & shopping/chef service avail.
**Recreation:** In-line skating; near tennis, swimming at health club, theater
**Amenities & Services:** Laundry (self-serve or pick-up service), BBQ, e-mail; optional ensuite fax & copier; shopping &/or cooking, secretarial, airport pick-up all avail.

## ACCOMMODATIONS

**Units:** 7 suites, 1–3 BRs each
**All Rooms:** Full kitchen, fireplace, TV/VCR, sound system, phone (private line w/ dataport, free local calls)
**Some Rooms:** Fireplace in master BR
**Bed & Bath:** Queens; private baths (most suites have 2 baths)
**Favorites:** All suites are comparable; specify preferred amenities for best fit
**Comfort & Decor:** Hardwood floors and extra-high ceilings enhance the spacious feeling of these large (1,200–1,500 sq. ft.) suites. Antique furnishings add a touch of class, while modern amenities ensure comfort. Kitchens include dishwashers, microwaves, gas ranges, coffeemakers, and all utensils.

## RATES, RESERVATIONS, & RESTRICTIONS

**Deposit:** Policy varies, call; 14-day cancellation
**Discounts:** Longer stays; sharing a suite from CDN $99/night (as avail.); suites CDN $225–425/night; monthly rates CDN $2,650–6,500
**Credit Cards:** V, MC, JCB
**Check-in/Out:** After 3 or by arrangement; earlier luggage drop-off OK/noon
**Smoking:** Outside only
**Pets:** Can be accommodated by arrangement
**Kids:** Welcome
**Minimum Stay:** 3 nights
**Open:** All year
**Hosts:** Rosemary & Boyd McConnell
1419 Pendrell St.
Vancouver, BC V6G 1S3
(604) 688-7983 or (604) 685-0715, reservations (888) 250-7211
Fax: (604) 685-8675
rosemary@pendrellsuites.com, boyd@pendrellsuites.com
www.pendrellsuites.com

## PENNY FARTHING INN, Vancouver

| Overall: ★★★½ | Room Quality: B | Value: B | Price: CDN $110–$165 |

This charming little Victorian welcomes you to a simpler, more relaxing era. Located in the fun, trendy Kitsilano district, where shopping and restaurants are plentiful, it's well established and professionally run. The smaller bedrooms and the common areas are snug but well laid out; the suites are a real treat, with room to stretch out a bit. You really gotta love cats to fully appreciate this place. Although they aren't allowed in the rooms, the presence of these three furry friends (one of which plays the piano—seriously) is an integral part of the inn's ambiance.

## SETTING & FACILITIES

**Location:** South of English Bay, in the Kitsilano district
**Near:** English Bay, beach, Univ. of British Columbia, Stanley Park
**Building:** 1912 heritage house
**Grounds:** Small, cheerful front yard; backyard w/ brick patio & tiny, manicured yard
**Public Space:** Guest lounge, front porch, back patio

**Food & Drink:** Self-serve tea, coffee, cookies (24 hours); bountiful full breakfast
**Recreation:** Parks nearby offer tennis, bike routes
**Amenities & Services:** Fireplace, stereo, TV/VCR, games, puzzles, CDs & videos, library; hostess's personal office avail. w/ computer, scanner, printer, fax, copier

## ACCOMMODATIONS

**Units:** 2 guest rooms, 2 suites
**All Rooms:** Phone, view, brass or four-poster bed(s)
**Some Rooms:** Sitting room, sofabed, skylight, TV/VCR, stereo/CD, ensuite tea/coffee, fireplace, porch/veranda, refrigerator
**Bed & Bath:** Suites have queen beds, others have a double or twin/king

conversion; private baths (3 ensuite)
**Favorites:** Abigail's, Bettina's (the suites)
**Comfort & Decor:** Rich, attractive, solid colors blend with mellow wood, antique furnishings, and floral wallpapers and bedding to create a cozy, decorator look.

## RATES, RESERVATIONS, & RESTRICTIONS

**Deposit:** Credit card; 15-day cancellation
**Discounts:** Single occupancy, off-season; CDN $25 add'l person
**Credit Cards:** For deposit only; payment via cash or check
**Check-in/Out:** After 2 (flexible; early luggage drop-off OK)/11
**Smoking:** No
**Pets:** No; host kitties

**Kids:** No
**Minimum Stay:** None
**Open:** All year
**Hosts:** Lyn Hainstock
2855 West 6th Ave.
Vancouver, BC V6K 1X2
(604) 739-9002
Fax: (604) 739-9004
farthing@uniserve.com
www.pennyfarthinginn.com

## A TREEHOUSE B&B, Vancouver

| Overall: ★★★★ | Room Quality: B | Value: B | Price: CDN $90–$140 |
|---|---|---|---|

This sophisticated home has a distinct Pacific Rim flavor we absolutely loved. While the stark, white-on-white-with-black-accents theme may not suit everyone, the first-class anticipation of guests' every need is sure to impress. The only thing that keeps the experience from being a "perfect 10" is the rather significant noise from 49th Avenue. Your unobtrusive hosts, who live in another part of the house, are fully available if you summon them. Breakfast is a celebration of tastes, colors, and presentation (sample menu: blueberry smoothie, fresh fruit skewers, yogurt with berries, orange-hazelnut oatmeal, fresh veggie frittata with exotic mushrooms).

## SETTING & FACILITIES

**Location:** Kerrisdale District, about 1.5 km. (1 mi.) west of Granville St.
**Near:** Beaches, airport, Anthropology Museum, botanical gardens, Queen Elizabeth Park, Univ. of B.C., Granville Island, Kitsilano district, downtown
**Building:** Ultra-modern Bauhaus-style contemporary home
**Grounds:** Private Japanese garden, large side yard, towering mature trees
**Public Space:** 2nd-floor, large, open living/dining room; covered deck
**Food & Drink:** Four-course breakfast; early cont'l or bag breakfast avail.
**Recreation:** Golf, tennis, swimming, hiking, museums
**Amenities & Services:** Slippers, umbrellas; chocolates on pillow

## ACCOMMODATIONS

**Units:** 2 suites, 1 guest room
**All Rooms:** Cable TV, VCR, phone w/ modem jack, small fridge, coffeemaker, kettle, robes, slippers, hairdryer, quality toiletries, sleep masks
**Some Rooms:** Extra futon, whirlpool, sitting room, closet, sound system, paperbacks, skylight bath
**Bed & Bath:** Queens; private baths
**Favorites:** Tree Top Suite
**Comfort & Decor:** Bright, airy, white-on-white decor with houseplants and modern art with a Pacific Rim flavor. Contemporary furnishings are, themselves, pieces of art. White Berber-style carpet. Radiant in-floor heating with individual room thermostats; fans provided, and windows open for ventilation.

## RATES, RESERVATIONS, & RESTRICTIONS

**Deposit:** Credit card; 2-week cancellation or forfeit unless rebooked
**Discounts:** Single occupancy; CDN $25 add'l person
**Credit Cards:** Ask
**Check-in/Out:** After 4 (earlier possible by arrangement); noon
**Smoking:** Deck & gardens only
**Pets:** No (boarding facil. nearby)
**Kids:** 10 & older only
**No-Nos:** Shoes in house
**Minimum Stay:** 2 nights preferred, weekends; single nights by chance
**Open:** All year
**Hosts:** Barb & Bob Selvage
2490 West 49th Ave.
Vancouver, BC V6M 2V3
(604) 266-2962
Fax: (604) 266-2960
bb@treehousebb.com
www.treehousebb.com

## WEST END GUEST HOUSE, Vancouver

| Overall: ★★★★ | Room Quality: B | Value: C | Price: CDN $157–$220 |

This popular downtown bed-and-breakfast hotel (est. 1984, current owner since 1991) emphasizes a gracious, social atmosphere. While the rooms are smaller than some comparably priced inns, they are surprisingly light and airy; even the smallest (and it's very small) is cheerful and makes the most of the space. The historic photos and Evan's knowledge of local history add to the enjoyment. Storage is very limited in most of the rooms. Rooms have many classy and thoughtful touches, and each is individually decorated. Having eight rooms gives West End Guest House the feel of a tasteful little hotel with a convivial, posh lobby.

### SETTING & FACILITIES

**Location:** Fashionable West End area between downtown & Stanley Park
**Near:** Robson Street, Denman Street, cruise ship terminal, English Bay (beach), Gastown, Chinatown, Granville Island
**Building:** Very pink 1906 Victorian
**Grounds:** Trim front lawn w/ lush border plantings on relatively quiet side street
**Public Space:** Front porch, LR/DR, garden, guest pantry
**Food & Drink:** Snacks & hot beverages; afternoon sherry or iced tea; full breakfast
**Recreation:** In-line skating at Stanley Park or along English Bay; tennis, swimming, theater
**Amenities & Services:** Guest directory w/ historical tidbits; dinner reservations, turndown, valet, personal note & chocolates greet you in your room

### ACCOMMODATIONS

**Units:** 6 guest rooms, 2 suites
**All Rooms:** Robes, carpet, TV, phones, feather mattress, foam and feather pillows
**Some Rooms:** Sitting area, closet, clawfoot tub, skylight
**Bed & Bath:** Queen, double, or twins; private baths
**Favorites:** 1, 2, & Terra Queen Suite
**Comfort & Decor:** Smallish rooms, but well laid out and decorated. Striking, rich colors; ornate patterns and textures. Antiques, attractive wallpapers, fine original woodwork, framed historical photographs. High-thread-count, hand-ironed sheets are one example of how the experienced innkeeper "goes the extra mile." Classical music completes the ambiance.

## RATES, RESERVATIONS, & RESTRICTIONS

**Deposit:** 1st night; 3-day cancellation or forfeit partial

**Discounts:** Extended stay, off-season (affiliate properties starting at CDN $125)

**Credit Cards:** V, MC, AE, D

**Check-in/Out:** 3 (early luggage drop-off accommodated)/11

**Smoking:** Outside only

**Pets:** No

**Kids:** 12 & older only, some exceptions by arrangement (affiliate properties can accommodate children—please call)

**Minimum Stay:** 2 nights, some weekends

**Open:** All year

**Host:** Evan Penner
1362 Haro St.
Vancouver, BC V6E 1G2
(604) 681-2889
Fax: (604) 688-8812
wegh@idmail.com
www.westendguesthouse.com

## BAYVIEW B&B, West Vancouver

Overall: ★★★★½    Room Quality: A    Value: B    Price: CDN $135–$250

Top-notch, all-suite B&B has it all: peaceful setting, great views, fabulous breakfasts, well-appointed rooms, and super hosts. Classy, clean, upscale—one of our favorite Vancouver properties. Gourmet breakfast, served at a common table with view of bay, includes freshly squeezed OJ, home-baked bread or muffins, choice of cold cereals, yogurt, fruit, a hot entree (such as sockeye salmon & eggs or mascarpone-stuffed French toast), and a heavenly dessert. Special diets accommodated graciously. Backyard is like your own private park. Adorable, well-behaved small pets on-site. We can't wait to go back.

## SETTING & FACILITIES

**Location:** North of Ambleside Beach and just south of Hwy. 1/99

**Near:** Ambleside district, parks, Stanley Park, downtown, Grouse Mountain, Whistler

**Building:** Modern home w/ traditional styling

**Grounds:** Exceptionally private, large backyard w/ garden areas, gazebo

**Public Space:** LR, DR, deck, gazebo

**Food & Drink:** Tea & cookies; abundant & delicious full breakfast

**Recreation:** Seaside walk, skiing, antiquing, golf, ferry to Vancouver Island (Victoria)

**Amenities & Services:** Library, videos, iron; office room with copier, computer, fax, Internet access

## ACCOMMODATIONS

**Units:** 3 suites
**All Rooms:** Three rooms, view of English Bay, sitting room, TV/VCR, small refrigerator, books, desk, hairdryer, phone, robes
**Some Rooms:** Sofa-sleeper, kitchenette, fireplace, balcony
**Bed & Bath:** Queens; private baths
**Favorites:** All 3 lovely & spacious; Bayview Suite is the largest

**Comfort & Decor:** Designer wallpaper and bedding, top-of-the-line mattresses, hardwood floors with sculpted, handmade rugs. Many special touches such as art-quality fixtures, handmade lamps, hand-painted sinks, antiques; original Canadian artwork throughout. Central heat (guests have thermostat access); house is quiet and well insulated.

## RATES, RESERVATIONS, & RESTRICTIONS

**Deposit:** 1st night; 7-day cancellation or forfeit
**Discounts:** Extended stays; seniors in the off-season
**Credit Cards:** V, MC, AE
**Check-in/Out:** Flexible/generally 11
**Smoking:** Outside only
**Pets:** By arrangement only; host pets on site
**Kids:** By arrangement only

**Minimum Stay:** None
**Open:** All year
**Hosts:** Jim & Gwen MacLean Cruickshank
1270 Netley Place
West Vancouver, BC V7T 2H2
(800) 208-2204, (604) 926-3218
Fax: (604) 926-3216
bayview@bayview-bb.com
www.BayView-BB.com

## BEACHSIDE B&B, West Vancouver

Overall: ★★★½    Room Quality: B    Value: C    Price: CDN $145–$250

Where else can you get a beachfront spa, immediate beach access, and proximity to all that Vancouver has to offer? This is a unique property. Located on a quiet cul-de-sac in a residential neighborhood, Beachside has been a bed-and-breakfast since 1985. Hosts and common areas are relaxed and unpretentious. The non-oceanfront rooms are, frankly, uninspired, but Oceanfront and Seaside are very special indeed. Just 20 minutes to downtown; good restaurants in nearby Ambleside.

## SETTING & FACILITIES

**Location:** On the waterfront on the north shore of English Bay
**Near:** BEACH!, Ambleside district shopping & dining
**Building:** Contemporary/Mediterranean brick & stucco home
**Grounds:** Small, grassy, oceanfront backyard w/ deck & spa
**Public Space:** Cathedral-ceilinged

LR & DR w/ near-180° oceanfront view
**Food & Drink:** Full breakfast
**Recreation:** Golf, antiquing, ship/storm watching, wildlife watching
**Amenities & Services:** Videos, oceanfront deck, guest phone; great local info (Gordon is a tour guide; both are natives)

## ACCOMMODATIONS

**Units:** 3 guest rooms, 1 suite
**All Rooms:** Coffeemaker, TV/VCR, hairdryer, curling iron, iron, mini-fridge
**Some Rooms:** Ocean view, whirlpool spa, private patio, kitchen, fireplace
**Bed & Bath:** Queens; private baths
**Favorites:** Oceanfront, Seaside
**Comfort & Decor:** Living room is

beam-ceilinged, contemporary, and open. "Oceanfront" has an incredible tile whirlpool spa with adjacent bathroom and shower; striking decor includes cobalt walls. "Seaside" is more traditionally deluxe, with a brick fireplace, kitchenette, and whirlpool tub. Other two rooms are standard. Individual heat control.

## RATES, RESERVATIONS, & RESTRICTIONS

**Deposit:** 50%; 2-week cancellation
**Discounts:** Weekly rate, off-season; CDN $30 add'l person
**Credit Cards:** V, MC
**Check-in/Out:** 5–6 (flexible)/noon
**Smoking:** No
**Pets:** No
**Kids:** OK in one unit, by arrangement
**Minimum Stay:** 2 nights in most cases (some flexibility)

**Open:** All year
**Hosts:** Gordon & Joan Gibbs
4208 Evergreen Ave.
West Vancouver, BC V7V 1H1
(800) 563-3311 or (604) 922-7773
Fax: (604) 926-8073
beach@uniserve.com
www.beach.bc.ca or www.vancouver-bc.com/BeachsideBB/

# Washington

Those who know little about Washington might be fooled by the homogeneous state nickname, "The Evergreen State," thinking Washington is one big rain forest centered around Seattle, that edgy, pioneering city that gave birth to grunge music, coffee culture, and Microsoft.

Upon closer inspection, Washington is clearly divided down the middle into two geologically, socially, and climatically different regions: the green, rainy West Side, with its urban hubs of Seattle, Tacoma, Olympia, Vancouver, and Bellingham; and the dry, sparsely populated deserts and basins of the East Side, with its irrigated agriculture and slower pace.

But—wait! The East Side isn't all arid desert or orchard acreage. The state's northeast corner is forested, and Spokane is an urban oasis. Neither is the West Side all microchips and interstates—here you'll find the deep rain forests of the Olympic Peninsula, the sleepy coastal towns, the charming seaports and islands. We've divided Washington into seven distinct regions. Zone 3, the coast and Olympic Peninsula, is an overall sleepy region, home to prodigious rain, quaint communities, and exquisite scenery. Zone 4, Northwest Washington, includes the San Juan Islands and the Interstate 5 communities sandwiched between Puget Sound (that's the big "bite" out of Washington's northwest corner) and the Cascade Mountains. Zone 5 is the urban area—Seattle, Tacoma, and surrounding communities at the southeast corner of Puget Sound. Zone 6 is the Interstate 5 corridor stretching south from Tacoma to the Oregon border, with the Olympic Peninsula to the west and the Cascade Mountains to the east. Zone 7 is the Cascades themselves—home of skiing, hiking, and exceptional beauty. Zones 8 and 9 cover the east side of the state. Zone 8 includes the forests of northeastern Washington and the city of Spokane, while Zone 9 takes in the high deserts, the Columbia River basin, and the agricultural communities.

Whether you can visit all seven "Washingtons" or just one, you'll find quality bed-and-breakfasts in each zone.

# Zone 3
# Washington Coast and
# Olympic Peninsula

Everything you've heard about the rain is true. The Olympic Peninsula is home to Olympic National Park and the Hoh Rain Forest, with 14 feet of annual rainfall. The storms along Washington's rugged, rocky coast are legendary. And with all these forces of nature comes a terrific beauty that entices hikers, birders, whale-watchers, hot-spring aficionados, and beach lovers from all over the world. But it's a gentler kind of tourist you'll find here, and fewer in numbers than the hordes that flock to Washington's flashier destinations like Mount Rainier or Seattle.

The little town of Forks is closest to the deep rain forest. Isolated and surrounded by lush greenery, it's an outpost just large enough to support its tourist trade. No boardwalks or amusement parks in this neck of the woods—just a few restaurants, personable innkeepers, savvy fishing guides, and a bit of logging and Native American history. Just outside town: prime fishing, wild and isolated beaches, and exceptional hiking. Easy daytrip distance to Clallam and Neah Bays and Sol Duc Hot Springs.

Farther north and east on Highway 101 are the more developed towns (restaurants, shopping, tourist infrastructure) of Port Angeles, Sequim, and Port Townsend. This corridor, on the north side of the Olympic Peninsula along the Strait of Juan de Fuca, enjoys a more temperate, drier, and sunnier "rain shadow" climate than other parts of the peninsula.

Port Angeles offers great access to some of Olympic National Park's most popular features, including Hurricane Ridge, with its panoramic vistas and hiking trails for all ability levels, and Sol Duc Hot Springs, where, in addition to therapeutic mineral pools, you'll find hiking trails and dining. Port Angeles also has a ferry terminal, with daily crossings to Victoria, British Columbia (see Zone 1).

Just east of Port Angeles is Sequim (pronounced "squim"), home to Dungeness Spit, the longest natural sand spit (over 5 miles) in the United

States, and its adjacent wildlife refuge. For those who'd rather drive than walk, Sequim's Olympic Game Park is a "drive-thru safari" with critters ranging from buffalo to retired movie bears to bored llamas. For a small additional fee, you can purchase bread to feed the inmates.

Victorian seaport Port Townsend is a treat, with historic homes, a working port, and a vibrant waterfront shopping district. It is also home to Fort Worden State Park and Conference Center (www.olympus.net/gov/ftworden/), with its lighthouse, historic buildings and gun batteries, hiking trails, and meeting and recreational facilities. Ferries run daily from Port Townsend to Keystone on Whidbey Island.

Farther south, the Grays Harbor area (Aberdeen, Hoquiam, Westport, Ocean Shores) is a historic deepwater port and migratory bird route, as well as a jumping-off place for exploring Olympic National Park from the south. Bowerman Basin National Wildlife Refuge (aka Grays Harbor NWR), comprising more than 100 acres of mudflats, comes alive with migratory birds, especially in April and May, and again (though more dispersed) from July through October. Hoquiam Castle is a 20-room lumber-baron mansion listed on the National Historic Register, built in 1897 and restored as a museum.

The Long Beach Peninsula is well developed for tourists. It offers fine lodging, dining, shopping, and a spectacular 26-mile sand beach. The communities of Long Beach and nearby Seaview offer many upscale creature comforts and typical "beach town" atmosphere (as does Ocean Park, to the north), while Ilwaco maintains more of a working port atmosphere and has the best access to some of the area's historical regions and a museum (e.g., Fort Canby and Fort Columbia State Parks, Lewis and Clark Interpretive Center, Ilwaco Heritage Museum). The Long Beach Peninsula hosts seasonal events, including a cranberry festival and an internationally renowned kite festival.

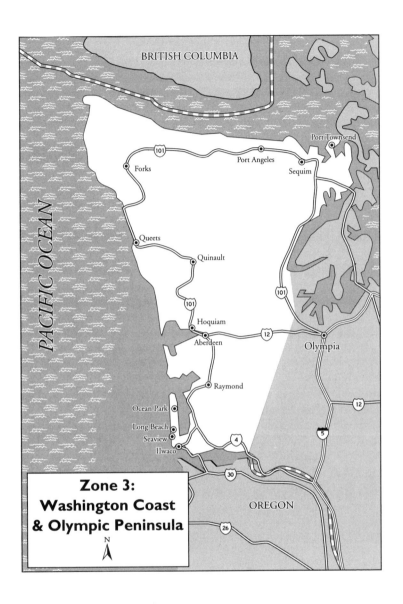

BRITISH COLUMBIA

Port Townsend

101

Forks

Port Angeles

Sequim

PACIFIC OCEAN

Queets

Quinault

101

101

Hoquiam

12

Olympia

Aberdeen

Raymond

12

Ocean Park

Long Beach

Seaview

Ilwaco

4

5

30

**Zone 3:
Washington Coast
& Olympic Peninsula**

N

OREGON

26

**Aberdeen**
Cooney Mansion B&B Inn, p. 82

**Forks**
Huckleberry Lodge, p. 83
Manitou Lodge, p. 84
Miller Tree Inn, p. 85

**Hoquiam**
Lytle House, p. 87

**Ilwaco**
Chick-ADee Inn, p. 88
China Beach B&B Retreat, p. 89

**Long Beach**
Boreas B&B Inn, p. 91

**Ocean Park**
The DoveShire B&B, p. 92

**Port Angeles**
BJ's Garden Gate, p. 94
Domaine Madeleine, p. 95
Maple Rose Inn, p. 97
The SeaSuns B&B, p. 98

**Port Townsend**
Ann Starrett Mansion, p. 99
The James House, p. 101
Lizzie's, p. 102
Ravenscroft Inn, p. 103

**Seaview**
The Shelburne Country Inn,
    p. 105

**Sequim**
Brigadoon B&B, p. 106
Greywolf Inn, p. 107
Simone's Groveland Cottage B&B
    Inn, p. 108
Toad Hall, p. 110

## COONEY MANSION B&B INN, Aberdeen

| Overall: ★★½ | Room Quality: D | Value: D | Price: $65–$165 |
|---|---|---|---|

This faded beauty hides in the hills above the working-class town of Cosmopolis (just outside Aberdeen), where gull cries and the scent of fresh-hewn timber fill the air. The venerable, somewhat down-at-the-heels bed-and-breakfast's bachelor–lumber baron charm seems ideally suited to innkeeper Jim's crusty style. (Signs read: "Unattended children will be sold as slaves," and "Public tours will be conducted for $3 at the innkeepers' convenience." We think the first one was a joke. . .) The many original fixtures will fascinate history buffs; those dependent upon modern amenities—like in-room showers—should look elsewhere.

### SETTING & FACILITIES

**Location:** On a hill above Cosmopolis
**Near:** Mill Creek Park, golf course, Hoquiam, Aberdeen, lakes, ocean beaches, Westport, Ocean Shores, Olympic N.P. (45 minutes)
**Building:** 1908 Craftsman-style mansion
**Grounds:** Lawns framed by flowers, a pine forest, a park, & a public golf course
**Public Space:** LR, DR, parlor/guest phone room, ballroom, balcony
**Food & Drink:** Tea (anytime); sodas (fee); full "Lumber Baron" breakfast; early cont'l by arrangement
**Recreation:** Short drive to boating, deep-sea charters, beach horseback riding, kayaking
**Amenities & Services:** Hot tub, sauna, beach towels, swimsuits, racquets, exercise equipment, player piano, phone, library, videos, VCRs, ice, gift shop, games; group dinners by arrangement, high teas, murder mysteries, business functions, weddings, parties (including Dickens Family Christmas)

### ACCOMMODATIONS

**Units:** 8 guest rooms
**All Rooms:** Robes, closet or armoire, radio
**Some Rooms:** TV, claw-foot tub, VCR, fireplace, fridge, micro.
**Bed & Bath:** Various, some w/ add'l bed or roll-away option; 5 private baths (shower rooms on lower level—most rooms have tub baths only), 3 share a bath
**Favorites:** Cooney Suite
**Comfort & Decor:** Built, decorated, and furnished with lumber baron Neil Cooney's own specialty: sitka spruce. Original Arts and Crafts period fixtures, furnishings, stained glass. Central heat plus individual room heaters. Masculine with comfortable touches; a bit musty, but undeniably regal and deserving of its National Historic Register designation.

## RATES, RESERVATIONS, & RESTRICTIONS

**Deposit:** Credit card; 5-day cancellation or subject to full charge unless rebooked; $20 cancellation fee
**Discounts:** Extended business stays, single occupancy; $20 add'l person
**Credit Cards:** V, MC, AE, D, DC
**Check-in/Out:** 4 or by arrangement/11 ($25/hr for late check-outs)
**Smoking:** Outside only
**Pets:** No
**Kids:** Under 12 only by prior arrangement

**Minimum Stay:** 2 nights some holidays
**Open:** All year
**Hosts:** Judi & Jim Lohr
1705 Fifth St.
Cosmopolis, WA 98537
(360) 533-0602
Fax: same as phone
cooney@techline.com
www.techline.com/~cooney/

## HUCKLEBERRY LODGE, Forks

Overall: ★★★½       Room Quality: B       Value: B       Price: $70–$110

As you drive under the grand, rustic log entry archway and follow the split-rail entry drive, you have a sense of finding a country estate. Inside, Huckleberry Lodge is modern but not pretentious. Relax with a game of pool, scratch the host cat behind the ears, or kick back with a wildlife magazine. Take an evening sauna or hot tub, then chat with your knowledgeable hosts or fellow guests in the living room or on the patio. A full breakfast (or extra-early box breakfast for sportsmen) sends you off in the morning.

## SETTING & FACILITIES

**Location:** On the Calawah River, off Hwy. 101 in Forks
**Near:** Olympic N.P., Hoh Rain Forest, rivers, beaches, Forks Timber Museum, lakes, Clallam & Neah Bays, Sol Duc Hot Springs
**Building:** Modern Pacific Northwest home & 1997 cabin
**Grounds:** Five acres; huge lawns, BBQ pit, paths, patio for al fresco dining
**Public Space:** LR, game room, DR, loft sitting area
**Food & Drink:** Coffee & tea; full breakfast

**Recreation:** Wildlife (whale, eagle, elk, bird) watching, scenic drives, art galleries & studios
**Amenities & Services:** Gazebo hot tub, sauna, pool table, games, fish cleaning station, wader dryers, BBQ pit, coin-op laundry, walking sticks, phone, videos, ice; showers avail. for late check-out sportsmen; work with local guide services for outdoor recreation packages: fishing, hunting, ATV & llama treks

## ACCOMMODATIONS

**Units:** 3 guest rooms, 3 cabins (incl. 1 duplex)

**All Rooms:** Down comforter, slippers, robes, TV/VCR, hairdryer, guest guide, ice bucket, quality linens, toiletries

**Some Rooms:** Phone, basic kitchen, coffeemaker, table & chairs

**Bed & Bath:** Queens in cabins; king, queen, or twins in main house; private baths (some detached)

**Favorites:** Master Room, Cabin 2

**Comfort & Decor:** Contemporary furnishings and decor have an emphasis on the outdoor life, including trophy heads. The duplex cabin was fashioned from helicopter-logged dead fir—recycled, glued, and laminated—for a 21st-century take on the old log cabin theme: beautiful, functional, environmentally responsible. In-house rooms have central heat; cabin guests control their own heat. Windows open in all units.

## RATES, RESERVATIONS, & RESTRICTIONS

**Deposit:** 1st night; 48-hour cancellation

**Discounts:** Off-season, single occupancy; $15 add'l person

**Credit Cards:** V, MC

**Check-in/Out:** 3/11 (later showers avail.)

**Smoking:** Outside only

**Pets:** No; host cats

**Kids:** No

**Minimum Stay:** None

**Open:** All year

**Hosts:** Kitty & Bill Sperry
1171 Big Pine Way, Forks, WA 98331
(888) 822-6008 or (360) 379-8079
Fax: (360) 385-6623
hucklodg@olypen.com
www.northolympic.com/huckleberry

## MANITOU LODGE, Forks

| Overall: ★★½ | Room Quality: D | Value: C | Price: $80–$100 |
|---|---|---|---|

A modern hunting lodge in a secluded, fern-filled wood, on a parcel far from anywhere. . . (or so it seems; the restaurants of Forks are just a short drive away). Built in the 1970s, the property has been a bed-and-breakfast since 1988 and owned by the Murphys since 1996.

## SETTING & FACILITIES

**Location:** About 10 mi. from Forks via Hwy. 110 & Quillayute Rd.

**Near:** Olympic N.P., Hoh Rain Forest, rivers, beaches, Forks Timber Museum, lakes, Clallam & Neah Bays, Sol Duc Hot Springs

**Building:** 1970s hunting/fishing lodge

**Grounds:** Eleven wooded acres w/ trails

**Public Space:** Great room, porch/deck, mezzanine sitting area

**Food & Drink:** Coffee, tea, cookies (in the p.m.); full breakfast

**Recreation:** Fishing, scenic driving, beachcombing, kayaking, art galleries & studios

**Amenities & Services:** Gift shop, large library, games, sound system

## ACCOMMODATIONS

**Units:** 6 guest rooms
**All Rooms:** Private entrances, coffeemakers
**Some Rooms:** Tub & shower bath, fireplace, desk, closet, bubble bath, carpet
**Bed & Bath:** Various, some with add'l beds; private ensuite baths
**Favorites:** Sacajawea
**Comfort & Decor:** Modern Native-American-cum-Southwest-cum-hunting-lodge results in a fresh, pleasant theme. The great room, taken by itself, would rate 4 stars, with its vaulted ceiling, huge fieldstone fireplace, sound system, comfortable couches and chairs, and extensive library. Rooms are functional and are being upgraded; some room decor is a bit dated, but homey touches including handmade quilts make them pleasant. Tasteful pottery and other artwork in common areas.

## RATES, RESERVATIONS, & RESTRICTIONS

**Deposit:** Check or credit card; 5-day cancellation, $10 fee May 1–Sept. 30
**Discounts:** See Web site for specials; $15 add'l person, under 3 free
**Credit Cards:** V, MC, AE, DC
**Check-in/Out:** 4–8/10:30
**Smoking:** No
**Pets:** Allowed in one room ($10/night add'l); host dogs & cats on site
**Kids:** Welcome
**Minimum Stay:** None
**Open:** All year
**Hosts:** Lynne & Ed Murphy
Kilmer Rd., P.O. Box 600
Forks, WA 98331
(360) 374-6295
Fax: (360) 374-7495
manitou@olypen.com
www.northolympic.com/manitou

## MILLER TREE INN, Forks

| Overall: ★★★ | Room Quality: C | Value: B | Price: $60–$115 |
|---|---|---|---|

The perfect combination: an established inn (with previous longtime owners still nearby and involved) and new, energetic hosts with local background. Bill and Susan, who took over the 12-year-old inn in 1998, are ideally suited to be innkeepers—they are relaxed yet enthusiastic, and genuinely care about their guests. Their able assistant, Guinness the cat, may assist you with your bags, for the price of a belly rub. Breakfasts are hearty and abundant. Bathroom facilities may sound confusing, but bottom line is: plenty for all. At most, two rooms share a full bath. This is a great little inn.

## SETTING & FACILITIES

**Location:** 6 blocks off Hwy. 101 in
Forks
**Near:** Olympic N.P., Hoh Rain Forest,
rivers, beaches, Forks Timber Museum,
lakes, Clallam & Neah Bays, Sol Duc
Hot Springs
**Building:** 1914 farmhouse
**Grounds:** Border plants, mature trees
(giant monkey puzzle tree—holy
cow!), swings, basketball hoop; pastoral
setting adjacent to grazing cattle
**Public Space:** Porch, front parlor, LR,
deck
**Food & Drink:** Hot beverages &

cookies; fresh coffee (6 a.m.);
all-you-can-eat breakfast (guests
choose time)
**Recreation:** Fishing, wildlife watching,
scenic driving, kayaking, art galleries &
studios
**Amenities & Services:** Hot tub,
robes, swimsuits, cable, library, games,
raingear, boot dryer, guest phone/fax,
data port, piano; excellent local touring
info, guide referrals, boat trailer shuttle
& hiking shuttle referrals, thermoses
filled

## ACCOMMODATIONS

**Units:** 6 guest rooms, 1 suite
**All Rooms:** Clean, homey, carpeted
**Some Rooms:** Desk, view
**Bed & Bath:** Queen, king, twin, some
with extra beds; 3 private baths (2
ensuite); 2 rooms have half-baths (toi-
lets), while 2 share 2 full baths (showers in the 2 shared full baths are also
shared by the 2 half-bath rooms)
**Favorites:** Blue Jay, Cedar Creek,
Orchard Suite

**Comfort & Decor:** Relaxed hospitality is the hallmark at Miller Tree Inn.
Common areas are spacious and comfortable, with warm knotty wood paneling. Wall and window treatments are
color-coordinated and attractive,
though not expensive. Lace, wicker, and
floral motifs predominate. Impeccably
clean. Rooms have heat controls; windows open and fans are available.

## RATES, RESERVATIONS, & RESTRICTIONS

**Deposit:** Credit card; 72-hour
cancellation
**Discounts:** Off-season, single in off-
season; $15 add'l person
**Credit Cards:** V, MC
**Check-in/Out:** 4:30–8:30/11
**Smoking:** Outside only
**Pets:** Welcome in some rooms, $10
fee per pet; host pets on site
**Kids:** Age 7 & older welcome in main
inn; any age welcome in Orchard Suite

**Minimum Stay:** None
**Open:** All year
**Hosts:** Bill & Susan Brager
654 East Division St
Forks, WA 98331
(360) 374-6806
Fax: (360) 374-6807
milltree@ptinet.net
www.northolympic.com/millertree

## LYTLE HOUSE, Hoquiam

| Overall: ★★★★ | Room Quality: B | Value: B | Price: $65–$135 |
| --- | --- | --- | --- |

What a wonderful place! The Historic Register building is a real stunner, and the decidedly uncommon hosts are a delight. Touches of whimsy are everywhere, from the coloring-crayons guest books (where you are encouraged to draw, not just write) to the eclectic gift shop to the free-roaming indoor bunny and living room aviary. The steep stairs (both within the house and from the street) will be difficult for some; a side driveway offering alternate access is in the works. Some guests might be befuddled by such period eccentricities as the tub-only bath in the Rose Room, but we found our stay comfortable in every way.

### SETTING & FACILITIES

**Location:** On the hill, adjacent to Hoquiam Castle
**Near:** Hoquiam Castle, Bowerman Basin Nat'l Wildlife Refuge, farmers' market, Riverside Dike Trail and other trails & parks, lakes, ocean beaches, Westport, Ocean Shores, Olympic N.P. (45 minutes)
**Building:** 1897 Queen Anne Victorian mansion
**Grounds:** Parklike, spacious (a state-certified Backyard Wildlife Sanctuary); private, ideal for picnicking; gardens (incl. rose garden)
**Public Space:** Lobby/gift shop, front parlor, back parlor/aviary, DR, library/TV room, porch
**Food & Drink:** Evening tea & dessert; in-room chocolates and honor basket; cold beverages (fee); morning coffee; elegant full breakfast
**Recreation:** Antiquing, deep-sea charters, beach horseback riding, golf, museums
**Amenities & Services:** Cordless guest phone, TV executive suite (avail. weekly/monthly), extra towels & toilet items upon request, iron, umbrellas, games, 1850 Chickering piano; fax/computer, catering, breakfast meetings, seminars, corporate billing; murder mystery, Victorian Christmas, and other parties; small weddings & showers; cocktail parties & high teas; picnic basket/supplies/ice avail. for on-site picnics

### ACCOMMODATIONS

**Units:** 6 guest rooms, 2 suites
**All Rooms:** Antique furnishings & fixtures, robes, honor basket, sitting area, closet or armoire
**Some Rooms:** Private balcony, seating alcove, desk, claw-foot tub, decorative woodstove, mini-library
**Bed & Bath:** Queens (some with extra bed/daybed), one with king & queen; 6 private baths, 2 share a full bath
**Favorites:** Balcony Suite, Windsor Room, Rose Room
**Comfort & Decor:** Quintessential Queen Anne Victorian mansion. Original woodwork, wall coverings, fixtures, and stained glass. The spacious, high-ceilinged rooms vary in decor from the lace-and-rose motifs of the Rose Room to the masculine jewel tones of the Harbor View Room. Windows open; rooms have individual baseboard heaters and room-darkening shades.

## RATES, RESERVATIONS, & RESTRICTIONS

**Deposit:** 1st night; 72-hour cancellation for refund (less $10 handling fee)
**Discounts:** Corporate; "Comfort Club" frequent business traveler program; single occupancy; $15 add'l person
**Credit Cards:** V, MC
**Check-in/Out:** 4–8/11 or by arrangement
**Smoking:** Front porch and gardens only (not on balconies or inside)
**Pets:** No

**Kids:** Call about accommodations for children under 10
**Minimum Stay:** None
**Open:** All year
**Hosts:** Robert & Dayna Bencala
509 Chenault Ave.
Hoquiam, WA 98550
(800) 677-2320 or (360) 533-2320
Fax: (360) 533-4025
benchmrk@techline.com
www.lytlehouse.com

## CHICK-ADEE INN, Ilwaco

Overall: ★★★     Room Quality: D     Value: D     Price: $76–$180

Formerly the Inn at Ilwaco, this Presbyterian-church-turned-high-school-turned-inn was taken over by the Hinkles in 1995. They refurbished the interior and exterior, redecorated, and fashioned the quaint, commodious, quiet Chick-ADee Inn. Your relaxed and friendly hosts live on-site and are happy to provide information about the peninsula in general, and what makes Ilwaco special in particular. Most rooms are modest in size, and each is unique. The church portion of the property is still intact, pews and all, providing a gathering place for local events as well as a most unusual setting for breakfast.

## SETTING & FACILITIES

**Location:** A few blocks from Baker Bay at the north end of Williams St.
**Near:** Museum, Fort Canby, Lewis & Clark Interpretive Center, lighthouses, boardwalk & dune trail, Fort Columbia
**Building:** 1879 church, later a high school
**Grounds:** Two-acre property next to wetland; front lawn, two patios
**Public Space:** Guest parlor with sitting areas

**Food & Drink:** 24-hour cran-oatmeal cookies (decadent), coffee & tea; full breakfast
**Recreation:** Kite flying, salmon fishing, horseback riding, galleries, beach driving
**Amenities & Services:** Library, CDs; kitchen avail. by arrangement; 1940 Cadillac touring car for special transport; weddings

## ACCOMMODATIONS

**Units:** 8 guest rooms, 1 suite
**All Rooms:** Basic toiletries
**Some Rooms:** Claw-foot tub, window seat, sitting area, river view, binoculars, tub baths
**Bed & Bath:** Queen or king; private bath
**Favorites:** Admiral Suite

**Comfort & Decor:** The huge parlor has extra-high ceilings and many places to lounge. Decor is a mix of romantic and nautical. Suite is truly fit for an Admiral, with king bed, double bed room, wet bar, fridge, vanity, sitting area, and 2 baths. Rooms and baths have individual heat controls.

## RATES, RESERVATIONS, & RESTRICTIONS

**Deposit:** 1st night; 7-day cancellation
**Discounts:** AAA, winter, AARP, military
**Credit Cards:** V, MC
**Check-in/Out:** After 1/11
**Smoking:** No
**Pets:** No
**Kids:** No

**Minimum Stay:** Major holidays only
**Open:** All year
**Hosts:** Chick and Delaine (DeeDee) Hinkle (get it?)
120 NE Williams
Ilwaco, WA 98624
(888) CHICKAD or (360) 642-8686
Fax: (360) 642-8642

## CHINA BEACH B&B RETREAT, Ilwaco

Overall: ★★★★★      Room Quality: A      Value: D      Price: $189–$229

David and Laurie, whose Shelburne Country Inn (see "Seaview, WA") has been a rave-review Long Beach Peninsula staple for years, have poured their love and experience into this exclusive property. Because of their backgrounds and the amount of effort already visible in this new endeavor at the time of our visit, we are confident in including it and giving it five stars. The China Beach site is adjacent to Fort Canby State Park, fronts acres of wetlands and Baker Bay, and has views of Cape Disappointment, its lighthouse, and the mouth of the mighty Columbia River.

## SETTING & FACILITIES

**Location:** South of Ilwaco off Robert Gray Dr. on Baker Bay
**Near:** Fort Canby, museum, lighthouses, boardwalk & dune trail, Fort Columbia, Lewis & Clark Interpretive Center
**Building:** 1907 Craftsman home, expanded & newly remodeled
**Grounds:** Parklike, secluded; bay view, fire pit, stream; plans for Japanese tea house
**Public Space:** Great room (living/dining area), deck

**Food & Drink:** Coffee & quality tea; full gourmet breakfast on-site or in town at Shelburne Country Inn (see separate profile)
**Recreation:** Clam digging, salmon fishing, beachcombing, horseback riding, festivals
**Amenities & Services:** Phones avail. for rooms, kayak (fee); policies/amenities still evolving, but certain to be exceptional; charter fishing arrangements, workshops, classes, retreats

## ACCOMMODATIONS

**Units:** 2 guest rooms, 1 suite
**All Rooms:** Jetted tubs, Berber carpets; exceptional antiques, stained glass, finish work, furnishings, mattresses, & linens
**Bed & Bath:** Queens; private ensuite baths
**Favorites:** Main floor suite
**Comfort & Decor:** This B&B retains the elegance of the past with its impressive antiques but is a picture of modern opulence. Each guest room is decorated in a surprising palette; baths feature exceptional tile work. Views are stunning, especially from the elegant great room, with its wrap-around glass and Asian antiques. Original paintings adorn the walls.

## RATES, RESERVATIONS, & RESTRICTIONS

**Deposit:** 1st night; 5-day cancellation or forfeit deposit unless rebooked; $10 cancellation fee
**Discounts:** Winter midweek
**Credit Cards:** V, MC, AE
**Check-in/Out:** After 2/11:30
**Smoking:** No
**Pets:** No
**Kids:** Only if entire house rented by same party
**Minimum Stay:** 2 nights most weekends & holidays

**Open:** All year
**Hosts:** David Campiche & Laurie Anderson
222 Captain Robert Gray Dr.
Ilwaco, WA 98624
(mailing: P.O. Box 250
Seaview, WA 98644)
(360) 642-5660
Fax: (360) 642-8904
innkeeper@theshelburneinn.com
www.chinabeachretreat.com

## BOREAS B&B INN, Long Beach

| Overall: ★★★★½ | Room Quality: B | Value: B | Price: $120–$135 |
|---|---|---|---|

Bill and Susie are among the most gracious innkeepers we've found. Their remodeled beach house looks out at beach grass, dunes, the beach, and the wide Pacific—a short walk along their private path takes you to the water's edge. Everything about this place lends an air of respite and tranquility, from the fresh, contemporary decor to the socially responsible (and delicious) coffee. "Boreas" is Greek God of the North Wind, homage to this kite-flying Mecca. Splendid breakfast is truly a celebration meal. (Sample menu: baked pears stuffed with brown sugar, cinnamon, fresh-grated nutmeg, pecan halves, dried cranberries, and Grand Marnier, served with crème Anglaise; frittata with smoked salmon, assorted wild mushrooms, and Tillamook sharp cheddar; rosemary-dill home fries; wild blackberry and apple kuchen; apricot-macadamia–white chocolate scone.)

### SETTING & FACILITIES

**Location:** Just north of downtown, a block west of Hwy. 103 on N. Boulevard at 6th
**Near:** Long Beach boardwalk & dune trail, Fort Columbia, Fort Canby, Lewis & Clark Interpretive Center, lighthouses, Ilwaco Heritage Museum
**Building:** Modernized 1920s beach house
**Grounds:** Back lawn, deck, & garden; dunes & ocean view; path to beach

**Public Space:** 2 LRs, DR/coffee bar
**Food & Drink:** Evening brownies, in-room chocolates; coffee, cocoa, tea; gourmet breakfast
**Recreation:** Clamming, salmon fishing, horseback riding, festivals
**Amenities & Services:** Cedar gazebo w/ hot tub, VCR, grand piano, library, games, CDs, binoculars; celebration extras, massage avail.

## ACCOMMODATIONS

**Units:** 5 guest rooms (beach house adjacent—ideal for families and those with pets)
**All Rooms:** View, feather bed, plush carpet, hairdryers, closet or armoire, seating
**Some Rooms:** Jetted tub, ocean/dune views, extra daybed, skylight(s), balcony, vaulted ceiling, desk, private deck or deck access
**Bed & Bath:** Queen or king; private bath

**Favorites:** Each is truly beautiful & unique
**Comfort & Decor:** White walls and warm woods are accented by elegant, contemporary fabrics, fine art, curious antiques, and international objets d'art. Fresh flowers, hypoallergenic bedding, and tons of pillows add to a sense of pampered ease. Rooms have individual heat control.

## RATES, RESERVATIONS, & RESTRICTIONS

**Deposit:** Credit card; 7-day cancellation
**Discounts:** Off-season; $15 add'l person
**Credit Cards:** V, MC, AE, D, DC
**Check-in/Out:** 4–6 or by arrangement/11
**Smoking:** Outside only
**Pets:** No, except service dogs; host pets on site
**Kids:** Welcome under parental control

**Minimum Stay:** 2 nights, high-season weekends; 3 nights during festivals
**Open:** All year
**Hosts:** Bill Verner & Susie Goldsmith
607 N. Boulevard
Long Beach, WA 98631
(888) 642-8069 or (360) 642-8069
Fax: (360) 642-5353
boreas@aone.com
www.boreasinn.com

## THE DOVESHIRE B&B, Ocean Park

Overall: ★★★★    Room Quality: B    Value: B    Price: $120

As you turn off Highway 103 onto the tree-lined drive, this elegant home promises peace and privacy. Gene and Sharon built the property—their own two-level home with separate guest common area and four ground-level rooms with private entrances and shared deck—in 1997. The thoughtful design incorporates the best of privacy with good access to common-area amenities. The spacious rooms and doorways enable accessibility for most mobility-impaired individuals, and provide a roomy, private retreat for anyone. Awaken to the soft morning calls of resident doves "Fred and Ginger."

## SETTING & FACILITIES

**Location:** 2 mi. south of Ocean Park, 7 mi. north of Long Beach, set back from Hwy. 103
**Near:** Long Beach boardwalk & dune trail, Fort Columbia, Fort Canby, Lewis & Clark Interpretive Center, lighthouses, Ilwaco Heritage Museum
**Building:** New home w/ traditional lines
**Grounds:** Sweeping front lawn, fairytale backyard: patio, deck, paths

**Public Space:** DR, kitchenette, library/sitting area
**Food & Drink:** Coffee, tea, cocoa, & cider; buffet-style full breakfast
**Recreation:** Wildlife watching, salmon fishing, horseback riding, beach driving, festivals
**Amenities & Services:** Fridge & micro., BBQ, hot tub (in the works when we visited); small weddings & special events

## ACCOMMODATIONS

**Units:** 4 guest rooms
**All Rooms:** Vaulted ceiling, sitting area, VCR, private entrance, deck, carpet, down comforters, heat controls
**Bed & Bath:** Queens; private ensuite baths
**Favorites:** Each is spacious and has same amenities; differ only in decor
**Comfort & Decor:** Entire property

is upscale and modern, yet traditional in its decor sensibilities. Room themes include Garden (whimsical mural, "rabbit hutch" TV armoire, "white-picket-fence" bed), Gibson (1920s style), Rose (wicker sleigh bed), Vanilla (romantic). Common area is comfortable, but rooms are also large enough for lounging.

## RATES, RESERVATIONS, & RESTRICTIONS

**Deposit:** Call
**Discounts:** None
**Credit Cards:** V, MC, AE
**Check-in/Out:** 3/11 or by arrangement
**Smoking:** Outside only
**Pets:** No
**Kids:** No
**Minimum Stay:** None

**Open:** All year
**Hosts:** Sharon & Gene Miller
21914 Pacific Hwy. 103
Ocean Park, WA 98640
(888) 553-2320 or (360) 665-3017
Fax: (360) 665-3017
doveshire@willapabay.org
www.willapabay.org/~doveshire

## BJ'S GARDEN GATE, Port Angeles

| | | | |
|---|---|---|---|
| Overall: ★★★★ | Room Quality: A | Value: C | Price: $130–$170 |

Just up the road from legendary Domaine Madeleine, this brand-new (1998) inn has drawn rave reviews from the outset. The attitude is Northwest casual—shorts and T-shirts welcome!—but the surroundings are European formal, complete with antiques and attention to luxurious detail. Gardens include volumes of bulbs, rhododendrons, roses, climbing and flowering plants, identified by labels, overlooking the strait. Hosts are seasoned B&B-goers but have new-B&B-owner enthusiasm for their work; they're attentive but never intrusive. A place for romance and pampering.

### SETTING & FACILITIES

**Location:** 6 mi. north of Sequim overlooking the Strait of Juan de Fuca
**Near:** Port Angeles and Sequim, Victoria ferries, Olympic Game Farm, Dungeness Spit, Hurricane Ridge/Olympic N.P., Port Townsend
**Building:** New Victorian-style inn
**Grounds:** Outstanding gardens, huge lawn with Victoria & Mt. Baker views
**Public Space:** Porch, parlor/DR

**Food & Drink:** In-room fresh cookies (the BEST!) & ice water; refreshments upon arrival; morning beverage tray to room; full formal breakfast
**Recreation:** Wildlife watching, kayaking, clamming, horseback riding, X-C skiing
**Amenities & Services:** Menus, ferry schedules, CDs, videos; turndown, reservations, massage by arrangement

## ACCOMMODATIONS

**Units:** 5 guest rooms
**All Rooms:** Water view, VCR, phone, CD, remote-control fireplace, down comforters
**Some Rooms:** Private porch, private hot tub, dbl. whirlpool, queen futon, table & chairs
**Bed & Bath:** Queen or king, excellent beds; private ensuite bath
**Favorites:** Maria Theresa Suite

**Comfort & Decor:** Eastlake and other antiques from the 18th & 19th centuries abound. Victorian sensibilities, but wide hallways, white-painted woodwork, jewel-tone and floral accents, and rich prints. Duvets, down comforters, exquisite linens. Extra-large showers, roomy baths. Excellent sound insulation. Individual room heat control via fireplaces; air-conditioning.

## RATES, RESERVATIONS, & RESTRICTIONS

**Deposit:** 1st night
**Discounts:** Packages, some extended stays, off-season; $25 add'l person
**Credit Cards:** V, MC, AE
**Check-in/Out:** 4–6 or by arrangement/11
**Smoking:** Designated outside areas only
**Pets:** No
**Kids:** No
**No-Nos:** Smoking on porches;
whirlpool tubs after 11 p.m.
**Minimum Stay:** None
**Open:** All year
**Hosts:** BJ & Frank Paton
397 Monterra Dr.
Port Angeles, WA 98362
(800) 880-1332 or (360) 452-2322
Fax: (360) 417-5098
bjgarden@olypen.com
www.bjgarden.com

## DOMAINE MADELEINE, Port Angeles

Overall: ★★★★★      Room Quality: A      Value: C      Price: $150–$175

It's not so much the furnishings or fixtures that make Madeleine legendary (although the giant double whirlpool tubs, fireplaces, and artwork are nice), as the hosts' anticipation of your every need. Sure, they have the hairdryer and the CDs and the toiletries basket, but they also prestamp their postcards and slip a fresh coffee filter into the basket of your immaculate in-room coffeemaker. There's nothing to distract you from l'amour. Breakfasts are a celebration meal of the highest order; plan to linger.

## SETTING & FACILITIES

**Location:** Just east of Port Angeles on the Strait of Juan de Fuca
**Near:** Port Angeles and Sequim, Victoria ferries, Olympic Game Farm, Dungeness Spit, Hurricane Ridge/Olympic N.P., Port Townsend
**Building:** Contemporary waterfront home w/ outbuildings
**Grounds:** 5 waterfront acres w/ riotous flowers, trees, picnic areas, Monet garden
**Public Space:** DR, LR (adjacent to Renoir; becomes part of Renoir's space in evenings); rooms are spacious suites

**Food & Drink:** Coffee, tea, cookies; in-room fruit basket, chocolates; multi-course, chef-prepared celebration breakfast
**Recreation:** Lawn games, wildlife watching, water/winter sports, horseback riding, biking
**Amenities & Services:** Videos, whale-watching telescope, games; weddings, concerts, celebration extras, multilingual hostess & staff (Madeleine speaks French, Spanish, Farsi; assistants Victor & Ann are from Thailand)

## ACCOMMODATIONS

**Units:** 5 suites
**All Rooms:** TV/VCR, CDs, fireplace, robes, hairdryer, phone, French perfume, extensive toiletries, flowers, sitting areas
**Some Rooms:** Kitchenette area with coffeemaker, micro., fridge; skylight, water view, dbl. whirlpool, private entrance, private deck
**Bed & Bath:** Queen or king; private ensuite baths

**Favorites:** Ming Room, Rendezvous Room
**Comfort & Decor:** Inviting and international, with Asian motifs mixing effortlessly with European, such as Provence and the Impressionists. Fourteen-foot basalt fireplace in the living room. Original art and fine reproductions. Top-of-the-line linens and beds, quality electronics.

## RATES, RESERVATIONS, & RESTRICTIONS

**Deposit:** $10 by credit card (non-refundable) or a check for 1st night; 7-day cancellation or forfeit charge for 1st night unless rebooked
**Discounts:** Off-season weekday, public school teachers, extended stays, cash; $25 add'l person
**Credit Cards:** V, MC, AE, D
**Check-in/Out:** 4–6 or by arrangement/11
**Smoking:** Outside only
**Pets:** No

**Kids:** Over 12 only
**Minimum Stay:** 2 nights weekends mid-April to mid-Oct.
**Open:** All year
**Hosts:** Madeleine & John Chambers
146 Wildflower Ln.
Port Angeles, WA 98362
(360) 457-4174
Fax: (360) 457-4174
romance@domainemadeleine.com
www.northolympic.com/dm

## MAPLE ROSE INN, Port Angeles

| Overall: ★★★★ | Room Quality: B | Value: B | Price: $79–$147 |
|---|---|---|---|

Traditionally styled, attractively decorated contemporary country inn. Host pets on site include friendly retriever, cute cat, and melodic finches. If you knew the Maple Rose before 1996, check it out again. New owners remodeled, redecorated, and are providing a first-class bed-and-breakfast experience. Remodeling still underway, but as of our visit Maple Rose was already a graciously appointed, congenially hosted lodging.

### SETTING & FACILITIES

**Location:** Just south of downtown Port Angeles on Reservoir Rd. off Black Diamond Rd.
**Near:** Downtown Port Angeles, ferries to Victoria, Hurricane Ridge/Olympic N.P., Dungeness Spit, Olympic Game Farm
**Building:** 1992 transitional Victorian replica
**Grounds:** Spacious lawn & garden, mature trees
**Public Space:** Decks, porch, LR, DR, library/snack area, solarium (exercise/massage)

**Food & Drink:** Tea, fresh bean coffee, & other beverages; 7 a.m. cont'l breakfast or 8 or 9 a.m. full breakfast
**Recreation:** Water sports, crabbing, antiquing, horseback riding, mountain biking
**Amenities & Services:** Hot tub (8 a.m.–10 p.m.), exercise room (6 a.m.–10 p.m.), Internet access, library, micro./wet bar/fridge, umbrellas, videos; airport & ferry pick-up, massage avail., day trip arrangements; weddings & occasions, celebration extras, ensuite breakfast

### ACCOMMODATIONS

**Units:** 5 guest rooms
**All Rooms:** Cable TV, coffeemakers w/ fresh bean coffee, tea, phone, closet, data port(s), plush carpet, guest guide, robes & nightshirts, designer linens
**Some Rooms:** Whirlpool, kitchenette, deck, ceiling fan, sitting area, desk, skylight(s), window seat w/ mountain view
**Bed & Bath:** King, queen, king/twin conversion (futon/roll-away avail.); private baths

**Favorites:** Master Suite, Junior Suites
**Comfort & Decor:** Floral wallpapers in bold tones are paired with wood wainscoting throughout much of the house. Furnishings mix comfortable modern pieces with period pieces and replicas. Lighting can be a bit dim. Individual heating controls; windows open. Central music system; rooms have volume controls. Judicious use of well-tended houseplants.

## RATES, RESERVATIONS, & RESTRICTIONS

**Deposit:** Credit card; 7-day cancellation
**Discounts:** Off-season, group, special packages; $15 add'l person
**Credit Cards:** V, MC, AE, D
**Check-in/Out:** 3–6 or by arrangement/11–12
**Smoking:** Outside only
**Pets:** Welcome in one room, $15; host pets on site
**Kids:** 10 & over welcome; younger by arrangement

**Minimum Stay:** 2 nights holiday weekends
**Open:** All year
**Hosts:** Geoff Shelton & Darryl Hayes
112 Reservoir Rd.
Port Angeles, WA 98363
(800) 570-2007 or (360) 457-ROSE
Fax: (360) 457-0176
maplerose@tenforward.com
www.northolympic.com/maplerose

## THE SEASUNS B&B, Port Angeles

| Overall: ★★★★ | Room Quality: B | Value: B | Price: $95–$125 |

Let's be honest—it's not in the best neighborhood. As you come up semi-seedy Lincoln Street, which is also US Highway 101 as it passes through Port Angeles, it doesn't seem likely that an elegant bed-and-breakfast will be nearby. But The SeaSuns is a surprise. The inside is gorgeous, the innkeepers are warm and gracious, and the breakfasts are creative and very special. Even the grounds, which take advantage of three city lots, are surprisingly peaceful for their busy corner location. For city and ferry access in Port Angeles, and for hospitality and restored-Colonial elegance, you can't beat The SeaSuns.

## SETTING & FACILITIES

**Location:** Corner of 10th & Lincoln
**Near:** Downtown Port Angeles, ferries to Victoria, Hurricane Ridge/Olympic N.P., Dungeness Spit, Olympic Game Farm
**Building:** 1926 Dutch Colonial
**Grounds:** Colonnade seating area w/ waterfall; spacious lawns
**Public Space:** LR
**Food & Drink:** Morning coffee/tea; full breakfast

**Recreation:** Water/winter sports, clamming, crabbing, antiquing, horseback riding
**Amenities & Services:** TV in LR, phones in entry hall & kitchen; ferry and airport pick-up, celebration extras, dinner & picnic lunches by arrangement, receptions and small gatherings, personal wake-up call

## ACCOMMODATIONS

**Units:** 4 guest rooms, 1 carriage house (ideal for families or extra privacy)
**All Rooms:** Closets or armoires, robes
**Some Rooms:** View of Mt. Baker, Victoria, Strait of Juan de Fuca; private deck or deck access
**Bed & Bath:** Queen or double; private baths
**Favorites:** Winter or Summer

**Comfort & Decor:** Common area: pale, fresh hues with comfortably elegant furnishings. Attractive wallpapers; original light fixtures; some bath items, such as the oversized soaking tub in Herfst, add charm. All new double-pane windows that vent; radiator heat has individual room controls. Carriage House unit: knotty-pine, contemporary style; queen bed and queen sofa-sleeper.

## RATES, RESERVATIONS, & RESTRICTIONS

**Deposit:** 1st night; 72-hour cancellation
**Discounts:** Single occupancy, off-season, business traveler, extended stay; $15 add'l person
**Credit Cards:** V, MC
**Check-in/Out:** 4–6 or by arrangement/11
**Smoking:** Outside only
**Pets:** No

**Kids:** 12 & over welcome
**Minimum Stay:** None
**Open:** All year
**Hosts:** Bob & Jan Harbick
1006 S. Lincoln
Port Angeles, WA 98362
(800) 708-0777 or (360) 452-8248
Fax: (360) 417-0465
seasuns@olypen.com
www.northolympic.com/seasuns

## ANN STARRETT MANSION, Port Townsend

| Overall: ★★★★½ | Room Quality: A | Value: D | Price: $98–$225 |
|---|---|---|---|

This Port Townsend fixture, currently painted a soft brick red with sage and cream trim, has drawn stares and tourists for years. A registered historic landmark, it's open for public tours 12–3 daily (tourists view rooms from the halls, across roped doorways; stayover guests may elect privacy by leaving doors closed), which may give you the feeling of overnighting in a museum. Yet this "Victorian of Victorians" is truly a deluxe experience in this most Victorian of seaports. Lighting is dim— hey, you don't come to a landmark to read. An innkeeper is on site to attend to your needs.

## SETTING & FACILITIES

**Location:** Corner of Adams & Clay
**Near:** Downtown Port Townsend and waterfront, ferries, Fort Worden S.P., Chevy Chase Golf Course, Olympic N.P., Port Angeles & Sequim
**Building:** 1889 four-story Victorian; 1930s cottage
**Grounds:** Corner lot, narrow lawns; profuse, colorful border plantings
**Public Space:** Front parlor, sitting room

**Food & Drink:** Full breakfast; box breakfast avail.; ensuite breakfast avail. (w/ notice; $20 fee)
**Recreation:** Kayaking, antiquing, golf, museums, galleries
**Amenities & Services:** Ice, guest phone, maps, ferry schedules, games; small retreats, weddings, conferences; eco-sensitive recycling & linens programs; rooms tidied during breakfast; massage/reflexology by arrangement

## ACCOMMODATIONS

**Units:** 6 guest rooms, 5 suites
**All Rooms:** Hairdryer, ornate bed
**Some Rooms:** Sitting area, view, antique tubs, robes
**Bed & Bath:** Various (roll-aways avail.); private baths (most ensuite)
**Favorites:** Gable Suite, Master Suite, Ann's Parlor, Drawing Room, Upper Cottage

**Comfort & Decor:** Extravagantly appointed; museum-quality antiques in every room. Grand spiral staircase, elegant frescoes. Sumptuous bedding, tapestries. Antique lighting and bath fixtures. Baseboard heaters have individual room controls. (Cottage rooms are more modern, with 1930s-era furnishings.)

## RATES, RESERVATIONS, & RESTRICTIONS

**Deposit:** Full payment in advance; 14-day cancellation for refund, less $10 fee
**Discounts:** Off-season, special mid-week promotions (vary); $35 add'l person
**Credit Cards:** V, MC, AE, D
**Check-in/Out:** 3–6 or by arrangement/11
**Smoking:** No

**Pets:** No
**Kids:** Welcome
**Minimum Stay:** None
**Open:** All year
**Hosts:** Innkeeping staff
744 Clay St.
Port Townsend, WA 98368
(800) 321-0644 or (360) 385-3205
Fax: (360) 385-2976
www.olympus.net/starrett

## THE JAMES HOUSE, Port Townsend

| Overall: ★★★★ | Room Quality: B | Value: C | Price: $75–$165 |
|---|---|---|---|

With its sweeping view of Port Townsend Bay and excellent walking access to downtown and the waterfront, The James House (which claims to have been the Northwest's first bed-and-breakfast) is a good base from which to explore Port Townsend. The atmosphere is more akin to a small hotel than a cozy bed-and-breakfast, and the authentic Victoriana comes with its share of quirks (rooms are a tad drafty and dim, furnishings a bit stilted), but it's exceptionally well-maintained and restored, and is a good value in its class.

### SETTING & FACILITIES

**Location:** On Washington overlooking the waterfront & ferry
**Near:** Downtown Port Townsend and waterfront, ferries, Fort Worden S.P., Chevy Chase Golf Course, Olympic N.P., Port Angeles & Sequim
**Building:** 1889 Victorian mansion
**Grounds:** Bay & inlet views; colorful border plantings
**Public Space:** Small porch, 2 parlors, DR

**Food & Drink:** Afternoon sherry & cookies; tea & coffee on request; breakfast
**Recreation:** Water sports, antiquing, historic touring, museums, galleries
**Amenities & Services:** Bear & bunny gift shop in parlor, discount golf coupons, eco-sensitive linens policy

### ACCOMMODATIONS

**Units:** 12 (8 guest rooms, 3 suites, 1 cottage), plus adjacent "Bungalow on the Bluff" (modern, w/ fireplace, whirlpool, TV/VCR, cont'l breakfast)
**All Rooms:** Antiques, guest directory, custom soaps & shampoo
**Some Rooms:** Private patio, deck, or balcony; fireplace, view, robes, desk, feather bed, sitting area
**Bed & Bath:** Mostly queens (some with add'l twin or double); 10 private baths, 2 share a bath
**Favorites:** Master/Bridal Suite,

Olympic Garden Suite, Cascade Garden Suite
**Comfort & Decor:** Elegant antiques; extensive original woodwork includes hand-carved cherry staircase and the cherry-oak-walnut parquet entry floor. The stained glass, lace, and brocade elegance is softened by relaxing informal touches. Windows open, small fans are provided, and rooms have individual heat controls via thermostat or space heaters.

## RATES, RESERVATIONS, & RESTRICTIONS

**Deposit:** Credit card or check confirmation; 7-day cancellation
**Discounts:** Single occupancy, off-season midweek; $20 add'l person
**Credit Cards:** V, MC, AE
**Check-in/Out:** 3–7 or by arrangement/11
**Smoking:** No
**Pets:** No
**Kids:** 12 & over welcome

**Minimum Stay:** None
**Open:** All year
**Hosts:** Carol McGough, owner;
Donna Kuhn & J.R. Terry, managers
1238 Washington St.
Port Townsend, WA 98368
(800) 385-1238
Fax: (360) 379-5551
info@jameshouse.com
www.jameshouse.com

## LIZZIE'S, Port Townsend

| Overall: ★★★ | Room Quality: D | Value: C | Price: $70–$135 |
|---|---|---|---|

It's no Ann Starrett Mansion—but neither are the prices. On the quiet residential corner of Pierce and Lincoln, Lizzie's is named for original 1888 owner Lizzie Grant. This less-expensive Victorian alternative is more homey than its showplace cousins and still within walking distance of downtown and the Water Street shops and activities. Don't be put off by the relative lack of curb appeal; the rooms are spacious and quite acceptable.

## SETTING & FACILITIES

**Location:** Corner of Pierce & Lincoln
**Near:** Downtown Port Townsend & waterfront, ferries, Fort Worden S.P., Chevy Chase Golf Course, Olympic N.P., Port Angeles & Sequim
**Building:** 1888 Italianate Victorian mansion
**Grounds:** Small fountain, rock pond; roses, other flowers are lit at night; miniature replica of the house (in backyard) serves as the owner's flower-drying workshop
**Public Space:** 2 parlors
**Food & Drink:** Cookies, coffee, & tea; full all-you-can-eat breakfast
**Recreation:** Kayaking, antiquing, historic touring, museums, galleries
**Amenities & Services:** Grand piano, library, guest phone, fireplace

## ACCOMMODATIONS

**Units:** 7 guest rooms
**All Rooms:** Closet &/or armoire, guest guide, teddy bears
**Some Rooms:** Claw-foot soaking tub, bubble bath, table & chairs, sitting area, fireplace, desk
**Bed & Bath:** Mostly queen, 1 king, 1 double (1 with queen & double); private baths
**Favorites:** Sarah's Room, Lizzie's Room
**Comfort & Decor:** A bit dim, but stately, with high ceilings, dark-stained wood, and period furnishings. Moderate quality but tidy linens, wall coverings, and window treatments; newer vinyls in most baths. Common rooms are elegant and comfortable. Room decor ranges from the chic dusty plum of Sarah's Room to the faded Old-World elegance of Lizzie's Room. Windows open. Downstairs rooms have central forced air heat; upstairs rooms have individual baseboard heaters.

## RATES, RESERVATIONS, & RESTRICTIONS

**Deposit:** Credit card; 4-day cancellation
**Discounts:** None
**Credit Cards:** V, MC, D
**Check-in/Out:** 4 or by arrangement/11
**Smoking:** No
**Pets:** No
**Kids:** Over 10 welcome
**Minimum Stay:** 2 nights during holidays, local festivals
**Open:** All year
**Hosts:** Patti & Bill Wickline
731 Pierce, Port Townsend, WA 98368
(800) 700-4168 or (360) 385-4168
Fax: (360) 385-9467
wickline@olympus.net
www.kolke.com/lizzies

## RAVENSCROFT INN, Port Townsend

Overall: ★★★★½     Room Quality: B     Value: B     Price: $70–$185

A welcoming, small-European-hotel atmosphere, in an excellent Port Townsend location. Relaxingly homey, yet professionally run. Leah has operated the successful inn since 1989 and was seeking to retire at our visit, so check for policy and host updates. (Our hunch is that Leah will find a like-minded buyer and continue to stay local and perhaps even involved with Ravenscroft.) Breakfasts are savory, innovative, and tasty, with an adventurous (adult) palate in mind. A solid recommendation for a relaxing stay.

## SETTING & FACILITIES

**Location:** Corner Quincy & Clay, overlooking Port Townsend Bay
**Near:** Downtown Port Townsend & waterfront, ferries, Fort Worden S.P., Chevy Chase Golf Course, Olympic N.P., Port Angeles & Sequim
**Building:** 1987-built 3-story inn
**Grounds:** Grassy lawn, attractive borders
**Public Space:** Porch, sitting area, library, DR

**Food & Drink:** Tea & refreshments; in-room candy; self-serve popcorn & cold beverages; morning coffee; full breakfast
**Recreation:** Antiquing, historic touring, golf, museums, galleries
**Amenities & Services:** Piano, newspaper, fridge, micro., "I forgot it" basket, gift shop, games, books, puzzles, VCR, phone, fax, ferry schedules; special packages, celebration extras

## ACCOMMODATIONS

**Units:** 6 guest rooms, 2 suites
**All Rooms:** Quality linens, guest directory
**Some Rooms:** Water view, mountain view, four-poster, window seat, sitting area, fireplace, towel dryer, deck access, dual whirlpool tub
**Bed & Bath:** Queen (7) or king/twin conversion; private ensuite baths
**Favorites:** Admiralty Suite, Rainier,

Fireside, Bay
**Comfort & Decor:** Common area decor has a Colonial-meets-contemporary-Country feel, in a brick red, cobalt, ivory, and teal palette. Individual room decor varies: sunny blue and yellow in one, romantic rose and teal in another, luxurious ivory and mint in a third. Accents include brick, dried flowers. Central heat plus auxiliary units.

## RATES, RESERVATIONS, & RESTRICTIONS

**Deposit:** 1st night; 7-day cancellation
**Discounts:** Off-season, single, some extended stays (ask), packages; $35 add'l person
**Credit Cards:** V, MC
**Check-in/Out:** 3–6 or by arrangement/11
**Smoking:** Outside only
**Pets:** No
**Kids:** Over 12 welcome

**Minimum Stay:** 2 nights during high season weekends, special events
**Open:** All year
**Hosts:** Leah Hammer
533 Quincy St.
Port Townsend, WA 98368
(800) 782-2691 or (360) 385-2784
Fax: (360) 385-6724
ravenscroft@olympus.net
www.ravenscroftinn.com

## THE SHELBURNE COUNTRY INN, Seaview

| Overall: ★★★★ | Room Quality: B | Value: C | Price: $109–$179 |

The Shelburne, originally built as a hotel in 1896, may be the oldest continuously operating hotel in Washington. David and Laurie have owned and operated the property since 1977. It is a romantic, true-to-the-period inn, professionally run with the assistance of a friendly, helpful staff. The inn's large size on a small lot results in a bit of a parking shortage and not a lot of common area; in fair weather, try for a room with a balcony or deck to enhance your sense of space. Lavish, herb-rich breakfasts.

### SETTING & FACILITIES

**Location:** Just south of Long Beach, on Hwy. 103 in Seaview
**Near:** Beach, dunes, Long Beach boardwalk & dune trail, Fort Columbia, Fort Canby, Lewis & Clark Interpretive Center, lighthouses, Ilwaco Heritage Museum
**Building:** 1896 hotel w/ extensive 1986 addition
**Grounds:** Lavish front flowers & garden path; side garden & small lawn, herb garden

**Public Space:** Lobby/dining area; award-winning restaurant & pub; library
**Food & Drink:** Coffee, tea, & cocoa; full breakfast (choice of entrees); restaurant & pub on premises
**Recreation:** Kite flying, salmon fishing, horseback riding, galleries, beach driving, festivals
**Amenities & Services:** Gift shop, games, puzzles, books, fitness center pass, phone; eco-sensitive linens policy

### ACCOMMODATIONS

**Units:** 15 guest rooms
**All Rooms:** Carpet, antiques, hairdryers, down comforters, extra pillows, fans
**Some Rooms:** Private deck or balcony, desk, disabled access, claw-foot tub
**Bed & Bath:** Queen or double (some w/ extra twin); ensuite private baths
**Favorites:** 17, 9, 5 & 6; 4 & 10 share small deck, as do 1 & 8
**Comfort & Decor:** Abundant warm, deep-toned woodwork, lavish period furnishings, stained glass, original art, lace. Quality old-growth fir graces many walls and ceilings. Forest and rose carpet, attractive wallpapers, brocade upholstery. Overall effect can be dark for modern sensibilities, but is undeniably period-correct and romantic. Individual heat controls and windows that open; avoid the third floor on hot summer days.

## RATES, RESERVATIONS, & RESTRICTIONS

**Deposit:** 1st night; 5-day cancellation or forfeit deposit unless rebooked; $10 cancellation fee
**Discounts:** Midweek off-season, extended stays, dining/room packages
**Credit Cards:** V, MC, AE
**Check-in/Out:** After 2/11:30
**Smoking:** Outside only
**Pets:** No
**Kids:** Welcome if well supervised

**Minimum Stay:** 2 nights, most weekends & holidays
**Open:** All year
**Hosts:** David Campiche & Laurie Anderson
4415 Pacific Way, Seaview, WA 98644
(800) INN-1896 or (360) 642-2442
Fax: (360) 642-8904
innkeeper@theshelburneinn.com
www.theshelburneinn.com

## BRIGADOON B&B, Sequim

| Overall: ★★★½ | Room Quality: C | Value: B | Price: $65–$95 |
|---|---|---|---|

Flower-bedecked, bird-friendly Brigadoon has country charm just outside the city. Whimsical and romantic: from the wicker buggy on the front porch (filled to overflowing with colorful container flowers) to the antique glider horse in the dining room to the hat and coat stand decked with vintage wear in the foyer. Marvelous, eclectic antiques are both aesthetic and integrated functionally (such as Marilyn's stove and actress Myrna Loy's four-poster bed). The spa area is a delightful oasis. The home is elegant, yet the atmosphere is relaxed.

## SETTING & FACILITIES

**Location:** 3.8 mi. north of Sequim, off Sequim-Dungeness Way
**Near:** Dungeness Spit, Olympic Game Farm, casino, Port Townsend, Port Angeles
**Building:** Craftsman-style country home
**Grounds:** Cutting garden, vegetable/herb garden, exuberant flowers; duck pen

**Public Space:** Porch, patio w/ hot tub, common room, DR
**Food & Drink:** Hot beverages & evening snacks; morning coffee & tea; full breakfast
**Recreation:** Festivals, wine-tasting, galleries, golf, kayaking, wildlife watching
**Amenities & Services:** Garden hot tub, stereo, TV/VCR

## ACCOMMODATIONS

**Units:** 2 guest rooms (a 3rd is possible)
**All Rooms:** Quality toiletries, hairdryer, antiques, flowers
**Some Rooms:** "Peek-a-boo" views of Strait of Juan de Fuca, cable
**Bed & Bath:** Queens; private baths
**Favorites:** Green Room
**Comfort & Decor:** The home, built from a Sears & Roebuck kit, boasts original woodwork and period light fixtures, and is decorated in soft hues with ornate, cheerful wallpapers and accents of lace and crystal. Rooms have individual thermostats and windows that open. Bedrooms and stairs are carpeted; other areas have hardwood and extra-thick area rugs.

## RATES, RESERVATIONS, & RESTRICTIONS

**Deposit:** 72-hour cancellation
**Discounts:** Single occupancy; $15 add'l person
**Credit Cards:** Not accepted
**Check-in/Out:** 3–6 or by arrangement/11
**Smoking:** No
**Pets:** No
**Kids:** 12 & over welcome
**Minimum Stay:** None
**Open:** All year
**Hosts:** Marilyn & Larry Cross
62 Balmoral Ct.
Sequim, WA 98382
(800) 397-2256 or (360) 683-2255
Fax: (360) 681-5285
brigadoon2@webtv.net
www.northolympic.com/brigadoon

## GREYWOLF INN, Sequim

Overall: ★★★½     Room Quality: C     Value: B     Price: $65–$120

Greywolf's peaceful location is convenient to Port Townsend as well as to Sequim and Port Angeles. Peggy and Bill have been operating their bed-and-breakfast for a decade and are delightful, relaxed hosts with much to offer. Their care shows throughout the home and grounds, including the thoughtful little extras that make your stay special. Plan to spend some time wandering the meditative trails. (One of the two big farm dogs is likely to share your walk.) Delicious breakfasts, attractively presented.

## SETTING & FACILITIES

**Location:** 1 mi. east of Sequim near Sequim Bay
**Near:** Dungeness Spit, Olympic Game Farm, Port Townsend, Port Angeles
**Building:** Secluded 2-story inn
**Grounds:** 5 acres; stream, views, paths, gazebo, patio, spacious deck
**Public Space:** LR, DR, decks
**Food & Drink:** Self-serve hot beverages; full breakfast
**Recreation:** Festivals, wine-tasting, antiquing, galleries, golf, water sports
**Amenities & Services:** TV, sound system, guest phone/fax, reading material, games, gift shop, outdoor enclosed hot tub (till 10:30 p.m.); reservations, celebration extras, picnic lunch by arrangement

## ACCOMMODATIONS

**Units:** 5 guest rooms
**All Rooms:** Toiletry/amenity selection, hairdryer, TV, quality linens, robes, spa slippers, extra pillows, guest guide
**Some Rooms:** VCR, phone, private entrance, deck, desk, sitting area
**Bed & Bath:** Various beds (roll-away avail.); private baths
**Favorites:** Marguerite

**Comfort & Decor:** Main LR, while essentially windowless, is cozy and pleasant. DR is cheerful and sunny, with a clever garden mural. Guest rooms vary in decor from pale mauve and beige (Marguerite) to dark wood and blue accents (Pamela) to black-and-white Asian motif (Nancy) to soft, springlike tones (Kimberleigh).

## RATES, RESERVATIONS, & RESTRICTIONS

**Deposit:** 1st night; 72-hour cancellation
**Discounts:** Off-season; $20 add'l person
**Credit Cards:** V, MC, AE, D
**Check-in/Out:** 4 or by arrangement/11
**Smoking:** Outdoors only
**Pets:** No; host pets on-site
**Kids:** Older children welcome

**Minimum Stay:** None
**Open:** All year
**Hosts:** Bill & Peggy Melang
395 Keeler Rd.
Sequim, WA 98382
(800) 914-WOLF (9653) or
(360) 683-5889
Fax: (360) 683-1487
info@greywolfinn.com
www.greywolfinn.com

## SIMONE'S GROVELAND COTTAGE B&B INN, Sequim

Overall: ★★★½    Room Quality: C    Value: B    Price: $80–$110

This 19th-century farmhouse is an established bed-and-breakfast (since 1987) with modern comforts and a wonderful lawn and gardens. Delicious breakfasts may include an entree featuring Pacific Northwest smoked salmon or crab and are sure to include Simone's homemade five-grain hot cereal along with a range of fresh and creative accompaniments. The quiet home is an easy, unpretentious mix of the old and the new. It's a happy, comfortable place, and Simone is a wonderful hostess—gracious without being intrusive.

## SETTING & FACILITIES

**Location:** North of Sequim, half a mile from the beach
**Near:** Dungeness Spit, Olympic Game Farm, casino, Port Townsend, Port Angeles
**Building:** Turn-of-the-century home with modern updates
**Grounds:** Small, lush side yard; large showplace backyard adjoins creek, w/ gazebo, BBQ patio, fruit/nut trees, flowers, views of Olympic Mountains
**Public Space:** Great room/banquet room, LR, porch, mezzanine sitting area

**Food & Drink:** Early morning coffee service; in-room chocolates; full breakfast
**Recreation:** Festivals, wine-tasting, antiquing, galleries, golf, water sports, crabbing
**Amenities & Services:** Videos, newspapers, BBQ, phone, stationary bike, games, sound system; weddings, meetings, events, catering, reunions; picnic/box lunches avail.; celebration dinners by arrangement

## ACCOMMODATIONS

**Units:** 5 guest rooms
**All Rooms:** TV/VCR, phone jack(s), robes, fans, carpet, hairdryers
**Some Rooms:** Mountain view, whirlpool, skylight, large private deck, kitchenette
**Bed & Bath:** Queen or king; private bath

**Favorites:** Mr. Seal's Room, Happy Room, Secret Room
**Comfort & Decor:** Victorian touches include stained glass and period furnishings. Decor is comfortable and attractive, never frilly or pretentious. Fresh flowers, touches of tile. Windows open, and rooms and baths have individual heaters.

## RATES, RESERVATIONS, & RESTRICTIONS

**Deposit:** Call; 72-hour cancellation
**Discounts:** Off-season, specials; $15 add'l person
**Credit Cards:** V, MC, AE, D
**Check-in/Out:** 4 or by arrangement/11
**Smoking:** No
**Pets:** Sometimes OK in detached cottage; host kitty on site
**Kids:** Over 6 welcome (younger in the detached cottage by arrangement)

**Minimum Stay:** 2 days on some holiday weekends
**Open:** All year
**Host:** Simone Nichols
4861 Sequim Dungeness Way
Dungeness, WA 98382
(800) 879-8859 or (360) 683-3565
Fax: (360) 683-5181
simone@olypen.com
northolympic.com/groveland

## TOAD HALL, Sequim

| Overall: ★★★★ | Room Quality: B | Value: B | Price: $85–$125 |
|---|---|---|---|

We don't often report on brand-new bed-and-breakfasts, but this one showed exceptional promise. Bruce, a retired Navy officer, and Linda, a transplanted Brit, are a delightful combination, and seem to be having a great time with this whimsical inn. Clever breakfast menus include delightful English specialties, many of which are as much fun to say as they are to eat, such as "bubble and squeak," "toad in the hole" (no frogs involved), and "chookie eggs and soldiers." It's a fantasy camp for grown-ups; we loved it.

### SETTING & FACILITIES

**Location:** 1 mi. from downtown Sequim at Sequim Ave. & Jesslyn Ln.
**Near:** Dungeness Spit, Olympic Game Farm, Seven Cedars Casino, Port Townsend, Port Angeles
**Building:** Northwest contemporary w/ traditional lines
**Grounds:** Landscaping promises to be splendid; in front, a pond, willows; side & backyard rose garden, croquet court, hedge maze, field of lavender

**Public Space:** Lounge, porch, conservatory/sunroom
**Food & Drink:** Refreshments/afternoon tea upon arrival; beverages, coffee, tea, & muffin room service (7–9 a.m.); full breakfast
**Recreation:** Festivals, wine tasting, antiquing, galleries, golf, water activities
**Amenities & Services:** TV/VCR & phone avail. for rooms, games; celebration extras; small weddings, special teas

### ACCOMMODATIONS

**Units:** 3 guest rooms (2 finished)
**All Rooms:** Fridge, quality linens, down comforter (hypoallergenic avail.), sitting area, closet, extra pillows, toiletries, TV/VCR, robes, CD player
**Some Rooms:** Bathroom skylight, vaulted ceiling, dual whirlpool, sofa-sleeper
**Bed & Bath:** Queen (3rd room, unfinished as of our visit, may have

2 twins); private baths
**Favorites:** Badger's Lair
**Comfort & Decor:** This mid-1990s home is upscale, fresh, and contemporary, with tasteful English collectibles and other eclectic and antique pieces. Colors are muted with rich accents of maroon, gold, and lace. The Wind-in-the-Willows theme is carried cleverly via adorable wall murals.

### RATES, RESERVATIONS, & RESTRICTIONS

**Deposit:** 1st night; cancellations forfeit if not rebooked
**Discounts:** Single occupancy, off-season, cont'l breakfast, business, extended stay (ask)
**Credit Cards:** V, MC, AE
**Check-in/Out:** 3–6/11 (or by arrangement)
**Smoking:** Outside only
**Pets:** No

**Kids:** No
**Minimum Stay:** 2 nights, high season weekends & holidays
**Open:** All year
**Hosts:** Linda & Bruce Clark
12 Jesslyn Ln., Sequim, WA 98382
(360) 681-2534
Fax: (360) 683-2002
toadhall@olympus.net
www.northolympic.com/toadhall

# Zone 4
# Northwest Washington

Some of Washington's best-loved touring destinations are found in this popular corner of the state. On the west side, it's studded with islands. To the east, it's bounded by the jewel-like North Cascades. In the middle, bucolic and fertile farmland soothes the senses. And throughout, top-notch bed-and-breakfasts are kept in business by proximity to the population centers of Seattle, Tacoma, and Vancouver, BC.

The temperate and scenic San Juan Islands are a step back in time; to reach them, take the ferry (www.wsdot.wa.gov/ferries) from Anacortes. The three islands featured are San Juan, Lopez, and Orcas. San Juan is the busiest island; its hub city, Friday Harbor, is home to many bed-and-breakfasts, as well as restaurants and shops. Island attractions include historic American Camp and British Camp, from the days when island ownership was contested. Lopez is the sleepiest, smallest, most agrarian island, as well as the flattest (bicyclists take note!). Orcas is home to several truly impressive bed-and-breakfasts, as well as Moran State Park, Mount Constitution, and Rosario resort. Its main "city" (using the term loosely!) is Eastsound. Each of the islands has its complement of bays, beaches, parks, and landforms such as points and spits.

Anacortes, along the north shore of Fidalgo Island and connected to mainland Skagit County by bridge, is a town with history and charm of its own. While its attractions include museums, parks, shopping, a waterfront, and proximity to Fidalgo Bay, it is best known as a jumping-off point (read: ferry terminal) for the San Juan Islands.

South of Anacortes, Whidbey Island is a favorite getaway for Puget Sounders. At its north end, Deception Pass offers a dramatic vista, a beautiful state park, and a much-photographed, engineering-marvel bridge. Communities include historic Coupeville toward the north, artsy Langley toward the south, and pastoral Greenbank in the middle. Attractions include Admiralty Head Lighthouse, Fort Casey State Park, and Ebey's Landing historic preserve.

On the mainland, just southeast of Everett, Snohomish is a quaint community developing a reputation as an antiquing paradise. Moving north along the Interstate 5 corridor, you'll come to the Skagit Valley. Here, in and around the communities of Mount Vernon, La Conner, and Bow, you'll find tulip fields, scenic driving, shops and galleries, and pastoral beauty.

Farther north, Bellingham is home to Western Washington University, Lake Whatcom, and some of the state's finest bed-and-breakfasts. Waterfront activities include passenger ferries to the San Juan Islands, whale-watching tours, shopping, and dining. Bellingham is within striking distance of Mount Baker and the North Cascades (see Zone 7) and is only about half an hour from Blaine at the U.S./Canada border. Blaine, besides being the closest U.S. town to the Peach Arch International Park border crossing on Interstate 5, is home to Semiahmoo resort and conference center and Birch Bay Beach and State Park.

Point Roberts is a tiny thumb of land attached to Canada but politically part of Washington and the United States. To reach it, you must drive into Canada and back through another border crossing. For more information, see the profile for Maple Meadows B&B on page 157.

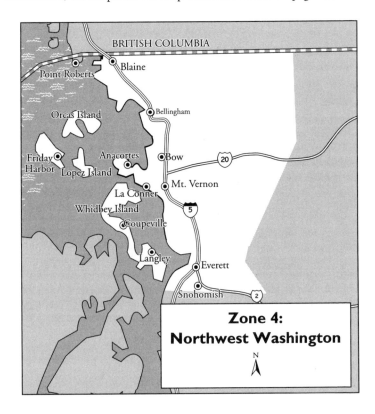

Zone 4:
Northwest Washington

**Anacortes**
Channel House, p. 114
Hasty Pudding House, p. 115
Nantucket Inn, p. 116

**Bellingham**
Big Trees B&B, p. 117
North Garden Inn, p. 118
Schnauzer Crossing, p. 119
South Bay B&B, p. 121
Stratford Manor, p. 122

**Blaine**
Harbor House B&B, p. 124

**Bow**
Benson Farmstead, p. 125
Chuckanut Manor B&B, p. 126
Samish Point by the Bay, p. 127

**Coupeville**
The Inn at Penn Cove, p. 129

**Friday Harbor**
Blair House, p. 130
Duffy House, p. 131
Olympic Lights, p. 132
Panacea, p. 133
Trumpeter Inn, p. 135
Wharfside B&B, p. 136
Wildwood Manor, p. 137

**La Conner**
Katy's Inn, p. 138
Ridgeway Farm B&B, p. 139
The Wild Iris, p. 140

**Langley**
Dove House, Chauntecleer House,
    & Potting Shed, p. 141
Log Castle B&B, p. 142

**Lopez Island**
Edenwild Inn, p. 144
Inn at Swifts Bay, p. 145
MacKay Harbor Inn, p. 146

**Mount Vernon**
The Colonial Manor, p. 147
The White Swan Guest House,
    p. 148

**Orcas Island**
Buck Bay Farm, p. 149
Chestnut Hill B&B, p. 150
Kangaroo House, p. 152
Otters Pond B&B, p. 153
Spring Bay Inn, p. 154
Turtleback Farm Inn, p. 156

**Point Roberts**
Maple Meadows B&B, p. 157

**Snohomish**
Redmond House B&B, p. 158
Susan's Surrey House, p. 160

**Whidbey Island**
Eagle's Nest Inn, p. 161
Guest House Cottages, p. 162
Island Tyme, p. 163

## CHANNEL HOUSE, Anacortes

| Overall: ★★★½ | Room Quality: C | Value: B | Price: $79–$109 |
|---|---|---|---|

Most convenient bed-and-breakfast to the ferry terminal. This water-view inn was established by the McIntyres in 1986, then expanded from four rooms to six when they remodeled the detached guest cottage in 1989. Cottage rooms are most modern; Island View has best view; Canopy Room has best antiques. Innkeepers were long-time restaurateurs before opening this bed-and-breakfast. Some furnishings tend toward threadbare, but the inn is spotless and emphasizes comfort and good food and service. The unusually flexible breakfast schedule and thorough guest-information packets are hallmarks of excellent hosts.

### SETTING & FACILITIES

**Location:** On main drag (Hwy. 20 is Oakes Ave. here), 1.5 mi. from ferry terminal
**Near:** Ferries, Washington Park, Anacortes attractions, Deception Pass/Whidbey Island
**Building:** 1902 Craftsman historic home
**Grounds:** Fruit trees, channel view, roses & perennials
**Public Space:** Sitting room, LR, DR

**Food & Drink:** Tea, coffee, and oatmeal-raisin cookies; full breakfast; cont'l option
**Recreation:** Golf, whale watching, scenic driving, fishing, kayaking
**Amenities & Services:** Outdoor hot tub, books, games, phone, travel library, umbrellas; excellent packet of local info/itineraries mailed to preregistered guests

### ACCOMMODATIONS

**Units:** 6 guest rooms (4 in main house, 2 in cottage)
**All Rooms:** Robes, abundant towels
**Some Rooms:** Jetted tub, fireplace, channel view, private deck or patio
**Bed & Bath:** Queen or king; private bath
**Favorites:** Rose Cottage rooms, Island View, or Canopy
**Comfort & Decor:** Lots of fire-

places, antiques, and cheerful stuffed toys. Period furnishings include fainting couches and window seats. Wallpapers and wood wainscoting; natural and painted wood floors sport area rugs. Main house has central heat (auxiliary heaters upstairs); cottage rooms have individual thermostats. Windows open for ventilation.

## RATES, RESERVATIONS, & RESTRICTIONS

**Deposit:** 1st night; 3-day cancellation or forfeit unless rebooked
**Discounts:** Off-season weekday or single, both main house only; $20 add'l person in Country Rose or Island View
**Credit Cards:** V, MC, AE, D
**Check-in/Out:** After 3/11
**Smoking:** Outside only
**Pets:** No
**Kids:** 12 & older

**Minimum Stay:** None
**Open:** All year
**Hosts:** Pat & Dennis McIntyre
2902 Oakes Ave.
Anacortes, WA 98221
(800) 238-4353 or (360) 293-9382
Fax: (360) 299-9208
beds@sos.net
www.channel-house.com

## HASTY PUDDING HOUSE, Anacortes

| Overall: ★★★★ | Room Quality: B | Value: A | Price: $79–$89 |
|---|---|---|---|

Cheerful, spotless, relaxed bed-and-breakfast combines best of yesteryear with contemporary comfort and more than a touch of whimsy. Innkeepers are delightful and experienced (since 1987), with a sense of style that makes you feel both pampered and at ease. While most of the decor is Victorian, an eclectic array of items includes a display case of impressive Native American artifacts, some of museum quality. Excellent breakfasts are attractively presented on festive and ever-changing tableware. Robyn's Nest, one of the two smaller rooms, is the best choice for tall people because of its large, detached bath; the other bathrooms are charming, funky retrofits with pitched ceilings. A super overall bed-and-breakfast experience!

## SETTING & FACILITIES

**Location:** 4 short blocks north of Hwy. 20 on 8th St. at N Ave.
**Near:** Anacortes Museum, Cap Sante Park & waterfront, downtown, Fidalgo Bay, ferries, Deception Pass/Whidbey Island
**Building:** 1913 Craftsman family home
**Grounds:** Backyard rockscaping w/ waterfall, decks, paths; flowers, shrubs

**Public Space:** Common room, DR
**Food & Drink:** Cider in p.m.; coffee & tea on request; full breakfast
**Recreation:** Golf, whale watching, ferry excursions, fishing, kayaking
**Amenities & Services:** Guest phone, musical instruments (piano, guitars), fireplace

## Accommodations

**Units:** 4 guest rooms (one w/ overflow-room option)
**All Rooms:** Robes
**Some Rooms:** Coffee & tea service, TV/VCR, claw-foot tub
**Bed & Bath:** Queen or king (one w/ extra twin); private baths, some ensuite
**Favorites:** Queen Anne's Lace, Victorian Garden

**Comfort & Decor:** Victorian antiques, collectibles, and touches of whimsy; modern and period furnishings. Rich original woodwork, including handsome corbeled ceilings. Fresh, intricate wallpapers. Excellent mattresses, quality linens, and heirloom quilts. Central heat; portable auxiliary heaters and electric fans; windows vent.

## Rates, Reservations, & Restrictions

**Deposit:** 1st night; 7-day cancellation or forfeit
**Discounts:** Call regarding off-season & specials; $20 add'l in adjoining room off Queen Anne
**Credit Cards:** V, MC, AE, D
**Check-in/Out:** 4–7 or by arrangement/11
**Smoking:** Outside only
**Pets:** No

**Kids:** By prior arrangement
**Minimum Stay:** None
**Open:** All year
**Hosts:** Mike & Melinda Hasty
1312 8th St.
Anacortes, WA 98221
(800) 368-5588 or (360) 293-5773
Fax: Same as local phone; call ahead
hasty@mail1.halcyon.com
www.hastypudding.net/hasty/

## NANTUCKET INN, Anacortes

| Overall: ★★★ | Room Quality: D | Value: C | Price: $75–$125 |
| --- | --- | --- | --- |

This easy-to-find inn provides great access to the ferry terminal, all Anacortes attractions, and Whidbey Island/Skagit Valley day trips. It was one of Anacortes' first guest houses and has been in operation since 1970. The Bransfords have operated the inn since 1996 and are in the process of updating furnishings and fixtures and adding landscaping and services such as weddings and high teas. Professionally run with help from a hired innkeeper. Buffet breakfast and reasonable rooms; some traffic noise.

## Setting & Facilities

**Location:** On Hwy. 20 as you enter Anacortes proper
**Near:** Entrance to Anacortes, Deception Pass/Whidbey Island, downtown, ferries
**Building:** 1925 Eastern Colonial-style
**Grounds:** Corner lot on busy Commercial Street; large back lawn w/ small pavilion

**Public Space:** Great room
**Food & Drink:** Buffet-style breakfast
**Recreation:** Golf, whale watching, scenic driving, fishing, kayaking, bicycling
**Amenities & Services:** TV/VCR, sound system, piano, library; weddings, high teas

## ACCOMMODATIONS

**Units:** 7 guest rooms
**All Rooms:** Sitting area, robes, phone
**Some Rooms:** Private entrance, TV
**Bed & Bath:** Queen (5), king (1), or twins (1), some w/ add'l sofa-sleeper; private baths (some adjacent, some ensuite)
**Favorites:** Fidalgo Bay Suite
**Comfort & Decor:** The redecoration

of this immense old inn is a work in progress. Stunning 19th-century antiques mingle with midquality modern furnishings and linens. Original artwork adds class, and the great room is quite elegant, with 9-foot ceilings, stylish furnishings, grand piano, library, and fireplace. Central steam heat; windows open for ventilation.

## RATES, RESERVATIONS, & RESTRICTIONS

**Deposit:** 1st night (50% for longer bookings); 7-day cancellation or forfeit unless rebooked; $15 late-cancellation fee
**Discounts:** Off-season; $20 add'l person
**Credit Cards:** V, MC, AE, D
**Check-in/Out:** 3–6 or by arrangement/11
**Smoking:** Outside only

**Pets:** No
**Kids:** 12 & older only
**Minimum Stay:** None
**Open:** All year
**Hosts:** Lynda & Doug Bransford
3402 Commercial
Anacortes, WA 98221
(888) 293-6007 or (360) 293-6007
Fax: (360) 299-4339
www.whidbey.com\nantucket

## BIG TREES B&B, Bellingham

| Overall: ★★★★ | Room Quality: B | Value: B | Price: $95–$115 |
|---|---|---|---|

A comfortable, artistic atmosphere prevails at Big Trees, where conversation is easy and food is abundant and delicious. The quiet location is like being in your own private park. Guests who enjoy pets will be charmed by the adorable and well-behaved resident canines and felines. While Jan's two guest rooms, Rhodie and Cedar, each have private baths, a third room, Maple, is available for guests who wish to rent two rooms with a shared bath. Maple is quite attractive in its own right, with a four-poster queen bed, window seat, and antique vanity. It rents for $75 but is only available paired with Rhodie ($160 for both) or Cedar ($180 for both).

## SETTING & FACILITIES

**Location:** Quiet neighborhood in eastern Bellingham
**Near:** Lake Whatcom, Mt. Baker
**Building:** 1907 Craftsman
**Grounds:** Towering cedars and maples, creek, paths, ivy, ferns, flowers, herb garden
**Public Space:** Front porch, LR, DR

**Food & Drink:** Plenty of snacks and beverages (24 hours); full breakfast
**Recreation:** Excellent porch sittin', croquet, strolling, boating, golf, hiking, antiquing
**Amenities & Services:** Travel info library, books, videos (VCRs avail.), fridge, sound system

## ACCOMMODATIONS

**Units:** 2 guest rooms (3rd room over-flow option for 2 parties wishing to share a bath)
**All Rooms:** TV, comfy chairs, robes, iron, copious toiletries, carpet, fan, phone, closet
**Some Rooms:** Window seat
**Bed & Bath:** King or queen; private baths (unless using overflow room)
**Favorites:** Either

**Comfort & Decor:** Eclectic mix of vintage furnishings, folk art, and rich fabrics. The home retains its Craftsman-era roots, with lots of woodwork and wainscoting, and the corbeled ceiling that trademarks the period. The living room sports a large stone fireplace. Central heat; baseboard supplement in Rhodie Room.

## RATES, RESERVATIONS, & RESTRICTIONS

**Deposit:** 1st night or 50%; 14-day cancellation or forfeit unless rebooked
**Discounts:** See 2-room option in introductory description
**Credit Cards:** V, MC
**Check-in/Out:** 4–6 or by arrangement/11
**Smoking:** No
**Pets:** No; host critters in residence

**Kids:** Please call
**Minimum Stay:** Holidays only
**Open:** All year
**Hosts:** Jan Simmons
4840 Fremont St.
Bellingham, WA 98226-2624
(800) 647-2850 or (360) 647-2850
bigtrees@nas.com
www.nas.com/~bigtrees

## NORTH GARDEN INN, Bellingham

| Overall: ★★ | Room Quality: D | Value: C | Price: $50–$99 |

Perfect for those who want a central, urban Bellingham location and appreciate an atmosphere where original art and good literature take precedence over expensive furnishings and lavish amenities. Frank and Barbara are relaxed, experienced hosts and accomplished musicians. North Garden Inn is in the unique position of being the only large bed-and-breakfast in the city limits, grandfathered in before Bellingham limited in-town bed-and-breakfasts to two rooms. The inn was up for sale at the time of our visit, but its longstanding reputation and central location suggest continued operation as a bed-and-breakfast. Expect some street noise in your room.

## SETTING & FACILITIES

**Location:** Urban Bellingham, near Western Washington University
**Near:** Ferry, parks, downtown
**Building:** 1897 Queen Anne Victorian
**Grounds:** Side yards w/ seating, roses, swings
**Public Space:** Guest lounge, DR

**Food & Drink:** Full breakfast
**Recreation:** Hiking, theater, museums, galleries, ferry trips
**Amenities & Services:** Guest phone, games, puzzles, books (good stuff!), TV in LR, 3 pianos, binoculars

## ACCOMMODATIONS

**Units:** 10 guest rooms

**All Rooms:** Robes, armoire or closet, sitting area

**Some Rooms:** Bay view, fainting couch, down comforter, private balcony

**Bed & Bath:** Mostly queens, 1 double, 1 w/ twins; 8 private baths, 2 share a bath

**Favorites:** Overture, Rhapsody, Adagio, Encore, Intermezzo

**Comfort & Decor:** Entire inn was painted, inside and out, in 1998. Hand-made afghans, embroidered runners, and quilts grace the sometimes-tired, always comfortable vintage and retro furnishings. Rooms are small but very clean. Much of the original woodwork remains.

## RATES, RESERVATIONS, & RESTRICTIONS

**Deposit:** Credit card; 24-hour cancellation

**Discounts:** Extended stays, AAA, senior; $10 add'l person

**Credit Cards:** V, MC, D

**Check-in/Out:** 3–7 or by arrangement/11

**Smoking:** No

**Pets:** No; host kitty

**Kids:** Welcome

**Minimum Stay:** None

**Open:** All year

**Hosts:** Barbara & Frank DeFreytas
1014 N. Garden St.
Bellingham, WA 98225
US (800) 922-6414
Canada (800) 367-1676
(360) 671-7828
ngi@northgardeninn.com
northgardeninn.com/ngi

## SCHNAUZER CROSSING, Bellingham

| Overall: ★★★★★ | Room Quality: A | Value: C | Price: $120–$200 |

Elegantly appointed contemporary lake-view home offers deluxe comfort with every conceivable amenity (oh, yes, and Schnauzers). Good access to downtown Bellingham (waterfront, urban services and amenities), yet the quiet suburban location is also near parks and rural/wilderness attractions. Rooms and common areas are welcoming, immaculate, and stylish. Hosts are gracious in the extreme but never intrusive. Breakfasts are scrumptious and served at your convenience. Unless you don't like animals—the resident Schnauzers are adorable, and the mini-aviary in the great room houses a melodic collection of doves, canaries, and finches—we can't recommend a better bed-and-breakfast experience.

## SETTING & FACILITIES

**Location:** Quiet neighborhood in eastern Bellingham overlooking Lake Whatcom
**Near:** Parks, Mt. Baker, North Cascades, San Juan Island passenger ferry
**Building:** Pacific Northwest contemporary home
**Grounds:** Thickly wooded site w/ cedars, maples, ferns, rhododendrons; back lawn with bamboo screening; new Japanese-inspired landscaping planned
**Public Space:** Great room, DR, deck

**Food & Drink:** In-room snack basket; tea or coffee; sumptuous full breakfast
**Recreation:** Outstanding on-site bird-watching, golf, swimming, tennis, skiing, boating, fishing, whale-watching tours, tours to San Juans, Seattle, or British Columbia
**Amenities & Services:** Vast library, videos, hot tub (plus robes, rubber sandals, towels), piano; turndown and daily room refresh upon request; massage avail.

## ACCOMMODATIONS

**Units:** 1 guest room, 2 suites
**All Rooms:** CDs, phone, hairdryer, "I Forgot It" toiletries basket, robes, slippers, skylight(s), view
**Some Rooms:** Oversized whirlpool, herbal bath grains, heated towel rack, fireplace, TV/VCR, desk, kitchenette, mini-fridge, reading lamps
**Bed & Bath:** Queen or king; private ensuite baths
**Favorites:** The Cottage (detached; clean-line, Pacific-Rim decor) or The

Garden Suite (romantic watercolorfloral motifs, dual sitting areas)
**Comfort & Decor:** Each well-lit, tastefully decorated room sports designer bedding and window treatments, original art, flowers and plants. Each greets you with a kimono on the wall; other subtle Asian-inspired motifs as well. The Great Room's glass panels open onto the Lake-Whatcom-view deck, creating a virtually open-walled room in pleasant weather.

## RATES, RESERVATIONS, & RESTRICTIONS

**Deposit:** 1st night; 5-day cancellation notice for refund
**Discounts:** $25 add'l adult, $10 child, $15 teen
**Credit Cards:** V, MC
**Check-in/Out:** 4–7 or by arrangement/11
**Smoking:** No
**Pets:** No; host dogs on premises
**Kids:** Welcome by arrangement

**Minimum Stay:** 2 nights, weekends & holidays
**Open:** All year
**Hosts:** Donna & Monty McAllister
4421 Lakeway Dr.
Bellingham, WA 98226
(800) 562-2808 or (360) 733-0055
Fax: (360) 734-2808
schnauzerX@aol.com
www.schnauzercrossing.com

## SOUTH BAY B&B, Bellingham

| Overall: ★★★★ | Room Quality: B | Value: C | Price: $150 |
|---|---|---|---|

Beautifully remodeled and expanded Craftsman perched on a hill over-looking pristine south Lake Whatcom—stunning views! Sally and Dan thoughtfully provide a range of amenities, including mountain bikes and a kayak, so you could really take off with just a change of clothes and a toothbrush and spend a fun, active weekend here. The historic, formerly 1,400-square-foot Craftsman home was moved to this site and nearly tripled in size through remodeling—a great story, complete with photos, if you're interested. It opened as an inn in 1997.

### SETTING & FACILITIES

**Location:** South end of Lake Whatcom
**Near:** Equidistant from Bellingham & Sedro Wooley
**Building:** 1910 Craftsman
**Grounds:** 5 acres with forest & lake view; campfire circle
**Public Space:** Wraparound porch, LR, DR/conservatory/sunroom
**Food & Drink:** Beverages & snack basket (24 hours); full breakfast

**Recreation:** Walking, hiking, bicycling, kayaking
**Amenities & Services:** Piano, canoe, kayak, mountain bikes, kitchenette w/ micro. & fridge, guest phone, games, binoculars, sound system; CD, iron, hairdryer, phone, roll-away bed; alternate dinner arrangements; weddings & other gatherings; fax, e-mail retrieval; gift items for sale; ensuite breakfast for special occasions

### ACCOMMODATIONS

**Units:** 5 guest rooms
**All Rooms:** Carpet, tile bath, armoire, top-quality toiletries, down comforters, quality ironed linens
**Some Rooms:** Gas fireplace, oversize jetted tub w/ lake view, patio access, wicker, desk or vanity, bubble bath, couch
**Bed & Bath:** Queens; private ensuite baths

**Favorites:** Tanglewood or Terrace
**Comfort & Decor:** Beamed ceilings and comfortable furnishings define the common areas, which have stunning, pale Swedish laminate and area rugs. Breakfast area is a sun-filled conservatory nook. The guest rooms are carpeted, with clean, spare, contemporary country decor. Radiant heat.

## RATES, RESERVATIONS, & RESTRICTIONS

**Deposit:** 1st night (50% for stays 3 days or longer); 72-hour cancellation for refund
**Discounts:** Single, off-season, extended stay; $25 add'l person ($15 for child)
**Credit Cards:** V, MC
**Check-in/Out:** After 4 or by arrangement/noon
**Smoking:** Designated outside areas only

**Pets:** No
**Kids:** 12 & older by arrangement
**Minimum Stay:** None
**Open:** All year
**Hosts:** Sally & Dan Moore
4095 South Bay Dr.
Sedro Woolley, WA 98284
(360) 595-2086
Fax: (360) 595-1043
southbay@gte.net
www.southbaybb.com

## STRATFORD MANOR, Bellingham

| Overall: ★★★★★ | Room Quality: A | Value: C | Price: $125–$175 |
| --- | --- | --- | --- |

This 6,500-square-foot estate home has enough common areas for each guest to have his or her own: casual living room with TV, guest fridge, and phone; formal parlor with upscale furnishings and fireplace; glass-walled, modernly furnished solarium/exercise area; cozy and plush library with leather couches. You're 15 minutes from downtown Bellingham, but the range of amenities and the in-room and living room snacks make the slight isolation factor a nonissue. Sprawling grounds are a delight. Pastoral setting makes for quiet sleeping. Gracious and spacious, this reproduction Tudor is a super-comfortable alternative to cramped Victorians and cookie-cutter hotels.

## SETTING & FACILITIES

**Location:** 15 minutes NE of Bellingham proper, off Hwy. 542 (Mt. Baker Hwy.)
**Near:** Bellingham, Mt. Baker, U.S./Canada border, North Cascades
**Building:** Tudor-style estate home
**Grounds:** 30-acre parcel, 5 landscaped acres; putting greens, pond, footbridge, lush garden; hillside trail into woods
**Public Space:** 2 LRs, solarium, DR, library, decks

**Food & Drink:** Coffee tray to your door (8 a.m.), full breakfast at 9; other times or ensuite breakfast by arrangement
**Recreation:** Golf, skiing, boating, fishing, whale-watching, tours
**Amenities & Services:** Satellite, videos, portable guest phone, stocked fridge, exercise equipment, outdoor hot tub, games, paddle boat (summer), tennis courts to come; celebration extras; fax & copier

## ACCOMMODATIONS

**Units:** 3–4 guest rooms (3 year-round, 4 summer)
**All Rooms:** Jetted tub, fireplace, robes, slippers, iron, hairdryer, fresh flowers, green plants, CD player/alarm clock, CDs, TV/VCR, down duvet
**Some Rooms:** Skylights
**Bed & Bath:** King or queen; private ensuite tile bath w/ jetted tub, shower, dual-sink vanity
**Favorites:** Garden Room or Master Suite

**Comfort & Decor:** Elegant in the extreme, yet never stuffy. Adult-only atmosphere. Expensive wallpapers in striking combinations. Extra-high ceilings lend an incredible sense of space to already spacious proportions. Traditional, romantic decor. Top-quality linens. Tile-floor, glass-wall solarium; oak-floor formal living room with windowed turret alcove; library with super-comfy leather sofas. Individual room heat control via thermostat gas fireplaces; AC in some.

## RATES, RESERVATIONS, & RESTRICTIONS

**Deposit:** 1st night; 7-day cancellation
**Discounts:** None
**Credit Cards:** V, MC
**Check-in/Out:** 4–7 or by arrangement/11
**Smoking:** No
**Pets:** No
**Kids:** No
**Minimum Stay:** None

**Open:** All year
**Hosts:** Leslie & Jim Lohse
4566 Anderson Way
Bellingham, WA 98226
(360) 715-8441
Fax: (360) 671-0840
llohse@aol.com
www.site-works.com/stratford/

## HARBOR HOUSE B&B, Blaine

| Overall: ★★★ | Room Quality: D | Value: B | Price: $75–$90 |
|---|---|---|---|

This relatively new bed-and-breakfast has all the necessary ingredients for success: great waterfront location, easy access, pleasant rooms, good breakfasts, and innkeepers who are no strangers to hard work. Both Tim and Jonni were commercial fishermen for years before opening their inn in 1997. Don't be afraid to try their outstanding halibut omelet if it's offered. Host kitties and astonishingly well-behaved dog on premises. Warm, friendly hosts enjoy their work.

### SETTING & FACILITIES

**Location:** Minutes from Canadian border on Drayton Harbor between I-5 and Semiahmoo
**Near:** I-5 (easy access), US/Canada Peace Arch border crossing, Semiahmoo resort/conf. center, Birch Bay Beach & State Park
**Building:** Waterfront c. 1900 farmhouse
**Grounds:** Large front lawn, roses, across from Drayton Harbor; side/back yard, deck, hot tub
**Public Space:** Rooms have private entrances, so guests spend most of their time there (but hosts are flexible and welcoming); front & back porches, hot tub area
**Food & Drink:** In-room coffee, small snack; in-room breakfast at chosen time (somewhat restricted on Sundays)
**Recreation:** Lawn games, golf, skiing, beach, kayaking, Canadian shopping
**Amenities & Services:** Hot tub, croquet, horseshoes, badminton; picnic lunches and family-style dinners by arrangement

### ACCOMMODATIONS

**Units:** 1 room, 1 suite
**All Rooms:** Coffeemaker, fridge, view, private entry, carpet, TV/VCR, videos
**Some Rooms:** Kitchen, gas fireplace, phone (portable avail. for other room)
**Bed & Bath:** Queens; private ensuite baths
**Favorites:** Drayton Harbor Suite
**Comfort & Decor:** Captain's Quarters is cheerful and homey, with nautical motif and small bathroom cleverly tucked under a staircase. Drayton Harbor Suite has more upscale decor, brick-and-forest accents, and an attractive pine bed; fully equipped kitchen with breakfast-bar seating. Original artwork. Gas fireplace or baseboard heat.

## RATES, RESERVATIONS, & RESTRICTIONS

**Deposit:** Credit card; please provide ample notice of cancellation
**Discounts:** Family & weekly rates, off-season, under age 6 free; $10 add'l person
**Credit Cards:** V, MC, D
**Check-in/Out:** Flexible; please call
**Smoking:** Outside only
**Pets:** By arrangement; host pets on site

**Kids:** Welcome
**Minimum Stay:** None
**Open:** All year
**Hosts:** Tim & Jonni Lukens
5157 Drayton Harbor Rd.
Blaine, WA 98230
(888) 705-9060 or (360) 371-9060
Fax: (360) 371-2787
harborhouse@Harbor-House.com
www.Harbor-House.com

## BENSON FARMSTEAD, Bow

| Overall: ★★★ | Room Quality: C | Value: B | Price: $75–$85 |

Picturesque working crop farm with home-style Scandinavian-hospitality atmosphere. Jerry and Sharon are descendants of Skagit Valley pioneers, and their knowledge of and ties to this area make them excellent hosts. The farmhouse was their family home for years. After raising their four boys, they decided to extend their natural hospitality by turning the place into a bed-and-breakfast in 1991. The result is a peaceful country atmosphere for either low-key relaxation or venturing out to a myriad of day-trip possibilities from Mt. Baker to the North Cascades to the San Juan Islands.

## SETTING & FACILITIES

**Location:** Less than a mi. east of Hwy. 11, about halfway between Mount Vernon & Bellingham
**Near:** Chuckanut Dr., La Conner, Mt. Vernon, Bellingham, Anacortes, N. Cascades Hwy.
**Building:** 1914 family farmhouse
**Grounds:** Bucolic farm; gardens, picnic area, playground, "antique machinery garden"
**Public Space:** Parlor, study, sunroom, music area, children's play cubby, porches
**Food & Drink:** Homemade dessert & coffee (evening); full breakfast
**Recreation:** Bicycling, shopping, scenic driving, ferry excursions
**Amenities & Services:** Games, music, puzzles, piano, hot tub, ice, fridge; reunions & gatherings (extra outbuilding rooms; up to 25)

## ACCOMMODATIONS

**Units:** 4 guest rooms
**All Rooms:** Reading chairs, reading material, flowers
**Some Rooms:** Claw-foot tub
**Bed & Bath:** Queens, some w/ trundle &/or daybed(s); private baths (3 of 4 ensuite)
**Favorites:** Wildflower, English Garden

**Comfort & Decor:** Period recreations mix with country antiques in a homey, warm atmosphere. Hardwood floors with area carpets, period light fixtures, attractive wallpapers, and handmade quilts. Central heat with auxiliary electric heaters in rooms.

## RATES, RESERVATIONS, & RESTRICTIONS

**Deposit:** 1st night; 3-day cancellation
**Discounts:** Extended stay, entire house; $15 add'l person, $10 child
**Credit Cards:** V, MC
**Check-in/Out:** 4–6 or by arrangement/noon
**Smoking:** Outside only
**Pets:** Outside only, by arrangement
**Kids:** Call; often accommodated

**No-Nos:** Coming in after 11 p.m. discouraged
**Minimum Stay:** None
**Open:** All year
**Hosts:** Sharon & Jerry Benson
10113 Avon-Allen Rd.
Bow, WA 98232
(800) 441-9814 or (360) 757-0578
www.bbhost.com/bensonbnb

## CHUCKANUT MANOR B&B, Bow

| Overall: ★½ | Room Quality: D | Value: D | Price: $100 |
|---|---|---|---|

If a beautiful water view and lively restaurant/bar adjacency are your main hot buttons, these units will appeal. Expect self-sufficiency, rough-around-the-edges finish work, and hosts who are very busy with their restaurant and lounge enterprises. Also expect car noise from Chuckanut Drive and train noise from the tracks behind the units. However, all of that being said, the location—on incredibly scenic Chuckanut Drive, with Samish Bay views—is such a plus that we really wanted to include these units. The restaurant and bar is a fun place with a great local and tourist reputation, and the Woolcocks seem like really nice folks. Wish we could be more complimentary of the lodgings.

## SETTING & FACILITIES

**Location:** Right on Chuckanut Dr. (Hwy. 11), just south of Bellingham
**Near:** Chuckanut Dr., Samish Bay, Samish Island, Edison & Bow, Skagit Valley activities, Fairhaven, Bellingham
**Building:** Apt. attached to funky "destination" seafood restaurant; adjacent cottage (former gas station)
**Grounds:** On busy, scenic Chuckanut Dr.; no "grounds," but super views

**Public Space:** Each unit is self-contained; restaurant/lounge adjacent
**Food & Drink:** Snacks, self-serve cont'l breakfast, bottled water provided; host-owned restaurant serves appetizers & full meals w/ seafood emphasis; full bar
**Recreation:** Scenic driving, day trips
**Amenities & Services:** Videos & sound system in Kristy's Cottage

## ACCOMMODATIONS

**Units:** 2 guest houses
**All Rooms:** Samish Bay views, LR, dining area, kitchen
**Bed & Bath:** Chuckanut Manor is a 2-BR, 1 bath apt. w/ water-view & whirlpool tub; Kristy's Cottage has a king bed, water-view deck, & hot tub

**Favorites:** Kristy's Cottage
**Comfort & Decor:** Some of the furnishings and appliances are decidedly 1970s vintage, but the views are great. Both units have a bit of the musty "aging beach house" flavor. Antiques and decorator touches in the Cottage unit.

## RATES, RESERVATIONS, & RESTRICTIONS

**Deposit:** Credit card; 48-hour cancellation or forfeit $50
**Discounts:** None
**Credit Cards:** V, MC, AE, DC
**Check-in/Out:** 3/noon
**Smoking:** OK in Chuckanut Manor; not allowed in Kristy's Cottage
**Pets:** No

**Kids:** Welcome
**Minimum Stay:** None
**Open:** All year
**Hosts:** Pat & Kristy Woolcock
3056 Chuckanut Dr., Bow, WA 98232
(360) 766-6191
Fax: (360) 766-8515
pawoolcock@aol.com

## SAMISH POINT BY THE BAY, Bow

| Overall: ★★★★½ | Room Quality: A | Value: C | Price: $175 |
|---|---|---|---|

This upscale Cape Cod replica offers a totally private lodging experience surrounded by the things that typify the Pacific Northwest: dense woodland, salt breezes from nearby beaches, countless bird species, nearby seafood restaurants, and farm-fresh produce. The house stands alone, separate from the hosts' nearby home. Once you are checked in and graciously shown the ropes, you're on your own in total privacy unless you need something. Daytrip to Bellingham, Anacortes, or the farmlands of the Skagit Valley, or stay on the Point, where miles of trails await you from your doorstep in the surrounding woods, leading to your choice of three rugged beaches.

## SETTING & FACILITIES

**Location:** Tip of Samish Point peninsula, NW of Mount Vernon & SW of Bellingham
**Near:** Community of Samish Island, Chuckanut Drive, community of Edison, Skagit Valley activities, Anacortes
**Building:** Fully modern 1940s-style shingle Cape Cod home
**Grounds:** Lawn surrounded by woods w/ trails; access to 3 rugged beaches
**Public Space:** Entire house

**Food & Drink:** Snacks, hot beverage service; self-serve breakfast
**Recreation:** Trails, beachcombing, scenic driving, bird-watching, bicycling
**Amenities & Services:** Private phone, cable, deck & picnic area, hot tub, complete modern kitchen, cassettes, videos, gas fireplace, umbrellas, desk, data port, robes, hairdryer

## ACCOMMODATIONS

**Units:** 1 guest house (overflow lodging may be avail.)
**All Rooms:** Quality beds & linens
**Bed & Bath:** King or queen; private baths
**Favorites:** King room on main floor
**Comfort & Decor:** Fresh, white walls with warm woods and upscale country fabrics. Slate entry and large river-rock gas fireplace in living room. Bedroom furnishings feature honey pine, wicker, quilts, and English chintz. Immaculately clean. Thermostat-controlled gas fireplace; individual room heat controls; windows open for ventilation.

## RATES, RESERVATIONS, & RESTRICTIONS

**Deposit:** 1st night; 5-day cancellation for stays of 3 or fewer nights (14-day cancellation for longer stays) or forfeit
**Discounts:** Sliding scale to $330 for as many as 6 guests; the 3-BR house is occupied by only one party at a time; price and number of accessible rooms is determined by number of guests
**Credit Cards:** V, MC, AE
**Check-in/Out:** 4–6 or by arrangement/11 (welcome to stay and enjoy surrounding property after vacating house)
**Smoking:** No

**Pets:** No
**Kids:** 7 & older only
**No-Nos:** Large groups or gatherings (registered guests only)
**Minimum Stay:** 2 nights (1 night by chance)
**Open:** All year
**Hosts:** Theresa & Herb Goldston
4465 Samish Point Rd.
Bow, WA 98232
(800) 916-6161 or (360)766-6610
samishpt@cnw.com
www.samishpoint.com

## THE INN AT PENN COVE, Coupeville

| Overall: ★★½ | Room Quality: D | Value: C | Price: $60–$125 |
|---|---|---|---|

These two cozy, adjacent Victorians have curb appeal, water views, and a great location for exploring the various sights of Coupeville and the island. While some guest rooms are small (Kineth House ones are larger) and lighting can be dim, the houses are overall homey and comfortable, with a European bed-and-breakfast feel. Kineth House parlor and sunroom are particularly comfortable common areas. The Howards have owned the inn since 1993 and live in the Kineth House.

## SETTING & FACILITIES

**Location:** On Main in downtown Coupeville
**Near:** Front St., Fort Casey, lighthouse, Ebey's Landing, Deception Pass S.P.
**Building:** Adjacent 1887 and 1891 Victorians
**Grounds:** Dbl. corner lot w/ water view
**Public Space:** Parlor, sunroom, TV/video lounge (Kineth); game room,

dual parlor (CG)
**Food & Drink:** Afternoon tea; full breakfast; early cont'l option
**Recreation:** Scuba, boating, wine touring, ferry to Port Townsend, golf, beachcombing
**Amenities & Services:** TV/VCR, guest fridge & phone, books, binoculars, games; kitchen avail. by special arrangement

## ACCOMMODATIONS

**Units:** 6 guest rooms (3 in each house)

**All Rooms:** Antique furnishings, ceiling fans, armoires

**Some Rooms:** Water view, fireplace, dbl. whirlpool, robes, claw-foot tub, fainting couch

**Bed & Bath:** Queen (5) or king, rollaway avail.; 4 private baths, 2 share a bath

**Favorites:** Desiree, Amanda, Elizabeth

**Comfort & Decor:** Authentic Victorian seaport homes, complete with a bit of the mustiness that age and salt spray provide. Amazing antiques mingle with modest contemporary accessories. Period velvets and brocades (some with mileage). Vinyl baths, green plants. Kineth House parlor includes fanciful and authentic accoutrements such as a Victorian pump organ and antique music box. Kineth has central heat plus fireplaces; Coupe-Gillespie has baseboards.

## RATES, RESERVATIONS, & RESTRICTIONS

**Deposit:** 1st night; 7-day cancellation

**Discounts:** Single occupancy; $15 add'l person

**Credit Cards:** V, MC, AE, D

**Check-in/Out:** 4–6/noon

**Smoking:** Outside only

**Pets:** No

**Kids:** Welcome under most circumstances

**Minimum Stay:** 2 nights, holidays

**Open:** All year

**Hosts:** Gladys & Mitchell Howard
702 N. Main St., P.O. Box 85
Coupeville, WA 98239
(800) 688-COVE or (360) 678-8000
Fax: Call
penncove@whidbey.net
www.whidbey.net/~penncove/pencv.htm

## BLAIR HOUSE, Friday Harbor

| Overall: ★★★ | Room Quality: D | Value: C | Price: $75–$155 |
|---|---|---|---|

Excellent location for downtown Friday Harbor access. Great views from porch and dining room. Modest and comfortable. Pool, deck, and porches are pleasant places to hang out in the summer. Not the ritziest bed-and-breakfast in the islands, but dependable, predictable, and the pool is a nice feature. Helpful and personable innkeeper and owner.

## SETTING & FACILITIES

**Location:** 5 blocks from ferry landing, on Blair off Spring

**Near:** Ferry landing, downtown Friday Harbor

**Building:** Circa 1900 farmhouse-style home, remodeled & expanded

**Grounds:** 2 wooded, landscaped acres; seasonal pool

**Public Space:** Porch, LR, DR

**Food & Drink:** Tea & coffee; full breakfast

**Recreation:** Wildlife watching, historic touring, kayaking, boating, fishing, galleries

**Amenities & Services:** Pool, hot tub, fridge, sound system, VCR, woodstove

## ACCOMMODATIONS

**Units:** 7 guest rooms, 1 cottage
**All Rooms:** Carpet
**Some Rooms:** Robes, down comforter, deck; cottage has LR, DR, kitchen, TV/VCR
**Bed & Bath:** Queen, king, or twins, roll-away avail.; 1 private bath, 2 have private half-bath and share full bath;

4 share a large full bath
**Favorites:** #3, #4, & "PB"
**Comfort & Decor:** Older home with modest finish work. Floral bedding and wallpapers, painted woodwork. Rooms are fairly large. Individually controlled baseboard heat with woodstove supplement.

## RATES, RESERVATIONS, & RESTRICTIONS

**Deposit:** Credit card; 2-week cancellation or 10%; 72-hour cancellation or forfeit
**Discounts:** Cottage $155; $20 add'l person
**Credit Cards:** V, MC, AE, D
**Check-in/Out:** After 2 or by arrangement/11
**Smoking:** Outside only
**Pets:** Cottage only or by arrangement off-season

**Kids:** 12 & over welcome; younger in cottage
**Minimum Stay:** None
**Open:** All year
**Hosts:** Bob Pittman, owner;
Margie Winkelman, innkeeper
345 Blair St.
Friday Harbor, WA 98250
(800) 899-3030 or (360) 378-5907
bobp2@webtv.net
www.friday-harbor.net/blair

## DUFFY HOUSE, Friday Harbor

| Overall: ★★★½ | Room Quality: B | Value: C | Price: $95–$115 |
|---|---|---|---|

Charming inside and out, this secluded bayview Tudor plays host to a bald eagle (who has made its home on the grounds for several years) and a loyal following of island tourists, as well as the Millers, who purchased it in 1992. Tucked into a fruit orchard with a commanding water view, the location is peaceful and private, and access to town is excellent. Transportation is provided if you choose not to drive. Breakfasts are bountiful, and rooms are comfortable and cheery, though not overlarge.

## SETTING & FACILITIES

**Location:** Less than 2 mi. from ferry landing on Pear Point Rd. overlooking Griffin Bay
**Near:** Friday Harbor, ferry landing, Griffin Bay, airport
**Building:** 1920s Tudor-style home
**Grounds:** 5 acres; bay-view lawn, flower/veg. gardens; private beach across road
**Public Space:** LR, DR
**Food & Drink:** Beverages; homemade

from-the-orchard fruit roll-ups & cookies; full breakfast; early cont'l or bag breakfast option
**Recreation:** Beachcombing, wildlife watching, historic touring, kayaking, boating, fishing
**Amenities & Services:** Sound system, books, woodstove, slippers, games, guest phone & fridge; special occasion extras, town & ferry transport

## ACCOMMODATIONS

**Units:** 5 guest rooms
**All Rooms:** Country furnishings & period reproductions
**Some Rooms:** Robes, hip roof, desk, armoire
**Bed & Bath:** Queen, one with daybed & trundle; private baths, 4 of 5 ensuite
**Favorites:** Sunset, Panorama
**Comfort & Decor:** Impeccably clean

and "farmhouse comfortable." Rich woodwork, contemporary country colors, traditional furnishings. Chintz, wicker, slipcovers, quaint quilts, cozy artifacts. Living room takes a Southwest turn, with Navajo artifacts and pottery. Central hot-water heat with auxiliary space heaters.

## RATES, RESERVATIONS, & RESTRICTIONS

**Deposit:** Credit card; 7-day cancellation, $15 fee
**Discounts:** Single occupancy, off-season; $20 add'l person
**Credit Cards:** V, MC
**Check-in/Out:** 3–6 or by arrangement/11
**Smoking:** Outside only
**Pets:** No
**Kids:** 8 & over welcome
**Minimum Stay:** 2 nights, peak season

weekends, some holidays and festival weekends
**Open:** All year
**Hosts:** Mary & Arthur Miller
760 Pear Point Rd.
Friday Harbor, WA 98250
(800) 972-2089 or (360) 378-5604
Fax: (360) 378-6535
duffyhouse@rockisland.net
www.san-juan.net/duffyhouse/

## OLYMPIC LIGHTS, Friday Harbor

| Overall: ★★★ | Room Quality: C | Value: B | Price: $75–$110 |
|---|---|---|---|

This striking yellow Victorian commands an open meadow, affording a broad sea panorama and views of the Olympic Peninsula. Inside, a peaceful retreat is so gentle and mellow as to defy description. The home has an intangible sense of tranquility. Soft, pale colors give a contemporary feel; laid-back pace and a few well-placed antiques evoke the turn-of-the-century. Christian and Lea have operated their bed-and-breakfast since 1986. A top pick for get-away-from-it-all value and pure relaxation.

## SETTING & FACILITIES

**Location:** South end of island, just outside American Camp National Historic Park; 5.5 mi. from Friday Harbor ferry landing
**Near:** Eagle Point/Eagle Cove, False Bay, Griffin Bay, Cattle Point
**Building:** 1895 Victorian farmhouse
**Grounds:** Peaceful gardens w/ paths in meadow w/ panoramic views

**Public Space:** LR, DR, porch
**Food & Drink:** Sherry, tea; full vegetarian breakfast, early bag breakfast option
**Recreation:** Croquet, bocci ball; wildlife watching, touring, boating, fishing
**Amenities & Services:** Binoculars, kites, sporting equipment, games, reading material

## ACCOMMODATIONS

**Units:** 5 guest rooms
**All Rooms:** View, high-quality linens, down comforters
**Some Rooms:** Bay window, sitting area, table & chairs, walk-in closet, armoire
**Bed & Bath:** King, queen, or queen & twin; 1 private bath, 4 share 2 baths

**Favorites:** Heart, Ra, Garden
**Comfort & Decor:** Light, airy, and sunny, the rooms are smallish but feel larger with shades of white and off-white and delicate accents of sage and pink. Super-clean. White-painted woodwork, pale carpet. Fresh flowers. Individually controlled thermostats.

## RATES, RESERVATIONS, & RESTRICTIONS

**Deposit:** 1st night; 7-day cancellation, $15 fee
**Discounts:** Single occupancy; $20 add'l person
**Credit Cards:** Not accepted
**Check-in/Out:** 2–5 or by arrangement/11
**Smoking:** No
**Pets:** No; host cats on premises
**Kids:** By arrangement only

**No-Nos:** Shoes on 2nd floor
**Minimum Stay:** 2 nights, high season & holidays
**Open:** All year
**Hosts:** Christian & Lea Andrade
4531-A Cattle Point Rd.
Friday Harbor, WA 98250
(360) 378-3186
Fax: (360) 378-2097
www.san-juan.net/olympiclights

## PANACEA, Friday Harbor

| Overall: ★★★★½ | Room Quality: B | Value: C | Price: $135–$165 |
|---|---|---|---|

Distinctive property is a textbook example of the bungalow style of the Craftsman era—clean lines, but accented with the more fanciful swooping curves and dormers. Rooms are individually decorated, with palettes as diverse as malachite and burgundy with Native American accents to peach, yellow, and red with classic wall quilt. Original woodwork and glass used to good advantage. The Schutte family took over this established bed-and-breakfast in 1997 and are creating a classic—in-town convenience and upscale ambiance. Great breakfasts, too: fresh, creative menus combine the traditional and the trendy with the inspiration of Pacific Northwest seasonal items. Worth checking out.

## SETTING & FACILITIES

**Location:** In town, on Park just off Blair across from high school; a few blocks from ferry
**Near:** Ferry landing, downtown Friday Harbor
**Building:** 1907 Craftsman bungalow
**Grounds:** Grassy lot; landscaping under way at our visit, to include waterscaping, gazebo
**Public Space:** Parlor, wraparound veranda

**Food & Drink:** Afternoon refreshments; full breakfast
**Recreation:** Wildlife watching, historic touring, kayaking, boating, fishing, galleries
**Amenities & Services:** Guest phone, covered bike parking, books, games, umbrellas; celebration packages & extras, breakfast in bed, picnic packages

## ACCOMMODATIONS

**Units:** 4 guest rooms
**All Rooms:** Private entrances, extra-high ceilings, high-quality beds & linens, carpet, TV, guest guide
**Some Rooms:** Dbl. whirlpool tub, private patio, robes, fireplace
**Bed & Bath:** Queen or king, roll-away avail.; private ensuite baths
**Favorites:** Trellis, Veranda

**Comfort & Decor:** Cozy parlor with arched doorways, stone fireplace, and original leaded glass. Lovely tile work, rich wood, and elegant decor throughout. Ralph Lauren bedding, period furnishings, lace curtains; florals mix with classic lines and intricate patterns. Ceiling fans and individual room thermostats.

## RATES, RESERVATIONS, & RESTRICTIONS

**Deposit:** 1st night; 7-day cancellation
**Discounts:** Midweek, off-season, extended stay, AARP; $25 add'l person
**Credit Cards:** V, MC
**Check-in/Out:** 2–6 or by arrangement/11
**Smoking:** Outside only
**Pets:** No
**Kids:** No
**Minimum Stay:** None

**Open:** All year
**Hosts:** Jessica Schutte, Bruce & Beverly Schutte, Rebecca Schutte
595 Park St., P.O. Box 2983
Friday Harbor, WA 98250
(800) 639-2762 or (360) 378-3757
Fax: (360) 378-8540
panacea@pacificrim.net
www.friday-harbor.net/panacea

## TRUMPETER INN, Friday Harbor

| Overall: ★★★★ | Room Quality: B | Value: C | Price: $95–$140 |
|---|---|---|---|

It's easy to see why the Trumpeter Inn (named for the swans that sometimes visit in winter) is a San Juan Island favorite. Set back from the road on its own pastoral acreage, it's just moments from town, but rural and peaceful, plus it's centrally located for accessing all other parts of the island. The atmosphere at Trumpeter is of gracious ease—comfortable, welcoming. Many little extras (hot tub flashlights and slippers, beverage access, great cookies, touring info) make the livin' easy. Your excellent hosts provide a thorough introduction to the premises, then interact as much or as little as you wish. They live in separate, adjacent quarters, and are always available by intercom. Excellent breakfasts.

### SETTING & FACILITIES

**Location:** 2 mi. from ferry landing, off San Juan Valley Rd.
**Near:** Friday Harbor, airport, all island attractions
**Building:** Contemporary 2-level small inn
**Grounds:** 5 sprawling, grassy acres with pond, gardens, rockscaping
**Public Space:** Upstairs parlor, TV room, guest pantry
**Food & Drink:** Self-serve hot beverages, juices, cookies; full breakfast; early coffee
**Recreation:** Wandering the grounds, bicycling, wildlife watching, boating, fishing
**Amenities & Services:** Hot tub, VCR, sound system, games, phone, woodstove, "I Forgot It" basket; morning "headline news," equipped picnic baskets avail.

## ACCOMMODATIONS

**Units:** 5 guest rooms
**All Rooms:** Robes, carpet, high-quality beds & linens, hairdryer, down comforter
**Some Rooms:** Desk, sitting area, private deck, disabled access
**Bed & Bath:** Queen, king, king & twin, or twins; private ensuite baths
**Favorites:** Bay Laurel, Rosemary, Sage

**Comfort & Decor:** Pale walls and carpets, traditional furnishings, soft contemporary colors. Tile entry, rich wood trim. Common areas are bright and airy. Guest rooms are fresh and romantic (not fussy), in palettes such as lavender and pink, burgundy and forest, blue and yellow. Local watercolor paintings enliven the walls.

## RATES, RESERVATIONS, & RESTRICTIONS

**Deposit:** 1st night; 7-day cancellation
**Discounts:** Off-season; $25 add'l person
**Credit Cards:** V, MC, AE, D
**Check-in/Out:** 2–5 or by arrangement/11
**Smoking:** Outside only
**Pets:** No; host dog & cat outside on premises
**Kids:** Over 12 by arrangement
**Minimum Stay:** 2 nights, summer

weekends & some holidays
**Open:** All year (may close some periods in winter)
**Hosts:** Bobbie & Don Wiesner
420 Trumpeter Way
Friday Harbor, WA 98250
(800) 826-7926 or (360) 378-3884
Fax: (360) 378-8235
swan@rockisland.com
www.friday-harbor.net/trumpeter/

## WHARFSIDE B&B, Friday Harbor

| Overall: ★★★½ | Room Quality: C | Value: D | Price: $155 |
| --- | --- | --- | --- |

Sleep and dine aboard the *Slow Season,* the San Juans' only floating bed-and-breakfast. Formerly the *Jacquelyn* (also operated as a bed-and-breakfast since the 1980s), the 60-foot motorsailer was purchased, renamed, and refurbished by Bob (also owner of Blair House) and Page in early 1999. The new owners plan to offer a luxurious experience, complete with fine-china dining and all the comforts of the finest yacht. When we saw the sumptuous upgrades (still in progress at the time of our visit), it was hard to believe this 45-ton beauty was a former tuna boat.

## SETTING & FACILITIES

**Location:** Main dock at the Port of Friday Harbor
**Near:** Ferry landing, downtown Friday Harbor
**Building:** 60-foot gaff-rigged ketch
**Grounds:** The dock & the harbor!

**Public Space:** Main salon
**Food & Drink:** Full breakfast
**Recreation:** Shopping, galleries, bicycling, wildlife watching, kayaking, fishing
**Amenities & Services:** TV/VCR; sunset cruises by arrangement (fee)

## ACCOMMODATIONS

**Units:** 2 staterooms
**All Rooms:** Fine fabrics, rich detailing, sitting area
**Some Rooms:** TV/VCR
**Bed & Bath:** Queen; private baths
**Favorites:** Either (see descriptions below)
**Comfort & Decor:** Nautical motifs with rich woodwork and elegant fab-rics. Upscale accoutrements include fine china. Aft suite has low headroom but ensuite head. (For the uninitiated, a ship's bathroom is called the "head.") Forward suite has higher ceiling and adjacency to shared main salon; its head is across the main salon. Bear in mind, tall folk, that this is a BOAT, and spaces are accordingly compact.

## RATES, RESERVATIONS, & RESTRICTIONS

**Deposit:** Call
**Discounts:** Call
**Credit Cards:** V, MC, AE, D
**Check-in/Out:** 2–5/11 or by arrangement
**Smoking:** No
**Pets:** No
**Kids:** No

**Minimum Stay:** None
**Open:** All year
**Hosts:** Bob Pittman & Page Sugg
P.O. Box 1212
Friday Harbor, WA 98250
(800) 899-3030 or (360) 378-5907
bobp@webtv.net
www.san-juan-island.net/wharfside/

## WILDWOOD MANOR, Friday Harbor

| Overall: ★★★★ | Room Quality: C | Value: D | Price: $155–$175 |
|---|---|---|---|

Grand, elegant home mixes whimsy with opulence. Hostess's paintings decorate some of the walls. Hosts are surprisingly laid-back for owners of such a majestic home; new to innkeeping, they like to treat guests like family. While they are not the island's most experienced innkeepers, they are gracious, intuitive, and well-intentioned. Rooms are small for the price. Breakfasts are rich and decadent. Those sensitive to smoke or cats may want to look elsewhere.

## SETTING & FACILITIES

**Location:** 5 mi. from Friday Harbor on Roche Harbor Rd.
**Near:** Roche Harbor Resort & Marina, English Camp
**Building:** 1980s Queen Anne–style Victorian
**Grounds:** 11 wooded acres w/ lawn, landscaping, wildlife
**Public Space:** LR, deck, guest sitting room

**Food & Drink:** Refreshments; coffee & light snack (7-ish); full breakfast
**Recreation:** Wildlife watching, bicycling, kayaking, boating, fishing, galleries
**Amenities & Services:** Games, phone, videos, desk, books; special occasion extras

## ACCOMMODATIONS

**Units:** 3 guest rooms
**All Rooms:** Fine furnishings, carpet
**Some Rooms:** Bay window, quilt, TV/VCR, robes
**Bed & Bath:** Double, king, or queen; 1 private bath, 2 rooms share a bath
**Favorites:** Depends on your needs
**Comfort & Decor:** Stately home has elegant furnishings and upscale decor,

blending French Renaissance with American Victorian with whimsy. Guest rooms are small and a bit dim (Blue Room has the best light, plus a bay window), with rich wallpapers, lace and cloth window treatments. Tile baths. Central heat and—rare on the island—air-conditioning.

## RATES, RESERVATIONS, & RESTRICTIONS

**Deposit:** Credit card
**Discounts:** None
**Credit Cards:** V, MC
**Check-in/Out:** Call
**Smoking:** Outside only
**Pets:** No; host cats on premises
**Kids:** Over 12 welcome
**No-Nos:** More than 2 sharing a room
**Minimum Stay:** None

**Open:** March–Nov. (approximately)
**Hosts:** Victoria & Richard Baker
P.O. Box 2255
3021 Roche Harbor Rd.
Friday Harbor, WA 98250
(360) 378-3447
Fax: (360) 378-6095
wildwdmanor@rockisland.com
www.rockisland.com/~wildwdmanor

## KATY'S INN, La Conner

| Overall: ★★★★ | Room Quality: B | Value: B | Price: $72–$120 |
|---|---|---|---|

Thought to be the first bed-and-breakfast in the Skagit Valley, Katy's Inn opened in 1984. The elegant Victorian inn has passed through several owners; Bruce and Kathie have owned it since 1994. Their improvements include extra loving care on the beautifully landscaped grounds, a real sense of hospitality with respect to amenities, and marvelous gourmet breakfasts served with pride and class. "Small rooms, big breakfasts!" Closest bed-and-breakfast to downtown, and our favorite.

## SETTING & FACILITIES

**Location:** Corner of Washington & Third, just uphill from downtown
**Near:** Downtown La Conner, Mount Vernon, Whidbey Island, Anacortes, San Juan Islands
**Building:** 1882 Victorian
**Grounds:** Spacious hillside; roses, rockscaping, waterfall, & pond
**Public Space:** Deck & patio, hot tub gazebo, parlor, DR, balcony
**Food & Drink:** Cookies, tea, cocoa,

cider (evening); full gourmet brunch (ensuite or in DR)
**Recreation:** Shopping, boating, kayaking, bicycling, galleries
**Amenities & Services:** Games, phone, hairdryer, amenities basket, extra shorts & T's for hot tub; silver tray full breakfast delivered to your room (optional—no charge), eco-sensitive towel policy

## ACCOMMODATIONS

**Units:** 4 guest rooms, I suite
**All Rooms:** Fresh flowers, robes
**Some Rooms:** Stained glass, claw-foot tub, sitting area, TV/VCR & videos, canopy bed, separate entrance, gas fireplace, soaking tub, bubble bath
**Bed & Bath:** Most queen (I double; 2 w/ extra daybed); 3 private baths, 2 share a bath
**Favorites:** Captain's Suite, Lilac Room

**Comfort & Decor:** Thoroughly Victorian, with florals, brocades, lace, wicker, and period furnishings. Softly intricate wallpapers, hardwood floors with area rugs. Hand-painted touches; historic photos and original artwork. Gas-forced air heat on main floor, augmented by individual space heaters upstairs. Captain's Suite has gas fireplace.

## RATES, RESERVATIONS, & RESTRICTIONS

**Deposit:** Credit card or check; 3-day cancellation
**Discounts:** Off-season midweek; $20 add'l person
**Credit Cards:** V, MC, D
**Check-in/Out:** 4–6/11 or by arrangement
**Smoking:** Outside only
**Pets:** No

**Kids:** Welcome in downstairs suite only
**Minimum Stay:** None
**Open:** All year
**Hosts:** Bruce & Kathie Hubbard
503 S. Third
La Conner, WA 98257
(800) 914-7767 or (360) 466-3366
home.ncia.com/katysinn/

## RIDGEWAY FARM B&B, La Conner

| Overall: ★★★½ | Room Quality: C | Value: C | Price: $75–$155 |
|---|---|---|---|

A comfortable farmhouse inn amidst famous Skagit Valley tulip fields. Louise and John have owned this relaxed, clean, and pleasant inn since 1991. Ambiance puts you in the mind of the Midwest—farms and heartland hospitality. Hosts live on the property in a separate cottage, so guests have the common rooms to themselves.

## SETTING & FACILITIES

**Location:** Between La Conner and Mount Vernon on McLean Rd.
**Near:** Whidbey Island, Anacortes, San Juan Islands
**Building:** 1928 brick-faced Dutch Colonial
**Grounds:** Expansive w/ a profusion of flowers in a relaxed country setting
**Public Space:** DR, LR, deck
**Food & Drink:** In-room chocolates; evening dessert; morning coffee, tea, or cocoa room service; hearty farm breakfast
**Recreation:** Boating, kayaking, bicycling, bird-watching, scenic flights, galleries
**Amenities & Services:** Travel library, books, sound system & CDs, videos, first-rate hot tub; concierge services incl. arrangement of scenic airplane or hot-air balloon rides; special occasions; meetings

## ACCOMMODATIONS

**Units:** 5 guest rooms, 1 suite
**All Rooms:** Flowers, tile bath, robes, bath amenities
**Some Rooms:** Sitting area, claw-foot or soaking tub, skylights; brass, iron, or wicker bed
**Bed & Bath:** Queen or king (1 w/ extra twin; roll-away avail.); 4 private baths, 2 share a bath

**Favorites:** Nicole, the skylight penthouse suite
**Comfort & Decor:** "Country casual." Florals, wallpapers, quilts, stuffed animals lend character. Newer carpet, wicker pieces, and period furnishings lend class. Penthouse suite (Nicole) has vaulted ceiling, pale decor with floral accents.

## RATES, RESERVATIONS, & RESTRICTIONS

**Deposit:** Credit card; 5-day cancellation
**Discounts:** Off-season midweek; $25 add'l person
**Credit Cards:** V, MC, D
**Check-in/Out:** 3–7 or by arrangement/11
**Smoking:** Outside only
**Pets:** No; host kitty
**Kids:** By arrangement

**Minimum Stay:** Only applicable during Tulip Festival
**Open:** All year
**Hosts:** John & Louise Kelly
14914 McLean Rd.
La Conner, WA 98257
(800) 428-8068 or (360) 428-8068
Fax: (360) 428-8880
ridgeway@halcyon.com
www.placestostay.com/LaCon-Ridge-wayFarm

## THE WILD IRIS, La Conner

| Overall: ★★★★ | Room Quality: B | Value: C | Price: $95–$180 |
| --- | --- | --- | --- |

Justifiably proud of its many guidebook listings, The Wild Iris is a hybrid hotel–bed-and-breakfast that pulls off the combination well—a perfect option for the person who's not ready for an in-home bed-and-breakfast. On-premises restaurant (where breakfast is served) also began offering dinner in 1998. Jointly managed with 12-unit, more casual Blue Heron next door. Managed by Susan since it opened in 1992.

## SETTING & FACILITIES

**Location:** Two blocks south of Main St.
**Near:** Downtown La Conner, waterfront, Whidbey Island, Anacortes, San Juan Islands
**Building:** Modern hotel w/ Craftsman & Victorian aspects
**Grounds:** Minimal; larger yard at adjacent Blue Heron
**Public Space:** Intimate parlor and wine bar (added winter 1999)

**Food & Drink:** Hot beverages; full chef-prepared buffet breakfast; restaurant on premises
**Recreation:** Shopping, boating, kayaking, bicycling, galleries
**Amenities & Services:** Umbrellas, many in-room amenities; celebration extras, concierge, desk staff 6 a.m.–11 p.m. (emergency staff adjacent 24 hours), meeting room

## ACCOMMODATIONS

**Units:** 7 guest rooms, 12 suites
**All Rooms:** Private-line phone, data port, remote TV w/ VCR jack, guest guide, hairdryer, closet
**Some Rooms:** Gas fireplace, dual whirlpool, sitting area, private entrance, patio, coffee service, canopy bed, outdoor whirlpool on private deck, ADA wheelchair access
**Bed & Bath:** King or queen (1 w/ 2 queens); all private ensuite baths

**Favorites:** Ivy Room, Cloud Room, Indonesian Room
**Comfort & Decor:** Tailored and crisp, with tile baths, wallpapers, carpet. Rooms individual and tastefully decorated, some with floral or quilt accents, others with more "masculine" jewel colors or tone-on-tone decor. Solid construction means very little noise. Radiant floor heating (nice in tile bath!) with individual room controls.

## RATES, RESERVATIONS, & RESTRICTIONS

**Deposit:** 1st night; 24-hour cancellation
**Discounts:** Off-season, extended stay; $15 add'l person
**Credit Cards:** V, MC, AE
**Check-in/Out:** After 3/11
**Smoking:** Outside only
**Pets:** No
**Kids:** No (only in adjacent property; call)

**Minimum Stay:** None
**Open:** All year
**Hosts:** Susan Sullivan, General Mgr.
121 Maple Ave.
La Conner, WA 98257
(800) 477-1400 (WA & BC only) or
(360) 466-1400
Fax: (360) 466-1221
info@wildiris.com
www.wildiris.com

## DOVE HOUSE, CHAUNTECLEER HOUSE, & POTTING SHED, Langley

| Overall: ★★★★★ | Room Quality: A | Value: C | Price: $175–$225 |
| --- | --- | --- | --- |

Those who appreciate life's finer things will love these three unique, self-contained lodgings. Each has been lovingly and lavishly decorated by the extraordinary Bunny Meals, whose interior design work is now requested far and wide. Exceptional finish work, surprising fabric and accessory choices, all tied together with the style of a real artist. These detached units with self-serve breakfasts are not as intimate as some inns, but you will feel pampered to the hilt and won't want to leave your wonderful home-away-from-home on its lovely, secluded grounds. Little touches make the difference—like the small but top-notch libraries in each unit.

## SETTING & FACILITIES

**Location:** Just off Saratoga Rd. on the Saratoga Passage waterway, w/in walking distance of Langley
**Near:** Clinton ferry to Mukilteo, Langley, Keystone ferry to Port Townsend
**Building:** 3 individual structures; incl. former pigeon coop & former garden shed
**Grounds:** 6.5 secluded acres; flowers, pond, Puget Sound views
**Public Space:** Each unit has living area(s)
**Food & Drink:** Full self-serve breakfast in your fridge
**Recreation:** Boating, scuba, wine touring, golf, clamming, beachcombing
**Amenities & Services:** see "All Rooms" and "Some Rooms" below

## ACCOMMODATIONS

**Units:** 3 cottages
**All Rooms:** TV, VCR, phone, library, sound system, stunning handicrafts/art, woodstove or fireplace, full kitchen or extended kitchenette
**Some Rooms:** Whirlpool tub, hot tub, water view
**Bed & Bath:** Queen (Dove House also has twins and twin bunks); private ensuite baths
**Favorites:** ANY!

**Comfort & Decor:** This place deserves a page of its own just for decor. Each of the 3 units is cute but classy. Dove House features rich wood, hand-hewn furnishings, Northwest artwork, stone, and tile. Chantecleer hearkens to the Eastern seaboard, with classic and nautical motifs. Potting Shed is a whimsical mix of garden motifs in shades of green, with brick, wormwood, and tile accents. Top-drawer all the way.

## RATES, RESERVATIONS, & RESTRICTIONS

**Deposit:** Full advance payment; 7-day cancellation
**Discounts:** Extended stays, rental of all 3 units; $25 add'l person
**Credit Cards:** V, MC
**Check-in/Out:** 4–7/noon
**Smoking:** No
**Pets:** No
**Kids:** 10 & over welcome in Dove House
**Minimum Stay:** 2 nights, weekends
**Open:** All year
**Hosts:** Bunny & Bob Meals
3557/5081 Saratoga Rd.
Langley, WA 98260
(800) 637-4436 or (360) 221-5494
Fax: (360) 221-0397
bunny@dovehouse.com
www.dovehouse.com

## LOG CASTLE B&B, Langley

| Overall: ★★★★½ | Room Quality: C | Value: B | Price: $95–$120 |
|---|---|---|---|

Astonishing log work-of-art hand-crafted by congressman Metcalf and his family. Third-story octagonal turret (Ann's Room) gives the structure a sort of lighthouse (or castle) appearance. Inside, the turret is a divine space, surrounded by glass and offering predictably awesome views of the water and Camano Island. The home incorporates driftwood, native stone, and beach artifacts in fanciful and dramatic ways—and every piece has its story. Furnishings are comfy, tending toward retro—sort of like staying in your wacky uncle's cabin, if your uncle was a master craftsman and four-star chef. Innkeepers are among the best in the business.

## SETTING & FACILITIES

**Location:** 1.5 mi. from downtown, off Saratoga Rd. on the Saratoga Passage waterfront
**Near:** Clinton ferry landing, Holmes Harbor, beaches
**Building:** Hand-crafted log home with octagonal turret
**Grounds:** 2.5 waterfront acres surrounded by family acreage; beachfront and hiking trails
**Public Space:** Great room, reading nooks

**Food & Drink:** Evening refreshments; in-room fruit & nuts; early coffee tray; full breakfast; early ferry breakfast upon request
**Recreation:** Rowing, fishing, scuba, ferry to Port Townsend, golf, wine touring
**Amenities & Services:** Games, binoculars, canoe, rowboat, tide charts, life jackets, phone, TV; weddings, meetings, retreats

## ACCOMMODATIONS

**Units:** 4 guest rooms
**All Rooms:** Water view, robes, log construction, private deck or balcony
**Some Rooms:** Sofa-sleeper, ceiling fan, balcony swing, woodstove, sitting area
**Bed & Bath:** Queen, king, double (2 w/ sofa-sleepers); private ensuite baths
**Favorites:** Ann, Marta, Lea
**Comfort & Decor:** Entire structure

was hand-crafted from on-site products: hand-peeled logs, hand-cut shingles, driftwood accents. Great room is awesome—sprawling and comfy, with cathedral ceiling. Reading nooks are like a fort for grown-ups. Tile baths. Green plants. Woodstove central heat, plus backup electric system. Each room has auxiliary wood or electric heat, individually controlled. Fans.

## RATES, RESERVATIONS, & RESTRICTIONS

**Deposit:** Credit card; 7-day cancellation
**Discounts:** $25 add'l person
**Credit Cards:** V, MC, D
**Check-in/Out:** 3–7/11 or by arrangement
**Smoking:** No
**Pets:** No
**Kids:** Over 10 welcome
**Minimum Stay:** 2 nights, holiday weekends

**Open:** All year
**Hosts:** Jack & Norma Metcalf, owners; Karen & Phil Holdsworth, innkeepers
4693 Saratoga Rd.
Langley, WA 98260
(360) 221-5483
Fax: (360) 221-6249 (call ahead)
innkeepr@whidbey.com
www.whidbey.com/logcastle

## EDENWILD INN, Lopez Island

| Overall: ★★★★ | Room Quality: B | Value: C | Price: $110–$165 |
|---|---|---|---|

This established, "in-town" inn offers an upscale, predictable atmosphere and walking-distance access to the various services of the island's only commercial center, Lopez Village. Ownership changed as this book went to press, so specifics are subject to change, but the basics are likely to remain the same. Landscaped grounds with brick patio are festooned with climbing roses. This property feels like a small European inn rather than an intimate bed-and-breakfast, with owners living adjacent. Where Inn at Swifts Bay is lush and inviting, and MacKay Harbor Inn is homey and cozy, Edenwild is clean-line and uncluttered.

### SETTING & FACILITIES

**Location:** NW part of island, in Lopez Village
**Near:** Lopez Village, Fisherman Bay, Saturday Market
**Building:** Contemporary farmhouse Victorian
**Grounds:** 1 acre, beautifully landscaped; herb beds, flowering shrubs, roses
**Public Space:** Front porch, patio, LR, DR
**Food & Drink:** Afternoon aperitif; in-room sherry, coffee service, chocolates; soft drinks; full breakfast; early sack breakfast option
**Recreation:** Croquet, bocci ball, beach, kayaking, golf, wildlife watching, photography
**Amenities & Services:** Piano, woodburning fireplace, umbrellas, guest phone & fridge; ferry landing, seaplane, or airport pick-up by arrangement; parties, reunions

### ACCOMMODATIONS

**Units:** 8 guest rooms
**All Rooms:** Garden view, down comforter, hairdryer, closet
**Some Rooms:** Disabled access, fireplace, sitting area, private entrance, desk, sofa-sleeper, soaking tub
**Bed & Bath:** Queen (6), double, king & queen; private baths
**Favorites:** #6 is Honeymoon Suite, #5 has great views, #2 has nice layout
**Comfort & Decor:** Leaded glass, pale hardwood floors, designer-palette (sage, sky, lavender) painted walls or wallpapers, painted woodwork. Original artwork by Northwest artists. Very clean. Individual thermostats.

### RATES, RESERVATIONS, & RESTRICTIONS

**Deposit:** Credit card; 14-day cancellation, $10 fee
**Discounts:** $25 add'l person
**Credit Cards:** V, MC, AE
**Check-in/Out:** After 3/11
**Smoking:** No
**Pets:** No
**Kids:** Welcome
**Minimum Stay:** None
**Open:** All year (may close some winter weeks/months)
**Hosts:** Clark Hailey & Mary Anne Miller
P.O. Box 271, Lopez Island, WA 98261
(360) 468-3238
Fax: (360) 468-4080
edenwildinn@msn.com
www.edenwildinn.com

## INN AT SWIFTS BAY, Lopez Island

| Overall: ★★★★½ | Room Quality: A | Value: C | Price: $95–$175 |
|---|---|---|---|

Our hands-down favorite Lopez Island property, Inn at Swifts Bay has it all—lush, welcoming decor, fabulous food, and a host of amenities, including don't-disturb-your-neighbor electronic headsets for viewing videos from their large collection and marvelous little cedar-scented exercise and sauna studio with back-to-nature "al fresco" shower. Reservation system ensures privacy in hot tub and exercise studio. Attic rooms (4 and 5), with their pitched ceilings and skylights, are secluded and romantic. Each room is beautifully decorated, as are common areas, in a sort of "Eddie Bauer visits the English countryside" fashion.

### SETTING & FACILITIES

**Location:** Between Swifts & Shoal Bays, NE end of island; 2 mi. from ferry landing
**Near:** Odlin Park, Spencer Spit Park
**Building:** Brick & wood-faced contemporary home
**Grounds:** Gardens and sitting areas set in the woods across from bay
**Public Space:** Library, LR, DR, exercise studio, patio
**Food & Drink:** Sherry, snacks, beverages; early coffee; full breakfast
**Recreation:** Kayaking, beach, wildlife watching, photography, golf, boating
**Amenities & Services:** Hot tub, TV/VCR, videos, exercise room, sauna, sound system, piano, games, guest phone, micro., newspaper, "I Forgot It" basket, walking sticks, hiking info; pick-up service by arrangement, group retreats

### ACCOMMODATIONS

**Units:** 2 guest rooms, 3 suites
**All Rooms:** Down or wool comforter, fresh flowers, robes, slippers, desk or writing area
**Some Rooms:** Sitting area, fireplace, private deck, private entrance, VCR, skylights, stained glass, fridge, sleigh or four-poster bed, sound system
**Bed & Bath:** Queen; 3 private baths, 2 share a bath
**Favorites:** #4, #5
**Comfort & Decor:** Traditional fabrics and furnishings; "weekend in the country" feeling. Upscale treatments such as brocades, wrought iron, antique beds, yet comfy in a Cape Cod/LL Bean manner. Soft classical music in common areas. Individual room thermostats.

## Rates, Reservations, & Restrictions

**Deposit:** 1st night; 10-day cancellation
**Discounts:** Special seasonal packages (call)
**Credit Cards:** V, MC, AE, D
**Check-in/Out:** 3–7 or by arrangement/11
**Smoking:** Outside only
**Pets:** No
**Kids:** No
**Minimum Stay:** Major holidays only

**Open:** All year except 12/24–25, 12/31–1/1
**Hosts:** Rob Aney & Mark Adcock, owners; on-site innkeepers
Rte. 2, Box 3402
Lopez Island, WA 98261
(360) 468-3636
Fax: (360) 468-3637
inn@swiftsbay.com
www.swiftsbay.com

## MACKAY HARBOR INN, Lopez Island

| Overall: ★★★ | Room Quality: D | Value: D | Price: $99–$159 |
|---|---|---|---|

Relax in the water-view living room, where a fire burns cheerily on a winter day, and several seating areas provide room for everyone. Wonderful views and a homey atmosphere. Kayaks for rent and a great little bay to use them on. Away-from-the-crowds location and private beach make this a good getaway for an active vacation, or one with older children.

### Setting & Facilities

**Location:** South end of island, about 10 mi. from ferry landing
**Near:** MacKay Harbor, Barlow Bay, Agate Beach, Aleck Bay, Iceberg Point
**Building:** 1904 orig. structure, extensively remodeled
**Grounds:** 2 waterfront acres; gardens, bay, & beach across street
**Public Space:** LR, DR
**Food & Drink:** Tea, coffee, snacks/chocolates (in p.m.); soft drinks; full breakfast
**Recreation:** Wildlife watching, photography, golf, historic touring, boating
**Amenities & Services:** Mountain bikes, binoculars, phone, fridge, books, games, sound system; kayak rentals, pick-up service (fee, by arrangement), weddings

### Accommodations

**Units:** 5 guest rooms
**All Rooms:** Hairdryers, carpet
**Some Rooms:** Water view, fireplace, separate entrance, robes, armoire
**Bed & Bath:** Various, some w/ more than 1 bed; 3 w/ private bath, 2 share a bath
**Favorites:** Harbor Suite, Captain's Room
**Comfort & Decor:** Fresh, simple, and modest. Homey quilts and fabric window treatments. Guest rooms dimly lit and smallish. Common areas welcoming and comfortable. Individual room thermostats.

## RATES, RESERVATIONS, & RESTRICTIONS

**Deposit:** 1st night; 14-day cancellation, $10 fee
**Discounts:** Off-season midweek; $25 add'l person
**Credit Cards:** V, MC
**Check-in/Out:** 3–7 or by arrangement/noon
**Smoking:** No
**Pets:** No
**Kids:** Age 10 & older welcome by arrangement
**No-Nos:** Food preparation in rooms

**Minimum Stay:** None
**Open:** All year
**Hosts:** Mike & Robin Bergstrom, owners; Sue & Arnie Johnson, winter innkeepers
949 MacKaye Harbor Rd.
Lopez Island, WA 98261
(360) 468-2253
Fax: (360) 468-2393
mckay@pacificrim.net
www.san-juan.net/mackayeharbor/

## THE COLONIAL MANOR, Mount Vernon

| Overall: ★★★½ | Room Quality: C | Value: C | Price: $95–$150 |
|---|---|---|---|

Colonial-style home in a rural setting. Enthusiastic new innkeepers Bonnie and Howard bought this inn in 1998 and were in the process of remodeling and redecorating when we visited. The rooms, named after family members, each have designated baths, not always ensuite. Some have only tubs, but shower access can be arranged easily, especially if it's not a full house. Decor and policies are evolving. Bonnie is very service-oriented and strives to make every guest's stay memorable.

## SETTING & FACILITIES

**Location:** Between La Conner and Mount Vernon on McLean Rd.
**Near:** Skagit River, Skagit Valley attractions, casino, Anacortes
**Building:** 1907 local pioneer's Colonial-style home
**Grounds:** 1.4 acres of fruit & nut trees, w/ grape arbor, fountain courtyard, barn, gazebo
**Public Space:** Front porch, library, parlor, DR

**Food & Drink:** Espresso drinks, mulled cider (seasonal), & other beverages; afternoon English tea avail.; evening dessert; extended cont'l breakfast
**Recreation:** Hiking, bird-watching, scenic driving, galleries
**Amenities & Services:** Hot tub, deck, videos, guest fridge, antique baby grand; celebration extras

## ACCOMMODATIONS

**Units:** 5 guest rooms
**All Rooms:** Down comforters, cotton quality sheets, TV/VCR, phone jacks (phones avail.), armoire, robes
**Some Rooms:** Sofa-sleeper, candles, bath salts, in-room champagne, desk, antique sink
**Bed & Bath:** Queen (4) or double (1); private baths (some ensuite)
**Favorites:** Bonnie Jean and Jamie Rebecca

**Comfort & Decor:** This work-in-progress inn combines antiques with a mix of midquality contemporary furnishings. Finer touches include period light fixtures, stained glass, brocade upholstery and bedding, and high-quality linens. Roomy attic suite (Bonnie Jean) has dormered alcoves and sitting area. Central heat and air-conditioning.

## RATES, RESERVATIONS, & RESTRICTIONS

**Deposit:** Credit card; 7-day cancellation
**Discounts:** Off-season extended stays
**Credit Cards:** V, MC
**Check-in/Out:** After 3 or by arrangement/11
**Smoking:** No
**Pets:** No
**Kids:** Welcome

**Minimum Stay:** None
**Open:** All year
**Hosts:** Bonnie & Howard Anderson
1556 McLean Rd.
Mount Vernon, WA 98273
(800) 893-1022 or (360) 424-3237
Fax: (360) 428-2009
cmanor@fidalgo.net
www.fidalgo.net/~cmanor

## THE WHITE SWAN GUEST HOUSE, Mount Vernon

| Overall: ★★★½ | Room Quality: B | Value: C | Price: $80–$135 |
|---|---|---|---|

Whimsy and artistry in a country setting; storybook Queen Anne surrounded by a riot of flowers and flowering plants. After a decade as an innkeeper, former interior designer Peter Goldfarb knows how to create a memorable, relaxing experience. The main inn is for adults only, with its bold color palette and profuse reading material. The cottage is self-contained with its kitchen and laundry facilities, and attractive with stained glass accents and subtle Native American motifs. Have a chocolate chip cookie (or 3 or 4) and relax into a simpler era. Four large, sweet dogs on premises.

## SETTING & FACILITIES

**Location:** Between La Conner and Conway on Fir Island
**Near:** Mount Vernon, La Conner, Skagit River, Skagit Valley attractions, Anacortes
**Building:** 1890s Queen Anne farmhouse
**Grounds:** 4 acres w/ extensive English flower garden, brick courtyard

**Public Space:** Sitting area, kitchen bar, DR, LR
**Food & Drink:** Cookies on arrival; large "country cont'l" breakfast
**Recreation:** Hiking, bicycling, birdwatching, scenic driving, shopping, galleries
**Amenities & Services:** Lots of fun & artsy reading material

## ACCOMMODATIONS

**Units:** 3 guest rooms, 1 cottage
**All Rooms:** Robes, reading material
**Some Rooms:** Window seat; cottage: deck, kitchen, futon couch, W/D
**Bed & Bath:** Queen or king; cottage has private bath; 3 rooms in main house share 2 baths
**Favorites:** Cottage or Yellow Room

**Comfort & Decor:** "Artistic Country" mixes well-chosen antiques with comfortable, slipcovered contemporary with wicker with simple, Shaker-like pieces. Bold colors; needlepoint samplers and gilt-framed prints; hardwood floors with handsome hooked rugs.

## RATES, RESERVATIONS, & RESTRICTIONS

**Deposit:** 1st night; 5-day cancellation
**Discounts:** Single occupancy, off-season, no breakfast option (cottage has kitchen); $20 add'l person; under age 5 free in cottage
**Credit Cards:** V, MC
**Check-in/Out:** 3–6 or by arrangement/11
**Smoking:** No
**Pets:** No; host dogs on site

**Kids:** Welcome in cottage only
**Minimum Stay:** 2 nights during Tulip Festival & Labor Day
**Open:** All year
**Hosts:** Peter Goldfarb
15872 Moore Rd.
Mount Vernon, WA 98273-9249
(360) 445-6805
www.cnw.com/~wswan/

## BUCK BAY FARM, Orcas Island

| Overall: ★★★½ | Room Quality: C | Value: C | Price: $85–$125 |
|---|---|---|---|

Here on the "quieter part of the island," you can really get away from it all at Buck Bay Farm. Local history has it that this property was originally the barn for Olga's town bull (?!), but you'd never know it today. Rick and Janet purchased it in 1991, remodeled extensively, and turned it into a quiet, clean bed-and-breakfast that's a cross between Grandma's house and country contemporary. Common areas are small and homey, with comfortable, if worn, period pieces. Guest rooms are a bit more upscale. Bucolic lawn (with sheep in one adjacent pasture, llamas and alpacas in another) invites picnicking.

## SETTING & FACILITIES

**Location:** Point Lawrence Rd., .75 mi. east of Olga
**Near:** Olga, Moran S.P., Mt. Constitution, Mt. Pickett; Buck, Buoy, & Doe Bays
**Building:** Historic farmhouse
**Grounds:** 5.5 acres; trees, pond, large lawn, fire pit, picnic areas
**Public Space:** LR, sunroom, porch
**Food & Drink:** Self-serve hot beverages; cookies or snack; family-style full breakfast
**Recreation:** Picnicking & strolling; beaches, wildlife watching, boating, fishing
**Amenities & Services:** TV, games, desk, sound system, hot tub, phone, piano

## ACCOMMODATIONS

**Units:** 4 guest rooms, 1 two-room suite
**All Rooms:** Down comforter, robes, period furnishings, carpet
**Some Rooms:** Vanity, TV, balcony, private entrance, sleeping loft, VCR, sitting area
**Bed & Bath:** Queen (3 w/ sleeper-sofa); private baths (unless 2 parties in Garden Suite)
**Favorites:** Garden Suite, Alder
**Comfort & Decor:** Period furnishings. Fresh woods accent walls painted white or rich hues such as moss green, burgundy, or rose. Tongue-and-groove pine ceilings. Lace curtains. Very clean and farmhouse-tidy, with a touch of the upscale. Zoned central heat.

## RATES, RESERVATIONS, & RESTRICTIONS

**Deposit:** 1st night or 50%
**Discounts:** Off-season extended stay; $20 add'l person
**Credit Cards:** V, MC, AE, D
**Check-in/Out:** 4–6 or by arrangement/11
**Smoking:** Outside only
**Pets:** No; host basset hound & kitties
**Kids:** Welcome by arrangement
**Minimum Stay:** None
**Open:** All year
**Hosts:** Janet & Rick Bronkey
Star Route 45, Olga, WA 98279
(888) 422-BUCK (2825) or
(360) 376-2908
www.buckbayfarm.com

## CHESTNUT HILL B&B, Orcas Island

| Overall: ★★★★½ | Room Quality: A | Value: C | Price: $145–$195 |
|---|---|---|---|

Where Turtleback embodies quality craftsmanship and the quintessential farmhouse, and Spring Bay is a haven for the outdoorsperson, Chestnut

Hill's hallmarks are romance, privacy, and pampering. Innkeepers are in the house 6 a.m. to 6 p.m., then retire to adjacent quarters, leaving guests the exclusive use of the house. Delicious breakfasts (and dinners, in the off-season by arrangement) are served at cozy tables for two in the dining room, which offers views of the meadow and pond. Chestnut Suite and Garden are the most spacious, with cathedral ceilings and skylights, but Chapel, Pond, and Stable have fabulous, expansive pastoral views (each with its namesake in sight).

## SETTING & FACILITIES

**Location:** About 1.5 mi. NE of the ferry landing
**Near:** Ferry landing, Orcas, West Sound
**Building:** 1960s Victorian-style farmhouse, extensively remodeled w/ addition
**Grounds:** 16 acres w/ pond, stables, meadows
**Public Space:** Library, parlor, veranda

**Food & Drink:** Sherry; in-room champagne, chocolates; full breakfast
**Recreation:** Catch-and-release trout fishing, golf, tennis, boating, galleries
**Amenities & Services:** Videos (Nov.–April only), bikes, games, sound system, phone, desk, fridge, rowboat; romantic packages w/ dinners (off-season), elopement & other packages, massage by appointment

## ACCOMMODATIONS

**Units:** 4 guest rooms, 1 suite
**All Rooms:** Quality beds & linens, robes, slippers, bath amenities, fireplace, feather bed
**Some Rooms:** Sitting area, claw-foot tub, whirlpool, slate bath, desk, TV/VCR, skylights, fridge, patio
**Bed & Bath:** Queen four-poster

canopy; private ensuite baths
**Favorites:** Chestnut Suite
**Comfort & Decor:** Classic country-home styling. Soft, lush wall colors accented by wide decorative moldings. Traditional furnishings throughout. Thermostat-controlled fireplaces heat each room individually.

## RATES, RESERVATIONS, & RESTRICTIONS

**Deposit:** Credit card; 7-day cancellation
**Discounts:** Off-season, single, packages
**Credit Cards:** V, MC
**Check-in/Out:** 2–6 (as soon as you arrive on island, arrange if after 6)/11
**Smoking:** No
**Pets:** No; host dog & cat outside
**Kids:** No
**No-Nos:** More than 2 in a room; shoes in house

**Minimum Stay:** 2 nights, peak season & holidays; 2 nights preferred, all weekends
**Open:** All year
**Hosts:** Marilyn & Dan Loewke
P.O. Box 399
Orcas, WA 98280
(360) 376-5157
Fax: (360) 376-5283
chestnut@pacificrim.net
www.chestnuthillinn.com

## KANGAROO HOUSE, Orcas Island

| Overall: ★★★ | Room Quality: C | Value: C | Price: $75–$125 |
|---|---|---|---|

Both house and hosts are folksy and comfortable; the latter are retired Sequoia National Park Service rangers. When the Allens found this established inn (so named for the pet kangaroo kept by the globe-trotting original owner), Australian-born Peter and wife Helen knew their purchase was fated. Excellent midisland location is close to Eastsound shopping and eateries. Airport adjacency can lead to noise. Hosts live on-site in their own quarters. Common areas are relaxing; breakfasts are fresh, delicious, and seasonally inspired.

### SETTING & FACILITIES

**Location:** 1 mi. north of village of Eastsound
**Near:** Airport, North Beach, Terrill Beach, Point Doughty
**Building:** 6,700-sq.-ft. 1907 Craftsman
**Grounds:** Mature trees, flowers, border plantings
**Public Space:** Porch, deck, LR, library
**Food & Drink:** Early coffee; full breakfast

**Recreation:** Golf, tennis, wildlife watching, touring, boating, fishing, galleries
**Amenities & Services:** Hot tub, phone, fridge, games, puzzles, covered bike racks; excellent activities guide, dinners by arrangement in off-season, celebrations

### ACCOMMODATIONS

**Units:** 4 guest rooms, 1 suite
**All Rooms:** Casual country decor, robes, spa towels, flashlight
**Some Rooms:** Hairdryer, sitting room, four-poster, sink, wicker, pitched ceiling, down comforter
**Bed & Bath:** Queen (4, some w/ extra bed), double and twin, roll-away avail.; 2 w/ private baths, 3 share 1.5 baths

**Favorites:** Kathleen's Suite, Anne's Room
**Comfort & Decor:** Embossed and beamed Craftsman-style ceilings in common areas. Guest rooms feature painted or stained hardwood floors (1 carpeted), pale paint, floral wallpapers, midquality mixed-period furnishings; some with wainscoting. Central heat plus auxiliary unit in each room.

### RATES, RESERVATIONS, & RESTRICTIONS

**Deposit:** 1st night; 10-day cancellation
**Discounts:** Single occupancy; $20 add'l person
**Credit Cards:** V, MC, AE, D
**Check-in/Out:** 2:30–7 or by arrangement/11
**Smoking:** No
**Pets:** No; host dog in host quarters
**Kids:** Welcome

**Minimum Stay:** None
**Open:** All year
**Hosts:** Peter & Helen Allen
P.O. Box 334
Eastsound, WA 98245
(888) 371-2175 or (360) 376-2175
Fax: (360) 376-2175
innkeeper@kangaroohouse.com
www.kangaroohouse.com

## OTTERS POND B&B, Orcas Island

| Overall: ★★★★ | Room Quality: B | Value: C | Price: $75–$150 |
|---|---|---|---|

Careful craftsmanship, attention to detail, and a sense of ease combine to give Otters Pond promise as a real contender in the fine bed-and-breakfast community of Orcas Island. The reedy pond, just outside, is a source of peace and beauty (especially lovely viewed from the hot tub gazebo), playing host to a wide community of island wildlife. Gourmet, Pacific Northwest–inspired breakfasts and upscale, adult-retreat atmosphere. This beautiful home began its bed-and-breakfast life in 1997–98 and was still undergoing finish work and expansion at our visit. (Main house holds four bed-and-breakfast rooms; hosts' living quarters and smallest room in adjacent house.)

### SETTING & FACILITIES

**Location:** Just off Horseshoe Hwy. between East Sound & Moran S.P.
**Near:** East Sound (the water), Eastsound (the town), Moran S.P., Mt. Constitution, Cascade Lake, Rosario
**Building:** 2 early 1990s Pacific Northwest contemporary homes
**Grounds:** 5 wooded acres on beautiful, marshy pond
**Public Space:** Sitting room, LR, library, reading area

**Food & Drink:** Self-serve tea & other beverages; full breakfast (early by arrangement)
**Recreation:** Wildlife watching, golf, tennis, historic touring, boating, fishing, galleries
**Amenities & Services:** Satellite, videos, gift area, telescope, desk, phone, data port, games, toiletry items on request; picnic lunches by arrangement, eco-sensitive linens policy

### ACCOMMODATIONS

**Units:** 5 guest rooms
**All Rooms:** Contemporary decor, flowers, CD players/CDs, quality beds & linens, robes
**Some Rooms:** Four-poster bed, claw-foot tub, skylight, sitting area, pond view, antique bath fixtures; in-room TV/VCR avail.
**Bed & Bath:** Queen or king; private ensuite baths
**Favorites:** Swan Room, Bluebird

**Comfort & Decor:** Quality woodwork finished in fresh, pale tones. Outstanding original island artwork. Guest rooms are small but bright and exquisitely appointed (some are being enlarged). Exceptional finish work. Sitting area is fresh and contemporary, with view of pond and lovely leather sofas; living room has cozy brick fireplace.

## RATES, RESERVATIONS, & RESTRICTIONS

**Deposit:** 1st night; 7-day cancellation
**Discounts:** Off-season, seasonal
**Credit Cards:** V, MC, D
**Check-in/Out:** 2:30–6 or by arrangement/11
**Smoking:** No
**Pets:** No; host Pomeranians occasionally on premises
**Kids:** Not usually; older children may be accommodated by arrangement
**No-Nos:** Shoes in house, more than 2 in a room
**Minimum Stay:** 2 nights, weekends &
peak season
**Open:** All year
**Hosts:** Carl & Sue Silvernail
6 Pond Rd., P.O. Box 1540
Eastsound, WA 98245-1540
(888) 893-9680 or (360) 376-8844
Fax: (360) 376-8847
otterbehere@otterspond.com
www.otterspond.com

## SPRING BAY INN, Orcas Island

Overall: ★★★★½         Room Quality: B         Value: C         Price: $195–$235

The active person's paradise, Spring Bay Inn's tariff includes a daily guided kayak trip and miles of on-site hiking trails, all in a secluded area that feels like your own private national park. It follows, then, that Carl and Sandy are former park rangers. The home is quintessential Pacific Northwest, with lots of windows, wood and stone, and great views of the kayak launch cove. Friendly, fun hosts opened their unique inn in 1993. If you like the outdoors, a wilderness environment, an ecosensitive vibe, and adorable (if a bit "in-your-face") Golden Retrievers, you're gonna love this place as much as we do.

## SETTING & FACILITIES

**Location:** South end of east "lobe" of island, 20 mi. from ferry landing
**Near:** Obstruction Pass S.P., Olga, Moran S.P., Lieber Haven, Doe Bay
**Building:** Pacific Northwest contemporary lodge
**Grounds:** 57 wilderness acres w/ trails & beachfront campfire area
**Public Space:** Great room
**Food & Drink:** NW wines in evening, hot beverages; 7:30 a.m. cont'l breakfast before kayaking, 10:30 full brunch
**Recreation:** On-site kayaking, hiking, bird/wildlife watching
**Amenities & Services:** Water's edge hot tub, kayaks, binoculars, 8 fireplaces, books, musical instruments, guest phone, BBQ supplies; daily guided kayak trips (weather permitting), morning "in-house newsletter," Sandy is licensed minister should you decide to marry while visiting

## ACCOMMODATIONS

**Units:** 5 guest rooms
**All Rooms:** Wood-burning fireplace, extra-high ceiling, feather bed, robes, data port, water view, fridge, tile bath, fresh flowers
**Some Rooms:** Ceiling fan, private deck or balcony, private hot tub, table & chairs, claw-foot tub
**Bed & Bath:** King or queen; private baths
**Favorites:** Forest, Driftwood
**Comfort & Decor:** Great room has soaring ceiling, glass front with view of private cove, dual Rumford stone-faced fireplaces, and hardwood floors—Pacific Northwest "rustic-cum-sumptuous." Guest rooms are roomy, with quilts, wood trim, flannels, lace. Marvelously quirky, overall fabulous. Central heating system plus in-room fireplaces and electric bathroom heaters.

## RATES, RESERVATIONS, & RESTRICTIONS

**Deposit:** 1st night; 14-day cancellation, $25 fee
**Discounts:** None
**Credit Cards:** V, MC, AE, D
**Check-in/Out:** 3:30–7 or by arrangement/noon
**Smoking:** Outside OK
**Pets:** No; host Golden Retrievers on premises
**Kids:** Welcome
**No-Nos:** More than 2 per room
**Minimum Stay:** 2 nights, April–Oct.
**Open:** All year
**Hosts:** Carl Burger & Sandy Playa
P.O. Box 97
Olga, WA 98279
(360) 376-5531
Fax: (360) 376-2193
info@springbayinn.com
www.springbayinn.com

## TURTLEBACK FARM INN, Orcas Island

| Overall: ★★★★½ | Room Quality: A | Value: C | Price: $80–$210 |
|---|---|---|---|

Other bed-and-breakfasts might rightly describe theirs as a "pastoral setting," but this 80-acre spread defines it. Since 1985, Bill and Susan's Turtleback Farm Inn has set the standard for San Juan Islands bed-and-breakfasts. It's a classic. Restored with loving kindness, respect for heritage, attention to detail, and exceptional craftsmanship, the building itself is a work of art. The new Orchard House, built in 1997, adds four luxury, king-bed rooms, each with fireplace, claw-foot tub, and other deluxe amenities. Common area in the main house is a bit small to serve 11 rooms, but that's a small complaint in an otherwise rave review. Location, hosts, grounds, accommodation—all are first-rate.

### SETTING & FACILITIES

**Location:** 6 mi. from ferry landing, 4 mi. from Eastsound, on Crow Valley Rd.
**Near:** Crow Valley, West Sound, Turtleback Mountain, Orcas Island Golf Course
**Building:** Restored late-1800s "folk national" farmhouse & 1997 outbuilding
**Grounds:** 80 acres of rolling hills, meadows, ponds, trees, & flowers
**Public Space:** Breakfast room, parlor, deck

**Food & Drink:** Sherry, fruit basket, wet bar, hot beverages; breakfast; ensuite option in Orchard House
**Recreation:** Strolling the farm, livestock "watching"; biking, tennis, fishing, galleries
**Amenities & Services:** Guest fridge & phone, games, fireplace, travel & other books; activities planning

## ACCOMMODATIONS

**Units:** 11 guest rooms

**All Rooms:** Classic furnishings, wool-filled comforters, hairdryer

**Some Rooms:** Sofa-sleeper, claw-foot tub, ADA disabled access, private deck, work table, gas fireplace, robes, fridge, in-room coffee/tea service, iron, sitting area, data port

**Bed & Bath:** Mostly queen, some king, 1 double; private ensuite baths

**Favorites:** Any Orchard House room, Valley View, Meadow View

**Comfort & Decor:** Exquisite craftsmanship. Warm, gleaming firm paneling & flooring with area rugs. Tongue-and-groove wood wainscoting. Antique hotel sinks and fixtures. Soft taupe walls with wallpaper trim and classic art prints. Classic, simple furnishings. Individual room thermostats; fans.

## RATES, RESERVATIONS, & RESTRICTIONS

**Deposit:** 1st night; 10-day cancellation

**Discounts:** Off-season, single occupancy; $25 add'l person

**Credit Cards:** V, MC

**Check-in/Out:** As soon as you arrive on island (call if after 7)/11

**Smoking:** Outside only

**Pets:** No

**Kids:** 8 & older, by arrangement

**Minimum Stay:** 2 nights, May–Oct.; 2 nights, weekends & holidays

**Open:** All year

**Hosts:** Bill & Susan Fletcher

650, 1981 Crow Valley Rd.

Eastsound, WA 98245

(800) 376-4914 or (360) 376-4914

Fax: (360) 376-5329

www.turtlebackinn.com

## MAPLE MEADOWS B&B, Point Roberts

| Overall: ★★★★ | Room Quality: B | Value: B | Price: $75–$125 |
|---|---|---|---|

A "make-yourself-at-home" bed-and-breakfast, with upscale period furnishings and serious hospitality. Terrie and her husband, Keith, are excellent ambassadors of the tiny peninsula of Point Roberts, an accident of geography and politics—a finger of U.S. land projecting south of the 49th parallel off the southern edge of British Columbia, Canada. Surrounded by water, charming Point Roberts boasts beaches, parks, and fabulous bird-watching. Highlights of your visit will probably include a brisk beach walk and relaxing in the hot tub with its view across the pasture, where three friendly horses hang out under the 200-year-old maple.

## SETTING & FACILITIES

**Location:** NE part of tiny peninsula of Point Roberts
**Near:** Everything! A block from Boundary Bay & Maple Beach, a short stroll to Lily Point; just across border from Tsawwassen, BC, and Victoria ferries; 30 min. from Vancouver, and even closer to its airport
**Building:** 1910 farmhouse, fully restored
**Grounds:** Towering maples, horse pasture, award-winning flower garden, duck pond
**Public Space:** Main parlor, wrap-around veranda

**Food & Drink:** Blackberry kir and snacks at check-in; fridge with cold beverages; candies in room; morning coffee, tea, or cocoa service; full breakfast
**Recreation:** Crabbing, agate hounding, mountain biking, whale watching, tidepooling
**Amenities & Services:** Bathroom amenities, VCR, CDs, hot tub, phone avail., dog kennel, piano; horse boarding, weddings & wedding/honeymoon packages

## ACCOMMODATIONS

**Units:** 4 guest rooms
**All Rooms:** Fresh flowers, robes
**Some Rooms:** Claw-foot tub, table & chairs, TV
**Bed & Bath:** King or queen (one w/ twin/king conversion); 2 private baths, 2 share a bath
**Favorites:** The Old Pumphouse, The Rosewood

**Comfort & Decor:** Each room features gorgeous, romantic decor, including original art, antique furnishings, and rich, contemporary fabrics. Pumphouse is a cozy detached unit with queen bed on a raised, carpeted platform; tile foyer with sitting area; private bath; and tiny deck overlooking garden. Central heat plus auxiliary heaters.

## RATES, RESERVATIONS, & RESTRICTIONS

**Deposit:** Credit card; 7-day cancellation for refund; 3-day for 50% refund; 1st night charge for no-show
**Discounts:** Off-season, extended stay, corporate rate (extended stays), entire house
**Credit Cards:** V, MC
**Check-in/Out:** 4–6/noonish
**Smoking:** Outside only
**Pets:** Case-by-case; by prior arrangement only; host pets on premises

**Kids:** No
**Minimum Stay:** None
**Open:** All year
**Hosts:** Terrie LaPorte
101 Goodman Rd.
Point Roberts, WA 98281
(360) 945-5536
Fax: (360) 945-2855
mplmedbb@whidbey.com
www.travel-wise.com/maple/index.html

## REDMOND HOUSE B&B, Snohomish

| Overall: ★★★½ | Room Quality: C | Value: C | Price: $95–$115 |
|---|---|---|---|

We were sorry to find that this established, four-room bed-and-breakfast was actively up for sale at our visit. We've included it because it's so well set-up to continue as a bed-and-breakfast, and because the Rileys have done a great job with it to date. A mix of Victorian and contemporary, the inn has a plethora of sitting areas for guests' comfort—one party could quietly enjoy a book in the formal Victorian parlor while another watched a movie or played a raucous board game in the contemporary, skylit family room. Note that the Tower Room, a shared-bath unit with twin beds, has an additional little room with a third twin bed up a flight of stairs in the tower. A nice option for a family, or three singles traveling together.

## SETTING & FACILITIES

**Location:** 4 blocks from Snohomish antique & commercial district
**Near:** Snohomish River, Everett
**Building:** 5,000-sq.-ft. 1890 Victorian w/ modern additions
**Grounds:** At dead-end of street; rhododendrons, trees, small lawn, flowers
**Public Space:** Parlor, sunroom, FR, sitting room, porch

**Food & Drink:** Self-serve beverages & snacks; full breakfast
**Recreation:** Antiquing, fishing, biking, golf, historic touring
**Amenities & Services:** Hot tub, fireplaces, VCR, games, guest phone, umbrellas, books

## ACCOMMODATIONS

**Units:** 4 guest rooms
**All Rooms:** Quilt, feather bed, robes, ceiling fan
**Some Rooms:** Period bath fixtures, claw-foot tub, four-poster bed, sitting area
**Bed & Bath:** Queen, king, or twins (latter w/ extra twin room attached upstairs); 2 private baths, 2 share a bath

**Favorites:** Pilchuck, Garden
**Comfort & Decor:** Floral wallpapers, wainscoting (tongue-and-groove woodwork or wallpapered). Eastlake and other antiques and reproductions maintain Victorian feel in guest rooms and parlor; family room is more contemporary. Intense, vibrant tones in guest rooms; soft and pale hues in parlor. Central heat, fans.

## RATES, RESERVATIONS, & RESTRICTIONS

**Deposit:** Credit card; 7-day cancellation ($15 fee)
**Discounts:** Off-season; $25 add'l adult
**Credit Cards:** V, MC
**Check-in/Out:** 2–5 or by arrangement/11
**Smoking:** Outside only

**Pets:** No; host kitty
**Kids:** Welcome
**Minimum Stay:** None
**Open:** All year
**Hosts:** Mary & Ken Riley
317 Glen Ave.
Snohomish, WA 98290
(360) 568-2042

## SUSAN'S SURREY HOUSE, Snohomish

| Overall: ★★★★ | Room Quality: B | Value: B | Price: $95 |
|---|---|---|---|

The little village of Snohomish, renowned for its antique shops and fine dining, is the site of two bed-and-breakfasts we profiled. This one is under new ownership, and is a work-in-progress by Susan and Gary, who are transitioning to full-time innkeeping. The building has operated as a bed-and-breakfast since 1982, but the new owners are remodeling, rethinking, and revising. As such, policies, pricing, and even room configuration are subject to change as they "work the bugs out." We included them because we think their instincts are good and we liked what we saw so far. Comfortable, upscale, with contemporary country ambiance, the home is beautiful inside and out. Has potential to go to 4.5 stars.

### SETTING & FACILITIES

**Location:** 9 blocks north of Snohomish antique & commercial district
**Near:** Snohomish River, Everett
**Building:** 1884 Victorian estate
**Grounds:** Gardens, pool, cabana, deck (encompass 6 city blocks)
**Public Space:** DR, reading room, entertainment room, deck

**Food & Drink:** Beverages & cookies; early coffee; full breakfast
**Recreation:** Antiquing, swimming, fishing, biking, golf, historic touring
**Amenities & Services:** Pool (seasonal), books, large-screen TV, VCR, sound system

### ACCOMMODATIONS

**Units:** 2 guest rooms (expansion underway for 3rd room)
**All Rooms:** High-quality linens, robes, heated towels
**Some Rooms:** Claw-foot tub, over-flow room adjoining
**Bed & Bath:** Queen (one with add'l twin); private ensuite baths
**Favorites:** Either
**Comfort & Decor:** Upscale contem-porary country. Sunny yellow-and-white in entertainment room; tone-on-tone deep green in reading room; beige with plum accents in dining room. Guest rooms have charm of hip roofs, transoms, brass or iron bed, and wood wainscoting, but modern tile work and fixtures. Central (zoned) heat, fans.

### RATES, RESERVATIONS, & RESTRICTIONS

**Deposit:** 1st night; 7-day cancellation
**Discounts:** Senior; $25 add'l person
**Credit Cards:** V, MC
**Check-in/Out:** 3–6 or by arrangement/11
**Smoking:** Outside only
**Pets:** No; host teacup poodle
**Kids:** Over 12 welcome
**Minimum Stay:** None

**Open:** Weekends, holidays, & by reservation all year
**Hosts:** Susan & Gary McDonald
425 Ninth St.
Snohomish, WA 98290
(360) 568-7081
Fax: (360) 568-7551
susanmcdon@aol.com
www.surreyhouse.com

## EAGLE'S NEST INN, Whidbey Island

Overall: ★★★★½     Room Quality: A     Value: B     Price: $95–$125

A bed-and-breakfast since 1989, current owners since 1994. Awesome Saratoga Passage/Mt. Baker views from deck. Grounds are lovely (the local birds think so, too!), with trails, hammock, bird feeders, and attractive landscaping blending into natural wooded surroundings. Inside, relax with tea and a board game in the library, or take a book to the window seat. Breakfasts are "Pacific Northwest gourmet," where Joanne's culinary background shines. A very comfortable place; an excellent value.

### SETTING & FACILITIES

**Location:** 1.5 mi. from "downtown" Langley, off Saratoga Rd.
**Near:** Saratoga Passage, Langley, Clinton ferry landing, Holmes Harbor, beaches
**Building:** Late-1980s Northwest contemporary octagon
**Grounds:** 3 hilltop acres abutting DNR lands

**Public Space:** LR, library/lounge
**Food & Drink:** Beverages & cookies; full breakfast
**Recreation:** Rowing, scuba, ferry to Port Townsend Victorian seaport, golf, wine touring
**Amenities & Services:** Hot tub, piano, sound system, videos, cards, games, phone, puzzles, fridge

### ACCOMMODATIONS

**Units:** 4 guest rooms (inquire about cottage unit w/ kitchen)
**All Rooms:** Private deck, hairdryer, robes, TV/VCR, flowers, guest guide
**Some Rooms:** Four-poster, view, skylights, private entrance, sitting area, fridge, sound system
**Bed & Bath:** King or queen (1 w/ extra single daybed); private ensuite baths
**Favorites:** Eagle's Nest, Forest

**Comfort & Decor:** Gracious common areas—living room has soaring cathedral ceiling, library/lounge has deluxe yet comfortable furnishings—with Northwest flair. Guest rooms feature plush or Berber carpet, elegant furnishings. (Forest Room has handmade furnishings crafted from storm-fallen wood.) Fanciful nature paintings on walls. Pacific Northwest artwork.

## RATES, RESERVATIONS, & RESTRICTIONS

**Deposit:** 1st night; 7-day cancellation
**Discounts:** $25 add'l person
**Credit Cards:** V, MC, D
**Check-in/Out:** 3:30–6 or by arrangement/11
**Smoking:** Outside only
**Pets:** No
**Kids:** Over 12 welcome
**No-Nos:** Shoes in house

**Minimum Stay:** 2 nights, high-season weekends
**Open:** All year
**Hosts:** Jerry & Joanne Lechner
4680 Saratoga Rd., Langley, WA 98260
(360) 221-5331
Fax: same as phone (call ahead)
eaglnest@whidbey.com
www.eaglesnessinn.com

## GUEST HOUSE COTTAGES, Whidbey Island

| Overall: ★★★★½ | Room Quality: B | Value: C | Price: $160–$295 |
|---|---|---|---|

These secluded, romantic, adult-only cottages aren't your typical bed-and-breakfast, but the self-serve breakfast, full amenities, and absolute privacy make for a getaway experience we consider "5-star Pacific Northwest" at its best. If you panic at the sight of a spider or insist on a gourmet breakfast served by your host, look elsewhere. But if you want a self-contained woodland experience with your sweetie, this is it. Our only complaint is that, for a place of this caliber, we found it odd that they expected you to do your own dishes and clean the kitchen—for the prices charged and level of other amenities offered, these services should be handled by staff.

## SETTING & FACILITIES

**Location:** About halfway between Coupeville & Langley on Hwy. 525; a mi. south of Greenbank
**Near:** Meerkirk Rhododendron Gardens, Greenbank Farm, Keystone Park, Honeymoon Bay, Ebey's Landing, lighthouse, Deception Pass, ferry to Port Townsend
**Building:** Separate storybook cottages & a luxurious log home
**Grounds:** 25 lush, wooded acres w/ paths & pond; meadows; outdoor pool & spa

**Public Space:** Each cottage has living area(s); shared rudimentary exercise room
**Food & Drink:** Abundant snacks, hot beverages, & self-serve breakfast in cottage (first 2 days)
**Recreation:** Bicycling & boating (rentals nearby), scuba, wine touring, golf, beachcombing
**Amenities & Services:** Videos, phone in pool house (no phones in units); massage avail., maid & turndown by request (extra towels/linens in unit)

## Accommodations

**Units:** 5 cottages, 1 log lodge (each double occupancy only)
**All Rooms:** Private, detached units; sitting room, DR/area, fireplace or woodstove w/ wood, TV/VCR, equipped kitchen, BBQ (BYO charcoal), robes & slippers, hairdryer, toiletries, guest info books
**Some Rooms:** Skylights, whirlpool tub, deck, desk
**Bed & Bath:** King or queen; private baths

**Favorites:** The Lodge
**Comfort & Decor:** "Luxurious rusticity" best describes these units. Most have log walls or knotty pine paneling, hardwood floors, featherbeds, and comfortable country furnishings. Rock fireplaces, ceiling fans, funky old light fixtures, and stained glass lend ambiance, yet modern comforts abound, including electric heat with separate controls for every room and luxurious bathrooms.

## Rates, Reservations, & Restrictions

**Deposit:** 1st night or 50%; 21-day cancellation or no refund unless rebooked; no early departure refunds; $25 fee for any cancellations
**Discounts:** Winter midweek; 10th night free (cumulative)
**Credit Cards:** V, MC, AE, D, NOVUS
**Check-in/Out:** 4–5/11 (office open 9–5 only; key arrangements made for later arrivals)
**Smoking:** No
**Pets:** No
**Kids:** Under 4 only
**No-Nos:** More than 2 people in a unit

**Minimum Stay:** 2 nights (single nights sometimes avail. by chance)
**Open:** All year
**Hosts:** Mary Jane & Don Creger & Staff
3366 South Hwy. 525
Greenbank, WA 98253
(360) 678-3115
Fax: (360) 321-0631
guesthse@whidbey.net
www.virtualcities.com/ons/wa/w/wawb601.htm or www.whidbey.net/logcottages

## ISLAND TYME, Whidbey Island

| Overall: ★★★★ | Room Quality: B | Value: C | Price: $95–$140 |

"Newly minted gingerbread," this inn (built and established 1995) was taken over by the Wismans in 1999. A bit impersonal and hotel-ish (even the host admits, "This ain't Grandma's house!"), Island Tyme excels at hands-off hospitality (but hosts live on-site and are always available at the touch of a buzzer). Guests have all the amenities to make themselves at home, and rooms contain items you'd expect from a quality hotel. Peaceful surroundings, just a short drive from Langley restaurants and shopping.

## SETTING & FACILITIES

**Location:** 8.5 mi. from Clinton ferry landing, 2 mi. outside Langley proper
**Near:** Clinton ferry landing, Holmes Harbor, beaches
**Building:** 1995 3-story Victorian-style
**Grounds:** 10 wooded acres w/ pond, swingset, goats; abuts protected wetlands
**Public Space:** DR, LR

**Food & Drink:** Beverages, cookies; in-room chocolates; full breakfast
**Recreation:** Rowing, touring, scuba, ferry to Port Townsend Victorian seaport, golf
**Amenities & Services:** Videos, sound system, telescope; weddings, parties

## ACCOMMODATIONS

**Units:** 4 guest rooms, 1 suite
**All Rooms:** TV/VCR, private or shared deck, phone, carpet
**Some Rooms:** Disabled access, fireplace, dbl. whirlpool, table & chairs, desk, sofa-sleeper, sitting room
**Bed & Bath:** Queen, 2 queens, or king; private ensuite baths

**Favorites:** Heirloom (suite), Masterpiece, Turrett
**Comfort & Decor:** Quilts, florals, hand-stenciling, pale tones, bold wallpaper accents. Nothing Victorian about the clean, tile-and-oak contemporary decor. Individually controlled thermostats.

## RATES, RESERVATIONS, & RESTRICTIONS

**Deposit:** Credit card; 7-day cancellation
**Discounts:** AAA
**Credit Cards:** V, MC, AE, D
**Check-in/Out:** 3–6/11
**Smoking:** Outside only
**Pets:** Keepsake Room only; host dog in host quarters
**Kids:** Well-mannered children welcome

**No-Nos:** No whirlpool tubs or loud noise after 10 p.m.
**Minimum Stay:** 2 nights, high-season weekends
**Open:** All year
**Hosts:** Carol & Cliff Wisman
4940 Bayview Rd., Langley, WA 98260
(800) 898-8963 or (360) 221-5078
islandty@whidbey.com
www.moriah.com/island-tyme

# Zone 5
# Greater Seattle and Tacoma

The Space Needle. Pike Place Market. Boeing Field. The Tacoma Dome. Pioneer Square. Point Defiance. Seattle—birthplace of grunge and coffee culture—and Tacoma—the identity-crisis stepsister—are Washington's undisputed urban hubs. Just 30 miles apart, they cling to Interstate 5 and the southeast shore of Puget Sound and attract suburbs (and Californians) like a rock star attracts groupies. Chic, edgy, rainy, the cities blend turn-of-the-century Old West and a fascination with technology: first the airplane, now software.

Most of Seattle's better bed-and-breakfasts cluster on Capitol Hill, but we also profile two on Queen Anne Hill, one in West Seattle, one on Mercer Island, one in the University of Washington district, one across from Woodland Park and Zoo, and one that floats on Lake Union. The Capitol Hill properties offer a neighborhood setting apart from the mainstream madness of downtown Seattle, including proximity to Olmstead-designed Volunteer Park, the Seattle Asian Museum, and shopping and dining along Broadway. Queen Anne is the closest profiled neighborhood to Seattle Center (Space Needle, Pacific Science Center), while West Seattle is nearest Boeing Field, Alki Beach (strolling, dining, beach activities), and the ferry to Vashon Island and Southworth (on the Kitsap Peninsula). The University of Washington district includes the University itself, with its academic and sporting venues, the University Avenue commercial district, the Burke-Gilman multiuse recreational trail, and Ravenna Park. Green Lake, a great place for jogging, is a short drive away. The Woodland Park and Zoo area is also near the Seattle Rose Garden, and a short drive to the fascinating marine drama of the Ballard Locks and Shilshole Bay activities. Upscale, residential Mercer Island offers a quiet bed-and-breakfast with good city access as well.

Tacoma is a city of beauty and history, often overlooked in the tourist rush to get to Seattle or Mount Rainier. Just 30 miles south of Seattle, Tacoma is filled with historic architecture and districts with charm and character, like the Proctor District, Stadium Historical District, "antique row," theater district, etc. The Tacoma Dome is the site for major concerts and events. Point Defiance's Zoo and Aquarium are excellent. Some visit Tacoma for the education (University of Puget Sound, Pacific Lutheran University) and military (McChord Air Force Base, Fort Lewis Army Base) venues. Whatever your reason, Tacoma's bed-and-breakfast offerings are excellent and distributed throughout the city.

Other urban inns profiled include those in Kent, Kirkland, and Redmond—good choices if your business or leisure pursuits take you along the I-5 corridor but outside the main cities.

As Seattle- and Tacoma-dwellers need quick getaways, we've profiled a selection of good choices on the Kitsap Peninsula, Bainbridge Island, and Vashon Island. Kitsap Peninsula, gateway to the Olympic Peninsula from Seattle or Tacoma, includes the communities of Belfair, Gig Harbor, Port Orchard, Seabeck, Bremerton, and Poulsbo. Natural and manmade history is preserved via many designated parks and museums, including the popular Naval Undersea Warfare Museum. Tiny Belfair, along Hood Canal, is a relaxed community near Theler Wetlands, a habitat preserve with freshwater and saltwater marshes where the Union River meets Hood

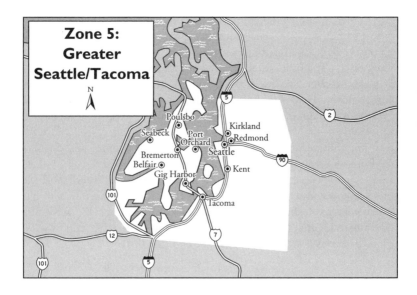

Canal. Bremerton is a Navy town, with the Puget Sound Naval Shipyard, Bremerton Naval Museum, and other reminders of marine matters past and present. Poulsbo is a tourist-friendly "Norwegian" village with activities for all seasons.

Bainbridge Island is just a short ferry hop from Seattle. Here, the community of Winslow offers a Saturday farmer's market and a waterfront park. Visit Bloedel Reserve, 150 acres of gardens, forest, and bird sanctuary.

Vashon Island is a surprisingly sleepy little island just north of Tacoma and easily accessed from either Seattle or Tacoma by ferry. Various harbors, a golf and country club, a small municipal airport, and the Tacoma Yacht club are located here.

**Bainbridge Island**
The Buchanan Inn, p. 168
Rockaway Beach Guest House, p. 169

**Belfair**
Cady Lake Manor, p. 171
Selah Inn, p. 172

**Bremerton**
Illahee Manor, p. 173

**Gig Harbor**
The Olde Glencove Hotel, p. 175

**Kent**
Victorian Gardens 1888 B&B, p. 176

**Kirkland**
Shumway Mansion, p. 177

**Mercer Island**
The Tree House B&B, p. 178

**Port Orchard**
Reflections, p. 179

**Poulsbo**
Foxbridge B&B, p. 181
Murphy House, p. 182

**Redmond**
A Cottage Creek Inn, p. 183

**Seabeck**
La Cachette B&B, p. 184

**Seattle**
Bacon Mansion, p. 185
The Blue Willow B&B, p. 186
Capitol Hill Inn, p. 187
Chambered Nautilus, p. 188
Chelsea Station, p. 190
Gaslight Inn, p. 191
The Green Gables Guesthouse, p. 192
Mildred's B&B, p. 194
Roberta's B&B, p. 195
Salisbury House, p. 197
Tugboat Challenger, p. 198
Villa Heidelberg, p. 199

**Tacoma**
Chinaberry Hill, p. 200
Commencement Bay B&B, p. 202
DeVoe Mansion, p. 203
The Green Cape Cod B&B, p. 204
Thornewood Castle, p. 206

**Vashon**
Angels of the Sea B&B, p. 207
Artist's Studio Loft B&B, p. 208

## THE BUCHANAN INN, Bainbridge Island

Overall: ★★★★½      Room Quality: A      Value: C      Price: $99–$159

Class act a short ferry hop from Seattle. Like All Season's River Inn in Leavenworth, the straightforward exterior belies the gracious, even elegant interior. You'd never know this place was a former fraternal organization's meeting hall once you're inside. Comfortable, contemporary common areas. Abundant and delicious breakfasts. Lovely garden path to hot tub building and deck; privacy ensured by a sign-up system.

### SETTING & FACILITIES

**Location:** 10 min. from ferry landing, at south end of island
**Near:** Winslow, Bloedel Nature Preserve, Waterfront Park, Sat. farmer's market, performing arts center, Blakely Harbor, Seattle
**Building:** 1912 former Oddfellows Hall
**Grounds:** 1.5 exceptionally lovely & private acres; greenhouse, paths, gardens, meadow
**Public Space:** Guest LR, DR, deck

**Food & Drink:** Self-serve wine & snacks; ensuite beverages; afternoon wine & hors d'oeuvres; full breakfast; ensuite extended cont'l option; early cont'l option
**Recreation:** Antiquing, wildlife watching, beachcombing, historic touring
**Amenities & Services:** Hot tub, videos, sound system, books, fireplace, guest phone, ice; conferences, weddings; check your e-mail

## ACCOMMODATIONS

**Units:** 3 guest rooms, 1 suite
**All Rooms:** Sitting area/room, CD, mini-fridge, coffeemaker, robes, high-quality linens, table & chairs, ferry & touring info, hairdryer
**Some Rooms:** Ceiling fan, window seat, whirlpool/soaking tub, private entrance, fireplace
**Bed & Bath:** Queen (1 w/ extra double or queen option) or king; private ensuite baths

**Favorites:** Bilberry, Buchanan
**Comfort & Decor:** Each of the spacious, designer-decor rooms offers a different mood. Buchanan: subtle, rich African motif, high ceilings. Clar Innes: sunny yellow, garden view. Bilberry: 2-room suite, mint walls. Loch Lomond: pale tan walls, Western art, another soaring ceiling. Central heat, auxiliary heat in baths, fans.

## RATES, RESERVATIONS, & RESTRICTIONS

**Deposit:** 1st night; 7-day cancellation
**Discounts:** Single occupancy, extended stay, off-season, corporate, special packages; $10 add'l person
**Credit Cards:** V, MC, AE
**Check-in/Out:** After 3 by arrangement (flexible)/11
**Smoking:** Outside only
**Pets:** No; host dogs on site
**Kids:** 16 & older welcome
**No-Nos:** Hot tub before 4 or after

11; quiet hours 10 p.m.–7 a.m.
**Minimum Stay:** None
**Open:** All year
**Hosts:** Ron & Judy Gibbs
8484 NE Oddfellows Rd.
Bainbridge Island, WA 98110
(206) 780-9258
Fax: (206) 842-9458
jgibbs@buchananinn.com
www.buchananinn.com

## ROCKAWAY BEACH GUEST HOUSE, Bainbridge Island

| Overall: ★★★★ | Room Quality: B | Value: C | Price: $95–$140 |
| --- | --- | --- | --- |

First—the view: a broad expanse of Puget Sound (often dotted with sailboats or a ferry) and a postcard-perfect Seattle skyline can be seen from living room, dining room, and either guest room. Unpretentious yet gracious, this retreat has a "family beach house" atmosphere of casual good cheer. It lacks the designer decor of the professionally run Buchanan Inn down the road, but has a charm of its own, from the slightly sloping floors (it does, after all, date back to 1906!) to the great stone fireplace to the rugged chinked log walls. If you're lucky, you might enjoy the occasional beach bonfire or whatever else is happening in this quiet residential beachfront neighborhood.

## SETTING & FACILITIES

**Location:** About 5 mi. from ferry landing, on waterfront
**Near:** Beach, Eagle Harbor, Blakely Harbor, Winslow, ferry landing, Waterfront Park, Sat. farmer's market, Performing Arts Center, Bloedel Nature Reserve, Seattle
**Building:** 1906 waterfront log home
**Grounds:** Landscaped beachfront lot w/ stunning Seattle skyline view

**Public Space:** LR, DR, TV/sitting room
**Food & Drink:** Full breakfast
**Recreation:** Beachcombing, antiquing, bird-watching, historic touring
**Amenities & Services:** Waterfront hot tub, bikes, puzzles, binoculars, TV, VCR, videos, games, micro., fridge, phone; eco-sensitive linens policy

## ACCOMMODATIONS

**Units:** 2 guest rooms
**All Rooms:** Seattle skyline/water view, down comforter, books, plush carpet, quality linens
**Some Rooms:** Mt. Rainier-view soaking tub, telescope, table & chairs, huge bath w/ spacious closet/vanity areas
**Bed & Bath:** King (option to extend to room w/ 2 twins) or queen w/ futon; private baths
**Favorites:** Master Suite

**Comfort & Decor:** Warm woods abound in this distinctly Pacific Northwest home, from the log walls of the common areas (nice and open, with lots of glass to take advantage of the awesome view) to the stained, beaded tongue-and-groove paneling throughout the upstairs halls. Guest rooms sport pale hues: Master Suite has mint carpet and linens, while Guest Room has rose-hued accents.

## RATES, RESERVATIONS, & RESTRICTIONS

**Deposit:** 1st night; please provide ample notice of cancellation
**Discounts:** Off-season extended stay; $10 add'l person
**Credit Cards:** Not accepted
**Check-in/Out:** 3–4 or by arrangement/noon
**Smoking:** No
**Pets:** No

**Kids:** Welcome
**Minimum Stay:** Some holidays
**Open:** All year
**Hosts:** Linda Hayes
5031 Rockaway Beach Rd.
Bainbridge Island, WA 98110
(206) 780-9427
Fax: (206) 780-0439
LHayes@aol.com

## CADY LAKE MANOR, Belfair

| Overall: ★★★★½ | Room Quality: B | Value: C | Price: $125–$185 |
|---|---|---|---|

A unique, self-contained resort with its own spring-fed, 15-acre fly-fishing lake. Everything the novice or expert fisherman needs is here—and many a BIG fish has been caught by the fishermen who come for the rainbow, brown, cutthroat, and steelhead. As with the kayaking-oriented Spring Bay Inn on Orcas Island (see Zone 4), those coming for the total package get the most value, but Cady Lake Manor is also a great place to relax with (or without) the family. Kids are welcome, the game room is relaxing and well equipped, and the surroundings are upscale but casual. Guest rooms tend toward sparse, but all furnishings and fixtures are high-quality, and common areas are commodious and comfortable.

### SETTING & FACILITIES

**Location:** 12.5 mi. west of Belfair
**Near:** Not much! Isolated, self-contained retreat
**Building:** 1996 custom brick home
**Grounds:** 53-acre natural wooded parcel w/ 15-acre fly-fishing lake
**Public Space:** LR, DR, deck, game room, library
**Food & Drink:** Self-serve soda or hot drinks upon request; full breakfast; huge, hearty, full-course dinners by arrangement ($20–25)

**Recreation:** On-site catch-and-release fly fishing, paddle/row/electric-motor boating
**Amenities & Services:** Fireplaces, paddle/row/electric-motor boats, float tubes, life vests, pool table, games, guest fridge, big-screen TV, huge video library; use of lake and all boating equipment complimentary; weddings, receptions (large banquet facil. w/ full catering infrastructure), meetings (small conf. room), parties; fly-fishing guide service by arrangement

## ACCOMMODATIONS

**Units:** 4 guest rooms
**All Rooms:** Sleigh bed, TV/VCR avail., private-line phone, toiletries, closet
**Some Rooms:** Sofa-sleeper, dual whirlpool tub, sitting area, disabled access
**Bed & Bath:** Queen (roll-away avail.); private ensuite baths
**Favorites:** 3 & 4
**Comfort & Decor:** Extensive art collection includes Northwest and European works: etched glass, paintings, drawings, sculpture. Antique-filled formal dining room for special dinners; most dining in sun-filled casual cafélike dining area overlooking lake. Well-executed fishing and outdoor motifs throughout. Leather and tapestry-upholstered furnishings. Common areas more opulent than guest rooms, which are rather simple with an over-all masculine sensibility.

## RATES, RESERVATIONS, & RESTRICTIONS

**Deposit:** 50% nonrefundable (credited to next visit w/ ample notice)
**Discounts:** Active military, off-season; $15 add'l adult; kids 14 & under free
**Credit Cards:** V, MC, AE, D
**Check-in/Out:** 3:30/11 (flexible)
**Smoking:** Outside only
**Pets:** No; host dog, Max
**Kids:** Welcome
**No-Nos:** Kids must wear life jackets on the water

**Minimum Stay:** None
**Open:** All year (weather permitting)
**Hosts:** Larry DePaul
P.O. Box 2190
Belfair, WA 98528 or 1471 NE
Dewatto Rd.
Tahuya, WA 98588
(360) 372-2673
cadylake@yahoo.com
www.cadylake.com

## SELAH INN, Belfair

Overall: ★★★★½      Room Quality: B      Value: C      Price: $90–$145

Don't let the semi-seedy approach neighborhood fool you—this is a class act. Where nearby Cady Lake Manor is a bit austere, Selah Inn's atmosphere is cozy and welcoming. Opened in 1997, the premises are cleverly designed with multiple-use areas that facilitate banquets, conferences, and other special events, but still provide an intimate feel. The inn sits toward the back (away from but within view of Hood Canal) of a grassy compound that includes the two cottages, the hosts' home, and a waterfront property in which lodgings (managed by the McCulloughs) are also available; more upscale, these run $135–175.

## SETTING & FACILITIES

**Location:** 3.5 mi. west of Belfair, on Hood Canal
**Near:** Theler Wetlands, world-class golf, Belfair S.P., ORV park
**Building:** 1996 Pacific Northwest contemporary
**Grounds:** Grassy w/ mature trees on Hood Canal
**Public Space:** LR, DRs, deck, library, sunroom
**Food & Drink:** Refreshments upon arrival, self-serve cold beverages (or beer & wine for purchase); in-room chocolates; full breakfast (early by arrangement); dinners by arrangement ($25)
**Recreation:** Water activities, clamming, crabbing, antiquing, galleries, bicycling
**Amenities & Services:** Fireplace, hot tub, guest fridge, canoe & light rowboat; business amenities include whiteboard, conf. table, A/V materials; conferences, events, high teas, dinners, brunches, catering

## ACCOMMODATIONS

**Units:** 4 guest rooms plus adjacent cottages & waterfront home lodgings
**All Rooms:** Quality beds & linens, closet, carpet, fresh flowers
**Some Rooms:** Canopy bed, sitting area, fireplace, CD sound system, whirlpool tub, dual-sink vanity, private deck, TV avail., desk
**Bed & Bath:** King or queen (3); private ensuite baths
**Favorites:** King suite
**Comfort & Decor:** Guest room styling varies from Mission to romance to upscale country. Quality vinyls, fixtures, furnishings. Contemporary finish work—rounded corners, painted woodwork. Upscale upholstered furnishings. Central heat and AC.

## RATES, RESERVATIONS, & RESTRICTIONS

**Deposit:** 1st night; 10-day cancellation, $10 fee
**Discounts:** Extended stay, midweek off-season, military, senior
**Credit Cards:** V, MC
**Check-in/Out:** 3/noon
**Smoking:** Outside only
**Pets:** No
**Kids:** Welcome in adjacent cottages
**Minimum Stay:** 2 nights in cottages
**Open:** All year
**Hosts:** Pat & Bonnie McCullough
130 NE Dulalip Landing
Belfair, WA 98528
(360) 275-0916
Fax: (360) 277-3187
innkeeper@selahinn.com
www.selahinn.com

## ILLAHEE MANOR, Bremerton

| Overall: ★★★★★ | Room Quality: A | Value: C | Price: $115–$195 |
|---|---|---|---|

Truly special, elegant retreat has a waterfront setting, exceptional hosts, private-park-style grounds, and a building with a sense of permanence overlaid with the contemporary and the eclectic. Glass-walled, stone-floored conservatory makes a delightful breakfast spot. Each room is loaded with character, belying the home's short life as a bed-and-breakfast (since 1997). While Penthouse and Tower are the most "over the top" guest rooms, each is special: Sunrise has an exceptional view, Library is charming and cozy (with a private sauna in its detached bath), and Gold's, with its antiques and view, would be the top suite at most inns!

## SETTING & FACILITIES

**Location:** 10 min. north of Bremerton ferry, off SR 303

**Near:** Illahee State Park, Rolling Hills Golf Course, Bremerton ferry landing, Bremerton, Silverdale, fairgrounds, Naval Undersea Warfare Museum, Puget Sound Naval Shipyard, Bremerton Naval Museum, Kitsap Historical Society Museum

**Building:** 1926 Russian-inspired estate

**Grounds:** About 6 acres w/ llamas, miniature deer, extensive landscaping, fruit trees, rose garden, picnic area, & 330 ft. of water frontage

**Public Space:** Wrap-around porch, conservatory, LR

**Food & Drink:** Refreshments; ensuite sodas; full breakfast (ensuite option avail.)

**Recreation:** Museums, antiquing, historic touring, casino, kayaking, boating

**Amenities & Services:** Picnic area, boat moorage; fax service, guest phone; retreats, small weddings, anniversaries, reunions; special occasion extras; gourmet dinners served on holidays, special occasions, & some Fridays

## ACCOMMODATIONS

**Units:** 2 guest rooms, 3 suites (also 2 cottages)

**All Rooms:** TV/VCR, books, robes, hairdryer, fridge, sitting area

**Some Rooms:** Fireplace, whirlpool, sauna, view, antiques, wet bar, private porch, private entrance, cathedral ceiling, claw-foot tub, table & chairs, four-poster bed, kitchen, fainting couch, desk, disabled access

**Bed & Bath:** Queen or king; private baths (4 ensuite)

**Favorites:** Penthouse, Tower Suite

**Comfort & Decor:** Common areas include original artwork and elegant furnishings. Themed rooms are exquisitely executed, from the book-lover whimsy of The Library to the leopard-print-and-brocade opulence of The Penthouse to the delicate blue, white, and ecru of the Tower Suite, complete with its grand Eastlake bedroom set. Touches throughout include stained glass, lace, oriental rugs, embossed ceilings, faux marble, delicate floral and tone-on-tone wallpapers. Central heat plus thermostat-controlled gas fireplaces.

## RATES, RESERVATIONS, & RESTRICTIONS

**Deposit:** Credit card; 7-day cancellation
**Discounts:** Extended stay; $5 add'l person (breakfast)
**Credit Cards:** V, MC, AE, D
**Check-in/Out:** 4–8 or by arrangement/11
**Smoking:** Outside only
**Pets:** Cottages only
**Kids:** Cottages only

**Minimum Stay:** None
**Open:** All year
**Hosts:** Doree & Jeff Pratt
6680 Illahee Rd. NE
Bremerton, WA 98311
(800) 693-6680 or (360) 698-7555
Fax: (360) 698-0688
illaheemanor@comstation.com
www.comstation.com/illaheemanor

## THE OLDE GLENCOVE HOTEL, Gig Harbor

Overall: ★★★          Room Quality: D          Value: B          Price: $65–$85

Character-filled old inn is suffused with pleasant light and located on an isolated-feeling cove. Proprietors have maintained historical integrity of the inn, including the shared bath in upstairs rooms. (Shared facilities include a spacious toilet/vanity room and separate bathing room.) Luciann and Larry raised their three daughters here and began offering lodging in the mid-1980s. A remodel was underway at our visit to upgrade the Ivy Room; new features likely to include whirlpool tub.

### SETTING & FACILITIES

**Location:** 12 mi. from Gig Harbor on the Longbranch Peninsula
**Near:** Port Orchard, Tacoma
**Building:** 1897 Nat'l Historic Landmark inn
**Grounds:** Gently sloping lawns overlooking cove; pond, gazebo, ivy
**Public Space:** Front & back parlors, DR, chimney room (office), deck
**Food & Drink:** Tissn & Ivy rooms

have in-room coffee service, stocked fridge, & fruit bowl; refreshments on arrival; full breakfast (honeymooners ensuite by arrangement)
**Recreation:** Historic touring, antiquing, wildlife & bird-watching
**Amenities & Services:** Big-screen TV, VCR, umbrellas, cordless guest phone; weddings

### ACCOMMODATIONS

**Units:** 4 guest rooms
**All Rooms:** Heirloom artifacts, phone jacks (phones avail.)
**Some Rooms:** Cove view, library, TV, VCR, games, mini-fridge, table & chairs, pitched ceiling, sitting area, private deck
**Bed & Bath:** Queens (roll-away avail.); 2 w/ private baths, 2 share a bath
**Favorites:** Ivy, Tissn, Baroque

**Comfort & Decor:** Care has been taken to preserve the historic ambiance throughout this National Landmark inn. Stained glass, antiques, lace, and the whimsy of period artifacts (hats, dressmaker dummy, old shoes) is clever and fun. Common areas sport rich original California redwood woodwork, hardwood floors with lovely old rugs, period furnishings, vintage light fixtures.

## Rates, Reservations, & Restrictions

**Deposit:** 1st night; 72-hour cancellation
**Discounts:** Extended stay, no breakfast; $10 add'l person
**Credit Cards:** V, MC
**Check-in/Out:** 3/11 or by arrangement
**Smoking:** Outside only
**Pets:** By arrangement
**Kids:** Welcome by arrangement

**Minimum Stay:** None
**Open:** All year
**Hosts:** Luciann & Larry Nadeau
9418 Glencove Rd. KPN
Gig Harbor, WA 98329
(253) 884-2835
Fax: (253) 884-4403
glencove@narrows.com
www.narrows.com/glencove

## VICTORIAN GARDENS 1888 B&B, Kent

Overall: ★★★★      Room Quality: B      Value: B      Price: $95–$125

The Kiels purchased this abandoned farmhouse 25 years ago, raised their family here, and turned the well-loved property into a bed-and-breakfast in 1994. These former educators have created three quite different guest rooms: Grand Suite has pale rose tones, floral prints, and a massive antique armoire; Victorian Suite has sloped ceilings and full-tilt Victorian decor; Up the Spiral Staircase is a fun, two-level unit with a garden-decor upstairs bedroom and bright, "Moulin Rouge" bath and claw-foot tub. Attractive grounds, great airport access. Property is elegant but not stuffy.

### Setting & Facilities

**Location:** Off 108 Ave. SE (a.k.a. Benson Hwy.) and Hwy. 167
**Near:** SeaTac Airport, freeway access, all urban Seattle/Tacoma venues
**Building:** 1888 Victorian farmhouse
**Grounds:** 2.5 acres; seating areas, gazebo
**Public Space:** Parlor, wraparound porch

**Food & Drink:** Refreshments on arrival; in-room ice water; morning coffee; full breakfast
**Recreation:** Lawn & garden activities; all Seattle/Tacoma attractions
**Amenities & Services:** Piano, BBQ pit; special occasion extras, weddings

### Accommodations

**Units:** 3 suitelike guest rooms
**All Rooms:** Sitting area, TV/VCR, table & chairs, fine linens, private balcony, dedicated data port, fridge
**Some Rooms:** Pitched ceiling, clawfoot tub, fainting couch
**Bed & Bath:** Queens (roll-away avail.); private baths

**Favorites:** See introductory comments above
**Comfort & Decor:** Beautifully restored farmhouse boasts rich, dark woods, fine antique and reproduction furnishings, elegant accent pieces, good light, and fun, upscale decor. Green plants, silk flowers.

## RATES, RESERVATIONS, & RESTRICTIONS

**Deposit:** 50%; 7-day cancellation
**Discounts:** Government, military, extended stay, corporate extended stay; $25 add'l person
**Credit Cards:** V, MC, AE
**Check-in/Out:** By arrangement/11
**Smoking:** Outside only
**Pets:** No; host kitty Lulu
**Kids:** Older children welcome

**Minimum Stay:** None
**Open:** All year
**Hosts:** Diane & Larry Kiel
9621 S. 200th St.
Kent, WA 98031-1492
(888) 850-1776 or (253) 850-1776
Fax: (253) 850-8590
innkeepers@victoriangardensbandb.com
www.victoriangardensbandb.com

## SHUMWAY MANSION, Kirkland

| Overall: ★★★½ | Room Quality: B | Value: B | Price: $70–$105 |
|---|---|---|---|

Lacking the history of Seattle, Kirkland is somewhat of a bedroom community, replete with housing developments and strip malls. Perched above it, and predating all around it, Shumway Mansion offers a deluxe venue for local soirees, as well as bed-and-breakfast rooms. Antique-filled but overlaid with whimsy (whose idea was the stuffed-animal theme?), the professionally run inn focuses on weddings and parties on the weekends, and on business travelers midweek. A reasonable choice if your travels center on Kirkland, Redmond, or Bellevue, but with so many fine city inns, it wouldn't be our top pick for a lodging from which to explore Seattle.

## SETTING & FACILITIES

**Location:** 1.5 mi. off Hwy. 405; 3 mi. north of downtown Kirkland
**Near:** Microsoft, Bastyr Univ., Juanita Bay, Bellevue, Seattle
**Building:** 1909 historic East Coast–style mansion
**Grounds:** Hillside lot w/ arbor, gazebo, duck pond, roses
**Public Space:** LR, sunroom, study, enclosed & open porches, DR, phone alcove

**Food & Drink:** Evening refreshments; in-room chocolates; full buffet breakfast
**Recreation:** Walking, jogging, shopping
**Amenities & Services:** Athletic club passes, piano, guest phone, ice & buckets, fireplace; conferences, weddings, parties, catering

## ACCOMMODATIONS

**Units:** 8 guest rooms
**All Rooms:** Phone/TV upon request, European antiques, stuffed (toy) animals
**Some Rooms:** Private entrance, disabled access, claw-foot tub, sofa-sleeper, sitting area or room, TV, four-poster bed, desk, private balcony, robes
**Bed & Bath:** Queens; private baths (7 ensuite)
**Favorites:** Kirkland, Redmond

**Comfort & Decor:** Common areas boast ornate, traditional European antiques in keeping with the rooms' grand scale. Dark wood, light walls, deep red and blue accents. Sunroom is a departure, with white wicker. Guest rooms also have traditional European antiques, with floral/patterned wallpapers and linens, lace window treatments, and incongruous (but cute) stuffed animal themes (cow, dog, duck, teddy bear. . .). Individual thermostats.

## RATES, RESERVATIONS, & RESTRICTIONS

**Deposit:** Credit card; 7-day cancellation
**Discounts:** Midweek corporate; $12 add'l person
**Credit Cards:** V, MC, AE
**Check-in/Out:** 3 (flexible)/11
**Smoking:** No
**Pets:** No; Dudley, the "P.R. Sheepdog," may be on premises
**Kids:** Over 12 welcome
**Minimum Stay:** None

**Open:** All year
**Hosts:** Richard & Salli Harris, Julie Blakemore
11410  99th Pl. NE
Kirkland, WA 98033
(425) 823-2303
Fax: (425) 822-0421
shumway@nwpages.com (not for reservations)
www.shumway.nwpages.com

## THE TREE HOUSE B&B, Mercer Island

Overall: ★★★★½    Room Quality: B    Value: C    Price: $115–$145

Bobbie Hanson's home is a very special bed-and-breakfast experience. Tucked into an exclusive neighborhood of private, water-view homes, you'll find a peace and ease that belies the few minutes' drive to downtown Seattle. Your hostess is casually gracious, with a flair for easy entertaining. The surroundings are Year-in-Provence-meets-Eddie-Bauer. Guest rooms are softly elegant, with pale tones and floral fabrics. Grand room is comfortably appointed in the manner of an upscale lodge, with contemporary upholstered furnishings, entertainment center, table and chairs, and three separate seating areas.

## SETTING & FACILITIES

**Location:** On west side of Mercer Island overlooking Lake Washington
**Near:** Seattle, Bellevue, Lake Washington
**Building:** Northwest contemporary home
**Grounds:** Thickly wooded & lush; gardens, decks, rhododendrons, water view
**Public Space:** Decks, grand room, main level LR
**Food & Drink:** In-room chocolates & flavored almonds; p.m. refreshments; full breakfast, w/ lattés afterward
**Recreation:** Museums, galleries, theater, cruises, tennis
**Amenities & Services:** Fireplace, books, TV, sound system; dinner meetings/parties, celebrations, workshops, seminars, reunions

## ACCOMMODATIONS

**Units:** 3 guest rooms
**All Rooms:** Phone, data port, hairdryer, down comforter, highest-quality linens, handmade soap, sink, view
**Some Rooms:** Deck access, settee, armoire, claw-foot tub, skylight, desk
**Bed & Bath:** Queen or twins; 1 private bath, 2 share a spacious, well-designed bath
**Favorites:** Any
**Comfort & Decor:** French and English country antiques. Lots of glass and light, airy spaces gently filled with soft music. Soaring cathedral ceilings. Fresh flowers and objets d'art. While elegant, formal living and dining areas are also "very Pacific Northwest," with broad barnwood paneling and Seattle cobblestones. Tile baths, deck with bentwood furniture.

## RATES, RESERVATIONS, & RESTRICTIONS

**Deposit:** 1st night; 2-week cancellation
**Discounts:** None
**Credit Cards:** V, MC
**Check-in/Out:** Flexible
**Smoking:** Designated outdoor areas only
**Pets:** No
**Kids:** Welcome if party takes entire house
**Minimum Stay:** 2 nights
**Open:** All year
**Hosts:** Bobbie Hanson
Street address not listed by request
(206) 230-8620
Fax: (206) 236-5274
www.moriah.com/treehouse

## REFLECTIONS, Port Orchard

| Overall: ★★★★ | Room Quality: C | Value: A | Price: $60–$95 |
| --- | --- | --- | --- |

Seasoned innkeepers Jim and Cathy have a great sense of humor and hospitality (not to mention a flair for decorating, gardening, and collecting New England 19th-Century antiques). They began offering their home as a bed-and-breakfast in 1990. Their pineapple logo—long a symbol for hospitality—repeats subtly throughout the inn. This hillside home offers expansive gardens and lovely views. A hearty and delicious breakfast entree is chosen by group consensus and accompanied by fruits, breads, and house special-blend coffee. Outstanding value.

## SETTING & FACILITIES

**Location:** 3.5 mi. from downtown Port Orchard, just off Beach Dr.
**Near:** Sinclair Inlet, ferry landings, McCormick Woods Golf Course, farmer's market, Bremerton
**Building:** Late-1970s Colonial-style home
**Grounds:** Terraced lawns and decks; gazebo, trees, roses, rhododendrons, extravagant gardens

**Public Space:** FR, LR, DR
**Food & Drink:** Refreshments upon arrival; family-style full breakfast
**Recreation:** Museums, antiquing, festivals, wildlife watching, boating
**Amenities & Services:** Hot tub, fireplace, telescope, TV, VCR, books, games; weddings (full range of allied services)

## ACCOMMODATIONS

**Units:** 3 guest rooms, 1 suite
**All Rooms:** Water view
**Some Rooms:** Four-poster, handmade quilt, private deck, mountain view, soaker tub w/ water view
**Bed & Bath:** Queen, double, twins (futon avail.); 2 w/ private baths, 2 share a bath
**Favorites:** Annette
**Comfort & Decor:** Overall Colonial feel. Upscale formal areas. Delightfully

casual family room cleverly decorated with eclectic antique toys and contemporary fabrics, and accented with wood and used brick (gotta love the adjacent powder room's antique bedpan collection!). Guest rooms (aside from Annette) aren't overlarge, but are attractively decorated with subtle wallpapers, quilts, and fabric window treatments, and furnished with 1840s antiques and reproductions.

## RATES, RESERVATIONS, & RESTRICTIONS

**Deposit:** Credit card; 5-day cancellation
**Discounts:** $20 add'l person
**Credit Cards:** V, MC
**Check-in/Out:** 4–9 or by arrangement/11
**Smoking:** Outside only
**Pets:** No; host dog on site
**Kids:** Over 15 welcome in separate room

**Minimum Stay:** None
**Open:** All year
**Hosts:** Cathy & Jim Hall
3878 Reflection Ln. E.
Port Orchard, WA 98366
(360) 871-5582
jimreflect@hurricane.net
www.bestinns.net/usa/wa/reflections.html

## FOXBRIDGE B&B, Poulsbo

Overall: ★★★★½          Room Quality: B          Value: A          Price: $85

This lovely home was built to be a bed-and-breakfast in 1993. Its many common areas are well designed and beautiful. Guest rooms each use deep green and burgundy, but in very different ways: Foxhunt Room has theme wallpaper, predominantly hunter green with burgundy and warm wood accents; Old World Room, with its sleigh bed, is gorgeous and traditional; Country Garden is the most feminine, combining pinks and a soft rose motif with green, burgundy, and pale wood. Beverly serves a three-course gourmet breakfast in the elegant dining room; specialties include home-grown-apple crisp, salmon quiche, eggs Benedict.

### SETTING & FACILITIES

**Location:** 8 mi. north of Poulsbo on Hwy. 3
**Near:** Poulsbo "Norwegian" village, Port Gamble, Hood Canal Bridge (Olympic Peninsula), Naval Undersea Warfare Museum, Port Gamble Historic Museum
**Building:** 1993 2-story Georgian-style manor house
**Grounds:** 5 country acres w/ trout pond, gazebo, orchard

**Public Space:** Library, DR, parlor, LR, patio
**Food & Drink:** Beverages upon request; full breakfast
**Recreation:** Trout fishing, wildlife watching, strolling; nearby festivals, boating, sport & craft classes, antiquing, casino
**Amenities & Services:** Fireplaces, TV, sound system, books, umbrellas, guest phone; small weddings

### ACCOMMODATIONS

**Units:** 3 guest rooms
**All Rooms:** Quality linens, fine furnishings, closets
**Some Rooms:** Sleigh, four-poster, or canopy bed
**Bed & Bath:** Queen; private ensuite baths
**Favorites:** Equally attractive, see

introductory comments above
**Comfort & Decor:** Elegant, traditional furnishings, with rich wood, chandeliers. Formal living and dining areas have plush, pale carpet with delicate floral motif. Library has deep green carpet and leather chairs.

## RATES, RESERVATIONS, & RESTRICTIONS

**Deposit:** 1st night; 72-hour cancellation
**Discounts:** Inquire about specials
**Credit Cards:** V, MC
**Check-in/Out:** 3–7/11
**Smoking:** Outside only
**Pets:** No
**Kids:** 16 & older welcome

**Minimum Stay:** None
**Open:** All year
**Hosts:** Beverly Higgins
30680 Hwy. 3 NE
Poulsbo, WA 98370
(360) 598-5599
foxbridge@sprintmail.com
www.sfox.com/foxbridge/

## MURPHY HOUSE, Poulsbo

| Overall: ★★★½ | Room Quality: C | Value: B | Price: $89–$98 |
|---|---|---|---|

Murphy House brings a little Irish to the Norwegian village of Poulsbo, where the lutefisk-loving Sons of Norway find a reason to celebrate nearly every month of the year. Besides celebrating the Viking Fest in May, the Yule Fest in December, and a dozen others, the town offers classes and entertainment and recreation enough for anyone seeking small-town charm in an attractive natural setting. Murphy House, an easy stroll from the marina and shopping district, is a perfect venue from which to explore Poulsbo. Opened 1994. On-site, personable hosts offer a relaxing stay.

## SETTING & FACILITIES

**Location:** Half-block up from marina, overlooking Liberty Bay
**Near:** Liberty Bay, Naval Undersea Warfare Museum, Port Gamble Historic Museum, Suquamish Museum
**Building:** 1950s 2-story home
**Grounds:** Corner lot w/ picnic areas & bay view
**Public Space:** LR, library

**Food & Drink:** Self-serve hot beverages & snacks; full breakfast
**Recreation:** Festivals, fishing, boating, bicycling, sport & craft classes, antiquing, casino
**Amenities & Services:** Umbrellas, games, phones, fridge, micro., icemaker, TV, VCR, sound system

## ACCOMMODATIONS

**Units:** 5 guest rooms
**All Rooms:** Iron, closets
**Some Rooms:** Table & chairs, four-poster bed, ceiling fan, separate entrance, water view
**Bed & Bath:** Queen or king (1 w/ add-on option of 2 twins in sep. room; roll-away avail.); 3 private baths,

2 share a bath
**Favorites:** #3
**Comfort & Decor:** Pale tones, contemporary furnishings. Some original 1950s fixtures (pink and mint green tile in upstairs baths), very retro, well maintained and attractive. Fresh, clean, restful. Individual thermostats.

## RATES, RESERVATIONS, & RESTRICTIONS

**Deposit:** 1st night; 72-hour cancellation
**Discounts:** Senior, extended stay; $25 add'l person
**Credit Cards:** V, MC
**Check-in/Out:** 4–6 or by arrangement/11
**Smoking:** Outside only
**Pets:** No
**Kids:** 16 & older welcome

**Minimum Stay:** None
**Open:** All year
**Hosts:** Barbara & Bob Lomas
425 NE Hostmark St., P.O. Box 1960
Poulsbo, WA 98370
(800) 779-1606 or (360) 779-1600
Fax: (360) 697-3832
bblomas78@aol.com
www.bbonline.com/wa/murphy/

## A COTTAGE CREEK INN, Redmond

| Overall: ★★★½ | Room Quality: B | Value: C | Price: $89–$127 |
|---|---|---|---|

A topiary deer and turquoise sign beckon you off busy Avondale Road—a major arterial in this Puget Sound bedroom community—down a gravel drive, through an evergreen canopy, over a one-lane bridge, and past a stream . . . to a world apart. The house itself has the typical Tudor Revival stucco-and-brick exterior, while the interior emphasizes romantic decor. Steve is an accomplished artist—his beautiful marine and wildlife paintings grace the common area walls. Grounds are truly stunning, from the formally landscaped areas to the serene little on-site nature walk.

## SETTING & FACILITIES

**Location:** Just off Avondale, a main Redmond arterial route
**Near:** Microsoft, Digital Systems, AT&T, Nintendo, and other major employers; Seattle
**Building:** 1970s English Tudor–style home
**Grounds:** 3.5 stunning, parklike acres; profuse flowers, gazebo, creek, pond

**Public Space:** Sitting room, DR
**Food & Drink:** Afternoon, evening tea on request; full breakfast
**Recreation:** On-site nature trail, wildlife watching
**Amenities & Services:** TV/VCR, fireplace, desk, piano, hot tub; small weddings, special occasion packages/ assistance, massage by appt.

## ACCOMMODATIONS

**Units:** 4 guest rooms
**All Rooms:** Robes, phone, quality beds, creek or garden view
**Some Rooms:** TV, VCR, mini-fridge, whirlpool, four-poster, private balcony, skylight, table & chairs, sitting area
**Bed & Bath:** Queen (1 w/ extra twin) or king; private baths (3 ensuite)
**Favorites:** Garden, Stephanotis

**Comfort & Decor:** Antique and reproduction furnishings mingle with romantic pinks and florals. Plush pink carpet, pale pink or yellow and floral-print wallpapers, bedding, window treatments. Lace, dark wood, pitched ceilings. Living room is very comfortable; dining room a bit dark and Gothic.

## RATES, RESERVATIONS, & RESTRICTIONS

**Deposit:** Varies; 2-week cancellation
**Discounts:** $20 add'l person
**Credit Cards:** V, MC, AE
**Check-in/Out:** After 3 or by arrangement/11
**Smoking:** Outside only
**Pets:** No; host outdoor kitty
**Kids:** By arrangement
**Minimum Stay:** 2 nights

(1 night by chance)
**Open:** All year
**Hosts:** Jeanette & Steve Wynecoop
12525 Avondale Rd. NE
Redmond, WA 98052
(425) 881-5606
Fax: same as phone
cotcreek@brigadoon.com
www.cottagecreekinn.com

## LA CACHETTE B&B, Seabeck

Overall: ★★★★★      Room Quality: A      Value: B      Price: $95–$195

Pastoral tranquility, Hood Canal view, and French country elegance are yours at La Cachette ("la kuh-SHETT," the "T" is pronounced), which means, "The Hideaway." Drs. Mike and Chris Robbins started this bed-and-breakfast in 1998, but they have all the right instincts, and have spared no expense in making your stay memorable. The grounds are private, peaceful, and lovely, but can be muddy, whereas the home is pale-toned and gorgeous—while your hosts don't insist, you'll want to use the slippers provided. Fresh and festive breakfasts include local fare served on a variety of rotating china and linens.

## SETTING & FACILITIES

**Location:** NW of Bremerton
**Near:** Poulsbo, Silverdale, Bainbridge Island, Olympic Peninsula
**Building:** 7,000-sq.-ft. estate home, built 1947
**Grounds:** 10 sprawling acres w/ flowering trees & shrubs, arbor, gazebo, ponds, creek, sheep
**Public Space:** LR, DR, decks
**Food & Drink:** Evening dessert &

beverages; morning silver coffee/tea service; full breakfast
**Recreation:** Kayaking, shrimping, boating, golf, local festivals
**Amenities & Services:** Fireplace, piano, video library, games, "I forgot it" items; weddings, special occasion extras, massages by arrangement, weekend dinners by arrangement

## ACCOMMODATIONS

**Units:** 4 suitelike guest rooms
**All Rooms:** TV, robes, slippers, fireplace, highest-quality linens, toiletries, hairdryer, closet
**Some Rooms:** VCR, sitting area, views, skylight, desk, four-poster bed, claw-foot tub, dual tile vanity, walk-in closet, down comforter, chaise lounge
**Bed & Bath:** Kings (1 opt. twin conversion); private ensuite baths
**Favorites:** Cezanne

**Comfort & Decor:** Gracious and elegant French Country surroundings blend period pieces with upscale contemporary fixtures. Recessed lighting, fresh and silk flowers, fine art, tile baths, sumptuous linens, designer palettes: eggplant, butter, and sage; peach and blue. Fine finish work includes elegant moldings. Lots of fireplaces. Individual room and bath thermostats; fans.

## RATES, RESERVATIONS, & RESTRICTIONS

**Deposit:** Credit card; 5-day cancellation
**Discounts:** Senior, active military
**Credit Cards:** V, MC, AE
**Check-in/Out:** 3–5/11 or by arrangement
**Smoking:** Outside only
**Pets:** No
**Kids:** No
**No-Nos:** More than 2 per room

**Minimum Stay:** None
**Open:** All year
**Hosts:** Mike & Chris Robbins
10312 Seabeck Hwy., P.O. Box 920
Seabeck, WA 98380
(888) 613-2845 or (360) 613-2845
Fax: (360) 613-2912
lacachette@moriah.com
www.bbhost.com/lacachettebnb

## BACON MANSION, Seattle

| Overall: ★★★ | Room Quality: C | Value: C | Price: $94–$154 |
|---|---|---|---|

This imposing mansion has been an inn since 1985, when it opened as The Broadway Guest House. Current owner Daryl King purchased it in 1993. Extra-large formal dining room and commodious living area make it comfortable for guests and also useful for parties and other occasions. Melange of styles isn't as pulled-together as, say, the Gaslight Inn, nor period-correct like Mildred's, nor opulent and extravagant like Capitol Hill Inn, but the spacious rooms with hotel-style amenities are pleasant and fairly priced. With ten rooms and a "kids welcome" policy, it's an important part of the Capitol Hill bed-and-breakfast scene.

## SETTING & FACILITIES

**Location:** Capitol Hill, Broadway East at Prospect
**Near:** Capitol Hill commercial district, Volunteer Park
**Building:** 4-level 1909 Edwardian-style tudor and carriage house
**Grounds:** Corner lot w/ courtyard
**Public Space:** Library, LR, DR, mezzanine sitting area, balcony

**Food & Drink:** Afternoon refreshments; early coffee/tea; extended cont'l breakfasts
**Recreation:** Museums, historic touring, all Seattle attractions
**Amenities & Services:** Fireplaces, guest fridge, piano; weddings, parties, receptions, meetings

## ACCOMMODATIONS

**Units:** 7 guest rooms, 3 suites
**All Rooms:** Phone (private line), data port, TV, sitting area or room, hairdryer
**Some Rooms:** Wet bar, sofa-sleeper, private entrance, fridge, wheelchair access, fireplace, view, desk, antique soaker tub, table & chairs, micro., walk-in closet, four-poster
**Bed & Bath:** Queen (9) or double,

some w/ extra bed, roll-away avail.; 8 private baths, 2 share a bath
**Favorites:** Capitol Suite
**Comfort & Decor:** Imposingly large (9,000 sq. ft. in main house), with Edwardian proportions. Decor mixes newer finish work (oak trims) with antique and reproduction furnishings of varying quality.

## RATES, RESERVATIONS, & RESTRICTIONS

**Deposit:** Credit card; 7-day cancellation
**Discounts:** Off-season, off-season single occupancy, off-season extended stay; $15 add'l person
**Credit Cards:** V, MC, AE, D
**Check-in/Out:** 3–5 or by arrangement/11
**Smoking:** Porches & patios only
**Pets:** No
**Kids:** Welcome

**Minimum Stay:** 2 nights, weekends or high season; 3 nights, holidays & high-season weekends
**Open:** All year
**Hosts:** Daryl J. King
959 Broadway East, Seattle, WA 98102
(800) 240-1864 or (206) 329-1864
Fax: (206) 860-9025
baconbanb@aol.com
www.site-works.com/bacon or
www.baconmansion.com

## THE BLUE WILLOW B&B, Seattle

| Overall: ★★★ | Room Quality: C | Value: B | Price: $75–$95 |
|---|---|---|---|

Kitties are key at this comfy, charming little three-unit guest house. The two sweet, loving felines are as much a part of the decor and ambiance as the impressive Blue Willow china collection. Kathy is a warm and winning hostess, and her inn is a great value (started in 1995; innkeepers live on-site). Stroll to parks and gardens or shopping and restaurants, or drop down Queen Anne to downtown. Of our two Queen Anne Hill choices (this and Green Gables), this is the homier, more folksy choice.

## SETTING & FACILITIES

**Location:** Queen Anne Hill, Comstock between 2nd & 3rd Ave. West
**Near:** Kerry Park, Queen Anne commercial district, downtown, Seattle Center, ferries
**Building:** 1910 "Seattle Box" foursquare
**Grounds:** Landscaped entry, screened side garden sitting area

**Public Space:** LR, DR, library
**Food & Drink:** Refreshments; in-room chocolates; full formal breakfast (early cont'l option)
**Recreation:** Museums, galleries, all Seattle attractions
**Amenities & Services:** Sound system, TV, games; picnics by arrangement; teas

## ACCOMMODATIONS

**Units:** 3 guest rooms
**All Rooms:** TV, seating, artwork & period artifacts
**Some Rooms:** View, window seat, robes, four-poster, vintage photos
**Bed & Bath:** Queen or double; private baths (2 ensuite)
**Favorites:** Rainier

**Comfort & Decor:** Living room features hardwood floors, leather and upholstered furnishings, cream walls, white-painted woodwork, antiques, Oriental rug, stained and leaded glass, plus an amazing collection of Blue Willow china. Guest rooms have pale walls (blue, beige, or floral), with iron, wicker, and lace.

## RATES, RESERVATIONS, & RESTRICTIONS

**Deposit:** 1st night; 7-day cancellation
**Discounts:** Extended stays; $15 add'l person
**Credit Cards:** V, MC
**Check-in/Out:** After 3/11
**Smoking:** Outside only
**Pets:** By arrangement; host kitties on site
**Kids:** Over 4 welcome

**Minimum Stay:** 2 nights, high season
**Open:** All year
**Hosts:** Kathy & Ken Cado
213 W. Comstock
Seattle, WA 98119
(206) 284-3730
Fax: (206) 284-3730
willowltd@aol.com
www.bluewillowbandb.com

## CAPITOL HILL INN, Seattle

| Overall: ★★★★ | Room Quality: B | Value: C | Price: $89–$170 |
|---|---|---|---|

The bustling (OK, noisy) immediate neighborhood is an unlikely place for this gracious old home. While its surroundings lack the charm of the historic neighborhoods of Roberta's and Salisbury House, the interior is richly detailed and the access to shopping, restaurants, the convention center, and downtown is excellent. Parking can be tricky (leave keys with owners). Well-read guests encouraged; Republicans might be more comfortable elsewhere (their words, not ours). Strongest asset is the fabulously inventive, eclectic decor. After a decade as owner-innkeepers, the mother-and-daughter team are transitioning to a less hands-on innkeeping style with an afternoon/evening hired innkeeper.

## SETTING & FACILITIES

**Location:** Capitol Hill on Belmont at Pine, 6 blocks from downtown
**Near:** Seattle Convention Center, downtown, Capitol Hill/Broadway commercial district, Seattle Univ.
**Building:** 1903 Queen Anne Victorian
**Grounds:** Very small lot w/ front landscaping

**Public Space:** Parlor, DR, foyer
**Food & Drink:** Afternoon refreshments; early coffee & muffins; full formal breakfast
**Recreation:** Museums, galleries, all Seattle attractions
**Amenities & Services:** Guest phone, fireplaces

## ACCOMMODATIONS

**Units:** 6 guest rooms
**All Rooms:** Bold, whimsical, designer decor
**Some Rooms:** Outside entrance, four-poster, fireplace, table & chairs, shared patio, claw-foot tub, desk
**Bed & Bath:** Queen or double; 4 private baths, 2 have half-baths & share shower room
**Favorites:** Room 3, Sherlock Holmes

**Comfort & Decor:** Eclectic, whimsical, deluxe, and custom all the way. Asian and European antiques abound. Stunning wallpapers and ceiling treatments, spandrel-detailed woodwork. Themed rooms (Sherlock Holmes, Western, "Chutney") boast vibrant wall colors: schoolbus yellow, cabbage red, deep slate. Tile and faux marble baths. Rooms can be a bit dark, but never dull.

## RATES, RESERVATIONS, & RESTRICTIONS

**Deposit:** 2 nights by check or money order; 7-day cancellation ($50 fee)
**Discounts:** Call for winter specials
**Credit Cards:** V, MC, AE
**Check-in/Out:** 4–6 or by arrangement/11
**Smoking:** Porch only
**Pets:** No; host toy poodles on site
**Kids:** Over 10 welcome
**Minimum Stay:** 3 nights, summer &

convention periods (single nights by chance)
**Open:** All year
**Hosts:** Katie Godmintz, Joanne Godmintz, staff
1713 Belmont Ave.
Seattle, WA 98122
(206) 323-1955
seattleabc@msn.com
www.capitolhillinn.com

## CHAMBERED NAUTILUS, Seattle

| Overall: ★★★½ | Room Quality: B | Value: C | Price: $94–$124 |

Welcoming ambiance, soaring hillside views, and University of Washington proximity are hallmarks. Feels casual and laid back, like a friend's home, but amenities are well thought out due to hosts' business travel experience. Bustling location comes with a measure of road noise. Great restaurant access, and nearby jogging trail helps you work it off. TV-free, book-and-game, adult-oriented ambiance. Steep exterior stairs may prove daunting for some. Permit system ensures ample free parking. "Chambered Nautilus" is a great name for such a warm, welcoming home-away-from-home.

## SETTING & FACILITIES

**Location:** 22nd Ave. NE off NE 54th St., overlooking University district
**Near:** Univ. of Washington, Burke-Gilman Trail, Ravenna Park, Green Lake, Woodland Park, University Way commercial district
**Building:** 1915 Georgian Colonial
**Grounds:** Landscaped hillside lot w/ flowers & side lawn sitting area
**Public Space:** DR, LR, sun porch
**Food & Drink:** Self-serve hot & cold (seasonal) beverages, cookies, fruit; in-room bottled water; full breakfast
**Recreation:** In-line skating, museums, all Seattle attractions
**Amenities & Services:** Games, books, daily newspaper, activity guides, guest fridge, travel library, iron, fireplace, umbrellas; receptions, retreats, seminars; catering avail. for luncheons & meetings

## ACCOMMODATIONS

**Units:** 6 guest rooms (ask about extended-stay suites nearby)
**All Rooms:** Phone w/ private lines & voice mail, data port, desk, library, robes, teddy bears, down comforters, earplugs
**Some Rooms:** Cascade Mountain view, semiprivate deck, fireplace, window seat, closet or armoire, claw-foot soaker tub, private porch
**Bed & Bath:** Queen (5) or king; private baths (5 ensuite)
**Favorites:** Scallop Chamber, Rose Chamber
**Comfort & Decor:** Hand-restored inn shows character. Framed prints, painted woodwork; furnishings mix funky, retro, antique, and contemporary. Common areas are inviting and comfortable, with wide sky blue, sea green, or shell pink moldings. Central heat.

## RATES, RESERVATIONS, & RESTRICTIONS

**Deposit:** 1st night; 7-day cancellation, $10 fee
**Discounts:** Off-season, U of W, single occupancy; $15 add'l person
**Credit Cards:** V, MC, AE
**Check-in/Out:** 4–6 or by arrangement/11
**Smoking:** No
**Pets:** No; host pets on site
**Kids:** 8 & older welcome by prior arrangement (inquire about nearby suites)
**Minimum Stay:** 2 nights, high season or weekends; 3 nights, holidays
**Open:** All year
**Hosts:** Joyce Schulte & Steve Poole, owner-innkeepers; Karen Carbonneau, innkeeper
5005 22nd Ave. NE
Seattle, WA 98105
(800) 545-8459 or (206) 522-2536
Fax: (206) 528-0898
chamberednautilus@msn.com
www.chamberednautilus.com

## CHELSEA STATION, Seattle

| Overall: ★★★½ | Room Quality: B | Value: C | Price: $95–$135 |
|---|---|---|---|

An established winner with an even brighter future. Carolanne and Eric purchased Chelsea Station in 1998. As new innkeepers, they are working hard to accommodate and make guests comfortable. While the premises are very cute and charming already, physical updates in progress at our visit promise even more deluxe accommodation. Good things are happening near the zoo!

### SETTING & FACILITIES

**Location:** Linden off 50th, just across from Woodland Park & Zoo
**Near:** Woodland Park & Zoo, Green Lake, Seattle Rose Garden, Univ. of Washington, Shilshole Bay, Ballard & locks
**Building:** Brick-faced 1927 Federal Colonial-style apt. building
**Grounds:** Corner lot across from park & zoo

**Public Space:** Parlor, DR
**Food & Drink:** Tea, coffee, soda, juice, cookies; full breakfast; early cont'l option
**Recreation:** Museums, galleries, historic touring, all Seattle attractions
**Amenities & Services:** Books, games, iron, menus; eco-sensitive linens policy

### ACCOMMODATIONS

**Units:** 3 guest rooms, 6 suites
**All Rooms:** Phones
**Some Rooms:** Private phone line, sitting area or room, piano, claw-foot or old-fashioned soaker tub
**Bed & Bath:** Queen or king (1 2-room suite, extra beds avail.); private baths
**Favorites:** Margaret, Woodland Park, Cedar, Morning Glory

**Comfort & Decor:** Mission-style and contemporary furnishings grace a coved-ceiling living room with arched doorways and pale mint walls. Hardwood floors with area rugs. Local artwork displayed and for sale. Guest room color schemes include tones of peach, rose, butter. Higher priced rooms are the better value.

### RATES, RESERVATIONS, & RESTRICTIONS

**Deposit:** Credit card; 7-day cancellation
**Discounts:** Off-season, off-season extended stay; $175 for 2-bedroom suite
**Credit Cards:** V, MC, AE, D, DC
**Check-in/Out:** 3–6 or by arrangement/noon
**Smoking:** Outside only
**Pets:** No

**Kids:** School-age by arrangement
**Minimum Stay:** 2 & 3 nights may apply during peak periods
**Open:** All year
**Hosts:** Carolanne & Eric Watness
4915 Linden Ave. N, Seattle, WA 98103
(800) 400-6077 or (206) 547-6077
Fax: (206) 632-5107
info@bandbseattle.com
www.bandbseattle.com

## GASLIGHT INN, Seattle

| Overall: ★★★★ | Room Quality: B | Value: C | Price: $78–$178 |
|---|---|---|---|

A sense of elegant style pervades this quality inn, where the purity of an Arts and Crafts heritage mingles with exceptional contemporary fabrics and original artwork. Designer colors—taupe, dusty lavender, deep turquoise—are offset by exquisite woodwork. The main inn is more charming and intimate, while the adjacent all-suite unit is more spacious and contemporary. Outstanding views from some units. Ideal for business travelers (hotel-style phone system, suite option), but also central for tourists wanting to experience the best of Seattle. Since 1982. Excellent hosts. Small-inn atmosphere.

### SETTING & FACILITIES

**Location:** Off Howell on 15th, at crest of Capitol Hill
**Near:** Volunteer Park, Capitol Hill/Broadway commercial district, Seattle Univ., Seattle Convention Center
**Building:** 2 adjacent prairie-style Craftsman homes
**Grounds:** Landscaped dbl. lot w/ small pond, pool, arbors, flowers

**Public Space:** LRs, DR, pool decks, porches, decks
**Food & Drink:** In-room fruit & coffee (suites); homemade cont'l breakfast
**Recreation:** Museums, historic touring, all Seattle attractions
**Amenities & Services:** Pool (seasonal), hairdryer, toiletries, ice, iron

## ACCOMMODATIONS

**Units:** 8 guest rooms, 6 suites
**All Rooms:** Phone, voice mail, TV
**Some Rooms:** Fridge, view, desk, private deck, private entrance, pitched ceilings; suites each have 700 sq. ft, LR, wet bar, dining area, fireplace, coffeemaker, micro.
**Bed & Bath:** Queen (most) or double; 11 w/ private baths, 3 share 2 baths
**Favorites:** Room 6 suite, Room 4, Room 6 shared bath is super value

**Comfort & Decor:** American Arts and Crafts antique furnishings, soothing designer wall colors, art-quality antique light fixtures, tile or slate baths, original stained and leaded glass, lots of rich woodwork. Accented by original Pacific Northwest artwork and Native American artifacts. Suites are more contemporary (heavily remodeled), but still echoing period elements. Central heat, some with gas fireplaces; fans.

## RATES, RESERVATIONS, & RESTRICTIONS

**Deposit:** 1st night; 7-day cancellation
**Discounts:** Long-term off-season
**Credit Cards:** V, MC, AE
**Check-in/Out:** 3–6 or by arrangement/11
**Smoking:** Outside only
**Pets:** No
**Kids:** No
**No-Nos:** Candles in rooms
**Minimum Stay:** 2 nights, weekends &

high season; 3 nights, holidays
**Open:** All year
**Hosts:** Trevor Logan, Steve Bennett, John Fox
1727 15th Ave.
Seattle, WA 98122
(206) 325-3654
Fax: (206) 328-4803
innkeepr@gaslight-inn.com
www.gaslight-inn.com

## THE GREEN GABLES GUESTHOUSE, Seattle

| Overall: ★★★★ | Room Quality: B | Value: C | Price: $109–$149 |

On a bustling and congested Queen Anne corridor, Green Gables is a vibrant inn in the thick of Seattle. Immediate access to restaurants and shopping, with the hub of Seattle (downtown, Seattle Center) just a short drive. Inside, a riot of style combines everything from classical to Victorian to Arts and Crafts to Deco to early Hollywood to contemporary. There was a sense of flux at our visit, as Reonn (who took over the established-late-1980s inn from his parents in 1996) updated and expanded. Of our two Queen Anne hill choices (this and Blue Willow), this is the more upscale, slightly less personal option. As with Capitol Hill Inn, decor is top-notch, inn is professionally run, and location is very busy.

## SETTING & FACILITIES

**Location:** Queen Anne hill, 2nd Ave. West at Galer
**Near:** Queen Anne commercial district, downtown, Seattle Center, ferries
**Building:** 1904 Craftsman & adjacent 1911 Sears & Roebuck kit home
**Grounds:** Dbl. corner lot; small, trellis-screened lawn and extensive flowerscaping
**Public Space:** Library, DR, porch, sunroom

**Food & Drink:** Tea & cookies upon request; early coffee; family-style full breakfast
**Recreation:** Historic touring, all Seattle attractions
**Amenities & Services:** Umbrellas, bus & ferry schedules, iron, travel library, piano, daily newspaper; store bags for late departure

## ACCOMMODATIONS

**Units:** 6 guest rooms
**All Rooms:** Phone w/ private line, TV/VCR
**Some Rooms:** Private balcony, off-street parking, four-poster, sitting area, kitchenette, window seat, stained & leaded glass, robes
**Bed & Bath:** Queen or king (some w/ extra single); private baths (5 ensuite)
**Favorites:** Rose Suite, Queen Anne Lace

**Comfort & Decor:** Heirloom antiques and whimsy meet in this artistic montage of over-the-top period pieces (chandeliers, fringed lamps, art glass, lace) and modern sensibilities (recessed can lighting, contemporary fabrics, carpet, tile). Douglas-fir and mahogany woodwork. Antique beds, beamed ceilings, wainscoting

## RATES, RESERVATIONS, & RESTRICTIONS

**Deposit:** 1st night, nonrefundable (transferable gift cert. issued in event of cancellation)
**Discounts:** Extended stay, single occupancy, corporate, off-season; $20 add'l person
**Credit Cards:** V, MC, AE, D
**Check-in/Out:** 3–7 or by arrangement/noon
**Smoking:** No
**Pets:** No

**Kids:** Welcome
**Minimum Stay:** 2 nights, peak season & weekends
**Open:** All year
**Hosts:** Reonn Rabon
1503 2nd Ave. W.
Seattle, WA 98119
(800) 400-1503 or (206) 282-6863
Fax: (206) 286-8525
greengab@wolfenet.com
www.greengablesseattle.com

## MILDRED'S B&B, Seattle

| Overall: ★★★½ | Room Quality: C | Value: C | Price: $90–$130 |
| --- | --- | --- | --- |

You couldn't ask for better access to beautiful, Olmstead-designed Volunteer Park, with its walking paths, tennis courts, flower conservatory, and more—it's right across somewhat-busy 15th Avenue from the inn. Mildred started this bed-and-breakfast in 1982 and was later joined by her daughter-in-law Melodee. Today, their bed-and-breakfast offers one of the few accommodations on Capitol Hill open to children. Bountiful breakfasts feature homemade jams and family-grown produce. Upstairs "butler's pantry" area with self-serve beverages helps you feel at home.

## SETTING & FACILITIES

**Location:** Capitol Hill, corner Highland & 15th, across from Volunteer Park
**Near:** Volunteer Park, Seattle Asian Museum, flower conservatory, Capitol Hill/Broadway commercial district, Washington Park Aboretum & Japanese Tea Garden
**Building:** 1890 Queen Anne Victorian
**Grounds:** Small, landscaped corner lot w/ small brick front patio
**Public Space:** Porch, LR, dining area, mezzanine butler pantry/phone area
**Food & Drink:** Self-serve coffee, tea, cookies; candy dishes; early coffee/juice tray to rooms; full breakfast
**Recreation:** Tennis, galleries, all Seattle attractions
**Amenities & Services:** Guest fridge, iron, phone, books, wet bar, piano, sound system, umbrellas; luggage storage for early check-in/late checkout; celebration extras, small group meetings w/ snacks

## ACCOMMODATIONS

**Units:** 3 guest rooms (4 in summer)
**All Rooms:** TV,VCR, desk, seating, robes, hairdryer, data port
**Some Rooms:** Skylight, four-poster, window seat, turret, chaise lounge
**Bed & Bath:** Queens (futon avail.); private baths (2 ensuite)
**Favorites:** Lace (w/ detached bath)
**Comfort & Decor:** Maintaining the

historic ambiance, the home features abundant woodwork, period light fixtures, red and gold figured carpets, high ceilings, leaded and stained glass, heirloom antiques, patterned and floral wallpapers, and lace window treatments. Rooms are good-sized for vintage. Central heat, fans.

## RATES, RESERVATIONS, & RESTRICTIONS

**Deposit:** Credit card; 7-day cancellation
**Discounts:** Single occupancy, off-season, extended stay; $20 add'l person
**Credit Cards:** V, MC, AE
**Check-in/Out:** Flexible/noon
**Smoking:** No
**Pets:** No; host cockatiel Lucky Louie
**Kids:** Welcome

**Minimum Stay:** 2 nights, weekends
**Open:** All year
**Hosts:** Mildred Sarver & Melodee Sarver
1202 15th Ave. E.
Seattle, WA 98112
(206) 325-6072
Fax: (206) 860-5907
mildredsbb@foxinternet.net
www.mildredsbnb.com

## ROBERTA'S B&B, Seattle

| Overall: ★★★★ | Room Quality: B | Value: C | Price: $95–$145 |
|---|---|---|---|

On a quiet, tree-lined side street just a block off 15th and Olmstead-designed Volunteer Park, this established (founded late 1980s) bed-and-breakfast is a centrally located oasis. The soft hues (pale plum, quiet rose, soft peach), clean lines, and stylish, traditional furnishings exude serenity. Bibliophiles will appreciate the eclectic in-room libraries, which include recent Northwest releases. Bring an open mind and an appreciation for life's simple pleasures: a cup of tea, a good book, a perfect strolling neighborhood. Your laid-back hostess (the soul of graciousness and gentle humor) is an excellent source of information for the many wonders of her native Seattle.

## SETTING & FACILITIES

**Location:** Capitol Hill, a block east of
Volunteer Park between Highland &
Prospect on 16th
**Near:** Seattle Asian Museum, flower
conservatory, Capitol Hill/Broadway
commercial district, Washington Park
Aboretum & Japanese Tea Garden
**Building:** 1903 Craftsman-era "classic
Seattle box"
**Grounds:** Small lot w/ mature trees &
profuse flowers on quiet, tree-lined
street

**Public Space:** Front porch, LR, DR
**Food & Drink:** Tea on arrival or in
evening; fresh cookies often out; morning coffee/tea to room; full vegetarian
breakfast
**Recreation:** Tennis, museums, galleries, historic touring, all Seattle
attractions
**Amenities & Services:** Fireplace,
piano, books, *New York Times,* irons,
hairdryers

## ACCOMMODATIONS

**Units:** 4 guest rooms, 1 suite
**All Rooms:** Phone, voice mail, high-
speed data port, books, seating, writing
desk
**Some Rooms:** Sitting area, window
seat(s)
**Bed & Bath:** Queen (1 w/ extra
futon); private baths (4 ensuite)
**Favorites:** Hideaway Suite
**Comfort & Decor:** Common areas

include hardwood floors with area
rugs, soft-hued walls with broad,
Craftsman-era painted moldings, lace
curtains, Mission furnishings and fixtures. Clean and uncluttered, giving a
spacious feeling. Guest rooms are
modest in size and simply but gracefully furnished with well-chosen pieces.
Excellent reading and natural light.

## RATES, RESERVATIONS, & RESTRICTIONS

**Deposit:** 1st night; 7-day cancellation
**Discounts:** Off-season, single occu-
pancy; $25 add'l person
**Credit Cards:** V, MC
**Check-in/Out:** Flexible/11
**Smoking:** No
**Pets:** No
**Kids:** No

**Minimum Stay:** None
**Open:** All year
**Host:** Roberta Barry
1147 16th Ave. E., Seattle, WA 98112
(206) 329-3326
Fax: (206) 324-2149
roberta@robertasbb.com
www.robertasbb.com

## SALISBURY HOUSE, Seattle

| Overall: ★★★★ | Room Quality: B | Value: C | Price: $89–$140 |
|---|---|---|---|

This stately, historic home in the city's most walkable neighborhood is lovely inside and out. Common areas—living, dining, library—are spacious, sunny, and welcoming. Bathrooms are full-sized. Contemporary fabrics mingle with attractive antique pieces in the open, airy, pale-hued spaces. The overall impression is one of clean lines—"no fringed lampshades in this Victorian!"—with a touch of modern art brightening the walls here and there. Innkeeper/owners live on third floor. Cute resident kitties are part of the ambiance, but inn is scrupulously clean.

### SETTING & FACILITIES

**Location:** Capitol Hill, corner 16th Ave. East & Aloha
**Near:** Volunteer Park, Seattle Asian Museum, flower conservatory, Capitol Hill/Broadway commercial district, Washington Park Arboretum & Japanese Tea Garden
**Building:** 1904 prairie-style Craftsman
**Grounds:** Dbl. corner lot w/ garden
**Public Space:** Front porch, LR, DR, deck, library, sunporch
**Food & Drink:** Self-serve tea; early coffee; family-style full breakfast
**Recreation:** Tennis, museums, galleries, historic touring, all Seattle attractions
**Amenities & Services:** Umbrellas, guest fridge, iron, fireplaces; luggage storage for afternoon flights

### ACCOMMODATIONS

**Units:** 4 guest rooms, 1 suite
**All Rooms:** Down comforter, phone, data port, voice mail, hairdryer, closet, in-room guest guide
**Some Rooms:** TV, canopy bed, desk, armoire, private deck, claw-foot soaking tub, whirlpool tub, wet bar, coffeemaker, fridge
**Bed & Bath:** Queen (1 w/ extra daybed); private ensuite baths
**Favorites:** Lavender Room, Rose Room, The Suite
**Comfort & Decor:** Extra-high ceilings (all rooms except suite), soft and pale tones, subtle wallpapers. Mary, an accomplished seamstress, has crafted lovely window treatments, bed canopies, and duvet covers. Common areas have hardwood floors with area rugs; guest rooms are carpeted. Suite, on lower level, is more modern and more isolated, with Berber-style carpet, recessed can lighting, and its own sitting room. Central heat, fans.

## RATES, RESERVATIONS, & RESTRICTIONS

**Deposit:** 1st night; 7-day cancellation
**Discounts:** Off-season midweek, single occupancy, off-season extended stay, weekly no-breakfast in suite; $20 add'l person
**Credit Cards:** V, MC, AE
**Check-in/Out:** 4–6 or by arrangement/11
**Smoking:** Outside only
**Pets:** No; host kitties in residence
**Kids:** Over 12 welcome

**Minimum Stay:** 2 nights, summer season; 3 nights, most holiday weekends
**Open:** All year
**Hosts:** Mary Weise & Cathryn Weise
750 16th Ave. E.
Seattle, WA 98112
(206) 328-8682
Fax: (206) 328-8682
sleep@salisburyhouse.com
www.salisburyhouse.com

## TUGBOAT CHALLENGER, Seattle

| Overall: ★★★ | Room Quality: C | Value: C | Price: $80–$170 |
|---|---|---|---|

It's a big ol' tugboat, OK? You're floating on Lake Union, in the thick of it all, with Space Needle views, water all around, and restaurants just up the dock. That's the fun of staying on *Challenger,* a longstanding Seattle bed-and-breakfast. The old dame had been up for sale for some time and had deteriorated in recent years. New owners' enthusiasm has improved appearance and comfort significantly. Watch for more improvements.

## SETTING & FACILITIES

**Location:** On Lake Union, at end of Yale St. Landing dock
**Near:** Seattle Center, Space Needle, Pacific Science Center, downtown
**Building:** 1944 Army tugboat
**Grounds:** Dock w/ benches & planters
**Public Space:** Solarium, main salon, sun deck

**Food & Drink:** Self-serve coffee, tea, & light snacks; extended cont'l buffet breakfast
**Recreation:** Museums, galleries, historic touring, all Seattle attractions
**Amenities & Services:** Fireplace, travel library, guest fridge, video library; fax, some Internet & email access

## ACCOMMODATIONS

**Units:** 8 staterooms (ask about other floating units)
**All Rooms:** Carpet, phone, radio
**Some Rooms:** TV, VCR, fridge, closet(s), view, sitting area, private deck, bathtub, sound system
**Bed & Bath:** Queen, double, or twin(s); 5 private baths, 3 share a bath
**Favorites:** Admiral's or Captain's cabin

**Comfort & Decor:** New carpet, paint, and wallpaper. Most rooms are small, as would be expected; cheapest are closetlike. Larger rooms (Admiral's Captain's, Master's) are well laid-out and comfortable. Shared bath units have sinks. Central heat.

## RATES, RESERVATIONS, & RESTRICTIONS

**Deposit:** Credit card; 2-week cancellation
**Discounts:** Single occupancy (some units), frequent-stay, corporate, extended-stay, off-season, midweek
**Credit Cards:** V, MC, AE, D, DC
**Check-in/Out:** 2–7 or by arrangement/11
**Smoking:** No
**Pets:** No
**Kids:** Over 8; other ages by arrangement

**No-Nos:** Shoes inside, candles in rooms
**Minimum Stay:** 2 nights on weekends
**Open:** All year
**Hosts:** Rick Anderson & Konstantin Fortrel, owners
1001 Fairview Ave. N., Suite 1600
Seattle, WA 98109-4416
(206) 340-1201
Fax: (206) 621-9208
ctugboat@uswest.net
www.challengerboat.com

## VILLA HEIDELBERG, Seattle

| Overall: ★★★★ | Room Quality: B | Value: B | Price: $80–$120 |
|---|---|---|---|

Stately, comfortable, well appointed. The best of the original home (embossed wallpapers, box-beam ceilings, original light fixtures and leaded glass), but brightened up and decorated with comfortable Mission furnishings. Called "Villa Heidelberg" by its original builder/owner, then purchased and started as a bed-and-breakfast in 1986. Hosts live on-site. Oberammergau is a delightful, pitched-ceiling third-floor hideaway that's not best for tall folk, but very charming, private, and roomy. Choose Munich for great views and more headroom. The four second-floor rooms are excellent values if you don't mind sharing a bath.

## SETTING & FACILITIES

**Location:** West Seattle off California, at 45th Ave. SW & Erskine Way
**Near:** Ferries, downtown, airport, Boeing Field, Lou Tice's Pacific Institute, Alki Beach
**Building:** 1909 Craftsman
**Grounds:** Hedge-screened corner lot; roses, monkey puzzle tree, gardens, waterscaping, Puget Sound view
**Public Space:** Porch, LR, DR, rooftop deck

**Food & Drink:** Self-serve coffee or tea; full breakfast
**Recreation:** In-line skating, bicycling, museums, all Seattle attractions
**Amenities & Services:** Fireplace, piano, guest phone, iron, sound system, umbrellas; business lunches, teas, retreats, small weddings/receptions

### ACCOMMODATIONS

**Units:** 5 guest rooms, 1 suite
**All Rooms:** TV, hairdryer
**Some Rooms:** Puget Sound & Olympic Mountain views, phone, fireplace, chandelier, sitting area, table & chairs, claw-foot tub, private deck, pitched ceiling
**Bed & Bath:** King (4, 1 w/ twin daybed, 1 w/ queen daybed), queen, or twins; 2 w/ private baths, 4 share 2 full baths

**Favorites:** Munich, Oberammergau, Heidelberg
**Comfort & Decor:** Staid Craftsman feel is maintained by the beaded and beamed ceilings, open staircase, period light fixtures/chandeliers, and leaded glass. Lots of king beds (4 of 6 rooms). Dark wood trim gives a masculine undertone despite lace window treatments, lovely quilts, and pale walls. Central radiator system, fans.

### RATES, RESERVATIONS, & RESTRICTIONS

**Deposit:** 1st night; 7-day cancellation
**Discounts:** Off-season, single occupancy, whole-house, off-season extended stay; $10 add'l person
**Credit Cards:** V, MC, AE, D
**Check-in/Out:** 3–6 or by arrangement/noon
**Smoking:** Outside only
**Pets:** No; host kitty in host quarters
**Kids:** Older children welcome with

prior approval
**Minimum Stay:** 2 nights, high season; 3 nights, some holidays
**Open:** All year
**Hosts:** Barb & John Thompson
4845 45th Ave. SW, Seattle, WA 98116
(800) 671-2942
Fax: (206) 935-7077
info@villaheidelberg.com
www.villaheidelberg.com

## CHINABERRY HILL, Tacoma

| Overall: ★★★★½ | Room Quality: A | Value: C | Price: $105–$195 |
|---|---|---|---|

This is one groovy place. The home itself is a stunner—from the oval window to the rounded porch—but Yarrow and Cecil have made it better-than-restored, with decor that's bold, eclectic, opulent, and inviting. Both romance and business travelers' needs are anticipated. And besides surrounding you with killer decor, the Waymans serve up a sumptuous gourmet breakfast. Connoisseurs of quirkiness won't be disappointed, nor will luxury-lovers. A delightful place, with secluded-garden, hilltop privacy, yet great urban access.

## SETTING & FACILITIES

**Location:** Stadium Historical District, on Tacoma Ave. between 3rd & 4th
**Near:** Antique Row, Tacoma Dome, downtown Tacoma, Univ. of Puget Sound, waterfront, historic Proctor District, Convention Center, theater district, Point Defiance Zoo & Aquarium
**Building:** 1889 Historic Register Victorian
**Grounds:** Small but attractive; old trees, cascading greenery, gardens, water views
**Public Space:** Guest kitchen, parlor, DR, porch
**Food & Drink:** Chocolate on pillow; beverages & snacks; full breakfast
**Recreation:** Bicycling, badminton, sport & cultural events, museums, historic touring
**Amenities & Services:** Fireplace, bicycles; celebration packages, weddings, seminars, meetings

## ACCOMMODATIONS

**Units:** 5 guest room/suites
**All Rooms:** Eclectic antique decor, claw-foot or whirlpool tub, TV, VCR, phone, data port, desk, top-quality beds & linens, robes
**Some Rooms:** Sitting room, bay window, water view, four-poster or canopy bed, roll-away avail.
**Bed & Bath:** Queen; private baths
**Favorites:** Each unique & stunning
**Comfort & Decor:** Each room is an artful montage; always opulent, always intriguing, never cluttered. Styles include Victorian, art deco, retro, and Asian, sometimes all in the same room. Some quirks from home's age. See Web site for accurate descriptions and good photos.

## RATES, RESERVATIONS, & RESTRICTIONS

**Deposit:** Credit card or full payment; 7-day cancellation
**Discounts:** Single occupancy, extended stays, special packages; $25 add'l person
**Credit Cards:** V, MC, AE
**Check-in/Out:** 4–6 or by arrangement/11 (extended 3 p.m. check-out $25)
**Smoking:** Outside only
**Pets:** No
**Kids:** 12 & older welcome (younger in cottage)
**Minimum Stay:** None
**Open:** All year
**Hosts:** Cecil & Yarrow Wayman
302 Tacoma Ave. N.
Tacoma, WA 98403
(253) 272-1282 (9 a.m. to 9 p.m.)
Fax: (253) 272-1335
chinaberry@wa.net
www.chinaberryhill.com

## COMMENCEMENT BAY B&B, Tacoma

| Overall: ★★★★½ | Room Quality: B | Value: B | Price: $90–$120 |
|---|---|---|---|

From its commanding perch above Commencement Bay, this imposing Colonial (set amidst other homes of weight and character) offers guests a deluxe business or romantic getaway. Experienced hosts anticipate every need with dozens of thoughtful extras. While the formal living room, with its fireplace and grand piano, is lovely, the downstairs game room, with its complementary beverages, games, video library, and adjacent exercise room, really makes you feel relaxed and at home. Alternative-lifestyle friendly.

### SETTING & FACILITIES

**Location:** North of Univ. of Puget Sound, overlooking Commencement Bay
**Near:** Univ. of Puget Sound, Commencement Bay, waterfront, historic Proctor District, downtown Tacoma, Tacoma Dome, Pt. Defiance Zoo & Aquarium
**Building:** 1937 Colonial-style historic home
**Grounds:** Landscaped, private backyard; front yard slopes steeply toward view of bay
**Public Space:** Formal LR, rec room, DR, exercise room, office work area, deck
**Food & Drink:** Espresso drinks on request; self-serve coffee, tea, & sodas; full breakfast; early cont'l option
**Recreation:** Sport & cultural events, museums, historic touring, antiquing
**Amenities & Services:** Exercise equipment, TVs, VCR, meeting area, bikes, iron, hot tub, video library, grand piano, games; same-day laundry & dry cleaning, copy/fax/e-mail, licensed massage therapy, limo & boat charter arrangements

### ACCOMMODATIONS

**Units:** 3 guest rooms
**All Rooms:** Phone, data port, TV
**Some Rooms:** Four-poster, desk, view, seating
**Bed & Bath:** Queen; private baths (2 ensuite)
**Favorites:** Myrtle's or Jessie's
**Comfort & Decor:** Upscale yet comfortable decor blends contemporary fabrics and plush carpet with restrained heirloom touches (antique quilt, chandelier). Myrtle's Room has awesome bay views, four-poster, chandelier, and green/rose/burgundy decor; Jessie's has bay, mountain, and lighthouse views and soft ecru and wood tones; Laurie's has a desk, chaise, and white iron bed. Exceptionally clean and well maintained.

## RATES, RESERVATIONS, & RESTRICTIONS

**Deposit:** Credit card; 7-day cancellation
**Discounts:** Off-season, frequent guest, extended stay
**Credit Cards:** V, MC, AE, D
**Check-in/Out:** 4–6/11
**Smoking:** No
**Pets:** No; host Cocker spaniel on premises
**Kids:** Over 12 welcome

**Minimum Stay:** 2 nights, some weekends & holidays
**Open:** All year
**Hosts:** Sharon & Bill Kaufmann
3312 N. Union Ave.
Tacoma, WA 98407
(253) 752-8175
Fax: (253) 752-4025
GREATVIEWS@aol.com
bestinns.net/usa/wa/cb.html

## DEVOE MANSION, Tacoma

| Overall: ★★★★½ | Room Quality: B | Value: B | Price: $90–$115 |
|---|---|---|---|

Thornewood has the castle, but this place has service down to an art. Built for tireless suffragette Emma Smith DeVoe and her devoted husband John Henry DeVoe, the mansion is not in the most appealing of neighborhoods, but you'll forget that once you're on the grounds or in the house. Cheryl and Dave's historic property blends traditional styling (e.g., columned front entrance porch) with modern amenities (e.g., back deck and hot tub). Vacationing couples will love the soaking tubs and classic in-room movies; business travelers will appreciate the early coffee tray and work space; everyone will love the fabulous gourmet breakfasts.

## SETTING & FACILITIES

**Location:** Southeast Tacoma near Pacific Lutheran Univ.
**Near:** Tacoma Dome, Western Washington Fairgrounds, Fort Lewis, McChord AFB, Point Defiance Zoo & Aquarium, Univ. of Puget Sound
**Building:** 1911 Historic Register Colonial
**Grounds:** 1.5 acre w/ mature trees, fruit trees
**Public Space:** LR, entry seating area, DR, front porch, back/side deck, upstairs porch

**Food & Drink:** Self-serve coffee/tea/cocoa & cookies; Almond Roca, bottled water, & ice in room; early coffee tray delivered to room; full breakfast
**Recreation:** Croquet, volleyball; day trips to Mt. Rainier, Tacoma attractions, antiquing
**Amenities & Services:** Hot tub, books, turn-of-20th-century newspapers, antique piano, sound system, games, gift shop; weddings, teas, luncheons, meetings, other celebrations

## ACCOMMODATIONS

**Units:** 4 guest rooms
**All Rooms:** TV/VCR, phone, down comforter, toiletries basket, hairdryer, curling iron, bath amenities, iron & board, fresh flowers, carpet, touring info
**Some Rooms:** Soaking tubs & bubble bath (3), sleigh or four-poster bed
**Bed & Bath:** Queen (add'l twin avail.); private baths (2 ensuite)
**Favorites:** Emma Smith DeVoe, Susan B. Anthony
**Comfort & Decor:** Common areas

have curious and effective combo of traditional and contemporary motifs: modern-feel, hand-painted black-and-white accents on gray walls, but turn-of-the-century embossed ceilings and splendid antiques; comfortable and stylish leather and upholstered furnishings. Guest rooms are more firmly traditional, from the fresh lilacs motif of Susan to the brocades of Emma and the Wedgwood blue-and-white of Henry. Carrie's private, detached bath, a former sun porch, is delightful.

## RATES, RESERVATIONS, & RESTRICTIONS

**Deposit:** 1st night; 7-day cancellation
**Discounts:** Extended stay, business traveler; $35 add'l person
**Credit Cards:** V, MC
**Check-in/Out:** 4–6 or by arrangement/11
**Smoking:** No
**Pets:** No; host kitty in residence
**Kids:** Over 12 welcome
**No-Nos:** Burning candles in room

**Minimum Stay:** PLU & UPS events & some holidays
**Open:** All year
**Hosts:** Cheryl & Dave Teifke
208 E. 133rd St.
Tacoma, WA 98445
(888) 539-3991 or (253) 539-3991
Fax: (253) 539-8539
devoe@wolfenet.com
www.wolfenet.com/~devoe

## THE GREEN CAPE COD B&B, Tacoma

| Overall: ★★★★ | Room Quality: B | Value: B | Price: $95–$105 |
| --- | --- | --- | --- |

A calm, stylish little oasis in urban Tacoma. Mary Beth, who purchased the well-located Cape Cod in 1989 and started the bed-and-breakfast in 1995, has a hospitality industry background and imparts a sense of gracious ease. Her quarters are on-site but separate. Rooms are quiet; needs of both the leisure and business traveler are anticipated. Main-floor Gibson Girl room is a nice option for those preferring not to climb stairs. Good value, excellent hostess.

## SETTING & FACILITIES

**Location:** North Tacoma's Univ. of Puget Sound neighborhood, on Warner off N. 30th St.
**Near:** Proctor district, downtown, Tacoma Dome, Pt. Defiance, Vashon ferries
**Building:** 1929 Cape Cod–style home
**Grounds:** Trim little front lawn w/ flowering shrubs; fenced backyard w/ patio
**Public Space:** LR, DR, porch, patio

**Food & Drink:** In-room Almond Roca; full or cont'l breakfast
**Recreation:** Antiquing, zoo/aquarium, galleries, theater
**Amenities & Services:** Games, separate-line cordless phone, fridge, YMCA passes, "I forgot it" items; concierge; laundry, ironing, dry cleaning by arrangement; office use by arrangement

## ACCOMMODATIONS

**Units:** 3 guest rooms
**All Rooms:** Guest guide, robes, TV, quality linens, toiletries, data port, closet, hairdryer
**Some Rooms:** Sofa-sleeper
**Bed & Bath:** King or queen; private baths (1 ensuite)
**Favorites:** Quite equal

**Comfort & Decor:** Hardwood floors and bentwood furnishings welcome you in a parlor that is graceful, uncluttered, with a calming, tailored feel that flows throughout the house. Tasteful palettes include taupe, ochre, Wedgwood blue, and pale sage.

## RATES, RESERVATIONS, & RESTRICTIONS

**Deposit:** 1st night; 7-day cancellation
**Discounts:** Senior, corporate extended stay; $20 add'l person
**Credit Cards:** V, MC, AE
**Check-in/Out:** After 3 or by arrangement/11
**Smoking:** Outside only
**Pets:** No
**Kids:** 12 & older welcome (younger if taking whole house or by arrangement)

**Minimum Stay:** 2 or 3 nights, some local university events
**Open:** All year
**Hosts:** Mary Beth King
2711 N. Warner
Tacoma, WA 98407
(253) 752-1977
Fax: (253) 756-9886
grncapecod@aol.com
www.tribnet.com/adv/bb/green-capecod/

## THORNEWOOD CASTLE, Tacoma

Overall: ★★★★★      Room Quality: A      Value: D      Price: $150–$200

While many places call themselves "Estate," "Mansion," or even "Castle," this one IS. It takes a real sophisticate to refrain from gawking at the grandeur of this Kirtland Cutter–designed estate. The castle's construction (involving imported building materials, artwork, and hand-painted glass dating from the 15th to 17th centuries) took three years and cost a million dollars in 1911. The Miraus, who live on-site in quarters of their own, have restored much of the grandeur of the castle and make many of the objets d'art available for purchase. The sunken garden and American Lake location complete the perfection, while amenities like the guest pantry help you feel at home in such over-the-top surroundings.

### SETTING & FACILITIES

**Location:** 10 min. south of Tacoma, 15 min. east of Olympia, on American Lake

**Near:** State capitol & attractions, Tacoma Dome, Pt. Defiance Zoo & Aquarium, cultural attractions, Lakewood Mall

**Building:** 28,000-sq.-ft. Gothic Tudor Historic Register mansion

**Grounds:** Expansive lawns, lush landscaping; stunning, walled, sunken English garden

**Public Space:** Music room, library, breakfast/game/history room, many sitting areas, guest pantry

**Food & Drink:** Snacks, treats, coffee (guest pantry); full breakfast

**Recreation:** Bird-watching, beach/lake activities; casino, military/historic touring, golf

**Amenities & Services:** Grand piano, sound system, games, pantry w/ ice & micro., coin-op laundry; massage by appt.; social events (50); seaplane hangar

## ACCOMMODATIONS

**Units:** 5 suites, plus overflow options
**All Rooms:** Robes, TV/VCR, sound system, sitting area, lots of storage, hotel-style amenities
**Some Rooms:** Lake view, kitchenette, desk, fireplace (4), window seat, couch, table & chairs, private balcony/deck, whirlpool, mini-fridge, antique soaker or claw-foot tub, coffee service, extra attached room w/ 2nd bed

**Bed & Bath:** Queen or king (cots avail.); private bath (4 ensuite)
**Favorites:** Each is amazing
**Comfort & Decor:** Grand and stunning. From the Welsh-brick exterior to the massive interior staircase, from the wide-plank English Oak paneling to the museum-quality art objects, you're surrounded by opulence. Ornate carpet and Oriental rugs over hardwood floors, extra-high ceilings with elaborate moldings.

## RATES, RESERVATIONS, & RESTRICTIONS

**Deposit:** 1st night; 7-day cancellation
**Discounts:** Business (Sun.–Thurs.), extended stay, off-season; $25 add'l person
**Credit Cards:** V, MC, AE
**Check-in/Out:** 4/11
**Smoking:** Outside only
**Pets:** No; host dog & cat on site
**Kids:** 12 & older welcome
**No-Nos:** Outside visitors, loud noise after 10 p.m.

**Minimum Stay:** 2 nights, high-season weekends
**Open:** All year
**Hosts:** Richard & Deborah Mirau
8601 N. Thorne Ln. SW
Lakewood, WA 98498
(253) 584-4393
Fax: (253) 584-4497
thornewood@mindspring.com
www.thornewoodcastle.com

## ANGELS OF THE SEA B&B, Vashon

| Overall: ★★★½ | Room Quality: C | Value: B | Price: $75–$125 |
|---|---|---|---|

What an unusual and peaceful place—first of all, the church architecture and ambiance is retained; second, the harp concerts by your hostess (included with breakfast!) are out of this world. Marnie has owned the building since 1992 and has offered lodgings since 1993. View the main salon ("sanctuary") on the Web site—the photo there gives a good sense of this unique room, with its multiple sitting areas, stage, and dining room all in one. Every nuance is designed for your comfort and ease. While the guest rooms are more humble than nearby Artist's Loft, the common area and overall experience ranks high. Child and pet-friendly policies are worth noting.

### SETTING & FACILITIES

**Location:** 15 min. SE of Vashon, on the edge of Dockton
**Near:** East Passage (Puget Sound), Tramp Harbor, Quartermaster Harbor, Tacoma Yacht Club, Vashon Golf & Country Club, Seattle, Tacoma
**Building:** 1917 Norwegian Lutheran Church
**Grounds:** Small yard w/ play area
**Public Space:** Sanctuary (great room), sitting room

**Food & Drink:** Beverages; full breakfast (or ensuite by guests' choice)
**Recreation:** Swimming (seasonal), boating, kayaking, hiking
**Amenities & Services:** Games, guest fridge, guest laundry, videos, sound system, country club passes; massage by arrangement, eco-sensitive linens policy

### ACCOMMODATIONS

**Units:** 3 guest rooms
**All Rooms:** Closet; pale, peaceful motifs
**Some Rooms:** Skylights, fridge, whirlpool tub, sitting area, TV/VCR
**Bed & Bath:** Queen (1 w/ sofa-sleeper & alcove futon) or twin/king conversion; 1 private bath, 2 share
**Favorites:** Ocean Suite

**Comfort & Decor:** Peace is the motif, with sea-creature art an overlying theme. Quality wood trim, original church windows. Pale, figured wallpapers create a clean, cheerful, homey atmosphere. Sanctuary is a lovely and meditative space. Individual electric heaters.

### RATES, RESERVATIONS, & RESTRICTIONS

**Deposit:** 1st night; 2-week cancellation
**Discounts:** Extended stays, Whale & Dolphin room together; $10 add'l person, free under 5
**Credit Cards:** V, MC
**Check-in/Out:** After 3/noon
**Smoking:** Outside only
**Pets:** Negotiable in some rooms; host pets in adjacent home

**Kids:** Welcome
**Minimum Stay:** None
**Open:** All year
**Hosts:** Marnie Jones
26431 99th Ave. SW
Vashon, WA 98070
(800) 798-9249 or (206) 463-6980
Fax: (206) 463-2205
AngelsSea@aol.com
www.angelsofthesea.com

## ARTIST'S STUDIO LOFT B&B, Vashon

| Overall: ★★★★½ | Room Quality: B | Value: B | Price: $85–$105 |
|---|---|---|---|

Peaceful, meditative gardens and private suites that are, themselves, works of art—that's Artist's Loft Bed & Breakfast. Where the best feature of our other profiled Vashon Island bed-and-breakfast, Angels of the

Sea, is the beautiful sanctuary common area, Artist's Loft's strength is the unique, tasteful, private spaces it creates for individuals and couples seeking a retreat. And the gardens are extraordinary and ever-evolving.

## SETTING & FACILITIES

**Location:** Just north of Vashon
**Near:** Vashon Municipal Airport, Tramp Harbor, Beals Point, Seattle, Tacoma
**Building:** Contemporary home & studio structures
**Grounds:** 5-acre wooded parcel w/ paths, ponds, gardens, fruit trees, arbors

**Public Space:** Fabulous gardens
**Food & Drink:** Extended cont'l breakfast (self-serve ensuite breakfast in Aerial Cottage kitchenette)
**Recreation:** Beachcombing, wildlife watching, kayaking, scenic flights
**Amenities & Services:** Outdoor spa; see also "All Rooms" and "Some Rooms" below

## ACCOMMODATIONS

**Units:** 2 guest rooms, 1 suite
**All Rooms:** Private entrance, robes, ceiling fans, TV
**Some Rooms:** Skylights, fireplace, kitchenette (coffeemaker, micro., fridge, cooktop), dual sinks, VCR, private deck, desk, sound system
**Bed & Bath:** Queen (plus daybed in Aerial); private ensuite baths
**Favorites:** Aerial Cottage

**Comfort & Decor:** Contemporary, artistic decor with special touches such as rag-painted walls, original artwork, art-quality fixtures. Stained glass, metal sculpture. Ivy Room has Southwest bent; Master has a peach and burgundy palette; Aerial Cottage is roomy and contemporary, with a Native American motif.

## RATES, RESERVATIONS, & RESTRICTIONS

**Deposit:** 1st night or 50%; 10-day cancellation
**Discounts:** Extended stay; $25 add'l person
**Credit Cards:** V, MC, AE, D
**Check-in/Out:** 4–6 or by arrangement/11
**Smoking:** Outside only
**Pets:** No
**Kids:** No

**Minimum Stay:** 2 nights, most weekends & holidays
**Open:** All year
**Hosts:** Jacqueline Clayton
16529 91st Ave. SW
Vashon Island, WA 98070
(206) 463-2583
Fax: (206) 463-3881
medowart@asl-bnb.com
www.asl-bnb.com

# Zone 6
# Washington's I-5 South

Between the Olympic Peninsula and the Cascade Mountains, Interstate 5 traces a path south from Puget Sound to Portland, Oregon.

At the north end of this zone is Olympia, the state capital. Olympia's geographic focus is the Capitol area and the city's waterfront areas. Evergreen State College is located here, and nearby Tenino is home to Wolf Haven, a sanctuary that promotes preservation of and education about wolves. As with Salem, Oregon's capital, this business-minded city's lodgings run to featureless hotels and motels and a smattering of one- and two-unit bed-and-breakfasts too small to include—only two made the cut. Another, a modest, family-friendly enterprise, is situated in nearby Rainier, offering access to both the Olympia area and the Cascade Mountains.

At the south end of the interstate corridor, Vancouver, Washington, sits immediately across the state line from Portland, Oregon, along the Columbia River. This city is rich in history, with attractions including the Fort Vancouver National Historic Site, but has a paucity of bed-and-breakfasts; its best one is profiled.

Between Olympia and Vancouver, towns like Toledo, Castle Rock, Silver Lake, and Woodland offer access to Mount St. Helens—Washington's westernmost Cascade peak, and its most infamous. Exceptional visitor centers tell the story of the 1980 eruption, hiking trails trace both the forested south and the blasted north sides, and a handful of bed-and-breakfasts join the motels and cabins in housing area visitors. Our two favorites are profiled: a grand one outside Castle Rock and a humble-quaint one outside Woodland.

Longview, a pretty community centered on a park and man-made lake, is home to an evolving bed-and-breakfast in a historic-home-turned-restaurant. Longview is also I-5's junction with scenic Highway 4, which leads to Long Beach Peninsula. En route, tiny Cathlamet, on the banks of the Columbia River, offers a piece of history, a ferry to Oregon, and an attractive bed-and-breakfast in a restored heritage home.

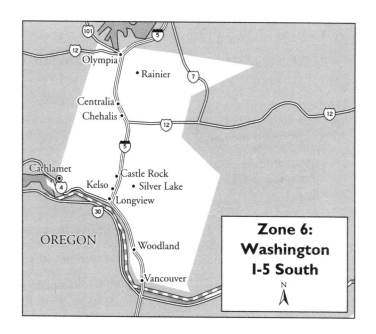

Zone 6:
**Washington
I-5 South**

N

---

**Castle Rock**
Blue Heron Inn, p. 212

**Cathlamet**
Bradley House, p. 213

**Longview**
Rutherglen Mansion, p. 214

**Olympia**
Harbinger Inn, p. 215
Swantown Inn, p. 216

**Rainier**
7C's Guest Ranch, p. 218

**Vancouver**
Vintage Inn, p. 219

**Woodland**
Grandma's House B&B, p. 220

## BLUE HERON INN, Castle Rock

Overall: ★★★★½    Room Quality: B    Value: C    Price: $145–$195

A first-class establishment on the most popular approach to Mount St. Helens, the Robards' Blue Heron Inn provides two much-needed services to the Highway 504 corridor: classy lodging and quality food. It's tough to find a good meal on this stretch of road, and lodgings tend toward motels. At Blue Heron Inn, you have views of the mountain and lake, a spacious deck, well-appointed living areas, and both your dinner and breakfast provided. Top off the day with a complimentary glass of wine or cup of tea. . .what more could you ask for as you visit the Pacific Northwest's most recently erupted volcano?

### SETTING & FACILITIES

**Location:** About 5 mi. east of I-5 on Hwy. 504
**Near:** Silver Lake, Seaquest Park, Mount St. Helens, Castle Rock, Toutle
**Building:** 7,700-sq.-ft. contemporary mountain lodge
**Grounds:** 5 acres w/ view of Silver Lake & Mount St. Helens; picnic area
**Public Space:** 3 living areas, DR, deck
**Food & Drink:** Coffee, tea, & wine; full-course dinner (family-style); full breakfast
**Recreation:** Hiking, fishing, boating, scenic driving, Mount St. Helens visitor centers, bicycling, helicopter tours, wildlife watching
**Amenities & Services:** Fireplace, library, games, koi pond, exercise equipment; weddings, business meetings

## ACCOMMODATIONS

**Units:** 7 guest rooms
**All Rooms:** TV, balcony
**Some Rooms:** Private video center, whirlpool tub, disabled access
**Bed & Bath:** Queen (5), two doubles, or king; private ensuite baths
**Favorites:** Jacuzzi Suite
**Comfort & Decor:** Guest rooms are clean, simple, fairly spacious (same size

except Jacuzzi Suite). Rooms are individually decorated: country quilts in one, sleigh bed and traditional decor in another, lacquered art nouveau in another. Common areas are graciously appointed with comfortable contemporary decor.

## RATES, RESERVATIONS, & RESTRICTIONS

**Deposit:** 1st night; 1-week cancellation
**Discounts:** Single occupancy, off-season; $30 add'l person, $20 add'l age 5–12
**Credit Cards:** V, MC
**Check-in/Out:** 2–6 or by arrangement/noon
**Smoking:** Outside (covered decks & balconies) only
**Pets:** No

**Kids:** Welcome 5 & older
**Minimum Stay:** None
**Open:** All year
**Hosts:** Jeanne & John Robards
2846 Spirit Lake Hwy.
Castle Rock, WA 98611
(800) 959-4049 or (360) 274-9595
Fax: (360) 274-2913
jeanne@blueheroninn.com
www.blueheroninn.com

## BRADLEY HOUSE, Cathlamet

| Overall: ★★★★ | Room Quality: C | Value: B | Price: $80–$100 |

Settled in 1846, Cathlamet is one of those sleepy, charming little "towns that time forgot"—a ferry ride away from Oregon and in between Longview and Long Beach off Washington's two-lane Highway 4. The Bradley House perches in its blue-and-white historic glory above Main Street across from the Court House. The home stayed with its longtime owners and namesakes, the Bradley family, until the 1970s, then became Cathlamet's library for several years before becoming a bed-and-breakfast known as Country Keeper. The Wests, pleasant and professional innkeepers, have owned and operated it since 1991.

## SETTING & FACILITIES

**Location:** On Main at Butler, just off Hwy. 4, 20 mi. west of Longview
**Near:** Marina, Columbia River, Wahkiakum Ferry, Puget Island, Longview/Kelso, Lewis & Clark Trail
**Building:** 1907 Eastlake-meets-foursquare
**Grounds:** Hillside lot w/ small lawn, border plantings; terraced backyard garden

**Public Space:** Two parlors, DR, front porch
**Food & Drink:** Tea, cocoa, port, sherry, cookies; full breakfast
**Recreation:** Boating, museum, historic touring, golf, tennis, windsurfing, bird-watching
**Amenities & Services:** Games, piano, puzzles, TV, sound system, guest phone; small wedding, receptions, seminars, meetings, reunions, parties

## ACCOMMODATIONS

**Units:** 4 guest rooms
**All Rooms:** Robes, desk or table & chairs, hairdryer, toiletries, closet
**Some Rooms:** River view, window seat, library
**Bed & Bath:** Queen (1 w/ extra daybed), king; 2 private baths, 2 share a bath
**Favorites:** Rose Room

**Comfort & Decor:** Lovely leaded and stained glass windows. Douglas fir wall and pillar woodwork, oak and mahogany floors. Period fixtures, many original. Guest rooms have pale walls, rich woodwork, delicate wallpapers, period furnishings, floral accents. Central heat plus auxiliary electric heaters; fans.

## RATES, RESERVATIONS, & RESTRICTIONS

**Deposit:** Credit card; 72-hour cancellation
**Discounts:** Single occupancy, gov't, extended stay; $15 add'l person
**Credit Cards:** V, MC
**Check-in/Out:** 4–7 or by arrangement/11
**Smoking:** Outside only
**Pets:** No
**Kids:** Older children welcome
**Minimum Stay:** 2 nights on 3-day weekends

**Open:** All year (except Christmas Eve & day; off-season Mon.–Tues. by reservation only)
**Hosts:** Barbara & Tony West
61 Main St., P.O. Box 35
Cathlamet, WA 98612
(800) 551-1691 or (360) 795-3030
Fax: (360) 795-0809 (call first)
bradleyhouse@transport.com
www.moriah.com/bradley

## RUTHERGLEN MANSION, Longview

| Overall: ★★ | Room Quality: D | Value: D | Price: $80–$100 |
| --- | --- | --- | --- |

This opulent mansion has a faded, semirestored elegance with enormous potential. In the meantime, it shows the attendant quirks of age. Additional guest rooms may include two with a shared bath and/or one grand Master Suite—plans still on the drawing board. The approach is via a not-so-promising heavy-industry section of Longview, and the twin-peaked, column-porched white mansion's hillside perch is a bit diminished by its view, which includes industrial smokestacks.

## SETTING & FACILITIES

**Location:** 2 blocks south of Hwy. 4 toward west end of Longview
**Near:** Lake Sacajawea & park, rivers, McClelland Arts Center, Columbia Theater
**Building:** 13,000-sq.-ft. 1929 National Historic Register mansion
**Grounds:** Hilltop location
**Public Space:** Mezzanine sitting area

**Food & Drink:** Property is also a restaurant; full breakfast (Sun. brunch for Sat. night guests)
**Recreation:** Hiking, fishing, hunting, windsurfing, boating, water skiing, golf, tennis
**Amenities & Services:** On-site restaurant; weddings, banquets, parties

## ACCOMMODATIONS

**Units:** 2 guest rooms
**All Rooms:** Phone, fireplace, table & chairs, down comforters
**Some Rooms:** Fridge, sitting area
**Bed & Bath:** King; private ensuite baths
**Favorites:** Sun Room is brighter, West Room more spacious & elegant

**Comfort & Decor:** Common areas boast original wood, tile, & plaster work. Large guest rooms have ornate furnishings and tile with a Mediterranean feel. Needs some TLC to restore its faded glory. Ladybug infestation at our visit.

## RATES, RESERVATIONS, & RESTRICTIONS

**Deposit:** Call
**Discounts:** Single occupancy, midweek; $10–15 add'l person
**Credit Cards:** V, MC, AE
**Check-in/Out:** After 3/11
**Smoking:** Outside only
**Pets:** No
**Kids:** Welcome

**Minimum Stay:** None
**Open:** All year
**Hosts:** Reuben Grendahl
420 Rutherglen Rd.
Longview, WA 98632
(360) 425-5816
Fax: (360) 636-3655

## HARBINGER INN, Olympia

| Overall: ★★★½ | Room Quality: C | Value: B | Price: $65–$125 |
|---|---|---|---|

In a location both convenient and attractive, this column-fronted home perches low on a hillside just above East Bay. Very business-friendly. A bit more polished than Swantown, and correspondingly less personal (where Swantown hosts are on-site and retired, Harbinger hosts are active professionals living adjacent). The professionally run inn was started in the 1980s and purchased by current owners in 1989. Ask to see the tunnel!

## SETTING & FACILITIES

**Location:** Just north of downtown on the East Bay of Budd Inlet
**Near:** State Capitol & campus, Evergreen State College, Wolf Haven
**Building:** 1910 concrete block Italianate American foursquare
**Grounds:** Hillside lot; flowers, water view, side patio, ivied back wall w/ natural spring

**Public Space:** Parlor, library, veranda, patio
**Food & Drink:** Afternoon/evening self-serve tea & cookies; complimentary wine, port, sherry; in-room bottled water; full breakfast
**Recreation:** Historic touring, farmer's market, theater, galleries
**Amenities & Services:** Sound system, TV/VCR

## ACCOMMODATIONS

**Units:** 4 guest rooms, 2-room suite (bungalow)
**All Rooms:** Robes
**Some Rooms:** Water/marina view, claw-foot tub, fridge, micro., sitting area, private deck, desk, fireplace, TV/VCR
**Bed & Bath:** Queen (1 w/ daybed), king, or double; private baths (4 ensuite)

**Favorites:** Innkeepers Suite, Blue Heron
**Comfort & Decor:** Victorian living room furnishings; Mission/Arts and Crafts library styling. Common areas include natural wood interior columns and lintels, lace, embossed ceiling. Guest rooms run to quilts, lace, and antiques, with floral wallpapers and tile baths.

## RATES, RESERVATIONS, & RESTRICTIONS

**Deposit:** 1st night; 72-hour cancellation
**Discounts:** Single occupancy, extended stay, off-season; $10 add'l person
**Credit Cards:** V, MC, AE
**Check-in/Out:** 4–6 or by arrangement/11

**Smoking:** Outside only
**Pets:** No; host dog Louis
**Kids:** 10 & older welcome
**Minimum Stay:** None
**Open:** All year
**Hosts:** Marisa & Terrell Williams
1136 East Bay Dr., Olympia, WA 98506
(360) 754-0389

## SWANTOWN INN, Olympia

| Overall: ★★★½ | Room Quality: C | Value: B | Price: $85–$115 |
|---|---|---|---|

This storybook Queen Anne (on multiple historic registers) is sage green with mustard-, ochre-, and brick-colored trim. Inside, it's a comfortable mix of the old and the new, with cozy common areas and rooms that are welcoming and unpretentious. Great breakfasts may include Lillian's signature scones. While the Astoria Room, with its double whirlpool tub, tile bath, and sitting area, is the feature room, Columbia is special as well. Its corner location provides good light, and its detached bath with claw-foot tub is delightful.

## SETTING & FACILITIES

**Location:** Near I-5 off Eastside on 11th
**Near:** State Capitol & campus, Evergreen State College, Wolf Haven
**Building:** 1893 Queen Anne/Eastlake Victorian
**Grounds:** Gazebo, rhododendrons; veggie, berry, and herb garden; fruit trees
**Public Space:** Parlor, drawing room, DR

**Food & Drink:** Afternoon refreshments; full breakfasts
**Recreation:** Historic touring, farmer's market, theater, galleries
**Amenities & Services:** Fax, modem, phone jack/data port, cable, fireplace, cordless guest phone, fridge; weddings, German-speaking hosts

## ACCOMMODATIONS

**Units:** 3 guest rooms
**All Rooms:** Capitol dome view, down comforters, couch or table & chairs
**Some Rooms:** Four-poster, dbl. whirlpool, tile bath, sofa-sleeper, closet/armoire, claw-foot tub, robes
**Bed & Bath:** Queen; private baths (2 ensuite)
**Favorites:** Astoria Room
**Comfort & Decor:** Antiques ranging from Eastlake through Arts and Crafts

periods grace this grand old home, lovingly restored by Ed, Lillian, and family. Original light fixtures, extra-high ceilings, stained glass, painted hardwood floors with area rugs. Rooms are open and airy for this vintage, with floral wallpapers, lace accents, and family heirlooms. Two zoned forced-air heating systems.

## RATES, RESERVATIONS, & RESTRICTIONS

**Deposit:** Credit card; 7-day cancellation
**Discounts:** Off-season, single occupancy, extended stays; $15 add'l person
**Credit Cards:** V, MC
**Check-in/Out:** 4–6 or by arrangement/11
**Smoking:** Outside only (gazebo & side veranda)
**Pets:** No

**Kids:** Over 12 welcome
**Minimum Stay:** None
**Open:** All year
**Hosts:** Ed & Lillian Peeples
1431 11th Ave. SE
Olympia, WA 98501
(360) 753-9123
Fax: (360) 943-8047
swantown@olywa.com
www.olywa.net/swantown

## 7C'S GUEST RANCH, Rainier

| Overall: ★★½ | Room Quality: D | Value: C | Price: $50–$100 |

A cross between "storybook farm" and "staying with well-loved cousins." Rural setting is peaceful and access to both city and mountains is good. Your well-traveled hostess has great stories, and provides a flexible, welcoming atmosphere. Home is also a working property with on-site ranch hands and rooms for the elderly; living areas are likely to be shared with others. Free-range-chicken eggs and organic fruit and veggies produced on-site. This casual guest house and ranch is the real thing.

### SETTING & FACILITIES

**Location:** 20 min. SE of Olympia near Hwy. 507
**Near:** Rainier; hub for daytrips to Olympia, Tacoma, Mt. Rainier
**Building:** 2-level private home
**Grounds:** 10 acres; pastures, barn, gardens, rhododendrons, fruit & nut trees
**Public Space:** Front porch, LR, sitting room, DR, library; game room under development

**Food & Drink:** Coffee bar, snacks on request; full breakfast
**Recreation:** On-site croquet, horseshoes, ranch strolling; nearby boating, casino, day trips
**Amenities & Services:** Big-screen TV, VCR, fireplace, huge video library, BBQ, hot tub, guest fridge, guest phone; horse barn & pasture avail., computer/e-mail access, RV hook-ups, Sea-Tac airport pick-up $20

### ACCOMMODATIONS

**Units:** 3 guest rooms
**All Rooms:** Sitting area, romantic decor
**Some Rooms:** TV, VCR, closet, vanity, table & chairs, sound system, phone, disabled access
**Bed & Bath:** Queens; 1 private bath, 2 share a bath
**Favorites:** Honeymoon Suite

**Comfort & Decor:** Eclectic and homey. The two smaller rooms have four-poster beds and stylish bedding, which makes up for the green shag carpet. Honeymoon Suite is all in black and white: plush white carpet, black lacquer furnishings, with mirror and glass accents and a private deck. Individual room heat control.

### RATES, RESERVATIONS, & RESTRICTIONS

**Deposit:** Varies
**Discounts:** Extended stay, single occupancy
**Credit Cards:** Not accepted
**Check-in/Out:** Flexible
**Smoking:** Outside (including covered porches) only
**Pets:** Not in house; inquire about outside facil.

**Kids:** Welcome
**Minimum Stay:** None
**Open:** All year
**Host:** Evelyn Cissna
11123 128th SE
Rainier, WA 98576
(360) 446-7957

## VINTAGE INN, Vancouver

| Overall: ★★★½ | Room Quality: C | Value: B | Price: $85 |
|---|---|---|---|

A great sense of Vancouver history is preserved throughout this lovely home. Not only are the woodwork, stained glass, and many fixtures original, the Hales (Vancouver natives) found many artifacts during their restoration process, and display them throughout the home (ask to see the butler's pantry). Room decor is charming. Despite the shared-bath situation, this place is top-notch. Walking distance to anything you need: restaurants, shopping, entertainment.

### SETTING & FACILITIES

**Location:** Downtown, West 11th St. between Columbia & Daniels
**Near:** All downtown venues, Amtrak, Columbia River, Vancouver Lake, Fort Vancouver Nat'l Historic Reserve, Portland
**Building:** 1903 National Historic Register Craftsman hybrid
**Grounds:** Rear gardens & small brick patio

**Public Space:** Two parlors, DR, porch, sunroom
**Food & Drink:** Early coffee/tea/cocoa service; full breakfast
**Recreation:** Antiquing, historic touring, theater, museums, sailing, rowing
**Amenities & Services:** Fireplace, TV, VCR, videos, games, piano; wedding night celebration extras; parties & teas

### ACCOMMODATIONS

**Units:** 4 guest rooms
**All Rooms:** Closet, robes, (shared) claw-foot tub, fresh flowers, guest guide
**Some Rooms:** Desk, fireplace, private porch
**Bed & Bath:** Queen (1 w/ daybed, roll-away avail.); share 1.5 baths
**Favorites:** Chumasero (summer),

Windsor (winter)
**Comfort & Decor:** Original woodwork (including pocket doors) and stained glass. Delicate floral and print wallpapers, antique (but comfortable) furnishings, lace, wine carpet. Historic photos in stairwell. Amazing amount of original fixtures; beautifully preserved.

### RATES, RESERVATIONS, & RESTRICTIONS

**Deposit:** 1st night; 7-day cancellation
**Discounts:** Extended stay, whole house, corporate; $20 add'l person
**Credit Cards:** V, MC
**Check-in/Out:** 3–7 or by arrangement/11
**Smoking:** Outside only
**Pets:** No
**Kids:** Welcome

**No-Nos:** Alcohol
**Minimum Stay:** None
**Open:** All year
**Hosts:** Mike & Doris Hale
310 W. 11th St.
Vancouver, WA 98660
(888) 693-6635
info@vintage-inn.com
www.vintage-inn.com/

## GRANDMA'S HOUSE B&B, Woodland

| Overall: ★★½ | Room Quality: D | Value: A | Price: $55 |
|---|---|---|---|

"Grandma's House" is the perfect name for this cozy, unpretentious, European-style (read: shared bath) bed-and-breakfast. It's funky and retro (just like Grandma!), with a mix of the old and the new. The Lewis River frontage makes for a peaceful retreat, whether you're passing by on Interstate 5 (just 8 miles away) or spending a few days exploring Mount St. Helens country. You can't beat the price, and you won't leave hungry after the simple but large farm breakfast. (Come during blackberry season for a special treat!)

### SETTING & FACILITIES

**Location:** About a mi. from Hwy. 503, 8 mi. east of Woodland/I-5, on the Lewis River
**Near:** Woodland, Ariel, Mount St. Helens
**Building:** Early 20th-century classic 2-level farmhouse
**Grounds:** 35 acres w/ pastures, garden, flowers, blackberries, shade trees

**Public Space:** Entire house (hosts live adjacent): LR, DR, kitchen, decks
**Food & Drink:** Hot beverages; full breakfast
**Recreation:** Hiking, fishing, scenic driving, Mount St. Helens touring
**Amenities & Services:** Excellent Mount St. Helens maps & info, kitchen privileges, TV, VCR, claw-foot tub, piano

### ACCOMMODATIONS

**Units:** 3 guest rooms
**All Rooms:** Simple country decor
**Some Rooms:** Sink, river view
**Bed & Bath:** Queen; shared bath
**Favorites:** Upstairs rooms have Lewis River view, main floor room has best bath access

**Comfort & Decor:** Floral wallpapers, practical period furnishings, and a sense of 1920s–1930s nostalgia. No AC; fans provided.

### RATES, RESERVATIONS, & RESTRICTIONS

**Deposit:** Credit card; 24-hour cancellation
**Discounts:** Single occupancy, whole house rental
**Credit Cards:** V, MC
**Check-in/Out:** I/11 flexible
**Smoking:** Outside only
**Pets:** No
**Kids:** Welcome

**Minimum Stay:** None
**Open:** All year
**Hosts:** Louise & Warren Moir
4551 Old Lewis River Rd.
Woodland, WA 98674
(360) 225-7002
gmasbb@pacifier.com
www.telltalesigns.com/grandmain.html

# Zone 7
# Washington's Cascades

The dramatic Cascade Mountain range separates Washington and Oregon's moist, green west sides from the dun-colored, sage-scented, high-desert basins of their east sides. Washington's Cascades include the celebrated peaks of Mount Baker, Mount Rainier, Mount St. Helens, and Mount Adams; recreation areas such as The Enchantments and Alpine Lakes; North Cascade and Mount Rainier National Parks; and Wenatchee, Okanogan, Gifford Pinchot, Mount Baker–Snoqualmie, and Mount Adams National Forests.

The northernmost major Washington Cascade peak is Mount Baker. With its record snowfalls, it's a skier's and snowboarder's paradise. Its high-country hiking trails and the glacier-fed Nooksack River are phenomenally beautiful. Mount Baker can be reached via Highway 542, an out-and-back highway that begins at Bellingham (see Zone 4) and ends at the mountain. En route, the hamlets of Maple Falls and Glacier offer lodgings included in our profiles.

Just south of Mount Baker, the northernmost route traversing Washington's Cascades is Highway 20, also known as North Cascades Highway, a rugged beauty open seasonally. Closures of the highway vary, but expect them November through April. To the west of the mountains on Highway 20 are the bed-and-breakfasts of Concrete and Rockport, with their proximity to popular Baker Lake and the Sauk and Skagit Rivers (prime bald eagle habitat), North Cascades National Park, and Ross and Diablo Lakes.

The second northernmost route across the Cascades is Highway 2, Stevens Pass. Stretching from Snohomish (see Zone 5) and Skykomish on the west side to Leavenworth and Wenatchee (see Zone 9) on the east side, this route was once a major railroad course. Travelers can combine Highway 2 with Highway 20 for a long, scenic drive known as the Cascade Loop. Wilderness activities and rail history dominate the western segment of this mountain pass, with lodgings featured in Index and Skykomish.

Stevens Pass Ski Area marks the summit. East of the pass, Leavenworth is a re-created Bavarian village with a healthy tourist infrastructure and a number of excellent bed-and-breakfast lodgings.

A town not accessible by any highway—or, for that matter, any road at all—is Stehekin. We've included this unique village and one of its lodgings. Isolated in a little valley at the head of 55-mile-long Lake Chelan, Stehekin can only be reached by boat or float plane.

The main east-west route across Washington's Cascades is Interstate 90, Snoqualmie Pass; featured bed-and-breakfasts can be found off I-90 in North Bend, Roslyn, and South Cle Elum. North Bend is situated between Seattle and Snoqualmie Pass Ski Area; its nearby attractions include Mount Si (Washington's most popular hiking trail, an eight-mile thigh-burner with 50,000 visitors annually) and Snoqualmie Falls.

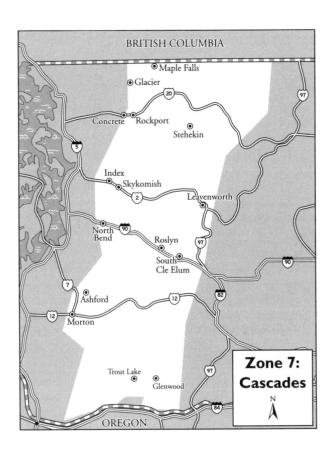

Mount Rainier, over 14,000 feet tall, is the crown jewel of the Cascades. Visible from both Seattle and Tacoma, it draws tourists like a magnet. The greatest concentration of bed-and-breakfast–style lodgings serving Mount Rainier are found in Ashford, near the Nisqually (west) entrance to Mount Rainier National Park along Highway 706. Ashford also offers access to surrounding Gifford Pinchot National Forest and its Glacier View Wilderness. Southwest of the mountain, along Highway 12, an excellent bed-and-breakfast is situated between Randle and Morton (listed in Morton); this property is within easy day-trip distance to Mount Rainier, Mount St. Helens (see also St. Helens access communities in Zone 6), and even Mount Adams.

When traveling across any Cascade Mountain pass in winter, be sure to check road conditions, closures, and required traction devices by calling (888) SNO-INFO.

**Ashford**
Alexander's Inn, p. 224
Growly Bear B&B, p. 225
Jasmer's at Mt. Rainier, p. 226
Mountain Meadows Inn, p. 227
Wellspring, p. 228

**Concrete**
Cascade Mountain Inn, p. 230
Ovenell's Heritage Inn, p. 231

**Glacier**
Glacier Guest Suite, p.232
Mt. Baker B&B, p. 233

**Glenwood**
Flying L Ranch, p. 234

**Index**
Bush House Country Inn, p. 235
A Stone's Throw B&B, p. 236

**Leavenworth**
All Season's River Inn, p. 237
Autumn Pond, p. 238
Blackbird Lodge, p. 240
Haus Lorelei, p. 241
Haus Rohrbach, p. 242
Pine River Ranch, p. 244
Run of the River, p. 245

**Maple Falls**
Country Hill B&B, p. 246
Yodeler Inn B&B, p. 248

**Morton**
St. Helens Manorhouse, p. 249

**North Bend**
Roaring River B&B, p. 250

**Rockport**
Brookhaven Lodge, p. 251

**Roslyn**
The Hummingbird Inn, p. 252

**Skykomish**
DeNonno's B&B, p. 253

**South Cle Elum**
Iron Horse Inn, p. 253

**Stehekin**
Stehekin Valley Ranch, p. 254

**Trout Lake**
The Farm, a B&B, p. 256
Llama Ranch B&B, p. 257

## ALEXANDER'S INN, Ashford

| Overall: ★★★★ | Room Quality: B | Value: C | Price: $99–$139 |
|---|---|---|---|

Less personal than a Mountain Meadows or a Growly Bear, Alexander's offers a small inn/historic hotel atmosphere. Attractively restored and ideally located just a mile from Mount Rainier National Park's Nisqually (west) entrance, it fills up early on summer weekends. The restaurant is a bit spotty, ranging from excellent to "Is this cook new?," but they're the best game in town for a celebration meal; seasonal outside dining is available. Tower suites, located in the signature turret, are fun; Upper Tower is for the youthful only, with a steep climb to the loft sleeping area.

### SETTING & FACILITIES

**Location:** On Hwy. 706, 12.1 mi. east of the Hwy. 7 junction and 1 mi. west of Mt. Rainier N.P. Nisqually entrance
**Near:** Ashford, Elbe, Glacier View Wilderness, Gifford Pinchot Nat'l Forest
**Building:** Historic hotel w/ turret
**Grounds:** Large lawn w/ trout pond, water wheel
**Public Space:** Guest lounge

**Food & Drink:** Wine at 5; full breakfast in restaurant
**Recreation:** Trout fishing for kids (catch their own breakfast); snowshoeing, mountain climbing, X-C skiing
**Amenities & Services:** Hot tub, fireplace, games, pay telephone; picnic lunches by arrangement; restaurant on premises

### ACCOMMODATIONS

**Units:** 12 guest rooms (some suites)
**All Rooms:** Standard hotel-style appointments
**Some Rooms:** Balcony or deck, sitting area
**Bed & Bath:** Queen; private baths, some ensuite
**Favorites:** Lower Tower Suite, Upper Tower Suite, Petite Suites

**Comfort & Decor:** Rooms are on the small side, but airy and well laid out; pale tones with wood accents and comfy quilts. Guest lounge is expansive, with many seating areas. Period reproduction and contemporary furnishings. Decorative woodwork and stained glass touches.

## RATES, RESERVATIONS, & RESTRICTIONS

**Deposit:** 1st night or 50%; 7-day cancellation
**Discounts:** Off-season, shoulder season; $15 add'l person
**Credit Cards:** V, MC
**Check-in/Out:** After 3/11
**Smoking:** No
**Pets:** No
**Kids:** Welcome

**Minimum Stay:** 2 nights, some holidays
**Open:** All year (except 12-24 & 25)
**Hosts:** Jerry & Bernadette Harnish, owners; Melinda Simpson, manager
37515 SR 706 East
Ashford, WA 98304
(800) 654-7615 or (360) 569-2300
Fax: (360) 569-2323

## GROWLY BEAR B&B, Ashford

Overall: ★★★½     Room Quality: C     Value: B     Price: $80–$110

This well-established bed-and-breakfast in one of the area's oldest historic buildings is a Mt. Rainier staple. Set back from the main road amidst the woods, you have a sense of quiet and privacy at Growly Bear, yet you're just a mile from the national park's west entrance. Attractive gardens, peaceful sunroom, and the soothing sounds of Goat Creek make for a pleasant retreat.

## SETTING & FACILITIES

**Location:** On Hwy. 706, 12 mi. east of the Hwy. 7 jct. and 1.1 mi. west of Mt. Rainier N.P. Nisqually entrance (just west of Alexander's Inn)
**Near:** Ashford, Elbe, Glacier View Wilderness, Gifford Pinchot Nat'l Forest
**Building:** Restored 1890 homestead
**Grounds:** 15 wooded acres w/ garden, adjoining Goat Creek

**Public Space:** Sunroom
**Food & Drink:** Coffee & tea; full breakfast
**Recreation:** Scenic driving, snowshoeing, mountain climbing, X-C skiing, photography, wildlife watching
**Amenities & Services:** Books, games

## ACCOMMODATIONS

**Units:** 4 guest rooms
**All Rooms:** Cozy country/Pacific Northwest decor
**Some Rooms:** Sitting area, futon, sofa-sleeper, balcony, hip-roof ceiling
**Bed & Bath:** Queen or double; 2 private baths, 2 share a bath
**Favorites:** The Mesler Room

**Comfort & Decor:** The common area and Mesler Room have the best light; Rainier Room is very spacious but a bit dark. Beljica and Nisqually, the shared-bath rooms, are small but cheerful, with slanted ceilings and cozy quilts. Woodsy, formerly rustic, homestead feel.

## RATES, RESERVATIONS, & RESTRICTIONS

**Deposit:** 1st night,;7-day cancellation, $10 fee

**Discounts:** $30 add'l person

**Credit Cards:** V, MC

**Check-in/Out:** After 4/11

**Smoking:** Outside (covered porch) only

**Pets:** No

**Kids:** Welcome

**Minimum Stay:** None

**Open:** All year (by reservation in off-season)

**Hosts:** Susan Jenny Johnson
37311 SR 706 East, P.O. Box 103
Ashford, WA 98304
(800) 700-2339 or (360) 569-2339

## JASMER'S AT MT. RAINIER, Ashford

| Overall: ★★★½ | Room Quality: B | Value: A | Price: $75–$95 |
|---|---|---|---|

While Jasmer's is only a two-unit bed-and-breakfast, we list them because (1) they also manage a selection of cabin/home rentals in the area, (2) they have their fingers on the pulse of everything that's going on in and around Ashford, and (3) we like their two bed-and-breakfast rooms a lot! The self-serve continental breakfast is a reasonable option to start an active day. The rooms are contemporary, with fine finish work and restful garden views. Even/odd-hour hot tub schedule assures privacy.

## SETTING & FACILITIES

**Location:** 7.2 mi. east of Hwy. 706/Hwy. 7 jct., 5.9 mi. west of Nisqually entrance to Mt. Rainier N.P.

**Near:** Ashford, Elbe, Glacier View Wilderness, Gifford Pinchot Nat'l Forest

**Building:** Structure separate from host's home

**Grounds:** Sprawling w/ flower garden surrounded by woods

**Public Space:** Units are self-contained

**Food & Drink:** Self-serve cont'l breakfast; snacks & coffee/tea supplies in room

**Recreation:** Historic touring, snowshoeing, mountain climbing, X-C skiing, wildlife watching

**Amenities & Services:** Hot tub

## ACCOMMODATIONS

**Units:** 2 guest rooms

**All Rooms:** TV, VCR, sound system, micro., fridge, dbl. shower, coffeemaker, private entrance, table & chairs

**Some Rooms:** Fireplace, bay window

**Bed & Bath:** Queen; private baths

**Favorites:** Songbird

**Comfort & Decor:** Upscale contemporary comfort includes romantic touches such as dimming wall sconces and classical/easy listening/jazz CDs. Decor in pale tones with wood and tile accents. Individually controlled heat, ceiling fans.

## RATES, RESERVATIONS, & RESTRICTIONS

**Deposit:** 1st night or 50%; 15-day cancellation
**Discounts:** Single occupancy, mid-week off-season
**Credit Cards:** V, MC
**Check-in/Out:** 4–8/11
**Smoking:** No
**Pets:** No
**Kids:** Over 10 welcome
**No-Nos:** More than 2 in a room (ask about cabin options)
**Minimum Stay:** None
**Open:** All year
**Hosts:** Tanna & Luke Osterhaus
30005 SR 706 East
Ashford, WA 98304
(360) 569-2682
Fax: (360) 569-8867
osterhaus1@juno.com
www.jasmers.com

## MOUNTAIN MEADOWS INN, Ashford

Overall: ★★★★½      Room Quality: A      Value: B      Price: $95–$125

This stylish inn has everything you look for in a bed-and-breakfast: upscale decor, fabulous food, personable hosts, and strong ties to the region it serves. Grounds are like a private park—very relaxing and secluded—yet just off the highway. Deluxe new hot tub. Michelle and Harry are the perfect hosts for your active Mt. Rainier–area visit: they are hikers and kayakers, they have food service backgrounds, and they are history buffs, with extensive knowledge of local history and the West in general. Highly recommended.

## SETTING & FACILITIES

**Location:** 6.5 mi. east of Hwy.
706/Hwy. 7 jct., 6.5 mi. west of Mt.
Rainier N.P.'s Nisqually entrance
**Near:** Ashford, Elbe, Glacier View
Wilderness, Gifford Pinchot Nat'l
Forest
**Building:** 1910 Craftsman home
**Grounds:** 10 acres surrounded by
woods; huge lawn, pond
**Public Space:** LR, DR, wraparound
porch

**Food & Drink:** Tea & coffee on
request; full breakfast
**Recreation:** Mountain climbing, X-C
skiing; stroll through woods to lumber
"ghost town"
**Amenities & Services:** Hot tub,
excellent library, guest phone, maps,
guidebooks, fireplace, sound system;
outstanding historic info

## ACCOMMODATIONS

**Units:** 5 guest rooms
**All Rooms:** Attractive appointments
**Some Rooms:** Brass bed, claw-foot
tub, extra bed(s), extra bedroom, table
& chairs, private entrance, simple
kitchen
**Bed & Bath:** Queen, queen & twin
(2), queen & double, 2 doubles, or king
plus daybed & trundle; private baths
**Favorites:** Chief Seattle, Mountain

Berry, Sunnybrook
**Comfort & Decor:** Common area
decor mixes Native American and
Northwest themes. Soft music
emanates from unseen speakers. Three
main-house guest rooms are quite
deluxe and upscale; adjacent guesthouse rooms are more motel-like but
quite serviceable, particularly for
families.

## RATES, RESERVATIONS, & RESTRICTIONS

**Deposit:** 1st night or 50%; 10-day
cancellation, $15 fee
**Discounts:** Off-season; $15 add'l
person
**Credit Cards:** V, MC
**Check-in/Out:** 4–6/11
**Smoking:** Outside only
**Pets:** By arrangement
**Kids:** Welcome in some rooms

**Minimum Stay:** 2 days, some rooms
during peak season
**Open:** All year
**Hosts:** Harry & Michelle Latimer
28912 SR 706 East, P.O. Box 291
Ashford, WA 98304
(360) 569-2788
mtmeadow@mashell.com
www.mtn-meadows-mt-rainier.com

| WELLSPRING, Ashford | | | |
| --- | --- | --- | --- |
| Overall: ★★★½ | Room Quality: C | Value: B | Price: $85–$125 |

Wellspring is so unique it almost defies description. Most units include a
simple breakfast basket, and all include beds (one hangs by huge ropes
from eye bolts in the ceiling. . .), so it's a "bed-and-breakfast," but it's
more than that. It's a holistic retreat, where access to hot tubs, saunas,

bodywork, and the woods provide a respite for mind and body. Lodgings are not for everyone. No telephone, only one unit has television (VCR in whimsical new Treehouse room). Pure Pacific Northwest, with metaphysical, back-to-the-land overtones. If that's your cup of herb tea, you'll love it—we do.

## SETTING & FACILITIES

**Location:** On Hwy. 706, 9.9 mi. east of the Hwy. 7 junction & 3.2 mi. west of Mt. Rainier N.P. Nisqually entrance (just west of Alexander's Inn)
**Near:** Ashford, Elbe, Glacier View Wilderness, Gifford Pinchot Nat'l Forest
**Building:** Collection of cabins & lodge-style buildings
**Grounds:** Wooded acreage w/ log gazebo

**Public Space:** N/A
**Food & Drink:** Simple cont'l breakfast & hot beverage service in most units
**Recreation:** Scenic driving, snowshoeing, mountain climbing, X-C skiing, photography
**Amenities & Services:** Hot tubs, saunas, BBQ; massage therapy by appointment (fee); weddings & retreats

## ACCOMMODATIONS

**Units:** 8 units (also large lodge that sleeps up to 14)
**All Rooms:** Unique Pacific Northwest atmosphere
**Some Rooms:** Cooking facil., disabled access
**Bed & Bath:** Various, private baths
**Favorites:** Depends on what you like!
**Comfort & Decor:** A one-of-a-kind Pacific Northwest original. Lodgings

are well-crafted but a bit rustic, and more than a bit quirky: one room has free-form waterfall shower, another shares its bath with the massage studio, another can't be occupied until after 9 p.m., another has no walls—just natural greenery—and a bed in the trees! Yet each is delightful if you're adventurous.

## RATES, RESERVATIONS, & RESTRICTIONS

**Deposit:** Credit card; 1-week cancellation
**Discounts:** Single occupancy, hot-tub discounts; $10 add'l person
**Credit Cards:** V, MC
**Check-in/Out:** After 3/11:30
**Smoking:** Outside only
**Pets:** No; host pets on premises
**Kids:** Welcome in some units

**Minimum Stay:** 2 nights on 3-day weekend
**Open:** All year
**Hosts:** Sunny Thompson-Ward
54922 Kernahan Rd.
Ashford, WA 98304
(360) 569-2514
Fax: (360) 569-2285

## CASCADE MOUNTAIN INN, Concrete

| Overall: ★★★ | Room Quality: C | Value: D | Price: $120 |
|---|---|---|---|

Off the west end of the North Cascades Highway (Hwy. 20), this five-room inn offers private baths and full breakfast in a serene Skagit Valley setting. Visitors to the North Cascades and Skagit River Valley in the 1980s may remember this well-loved inn under founders Ingrid and Gerhard Meyer. After a few years' closure, the inn reopened in 1998 under the ownership of enthusiastic Northwest hosts John and Sally Brummett, who live on-site in their own quarters. The Brummetts offer a country comfortable atmosphere in which guests can feel at home. Decadent desserts!

### SETTING & FACILITIES

**Location:** 24 mi. east of I-5 & 5 mi. west of Concrete just off Hwy. 20
**Near:** Baker Lake, Skagit River, North Cascades N.P.
**Building:** Gambrel-roofed (barn-shaped) country home built as B&B in 1984
**Grounds:** An acre of lawn amidst several acres w/ barn & orchard
**Public Space:** LR, DR, back patio, breezeway

**Food & Drink:** Evening dessert; beverages on request; full breakfast
**Recreation:** Bird-watching (including bald eagles), rafting, golf, hunting, winter sports
**Amenities & Services:** Guest fridge, games, sound system, fireplace; retreats, meetings, gatherings; lunches prepared (small fee; request)

### ACCOMMODATIONS

**Units:** 5 guest rooms
**All Rooms:** Robes, quality linens & toiletries, hairdryers
**Some Rooms:** Down comforters, feather beds, antique &/or custom furniture
**Bed & Bath:** Double (3), queen, or twins; private ensuite baths
**Favorites:** Sauk Mountain Room
**Comfort & Decor:** Living room has fireplace and comfy seating. Guest rooms are simply and tastefully furnished, with varied mountain-based themes. Most unusual is Scottish-theme Ben Nevis Room. Sauk has an impressive, rustic queen bed, plus bentwood furniture. Rainier has antiques, whimsy. Baker is yellow and pale pine.

## RATES, RESERVATIONS, & RESTRICTIONS

**Deposit:** 1st night; 72-hour cancellation
**Discounts:** $20 add'l person, roll-away & breakfast included
**Credit Cards:** V, MC
**Check-in/Out:** 4 or by arrangement/11
**Smoking:** Outside only
**Pets:** No; host pets on site
**Kids:** 10 & older welcome

**Minimum Stay:** None
**Open:** All year
**Hosts:** Sally & John Brumett
40418 Pioneer Ln.
Concrete-Birdsview, WA 98237
(360) 826-4333
Fax: (360) 826-3623
casmi1@gte.net
home1.gte.net/casmi1

## OVENELL'S HERITAGE INN, Concrete

Overall: ★★★½    Room Quality: C    Value: B    Price: $80–$115

Sitting in your plush terry robe, gazing across vast Skagit Valley acreage dotted with Maine-Anjou range cattle, listening to roosters competing to announce the sunrise over Mt. Baker—that's morning at Ovenell's. The in-home, old-fashioned bed-and-breakfast experience, complete with shared bathrooms for three of the rooms, is not for everyone, but those who appreciate the welcoming ambiance of a clean, well-run bed-and-breakfast on a busy working ranch will love it. Breakfast includes fresh-from-the-hen eggs and other hearty farm fare served in the antique-filled Mt.-Baker-view dining room on silver service. Do yourself a favor and stay a few days.

## SETTING & FACILITIES

**Location:** Just outside Concrete, south of Hwy. 20
**Near:** Concrete, Skagit & Sauk Rivers, North Cascades N.P., Baker Lake
**Building:** 1915 ranch house & 2-room guest house
**Grounds:** 500-acre cattle ranch; garden, fenced playground, river access, beaver ponds, pastures
**Public Space:** LR, DR

**Food & Drink:** In-room chocolate & candy dish; evening coffee or tea & dessert; full breakfast
**Recreation:** Wildlife (& farm animal) watching, fishing, X-C skiing; nearby mountain hiking, rafting, golf, hunting
**Amenities & Services:** TV/VCR, library, wood stove; horse boarding avail.; evening turndown; weddings, other gatherings; special occasion extras

## ACCOMMODATIONS

**Units:** 6 guest rooms (4 in main house, 2 in guest house)
**All Rooms:** Robes, fresh flowers, closet, carpet, quality linens & beds
**Some Rooms:** Guest house has laundry facil., full kitchen w/ appliances/ cookware/tableware, LR w/ TV/VCR/ sound system, sofa-sleeper, & private deck
**Bed & Bath:** 3 private baths (1 in main house & both in guest house); 3 share a bath

**Favorites:** Heirloom, Heritage, Windsor
**Comfort & Decor:** Heirloom antiques mingle with relaxed farmhouse charm in main house. Rooms are smallish but comfortable, and surprisingly well-lit for a house of this vintage. Softly ornate wallpapers with dark wood trim. Guest house is actually a trailer; its rooms are decorated in pleasant contemporary country comfort, with a few heirloom pieces.

## RATES, RESERVATIONS, & RESTRICTIONS

**Deposit:** Credit card; 24-hour cancellation
**Discounts:** Off-season
**Credit Cards:** V, MC, AE
**Check-in/Out:** 2 or by arrangement/11
**Smoking:** No
**Pets:** Welcome
**Kids:** Welcome
**Minimum Stay:** None

**Open:** All year
**Hosts:** Eleanor & Norm Ovenell, Cindy Ovenell, Helen Ovenell, Kris Hansen
46276 Concrete-Sauk Valley Rd.
Concrete, WA 98237
(360) 853-8494
Fax: (360) 853-8279
breakfast@ovenells-inn.com
www.ovenells-inn.com

## GLACIER GUEST SUITE, Glacier

| Overall: ★★★★½ | Room Quality: A | Value: B | Price: $95–$125 |
| --- | --- | --- | --- |

Private mountain hideaway on 100-acre homestead with stunning view of Mt. Baker and North Fork Nooksack River valley. The dirt drive up is a bit bumpy but short. Hosts also own nearby Alpenglow Farms produce and goodies stand, which offers travelers on Highway 542 scrumptious berry milkshakes, sundaes and such, plus bakery items (such as those in your generous continental breakfast) and specialty foods featuring Northwest ingredients. Your classy single-unit suite has fabulous view, beautiful craftsmanship, and upscale rustic ambiance.

## SETTING & FACILITIES

**Location:** Just above Hwy. 542 between Maple Falls & Glacier
**Near:** Glacier, Maple Falls, Mt. Baker
**Building:** Private hillside home w/ attached guest suite
**Grounds:** Hillside, natural wooded setting
**Public Space:** Entire 500-sq.-ft. suite for your use

**Food & Drink:** Hot beverages, popcorn; generous self-serve cont'l breakfast
**Recreation:** Winter sports, rafting, bird-watching, wildlife watching, photography, hunting
**Amenities & Services:** See "All Rooms" below

## ACCOMMODATIONS

**Units:** 1 suite
**All Rooms:** Studio suite has wet bar w/ mini-fridge, micro., toaster oven, & coffee press; TV/VCR & a few videos (rentals nearby); gas fireplace; sofa-sleeper, couch, table & chairs; alarm clock; private entry; guest guide; quality toiletries

**Bed & Bath:** Queen; shower/tub unit
**Comfort & Decor:** Beamed, vaulted, knotty pine ceiling emphasizes the awesome view. Teal carpet, rustic-chic log-post bed. "Pacific Northwest meets Southwest" decor. Lovely cedar bath with view, dimmer switch. Gas fireplace controlled by thermostat.

## RATES, RESERVATIONS, & RESTRICTIONS

**Deposit:** 50%; 14-day cancellation
**Discounts:** Weekdays; $10 add'l person
**Credit Cards:** Taken for deposit only
**Check-in/Out:** After 4 (please call w/ arrival time)/ noon
**Smoking:** No
**Pets:** No
**Kids:** Call (unit best suited for two adults)

**Minimum Stay:** None
**Open:** All year
**Hosts:** Bill Devine & Monica Gowen
P.O. Box 5237
Glacier, WA 98244
(360) 599-2927 (no phone in suite)
Fax: Same as phone
mgowan@pacificrim.net,
www.alpenglowfarms.com

## MT. BAKER B&B, Glacier

| Overall: ★★½ | Room Quality: D | Value: C | Price: $75–$95 |
|---|---|---|---|

Home and hosts are young and hip; property appeals to the active crowd. Decor is sparse and not of highest quality, but everything is fresh and clean, and the guest book comments show that people love the casual, upbeat atmosphere. Two Rottweilers on premises; guest interaction optional. Opened December 1997. Vel and Jacques bill their inn as "the closest bed-and-breakfast to Mt. Baker with a view of the mountain."

## SETTING & FACILITIES

**Location:** Half-mile off Hwy. 542, 1 mi. west of Glacier
**Near:** Maple Falls, Mt. Baker
**Building:** Chalet-style private residence
**Grounds:** Natural, wooded setting

**Public Space:** Living/dining room
**Food & Drink:** Full breakfast
**Recreation:** Hiking, winter/water activities, mushrooming, berry picking
**Amenities & Services:** Hot tub, videos, fridge access, phone access

## ACCOMMODATIONS

**Units:** 3 guest rooms
**All Rooms:** TV/VCR, carpet, chairs, robes, & rubber sandals (for hot tub), phone jacks (phones avail.)
**Some Rooms:** Private entrance, private patio
**Bed & Bath:** Queens; 1 private bath, 2 share a bath
**Favorites:** Room w/ private bath & deck

**Comfort & Decor:** Southwestern theme to "warm you up" here in snow country. Living/dining area has vaulted ceiling and woodstove. Furnishings and fixtures are modest but new and fresh. Rooms are a bit dim and lack good reading light. Central forced-air furnace plus wood heat; rooms also have auxiliary electric heaters.

## RATES, RESERVATIONS, & RESTRICTIONS

**Deposit:** Credit card; 5-day cancellation
**Discounts:** Midweek off-season; $15 add'l person
**Credit Cards:** V, MC
**Check-in/Out:** 4–5 or by arrangement/11
**Smoking:** Outside only
**Pets:** By prior arrangement (case-by-case); host dogs on site

**Kids:** Welcome
**Minimum Stay:** Major holidays only
**Open:** All year
**Hosts:** Vel Dearman & Jacques Massie
9447 Mt. Baker Hwy.
Glacier, WA 98244
(360) 599-2299
Fax: Same as phone
Mtbakerbnb@aol.com
members.aol.com/mtbakerbnb/index.html

## FLYING L RANCH, Glenwood

| Overall: ★★★ | Room Quality: C | Value: C | Price: $70–$140 |
|---|---|---|---|

This longstanding guest ranch, dating back to the 1940s, survives as an eco-sensitive nature preserve under the able stewardship of Jacquie Perry and Jeff Berend, who purchased it from the Lloyd family in 1997. Fabulous location for accessing the wonders of Mt. Adams. Flying L makes a great group retreat center but is also a pleasant place for a couple or family. Enjoy a hearty breakfast at long, picnic-style tables with your fellow guests. Not fancy, but great energy and a beautiful location.

## SETTING & FACILITIES

**Location:** A mi. NE of Glenwood, which is 31 mi. NE of White Salmon, WA (just across the river from Hood River, OR)
**Near:** Mt. Adams, Glenwood, Trout Lake, Conboy Nat'l Wildlife Refuge, rivers, Indian Heaven Wilderness, Columbia Gorge Nat'l Scenic Area
**Building:** 4,000-sq.-ft. 1945 ranch house; 2-story 1948 guest house; 3 cabins
**Grounds:** 80 wooded & meadowed acres w/ pond, wildflowers, wildlife, trails
**Public Space:** Cookhouse (DR), lodge LR, kitchens; cabins have individual living/dining/kitchen areas
**Food & Drink:** Tea; early coffee; full breakfast
**Recreation:** On-site X-C skiing, lawn games, ice skating in season; nearby rafting, horseback riding, llama pack trips
**Amenities & Services:** Hot tub, kitchen facil., lodge fireplace, library, piano, stereo, bicycles, games, puzzles, cots, cribs, high chairs, maps, BBQs, horse corral, yurt (meeting tent); group retreats & meetings, catered meals/sack lunches by arrangement

## ACCOMMODATIONS

**Units:** 8 guest rooms, 1 suite, 3 cabins
**All Rooms:** Clean & comfortable
**Some Rooms:** Mt. Adams view, fireplace, desk, sitting area, mini-fridge
**Bed & Bath:** Double or queen, several w/ extra bed; private baths
**Favorites:** Charles Russell Room, Mt. Adams Suite, The Log Cabin
**Comfort & Decor:** Simple, clean, high-country living. Room decor ranges from woodsy and humble to sort of Country Gentleman, with wood paneling, artwork, and Western artifacts. Electric and woodstove heat.

## RATES, RESERVATIONS, & RESTRICTIONS

**Deposit:** 1st night; 7-day cancellation (groups 50%, 1-month cancellation); refunds contingent upon rebooking
**Discounts:** Midweek Dec.–March; $10 add'l person
**Credit Cards:** V, MC, AE
**Check-in/Out:** 3–8 or by arrangement/11
**Smoking:** Outside only
**Pets:** No; horse corral & host dogs on site
**Kids:** Welcome
**Minimum Stay:** 2 nights in cabins & most Sat.; 3 nights, some holidays
**Open:** All year
**Hosts:** Jacquie Perry & Jeff Berend
25 Flying L Ln.
Glenwood, WA 98619
(888) MT ADAMS or (509) 364-3488
Fax: (509) 364-3634
flyingl@mt-adams.com
www.mt-adams.com

## BUSH HOUSE COUNTRY INN, Index

| Overall: ★★½ | Room Quality: D | Value: B | Price: $59–$80 |
|---|---|---|---|

Historic ambiance is yours at this restored turn-of-the-century inn. Not for those who need the predictable surroundings of a modern chain hotel—the place has its quirks (see "Comfort & Decor"), but is charming, and the food is good. Bring earplugs for the train noise. Beautiful setting, great hiking access. Not as deluxe as nearby "A Stone's Throw," but more rooms, and children are welcome.

## SETTING & FACILITIES

**Location:** From the bridge into Index, 2 blocks straight ahead on your left
**Near:** Hwy. 2, Skykomish, Gold Bar, Monroe, Stevens Pass ski area
**Building:** 1898 historic hotel
**Grounds:** Abundant roses
**Public Space:** Parlor, lounge, TV room, restaurant
**Food & Drink:** Cont'l breakfast, or apply toward purchase of full breakfast at restaurant
**Recreation:** Hiking, skiing, rafting
**Amenities & Services:** TV, on-site restaurant & full bar

## ACCOMMODATIONS

**Units:** 11 guest rooms
**All Rooms:** Period furnishings
**Some Rooms:** Garden view
**Bed & Bath:** Double, queen, or king; 2 shared bathrooms (1 room has private toilet & sink)
**Favorites:** #1 is largest, most deluxe; #11 has private half bath
**Comfort & Decor:** Carpet & wainscoting in common areas. Guest rooms are small (except #1, a studio suite with king bed and sitting area), with brass or wicker period furnishings, lace curtains. Individually controlled baseboard heat; no AC. "Historic ambiance" includes slightly uneven floors, sometimes-quirky pipes and fuses, and a loud train nearby.

## RATES, RESERVATIONS, & RESTRICTIONS

**Deposit:** Credit card; 48-hour cancellation
**Discounts:** Entire building, extended stays; $10 add'l person
**Credit Cards:** V, MC
**Check-in/Out:** After 3 or by arrangement/noon
**Smoking:** Outside only
**Pets:** No
**Kids:** Welcome
**Minimum Stay:** None
**Open:** All year
**Hosts:** Staff
300 Fifth St., Index, WA 98256
(360) 793-2312
Fax: (360) 793-3673

## A STONE'S THROW B&B, Index

| Overall: ★★★★ | Room Quality: A | Value: A | Price: $81 |
|---|---|---|---|

The loving craftsmanship of this hand-restored home shows in every luminous detail. The hardwoods gleam, the sun streams in through the windows, and all the amenities you might require are thoughtfully available. Outside, the gardens are thick with vegetables, herbs, and flowers; the hot tub beckons for a posthike or prebreakfast soak. Breakfasts are a delight for the senses—gourmet, organic, and mindful of your dietary needs and preferences. This single-unit inn is one of our Cascade Mountain favorites.

## SETTING & FACILITIES

**Location:** West of Bush House, just past the railroad tracks
**Near:** Bush House Restaurant, Highway 2, Skykomish, Gold Bar, Monroe, Stevens Pass ski area
**Building:** Restored 1912 home
**Grounds:** Beautiful organic gardens w/ waterfall, raised beds, paths, rock work

**Public Space:** Plenty of sitting space in private suite (see below); also DR, sun porch
**Food & Drink:** Coffee/tea; full breakfast
**Recreation:** Hiking, skiing, rafting
**Amenities & Services:** Outdoor spa

## ACCOMMODATIONS

**Units:** 1 suite
**All Rooms:** Fresh flowers, garden & Mt. Index views, elegant antiques, TV, VCR, videos, sound system, coffee bar, writing desk
**Bed & Bath:** Queen, private bath
**Comfort & Decor:** The entire 2nd

floor is your guest suite, including a bedroom, sitting room, and private bath. Natural fir paneling, hardwood floors, hip roof, tile bath. Modern amenities, old-fashioned warmth. Elegant, peaceful, very comfortable. Expect noise from the adjacent train.

## RATES, RESERVATIONS, & RESTRICTIONS

**Deposit:** $25/night; 48-hour cancellation
**Discounts:** Single occupancy, no breakfast; price includes tax
**Credit Cards:** Not accepted
**Check-in/Out:** After 2/11 or by arrangement
**Smoking:** No
**Pets:** No

**Kids:** No
**No-Nos:** Shoes in the house
**Minimum Stay:** 2 nights preferred on holidays
**Open:** All year
**Hosts:** David & Lynn
P.O. Box 164, Index, WA 98256
(360) 793-0100
Fax: Same as phone

## ALL SEASON'S RIVER INN, Leavenworth

Overall: ★★★★★     Room Quality: A     Value: B     Price: $100–$150

Spectacular river views are yours from every room of this gracious inn. Far more attractive inside than out, this built-to-be-a-B&B building is sumptuously decorated and filled with amenities to anticipate your every need. Where our other local favorite (Run of the River) is "Pacific Northwest upscale rustic," All Seasons River Inn is elegant and posh—a delightful place to pamper yourself. Kathy and Jeff are marvelous hosts—warm and accommodating, never intrusive. Rooms are spacious and private.

## SETTING & FACILITIES

**Location:** I mi. from Hwy. 2/Icicle Rd. intersection
**Near:** "Bavarian" village, rivers, ski areas, Lake Wenatchee, Wenatchee, The Enchantments, Alpine Lakes
**Building:** Contemporary 2-level home built as a B&B in 1991
**Grounds:** On the banks of the Wenatchee River
**Public Space:** LR, DR, TV lounge, deck

**Food & Drink:** In-room truffles; hot beverages & soft-drink honor bar; full breakfast
**Recreation:** Skiing, rafting, fishing, golf, sleigh rides, snowmobiling, festivals
**Amenities & Services:** Binoculars, bicycles, birding (and other) books, fridge, TV/VCR, videos, guest phones; dining/sight-seeing arrangements, celebration extras

## ACCOMMODATIONS

**Units:** 4 guest rooms, 2 suites
**All Rooms:** Robes, sitting area, teddy bears, central music
**Some Rooms:** Whirlpool (5), sitting room, fireplace, fridge, deck, ceiling fan, glider swing
**Bed & Bath:** Queen, roll-away avail.; private ensuite baths
**Favorites:** Evergreen Suite, River Bend Suite

**Comfort & Decor:** Airy and contemporary, with fine fabrics and furnishings both ornate and comfortable. Varied motifs. Pale backgrounds accented with contemporary tones and furnished with traditional styling. Hand-stenciling is subtle and attractive. Fine antique furnishings. Top-of-the-line fixtures.

## RATES, RESERVATIONS, & RESTRICTIONS

**Deposit:** 1st night; 10-day cancellation (30 days peak season)
**Discounts:** Special packages; $20 add'l person
**Credit Cards:** V, MC
**Check-in/Out:** After 3/11
**Smoking:** No
**Pets:** No
**Kids:** 16 & older only
**No-Nos:** Shoes in house

**Minimum Stay:** 2 nights weekends, festivals, holidays
**Open:** All year
**Hosts:** Kathy & Jeff Falconer
8751 Icicle Rd., P.O. Box 788
Leavenworth, WA 98826
(800) 254-0555 or (509) 548-1425
allriver@rightathome.com
www.allseasonsriverinn.com

## AUTUMN POND, Leavenworth

| Overall: ★★★ | Room Quality: C | Value: B | Price: $69–$89 |
| --- | --- | --- | --- |

This clean, contemporary home was built as a bed-and-breakfast in 1992. Current owners purchased in 1998. Large pond is home to many trout and a friendly cadre of hand-fed ducks. Surroundings are comfortable, fresh, and uncluttered. The guest lounge, with its woodstove, upholstered furnishings, and several tables, makes a pleasant place to hang out and enjoy a board game and a cup of tea. No TV; soft music. Hosts live on site but in separate quarters. Your host has a culinary background; his fresh baguettes are heavenly.

## SETTING & FACILITIES

**Location:** .75 mi. uphill from downtown, on Titus north of Pine
**Near:** Club West Health Club, outdoor amphitheater, "Bavarian" village, rivers, ski areas, Lake Wenatchee, Wenatchee, The Enchantments, Alpine Lakes
**Building:** Contemporary 2-level home
**Grounds:** 3 acres w/ trout/duck pond, deck, & Tumwater Mountain view
**Public Space:** Guest lounge

(living/dining area)
**Food & Drink:** Tea, cider, cocoa; coffee on request; full breakfast, early cont'l option
**Recreation:** On-site catch-and-release fishing; rafting, sleigh rides, festivals, golf
**Amenities & Services:** Hot tub, guest fridge, games, woodstove, BBQ, binoculars, health club passes ($6), cookbook library; dining & activity arrangements

## ACCOMMODATIONS

**Units:** 6 guest rooms
**All Rooms:** Carpet, artwork
**Some Rooms:** Themes, quilts
**Bed & Bath:** Queen (roll-away avail.); private ensuite baths
**Favorites:** 1 ("Bear" theme) & 2
**Comfort & Decor:** Contemporary

country/rustic, with newer upholstered furnishings, art prints. Guest rooms are smallish and motel-like but nicer, with pine beds, quilts or printed spreads, art prints, and rustic or country themes (e.g., Bear, Duck, Birdhouse). Central heat, AC.

## RATES, RESERVATIONS, & RESTRICTIONS

**Deposit:** Credit card; 7-day cancellation
**Discounts:** Off-season
**Credit Cards:** V, MC
**Check-in/Out:** 3–6 or by arrangement/11
**Smoking:** Outside only
**Pets:** No; host cats & Golden Retriever on site (outside)
**Kids:** 5 & older welcome; younger by arrangement

**Minimum Stay:** 2 nights, festivals & holidays
**Open:** All year
**Hosts:** John & Jennifer Lorenz
10388 Titus Rd.
Leavenworth, WA 98826
(800) 222-9661 or (509) 548-4482
info@autumnpond.com
www.autumnpond.com

## BLACKBIRD LODGE, Leavenworth

| Overall: ★★★½ | Room Quality: B | Value: B | Price: $79–$98 |
|---|---|---|---|

More a contemporary small hotel than a bed-and-breakfast (though breakfast is served, it's neither the focus nor the forté), Blackbird Lodge provides a predictable, upscale experience for the traveler wanting to be "in the middle of it all" in Leavenworth. You're a short stroll to all the town has to offer, from shopping and dining to exploring the trails of Blackbird Island. The attractive, clean-line decor and professional staff will make city-hotel denizens comfortable; lacking are the warmth, intimacy, and landscaped grounds of the more traditional bed-and-breakfasts.

### SETTING & FACILITIES

**Location:** Corner of 8th & Commercial in the heart of "Bavarian" downtown

**Near:** Blackbird Island, Wenatchee River, Front St.; Icicle River, ski areas, Lake Wenatchee, Wenatchee, The Enchantments, Alpine Lakes

**Building:** 1993 four-story hotel

**Grounds:** N/A

**Public Space:** Guest lounge

**Food & Drink:** Honor basket snacks & beverages in rooms; extended cont'l (w/ hot entree) delivered to room

**Recreation:** Rafting, fishing, golf, bird-watching, sleigh rides, snowmobiling, festivals

**Amenities & Services:** Gas log fireplace, elevator, hot tub; meeting room avail.

### ACCOMMODATIONS

**Units:** 20 guest rooms (remodel in progress to 15 rooms, 5 suites)

**All Rooms:** Phone, TV

**Some Rooms:** Whirlpool, private deck, fireplace

**Bed & Bath:** Queen or 2 queens, several w/ extra twin(s); private ensuite baths

**Favorites:** Ask about new suites

**Comfort & Decor:** Artistic, contemporary European Inn. Slate entry, pale olive walls, rich wood trim, contemporary artwork. While self-described as "rustic Bavarian," we'd call it a clean, crisp, slightly avant garde hotel, very unlike the "tourist Bavarian" kitsch of the village. Some sound transference from adjoining rooms and halls.

### RATES, RESERVATIONS, & RESTRICTIONS

**Deposit:** Credit card; 72-hour cancellation, 30 days in Dec.

**Discounts:** Sun.–Thurs., AAA, military, AARP, special packages; $10 add'l person, $2.50 kids under 12

**Credit Cards:** V, MC, AE, D

**Check-in/Out:** After 3/11

**Smoking:** No

**Pets:** No

**Kids:** Welcome

**Minimum Stay:** 2 nights, weekends; 2–3 nights, festivals & holidays

**Open:** All year

**Hosts:** Bill Brownlee & staff
305 8th St., Leavenworth, WA 98826
(800) 446-0240 or (509) 548-5800
Fax: (509) 548-7134
bedfindr@televar.com
http://www.bedfinders.com/lodging/lea venworth/ (listed under "hotels")

## HAUS LORELEI, Leavenworth

| Overall: ★★★★ | Room Quality: B | Value: C | Price: $95–$109 |

What a marvelous location—quiet and wooded, overlooking the river, yet a short stroll to the excitement of downtown Leavenworth. Behind-the-scenes precision ensures a professional-quality stay, but a "no-keys" casualness makes you feel at home. "Hands-on" heirloom European antiques are stunning. Large inn does an excellent job of providing areas for families and areas for adults. Large house dog and very authoritative cat. A unique place; very well suited to Leavenworth. Breakfast room is large and sunny, with many tables.

### SETTING & FACILITIES

**Location:** End of Division St., overlooking Wenatchee River
**Near:** "Bavarian" village, rivers, ski areas, Lake Wenatchee, Wenatchee, The Enchantments, Alpine Lakes
**Building:** 1903 three-story river-rock & shingle-faced lumber company property
**Grounds:** Quiet, wooded setting; spacious lawn; overlooks Wenatchee River & trails
**Public Space:** LR, billiards room, dining sunroom, upstairs TV/sitting room

**Food & Drink:** Afternoon tea & snack; early coffee; full breakfast
**Recreation:** Fishing, golf, bird-watching, sleigh rides, snowmobiling, festivals
**Amenities & Services:** Hot tub (8 a.m.–10 p.m.), 1886 billiards table (10 a.m.–9 p.m., adults only), river rock fireplace, tennis court (seasonal), tennis racquets & balls, mountain bikes, boats for rafting, games, guest phone, TV, fridge/ice, gift shop; wedding receptions, reunions, meetings, retreats

### ACCOMMODATIONS

**Units:** 10 guest rooms
**All Rooms:** Mountain or river view, robes
**Some Rooms:** Extra-high ceiling, private balcony, outside entrance, extra bed(s), bay window seat, sitting area, antique bed(s), TV
**Bed & Bath:** King or queen, many w/ add'l bed(s); private ensuite baths
**Favorites:** Prinzessin or Rotkäppchen

for 2, Schnee Wittchen for family
**Comfort & Decor:** Homey touches mix with contemporary furnishings and stunning antiques. Spacious rooms. Warm, homey European feel, yet professionally run. Elaborate wallpapers. Extra-high ceilings in downstairs (more romantic) rooms; pitched & dormered ceilings in upstairs (more family-oriented) rooms. Baseboard heat.

## RATES, RESERVATIONS, & RESTRICTIONS

**Deposit:** Full amount; 14-day cancellation
**Discounts:** $20 add'l person, $10 child
**Credit Cards:** Not accepted
**Check-in/Out:** 3–9/11
**Smoking:** No
**Pets:** No; host pets on site
**Kids:** Welcome in upstairs rooms
**No-Nos:** After-hours use of hot tub or billiards table; kids using billiards table; running/horseplay in house
**Minimum Stay:** 2 nights, weekends
**Open:** All year
**Hosts:** Elisabeth & Richard Saunders
347 Division St.
Leavenworth, WA 98826
(800) 514-8868 or (509) 548-5726
Fax: (509) 548-6548
info@hauslorelei.com
www.hauslorelei.com

## HAUS ROHRBACH, Leavenworth

| Overall: ★★★½ | Room Quality: C | Value: C | Price: $75–$165 |
|---|---|---|---|

Established in 1978, this clean, comfortable, easygoing inn is perched on a hillside overlooking the Wenatchee Valley and backed up to Tumwater Mountain. The huge, gently sloping front lawn makes a great winter sledding hill. Experienced hosts offer an unpretentious atmosphere free of TV and telephones. Breakfast may include sourdough pancakes, Dutch babies, omelettes, or eggs and seasoned potatoes—delicious and abundant.

## SETTING & FACILITIES

**Location:** 1.5 mi. from downtown, at end of Ranger Rd. off Ski Hill Rd.
**Near:** Leavenworth Ski Hill, Tumwater Mountain, "Bavarian" village, rivers, ski areas, Lake Wenatchee, Wenatchee, The Enchantments, Alpine Lakes
**Building:** 1975 three-level Bavarian-style hillside home
**Grounds:** 14 acres on gentle hillside
**Public Space:** Common room (living/dining) w/ seating areas, kids' playroom, balcony

**Food & Drink:** Tea, coffee, cider, cocoa, ice water; desserts avail. for purchase in evening; full breakfast; feature suites have ensuite dining option
**Recreation:** Sledding, drive or hike up mountain; nearby rafting, fishing, golf, sleigh rides, snowmobiling, festivals
**Amenities & Services:** Hot tub, heated pool (summer), games, sound system, X-C ski trail pass sales

## ACCOMMODATIONS

**Units:** 5 guest rooms, 5 suites
**All Rooms:** Deck, fresh flowers
**Some Rooms:** View, balcony, sitting area/room, fireplace, sound system, dbl. whirlpool, table & chairs, micro., fridge, coffeemaker, separate entrance, robes
**Bed & Bath:** Various, several w/ more than 1 bed; 8 private baths, 2 share a bath
**Favorites:** Snowberry, Larkspur, Wildflower

**Comfort & Decor:** Casual, homey, very clean, uncluttered. Fresh carpet, vinyls, & wallpaper throughout. Wood-stove heat; individual room AC & auxiliary baseboard heat. Feature suites (detached Snowberry & Larkspur, attached Wildflower) offer extra amenities, a stone-backed fireplace, and tile bath with dual-headed shower.

## RATES, RESERVATIONS, & RESTRICTIONS

**Deposit:** 1st night; 14-day cancellation (30 days in Dec. or for groups)
**Discounts:** Off-season Thurs., off-season 3-for-2; $20 add'l person; $10 kids under 12
**Credit Cards:** V, MC, AE, D
**Check-in/Out:** 2–9 or by arrangement/11
**Smoking:** Outdoors only
**Pets:** No
**Kids:** Welcome
**No-Nos:** Noise 11 p.m.–7:30 a.m.

**Minimum Stay:** Winter weekends, holidays, festivals
**Open:** All year (except 2 weeks in Nov.)
**Hosts:** Bob & Kathryn Harrild
12882 Ranger Rd.
Leavenworth, WA 98826
(800) 548-4477 or (509) 548-7024
Fax: (509) 548-5038
rkh@rightathome.com
www.hausrohrbach.com

## PINE RIVER RANCH, Leavenworth

| Overall: ★★★★ | Room Quality: B | Value: C | Price: $95–$160 |
| --- | --- | --- | --- |

We have nothing but praise for this ranch bed-and-breakfast. All of its rooms are pleasant and well-appointed, with upgrades constantly in progress, moving this solid 4-star property toward the 4.5 luxury category. The grounds are rural and great for strolling. The dog and cat are well behaved (trained to stay out of guest quarters) and sweet; the horses, llama, and goat complete the hobby-ranch atmosphere. Your hosts' food-service background means good eats!

### SETTING & FACILITIES

**Location:** On Hwy. 207, 1.8 mi. off Hwy. 2, 16 mi. west of Leavenworth
**Near:** Ski area, golf course, "Bavarian" village, Lake Wenatchee, rivers, The Enchantments, Alpine Lakes
**Building:** 1941 dairy farmhouse & outbuildings
**Grounds:** 32 acres w/ creek, pond, wildlife, forest, meadow, horse barn
**Public Space:** Sitting room, DR, front porch (suites have own sitting rooms)
**Food & Drink:** Hot beverages & ice; early coffee; full breakfast (ensuite for Lodgepole & Ponderosa suites); optional cont'l on request
**Recreation:** On-site animal watching (wild & domestic), river swimming, X-C skiing, snowshoeing, horseshoes, croquet; rafting, sleigh rides, dog sledding, fishing, mountain biking, festivals
**Amenities & Services:** Hot tub, fireplace, videos, games, snowshoes, guest pantry, amusing guest guide; recreational (horseback riding, rafting, skiing) packages

## ACCOMMODATIONS

**Units:** 3 guest rooms, 2 suites (plus 2 new suites in progress)
**All Rooms:** Robes, TV/VCR, sound system, hot tub thongs
**Some Rooms:** View, sitting area, deck, fireplace, dbl. whirlpool, private entrance, canopy bed, kitchenette (mini-fridge, wet bar, micro., coffee/espresso maker), ceiling fan, sofabed, binoculars
**Bed & Bath:** Queen; private ensuite baths

**Favorites:** Ponderosa Suite, Lodge-pole Suite
**Comfort & Decor:** Main house and rooms within it are contemporary upscale country. Outside suites are Pacific Northwest rustic-elegant, with pine pole beds, tile baths, stone-hearthed fireplaces, and deluxe fix-tures. Rooms have individual heat control (thermostat-controlled gas fireplaces in some).

## RATES, RESERVATIONS, & RESTRICTIONS

**Deposit:** 1st night; 14-day cancella-tion, 10% fee
**Discounts:** Single occupancy, extended stay, special packages; $15 add'l person
**Credit Cards:** V, MC, AE, D
**Check-in/Out:** After 3/11
**Smoking:** Outside only
**Pets:** No; host pets on site
**Kids:** 12 & older welcome
**No-Nos:** Noise after 10 p.m. &

before 8 a.m.
**Minimum Stay:** 2 nights
**Open:** All year
**Hosts:** Michael & Mary Ann Zenk
19668 Highway 207
Leavenworth, WA 98826
(800) 669-3877 or (509) 763-3959
Fax: (509) 763-2073
lodger@televar.com
www.lakewenatchee.com

## RUN OF THE RIVER, Leavenworth

| Overall: ★★★★★ | Room Quality: A | Value: B | Price: $100–$155 |
| --- | --- | --- | --- |

You've never seen "rustic" like this! Monty and Karen Turner's Run of the River takes the natural materials and outdoor beauty of the Pacific Northwest and turns them into an upscale experience you'll long remember. The grounds are a great place to watch birds and butterflies; adjacency to state-protected land enhances sense of isolation. Lots of amenities and services for the outdoor-minded; great food, attractively presented. We love the way the Turners have integrated nature into their bed-and-breakfast inside and out, yet provide an experience that's decidedly deluxe.

## SETTING & FACILITIES

**Location:** A mi. down E. Leavenworth Rd. from Hwy. 2 (just east of Wenatchee River bridge east of downtown)
**Near:** "Bavarian" village, rivers, ski areas, Lake Wenatchee, Wenatchee, The Enchantments, Alpine Lakes
**Building:** Elegant-rustic Pacific Northwest lodge-style home
**Grounds:** 2 acres of wildflowers & natural vegetation along Wenatchee River
**Public Space:** Guest LR/lounge, 2nd floor sitting/phone room
**Food & Drink:** Evening coffee, tea, treats; early coffee; full breakfast
**Recreation:** Rafting, fishing, golf, bird-watching, sleigh rides, snowmobiling, festivals
**Amenities & Services:** Bicycles (including a tandem), snowshoes, binoculars, guest phone, library, TV, hot tub, *Seattle PI & NY Times*, gift shop, piano; in-room licensed massage avail.; in-room flowers &/or treats avail.

## ACCOMMODATIONS

**Units:** 5 guest rooms, 1 suite
**All Rooms:** TV, fridge, binoculars, hairdryers, tile bath, private or semi-private deck
**Some Rooms:** Whirlpool, woodstove, river view, reading loft, table & chairs, porch swing
**Bed & Bath:** Queens; private ensuite baths
**Favorites:** Tumwater Suite
**Comfort & Decor:** Uniquely Northwest decor features craftsmanship of local artisans. Hand-hewn log furniture; subtle handiwork like birchbark trash baskets, buckwheat-filled neck pillows. Fabrics & textures blend denim, coarse-weave textiles, leather, plaid. "LL Bean meets Northern Exposure." Lots of natural wood.

## RATES, RESERVATIONS, & RESTRICTIONS

**Deposit:** 1st night; 10-day cancellation
**Discounts:** Special packages
**Credit Cards:** V, MC, D
**Check-in/Out:** 3–8 or later by arrangement/11
**Smoking:** No
**Pets:** No; host dog on site
**Kids:** No
**No-Nos:** More than 2 in a room; noise after 10
**Minimum Stay:** 2 days weekends, holidays, & peak seasons
**Open:** All year
**Hosts:** Monty & Karen Turner
9308 E. Leavenworth Rd., P.O. Box 285
Leavenworth, WA 98826
(800) 288-6491 or (509) 548-7171
Fax: (509) 548-7171
rofther@runoftheriver.com
www.runoftheriver.com

## COUNTRY HILL B&B, Maple Falls

| Overall: ★★★ | Room Quality: C | Value: B | Price: $75–$95 |
| --- | --- | --- | --- |

This contemporary hillside home offers good value and two spacious, private rooms. The steep, narrow quarter-mile drive up the hill is not for the faint of heart, but rest assured that Cliff and Dolores keep it graded and accessible to passenger cars at all times. The two-room Mountain View Suite is cozy, deluxe, and romantic; the Garden Terrace Room is spacious, light, and especially well suited to longer stays, with its large closet, lots of seating, and plenty of elbow room. Abundant in-room continental breakfast.

## SETTING & FACILITIES

**Location:** On a hill just outside Maple Falls toward Silver Lake
**Near:** Mt. Baker, Glacier, Bellingham
**Building:** Contemporary hillside home
**Grounds:** Perched high on a hill; gardens, picnic areas, surrounded by woods
**Public Space:** Besides your ample room/suite, enjoy deck & patio access
**Food & Drink:** In-room coffeemakers; generous cont'l breakfast
**Recreation:** Winter sports, rafting, mushrooming, berry picking, wildlife watching, hunting
**Amenities & Services:** Extensive! See below

## ACCOMMODATIONS

**Units:** 1 two-room suite, 1 large deluxe room
**All Rooms:** Satellite TV, VCR, videos, books, coffeemaker, sitting area, private entrance, games, closet, robes, hairdryer
**Some Rooms:** Sofa-sleeper, breakfast bar (micro., kettle, mini-fridge) w/ snacks, heated towel rack, patio access
**Bed & Bath:** King, private baths (1 ensuite, 1 accessed via hosts' laundry room)
**Favorites:** Mountain View
**Comfort & Decor:** Mountain View (detached, two-room suite with sofa-sleeper, breakfast bar, ensuite bath) has rose hues. Garden Terrace (one large, sunny room with seating area, designated bath) has sea-green carpet, floral bedding. Furnishings are midquality, but amenities are abundant and very thoughtful.

## RATES, RESERVATIONS, & RESTRICTIONS

**Deposit:** 50% (full amount for 1-night stays); 30-day cancellation, $10 fee
**Discounts:** Extended stays, weekdays; $15 add'l person
**Credit Cards:** Not accepted
**Check-in/Out:** 2–9/noon
**Smoking:** No
**Pets:** No
**Kids:** No
**Minimum Stay:** None
**Open:** All year
**Hosts:** Dolores & Cliff LaBounty
7968 Silver Lake Rd.
Maple Falls, WA 98266
(360) 599-1049
Fax: (360) 599-3018
LaBountyRebore@compuserve.com

## YODELER INN B&B, Maple Falls

| Overall: ★★½ | Room Quality: D | Value: B | Price: $65–$75 |
|---|---|---|---|

In a good location at the crossroads of Highway 542 and Silver Lake Road in Maple Falls, Yodeler Inn has great access to services and natural areas. Close enough to Mt. Baker, yet still a short drive back to Bellingham. Accommodations are basic but cheerful, and the convenience store offerings include espresso drinks, fruit, yogurt, pastries, and even breakfast (and other) sandwiches.

### SETTING & FACILITIES

**Location:** Hwy. 542 in Maple Falls
**Near:** Silver Lake, Mt. Baker, Glacier, Bellingham
**Building:** Private residence & 2 outbuildings
**Grounds:** Shares large corner lot w/ host-owned convenience store
**Public Space:** Each unit is self contained; no shared space
**Food & Drink:** Coffeemaker/hot beverages in each unit; self-serve cont'l breakfast from convenience store offerings
**Recreation:** Winter sports, rafting, mushrooming, berry picking, wildlife watching, hunting
**Amenities & Services:** Hot tub, adjacent to convenience/gas & liquor stores; touring packages; copier & fax; ATM

### ACCOMMODATIONS

**Units:** 2 cabins, 1 room
**All Rooms:** Cable TV, alarm clock, coffee service, games
**Some Rooms:** Deck access, kitchenette
**Bed & Bath:** Queen (some w/ extra single or futon); private ensuite baths
**Favorites:** The new cabin
**Comfort & Decor:** Unpretentious but clean and cozy. New cabin has a bedroom, futons in the living area (sleeping capacity 6), a small kitchen, a fireplace, a bath with tub and shower, and covered parking. Furnishings are fresh, attractive pine, and the walls have wood wainscoting and country-motif wallpaper trim. Other units' furnishings are midquality and a bit dated, but clean and very serviceable.

### RATES, RESERVATIONS, & RESTRICTIONS

**Deposit:** Credit card; 48-hour cancellation
**Discounts:** Extended stays, packages; $10 add'l person
**Credit Cards:** V, MC, AE, D
**Check-in/Out:** 2 or by arrangement; early luggage drop-off possible/11
**Smoking:** Outside only
**Pets:** Welcome in most cases; host pets on site
**Kids:** Welcome
**Minimum Stay:** None
**Open:** All year
**Hosts:** Bethnie & Jeff Morrison
7485 Mt. Baker Hwy.
Maple Falls, WA 98266
(800) 642-9033 or (360) 599-1716
Fax: (360) 599-1389
yodelerinn@gtemail.net

## ST. HELENS MANORHOUSE, Morton

| Overall: ★★★½ | Room Quality: B | Value: B | Price: $85–$105 |
|---|---|---|---|

We adore this place. Bordered by its chestnut stand, a wildlife preserve boasting 400 varieties of birds, and Riffe Lake, it's peaceful and serene. Add the sprawling yard and gardens, with its white wrought iron and wicker furniture, and you have the feeling you're relaxing in the English countryside. Conveniently located for exploring Mt. Rainier and Mount St. Helens, the Manorhouse is even close enough for daytrips to Mt. Adams, making it an ideal hub for a longer stay in Washington's Cascades. Susyn, natural-born hostess and intuitive chef, puts out a breakfast that rivals any in the Northwest—it's abundant, inventive, seasonally inspired, and delicious.

### SETTING & FACILITIES

**Location:** Between mileposts 103 & 104 on Hwy. 12 between Morton & Randle
**Near:** Mount St. Helens, Mt. Rainier, Riffe Lake
**Building:** 1910 country home
**Grounds:** Herb garden, fruit trees, American chestnut trees

**Public Space:** Parlor, DR, porch
**Food & Drink:** Refreshments; hot beverages on request; sumptuous full breakfast
**Recreation:** Fishing, swimming, boating, scenic driving, wildlife watching
**Amenities & Services:** Hot tub; gatherings, parties, reunions

### ACCOMMODATIONS

**Units:** 4 guest rooms
**All Rooms:** Antiques, collectibles
**Some Rooms:** Claw-foot tub
**Bed & Bath:** Queen (3) or twins; 2 private baths, 2 share a bath
**Favorites:** Limoges, Winterthur
**Comfort & Decor:** A sensuous combination of Victorian, French country,

and English manor house styles. Parlor is cozy and inviting, with local millwork, vintage decor. Guest rooms are spacious, each with its own color palette. Numerous period artifacts strewn about create an atmosphere of abundance and ease.

### RATES, RESERVATIONS, & RESTRICTIONS

**Deposit:** Credit card; 7-day cancellation
**Discounts:** Single occupancy, off-season, extended stay
**Credit Cards:** V, MC, AE, D
**Check-in/Out:** Flexible, call
**Smoking:** Outside only
**Pets:** By arrangement
**Kids:** By arrangement

**Minimum Stay:** None
**Open:** All year
**Hosts:** Susyn Dragness
7476 Highway 12
Morton, WA 98356
(360) 498-5243
innkeeper@myhome.net
www.mountsthelens.com/st.helens-manorhouse.html

## ROARING RIVER B&B, North Bend

Overall: ★★★★½      Room Quality: A      Value: C      Price: $85–$150

This peaceful property is the perfect getaway for harried Seattleites or those wishing to visit the Seattle-Snoqualmie Pass corridor without the bustle of the city or the crowds at the summit. Easy (half-hour) access to the city. Great hiking trails nearby, and countless more just up the highway. Rooms are private, for minimal mingling and maximum romance. Decor is contemporary, fresh, and deluxe, and breakfasts are rich and delicious. Peggy and Hersch are gracious and knowledgeable hosts; see as much or as little of them as you like. This is one of our favorite Seattle-area escapes.

### SETTING & FACILITIES

**Location:** Overlooking Middle Fork Snoqualmie River, outside North Bend off Mt. Si Rd.
**Near:** Mt. Si & Little Si, Snoqualmie Pass ski area, Twin Falls S.P., Snoqualmie Falls
**Building:** Pacific Northwest home & outbuildings

**Grounds:** Private wooded parcel; rose garden
**Public Space:** Rooms have sitting areas
**Food & Drink:** Full breakfast delivered to rooms
**Recreation:** Skiing, fishing, antiquing, outlet mall, golf, Seattle day trips
**Amenities & Services:** Gift shop

### ACCOMMODATIONS

**Units:** 4 guest rooms
**All Rooms:** Coffee bar, mini-fridge, private deck, local info
**Some Rooms:** Wet bar, micro., sauna, whirlpool, dbl. shower, sitting area, kitchenette w/ stove, sleeping loft
**Bed & Bath:** King, queen, or full plus twins; private ensuite baths
**Favorites:** Each is unique & wonderful, depending on your needs

**Comfort & Decor:** Mountain Room: kitchenette, huge bath, sitting area, modern decor, hip roof. Newest room, Bear Iris: country-meets-Oriental flavor, deep soaking tub, dual shower, queen feather bed. Rock and Rose: amazing in-room boulder (ivy-strewn), private sauna. Herb's Place: detached, self-contained unit with sleeping loft, living room, kitchen.

### RATES, RESERVATIONS, & RESTRICTIONS

**Deposit:** Credit card; 7-day cancellation
**Discounts:** AAA, AARP, Sun.–Thurs. off-season; $25 add'l person
**Credit Cards:** V, MC, AE
**Check-in/Out:** 4–7 or by arrangement/11
**Smoking:** Outside only
**Pets:** No
**Kids:** Older children welcome

**Minimum Stay:** 2 nights, some holidays
**Open:** All year
**Hosts:** Hersch & Peggy Backues
46715 SE 129th St.
North Bend, WA 98405
87-ROARING-7 or (425) 888-4834
roaring@ptinet.net
www.azl.com/roaringriv

## BROOKHAVEN LODGE, Rockport

| Overall: ★★½ | Room Quality: C | Value: A | Price: $63 |
|---|---|---|---|

The sprawling grounds of Clark Skagit River Resort contain everything folks need for a semirustic mountain getaway in the North Cascades: cabins (from primitive to upscale), a restaurant with delicious home-style cooking, laundry, plus tent and RV sites. And as of 1998, the Clarks (whose predecessors settled this area in 1889) have a bed-and-breakfast, too. This is a family-run, bootstrap operation with heart, in a superb location for exploring the North Cascades high country.

### SETTING & FACILITIES

**Location:** Hwy. 20 between Rockport & Marblemount
**Near:** Skagit River, Marblemount, Rockport, North Cascades N.P., Glacier Peak Wilderness, Ross Lake, Diablo Lake
**Building:** Metal-roof cedar-siding lodge
**Grounds:** Expansive; volleyball area, cabins, RV & tent sites, lots of bunnies

**Public Space:** Great room, exercise room
**Food & Drink:** Full breakfast at on-site restaurant
**Recreation:** Lawn games, volleyball, badminton, scenic driving
**Amenities & Services:** TV/VCR, Skagit River jade fireplace; The Eatery restaurant w/ delicious homemade fare, video rentals

### ACCOMMODATIONS

**Units:** 5 guest rooms
**All Rooms:** Country wreaths
**Some Rooms:** Down comforter, skylight
**Bed & Bath:** Double, queen, or twin; 2 shared baths (1 w/ private half bath)
**Favorites:** #1 for size; #2 for antiques; #5 has private half bath

**Comfort & Decor:** Rustic but clean and comfortable. Seafoam green carpet throughout (#5 has gray). "Country Comfortable" motifs include: patchwork and wicker, early American antique, floral print. "Skagit River Jade" (river rock) fireplace warms the great room.

### RATES, RESERVATIONS, & RESTRICTIONS

**Deposit:** Credit card; 24-hour cancellation
**Discounts:** Single occupancy, cont'l breakfast, no breakfast
**Credit Cards:** V, MC, AE, D
**Check-in/Out:** 3/noon
**Smoking:** Outside only
**Pets:** Not at B&B (leashed pets in other properties at resort)
**Kids:** Not at B&B (ask about other properties at resort)

**Minimum Stay:** None
**Open:** All year
**Hosts:** Tootsie Clark, Bob & Judi Brooks, Don Clark
Skagit River Resort/Clark's Cabins, 58468 Clark Cabin Rd.
Rockport, WA 98283
(800) 273-2606 or (360) 873-2250
Fax: (360) 873-4077
info@northcascades.com
www.northcascades.com

## THE HUMMINGBIRD INN, Roslyn

| Overall: ★★★½ | Room Quality: C | Value: A | Price: $65–$75 |
|---|---|---|---|

This cute little house is "the" place to stay when visiting *Northern Exposure* country or pursuing the exceptional hiking of the Salmon la Sac area. While the TV hit is history now, many still visit Roslyn because it was the town used to fashion the mythical Cicely, Alaska. Roberta's clean, cozy, quaint inn is a comfortable blend of history and modern conveniences, with good food, airy rooms, and a quiet location. Not far from the interstate but close to a plethora of outdoor recreation.

### SETTING & FACILITIES

**Location:** Just east of Pennsylvania Ave. & Hwy. 903 crossroads in "downtown"
**Near:** Roslyn (home of TV hit *Northern Exposure*), Cle Elum, I-90, Salmon la Sac
**Building:** 2-story turn-of-the-20th-century home

**Grounds:** Pleasant white-picket-fenced yard w/ pond
**Public Space:** Foyer/LR, DR, porch
**Food & Drink:** Full breakfast
**Recreation:** Skiing, antiquing, fishing, *Northern Exposure* touring
**Amenities & Services:** Porch swing, X-C skis, snowshoes, gas fireplace; light supper by arrangement (winter)

### ACCOMMODATIONS

**Units:** 3 guest rooms
**All Rooms:** Sun-dried sheets, light & airy
**Some Rooms:** Tailored or floral decor
**Bed & Bath:** Queens, roll-away ($10); 3 rooms share 2 baths, or 1 has private bath option

**Favorites:** Newest room, w/ private bath option
**Comfort & Decor:** Turn-of-the-20th-century country is the main motif, with hummingbird accents throughout. Original brick and wood, hardwood floors softened by oriental rugs. Dormers, quilts, and antiques give a quaint feel.

### RATES, RESERVATIONS, & RESTRICTIONS

**Deposit:** Call
**Discounts:** Mon.–Thurs., special packages; $10 roll-away
**Credit Cards:** V, MC, D
**Check-in/Out:** 4 or by arrangement/11
**Smoking:** No
**Pets:** No

**Kids:** Welcome
**Minimum Stay:** None
**Open:** All year
**Hosts:** Roberta Spinazola
P.O. Box 984, 106 Pennsylvania Ave. E
Roslyn, WA 98941
(509) 649-2758
blueplanet-group.com/hummingbirdinn

## DENONNO'S B&B, Skykomish

| Overall: ★★★½ | Room Quality: B | Value: A | Price: $55–$75 |
|---|---|---|---|

Pat and Lou (Mrs. and Mr., respectively) DeNonno are New Jersey expatriates who have assimilated the Pacific Northwest in a big way. Their delightful bed-and-breakfast is a celebration of the best of the Cascades: the sound of the rippling Skykomish river, the lush flower gardens surrounded by quiet woods, the artistic breakfasts featuring Northwest fare. As hosts, they are relaxed, gracious, and great fun. Join them for music and conversation, if you wish, or just appreciate the solitude of the deck, the hot tub, and a night's sleep on a good bed.

### SETTING & FACILITIES

**Location:** Just east of milepost 49 off Hwy. 2 on Skylane
**Near:** Highway 2, Index, Stevens Pass ski area, Leavenworth "Bavarian" village
**Building:** Contemporary riverfront home
**Grounds:** Flowers, herb garden, multi-level deck, on Skykomish River
**Public Space:** LR, DR, decks
**Food & Drink:** Full breakfast
**Recreation:** Hiking, skiing
**Amenities & Services:** Hot tub, extra towels

### ACCOMMODATIONS

**Units:** 3 guest rooms
**All Rooms:** Original artwork, fresh flowers
**Some Rooms:** Sitting area
**Bed & Bath:** Queen, 1 w/ extra queen hideabed; 1 private bath, 2 share
**Favorites:** Room w/ outside entrance, sitting area, private bath
**Comfort & Decor:** French country style blends sensuous florals with a variety of colors and textures in a casual elegance

### RATES, RESERVATIONS, & RESTRICTIONS

**Deposit:** V, MC
**Discounts:** $10 add'l person
**Credit Cards:** V, MC
**Check-in/Out:** After 3 or by arrangement/11
**Smoking:** Outside only
**Pets:** Welcome by arrangement
**Kids:** Welcome
**Minimum Stay:** None
**Open:** All year
**Hosts:** Lou & Pat DeNonno
P.O. Box 219, 527 Skylane
Skykomish, WA 98288
(360) 677-2518

## IRON HORSE INN, South Cle Elum

| Overall: ★★½ | Room Quality: D | Value: C | Price: $50–$125 |
|---|---|---|---|

A fun, historic ambiance is the main attraction at this clever inn, housed in a National Historic Register railroad bunkhouse. Many original objects remain from the railroad days and have been worked into the decor in guest rooms and common areas: lanterns, signals, rail spike doorstops, original duty roster board in lobby. Breakfasts are simple and honest, served on antique Hiawatha Dining Car china when available. Rooms are bright and airy, furnished more lovingly than lavishly. Families will enjoy the cabooses, while the inside, shared-bath rooms are an exceptional bargain. Formerly "The Moore House," the inn was purchased by Doug and Mary in 1999.

## SETTING & FACILITIES

**Location:** South under I-90 from Cle Elum, near Iron Horse S.P.
**Near:** Yakima River, Roslyn, I-90, Snoqualmie Pass, Alpine Lakes Wilderness Area
**Building:** 1909 Milwaukee Railroad historic bunkhouse
**Grounds:** Nearly 2 acres w/ year-round creek, trees, horse paddock
**Public Space:** Lobby/LR
**Food & Drink:** Full breakfast
**Recreation:** Skiing, antiquing, historic touring, horseback riding, fishing
**Amenities & Services:** Group meetings w/ lunches or dinners by arrangement

## ACCOMMODATIONS

**Units:** 8 guest rooms, 3 suites (2 are cabooses)
**All Rooms:** Period decor
**Some Rooms:** Writing desk, sitting room, view, four-poster, whirlpool; TV, fridge, coffeemaker, & deck in cabooses
**Bed & Bath:** Various; 5 private baths, 6 rooms share 2 baths
**Favorites:** Brady Suite or cabooses
**Comfort & Decor:** Antique flair and railroad memorabilia galore. Masculine tones and textures predominate; lace curtains, quilts, and antiques soften the edges. The Brady Suite, with satin sheets and whirlpool tub, is the room for romance, while the remodeled cabooses are novel and fun for families (they sleep up to 5).

## RATES, RESERVATIONS, & RESTRICTIONS

**Deposit:** Credit card; 7-day cancellation or subject to $10 fee
**Discounts:** Extended stays; $10 add'l person
**Credit Cards:** V, MC
**Check-in/Out:** 4/11
**Smoking:** Outside only
**Pets:** No (horse paddock avail.)
**Kids:** Welcome
**Minimum Stay:** 2 nights, holiday weekends
**Open:** All year
**Hosts:** Mary & Doug Pittis
526 Marie St., P.O. Box 629
South Cle Elum, WA 98943
(509) 674-5939 or (in WA & OR only)
(800) 22-TWAIN
Fax: (509) 674-1708
maryp@cleelum.com
ironhorseinn.uswestdex.com

## STEHEKIN VALLEY RANCH, Stehekin

| Overall: ★★ | Room Quality: D | Value: A | Price: $130–$150 |

We're stretching the definition of "bed-and-breakfast" a bit to include this outstanding guest ranch. After all, it's a bed (albeit in a clean but

---

decidedly rustic cabin or log-walled tent cabin), and you get a whale of a breakfast, plus lunch and dinner. On a motel scale, the sleeping quarters may rate low because they're rustic, but the overall value of this high country lodging and dining experience is tops. Don't come with big-city expectations or your mind on "must-see TV," bring a flashlight for late-night excursions to the bathroom, and you just might be surprised at how comfortable "rustic" can be.

## SETTING & FACILITIES

**Location:** 9 mi. up valley from the Lake Chelan boat landing
**Near:** Stehekin River, Agnes Gorge & other hiking trails, Cascade Corrals
**Building:** Regular & canvas-roofed log cabins w/ log bath/meal house
**Grounds:** Wooded acreage w/ corrals
**Public Space:** Large log lodge w/ game loft

**Food & Drink:** Coffee, tea, cocoa; three complete meals included
**Recreation:** Fishing, horseback riding, river rafting, mountain biking
**Amenities & Services:** Games, fireplace, hammocks; transportation throughout the lower valley (between boat landing & ranch; it's only accessible by boat & plane); history info

## ACCOMMODATIONS

**Units:** 12 cabins
**All Rooms:** Clean, simple, rustic; kerosene lamps
**Some Rooms:** Metal roof & private bath; canvas roof & shared bath house
**Bed & Bath:** Various multiple-bed configurations; 5 private baths, 7 share main bath house
**Favorites:** N/A

**Comfort & Decor:** Make no mistake—this is rustic living. No electricity or heat; no bathrooms in many units. Screened windows provide a breeze. Simple furnishings and bedding. Surprisingly cozy and comfortable, the ranch is somewhere between "rustic resort" and "fancy campground." No TVs, no telephone service.

## RATES, RESERVATIONS, & RESTRICTIONS

**Deposit:** 50% (25% nonrefundable); 21-day cancellation
**Discounts:** Single occupancy, extended stay, BYO bedding; ALL meals included in price; children $10–55 add'l person
**Credit Cards:** V, MC (by phone only; on-site payment must be by check)
**Check-in/Out:** Tied in w/ Lady of the Lake boat schedule
**Smoking:** Outside only

**Pets:** No
**Kids:** Welcome
**Minimum Stay:** None
**Open:** Mid-June to end of first week in Oct.
**Hosts:** Cliff & Kerry Courtney & staff
P.O. Box 36, Stehekin, WA 98852
(800) 536-0745 or (509) 682-4677
Fax: (509) 682-4705
info@courtneycountry.com
www.courtneycountry.com

## THE FARM, A B&B, Trout Lake

| Overall: ★★★½ | Room Quality: C | Value: B | Price: $75–$85 |
|---|---|---|---|

Rosie and Dean have offered lodging at their idyllic country farmhouse since 1995. It's a beautiful property, with lovingly tended gardens and breathtaking views of both Mt. Adams and Mt. Hood. Homey and unpretentious, yet clean and comfortable, those who enjoy good conversation and a beautiful setting will get the most out of The Farm. Don't bother asking about Jacuzzi tubs and room service here—this is a place for life's simpler pleasures: a hearty breakfast, world-class hiking, and a good book and classical music in the evening.

### SETTING & FACILITIES

**Location:** Just SW of Trout Lake "proper," about 20 mi. north of White Salmon
**Near:** Glenwood, Mt. Adams, Conboy Nat'l Wildlife Refuge, Indian Heaven Wilderness, Columbia Gorge Nat'l Scenic Area
**Building:** 1890 farmhouse
**Grounds:** 6 idyllic acres; flower/veg gardens, decks, barn, exceptional

Mt. Adams view
**Public Space:** LR, parlor, decks
**Food & Drink:** Afternoon refreshments; full breakfast
**Recreation:** Snowmobiling, X-C skiing, huckleberry picking, rafting, fishing, scenic flights
**Amenities & Services:** Mountain bikes, TV; weddings, receptions, reunions; box lunches by arrangement

### ACCOMMODATIONS

**Units:** 2 guest rooms; ask about overflow options
**All Rooms:** Robes, quilts, antique furnishings
**Some Rooms:** Extra bed, vanity
**Bed & Bath:** Double, queen and twin; shared bath
**Favorites:** 1890 Room

**Comfort & Decor:** Antiques and collectibles fill the rooms and common areas in a manner comfortable rather than cluttered. Abundant fresh flowers from on-site cutting garden in season. Shared bathroom has an extra-large tile-and-glass-block shower.

### RATES, RESERVATIONS, & RESTRICTIONS

**Deposit:** Call
**Discounts:** $10 add'l person
**Credit Cards:** Not accepted
**Check-in/Out:** By arrangement
**Smoking:** Outside only
**Pets:** No; host dog on premises (outside)
**Kids:** By arrangement
**No-Nos:** Drop-ins (reservations requested)

**Minimum Stay:** None
**Open:** All year
**Hosts:** Rosie & Dean Hostetter
490 Sunnyside Rd.
Trout Lake, WA 98650
(509) 395-2488
Fax: (509) 395-2127
farmbnb@gorge.net
www.gorge.net/business/farmbnb

## LLAMA RANCH B&B, Trout Lake

| Overall: ★★½ | Room Quality: D | Value: C | Price: $79–$99 |
|---|---|---|---|

Convenient location (right on Highway 141), great Mt. Adams view, interesting and knowledgeable hosts, and a chance to get up close and personal with a llama—these are the strengths of Trout Lake's Llama Ranch B&B. Guest rooms are simple affairs, retrofit into an old Montessori school, and most share a bath. Breakfast is modest but filling. Jerry and Dee are great sources of local trail and other touring information, and fun to talk with. But the real stars of this experience are the 60 wooly critters outside. Enjoy a complimentary llama walk on the expansive grounds, or sneak a hug. Kids and kids-at-heart will love it.

### SETTING & FACILITIES

**Location:** Just south of Trout Lake on Hwy. 141 (east side); 19 mi. north of White Salmon

**Near:** Glenwood, Mt. Adams, White Salmon river, Conboy Nat'l Wildlife Refuge, Indian Heaven Wilderness, Columbia Gorge Nat'l Scenic Area

**Building:** Converted Montessori school

**Grounds:** Acreage w/ llama pastures, barn

**Public Space:** Living, dining, kitchen areas

**Food & Drink:** Self-serve hot beverages; simple full breakfast

**Recreation:** Llama walking & hiking, huckleberry picking, rafting, fishing, snowmobiling, X-C skiing

**Amenities & Services:** Kitchen privileges; excellent local trail advice, free llama boarding & on-site llama walks

### ACCOMMODATIONS

**Units:** 7 guest rooms

**All Rooms:** Clean & comfortable

**Some Rooms:** Private kitchen, sofa-sleeper

**Bed & Bath:** Queen (5), 2 queens, or king plus queen sofabed; 2 private

baths, 5 share 2 baths

**Favorites:** Private-bath units

**Comfort & Decor:** Simple and straightforward. Modest furnishings, bedding, and linens.

### RATES, RESERVATIONS, & RESTRICTIONS

**Deposit:** Credit card; 48-hour cancellation requested

**Discounts:** Single occupancy, whole house rental; $10 add'l person

**Credit Cards:** V, MC, D

**Check-in/Out:** Flexible

**Smoking:** No

**Pets:** Welcome

**Kids:** Welcome

**Minimum Stay:** None

**Open:** All year

**Hosts:** Jerry Stone & Dee Kern
1980 Hwy. 141
Trout Lake, WA 98650
(877) 800-5262 or (509) 395-2786
lama1@gorge.net

# Zone 8
# Northeast Washington

Wild and sparsely populated, northeast Washington is thick with forests such as the Okanogan, Colville, and Kaniksu. Large areas are given over to the Colville and Spokane Indian reservations. Tiny towns like Okanogan, Republic, Omak, and Kettle Falls are sprinkled at intervals along the region's winding, two-lane highways. Long winters and low tourism means bed-and-breakfasts are small, few, far between, and not always as richly appointed as their west-side counterparts. We've chosen a few that offer genuine hospitality and superb recreation access.

The state's far northeast corner is rugged and thinly populated. Single-unit bed-and-breakfasts in Colville and Inchelium are featured, plus a funky old hotel in Usk. In a class by themselves, these lodgings offer such extras as homemade dinner by arrangement and guided hunting trips (try getting *that* in Seattle).

The area surrounding Grand Coulee Dam is one of amazing natural and man-made splendor (regardless of your political opinion of dams, this one will impress you). Two humble bed-and-breakfasts, one in Coulee Dam and one in Grand Coulee, serve this area. Additional area attractions include the geologic wonder Dry Falls, recreational Lake Roosevelt and Banks Lake, and Steamboat Rock State Park.

The resort town of Chelan is featured in this section. It provides water recreation on Lake Chelan, access to isolated Stehekin (see Zone 7), and seasonal events, as well as shopping and a solid tourism infrastructure.

Spokane is the urban center of northeastern Washington. Its shopping, industry, and elegant architecture have given rise to several fine bed-and-breakfasts we heartily recommend. It is also home to Gonzaga University, excellent parks (Riverside, Riverfront, Manito, and others), museums, shopping, recreation (including the multiuse Centennial Trail), historic neighborhoods (Browne's Addition, South Hill), and fine dining (including historic Patsy Clark's).

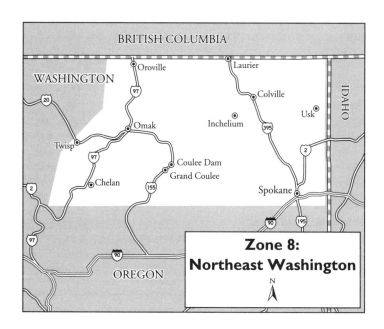

BRITISH COLUMBIA

WASHINGTON

Oroville

Laurier

Colville

Usk

Omak

Inchelium

Twisp

Coulee Dam
Grand Coulee

Chelan

Spokane

IDAHO

Zone 8:
Northeast Washington

N

OREGON

**Chelan**
Mary Kay's Romantic Whaley
    Mansion Inn, p. 260
A Quail's Roost Inn, p. 261

**Colville**
The Whitetail Inn, p. 262

**Coulee Dam**
Four Winds Guest House, p. 263

**Grand Coulee**
The Gold House Inn, p. 264

**Inchelium**
The Log House, p. 265

**Spokane**
Angelica's B&B, p. 266
Cobblestone B&B Inn, p. 267
Fotheringham House B&B, p. 268
Love's Victorian B&B, p. 270
Marianna Stoltz House, p. 271
Oslo's B&B, p. 272
Waverly Place B&B, p. 273

**Usk**
The Hotel Usk, p. 274

## MARY KAY'S ROMANTIC WHALEY MANSION INN, Chelan

| Overall: ★★★★ | Room Quality: B | Value: C | Price: $105–$135 |

For over 15 years, Mary Kay has offered whimsy and old-world elegance at her romantic, restored Edwardian mansion. A short block from Lake Chelan, and a few minutes' stroll to downtown, this bed-and-breakfast is ideally located for exploring Chelan. Mary Kay is a born hostess, welcoming and motherly, while Carol is responsible for the behind-the-scenes infrastructure, including record-keeping and producing their signature truffles and other decadent delights. The home is a melange of styles and themes, resulting in an amusing and fanciful escape from real life.

### SETTING & FACILITIES

**Location:** On Third, just across the bridge from downtown
**Near:** Lake Chelan, restaurants, shopping, Riverwalk Park, *Lady of the Lake* dock
**Building:** 1919 historic Edwardian foursquare mansion
**Grounds:** Bulbs, flowering shrubs, border plantings, dogwoods, rhododendrons

**Public Space:** Front porch, TV room, 2nd floor sitting room, parlor, LR, DR
**Food & Drink:** Early coffee; full breakfast
**Recreation:** Water/winter sports, boat/plane excursions to Stehekin, golf, casino, festivals
**Amenities & Services:** Player piano, books, videos, phones; celebration extras, eco-sensitive linens policy

### ACCOMMODATIONS

**Units:** 6 guest rooms
**All Rooms:** TV/VCR, mini-fridge, hairdryers, carpet, ceiling fans
**Some Rooms:** Antiques, closets
**Bed & Bath:** 3 queen, 2 king, 1 double; private ensuite baths
**Favorites:** Mary Kay Suite, Frances Room
**Comfort & Decor:** Edwardian splendor with heirloom antiques, whimsical

touches (a Carnivale theme at our visit), and a few incongruous department-store pieces. Flocked and floral wallpapers, lace and tasseled window treatments. Oak and Southern yellow pine woodwork. Small but serviceable ensuite baths. Central (hot water) heat; window AC units.

### RATES, RESERVATIONS, & RESTRICTIONS

**Deposit:** Call; 72-hour cancellation requested
**Discounts:** Off-season
**Credit Cards:** V, MC
**Check-in/Out:** After 3/11
**Smoking:** Outside only
**Pets:** No; host kitty on site
**Kids:** Not appropriate in most circumstances
**No-Nos:** Shoes in house (flexible)

**Minimum Stay:** 2 nights preferred weekends; 3 nights holidays
**Open:** All year
**Hosts:** Mary Kay & Carol
415 Third St.
Chelan, WA 98816
(800) 729-2408 or (509) 682-5735
Fax: (509) 682-5385
whaley@televar.com
www.lakechelan.com/whaley.htm

## A QUAIL'S ROOST INN, Chelan

| Overall: ★★★½ | Room Quality: B | Value: B | Price: $80–$114 |
| --- | --- | --- | --- |

Formerly Highland Guest House, this gingerbread-pretty National Historic Register Victorian has great curb appeal, in yellow and white with lavender scrollwork accents. Inside, it retains its period feel, but is very comfortable and relaxed. Marilee and Brad, who have had the inn since 1990, are super hosts. They make you feel instantly at home with an innkeeping style that is relaxed and intuitive. Great breakfasts, serious coffee, pleasant rooms. We liked this place a lot—it's the essence of a good bed-and-breakfast.

### SETTING & FACILITIES

**Location:** 4 blocks up from Don Morse City Park, overlooking Chelan
**Near:** Lake Chelan, restaurants, shopping, Riverwalk Park, *Lady of the Lake* dock
**Building:** 1889 Queen Anne Victorian
**Grounds:** Town, valley, & lake view
**Public Space:** Parlor, DR, porch
**Food & Drink:** Ice water & fruit in rooms; full breakfast

**Recreation:** Water/winter activities, boat & plane excursions to Stehekin, golf, casino
**Amenities & Services:** TV/VCR, guest fridge access, arts & crafts gift shop; gourmet picnic baskets by arrangement, celebration extras, private porch breakfast by arrangement

### ACCOMMODATIONS

**Units:** 3 guest rooms
**All Rooms:** Fresh flowers, ceiling fans
**Some Rooms:** Private porch, view, closet, armoire, canopy bed
**Bed & Bath:** Queen, double, or queen & double; private baths (1 ensuite)
**Favorites:** Rose & Wicker
**Comfort & Decor:** Elegant if weath- ered antiques grace the main parlor, along with elaborate original woodwork including beaded molding and spandrels. Hand stenciling, striped & floral wallpapers, stained glass. Rooms feature wicker, white iron, lace, florals, quilts; all are carpeted. Individual room heaters and window AC units. Fresh, charming, "like Grandma's."

### RATES, RESERVATIONS, & RESTRICTIONS

**Deposit:** 1st night; 10-day cancellation, $10 fee
**Discounts:** Off-season, off-season corporate, extended stays; $10 add'l person
**Credit Cards:** V, MC
**Check-in/Out:** 3–5 or by arrangement/11
**Smoking:** No
**Pets:** No

**Kids:** By arrangement
**No-Nos:** Noise after 10 p.m.
**Minimum Stay:** 2 nights, some rooms on summer weekends
**Open:** All year
**Hosts:** Marilee & Brad Stolzenburg 121 E. Highland Ave., P.O. Box 2089 Chelan, WA 98816
(800) 681-2892 or (509) 682-2892
www.lakechelan.com/quailinn

## THE WHITETAIL INN, Colville

| Overall: ★★★ | Room Quality: C | Value: B | Price: $75 |
|---|---|---|---|

Clean, tidy, and cute, this little cabin is a step above "rustic," but has all the charm of a wooded, rural setting. The square footage is quite tiny, but the layout is good. The cabin would be tight for more than 2 (OK for 2 adults and an older child), but it could sleep 4 (additional bunks in outbuilding offer overflow potential for hunters). Hosts are avid horsepeople, hunters, and outdoor folk; ask about personalized semi-guided hunting packages. The cabin is a short (150-foot) path away from the main house, where you can arrange dinner with your hosts ($30 for two, complete). Alternately, cook in your cabin or drive into town to a restaurant.

### SETTING & FACILITIES

**Location:** Off Hwy. 395 about an hour north of Spokane
**Near:** Colville, Kettle Falls, Addy, Chewelah, 49° North ski area, Colville Nat'l Forest
**Building:** 1986-built log cabin
**Grounds:** 22 acres w/ pond & horse pastures in timbered mountain setting
**Public Space:** Cabin fully self-contained
**Food & Drink:** Full breakfast (when avail.) served in host home; otherwise cont'l breakfast (price reduced); dinner avail.
**Recreation:** Horseback riding, hunting, skiing, snowmobiling, fishing, wildlife watching
**Amenities & Services:** Fee items include guided horseback rides, semi-guided hunting trips, dinners, game packing

### ACCOMMODATIONS

**Units:** 1 cabin
**All Rooms:** Full kitchen (range, coffeemaker, mini-fridge, supplies), front porch w/ rockers, table & chairs
**Bed & Bath:** Double plus 2 twin mattresses in loft; private bath
**Comfort & Decor:** "Country comfortable" log cabin mixes patchwork and chintz with bearskins and antlers for a rural charm that's fresh and updated. Braided rugs on plank floor. Reading lamps. Woodstove heat plus small electric heater. Very cozy—bordering on tiny—including the bitsy bathroom. Solid craftsmanship, well-supplied kitchen, and clean as a whistle. Loft is very low-ceilinged—strictly a crawl-in-to-sleep affair—and accessed by a ladder, making it inappropriate for young children.

## RATES, RESERVATIONS, & RESTRICTIONS

**Deposit:** 50%; 48-hour cancellation
**Discounts:** 2 or more nights; $67.50 w/ cont'l; $60 w/ no breakfast; $10, add'l person
**Credit Cards:** Not accepted
**Check-in/Out:** After 2 or by arrangement/11
**Smoking:** Outside only
**Pets:** By arrangement only

**Kids:** See loft description above; not appropriate for small children
**Minimum Stay:** None
**Open:** All year
**Hosts:** Pat & Galen Thompson
1140 Basin Rd., Colville, WA 99114
(509) 684-8856
pthompson@plix.com
www.bestinns.net/usa/wa/whitetail.html

## FOUR WINDS GUEST HOUSE, Coulee Dam

| Overall: ★★½ | Room Quality: D | Value: B | Price: $66–$85 |
|---|---|---|---|

The historic building housing Four Winds Guest House was once a 26-room dormitory used to house engineering workers for the Grand Coulee Dam. Dick and Fe took over the property in 1986 and turned it into a basic, simple, historic, and clean ten-room guest house. The guest rooms are upstairs, while the hosts live downstairs. Hosts are exceptionally knowledgeable and friendly, and have a great sense of humor and fun.

### SETTING & FACILITIES

**Location:** .25 mi. uphill from dam visitor center, at end of Lincoln, across from City Hall
**Near:** Grand Coulee Dam, Historical Walk footpath; Lake Roosevelt, Banks Lake
**Building:** 1935 dam engineers' dormitory
**Grounds:** Porches, deck, herb garden
**Public Space:** Guest lounge/LR, porches, DR/lounge
**Food & Drink:** Morning coffee & tea; full breakfast
**Recreation:** Dam tours, laser light show, Indian cultural museum, hunting, fishing, boating
**Amenities & Services:** TV/VCR, piano, pay phones; excellent historical info; personal welcome & orientation

### ACCOMMODATIONS

**Units:** 10 guest rooms
**All Rooms:** Sink, closet (most)
**Some Rooms:** Theme decor (e.g. Native American), four-posters, deck access, 2-room units w/ shared semi-private baths
**Bed & Bath:** Mostly queen, some double & twin, 2 doubles, or 2 twins; 2 private or semiprivate baths (shared by 2 rooms), 2 sex-segregated multiple-stall baths for other 6 rooms
**Favorites:** 4–6, 12, 30

**Comfort & Decor:** Original fixtures promote the historic authenticity of the unique building (sinks, lighting, medicine cabinets). Quilts and host's cross-stitching make rooms homey and quaint; period memorabilia adds interest. Rooms/baths are super-clean. Baseboard electric heat offers individual room control. No AC can make for hot summer days, but nights are comfortable with venting windows and fans.

## RATES, RESERVATIONS, & RESTRICTIONS

**Deposit:** Credit card; 48-hour cancellation
**Discounts:** Groups, advance payment, gift cert.; no charge for add'l sharing room, as bed capacity allows
**Credit Cards:** V, MC, AE, D
**Check-in/Out:** 3–4 or by arrangement/11
**Smoking:** No
**Pets:** No

**Kids:** Over 8 welcome
**Minimum Stay:** None
**Open:** All year
**Hosts:** Dick & Fe Taylor
301 Lincoln St.
Coulee Dam, WA 99116
(800) 786-3146 or (509) 633-3146
Fax: (509) 633-2454
fourwind@televar.com

## THE GOLD HOUSE INN, Grand Coulee

Overall: ★½       Room Quality: D       Value: D       Price: $75

Casual, relaxed home offers modest furnishings and sincere hospitality. Bob is a longtime area resident who is intimately familiar with the sights and activities of the area, and goes out of his way to make your stay pleasant. While The Gold House Inn would never be accused of being "upscale," the rooms are a reasonable lodging alternative, and a good value, especially for parties of 3–4 sharing a room.

## SETTING & FACILITIES

**Location:** On a hillside .5 mi. east of Hwy. 155/174 crossroads
**Near:** Steamboat Rock S.P., Lake Roosevelt, Grand Coulee Dam, Banks Lake
**Building:** 5,400-sq.-ft., 2-level host-built private home
**Grounds:** None; house sits on a patch of dirt

**Public Space:** LR, DR
**Food & Drink:** Full breakfast
**Recreation:** Fishing, boating, dam tours, visitor center, light show, hiking, hunting
**Amenities & Services:** Big-screen TV, piano, boat/RV parking

## ACCOMMODATIONS

**Units:** 7 guest rooms
**All Rooms:** Carpet, closet
**Some Rooms:** Library, TV, separate entrance, tub/shower units, 2 rooms can join as suite
**Bed & Bath:** Various (several w/ 2 beds); all private baths (6 of 7 ensuite)
**Favorites:** Gold, Angie/Diedra

**Comfort & Decor:** Four outside-entrance rooms are more "1980s-motel" decor—fresher carpet and vinyls. Three inside rooms are very 1970s. Living room has rust carpet, sectional couch, and large TV. Taxidermy in entryway. Central heat, some with auxiliary baseboard units; AC.

## RATES, RESERVATIONS, & RESTRICTIONS

**Deposit:** Credit card; 24-hour cancellation
**Discounts:** Weekday (Mon.–Thurs.), senior, AAA; $7.50 add'l person
**Credit Cards:** V, MC, AE
**Check-in/Out:** After 4/flexible check-out
**Smoking:** Outside only
**Pets:** No

**Kids:** Welcome
**Minimum Stay:** None
**Open:** All year
**Hosts:** Bob Pachosa
411 Partello Park
Grand Coulee, WA 99133
(800) 835-9369 or (509) 633-3276
members.aol.com/coug89/gold.htm

## THE LOG HOUSE, Inchelium

| Overall: ★★★½ | Room Quality: C | Value: B | Price: $85 |

Exceptional setting and quality craftsmanship. Midquality furnishings and vinyls. Top-quality hosts are friendly, gracious, and casual—they're just down the road if you need them, but basically, you're on your own at your private cabin-in-the-woods. Enjoy dynamite blufftop river views from living and dining rooms and the spacious deck. Adventure bonus: from most locations, you'll have to take the free-of-charge, ten-minute Gifford-Inchelium ferry to get to Inchelium. It runs every half-hour. Call or write for excellent directions to this out-of-the-way retreat.

## SETTING & FACILITIES

**Location:** South of Inchelium (north of Davenport) overlooking the Columbia River
**Near:** Twin Lakes Resort, Lake Roosevelt, Stone Rose Interpretive Center; day trip to: Kettle Falls, Colville, Davenport, Grand Coulee Dam, Fort Spokane
**Building:** 30' x 40', 2-level 1990s log home
**Grounds:** Wooded lot w/ picnic area on 60-acre parcel

**Public Space:** Self-contained house: kitchen, LR, deck, dining area, TV/library/den
**Food & Drink:** Cont'l breakfast basket (first day); coffee, cocoa, & kitchen basics
**Recreation:** Boating, fishing, water skiing, swimming, museums, antiquing, historic touring
**Amenities & Services:** Innkeepers are just up the road if you need them

## ACCOMMODATIONS

**Units:** One self-contained 3-BR log home
**All Rooms:** TV/VCR, full kitchen (range, oven, micro., coffeemaker, fridge, cookware & tableware)
**Bed & Bath:** Queen, double, 2 twins, & queen sofa-sleeper in den; 2 full baths
**Favorites:** 2 BRs have river views; master has queen & window seat; biggest room has 2 twins

**Comfort & Decor:** Casual furnishings in country and floral motifs. Fine knotty-wood paneling. Upstairs bath has soaker claw-foot tub, while downstairs has tub/shower combo. Bedrooms are simple but comfortable, with pitched roofs, carpet, fresh flowers, quilts, and reading lamps. Wood heat for winter, fans for summer

## RATES, RESERVATIONS, & RESTRICTIONS

**Deposit:** 50% nonrefundable; single-night stays require full nonrefundable payment
**Discounts:** Extended stays; $15 add'l, 2 persons up to 8
**Credit Cards:** Not accepted
**Check-in/Out:** 3–6 or by arrangement/noon
**Smoking:** Outside only

**Pets:** Sometimes can be accommodated by arrangement
**Kids:** OK
**Minimum Stay:** 2 nights, weekends
**Open:** All year
**Hosts:** Sue Jacobsen
HC1 Box 367, Inchelium, WA 99138
(509) 722-3784
Fax: Call

## ANGELICA'S B&B, Spokane

| Overall: ★★★★ | Room Quality: B | Value: B | Price: $95–$110 |
|---|---|---|---|

In a mixed neighborhood of fading, restored, and semirestored heritage homes, this Historic Register property might not stand out to the untrained eye, despite its architectural pedigree (built by Spokane turn-of-the-century celebrity architect Kirtland Cutter). The simple brick facade belies an interior of exceptional elegance. New proprietor Lynette

White purchased the home in 1998 and used her interior design background to create the deluxe surroundings guests enjoy today. A stylish, elegant, upscale Spokane experience.

## SETTING & FACILITIES

**Location:** Just east of downtown, near junction of Hwy. 195 and I-90/Hwy. 2/Hwy. 395.
**Near:** High Bridge & other parks, Spokane Airport, museums
**Building:** 1907 Arts and Crafts home
**Grounds:** Large, private, landscaped corner lot w/ seating areas
**Public Space:** LR, sunroom, library, large porch

**Food & Drink:** Early coffee in sunroom; full breakfast; evening snack & beverages
**Recreation:** Golf, museums, all Spokane attractions
**Amenities & Services:** Games, books, TV/VCR, videos, sound system, piano, gas fireplace; small guest office w/ phone, data port; receptions, dinner parties, meetings

## ACCOMMODATIONS

**Units:** 4 guest rooms
**All Rooms:** Big closets, robes, designer decor
**Some Rooms:** Sitting area, fireplace, canopy, wicker, or iron bed
**Bed & Bath:** Queen; 2 private baths, 2 share a bath
**Favorites:** Yvonne's & Jennifer's
**Comfort & Decor:** Elegant and plush, blending quality contemporary fabrics with the dark wood and inherent elegance of the period. Stained glass, antique light fixtures. Living room's elegance enhanced by grand piano and gas fireplace. Impressive silk and fresh flowers, designer decor with seasonal accents. Hardwood floors with hooked or sculpted area rugs.

## RATES, RESERVATIONS, & RESTRICTIONS

**Deposit:** 1st night; 7-day cancellation
**Discounts:** None
**Credit Cards:** V, MC
**Check-in/Out:** 4 or by arrangement/10:30
**Smoking:** No
**Pets:** No; host kitty
**Kids:** 12 & older only

**Minimum Stay:** Month of May only
**Open:** All year
**Hosts:** Lynette White
1321 W. 9th Ave.
Spokane, WA 99204
(800) 987-0053 or (509) 624-5598
Fax: (509) 624-5598
www.angelicasbb.com

## COBBLESTONE B&B INN, Spokane

| Overall: ★★ | Room Quality: D | Value: D | Price: $79–$99 |
| --- | --- | --- | --- |

This little bootstrap operation lacks the polish of other Spokane bed-and-breakfasts, as it is obviously a sideline to the proprietors' main business, The Cobblestone Bakery. The two rooms and the shared living and dining area (plus a kitchen, which guests are not allowed to use, except for the fridge) are above the bakery. Hosts live off-premises. The bakery features European pastries, a full line of wholegrain and standard yeast breads, and specialty breads. If you seek a pet- or child-friendly accommodation within walking distance of downtown, and if you don't mind sparsely furnished quarters on a busy main street, this could work for you.

## SETTING & FACILITIES

**Location:** Near downtown, just south of I-90 on Washington at 6th
**Near:** Riverfront Park, Opera House, Manito Park, Convention Center, hospitals
**Building:** Turn-of-the-20th-century home
**Grounds:** None per se—on busy street

**Public Space:** LR, DR, sunroom in progress
**Food & Drink:** Super-fresh cont'l breakfast from Cobblestone Bakery downstairs
**Recreation:** Walking, bicycling, historic touring
**Amenities & Services:** Remote TV, guest fridge; meeting area, cafe

## ACCOMMODATIONS

**Units:** 2 guest rooms
**All Rooms:** Carpet
**Some Rooms:** 2 beds
**Bed & Bath:** Queens (1 or 2); private baths (1 ensuite)
**Favorites:** Roubaix is larger and has ensuite bath

**Comfort & Decor:** Rooms are very large and sparsely furnished with modest pieces, including some period reproductions. Common areas are even more sparse. Dim lighting. Local original art in living area.

## RATES, RESERVATIONS, & RESTRICTIONS

**Deposit:** 1st night; 7-day cancellation or deposit is subject to forfeiture unless rebooked; $10 cancellation fee
**Discounts:** Single occupancy, extended stays, seniors; $10 add'l person
**Credit Cards:** V, MC
**Check-in/Out:** 2–4 (Sun. noon–2)/11
**Smoking:** No

**Pets:** Welcome
**Kids:** Welcome
**Minimum Stay:** None
**Open:** All year
**Hosts:** Matt & Robin Doval
S. 620 Washington St.
Spokane, WA 99204
(509) 624-9735
Fax: (509) 363-1745

## FOTHERINGHAM HOUSE B&B, Spokane

| Overall: ★★★★ | Room Quality: B | Value: B | Price: $80–$105 |
| --- | --- | --- | --- |

Relaxed and gracious hosts seem even more experienced than their several years as innkeepers would imply. Graham and Jackie purchased the historic home (built by prominent contractor and Spokane's first mayor, David B. Fotheringham) in 1993 and restored its interior and exterior to the storybook Victorian you see today. Guests are provided with a detailed self-guided walking tour of the fascinating historic neighborhood. Excellent location, wonderful hosts, outstanding food and attention to detail.

## SETTING & FACILITIES

**Location:** A mi. east of downtown in historic Browne's Addition neighborhood
**Near:** Patsy Clark's ("destination" restaurant), historic homes, Coeur d'Alene Park, downtown, High Bridge & other parks, Spokane Airport, museums
**Building:** 1891 Queen Anne Victorian
**Grounds:** Rose-entwined fence; lavishly landscaped corner lot across from public park
**Public Space:** Parlor, DR, veranda
**Food & Drink:** Morning coffee & tea; full breakfast; evening tea & truffles
**Recreation:** Golf, bicycling, museums, special events
**Amenities & Services:** Gift shop, guest phone/fax/data port, guest fridge; group teas by reservation, club & business meetings, limited catering

## ACCOMMODATIONS

**Units:** 4 guest rooms
**All Rooms:** Sink, hairdryer, robes, down comforter, dimmer switches
**Some Rooms:** Park view, desk, feather bed, four-poster
**Bed & Bath:** Queens; 1 private bath, 3 share 2 full baths
**Favorites:** Mayor's Room
**Comfort & Decor:** Exceptional restored antiques; living room player piano. Original light fixtures, stunning woodwork, embossed tin ceilings, heirloom quilts. Ornate floral wallpapers in common areas, soft tone-on-tone rag-rolled hues in guest rooms. Window AC units are nice on hot summer nights. Shared bathrooms: in-room sinks; both shared baths have claw-foot tubs (one full-sized, one 4-foot-long) and showers.

## RATES, RESERVATIONS, & RESTRICTIONS

**Deposit:** 1st night; 7-day cancellation
**Discounts:** Special packages (ask)
**Credit Cards:** V, MC, AE, D
**Check-in/Out:** 2–4/11
**Smoking:** On the veranda only
**Pets:** No
**Kids:** In most cases, none under 12
**Minimum Stay:** 2 nights, some holidays & festivals
**Open:** All year
**Hosts:** Jackie & Graham Johnson
2128 W. 2nd Ave., Spokane, WA 99204
(509) 838-1891
Fax: (509) 838-1807
innkeeper@fotheringham.net
www.fotheringham.net

## LOVE'S VICTORIAN B&B, Spokane

| Overall: ★★★★½ | Room Quality: A | Value: B | Price: $85–$125 |
|---|---|---|---|

Close enough to Spokane to be your base for exploring the city, yet just far enough out of town for absolute peace and quiet. Bill and Leslie have built and decorated a Victorian replica that is gracious and elegant in the extreme. The grounds and common areas are spacious and comfortable. Antiques, fine lace, ornate woodwork, and old-world hospitality combine to make you feel truly pampered. A highly recommended Spokane area experience.

### SETTING & FACILITIES

**Location:** 15 mi. north of Spokane
**Near:** Deer Park airport, Mt. Spokane, game park, 49° North ski area
**Building:** 1996-built (1896 plans) Victorian
**Grounds:** Fairytale landscaping: planters, arbors, statuary, rockery, gazebo
**Public Space:** Front parlor, DR, sunroom, back deck, great room

**Food & Drink:** Full breakfast; afternoon tea & cookies; morning coffee
**Recreation:** Croquet, bicycling, skiing, Spokane sights
**Amenities & Services:** Hot tub (extra suits & towels), games, satellite, videos, in-room sparkling cider; teas, weddings, receptions, luncheons & dinners, meetings, parties, Deer Park Airport pick-up, vintage car rides

## ACCOMMODATIONS

**Units:** 3 guest rooms
**All Rooms:** Robes, slippers, feather mattress, hairdryers
**Some Rooms:** Sitting area, balcony, turret, fireplace, claw-foot tub
**Bed & Bath:** Queens; private baths
**Favorites:** Turret Suite
**Comfort & Decor:** You'd never guess this Victorian was built in 1996!

Besides using 100-year-old houseplans (with updated plumbing and electrical), hosts brought in antique fretwork, moldings, and furnishings from old homes in Spokane to add to the authenticity. High ceilings, exceptional wallpapers, sponge-painted ceilings, lots of fireplaces.

## RATES, RESERVATIONS, & RESTRICTIONS

**Deposit:** Credit card; 10-day cancellation for refund less $10 fee; cancellations within 10 days have option of using their reservation within 30 days, Sun.–Thurs.
**Discounts:** Weekdays
**Credit Cards:** V, MC
**Check-in/Out:** After 4:30/11 or by arrangement
**Smoking:** Outside only
**Pets:** By arrangement

**Kids:** By arrangement
**Minimum Stay:** None
**Open:** All year
**Hosts:** Bill & Leslie Love
31317 N. Cedar Rd.
Deer Park, WA 99006
(509) 276-6939
Fax: Same as phone
lovesBandB@juno.com
www.bbhost.com/lovesvictorian

## MARIANNA STOLTZ HOUSE, Spokane

| Overall: ★★★½ | Room Quality: C | Value: B | Price: $69–$99 |
|---|---|---|---|

Closest bed-and-breakfast to Gonzaga University, this Historic Register home is in a pleasant walking neighborhood with century-old trees lining the sidewalks. Friendly, casual hosts put you at ease, yet common areas are uncommonly formal, with stunning antique furnishings. Maguires have run the Marianna Stoltz House since 1987, and their experience shows in the way they anticipate guests' needs: 24-hour beverages, extensive amenities basket for things you forgot, lots of extra towels, etc. Safe bicycle storage for those who arrive via the nearby Centennial Trail!

## SETTING & FACILITIES

**Location:** Central Spokane, 5 blocks east of Hwy. 395
**Near:** Gonzaga Univ., Riverfront Park, Centennial Trail, downtown, Northtown shopping center
**Building:** 1908 American foursquare
**Grounds:** Grassy lawn on corner lot w/ hedge border
**Public Space:** Parlor, den, LR, wrap-around veranda
**Food & Drink:** Tea & cookies, chilled water, & other drinks; formal breakfast (early to-go cont'l option)
**Recreation:** Golf, bicycling, museums, special events
**Amenities & Services:** Games, books, phone/fax, piano, fridge, umbrellas, amenities basket

## ACCOMMODATIONS

**Units:** 1 suite, 3 guest rooms
**All Rooms:** Remote cable TV, robes, hairdryer, desk or vanity
**Some Rooms:** Claw-foot tub
**Bed & Bath:** Mostly queens, 1 king plus twin; 2 private baths, 2 share a bath
**Favorites:** Ivy Suite (biggest bath, claw-foot tub for 2, brass bed); Blue

Room has king plus twin & great light
**Comfort & Decor:** Dark wood trims and moldings, pale maple and fir flooring. Common areas have Persian carpets, exceptional French antiques, archways, ornate tone-on-tone wallpapers with accent trims. Guest rooms have hardwood floors and mixed period furnishings.

## RATES, RESERVATIONS, & RESTRICTIONS

**Deposit:** 1st night; 7-day cancellation for refund less 15%
**Discounts:** Single occupancy, corporate; $10 add'l person
**Credit Cards:** V, MC, AE, D
**Check-in/Out:** 3–7/11
**Smoking:** Veranda only
**Pets:** No
**Kids:** By arrangement
**Minimum Stay:** Local festival weekends only

**Open:** All year
**Hosts:** Phyllis & Jim Maguire
427 E. Indiana
Spokane, WA 99207
(800) 978-6587 or (509) 483-4316
Fax: (509) 483-6773
mstoltz@aimcomm.com (MUST include your phone number on e-mail!)
aimcomm.com/stoltzhouse/

## OSLO'S B&B, Spokane

| Overall: ★★★ | Room Quality: C | Value: A | Price: $60–$80 |
|---|---|---|---|

Away from the panoply of historic homes, from the Victorians and brick edifices that define downtown Spokane and its heritage neighborhoods, one will find quiet, residential neighborhoods like this tidy, well-tended one in which Oslo's sits amongst similar single-level, ranch-style homes. Mrs. Stevenson has been offering two rooms in her home for several years. It's a homestay bed-and-breakfast, in which you are welcome to relax with the TV or a book in your hostess' living room or on her spacious brick patio overlooking her exceptional garden. Susy, a busy little pug, is an integral part of the stay, as is the delicious breakfast, which might include one of Mrs. Stevenson's special Scandinavian dishes, such as wafer-thin Norwegian pancakes, puff pancakes, or *eggerand*, a basted, custard-type dish.

## SETTING & FACILITIES

**Location:** Spokane's South Hill, 10 min. from downtown
**Near:** Manito Park; short drive to downtown attractions
**Building:** Single-level brick 1960 ranch house
**Grounds:** Attractively landscaped tidy lawn in comfortable residential neighborhood
**Public Space:** LR, DR, brick patio
**Food & Drink:** Breakfast
**Recreation:** Walking, jogging, tennis in the nearby park
**Amenities & Services:** TV/VCR, Susy (the resident pug dog), maps; gardening/landscaping advice

## ACCOMMODATIONS

**Units:** 2 guest rooms
**All Rooms:** Quiet, comfortable
**Some Rooms:** Robes, garden view
**Bed & Bath:** Queen or double; private baths, (1 ensuite)
**Favorites:** Front room (largest, ensuite bath, queen bed, garden view)
**Comfort & Decor:** Super-clean guest rooms and common areas, with newer, homey furnishings and nicely updated fixtures and decor. Exceptionally high-quality linens, down comforters. Norwegian theme is more about hospitality than decor; nothing kitschy here. AC.

## RATES, RESERVATIONS, & RESTRICTIONS

**Deposit:** 1st night; 1-week cancellation, $10 fee
**Credit Cards:** Not accepted
**Check-in/Out:** After 3/11
**Smoking:** Outside only
**Pets:** No; small host dog
**Kids:** 12 & over only
**Minimum Stay:** None
**Open:** All year
**Hosts:** Aslaug Stevenson
1821 E. 39th Ave., Spokane, WA 99203
(888) 838-3175 or (509) 838-3175

## WAVERLY PLACE B&B, Spokane

| Overall: ★★★★ | Room Quality: B | Value: B | Price: $75–$105 |
| --- | --- | --- | --- |

Terrific curb appeal—an immaculate Victorian in mint green, dark green, brick red, and white—and the interior lives up to the charming exterior's promise. Rooms are surprisingly spacious, with roomy, windowed closets. One of the few Spokane properties that allows more than two to occupy a room. While Waverly and Skinner are the premiere rooms, it should be noted that Anna's room has a turret reading alcove and four-poster bed, and that the shared upstairs bath has a dual whirlpool tub, plus there's another bath with shower downstairs. Same owners since 1986. We really liked this place; perhaps our Spokane favorite overall, in terms of value, hostesses, ambiance, neighborhood, and property.

## SETTING & FACILITIES

**Location:** North of downtown in the Corbin Park Historical District
**Near:** Riverside S.P., Northtown shopping center, downtown
**Building:** 1902 Victorian
**Grounds:** Corner lot across from Corbin Park; spacious backyard w/ flowers, pool
**Public Space:** Two parlors, DR, front porch

**Food & Drink:** Morning coffee delivered; full breakfast; afternoon tea & cookies
**Recreation:** Golf, bicycling, museums, events
**Amenities & Services:** Pool, guest phone w/ separate line, fridge; special events

## ACCOMMODATIONS

**Units:** 1 suite, 3 guest rooms
**All Rooms:** Chairs, down comforters
**Some Rooms:** Desk, sitting area, robes, turret alcove, four-poster
**Bed & Bath:** Queens (some w/ sofa-sleeper or trundle option); 2 private baths, 2 share 2 baths
**Favorites:** Waverly Suite (multiroom,

2-level suite); Skinner Suite (extra-large room w/ great light)
**Comfort & Decor:** Quality antiques and reproduction pieces, stained glass. Brocades, lace, embossed ceilings, window seats. Attractive woodwork. Central heat and AC

## RATES, RESERVATIONS, & RESTRICTIONS

**Deposit:** 1st night; 1-week cancellation
**Discounts:** Single occupancy, extended stays; $15 add'l person
**Credit Cards:** V, MC, AE, D
**Check-in/Out:** 3–6/11
**Smoking:** Outside only
**Pets:** No; host kitty
**Kids:** OK
**Minimum Stay:** 2 nights, some

holidays & festivals
**Open:** All year
**Hosts:** Marge & Tammy Arndt
709 W. Waverly Place
Spokane, WA 99205
(509) 328-1856
Fax: (509) 326-7059
waverly@ior.com
www.waverlyplace.com

## THE HOTEL USK, Usk

| Overall: ★★ | Room Quality: D | Value: B | Price: $37–$64 |
|---|---|---|---|

The Hotel Usk offers reasonable rates and a peaceful, quiet experience. It's not fancy, but the hosts are warm and knowledgeable, and the pet-and-child-friendly atmosphere is casual and laid-back. The hotel is just 300 yards from the Pend Oreille River and boat ramp and adjacent to a laundromat and video rentals, with restaurant and grocer nearby. Host kitties on premises.

## SETTING & FACILITIES

**Location:** On the Pend Oreille River about an hour north of Spokane
**Near:** Newport, Cusick, Idaho, 49° North ski area, lakes, Colville Nat'l Forest
**Building:** 1910 Hotel
**Grounds:** Fenced back lawn w/ picnic area, flowers, & border plantings
**Public Space:** LR/guest lobby, sun-deck, DR

**Food & Drink:** Full breakfast offered April–Sept. (fee)
**Recreation:** Hunting, boating, skiing, snowmobiling, ORV trails, festivals
**Amenities & Services:** TV/VCR, videos, piano, games, books; cyclist campground in back

## ACCOMMODATIONS

**Units:** 8 guest rooms
**All Rooms:** Sinks
**Some Rooms:** Four-poster, desk
**Bed & Bath:** Double or twins; most w/ bath, one w/ toilet only; hall bath w/ shower avail. to all
**Favorites:** #1 & # 2 as 2-BR suite; #3 is largest, has TV/VCR; #5 is most stylish

**Comfort & Decor:** Furnishings and decor can tend toward worn, but property is clean and comfortable. Carpet, electric heat, wallpapers. Dining room is stylish and cheerful, brick red in color, where the "country formal" breakfast is served in season. Smoking in some rooms results in a bit of mustiness overall.

## RATES, RESERVATIONS, & RESTRICTIONS

**Deposit:** 2 nights' deposit; 24-hour cancellation, 48 hours in summer
**Discounts:** Winter; $5 add'l person; breakfast $6 in season
**Credit Cards:** V, MC, AE, D
**Check-in/Out:** After 3/11
**Smoking:** OK in some rooms
**Pets:** Welcome
**Kids:** Welcome

**No-Nos:** Cooking in rooms; noisiness after 9 in rooms, 11 in lobby
**Minimum Stay:** None
**Open:** All year (breakfast offered April–Sept. only)
**Hosts:** Stan & Andrea
410 River Road, P.O. Box 100
Usk, WA 99180
(888) 423–8084 or (509) 445-1526

# Zone 9
# Southeast Washington

Welcome to Washington's "dry side": the lava plateaus, high deserts, rolling farmlands, and river basins of southeastern Washington. Here, visitors find the award-winning wineries of the Yakima Valley, the high-tech industry of the Tri-Cities, the apple orchards of the Wenatchee Valley, and the agricultural growing, processing, and distribution areas of Walla Walla, Dayton, Clarkston, Ritzville, and Moses Lake. The sun-drenched communities in this region are surrounded by vast acreage more fertile for crops than tourism, but several of the bed-and-breakfasts here are real gems.

Wenatchee is world-famous for its apple orchards and locally popular for its Mission Ridge Ski Area, where the powder tends to be light and dry and the weather better than west-side slopes. Other attractions include Ohme Gardens (a re-created alpine botanical touring garden), nearby Cashmere (home of the native-fruit confection "aplets and cotlets"), and tourist haven Leavenworth (see Zone 7).

The Yakima Valley is perhaps best known for its wines and microbrew beers, and bed-and-breakfasts have sprouted up not only in Yakima itself, but also in the nearby communities of Grandview, Outlook, and Sunnyside. Yakima's other attractions include its historic Capitol Theater (concert venue), Sundome (sports arena), museums, the Yakima Greenway (recreation trail and park), and Native American attractions.

At the other end of the Yakima Valley, where the Snake, Columbia, and Yakima Rivers converge, you'll find the Tri-Cities (Richland, Pasco, and Kennewick). These three towns form a retail hub, featuring the Columbia Center shopping district, Tri-Cities Coliseum, and seasonal events like the Columbia Cup hydroplane races.

East of the Tri-Cities, toward the Blue Mountains, Dayton and Walla Walla are charming communities steeped in history. Dayton is rich in railroad lore, including its Depot Museum, and has a surprising four-star restaurant. Walla Walla features a refurbished downtown with turn-of-the-20th-century buildings, plus many beautiful parks, three colleges, and the historic Whitman Mission.

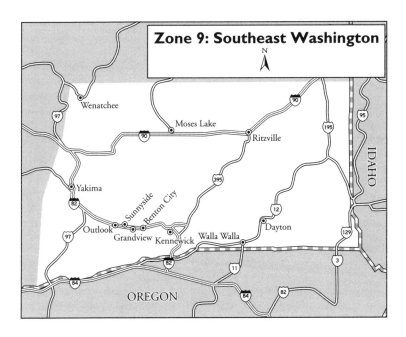

## Zone 9: Southeast Washington

N

Wenatchee

Moses Lake

Ritzville

IDAHO

Yakima

Sunnyside

Benton City

Outlook

Grandview

Kennewick

Walla Walla

Dayton

OREGON

**Benton City**
Palmer Farm B&B, p. 278

**Dayton**
The Purple House, p. 279
Weinhard Hotel, p. 280

**Grandview**
Cozy Rose Inn, p. 281

**Kennewick**
Casablanca, p. 282

**Moses Lake**
Carriage House B&B, p. 283

**Outlook**
Outlook Inn, p. 285

**Ritzville**
The Portico Victorian B&B,
    p. 286

**Sunnyside**
Sunnyside Inn B&B, p. 287

**Walla Walla**
Green Gables Inn, p. 288
Stone Creek Inn, p. 289

**Wenatchee**
Rimrock Inn, p. 290
Warm Springs Inn, p. 291

**Yakima**
Birchfield Manor, p. 293
A Touch of Europe B&B Inn,
    p. 294

## PALMER FARM B&B, Benton City

| Overall: ★★★½ | Room Quality: C | Value: A | Price: $70–$75 |
|---|---|---|---|

You won't find TVs or hot tubs at Palmer Farm. Instead, you'll find a cheerful, renovated turn-of-the-20th-century farmhouse with fresh, attractive decor, sunny rooms, and a wraparound porch that invites you to "sit a spell." Stroll the spacious grounds, where profuse flowers and iron arbors and a gazebo lend cheer near the house, and rambling lawns offer peace and quiet and a trail to the Yakima River. A score of wineries are just minutes away, as are the Columbia Center shopping district and the Columbia and Snake Rivers.

### SETTING & FACILITIES

**Location:** On River Rd. between Ellen & Dimmick, near the banks of the Yakima River
**Near:** Benton City, Tri-Cities (Richland, Pasco, Kennewick), 23 wineries
**Building:** 1902 family farmhouse
**Grounds:** 10-acre parcel w/ 2 acres of lawn & landscaped grounds with arbors & gazebo
**Public Space:** Living/dining area, sunroom, library, wraparound porch
**Food & Drink:** Full breakfast
**Recreation:** Fishing, boating
**Amenities & Services:** Picnic lunch, afternoon tea, light dinner by arrangement; weddings, reunions

### ACCOMMODATIONS

**Units:** 4 guest rooms
**All Rooms:** Sink, armoire or closet, AC, antiques
**Some Rooms:** Carpet, garden view
**Bed & Bath:** Queens; 1 private half-bath, 2 shared baths
**Favorites:** Addie's
**Comfort & Decor:** This quaint farmhouse, with its quilts and heirloom treasures, was fully modernized in the 1990s, yet retains the gracious feel of a 1902 homestead with 1942 updates. Attractive floral wallpapers back Palmer family photos; "excavated" 1940s linoleum mingles with fresh 1990s vinyls. Sunny, cheerful, with vintage flair.

### RATES, RESERVATIONS, & RESTRICTIONS

**Deposit:** N/A; please notify if you must cancel your reservation
**Discounts:** Group, single occupancy, whole house rental
**Credit Cards:** Not accepted
**Check-in/Out:** 4–7/11 or by arrangement
**Smoking:** No
**Pets:** No
**Kids:** No
**Minimum Stay:** None
**Open:** All year
**Hosts:** Virginia McKenna
42901 N. River Rd.
Benton City, WA 99320
(800) 635-3131 or (509) 588-4011

## THE PURPLE HOUSE, Dayton

Overall: ★★★     Room Quality: C     Value: C     Price: $85–$125

You can't help but smile when you see this charming, gingerbread, decidedly purple house on a quiet (is there any other kind?) Dayton side street. Your interesting, well-traveled hostess wants you to feel totally at home: play the piano, bring your friends, hang out. Her dogs, two adorable Shih Tzus, are cute and clean, but you gotta like dogs to be truly happy here. Makes a great home base for outdoor recreation in the Blue Mountains or for the antique shops and ambiance of Dayton's historic districts.

### SETTING & FACILITIES

**Location:** Quiet side street a block south of Hwy. 12
**Near:** Dayton Depot Museum, Patit Creek "destination" restaurant; half-hour from historic Walla Walla arts, festivals, Whitman Mission; Blue Mountains
**Building:** 1882 Queen Anne mansion
**Grounds:** Shady patio, pool, small landscaped front

**Public Space:** Library, parlor, TV room, deck
**Food & Drink:** Full breakfast; dinner by arrangement
**Recreation:** Fishing, hunting, skiing, picnicking, antiquing, bicycling, galleries
**Amenities & Services:** Heated pool, piano, phones (some ensuite, others extension reaches); Carriage House is a self-contained apartment; dinners by arrangement

### ACCOMMODATIONS

**Units:** 2 rooms, 2 suites
**All Rooms:** Airy, high ceilings
**Some Rooms:** Ensuite phone, TV, sunken tub & sep. shower, bidet, writing desk, armoire
**Bed & Bath:** King, queen, or double; 2 private baths, 2 share a bath
**Favorites:** Master Suite, Carriage House

**Comfort & Decor:** Rooms have high ceilings and are very clean and cheerfully decorated, with thoroughly modern fixtures. Common areas mix eclectic furnishings and art ranging from Victorian to Asian, reflecting the refined ease and tastes of your well-traveled hostess. Quality mattresses, attention to detail.

### RATES, RESERVATIONS, & RESTRICTIONS

**Deposit:** 1st night, 7-day cancellation
**Discounts:** Extended stays
**Credit Cards:** V, MC
**Check-in/Out:** 2:30/11
**Smoking:** Outside only
**Pets:** Small, well-behaved pets may be accommodated by arrangement
**Kids:** None under 16 except by

arrangement
**No-Nos:** Shoes in the house
**Minimum Stay:** None
**Open:** All year
**Hosts:** D. Christine Williscroft
415 E. Clay St., Dayton, WA 99328
(800) 486-2574 or (509) 382-3159
Fax: Same as phone

## WEINHARD HOTEL, Dayton

| Overall: ★★★★ | Room Quality: B | Value: C | Price: $70–$125 |
|---|---|---|---|

Built as Weinhard Saloon & Lodge Hall by local brewer Jacob Weinhard in 1889, this building has been beautifully restored by proprietors Dan and Ginny Butler to retain the charm of the era but embrace modern amenities. Luxurious rooms are spacious and super-clean. Large, comfortable lobby with grand piano is made cozier by a variety of seating groups. Try to catch their eclectic music and wine nights on Fridays and Saturdays. Not as intimate as nearby Purple House, and lacks the full breakfast, but this small inn will be more comfortable for those accustomed to hotels.

### SETTING & FACILITIES

**Location:** On Dayton's Main St. between 1st & 2nd
**Near:** Dayton Depot Museum, Patit Creek "destination" restaurant; half-hour from historic Walla Walla, w/ arts, festivals, Whitman Mission; Blue Mountains
**Building:** 1889 Victorian hotel & saloon
**Grounds:** None per se; delightful Victorian roof garden
**Public Space:** Spacious lobby, rooftop garden

**Food & Drink:** Cont'l breakfast; quality Italian restaurant adjacent, others nearby
**Recreation:** Fishing, hunting, skiing, picnicking, antiquing, galleries
**Amenities & Services:** In-room phones, TVs, toiletries, data ports, writing desks; chess, cribbage; wine & live music Fri. & Sat. in gracious lobby; romantic getaway packages (incl. roses, champagne, 5-course ensuite dinner)

### ACCOMMODATIONS

**Units:** 15 guest rooms
**All Rooms:** All-cotton bedding, spacious
**Some Rooms:** Whirlpool spa, balcony access, disabled access
**Bed & Bath:** Queen (13 rooms), 2 queens (Room 9), two twins (Room 8); full private bath w/ tub/shower unit
**Favorites:** 10, 15

**Comfort & Decor:** Ornate carpet, abundant woodwork (some original), and American Victorian furnishings. Original colored glass; fresh flowers. Upstairs rooms are more upscale, with better views and central AC (slightly more expensive). Downstairs $70 rooms have window-unit AC. Individual temperature controls. High ceilings.

## RATES, RESERVATIONS, & RESTRICTIONS

**Deposit:** 1st night; 7-day cancellation (unless emergency)
**Discounts:** AAA, commercial, gov't; $10 add'l person (antique cribs, child beds, roll-aways avail.)
**Credit Cards:** V, MC, AE
**Check-in/Out:** After 4/11
**Smoking:** No
**Pets:** Welcome
**Kids:** Welcome

**Minimum Stay:** 2 nights during certain major festivals
**Open:** All year
**Hosts:** Dan & Ginny Butler
235 E. Main St.
Dayton, WA 99328
(509) 382-4032
Fax: (509) 382-2640
www.weinhard.com

## COZY ROSE INN, Grandview

Overall: ★★★★★     Room Quality: A     Value: B     Price: $98–$129

A pastoral, romantic setting for your tour of the Yakima Valley wine country. Jennie and Mark have done their homework, and this labor-of-love bed-and-breakfast shows it. Beginning in 1994, they handcrafted a room at a time, bringing touches from their favorite Northwest bed-and-breakfasts to this quiet little corner of Washington. Each suite is a private retreat, and your hosts' exceptional service includes working with you on every detail to make your stay perfect (dinner by arrangement, late check-out, romantic "extras"). Fresh breakfasts incorporate local and site-grown produce. Beautiful grounds make an exquisite wedding or party setting.

## SETTING & FACILITIES

**Location:** 5 mi. off I-82's Exit 69, between Sunnyside & Prosser
**Near:** Wineries, microbreweries, Grandview, Sunnyside, Prosser, Yakima, Toppenish
**Building:** Cape Cod–style home & adjacent farmhouse
**Grounds:** Large lawns, extensive flowers, greenery; pond, fountain, picnic area; hobby farm includes cow, llamas; across from hop field
**Public Space:** Self-contained suites

**Food & Drink:** Evening cookies; in-room coffee/tea service; full breakfast delivered to room about 9 (early cont'l option)
**Recreation:** Wine touring, walking (w/ or w/out llamas), bicycling, golf, historic touring
**Amenities & Services:** (See "All Rooms" and "Some Rooms"); weddings, receptions, reunions; celebration packages by arrangement; hors d'oeuvres or dinners by arrangement

## ACCOMMODATIONS

**Units:** 4 self-contained suites
**All Rooms:** LR, fireplace, private entrance, sound system, fridge, down comforter, iron, toiletries & perfumes, robes, deck/patio, inside & outside dining areas
**Some Rooms:** TV, dual whirlpool, sofabed, full kitchen, big-screen TV, VCR, games, desk, phone

**Bed & Bath:** King (3) or queen; private baths
**Favorites:** Each is unique & wonderful
**Comfort & Decor:** French country ambiance. Pale background tones with deep, lush accents. Lots of florals, gauze, lace, silk, green plants. Very romantic. Fireplaces provide individual heat control. AC.

## RATES, RESERVATIONS, & RESTRICTIONS

**Deposit:** 1st night; 7-day cancellation
**Discounts:** Extended stay, single occupancy, corporate; $20 add'l person
**Credit Cards:** Not accepted
**Check-in/Out:** By arrangement
**Smoking:** Outside only
**Pets:** No; host dogs, cat, livestock on premises
**Kids:** Welcome in some rooms
**No-Nos:** Shoes in some units

**Minimum Stay:** 2 nights in Secret Garden
**Open:** All year
**Hosts:** Jennie & Mark Jackson
1220 Forsell Rd.
Grandview, WA 98930
(509) 882-4669
Fax: (509) 882-4234
www.virtualcities.com/ons/wa/c/wac67010.htm

## CASABLANCA, Kennewick

| Overall: ★★★★ | Room Quality: B | Value: A | Price: $65–$85 |
|---|---|---|---|

Conveniently located for accessing all points in the Tri-Cities (Richland, Pasco, Kennewick), Casablanca is appropriate for business, leisure, or family lodging. The emphasis is on rural peace and quiet and flexible accommodation packages to meet your needs. (Retreats, catered meals, extended stays, overflow sleeping areas can be configured by arrangement.) Business travelers will appreciate the self-sufficiency of the large kitchenette and whenever-you-want-it breakfast and snacks. Families will love the friendly horses, goats, sheep, dogs, cats, and whatever else the Dillmans are raising at their pristine, storybook hobby farm at the time of your visit.

## SETTING & FACILITIES

**Location:** Less than 3 mi. off I-82's Exit 109
**Near:** Columbia Center retail area, Hanford site, WSU Tri-Cities, Tri-Cities Coliseum, TRAC, Kennewick, Pasco, Richland
**Building:** 2-level ranch w/ daylight basement
**Grounds:** 5.25-acre hobby farm w/ huge lawns, roses, vineyard, barn, farm animals
**Public Space:** Main LR, deck, patio, guest LR, guest kitchenette

**Food & Drink:** Self-serve cold beverages, popcorn, cereal; breakfast is generally self-serve cont'l in guest kitchenette; full breakfast avail.
**Recreation:** Wine touring, golf, boating, water skiing
**Amenities & Services:** Big-screen TV, VCR, fireplaces, fridge, micro., coffeemaker, phone & fax, hammock, library, friendly animals; weddings, dinners, small retreats, on-site catering, celebration extras

## ACCOMMODATIONS

**Units:** 3 guest rooms w/ overflow potential
**All Rooms:** Deck/patio access, sep. entrance, deck table & chairs, phone avail.
**Some Rooms:** Oversize soaking tub, sound system, sitting area
**Bed & Bath:** King or queen; private baths (2 ensuite)

**Favorites:** Italian-American
**Comfort & Decor:** Blending American equestrian with French-English country, this casually gracious home has rich brocade furnishings, tile floors, plush carpet, and two fireplaces (one stone, one brick). Guest rooms have theme decor: American Outdoor, French Country, Italian-American.

## RATES, RESERVATIONS, & RESTRICTIONS

**Deposit:** 1st night; 3-day cancellation
**Discounts:** Gov't, extended corporate; inquire about add'l person(s)
**Credit Cards:** V, MC
**Check-in/Out:** 4/11 or by arrangement (flexible)
**Smoking:** No
**Pets:** No; host pets (adorable basset hounds, etc.); horse boarding
**Kids:** Welcome

**Minimum Stay:** None
**Open:** All year
**Hosts:** Dave & Candace Dillman
94806 E. Granada Ct.
Kennewick, WA 99337
(888) 627-0676 or (509) 627-0676
Fax: (509) 627-0768
casab-b@oneworld.owt.com
www.owt.com/casablancabb

## CARRIAGE HOUSE B&B, Moses Lake

| Overall: ★★★★ | Room Quality: B | Value: C | Price: $95–$130 |
|---|---|---|---|

A surprise in the desert, this gingerbread-pretty nouveau Victorian is an anomaly at the edge of a middle-class ranch-house neighborhood. Besides being pretty outside, with its mint-and-rose exterior, it's well built (road noise well muffled) and attractively appointed. Unfortunately, it was also for sale at this writing; call for possible policy changes. Current owners have collected beautiful antiques, many with family or other histories (a brass brothel bed in The Hunt Room, a living room chair in which presidents Woodrow Wilson and Gerald Ford have both sat).

## SETTING & FACILITIES

**Location:** Just off I-90, Exit 176, on Peninsula Dr. at Interlake Rd.
**Near:** The Gorge Amphitheatre, Champs de Brionne winery, Moses Lake (town & lake); Grand Coulee Dam (1 hour)
**Building:** 1995 storybook Victorian-style
**Grounds:** Lawn & lake view (albeit across the interstate)
**Public Space:** LR, deck, breakfast room

**Food & Drink:** Hot beverages; snacks; self-serve cont'l breakfast weekdays; full breakfast weekends & holidays
**Recreation:** Lake activities, golf, concerts, water slides, wine touring, historic touring
**Amenities & Services:** Piano; community events, mystery dinners, meetings, weddings

## ACCOMMODATIONS

**Units:** 4 guest rooms
**All Rooms:** TV, whirlpool or claw-foot tub, hairdryers, curling irons, toiletries
**Some Rooms:** Ceiling fan, water view
**Bed & Bath:** Queen or double (trundle avail. 1 room); private ensuite baths
**Favorites:** Hunt, Bridal Turret

**Comfort & Decor:** Forest and rose tones predominate. Plush carpet throughout. Wainscoting, attractive wallpapers, antique furnishings, lots of beautifully restored family heritage pieces. Chandeliers and other elegant period light fixtures. Quality bathrooms. Central heat and AC.

## RATES, RESERVATIONS, & RESTRICTIONS

**Deposit:** Credit card or full advance payment; 7-day cancellation
**Discounts:** Corporate, extended stay; $20 add'l person
**Credit Cards:** V, MC
**Check-in/Out:** After 5/11
**Smoking:** Outside only
**Pets:** No
**Kids:** Well-behaved 12 & older welcome

**Minimum Stay:** None
**Open:** All year
**Hosts:** Donna & Bill Hoyt
2801 W. Peninsula Dr.
Moses Lake, WA 98837
(800) 761-7466 or (509) 766-7466
www.carriagehouse.nu

## OUTLOOK INN, Outlook

| Overall: ★★ | Room Quality: D | Value: B | Price: $45–$75 |
|---|---|---|---|

Immediately adjacent to Tefft Cellars, this modest little three-bedroom ranch was converted from the Tefft's home to a bed-and-breakfast in 1997. (Hosts now live in a separate house behind the winery.) The casual atmosphere is like staying in a friend's vacation home. Extremely quiet and surrounded by vineyards, the little house provides a great base for touring wine country. Bit of a drive to services and restaurants. Ideally suited for a group traveling together: with the living room sofa-sleeper, the house sleeps eight, plus sleeping bags are allowed.

### SETTING & FACILITIES

**Location:** 4.5 mi. off I-82's Exit 63, between Sunnyside & Zillah
**Near:** Tefft Cellars Winery, Toppenish, wineries, Yakama Indian Reservation
**Building:** 1977 single-level home
**Grounds:** Small back lawn w/ deck, surrounded by vineyards
**Public Space:** Deck, LR, kitchen, dining area, den

**Food & Drink:** Wines avail.; self-serve cont'l breakfast
**Recreation:** Wine touring, historic touring, museums, golf, antiquing
**Amenities & Services:** Seasonal BBQ, full kitchen, iron, hairdryer, TV; wine & hors d'oeuvres by arrangement, eco-sensitive linens policy

### ACCOMMODATIONS

**Units:** 3 guest rooms
**All Rooms:** Electric blankets, robes, phone avail.
**Some Rooms:** Vanity, antiques
**Bed & Bath:** Queen or double; 1 private bath, 2 share a bath
**Favorites:** Champagne

**Comfort & Decor:** Midquality furnishings, 1970s decor & fixtures. Not fancy, but clean, serviceable, homey. Champagne is done in ivory tones, Vineyard with grapevine fabric, Bordeaux has red accents and is the smallest. Several antique radios. Central heat; kitchen window AC unit.

### RATES, RESERVATIONS, & RESTRICTIONS

**Deposit:** Credit card; 7-day cancellation
**Discounts:** Whole house, extended stay; $5–10 add'l person
**Credit Cards:** V, MC
**Check-in/Out:** 3–5 or by arrangement/noon
**Smoking:** Outside only
**Pets:** Welcome w/ whole-house rental or by arrangement

**Kids:** Welcome w/ whole-house rental or by arrangement
**Minimum Stay:** None
**Open:** All year
**Hosts:** Joel & Pam Tefft
1320 Independence Rd.
Outlook, WA 98938
(888) 303-7651 or (509) 837-7651
Fax: (509) 839-7337
tcwinery@aol.com
www.winesnw.com/OutlookInn.htm

## THE PORTICO VICTORIAN B&B, Ritzville

| Overall: ★★★★ | Room Quality: B | Value: A | Price: $59–$74 |
|---|---|---|---|

Incredibly beautiful inside and out, this National Historic Register house is faced with a combination of smooth and rough-faced salmon-colored bricks, and trimmed in jade green. The facade is accented by a sweeping, rounded "portico" porch with neo-classical Ionic columns. Interior decor is voluptuously Victorian—a real showcase. Please note that owners (who raised their ten children here) have The Portico up for sale at this writing, so prices, policies, and other details may change.

### SETTING & FACILITIES

**Location:** Corner of Adams & 5th
**Near:** Community pool, park, 9-hole golf course; 1 hour from Spokane; minutes from I-90
**Building:** 1902 combination Neoclassical/Queen Anne Victorian
**Grounds:** Grassy corner lot w/ mature trees, roses, patio, fruit trees, vegetable garden

**Public Space:** Parlor, library, wrap-around porch
**Food & Drink:** Evening coffee or tea; full breakfast
**Recreation:** Bicycling, historic touring, tennis
**Amenities & Services:** Cable TV, fireplace; luncheons, dinners, celebrations, receptions, meetings

### ACCOMMODATIONS

**Units:** 2 guest rooms
**All Rooms:** Serious antiques
**Bed & Bath:** Double or queen; private ensuite baths
**Favorites:** O.H. Greene
**Comfort & Decor:** Stunning

antiques fill this elegant home. Elaborate window treatments, embossed ceilings and wallpapers, rich dramatic woodwork. Florals, velvets, gilt-framed photos. Inlaid wood foyer floor.

### RATES, RESERVATIONS, & RESTRICTIONS

**Deposit:** 1st night; 72-hour cancellation
**Discounts:** Extended stay; single occupancy; $6 add'l person
**Credit Cards:** V, MC, D
**Check-in/Out:** 5–6 or by arrangement/11
**Smoking:** Outside only
**Pets:** No

**Kids:** Well-tended, well-behaved children welcome
**Minimum Stay:** None
**Open:** All year
**Hosts:** Mary Anne & Bill Phips
502 S. Adams St.
Ritzville, WA 99169
(509) 659-0800

## SUNNYSIDE INN B&B, Sunnyside

| | | | |
|---|---|---|---|
| Overall: ★★★½ | Room Quality: C | Value: A | Price: $59–$89 |

One of the Yakima Valley's first bed-and-breakfasts (founded 1989), Sunnyside Inn is a casual, comfortable property with motel-style amenities and a great location for exploring both the upper and lower valley. Your pleasant, hard-working hosts live off-site with their family, giving you the run of the house (the term "Manager's House" refers to an earlier time, when the Vliegers lived on site). "Big House" (original inn) rooms have signature double whirlpool tubs and are more upscale; rooms in both houses are excellent values. Snack lovers will appreciate the range of freebies in the Big House guest kitchen.

### SETTING & FACILITIES

**Location:** Near city center, corner of Edison & 8th; Exit 63 or 69 off I-82
**Near:** Over 20 Yakima Valley wineries, downtown, Yakima Valley agricultural areas
**Building:** 1919 "Big House" (original inn) & adjacent 1920s "Manager's House"
**Grounds:** Small, grassy corner lot w/ mature landscaping at edge of commercial district

**Public Space:** Manager's House LR, Big House guest kitchen & dining areas
**Food & Drink:** Popcorn, ice cream, cookies, baked goods, beverages; full breakfast
**Recreation:** Bicycling, golf, historic touring
**Amenities & Services:** Common snack kitchen, full kitchen privileges by arrangement; special occasion extras (gratis), banquets, catering, parties

### ACCOMMODATIONS

**Units:** 12 guest rooms
**All Rooms:** Premium TV channels, private phone line, hairdryer, coffeemaker or access
**Some Rooms:** Dbl. whirlpool (7), VCR, table & chairs, private entrance, fireplace, four-poster
**Bed & Bath:** Queen or king, some w/ extra bed; private baths (11 ensuite)
**Favorites:** Karen, Jean, Alice

**Comfort & Decor:** Overall warm country style. Big House: spacious rooms, antique reproduction decor, wallpapers, wainscoting, brick, tile; extra touches may include glider rocker, hand-stenciling. Manager's House rooms: more modest/motel-like, but wallpaper touches, some dormered ceilings. Central heat and AC, plus individual auxiliary in most.

## RATES, RESERVATIONS, & RESTRICTIONS

**Deposit:** Credit card; 2-week cancellation
**Discounts:** Weekday corporate, AAA, whole house (8 rooms); $10 add'l person
**Credit Cards:** V, MC, AE, D
**Check-in/Out:** After 2/11
**Smoking:** Outside only
**Pets:** No
**Kids:** Welcome

**Minimum Stay:** 2 nights, some holidays & local festivals
**Open:** All year
**Hosts:** Karen & Don Vlieger
804 E. Edison Ave.
Sunnyside, WA 98944
(800) 221-4195 or (509) 839-5557
Fax: (509) 839-3520
suninn@bentonrea.com
www.bbhost.com/sunnysideinn

## GREEN GABLES INN, Walla Walla

Overall: ★★★★½      Room Quality: A      Value: B      Price: $85–$110

Seasoned hosts Margaret and Jim Buchan, who live adjacent to the inn, purchased this property in 1990 and turned it into the award-winning bed-and-breakfast it is today. Green Gables Inn, with room names from L. M. Montgomery's *Anne of Green Gables*, opened for business in 1991. The Buchans take well-earned pride in their stringent standards of cleanliness, quality, safety, and their anticipation of guests' needs. Breakfast is served by candlelight on fine china and crystal.

## SETTING & FACILITIES

**Location:** Near Whitman College in north-central Walla Walla
**Near:** Historic Main Street, Whitman Mission, hospitals, wineries
**Building:** 1909 Craftsman-style mansion
**Grounds:** Small yard on a quiet street; parking lot
**Public Space:** Library, porch, 2 living/sitting rooms, DR
**Food & Drink:** Beverages; coffee & light snack set out early; full, formal breakfast

**Recreation:** Walking tours of historic homes or (believe it or not) historic trees, museums, golf, festivals, arts activities
**Amenities & Services:** Candy & coffee upon arrival, robes, games, extra pillows, extra-large towels, toiletries, hairdryer, tandem bikes, phones in common areas (not in rooms), fireplaces

## ACCOMMODATIONS

**Units:** 5 rooms, Carriage House apt.
**All Rooms:** Mini-fridge, cable TV, fresh flowers, artwork
**Some Rooms:** Claw-foot tub, private deck, fireplace, sitting area, writing desk; Carriage House has full kitchen, two TVs, LR
**Bed & Bath:** King, queen, or twin bed(s); private baths; Carriage House has king bed, queen sofabed, daybed, & bath-and-a-half

**Favorites:** Idlewild
**Comfort & Decor:** Hardwood floors downstairs and in common areas; plush carpet in guest rooms for sound-muffling. Fine period furnishings include mahogany, burled walnut, and bird's-eye maple. Top-quality mattresses and linens. Central AC, gas furnace. Lots of windows; each room has windows that vent.

## RATES, RESERVATIONS, & RESTRICTIONS

**Deposit:** Credit card or check; 7-day cancellation
**Discounts:** Single occupancy Mon.–Thurs., extended stays; add'l person $25; Carriage House $160 for 4
**Credit Cards:** V, MC, AE, D
**Check-in/Out:** 3–8/11
**Smoking:** No
**Pets:** No
**Kids:** Over 12, main house; younger in Carriage House (crib avail.)

**Minimum Stay:** A few special event weekends
**Open:** All year
**Hosts:** Jim & Margaret Buchan
922 Bonsella
Walla Walla, WA 99362
(888) 525-5501 or (509) 525-5501
greengables@wwics.com
www.greengablesinn.com

## STONE CREEK INN, Walla Walla

Overall: ★★★½     Room Quality: C     Value: C     Price: $95–$125

Elegant old mansion retains its historic character exceptionally well, if a bit at the expense of ultramodern amenities (closets small, storage limited, hot water limited). Decor and breakfasts (often incorporating famous Walla Walla Sweet onions) are exceptional. Current owner has run this bed-and-breakfast since 1995; previous owners' bed-and-breakfast was not universally well liked. Host's dog on property. Spacious, tree-filled grounds and pool are pleasant, restful amenities.

## SETTING & FACILITIES

**Location:** Due north of Tietan Park in eastern Walla Walla, about 1 mi. from downtown
**Near:** Pioneer Park, historic downtown, wineries, Whitman Mission
**Building:** 1883 Queen Anne Victorian, former Territorial Governor's Mansion
**Grounds:** 4 acres, sprawling lawns, 100-year-old trees
**Public Space:** Formal DR, two LRs, small upstairs sitting area
**Food & Drink:** Morning coffee/tea; full formal breakfast
**Recreation:** Swimming, Walla Walla attractions
**Amenities & Services:** Pool (seasonal), hot tub, library, two grand pianos, robes, iron, phones in common areas & avail. for (but not situated in) each room, fireplaces; weddings (incl. grand-scale); limousine (free airport service, also avail. to rent for wine touring, restaurant service, etc.); fax avail.

## ACCOMMODATIONS

**Units:** 4 guest rooms
**All Rooms:** 12-foot ceilings
**Some Rooms:** TV/VCR, porch/balcony, sitting room, fireplace
**Bed & Bath:** Queens; up to 3 private baths—if 4th room rented, 2 rooms have private bath & 2 rooms share (Governor's Room & Terrace Room)
**Favorites:** Veranda Room, Governor's Room
**Comfort & Decor:** Elaborate moldings and exquisitely decorated with period furniture. Lively color schemes (terra cotta & blue in Governor's Room). More Victorian-period feel than spit-and-polish modernization. Downstairs (incl. Garden Room) has central AC; other rooms have window AC.

## RATES, RESERVATIONS, & RESTRICTIONS

**Deposit:** First night; 7-day cancellation or forfeit unless room can be rebooked
**Discounts:** $25 add'l person on rollaway; $10 breakfast for outside guests
**Credit Cards:** V, MC
**Check-in/Out:** 3–8/11
**Smoking:** Outside only
**Pets:** No; host dog
**Kids:** 12 & over only
**Minimum Stay:** None
**Open:** All year
**Hosts:** Patricia Johnson
720 Bryant Ave.
Walla Walla, WA 99362
(509) 529-8120
Fax: (509) 529-8120
stonecrk@internetnw.net

## RIMROCK INN, Wenatchee

| Overall: ★★★ | Room Quality: D | Value: B | Price: $70 |
|---|---|---|---|

This homestay-style bed-and-breakfast is the closest lodging to Mission Ridge ski area. Tucked in a classic eastern Washington sagebrush steppe canyon that serves as a rich bird and wildlife habitat, the attractive home has been open to guests since 1996. Mary and Doug are warm, pleasant hosts who also have quarters on the lower level and tend to vacate the living areas when guests are inclined to privacy. Good value for skiers, business travelers, or anyone touring the Wenatchee valley.

## SETTING & FACILITIES

**Location:** 10 mi. from Mission Ridge, 3 mi. from south end of Wenatchee in Pitcher Canyon
**Near:** Mission Ridge ski area, Ohme Gardens, Rocky Reach Dam, Cashmere, Leavenworth "Bavarian" village
**Building:** Contemporary double-gambrel-roofed, 3-level cedar home
**Grounds:** Flowers & landscaping

**Public Space:** LR, DR, deck
**Food & Drink:** Refreshments; full breakfast
**Recreation:** Bird/wildlife watching, bicycling, skiing, hiking, golf, rafting
**Amenities & Services:** Hot tub, games, fireplace, TV/VCR, sound system, books; ski packages, activity/restaurant reservations

## ACCOMMODATIONS

**Units:** 3 guest rooms (one 2-room unit)
**All Rooms:** Robes, menus, touring info
**Some Rooms:** Desk, sitting area, Amish quilt

**Bed & Bath:** King (1) or queen & twin (2); private baths
**Favorites:** Columbia Room
**Comfort & Decor:** Attractive contemporary country wallpapers. Cedar-paneled ceiling. Carpet. Central heat and woodstove.

## RATES, RESERVATIONS, & RESTRICTIONS

**Deposit:** 50%; 14-day cancellation
**Discounts:** Extended stay; ski packages; $10 add'l person
**Credit Cards:** V, MC
**Check-in/Out:** After 2/11
**Smoking:** No
**Pets:** No
**Kids:** 10 & older welcome

**Minimum Stay:** None
**Open:** All year
**Hosts:** Doug & Mary Cook
1354 Pitcher Canyon Rd.
Wenatchee, WA 98801
(888) 664-5113 or (509) 664-5113
Fax: Same as phone; call ahead
www.rimrockinn.com

## WARM SPRINGS INN, Wenatchee

| Overall: ★★★½ | Room Quality: B | Value: B | Price: $85–$110 |
|---|---|---|---|

The house is massive and grand, the decor homey and vaguely quirky, mixing eras and styles companionably. Lots of rich knotty plank paneling and brick. Quiet riverfront location offers great access to both Leavenworth and Wenatchee. Common areas offer many elegant yet comfortable options for relaxation, as do the sprawling grounds, which are especially lovely in spring and summer. Great place for a group gathering.

### SETTING & FACILITIES

**Location:** End of Love Lane, off Hwy. 2 at Lower Sunnyslope Rd., just west of Wenatchee
**Near:** Ohme Gardens, Cashmere, Mission Ridge ski area, Leavenworth "Bavarian" village
**Building:** 9,000-sq.-ft. 1917 Southern Colonial–style estate
**Grounds:** 10 riverfront acres w/ mature trees, roses, gardens, adjacent orchard

**Public Space:** Great room, LR, DR, porch, deck
**Food & Drink:** Tea & coffee; full breakfast
**Recreation:** Bicycling, skiing, hiking, golf, rafting
**Amenities & Services:** Sound system, fireplaces, games, guest phone, iron, hairdryer, hot tub; weddings, parties, retreats, business meetings, catering

### ACCOMMODATIONS

**Units:** 4 guest rooms (plus overflow loft sleeping area)
**All Rooms:** Robes, TV
**Some Rooms:** View, sitting area, VCR
**Bed & Bath:** Queens (one w/ extra twin); private ensuite baths
**Favorites:** Chandelier Room or White River Room

**Comfort & Decor:** Textured wallpapers, custom-made (by Dennis) or antique beds, rich hues, artwork. Furnishings are of mixed vintages and quality. Bath fixtures a bit dated. Common areas spacious, numerous, beautiful. Central radiator heat plus auxiliary room units; window AC units.

### RATES, RESERVATIONS, & RESTRICTIONS

**Deposit:** 1st night; 10-day cancellation
**Discounts:** Off-season, corporate; $15 add'l person
**Credit Cards:** V, MC, AE, D
**Check-in/Out:** 3–6 or by arrangement/11
**Smoking:** Designated outside areas only
**Pets:** No; schnauzer in residence (primarily host quarters)
**Kids:** Over 6 accommodated by arrangement

**No-Nos:** Sleeping bags on floor (ask about overflow sleeping options)
**Minimum Stay:** 2 nights, holidays
**Open:** All year
**Hosts:** Dennis & Janice Whiting
1611 Love Ln.
Wenatchee, WA 98801
(800) 543-3645 or (509) 662-8365
Fax: (509) 663-5997
warmsi@warmspringsinn.com
www.warmspringsinn.com

## BIRCHFIELD MANOR, Yakima

| Overall: ★★★★½ | Room Quality: A | Value: C | Price: $95–$195 |
|---|---|---|---|

Starting as a restaurant in 1979, adding bed-and-breakfast facilities in 1989, Birchfield Manor is one of eastern Washington's claims to fame in the world of fine dining and lodging experiences. The Massets' little project in the countryside just two miles from Yakima has been critically acclaimed nationwide. Their multicourse dinners have become a traditional way to celebrate the end of a Thursday, Friday, or Saturday Yakima Valley wineries tour. The Cottage was built in the mid-1990s, doubling overnight occupancy, and the Manor rooms were remodeled and made even more beautiful and deluxe in 1999.

### SETTING & FACILITIES

**Location:** 2.5 mi. east of Yakima, off I-82's Exit 34
**Near:** Over 20 wineries, Yakima Valley agriculture, all Yakima venues (see zone intro)
**Building:** 1910 brick-and-stucco manor house & matching 1990s-built cottage
**Grounds:** 14 countryside acres w/ trees & pond, rangeland adjacent
**Public Space:** N/A

**Food & Drink:** Snack & beverage basket in rooms; hors d'oeuvre plates & ensuite dinners avail.; gourmet restaurant on site (dinner Thurs.–Sat. only); full breakfast (ensuite option)
**Recreation:** Historic touring, local festivals & concerts, golf, bicycling
**Amenities & Services:** Pool, ice-maker, guest phone, games, books; parties, receptions, dinners by reservation Thurs.–Sat.

## ACCOMMODATIONS

**Units:** 11 guest rooms
**All Rooms:** Exceptional antiques, robes, carpet, sitting area, desk/vanity/table, TV avail., beverage service
**Some Rooms:** Dbl. whirlpool, private deck/patio, window seat, ceiling fan, skylight, gas fireplace, mini-fridge, disabled access, private-line phone, steam sauna shower
**Bed & Bath:** Mostly king, 1 queen, some w/ sofa-sleepers; private ensuite baths
**Favorites:** Hunter's Glen, Vineyard

**Comfort & Decor:** Each room is uniquely decorated; all have great light, top-quality fixtures, and traditional sensibilities overlaid with modern, hotel-style amenities. Softly ornate wallpapers, bedding, and window treatments. Some rooms have Sandy's exceptional handmade quilts. Manor rooms have central heat and AC, plus auxiliary room units; cottage rooms have individual, remote-controlled heat and AC units.

## RATES, RESERVATIONS, & RESTRICTIONS

**Deposit:** Credit card; 7-day cancellation
**Discounts:** Off-season, single occupancy; $20 add'l person
**Credit Cards:** V, MC, AE, DC
**Check-in/Out:** After 2/11
**Smoking:** Outside only
**Pets:** Small pets in some rooms by arrangement
**Kids:** Over 8 welcome

**Minimum Stay:** None
**Open:** All year
**Hosts:** Will & Sandy Masset, sons Brad & Greg Masset, innkeeper Tim Newbury
2018 Birchfield Rd., Yakima, WA 98901
(800) 375-3420 or (509) 452-1960
Fax: (509) 452-2334 (call ahead)
reservations@birchfieldmanor.com
www.birchfieldmanor.com

## A TOUCH OF EUROPE B&B INN, Yakima

Overall: ★★★★½      Room Quality: A      Value: A      Price: $75–$110

Where Yakima's famous Birchfield Manor emphasizes contemporary comfort in its historic setting, A Touch of Europe emphasizes grand, historic elegance. Jim and Erika offer an exceptional, deluxe Old World experience that's very posh, pampering, and original. The home itself is a stunner, as is the rich, subtle decor: picture gold, brass, pewter fixtures against tones of green, silver, rose, brick. But the real star is Chef Erika's cuisine. From ingredient selection to creative, fresh, from-scratch preparation, it's absolutely stupendous. Arrange a dinner for yourself and your friends during your stay.

## SETTING & FACILITIES

**Location:** N. 16th off Summitview
**Near:** All Yakima venues; over 20 wineries, Yakima Valley agriculture
**Building:** National Historic Register 1889 Queen Anne Victorian
**Grounds:** Parklike acre has mature trees, lawn, & private feel
**Public Space:** Sitting room, library, formal DR, parlor DR, turret sitting room

**Food & Drink:** Fresh fruit, beverage, & chocolates in rooms; full multicourse breakfast
**Recreation:** Festivals & concerts, golf, bicycling
**Amenities & Services:** Fireplaces, desk, stationery, games; high teas, luncheons, dinners, & parties; celebration extras; meeting rooms

## ACCOMMODATIONS

**Units:** 3 guest rooms
**All Rooms:** Exceptional antiques, period light fixtures, down comforter/duvet, phone
**Some Rooms:** Desk or vanity, gas fireplace, claw-foot soaker tub, fainting couch, robes
**Bed & Bath:** Queen or twins; private baths (1 ensuite)
**Favorites:** Prince & Princess

**Comfort & Decor:** Guest rooms, while not large, are exquisitely decorated with an "old money" feel—subtle, rich, elegant. Fine woodwork, ornate carpet, unique European wallpapers. Think brocade, damask, velvet. Top-quality linens and fixtures. Common areas are posh and plentiful. Radiator heat.

## RATES, RESERVATIONS, & RESTRICTIONS

**Deposit:** Credit card or 50%; 7-day cancellation
**Discounts:** Single occupancy, corporate
**Credit Cards:** V, MC, AE
**Check-in/Out:** 3–8/11
**Smoking:** Outside only
**Pets:** No

**Kids:** No
**No-Nos:** More than 2 per room
**Minimum Stay:** None
**Open:** All year
**Hosts:** Erika & Jim Cenci
220 N. 16th Ave., Yakima, WA 98902
(888) 438-7073 or (509) 454-9775
www.winesnw.com/toucheuropeb&b.htm

# Oregon

Once upon a time, Californians crossing the border into Oregon were greeted by a road sign: WELCOME TO OREGON, NOW GO HOME.

The hospitality has improved, but the quirks remain in this land of the pioneering individualist at the end of the Oregon Trail. Even today, Oregonians break new ground, marching to their own drummers. They've leaped ahead with controversial laws. They've elected unusual politicians. They do things *their way* in Oregon.

In a state that never fails to surprise, the bed-and-breakfasts here are among the pleasant surprises. From upscale urban to cattle-ranch rural, from majestic oceanfront to humble farmhouse, there is something here for every taste.

Probably the most popular tourist destination in Oregon is its Pacific coastline. Here, in the region we call Zone 10, you'll find a plethora of fine bed-and-breakfasts tucked between the sandy beaches and the coastal mountain range.

Between the Coast Range and the Cascade Range, the Interstate 5 corridor runs north-south through the state's larger cities. At its north end is Portland, Oregon's largest city and cultural hub, Zone 11. South of Portland is the Willamette Valley, Zone 12, with its agriculture, wineries, and university towns. The southern segment of the I-5 corridor, Zone 13, provides access to the southern Oregon Cascades, wilderness recreation, and the northern California redwoods.

Zone 14 encompasses the north part of Oregon's Cascades, namely Mt. Hood and the Columbia Gorge. Zone 15 is the heart of the Oregon Cascades. Rugged and scenic, these two areas are becoming increasingly tourist-savvy, with a fine and growing selection of bed-and-breakfasts.

East of the Cascades (Oregon's "dry side") are tens of thousands of acres of high desert and rangeland, plus pockets of forest and pristine mountains. This vast region—one of America's true frontiers—is Zone 16.

# Zone 10
# Oregon Coast

Wild, beautiful, yet developed for tourism, the Oregon Coast is a five-star destination for anyone living in or visiting the Pacific Northwest. Highway 101 runs north-south along the coast, accessible by half a dozen feeder routes from Interstate 5 on the other side of the coastal mountain range. We found the charm of the Oregon Coast to be enhanced by the tiny villages and pocket-sized lodgings, so we concentrate on intimate bed-and-breakfast experiences and pass over much-touted larger inns such as Tu Tu' Tun Lodge in Gold Beach and Stephanie Inn in Cannon Beach.

Beginning at the north end of the coast, at the mouth of the mighty Columbia River, you'll find Astoria, a city of Victorian and maritime heritage. Its many attractions include museums, parks, and monuments dedicated to military, seafaring, and general Oregon history. A 4.1-mile bridge connects Oregon to Washington at Astoria.

Moving south, Seaside is an old-fashioned bumper-cars-and-saltwater-taffy beach town; great fun for families. Nearby Cannon Beach is more upscale and adult-oriented. It's home to Haystack Rock, a photogenic monolith surrounded by tidepools, and Ecola State Park, an impressive bird refuge.

Rather than feature the too-developed tourist magnets of Tillamook and Lincoln City (the former has an interesting cheese factory tour, the latter is a good place to buy a kite), we selected bed-and-breakfasts in the nearby Three Capes area. Named for Cape Lookout, Cape Meares, and Cape Kiwanda, this scenic side route includes two excellent bed-and-breakfasts (one in Pacific City and one near Sandlake) off the beaten path of Highway 101.

Depoe Bay and Newport are established marina communities. Depoe Bay sports a dramatic, rocky channel, along which one of our featured properties is situated. The channel leads from the ocean to a small, protected harbor that's home to our other profiled Depoe Bay inn. Newport is a thriving center of activity, with a full complement of restaurants and shopping, plus science and activity centers, parks and natural areas, and an excellent aquarium.

Waldport and Yachats (pronounced "yuh-HOTS") boast great beach access and some of the best bed-and-breakfasts on the coast. Nearby attractions include Sea Lion Caves and the Alsea Bay Bridge Interpretive Center, magnificent landforms such as Devil's Churn and Strawberry Hill, and lighthouses. Plus, you're still within easy striking distance of Newport to the north and Florence to the south.

Florence is charming, historic, and adjacent to Oregon Dunes National Recreation Area. Its restored Old Town shopping area is a big draw, and its location makes a good base for exploring much of the south-central coast.

Coos Bay is a major port and retail center for the southern coast. Other south coast communities (Bandon, Langlois, Port Orford, Gold Beach, Brookings) are sparsely populated, with rugged beaches and the occasional fine restaurant. Bandon is home to the West Coast Game Farm, a wild-animal preserve promoted as a walk-through safari, where visitors can interact with animal babies (we've played with bear cubs, tussled a jaguar, and picked up a 'possum here). Port Orford is an artisan hub (glass, scrimshaw, basketry, quilting, native myrtlewood crafts) and the address for Prehistoric Gardens, a collection of life-size dinosaur replicas set amongst the woods along Highway 101.

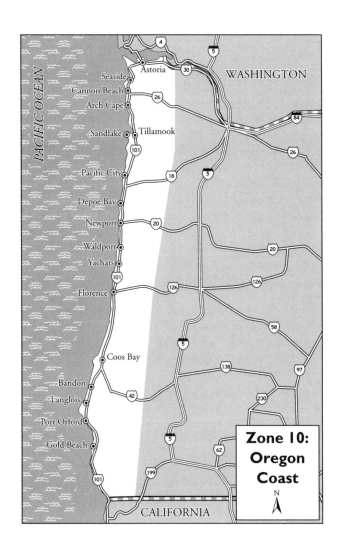

PACIFIC OCEAN

WASHINGTON

Astoria

Seaside

Cannon Beach

Arch Cape

Sandlake

Tillamook

Pacific City

Depoe Bay

Newport

Waldport

Yachats

Florence

Coos Bay

Bandon

Langlois

Port Orford

Gold Beach

CALIFORNIA

**Zone 10: Oregon Coast**

N

**Arch Cape**
St. Bernards, p. 302

**Astoria**
Clementine's B&B, p. 303
Franklin Street Station, p. 304
Grandview B&B, p. 306
Rosebriar Hotel, p. 307

**Bandon**
Bandon Beach House, p. 308
Lighthouse B&B, p. 309

**Cannon Beach**
Cannon Beach Hotel, p. 310
The Courtyard, p. 311
Hearthstone Inn, p. 312

**Coos Bay**
Coos Bay Manor, p. 313

**Depoe Bay**
Channel House, p. 314
Gracie's Landing, p. 315

**Florence**
The Edwin K B&B, p. 316
The Johnson House, p. 318

**Gold Beach**
Inn at Nesika Beach, p. 319

**Langlois**
Floras Lake House B&B, p. 320
Marsh Haven Farm B&B, p. 321

**Newport**
Newport Belle B&B, p. 321
Oar House B&B, p. 323
Sylvia Beach Hotel, p. 324

**Pacific City**
Eagle's View B&B, p. 325

**Port Orford**
Home by the Sea B&B, p. 326

**Sandlake**
Sandlake Country Inn, p. 327

**Seaside**
Anderson's Boarding House,
    p. 328
Gilbert Inn , p. 329

**Waldport**
Cliff House B&B, p. 330

**Yachats**
Morning Star, p. 331
Sea Quest B&B, p. 332
Serenity B&B, p. 333

## ST. BERNARDS, Arch Cape

| Overall: ★★★★★ | Room Quality: A | Value: D | Price: $139–$199 |

For a memorable bed-and-breakfast experience near Cannon Beach, St. Bernards is our top pick. Don and Deanna Bernard have crafted a story-book inn for grownups. Their collection of museum-quality European antiques is impressive, and their sense of style and drama is contagious. Where "European-style" can mean "funky and strange" in bed-and-breakfast parlance (hand-held showers, shared baths, etc.), here it means exotic, evocative, and enchanting. Plan a full hour to enjoy the elegant presentation and creative fare at breakfast—a celebration of the senses for the discriminating traveler.

### SETTING & FACILITIES

**Location:** 4 mi. south of Cannon Beach, just uphill on the east side of Hwy. 101

**Near:** Beaches: Hug Point, Oswald West, Ecola, & Arcadia Beach State Parks; Haystack Rock, Cannon Beach, & Manzanita

**Building:** New European-style chateau

**Grounds:** 1.5 acres w/ gardens, topiary, pond, greenhouse

**Public Space:** LR, patio, DR/conservatory, front balcony

**Food & Drink:** Afternoon cocktails; full gourmet breakfast

**Recreation:** Tidepooling, kite flying, bird-watching

**Amenities & Services:** Workout room, sauna, conf. room, video library; meetings, weddings, small conferences

## ACCOMMODATIONS

**Units:** 7 guest rooms/suites
**All Rooms:** Gas fireplace, phones, cable TV/VCR, fridge, seating
**Some Rooms:** Whirlpool or soaking tub, window seat, vaulted ceiling, private patio/deck
**Bed & Bath:** King or queen; private ensuite baths
**Favorites:** Tower, Provence

**Comfort & Decor:** Rich and whimsical color schemes. Original artwork, amazing antiques, unusual architecture (turrets, vaulting, dormers), rough-plastered walls, tile floors, tapestry furnishings. Like a European castle, but without the drafts and quirks. Individual heat controls in each room; venting windows.

## RATES, RESERVATIONS, & RESTRICTIONS

**Deposit:** Credit card; 7-day cancellation
**Discounts:** Midweek winter
**Credit Cards:** V, MC, AE
**Check-in/Out:** 3–6 or by arrangement/11
**Smoking:** Outside only
**Pets:** No
**Kids:** 12 & older welcome
**Minimum Stay:** 2 nights on weekends; some holidays

**Open:** All year
**Hosts:** Don & Deanna Bernard
3 East Ocean Rd.
Arch Cape, OR 97102
(800) 436-2848 or (503) 436-2800
Fax: (503) 436-1206
bernards@pacifier.com
www.pacifier.com/~bernards

## CLEMENTINE'S B&B, Astoria

| Overall: ★★★ | Room Quality: C | Value: C | Price: $65–$105 |
|---|---|---|---|

Homey, comfortable Victorian with a weathered charm and relaxed atmosphere. Judith, a master gardener, former professional singer, and gourmet chef, is a splendid hostess, delivering on her promise of "friendly, nurturing service." She and her husband purchased this grand old home in 1993, then gutted it, renovated, remodeled, and opened as a bed-and-breakfast in 1994. Comfortable, laid-back atmosphere invites you to relax. After a day of touring the many delights of Astoria, enjoy the collection of gardening and other lovely books in the parlor before turning in and waking to a memorable breakfast.

## SETTING & FACILITIES

**Location:** Across from Flavel House museum on Exchange near 8th
**Near:** Heritage Center Museum, Flavel House, Uppertown Fire Fighters Museum, Columbia River Maritime Museum, piers & waterfront, Fort Clatsop Nat'l Memorial, Fort Stevens S.P., Fort Astoria, Astoria Column
**Building:** 1888 classic Italianate Victorian
**Grounds:** Moss, ivy, flowers in steep front yard; side yard

**Public Space:** Parlor, DR, garden seating
**Food & Drink:** Tea & cookies; full breakfast
**Recreation:** Mushrooming, festivals, ship viewing & touring, clamming, beach, golf
**Amenities & Services:** Icemaker, fridge access, books, games, piano; cooking classes, fax avail., "concierge of the North Coast"

## ACCOMMODATIONS

**Units:** 5 guest rooms (also 2 multibed suites adjacent—ideal for families)
**All Rooms:** Hairdryers, toiletries, robes, feather beds, armoire or closet, fresh flowers
**Some Rooms:** Disabled access, view, balcony, gas fireplace
**Bed & Bath:** Queen (1 w/ queen & double); private baths (4 of 5 ensuite)

**Favorites:** Clementine's Suite, Garden Room
**Comfort & Decor:** This charming century-old house shows some signs of time's passage as well as the limitations of her era (delicate plumbing, dim lighting). Beyond that, it's a jewel. And the extra in-room amenities are the mark of a good hostess.

## RATES, RESERVATIONS, & RESTRICTIONS

**Deposit:** 1st night; 7-day cancellation
**Discounts:** Off-season, extended stays, whole house; $15 add'l person— ask about suites next door
**Credit Cards:** V, MC, AE, D
**Check-in/Out:** 4–7/11 or by arrangement
**Smoking:** No
**Pets:** No; canary in residence
**Kids:** OK; best-suited for multibed

suites next door
**Minimum Stay:** None
**Open:** All year
**Hosts:** Judith Taylor
847 Exchange St.
Astoria, OR 97103
(800) 521-6801 or (503) 325-2005
Fax: (503) 325-7056
jtaylor@clementines-bb.com
www.clementines-bb.com

## FRANKLIN STREET STATION, Astoria

| Overall: ★★★★ | Room Quality: B | Value: B | Price: $80–$135 |
|---|---|---|---|

Offering the best of the old and the new, this well-established inn has been a bed-and-breakfast since the mid-1980s but was purchased by enthusiastic new owners in 1998. Maurizio and Darcy spend the off-season in their other residence in Milan, Italy. As their guests, you reap the benefits—their Astoria kitchen is filled with hand-imported candies, cheeses, and Torrefazione coffee. The home has a gracious, genteel feel, and the hosts (who live in a separate residence nearby) are ardent in their desire to make your stay memorable. Attractive, super-clean rooms; excellent service and cuisine. Hosts are still very new, and time will tell, but we think the whole package looks tremendously promising.

## SETTING & FACILITIES

**Location:** Franklin between 11th & 12th, a few blocks uphill from downtown
**Near:** Flavel House, museums, piers & waterfront, Fort Clatsop Nat'l Memorial, Fort Stevens S.P., Fort Astoria, Astoria Column
**Building:** 1900 Victorian
**Grounds:** Small lot w/ stone front patio

**Public Space:** Parlor, DR
**Food & Drink:** Refreshments (coffee, chilled beverages) on arrival; Italian chocolates & candies; in-room coffee/tea service; full breakfast
**Recreation:** Mushrooming, galleries, festivals, ship viewing & touring, beachcombing, golf
**Amenities & Services:** Exceptional treats; small weddings

## ACCOMMODATIONS

**Units:** 3 guest rooms, 2 suites (also non-B&B apt.)
**All Rooms:** Tasteful decor, carpet
**Some Rooms:** Canopy bed, claw-foot tub (4 of 5), wet bar w/ fridge, deck access, table & chairs, TV, VCR, sound system, fireplace, telescope, river view
**Bed & Bath:** Queen (1 w/ daybed & trundle); private baths

**Favorites:** Captain's Quarters, Astor Suite
**Comfort & Decor:** Original woodwork; roses, lace, period fixtures, fine furnishings, fresh flowers, stained glass. Immaculate. Central heat plus auxiliary baseboard units. Top-floor suite (Captain's Quarters) may be overwarm on hottest days.

## RATES, RESERVATIONS, & RESTRICTIONS

**Deposit:** 1st night; 48-hour cancellation
**Discounts:** Single occupancy; $10 add'l person
**Credit Cards:** V, MC
**Check-in/Out:** 3–7 or by arrangement/11
**Smoking:** No
**Pets:** No

**Kids:** No
**Minimum Stay:** 2 nights preferred, holidays & festival weekends
**Open:** March–Oct. (subject to change; call)
**Hosts:** Darcy Urell & Maurizio Bassini
1140 Franklin St.
Astoria, OR 97103
(800) 448-1098 or (503) 325-4314

## GRANDVIEW B&B, Astoria

| Overall: ★★½ | Room Quality: D | Value: B | Price: $45–$159 |
|---|---|---|---|

Somewhat dated and not exactly spic 'n' span, but cheerful and bright. Those accustomed to budget European accommodations will be very comfortable and pleased at the value. Breakfast room is fresh, bright, and pleasant, with china service and fresh flowers. Guest rooms and parlor are a bit down-at-the-heels. Exceptional Columbia River views. Practical, good location, lots of space. Several rooms adjoin for two-rooms-sharing-one-bath configuration possibilities.

### SETTING & FACILITIES

**Location:** Grand, west of 16th, 3 blocks uphill from Marine Dr. & Columbia River
**Near:** Flavel House, museums, piers & waterfront, Fort Clatsop Nat'l Memorial, Fort Stevens S.P., Fort Astoria, Astoria Column
**Building:** Circa 1900 3-story Victorian
**Grounds:** Bulbs, trees, water view, ivy
**Public Space:** Parlor, DR
**Food & Drink:** Self-serve hot beverages & light snacks; full or extended cont'l breakfast
**Recreation:** Mushrooming, kayaking, sailing, festivals, ship touring, golf
**Amenities & Services:** Games, binoculars

### ACCOMMODATIONS

**Units:** 3 guest rooms, 3 2-BR units (configurations vary)
**All Rooms:** Reading material, electric kettle
**Some Rooms:** Games, bay window, canopy bed, reading nook, fireplace
**Bed & Bath:** Queen (2 w/ extra daybed); some private baths, some shared
**Favorites:** Gazebo, The Treetops
**Comfort & Decor:** Cheerfully, though not expensively decorated & furnished. Pale wallpapers; hardwood floors or indoor/outdoor–type carpet, not always in the best of repair. Wicker, iron beds. Central heat with auxiliary units avail.

### RATES, RESERVATIONS, & RESTRICTIONS

**Deposit:** Credit card; 24-hour cancellation
**Discounts:** Off-season, group; $15 add'l person
**Credit Cards:** V, MC, D
**Check-in/Out:** 4–8 or by arrangement/11
**Smoking:** Outside only
**Pets:** No; host dog (elderly & harmless but has a big bark)
**Kids:** In some rooms
**No-Nos:** Alcohol, unmarried couples
**Minimum Stay:** None
**Open:** All year
**Hosts:** Charleen Maxwell
1574 Grand Ave.
Astoria, OR 97103
(800) 488-3250
www.bbonline.com/or/grandview/ or
www.pacifier.com/–grndview

## ROSEBRIAR HOTEL, Astoria

| Overall: ★★★★ | Room Quality: C | Value: C | Price: $65–$135 |
|---|---|---|---|

Those who want a "historic Astoria" lodging experience but are more comfortable with the predictability of a hotel-type atmosphere should consider the Rosebriar. Managed by the same folks who handle the Cannon Beach Hotel and its many affiliated properties, Rosebriar is a larger, staff-run establishment and, as such, less personal than, say, Clementine's. Breakfast served at individual tables, more restaurant-style than most bed-and-breakfasts. Private phone lines make this a good business traveler choice.

### SETTING & FACILITIES

**Location:** Corner of Franklin & 14th, 3 blocks from downtown
**Near:** Flavel House, museums, piers & waterfront, Fort Clatsop Nat'l Memorial, Fort Stevens S.P., Fort Astoria, Astoria Column
**Building:** 1902 Neoclassic residence
**Grounds:** Ivied slope, small side yard w/ bench, front patio, courtyard, & herb garden
**Public Space:** Front patio, small front porch, LR, courtyard

**Food & Drink:** Morning tea & coffee; full breakfast
**Recreation:** Bird-watching, whale watching, fishing, sailing, festivals, ship touring, clamming, golf
**Amenities & Services:** Cribs avail., 70-person conf. room w/ tables & piano, gas fireplace; receptions, banquets, catering, business meetings

### ACCOMMODATIONS

**Units:** 10 guest rooms plus carriage house
**All Rooms:** Phone w/ private extension, TV w/ remote, lots of pillows
**Some Rooms:** View, whirlpool tub, sitting area, gas fireplace, sofabed, table & chairs, sitting room, private entrance, disabled access
**Bed & Bath:** Double or queen; ensuite private baths

**Favorites:** The Carriage House, Room 2
**Comfort & Decor:** High ceilings, mahogany wood tones, olive-taupe paint, stained glass. Furnishings are elegant and masculine. Lighting is dim. Central heating can be supplemented by individually controlled baseboard heaters.

## RATES, RESERVATIONS, & RESTRICTIONS

**Deposit:** Required; call
**Discounts:** Off-season, 3-night (week-night) special; $10 add'l person
**Credit Cards:** V, MC, AE, D
**Check-in/Out:** After 3 (desk staffed til 10 p.m.)/11
**Smoking:** No
**Pets:** No
**Kids:** Welcome
**Minimum Stay:** 2 nights summer

weekends & special event/holiday weekends
**Open:** All year
**Hosts:** Anthony & Teresa Tavoloni
636 Fourteenth St.
Astoria, OR 97103
(800) 487-0224 or (503) 325-7427
Fax: (503) 325-6937
www.oregoncoastlodgings.com/rosebriar

## BANDON BEACH HOUSE, Bandon

| Overall: ★★★½ | Room Quality: A | Value: C | Price: $160 |
|---|---|---|---|

Contemporary beachfront home offers two spacious king-bed rooms, panoramic ocean views, and superb hosts. Steve and Adrienne built this very quiet, well-built home in 1996 and opened it to guests as a bed-and-breakfast in 1997. Situated in a neighborhood of newer homes on a quiet beachfront loop, Bandon Beach House is conveniently close to Highway 101 and the surprisingly good dining and shopping of tiny Bandon.

## SETTING & FACILITIES

**Location:** On the ocean, just south of Bandon
**Near:** Beach, restaurants, West Coast Game Farm ("walk-through safari"), riding stable, Cape Blanca lighthouse, Cape Arago, Shore Acres S.P., Coos Bay
**Building:** Contemporary cedar-shake beach lodge w/ Craftsman-style appointments
**Grounds:** Large, rockscaped front yard; on 40-foot bluff overlooking the ocean

**Public Space:** DR, LR, outside decks, front porch
**Food & Drink:** Tea, coffee, & cookies at check-in; in-room refreshments w/ turndown; morning coffee & juice; full breakfast; early by arrangement
**Recreation:** Beach/ocean activities, galleries, golf, horseback riding
**Amenities & Services:** Portable phone avail., TV in LR (in-room portable avail.), library; turndown, local masseuse avail.

## ACCOMMODATIONS

**Units:** 2 deluxe guest rooms (could be called suites)
**All Rooms:** Lounging area, stone fireplace, robes, quality toiletries, iron, desk, binoculars, armoire, vanity, large showers, natural light on 3 sides
**Some Rooms:** Vaulted ceiling, stereo/CD
**Bed & Bath:** Kings; ensuite private baths

**Favorites:** Quite similar
**Comfort & Decor:** Open architecture, beamed ceilings, lack of clutter; well-placed, attractive antique and reproduction furnishings. Striking, pale blonde Canadian maple flooring. Windows open; individual controls for radiant in-floor water-based heat system.

## RATES, RESERVATIONS, & RESTRICTIONS

**Deposit:** 1st night; 7-day cancellation
**Discounts:** Off-season
**Credit Cards:** Not accepted
**Check-in/Out:** 3–6 or by arrangement/11
**Smoking:** Outside only
**Pets:** No
**Kids:** No
**Minimum Stay:** 2 nights for advance

reservations
**Open:** All year
**Hosts:** Steve & Adrienne Casey
2866 Beach Loop
Bandon, OR 97411
(541) 347-1196
Fax: (541) 347-1204
beachhouse@harborside.com
www.bandonbeach.com

## LIGHTHOUSE B&B, Bandon

| Overall: ★★★ | Room Quality: D | Value: D | Price: $100–$155 |
|---|---|---|---|

Conveniently located within easy strolling distance to the quaint shopping and excellent restaurants of Old Town. Jetty location offers unique views (mouth of the river, ocean, lighthouse) and privacy due to the lay of the adjacent land. Shirley is a gracious, fun hostess with a "forever" background in the hospitality industry; she has operated the Lighthouse B&B since 1994 (previous owners also operated the home as a popular bed-and-breakfast). She has her own apartment downstairs and "makes herself scarce unless needed" from check-in to breakfast, giving guests privacy and the run of the common areas.

## SETTING & FACILITIES

**Location:** At mouth of Coquille River across from lighthouse near Old Town
**Near:** West Coast Game Farm ("walk-through safari"), beach, Cape Blanca lighthouse, Cape Arago, Shore Acres S.P., Coos Bay
**Building:** 3-level beach house
**Grounds:** Unique view of lighthouse, surrounded by undeveloped & protected land
**Public Space:** Guest LR, deck, dining area
**Food & Drink:** Evening wine; in-room chocolate kisses; tea, soda, juices; full breakfast
**Recreation:** Agate hunting, Old Town shopping & galleries, kayaking, golf, horseback riding, surfing, tidepooling, whale watching
**Amenities & Services:** Travel library, sound system & CDs, telescope, binoculars, TV

## ACCOMMODATIONS

**Units:** 5 guest rooms
**All Rooms:** View
**Some Rooms:** Dbl. whirlpool tub, TV, woodstove, fireplace, private deck, skylit bath, robes, sitting area
**Bed & Bath:** Queen or king; private baths (most ensuite)
**Favorites:** Gray Whale, Greenhouse

**Comfort & Decor:** Furnishings are comfortable but not new. All rooms are carpeted. Decor has a "bit of the '70s thing goin' on," so *Architectural Digest* fans may be disappointed; the rest of us feel an atmosphere of ease and "family." Central heat; fans in rooms.

## RATES, RESERVATIONS, & RESTRICTIONS

**Deposit:** 1st night; 7-day cancellation
**Discounts:** Off-season midweek, single occupancy
**Credit Cards:** V, MC
**Check-in/Out:** 3–6/11
**Smoking:** Outdoors only
**Pets:** No
**Kids:** Over 12 welcome; under 12 by arrangement only
**Minimum Stay:** None
**Open:** All year
**Hosts:** Shirley Chalupa
650 Jetty Rd., Bandon, OR 97411
(541) 347-9316
lthousebb@harborside.com
www.moriah.com/lighthouse

## CANNON BEACH HOTEL, Cannon Beach

| Overall: ★★★½ | Room Quality: B | Value: C | Price: $59–$149 |
|---|---|---|---|

Self-described "petite European hotel" has contemporary decor, modern amenities, and extremely convenient location. However, doorstep access to a world-class beach, restaurants, galleries, and shops comes at a price: the beach town is noisy, and opening your well-crafted windows for a breeze will result in more noise than makes for a good night's rest. Work space in some rooms and individual phone lines make CBH great for business travel. Breakfast is really just a snack.

## SETTING & FACILITIES

**Location:** In the middle of Cannon Beach's main commercial street, on the west side
**Near:** Beach, Haystack Rock, downtown Cannon Beach, Ecola S.P., Seaside
**Building:** Historic logger's boarding house
**Grounds:** Border plantings
**Public Space:** Lobby w/ fireplace
**Food & Drink:** Coffee, tea, & fruit; light cont'l breakfast delivered to room; restaurant adjacent
**Recreation:** Tidepooling, kite flying, bird-watching, galleries, theater
**Amenities & Services:** Ice & beverage machines, variety of newspapers, daily *Oregonian* delivered to rooms; fax avail., eco-sensitive towel option, massage avail.

## ACCOMMODATIONS

**Units:** 9 guest rooms
**All Rooms:** Phones w/ direct ext., pillows, remote TV/VCR, carpet, bureau, closet, quality toiletries
**Some Rooms:** Gas fireplace, whirlpool spa, sitting area, table & chairs, partial ocean/Haystack rock view, disabled access, sofa-sleeper
**Bed & Bath:** Various (double, queen, king), some w/ more than 1 or a sofabed; private ensuite baths
**Favorites:** 7
**Comfort & Decor:** Contemporary midquality furnishings; accents in deep earth tones. Mahogany-hued tables and bureaus; Northwest art. Individual heat controls; windows open.

## RATES, RESERVATIONS, & RESTRICTIONS

**Deposit:** 2 nights (1st night only off-season); 7-day cancellation required for refund (less $10 service fee)
**Discounts:** Off-season, shoulder season, 3-night specials; $10 add'l person
**Credit Cards:** V, MC, AE, D
**Check-in/Out:** 3–10/11 (lobby staffed 8 a.m.–10 p.m.)
**Smoking:** No
**Pets:** No
**Kids:** Welcome
**Minimum Stay:** 2 nights, most weekends
**Open:** All year
**Hosts:** Linda Toler, manager
1116 S. Hemlock St.
Cannon Beach, OR 97110
(800) 238-4107 or (503) 436-1392
Fax: (503) 436-1396
cbh@oregoncoastlodgings.com
www.oregoncoastlodgings.com/cannonbeach/cbhl/

## THE COURTYARD, Cannon Beach

| Overall: ★★★★ | Room Quality: B | Value: C | Price: $99–$159 |
| --- | --- | --- | --- |

Set off the main street, The Courtyard is the luxury affiliate of the Cannon Beach Hotel Lodgings group. Duvet bedding, gas fireplaces, kitchenettes, tile baths, and quality furnishings. As with the Cannon Beach Hotel, breakfast is really just a snack. Upscale, romantic rooms with a European flair. Great access to beach, shopping, galleries, restaurants.

## SETTING & FACILITIES

**Location:** Set back from Cannon Beach's main street, just north of Cannon Beach Hotel
**Near:** Beach, Haystack Rock, downtown Cannon Beach, Ecola S.P., Seaside
**Building:** 2-story U-shaped building
**Grounds:** Brick courtyard w/ fountain
**Public Space:** Library
**Food & Drink:** Light cont'l breakfast delivered; some rooms include kitch-enettes w/ coffee/tea supplies & microwaves w/ popcorn.
**Recreation:** Tidepooling, kite flying, bird-watching
**Amenities & Services:** Guest fridge in library, ice maker, *Oregonian* newspaper delivered to rooms daily; fax avail., eco-sensitive towel option, massage avail.

## ACCOMMODATIONS

**Units:** 13 guest rooms
**All Rooms:** Phones w/ direct ext., gas fireplace, private deck/patio, TV/VCR, carpet, closet, quality toiletries, duvets
**Some Rooms:** Kitchenette, sitting area, dual whirlpool spa, disabled access
**Bed & Bath:** Queen or king, some w/ sofabeds; private ensuite baths
**Favorites:** Corner units are best; try for one w/ a dual spa &/or kitchenette
**Comfort & Decor:** This upscale cousin to the Cannon Beach Hotel takes European elegance one step far-ther. A newer building, it is also quieter. Quality furnishings and bedding, tile baths. Library looks out at the brick courtyard and fountain.

## RATES, RESERVATIONS, & RESTRICTIONS

**Deposit:** 2 nights (1st night only off-season); 7-day cancellation required for refund (less $10 service fee)
**Discounts:** Off-season, shoulder season, 3-night specials; $10 add'l person; rollaways $10; kids under 2 free
**Credit Cards:** V, MC, AE, D
**Check-in/Out:** 3–10/11 (lobby staffed 8 a.m.–10 p.m.)
**Smoking:** No
**Pets:** No
**Kids:** Welcome
**Minimum Stay:** 2 nights, most weekends
**Open:** All year
**Hosts:** Linda Toler, manager
1116 S. Hemlock St.
Cannon Beach, OR 97110
(800) 238-4107 or (503) 436-1392
Fax: (503) 436-1396
courtyard@oregoncoastlodgings.com
www.oregoncoastlodgings.com/
cannonbeach/cbhl/courtyard/

## HEARTHSTONE INN, Cannon Beach

| Overall: ★★★½ | Room Quality: B | Value: C | Price: $89–$105 |
|---|---|---|---|

Handcrafted, woodsy, self-contained lodgings offer a romantic retreat. Operated by Cannon Beach Hotel Lodgings, these units are more like private vacation condos than a bed-and-breakfast, but do include the same continental breakfast basket as CBH. Hearthstone offers a little more privacy, meal flexibility, and elbow room than the other CBH properties, at a reasonable price. Rooms 25 and 27 sleep two; rooms 24 and 26 sleep four. Of the latter, Room 24 is perhaps the more stylish, while Room 26 is a two-room suite, offering more privacy

## SETTING & FACILITIES

**Location:** Across the street from Cannon Beach Hotel on main thoroughfare
**Near:** Beach, Haystack Rock, downtown Cannon Beach, Ecola S.P., Seaside
**Building:** Constructed by local artisans
**Grounds:** Landscaped borders
**Public Space:** None; self-contained units have living areas

**Food & Drink:** Coffee/tea in kitchen; cont'l breakfast basket delivered each morning
**Recreation:** Tidepooling, kite flying, bird-watching, shopping, galleries, theater
**Amenities & Services:** Equipped kitchenette (stove, oven, coffeemaker, toaster)

## ACCOMMODATIONS

**Units:** 4 units
**All Rooms:** Phone, TV, table & chairs, duvet
**Some Rooms:** Skylit bath, wraparound porch, sofa-sleeper
**Bed & Bath:** Queens; private ensuite baths
**Favorites:** 24 (depends; see above)

**Comfort & Decor:** Vaulted ceilings, cedar paneling, hand-hewn furnishings, and stone fireplaces give these rooms rustic flavor. Kitchen units make them ideal for longer stays. Cobalt blue tile in kitchens and baths. Individual heat control and ceiling fans.

## RATES, RESERVATIONS, & RESTRICTIONS

**Deposit:** 2 nights (1st night only off-season); 7-day cancellation required for refund (less $10 service fee)
**Discounts:** Off-season, shoulder season, 3-night specials; $10 add'l person; $10 for roll-away
**Credit Cards:** V, MC, AE, D
**Check-in/Out:** 3–10/11 (check in at Cannon Beach Hotel; lobby staffed 8 a.m.–10 p.m.)
**Smoking:** No
**Pets:** No
**Kids:** Welcome

**Minimum Stay:** 2 nights, most weekends
**Open:** All year
**Hosts:** Linda Toler, manager
Mail to Cannon Beach Hotel
1116 S. Hemlock St.
Cannon Beach, OR 97110
(800) 238-4107 or (503) 436-1392
Fax: (503) 436-1396
hearthstone@oregoncoastlodgings.com
www.oregoncoastlodgings.com/
cannonbeach/cbhl/hearthstone/

## COOS BAY MANOR, Coos Bay

| Overall: ★★★ | Room Quality: C | Value: C | Price: $79–$100 |
|---|---|---|---|

Grand old Colonial Manor is a regal slice of yesteryear in historic shipping town. The entire home is a work of art, but is also showing its age (albeit gracefully). Come for the romance of the turn of the 20th century, not for Best Western's sterile, predictable style. The house is located on a very walkable old street in a historic neighborhood. Patricia, your down-to-earth hostess, has operated the Manor since 1990.

## SETTING & FACILITIES

**Location:** 3 blocks west of Broadway, in a historic neighborhood
**Near:** Oregon Dunes N.R.A., Golden & Silver Falls, state parks, beaches
**Building:** National Historic Register 1912 Colonial
**Grounds:** Sloping front lawn, back garden

**Public Space:** Front porch, parlor, DR
**Food & Drink:** Full breakfast
**Recreation:** Deep-sea fishing, crabbing, dunes driving, theaters, museums
**Amenities & Services:** Games, 1872 Weber piano, cordless guest phone; weddings, meetings, gatherings, airport pick-up

## ACCOMMODATIONS

**Units:** 5 guest rooms
**All Rooms:** Toiletries, robes, bathroom nightlights
**Some Rooms:** TV, tub baths, coffee service, desk, library
**Bed & Bath:** Queen or twin/king conversion; 3 private baths, 2 share a bath

**Favorites:** The Victorian
**Comfort & Decor:** The romance of another era, with rich tones and textures. Grand entry w/ parquet oak floor; second level has inside balcony. Antiques and comfortably upholstered pieces of varying vintages. Portable heaters in rooms; windows open.

## RATES, RESERVATIONS, & RESTRICTIONS

**Deposit:** Check or credit card; 5-day cancellation for refund less $15
**Discounts:** Call; $15 add'l person with roll-away
**Credit Cards:** V, MC, D
**Check-in/Out:** After 3/11
**Smoking:** Outside only
**Pets:** Well-mannered guest dogs

allowed; host kitties on site
**Kids:** 4 & older welcome
**Minimum Stay:** None
**Open:** All year
**Hosts:** Patricia Williams
955 S. Fifth St., Coos Bay, OR 97420
(800) 269-1244 or (541) 269-1244
Fax: Same as phone

## CHANNEL HOUSE, Depoe Bay

Overall: ★★★½    Room Quality: B    Value: D    Price: $160–$235

This place really has two selling points: the view and the sexy outdoor whirlpool tubs (with view). The accommodations are contemporary and private; certainly not the intimate, bonding-with-hosts-and-other-guests experience of many bed-and-breakfasts or small inns. The breakfasts are nothing to set your alarm for, but they fill the belly for a day of touring.

So come for romance and knock-your-socks-off views, and you won't be disappointed. The spacious, no-frills, modern rooms (combined with the easy on-the-run breakfast, private phone line, wet bar, and a.m. newspaper) make good business traveler accommodations, too.

## SETTING & FACILITIES

**Location:** Just east of Hwy. 101 at south side of Depoe Bay; overlooks "world's narrowest rocky channel"
**Near:** Historic Depoe Bay Bridge, Newport
**Building:** Contemporary bluff-top tri-level
**Grounds:** Brick courtyard entry w/ flowerbed

**Public Space:** Breakfast room/library also functions as guest lounge
**Food & Drink:** Bottled water, tea, & coffee in room; beverages also in breakfast room; cont'l breakfast buffet
**Recreation:** Deep sea fishing, whale watching, diving, shopping, festivals
**Amenities & Services:** Gift shop, ice machine; morning newspaper delivered

## ACCOMMODATIONS

**Units:** 3 guest rooms, 7 suites (overflow rooms: 2 at nearby property & 2 discount on-site rooms w/o spas or views)
**All Rooms:** Outdoor deck w/ whirlpool tub, private phone line, hairdryer, binoculars, guest guide, gas fireplace, fridge, wet bar, remote TV, robes

**Some Rooms:** Sitting room, kitchenette, 2 TVs, table & chairs
**Bed & Bath:** Queen (1 king); private baths (whirlpool on deck)
**Favorites:** 1, 8, 12
**Comfort & Decor:** The contemporary decor is basic, with slate, mauve, and wood tones. Rooms are spacious and open, and are pleasantly, though not expensively, furnished.

## RATES, RESERVATIONS, & RESTRICTIONS

**Deposit:** 1st night; 2-week cancellation required for refund less $25 service fee
**Discounts:** Off-season; $30 add'l person
**Credit Cards:** V, MC, AE, D
**Check-in/Out:** 4–8/11
**Smoking:** No
**Pets:** No

**Kids:** 12 & older welcome
**Minimum Stay:** None
**Open:** All year
**Hosts:** Vicki Mix
35 Ellingson St., Depoe Bay, OR 97341
(800) 447-2140 or (541) 765-2140
Fax: (541) 765-2191
cfinseth@newportnet.com
www.channelhouse.com

## GRACIE'S LANDING, Depoe Bay

| Overall: ★★★ | Room Quality: C | Value: C | Price: $90–$120 |
|---|---|---|---|

Accommodations are perfectly comfortable, if a bit impersonal; rooms are motel-ish by design, but innkeepers do a good job in adding homey touches such as seasonal decorations in the common areas. Harbor views are nice, and the inn is impeccably clean. Two smoking rooms are available, a rarity in the world of bed-and-breakfasts and small inns. The property was up for sale at the time of our visit, and a change in ownership could affect prices and policies, but the inn is well established, well located, and likely to endure.

## SETTING & FACILITIES

**Location:** Just east of Hwy. 101, right on Depoe Bay harbor
**Near:** Historic Depoe Bay Bridge, Newport
**Building:** Harborside hotel built 1989
**Grounds:** Parking in front, decks overlooking water in back
**Public Space:** Parlor, deck, library
**Food & Drink:** Coffee, tea, cookies in

p.m.; full breakfast (ensuite, add'l $3.50 each)
**Recreation:** Deep sea fishing, whale watching, diving, shopping, festivals
**Amenities & Services:** Piano, guest phone, games, TV in library, ice machine, fireplace; group functions, celebration extras by arrangement

## ACCOMMODATIONS

**Units:** 13 guest rooms
**All Rooms:** Patio or deck w/ view, remote TV & VCR, closet
**Some Rooms:** Whirlpool tub, robes
**Bed & Bath:** Queen or king; private ensuite baths

**Favorites:** Admiral's Suites
**Comfort & Decor:** Fresh, contemporary furnishings in mauves and grays with wood accents. Individual room thermostats.

## RATES, RESERVATIONS, & RESTRICTIONS

**Deposit:** 1st night; 2-week cancellation requested, 7-day cancellation required for refund if rebooked, less $15 service fee
**Discounts:** Off-season, midweek
**Credit Cards:** V, MC, AE, D
**Check-in/Out:** 3:30–7:30 or by arrangement/11
**Smoking:** Allowed in some rooms
**Pets:** No

**Kids:** No
**No-Nos:** More than 2 per room
**Minimum Stay:** 2 nights, July–Sept. & holidays
**Open:** All year
**Hosts:** Dale & LaRona (Lee) Hoehne, innkeepers
235 SE Bay View Ave.
Depoe Bay, OR 97341
(800) 228-0448 or (541) 765-2322

## THE EDWIN K B&B, Florence

| Overall: ★★★★½ | Room Quality: A | Value: B | Price: $85–$125 |
|---|---|---|---|

This established bed-and-breakfast has a well-deserved reputation for elegance. The new owners (May 1998) are continuing the tradition. Vic and Inez love cooking, entertaining, and doing whatever it takes to make their guests' stays enjoyable. They have staff to do the drudgery (grounds, housekeeping), so they can concentrate on food, atmosphere, and interacting with guests ("we're being paid to give parties!" they enthuse). While the ambiance is luxurious, The Edwin K is also relaxed and comfortable. Breakfast is a "celebration meal," sinful and elaborate (dietary needs cheerfully and creatively accommodated), beginning with dessert and soaring from there.

## SETTING & FACILITIES

**Location:** On the Siuslaw River, just west of Hwy. 101
**Near:** Old Town Florence, Siuslaw River, Oregon Dunes N.R.A., beaches, lakes, Cape Perpetua, Heceta Head Lighthouse
**Building:** 1914 Craftsman, resited and extensively remodeled
**Grounds:** Rock patio, deck, & back garden w/ waterfall; small, very lovely; side yard
**Public Space:** Guest LR, DR, front porch, back patio

**Food & Drink:** Snacks & sherry in p.m.; in-room truffles or similar; full breakfast
**Recreation:** Fishing (saltwater or fresh), crabbing, clamming, horseback riding, dune buggy riding, riverboat tours, golf, antiquing
**Amenities & Services:** Toiletries basket, games, phone avail., TV in apt. unit (host big-screen TV gladly shared for major broadcast events!); dinner reservations, local airport pick-up, celebration extras, special events

## ACCOMMODATIONS

**Units:** 6 guest rooms, 1 apt.
**All Rooms:** Hairdryer, quality linens, armoires
**Some Rooms:** TV, kitchen (apt. only); private patio, dbl. whirlpool, claw-foot tub
**Bed & Bath:** Queen (5) or king (1), one w/ 2 extra twin daybeds; private ensuite baths

**Favorites:** Winter, Spring
**Comfort & Decor:** Upscale, elegant, sumptuous. Pale-toned paints and subtle wallpapers are accented with tasteful window treatments and fine, yet comfortable furnishings and antiques. Quality, ironed linens; fresh flowers. Windows open.

## RATES, RESERVATIONS, & RESTRICTIONS

**Deposit:** 72-hour cancellation or forfeit full reservation unless rebooked
**Discounts:** Off-season; $25 per add'l bed (in "Summer," w/ its queen plus 2 twins, & in apt.)
**Credit Cards:** V, MC, D
**Check-in/Out:** 3–7/11 or by arrangement
**Smoking:** Outside only
**Pets:** No; dander-free "pixibobcat" on site

**Kids:** 12 & older welcome (under 12 OK in apt. unit)
**Minimum Stay:** None
**Open:** All year
**Hosts:** Inez & Victor West
1155 Bay St.
Florence, OR 97439
(800) 8-EDWIN K or (541) 997-8360
Fax: (541) 997-1424
www.edwink.com

## THE JOHNSON HOUSE, Florence

| Overall: ★★★½ | Room Quality: C | Value: C | Price: $95–$125 |

The oldest house in Florence, originally built for a doctor, but named for Milo and Cora Johnson, who called it home for 60 years. Today, the cheerful white Victorian has a great location in historic Old Town, with shopping and dining a short walk away. Delicious breakfasts, attractively presented, feature local ingredients. Jayne and Ron renovated the home and have operated the bed-and-breakfast since 1984. These experienced hosts take obvious joy in their work—not the over-eager enthusiasm of brand-new proprietors, but the abiding pleasure of those who enjoy what they do. You'll enjoy it, too.

### SETTING & FACILITIES

**Location:** Historic Old Town waterfront district
**Near:** Siuslaw River, Oregon Dunes Nat'l Rec. Area, beaches, lakes, Cape Perpetua, Heceta Head Lighthouse
**Building:** 1892 Victorian home
**Grounds:** Attractive garden in back; border plantings, picket fence in front
**Public Space:** Parlor, DR

**Food & Drink:** Morning coffee; full breakfast
**Recreation:** Fishing (saltwater or fresh), crabbing, clamming, horseback riding, dune buggy riding, riverboat tours, bird/whale watching, golf, antiquing
**Amenities & Services:** Library, umbrellas, security system

### ACCOMMODATIONS

**Units:** 3 guest rooms plus overflow options (also retreat home; ask about "MoonSet")
**All Rooms:** Fresh flowers, armoire
**Some Rooms:** Claw-foot tub
**Bed & Bath:** Double or queen; private baths ("overflow" rooms w/ shared baths avail. by arrangement)
**Favorites:** The Rose Cottage

**Comfort & Decor:** Plain, comfortable living in a more genteel time. Antiques, original details and fixtures. High ceilings; ornate, old-fashioned wallpapers; painted wood floors. Special touches like the all-cotton, quality linens, crisply ironed, make you feel pampered.

### RATES, RESERVATIONS, & RESTRICTIONS

**Deposit:** Credit card; 7-day cancellation
**Discounts:** Off-season
**Credit Cards:** V, MC, D
**Check-in/Out:** 3 or by arrangement)/11
**Smoking:** No
**Pets:** No
**Kids:** 12 & over welcome

**Minimum Stay:** None
**Open:** All year
**Hosts:** Jayne & Ronald Fraese
P.O. Box 1892, Florence, OR 97439
(541) 997-8000
Fax: (541) 997-2364
fraese@presys.com
www/touroregon.com/TheJohnsonHouse

## INN AT NESIKA BEACH, Gold Beach

| Overall: ★★★★ | Room Quality: B | Value: C | Price: $100–$130 |
|---|---|---|---|

We were devastated to learn that this exceptional property—our choice for southernmost luxury bed-and-breakfast on the Oregon coast—was up for sale, but decided to include it anyway. The huge, new Victorian-style home was built as a top-of-the-line bed-and-breakfast, and will doubtless be operated as one even if new owners take over. The exceptional kitchen should ensure purchase by a party who enjoys cooking. Inquire as to new prices and policies. Setting, house, and rooms are wonderful.

### SETTING & FACILITIES

**Location:** Just west of Hwy. 101, 5.5 mi. north of Gold Beach and 20 mi. south of Port Orchard
**Near:** Mouth of Rogue River
**Building:** Victorian-styled contemporary home
**Grounds:** 270° ocean view
**Public Space:** Fireside room, formal parlor, DR, enclosed sun porch, wraparound exterior porch

**Food & Drink:** Full breakfast; early breakfast can be arranged
**Recreation:** Beach jet boating, golf, whale watching, windsurfing, horseback riding, tidepooling
**Amenities & Services:** Games, puzzles, umbrellas, library, fireplaces, piano, TV, built-in music system (w/ room volume controls); special occasion extras, reservations

### ACCOMMODATIONS

**Units:** 4 guest rooms
**All Rooms:** Ocean view, feather bed, whirlpool tub w/ European-style (hand-held) shower
**Some Rooms:** Ceiling fan, roll-away, private deck
**Bed & Bath:** Twins, queen, or king

(roll-away avail.); private ensuite baths
**Favorites:** Sans Souci, Beau Soleil
**Comfort & Decor:** High ceilings, oak floors with inlay. Antiques and quality reproduction furnishings; airy, open rooms. Main floor has AC; each room has individual thermostat.

### RATES, RESERVATIONS, & RESTRICTIONS

**Deposit:** 1st night; 72-hour cancellation, $10 fee
**Discounts:** Multiple night, single occupancy; $20 add'l person
**Credit Cards:** Not accepted
**Check-in/Out:** 3–6 or by arrangement/11
**Smoking:** No
**Pets:** No

**Kids:** No
**Minimum Stay:** None
**Open:** All year
**Hosts:** Ann Arsenault
33026 Nesika Rd.
Gold Beach, OR 97444
(541) 247-6434
www.virtualcities.com/ons/or/y/ory360 2.htm

## FLORAS LAKE HOUSE B&B, Langlois

| Overall: ★★★★ | Room Quality: B | Value: C | Price: $100–$130 |
|---|---|---|---|

Owners Liz and Will Brady, a dynamic young couple from southern California, are living their dream with this combination windsurfing school/bed-and-breakfast. Floras Lake is a windsurfer's paradise, separated from the ocean by only a small ridge of sand, with steady north-south wind. The full-service windsurfing school and rental outlet can outfit beginners to experts. Liz and Will live with their two young sons and adorable dog in a home separate from the bed-and-breakfast; assistant innkeepers live downstairs at the inn. Each guest room has a view of Floras Lake and the ocean.

### SETTING & FACILITIES

**Location:** About 3 mi. west of Hwy. 101, 25 mi. south of Bandon, 9 mi. north of Port Orford
**Near:** Beach, Blacklock S.P., Cape Blanco S.P. & Lighthouse
**Building:** Pacific Northwest contemporary
**Grounds:** Acre-plus grounds are like a private park
**Public Space:** Great room (LR, DR, guest wet bar)
**Food & Drink:** Coffee, tea, cocoa; morning coffee by 6:30; buffet full breakfast
**Recreation:** Windsurfing (see below), mountain biking, canoeing/kayaking, fishing, golf
**Amenities & Services:** BBQ, wet bar w/ mini-fridge, ice maker, sound system & CDs, books, games, sauna w/ view of lake; canoes & small paddle craft avail. for use on lake; windsurfing lessons & equipment rental (reasonable rates)

### ACCOMMODATIONS

**Units:** 4 guest rooms
**All Rooms:** Vaulted ceiling, ceiling fan, vanity area, carpet, sitting area, private deck entrance
**Some Rooms:** Window seat, tile fireplace
**Bed & Bath:** King (one with extra twin) or 2 doubles; private ensuite baths
**Favorites:** North, South
**Comfort & Decor:** Comfortable, contemporary decor with relaxed, modern furnishings. Fresh flowers and plants; new-looking paint and wallcoverings. Central heat and AC.

### RATES, RESERVATIONS, & RESTRICTIONS

**Deposit:** 1st night; 7-day cancellation
**Discounts:** Single occupancy, extended stays; add'l person, $15; children 3–12, $8; under 2 free
**Credit Cards:** V, MC, D
**Check-in/Out:** 3–6/noon
**Smoking:** Outside only
**Pets:** No
**Kids:** Welcome
**Minimum Stay:** 2 nights on major holidays
**Open:** Mid-Feb. to mid-Nov.
**Hosts:** Liz & Will Brady
92870 Boice Cope Rd.
Langlois, OR 97450
(541) 348-2573
floraslk@harborside.com
www.floraslake.com

## MARSH HAVEN FARM B&B, Langlois

| Overall: ★★½ | Room Quality: D | Value: A | Price: $65 |
|---|---|---|---|

What a peaceful place. A small, rustic, homestay on a working organic farm (certified to strict Oregon tilth standards) is not going to be everyone's cup of tea. (As in, "no TV," got it?) But if you're comfortable sharing space and like the idea of hanging out with folks who dry flowers, make bent willow furniture, and produce happy chickens and healthy produce . . .you might find this tiny homestead an absolute gem. We did.

### SETTING & FACILITIES

**Location:** A mi. or so west of Hwy. 101, 25 mi. south of Bandon, & 9 mi. north of Port Orford
**Near:** Floras Lake, Blacklock S.P., beach, Cape Blanco S.P. & Lighthouse
**Building:** 1880s homestead
**Grounds:** 23 acres, mostly wetland; guests may wander the farm
**Public Space:** You share living areas & shower w/ hosts

**Food & Drink:** Full breakfast; dinners by arrangement (naturally raised chickens, organic fruits & veg., $15–$25)
**Recreation:** Bird-watching, "farm animal watching," u-pick fruit, short drive (or long walk!) to ocean, Floras Lake windsurfing
**Amenities & Services:** Plenty of storage, phone avail.; dried flower classes & workshops (inquire)

### ACCOMMODATIONS

**Units:** 1 guest room
**Bed & Bath:** Four-poster double; private half bath (share shower in hosts' main bathroom)
**Comfort & Decor:** Small, cute room has whitewashed walls, lace trimmings, and painted wood floor with woven rug. Window seat overlooks marsh. Spotlessly clean. This is authentic country, not that slate-blue-and-stenciled-goose motif that passes for "country" in the suburbs! Woodstove heat (space heater avail. if really cold).

### RATES, RESERVATIONS, & RESTRICTIONS

**Deposit:** By arrangement
**Discounts:** $30 add'l person
**Credit Cards:** Not accepted
**Check-in/Out:** By arrangement
**Smoking:** No
**Pets:** Not in house; allowed on property on leash by arrangement
**Kids:** By arrangement

**Minimum Stay:** None
**Open:** All year
**Hosts:** Eileen Mulligan & Michael Murphy
47815 Floras Lake Loop
Langlois, OR 97450
(541) 348-2564

## NEWPORT BELLE B&B, Newport

| Overall: ★★★½ | Room Quality: C | Value: C | Price: $125–$145 |
|---|---|---|---|

You're King of the Harbor in your stateroom on this elegant stern-wheeler, featuring made-from-scratch breakfasts and delightful hostess.

Let the ever-so-slight motion of the harbor's waters lull you to sleep. Beautifully appointed and built to be a bed-and-breakfast, the *Salmon Harbor Belle* combines the best of nostalgic, turn-of-the-20th-century nautical ambiance with fully modern amenities. Rooms are spacious by ship standards. The main salon, housed in the bow of the boat, with 180° view through wrap-around glass, is a comfortable place to lounge. The deluxe, novel quarters will make your trip memorable.

## SETTING & FACILITIES

**Location:** Floating alongside "H" Dock at Newport's South Beach Marina
**Near:** Yaquina Bay, Yaquina Head Outstanding Natural Area, Yaquina Bay Lighthouse Museum, Hatfield Marine Science Center, South Beach, downtown Newport, Oregon Coast Aquarium, Nye Beach, Agate Beach
**Building:** 97-foot-long new sternwheel riverboat, with 3,100 sq. ft. of living space on 3 decks
**Grounds:** Does the whole harbor count? Plus dock, w/ tables, chairs, & container plants (like a patio)
**Public Space:** Dock, main salon
**Food & Drink:** Coffee, tea, & wine; snacks on arrival; full breakfast
**Recreation:** Crabbing off the dock, off-road (dune) driving (rental shops nearby), wildlife (whale, bird, sea lion) watching, sport fishing, rockhounding, clamming, sailing, golf
**Amenities & Services:** Binoculars, pellet stove, library, games; recipes printed out

## ACCOMMODATIONS

**Units:** 5 staterooms
**All Rooms:** Table & chair, roomy shower, bottled water, alarm clock, plants, life jackets, private entrances
**Some Rooms:** Theme decor
**Bed & Bath:** 1 king, 3 queens, 1 w/ double plus twin daybed
**Favorites:** Room 5: king bed, windows on 2 sides; Room 1 ("Montana Room"): a little more spacious, queen bed, subtle Western art.
**Comfort & Decor:** Stained fir decking, wainscoting, and ceilings; clean white walls and forest, burgundy, and gold bedding. Down comforters and lots of pillows. Each room has its own thermostat for heat, and at least one venting window.

## RATES, RESERVATIONS, & RESTRICTIONS

**Deposit:** 1st night; 5-day cancellation for full refund; cancellation less than 5 days will result in refund if rebooked
**Discounts:** Off-season, extended stays
**Credit Cards:** V, MC, AE
**Check-in/Out:** 3–6/11
**Smoking:** No
**Pets:** No
**Kids:** Older children welcome
**No-Nos:** Hard-soled shoes
**Minimum Stay:** Major holidays only
**Open:** All year
**Hosts:** Sherry Porter
P.O. Box 685, South Beach, OR 97366
(800) 348-1922 or (541) 876-6290
sporter@newportbelle.com
www.newportbelle.com

## OAR HOUSE B&B, Newport

| Overall: ★★★½ | Room Quality: B | Value: C | Price: $95–$125 |
|---|---|---|---|

Nautical-themed five-room guest house with colorful past offers a restful present for the weary, hungry traveler. Architecturally unique, the house sports nooks and crannies and quirks all integrated into the scheme of things by Jan, who remodeled extensively when she took over the property in 1992. Pleasant innkeeper, warm and inviting home.

### SETTING & FACILITIES

**Location:** Nye Beach district on SW 2nd between Hurbert & Brook
**Near:** Agate Beach, bayfront, downtown, Yaquina Head Outstanding Natural Area, Yaquina Bay Lighthouse Museum, Hatfield Marine Science Center, Oregon Coast Aquarium
**Building:** Craftsman-derivative boarding house from shipwreck lumber
**Grounds:** Off-street parking lot
**Public Space:** Guest sitting room, guest LR, 360° cupola viewing area
**Food & Drink:** Soft drinks, hot beverages; morning coffee; full breakfast
**Recreation:** Sports fishing, rockhounding, crabbing, clamming, sailing, golf
**Amenities & Services:** Phone, games, binoculars, beverage bar & fridge, cable & movie channels, fireplace, sound system

### ACCOMMODATIONS

**Units:** 4 guest rooms, 1 suite
**All Rooms:** Plenty of storage, toiletries
**Some Rooms:** Ceiling fan, view, desk, claw-foot tub, sitting room
**Bed & Bath:** Queens; private baths (4 of 5 ensuite)
**Favorites:** Captain's Quarters, Crow's Nest (for guests 5'8" & shorter)
**Comfort & Decor:** Nice sound system plays relaxing music in common areas. Guest rooms are carpeted, with modern fixtures and furnishings in fresh, contemporary colors. Unpretentious, attractive, well laid out. Individual heat controls.

### RATES, RESERVATIONS, & RESTRICTIONS

**Deposit:** 1st night, 72-hour cancellation or forfeit unless rebooked ($20 handling charge)
**Discounts:** Off-season, two or more nights, midweek off-season, single occupancy
**Credit Cards:** V, MC, D
**Check-in/Out:** 4–6 or by arrangement/ 11
**Smoking:** No
**Pets:** No
**Kids:** Older children OK by arrangement
**Minimum Stay:** 2 nights when staying a Sat. in summer; 2 nights during holidays & Newport's Seafood & Wine Festival
**Open:** All year
**Hosts:** Jan LeBrun
250 SW Second St.
Newport, OR 97365
(800) 252-2358 or (541) 265-9571
oarhouse@newportnet.com
www.newportnet.com/oarhouse

## SYLVIA BEACH HOTEL, Newport

| Overall: ★★★ | Room Quality: D | Value: C | Price: $69–$152 |
|---|---|---|---|

Named not for a particular stretch of sand, as one might reasonably expect for an oceanfront property, but for bookseller Sylvia Beach, owner of Shakespeare & Co. in Paris during the 1920s and 1930s. On the whole, it is worn and tousled around the edges, but charming and very evocative for bibliophiles. The front desk is staffed 24 hours; the staff is warm and pleasant. Author motifs are cleverly executed for each room. "Extremes" include Edgar Allan Poe room (predictably psychotic with its black wallpaper, red velvety bedspread, stuffed raven, and the curved blade from *The Pit and the Pendulum* swinging cheerfully above the bed) and the Dr. Seuss room (in primary colors, with twin trundle beds, hat rack with many hats—you gotta love it!). Others, like Dickinson, Fitzgerald, Melville, and Williams are clever but more "normal."

### SETTING & FACILITIES

**Location:** On the waterfront
**Near:** Nye Beach, Agate Beach, ocean, bayfront, downtown Newport, Yaquina Head Outstanding Natural Area, Yaquina Bay Lighthouse Museum, Hatfield Marine Science Center, Oregon Coast Aquarium
**Building:** Early 1900s oceanfront hotel
**Grounds:** Beachfront; flower-lined entry walk
**Public Space:** Lounge on 3rd floor, attic-level (4th floor) library
**Food & Drink:** Coffee & tea; hot mulled wine (10 p.m. nightly); pop & bottled water (fee); room service snack tray avail. for purchase 24 hours; breakfast; popular fixed-price dinners offered weekend evenings (reservations required)
**Recreation:** Sports fishing, rockhounding, crabbing, clamming, sailing, golf, bird/whale/sea lion watching, storm watching from 3rd-floor lounge
**Amenities & Services:** Local entertainment bulletin board, phones, ice machine, pop machine, gift shop, puzzles, books galore, games, fireplace, deck; book club retreats

### ACCOMMODATIONS

**Units:** 20 guest rooms, plus 8-bunk women's dorm & 4-bunk men's dorm
**All Rooms:** Books, period furnishings, carpet, high ceilings; theme-author books, decor, quotes, & memorabilia
**Some Rooms:** Deck, fireplace, ocean view, plants
**Bed & Bath:** Various bed configurations; private baths (except dorm rooms)
**Favorites:** Agatha Christie, Mark Twain, Colette
**Comfort & Decor:** Big and old, the hotel is a combination "genteel-shabby" European hotel and B&B. Author-motif theme decor in each room is delightful. Rooms tend toward drafty in the winter and overwarm on the hottest summer days on the upper levels. Rooms have individual thermostats.

## RATES, RESERVATIONS, & RESTRICTIONS

**Deposit:** 1st night; 48-hour cancellation
**Discounts:** Single occupancy, off-season weekdays; $15 add'l person; $22/night for bed in one of the dorm rooms w/ showers down the hall, breakfast included
**Credit Cards:** V, MC, AE
**Check-in/Out:** After 2/11
**Smoking:** No

**Pets:** No; cat in residence
**Kids:** Older children welcome
**Minimum Stay:** 2 nights when staying on a Sat.
**Open:** All year
**Hosts:** Goody Cable & Sally Ford, owners; Ken Payton, manager; Charlotte Dinolt, assistant manager
267 NW Cliff, Newport, OR 97365
(541) 265-5428

## EAGLE'S VIEW B&B, Pacific City

| Overall: ★★★★ | Room Quality: B | Value: B | Price: $95–$115 |
|---|---|---|---|

Country hospitality, bird's-eye bay views, plenty of tasty food, and comfortable, modern rooms. Mike and Kathy Lewis aren't faking their warmth and enthusiasm. The day we arrived, a young couple was sitting at the dining room table, eating cookies and drinking iced tea. Turns out they weren't guests at all—their car had broken down nearby, and Mike and Kathy had not only let them use the phone, but fed them and gave them a comfortable place to wait. "These guys are so nice!" the young man confided when the hosts left the room, "You oughta stay here!" We agree.

## SETTING & FACILITIES

**Location:** West of Hwy. 101 near the southern end of the Three Capes Scenic Loop drive
**Near:** Lincoln City, Nestucca Bay, Tillamook, beaches, Cape Kiwanda, Cape Lookout, & lighthouse
**Building:** Contemporary country home
**Grounds:** 4-acre parcel; splendid view of Nestucca Bay & Nestucca Nat'l Wildlife Refuge; pond and waterfall
**Public Space:** Multilevel front & side

decks, great room
**Food & Drink:** Teas, cocoa, baked goods; breakfast, ensuite or dining area
**Recreation:** Wildlife watching; sailing, crabbing, kite flying; in Tillamook, cheese factory tours & museums; in Lincoln City, shopping & gambling
**Amenities & Services:** Ice maker & micro., laundry facil., full-size beverage-stocked fridge, videos & CDs; retreats & small business meetings

## ACCOMMODATIONS

**Units:** 5 guest rooms
**All Rooms:** Remote TV/VCR, phone, table & chairs, European armoires, carpet, sound system, quality mattresses
**Some Rooms:** Priv. entrance, disabled access, vaulted ceiling, whirlpool tub
**Bed & Bath:** Queens (1 w/ extra twin trundles); private ensuite baths

**Favorites:** Love Spoken Here
**Comfort & Decor:** Clean, bright, contemporary country, with fine handmade quilts. Floral print bedding and window treatments. Individual thermostats in each room and each bath; AC on main level.

## RATES, RESERVATIONS, & RESTRICTIONS

**Deposit:** 1st night; 7-day cancellation
**Discounts:** Winter months, weekdays; $20 add'l person
**Credit Cards:** V, MC, D
**Check-in/Out:** 3–8 or by arrangement/11
**Smoking:** No
**Pets:** No; host dogs on site in separate quarters
**Kids:** 12 & older welcome

**Minimum Stay:** 2 nights, holiday weekends
**Open:** All year
**Hosts:** Mike & Kathy Lewis
37975 Brooten Rd.
Pacific City, OR 97135
(888) 846-3292 or (503) 965-7600
eagle@wcn.net
www.moriah.com/eaglesview/

## HOME BY THE SEA B&B, Port Orford

| Overall: ★★½ | Room Quality: D | Value: D | Price: $95–$105 |

The loquacious Mr. Mitchell designed and built this home, and has offered it as a bed-and-breakfast since the late 1980s. The home is a bustle of motifs, and the hosts are multifaceted, knowledgeable, down-to-earth people with many interests and a genuine affection for people. Breakfasts feature quality local ingredients. The unique peninsular location affords one of the few east-facing views on the west coast—watch the sun rise over the cove!

## SETTING & FACILITIES

**Location:** Just west of Hwy. 101 on the beach in Port Orford
**Near:** Restaurants, Humbug Mountain, Cape Blanco S.P. & Lighthouse, Elk River Salmon Hatchery, Prehistoric Gardens
**Building:** Ocean-view tri-level home
**Grounds:** Direct beach access
**Public Space:** Casual sitting area w/ ocean cove view

**Food & Drink:** Full breakfast
**Recreation:** Shopping (tiny town is a "quilting Mecca" and home to fine artisans & craftsmen), photography, whale/bird watching
**Amenities & Services:** Laundry privileges, travel books; e-mailing, faxing, hiking shuttle for downwind beach walking (this is a GREAT service!)

## ACCOMMODATIONS

**Units:** 2 guest rooms
**All Rooms:** Phone jack (phone avail.), mini-fridge, cable TV, ocean view, binoculars
**Bed & Bath:** Queens (roll-away avail.); private baths (1 ensuite, 1 across hall)
**Favorites:** The Blue Suite

**Comfort & Decor:** Eclectic, unpretentious, nautical. Oregon-crafted myrtlewood beds with quality mattresses w/ electric blankets and lighthouse quilts. Common areas are chockablock with books and information. Tropical fish and birds.

## RATES, RESERVATIONS, & RESTRICTIONS

**Deposit:** Credit card; 72-hour
cancellation
**Discounts:** $20 add'l person
**Credit Cards:** V, MC
**Check-in/Out:** 4–6 or by arrange-
ment/11
**Smoking:** Outside only
**Pets:** No

**Kids:** By arrangement
**Minimum Stay:** None
**Open:** All year
**Hosts:** Alan & Brenda Mitchell
P.O. Box 606, Port Orford, OR 97465
(541) 332-2855
alan@homebythesea.com
www.homebythesea.com

## SANDLAKE COUNTRY INN, Sandlake

| Overall: ★★★★½ | Room Quality: A | Value: B | Price: $90–$135 |
|---|---|---|---|

Enjoy the romantic seclusion and attention to detail provided by Femke
and her staff. This is the type of bed-and-breakfast where you feel pampered and leave renewed. While beaches and touring attractions are very
nearby, you might want to save some time for just lingering on the
grounds and enjoying your hideaway room. The sumptuous ensuite
breakfasts are elegantly presented as well as delicious.

## SETTING & FACILITIES

**Location:** About 6 mi. west of Hwy.
101 via Sandlake Rd., just off Three
Capes Scenic Loop
**Near:** Sandlake Rec. Area, Cape Lookout, Cape Kiwanda, Cape Meares &
lighthouse, Tillamook, Lincoln City
**Building:** 1894 shipwreck-timbered
farmhouse
**Grounds:** Parklike 2 acres w/ stream;
weathered, relaxed, & "happy"
**Public Space:** If you ever leave your
room, the LR is avail.

**Food & Drink:** Chocolate mints in
room; hot, spiced cider, tea, & sinful
homemade cookies; full breakfast
delivered
**Recreation:** Wildlife-, whale-, &
bird-watching; crabbing, kite flying;
Tillamook cheese factory tours/muse-
ums; Lincoln City shopping & gambling
**Amenities & Services:** Chess,
croquet, vintage videos, gift pantry;
deluxe romantic picnic baskets ($34
on request)

## Accommodations

**Units:** 4 guest rooms
**All Rooms:** Private deck, fridge, whirlpool tub, quality toiletries, fresh fruit, water carafe
**Some Rooms:** TV/VCR, dbl. whirlpool tub
**Bed & Bath:** King or queen; private ensuite baths

**Favorites:** Each is special & romantic; we liked Timbers & Rose Garden
**Comfort & Decor:** Abundant fresh flowers and/or dried arrangements. Decor is exuberant but never "foofy" or oppressive. Exceptional attention to details. Rooms have individual heat controls.

## Rates, Reservations, & Restrictions

**Deposit:** 1st night; 7-day cancellation, $15 fee
**Discounts:** Single occupancy; $20 add'l person
**Credit Cards:** V, MC, AE, D
**Check-in/Out:** 3–6/11
**Smoking:** Outside only
**Pets:** No

**Kids:** 14 & older only
**Minimum Stay:** 2 nights, weekends; 3 nights, holidays
**Open:** All year
**Hosts:** Femke & David Durham
8505 Galloway Rd.
Cloverdale, OR 97112
(503) 965-6745

---

## ANDERSON'S BOARDING HOUSE, Seaside

| Overall: ★★★½ | Room Quality: B | Value: B | Price: $80–$90 |
|---|---|---|---|

Anderson's Boarding House is an established bed-and-breakfast named for the house's longstanding resident and local character Babe Anderson, whose stuffed parrot resides unobtrusively in the dining room. Its location is convenient to downtown (an easy walk), yet a tad removed from the carnival atmosphere of Broadway. Barb purchased the property in 1988 (previous owners also operated it as a bed-and-breakfast) and redecorates periodically for a well maintained appearance. The professionally landscaped front garden is tidy and colorful. Located just off downtown corridor with deck overlooking the Necanicum River.

## Setting & Facilities

**Location:** 3 blocks north of Broadway on the Necanicum River
**Near:** Downtown, beach, arcade, aquarium, Ecola S.P., Cannon Beach, Astoria
**Building:** 1898 Transitional Victorian (w/ Craftsman aspects)
**Grounds:** Rhododendrons, porch

**Public Space:** Parlor, DR, 2nd-floor deck
**Food & Drink:** Tea, coffee, & cocoa at check-in; full breakfast
**Recreation:** Walking, in-line skating, or bicycling along "the Prom"; kite flying, crabbing, horseback riding, golf
**Amenities & Services:** Games, guidebooks, gas log fireplace

## ACCOMMODATIONS

**Units:** 5 guest rooms
**All Rooms:** Carpet, starched &
ironed sheets, fresh flowers
**Some Rooms:** River view, claw-foot
tub
**Bed & Bath:** Queen, 1 double (trundles in 3 rooms); private baths (tub &
shower)

**Favorites:** 5, 6
**Comfort & Decor:** "Decade theme"
rooms from 1890s Eastlake to 1930s
Art Deco. Eclectic antiques; well cho-
sen wallpapers. Old photos, Wallace
Nutting hand-tinted photographs.
Parlor has beamed ceiling and old-
growth-fir paneling.

## RATES, RESERVATIONS, & RESTRICTIONS

**Deposit:** 1st night; 5-day cancellation
**Discounts:** Single occupancy; $15
add'l person
**Credit Cards:** V, MC
**Check-in/Out:** 4–6/11 or by
arrangement
**Smoking:** Outside only
**Pets:** No

**Kids:** Over age 2 welcome
**Minimum Stay:** None
**Open:** All year
**Hosts:** Barb Edwards
208 N. Holladay Dr.
Seaside, OR 97138
(800) 995-4013 or (503) 738-9055
www.moriah.com/andersons/

## GILBERT INN, Seaside

| Overall: ★★★★ | Room Quality: B | Value: B | Price: $89–$105 |
|---|---|---|---|

This classy, remodeled, and expanded Queen Anne offers upscale decor and modern amenities in an elegant setting that's walking distance to the beach and Seaside attractions. Contemporary furnishings and the extensive 1988 addition give the feeling of a modern hotel despite the building's vintage. Sunny, cafe-style dining room with its small, white-iron tables is an unusual and memorable breakfast venue; not open to guests aside from mealtime. (In truth, the property is a little short on common areas for its 10-room capacity.) Upscale, comfortable, good location.

## SETTING & FACILITIES

**Location:** A block south of Broadway,
close to everything
**Near:** Downtown, beach, arcade,
aquarium, Ecola S.P., Cannon Beach,
Astoria
**Building:** 1892 Queen Anne Victorian,
restored & expanded
**Grounds:** Lovely front grounds
**Public Space:** Parlor, "Gilbert's

Gallery" sitting room
**Food & Drink:** Evening sherry;
morning coffee; full breakfast
**Recreation:** In-line skating or
bicycling along "the Prom," kite flying,
horseback riding, golf
**Amenities & Services:** Small
retreats, meetings, weddings,
receptions

## ACCOMMODATIONS

**Units:** 10 guest rooms (also 2 adjacent duplexes w/ kitchens)
**All Rooms:** Remote TVs, phone w/ private ext., carpet
**Some Rooms:** Sitting area, "peek-at-the-ocean" view
**Bed & Bath:** Queens (The Garret also has 2 twins); ensuite baths w/ tub

**Favorites:** The Garret, 1880 Suite
**Comfort & Decor:** Emerald green carpet, old-growth fir paneling, and a brick fireplace greet you in the parlor. Decor is kept updated and upscale, plus a few well-placed antiques. Individual heat controls in rooms.

## RATES, RESERVATIONS, & RESTRICTIONS

**Deposit:** 1st night; 5-day cancellation
**Discounts:** Single occupancy; $10 add'l person
**Credit Cards:** V, MC, AE, D
**Check-in/Out:** After 3/11
**Smoking:** No
**Pets:** No
**Kids:** By arrangement; best suited for adjacent duplex units

**Minimum Stay:** 2 nights, weekends; 3 nights, some holidays
**Open:** All year
**Hosts:** Carole & Dick Rees
341 Beach Dr., Seaside, OR 97138
(800) 410-9770 or (503) 738-9770
Fax: (503) 717-1070
gilbertinn@clatsop.com
www.clatsop.com/gilbertinn

## CLIFF HOUSE B&B, Waldport

Overall: ★★★★★     Room Quality: A     Value: C     Price: $99–$229

Gabrielle Duvall thinks of everything; "You need bring nothing but your sweetheart!" when you visit Cliff House. Outstanding oceanfront views and eight-mile walking beach immediately adjacent. The ten-jetted hot tub and the sauna/steam room are open to guests 24 hours a day, and an Esalen-trained masseur is avail. by appointment for therapeutic massage in the private, ocean-view gazebo. Breakfast fare is gourmet, and the presentation is opulent: candlelight, china, crystal, linen, silver. The best of Old World elegance and New Age relaxation. One of our favorite inns.

## SETTING & FACILITIES

**Location:** Just south of Waldport, overlooking Alsea Bay
**Near:** Beach, Alsea Bay Bridge Interpretive Center, Yachats, Cape Perpetua (visitors center, hiking, viewing), Devil's Churn, Sea Lion Caves, Strawberry Hill (tide pools & sea lion viewing), Heceta Head Lighthouse, Florence, Newport
**Building:** 1932 historic beach house
**Grounds:** Back lawn w/ panoramic beach/ocean view
**Public Space:** Great room, upstairs window seat & library, enormous back

deck w/ glass windbreak
**Food & Drink:** In-room chocolates & port or sherry; tea & other beverages; weekdays, cont'l breakfast; weekends, full gourmet breakfast; Bridal Suite guests dine ensuite
**Recreation:** Tidepooling, kite flying, croquet, bird/sea lion/seal watching, golf
**Amenities & Services:** Phone & fax, hot tub & wet-dry sauna, ocean-view massage gazebo, indoor & outdoor games, binoculars, piano, fireplace; massage by appointment

## ACCOMMODATIONS

**Units:** 3 guest rooms, 1 suite
**All Rooms:** Ocean views, antiques, chandeliers, TV/VCR, books, deluxe hooded robes, hairdryer, curling iron, binoculars, sitting area
**Some Rooms:** Writing desk, fridge, woodstove, private balcony, jetted tub
**Bed & Bath:** Queen or king; private cedar baths (most ensuite, one adjacent)

**Favorites:** The Bridal Suite
**Comfort & Decor:** Whimsical, eclectic mix of motifs, all overlaid with a hint of the mystic. Great room is a lavish work of art, with massive stone fireplace. Fir and oak flooring. Rooms include plush carpet and rich, elegant decor with bold, jewel colors.

## RATES, RESERVATIONS, & RESTRICTIONS

**Deposit:** Check or credit card; 14-day cancellation, $20 cancellation fee
**Discounts:** None
**Credit Cards:** Cash preferred; V, MC, D
**Check-in/Out:** 3–7/11
**Smoking:** No
**Pets:** No
**Kids:** No
**Minimum Stay:** 2 nights, weekends; 3

nights, holidays
**Open:** All year
**Hosts:** Gabrielle Duvall
1450 Adahi Rd., P.O. Box 436
Waldport, OR 97394
(541) 563-2506
Fax: (541) 563-4393
clifhos@pioneer.net
www.virtualcities.com/ons/or/z/orzb50 1.htm

## MORNING STAR, Yachats

| Overall: ★★★★ | Room Quality: B | Value: C | Price: $85–$150 |
|---|---|---|---|

You can't miss this bright, contemporary, romantic beach house—its right on the highway. Fortunately, it's also right on the ocean. Artist Susan Hanson built Morning Star in 1995. Her plan for a "quiet establishment of fine taste overlooking a spectacular oceanfront bluff," has been realized. Rooms are artistic, common areas are small but comfortable (and ample for only 3 guest rooms), and views are spectacular. Next door, Susan's gallery serves as her studio for her painting, sculpture, and jewelry work and is open for viewing by appointment.

## 332   Yachats, Oregon

### SETTING & FACILITIES

**Location:** 6 mi. south of Yachats & 19 mi. north of Florence on Hwy. 101
**Near:** Beach, ocean, Yachats, Cape Perpetua (visitors center, hiking, viewing), Devil's Churn, Sea Lion Caves, Strawberry Hill (tidepools & sea lion viewing), Heceta Head Lighthouse, Florence (Old Town)
**Building:** Contemporary oceanfront beach house
**Grounds:** Cheerful front flower beds; large backyard on bluff w/ stairs to beach
**Public Space:** Den, LR, deck
**Food & Drink:** Full breakfast
**Recreation:** Horseback riding, golf, storm watching, kite flying, sand castle building
**Amenities & Services:** Library, ocean-view hot tub w/ wind break, satellite TV/VCR, sound system, cordless guest phone; massage avail.

### ACCOMMODATIONS

**Units:** 3 guest rooms
**All Rooms:** Roomy closets, plush carpet, ocean views, unique beds, sitting area or vanity
**Some Rooms:** Dbl. whirlpool tub, mini-library
**Bed & Bath:** King or queen; private ensuite baths
**Favorites:** Icart
**Comfort & Decor:** Slate entry, comfortable furnishings, unusual and fun mix of art and antiques. Icart has a groovy mix of antique French elegance, Asian motifs, and jungle prints, plus original etchings, and a huge, festive tile bath. O'Keefe and Matisse sport reproductions of their namesakes' work.

### RATES, RESERVATIONS, & RESTRICTIONS

**Deposit:** 1st night; 7-day cancellation
**Discounts:** Winter midweek packages
**Credit Cards:** V, MC, AE
**Check-in/Out:** 3–7 or by arrangement/11
**Smoking:** No
**Pets:** No; tiny dog on premises
**Kids:** No
**Minimum Stay:** 2 nights preferred on weekends
**Open:** All year
**Hosts:** Susan Hanson
95668 Highway 101, Yachats, OR 97498
(541) 547-4412
Fax: (541) 547 4335
artgal@teleport.com
www.teleport.com/~artgal

### SEA QUEST B&B, Yachats

| Overall: ★★★★★ | Room Quality: A | Value: B | Price: $140–$up |

"The beach house you wish you had"—contemporary comfort, superb ocean views, and immediate beach access are yours, plus a wonderful breakfast and warm, winning hosts. A telling statistic: since their opening in 1991, over 1,000 of Elaine and George's guests have come back to Sea Quest three or more times. Maybe it's because no one surpasses the mix of upscale contemporary decor and relaxed comfort you'll find at Sea Quest. And the oceanfront setting is nothing short of sublime. Attention to detail is phenomenal. We've booked our return trip.

## SETTING & FACILITIES

**Location:** On the ocean 7 mi. south of Yachats & 18 mi. north of Florence
**Near:** Cape Perpetua (visitors center, hiking), Devil's Churn, Sea Lion Caves, Strawberry Hill (tidepools & sea lion viewing), Heceta Head Lighthouse, Florence (Old Town)
**Building:** Pacific Coast contemporary
**Grounds:** Back lawn, beach access, decks, front patio/entry
**Public Space:** Great room, deck, library/phone room/guest pantry
**Food & Drink:** Coffee, tea, bottled water, & snacks; buffet-style full breakfast
**Recreation:** Tidepooling, horseback riding, golf, storm watching, kite flying, sand castle building
**Amenities & Services:** Books, games, binoculars, telescope, gift shop, guest fridge & micro., piano, sound system; "General Mess" mud room: caps, jackets, rubber boots, lanterns, scruffy towels, croquet, kites, pails & shovels, & other fun "kid-in-all-of-us" toys; reservations, celebration extras

## ACCOMMODATIONS

**Units:** 5 guest rooms
**All Rooms:** Lots of pillows, ocean view, custom toiletries, oil lamps, private entrance
**Some Rooms:** Whirlpool tub, private deck, comfortable chairs
**Bed & Bath:** Queens (one w/ twin daybed); private ensuite baths
**Favorites:** One w/ a dbl. spa tub (but each is a treat)
**Comfort & Decor:** Soft, contemporary tones, mixed patterns and textures. Rooms arranged with casual charm that affects a "lived-in" look, while all is flawlessly clean. Soft music in the great room and healthy houseplants throughout.

## RATES, RESERVATIONS, & RESTRICTIONS

**Deposit:** 1st night; 7-day cancellation
**Discounts:** None
**Credit Cards:** V, MC
**Check-in/Out:** 3–7/11
**Smoking:** Outside only
**Pets:** No
**Kids:** 14 & older welcome
**Minimum Stay:** 2 nights, weekends; 3 nights, holidays
**Open:** All year
**Hosts:** George & Elaine
95354 Highway 101, Yachats, OR 97498
(800) 341-4878 or (541) 547-3782
Fax: (541) 547-3719
seaquest@newportnet.com
www.seaq.com

## SERENITY B&B, Yachats

Overall: ★★★★★    Room Quality: A    Value: B    Price: $80–$145

European-themed bed-and-breakfast pampers guests with spacious, luxurious rooms and delicious breakfasts. We never thought Germany could be so romantic. Baerbel brings the best of the Old Country to her sumptuously decorated rooms (which could easily be considered suites, sizewise) and her decadent breakfasts. Sample menu: baked spiced apples

(Bratapfel), cheese blintzes with homemade berry sauce (Käseblintzen mit Himbersaft), melt-in-your-mouth roasted potatoes (Bratkartoffel), and smoked turkey breast (geräucherte Truthahnbrust).

## SETTING & FACILITIES

**Location:** 6 mi. inland from Hwy. 101 at Yachats

**Near:** Upper Yachats covered bridge, Siuslaw Nat'l Forest, Yachats River, ocean beaches, Waldport, Cape Perpetua (visitors center, hiking), Devil's Churn, Sea Lion Caves, Strawberry Hill (tidepools & sea lion viewing), Heceta Head Lighthouse

**Building:** Contemporary ranch house & remodeled outbuilding

**Grounds:** 10 acres of lawn w/ exceptional flowers, mature trees, elk visitors

**Public Space:** Rooms are commodious, but host LR is open as well

**Food & Drink:** In-room chocolates, bottled water, & sodas; full breakfast

**Recreation:** Crabbing, tidepooling, horseback riding, golf, kite flying, sand castle building

**Amenities & Services:** Large video library; hairdryers, etc., avail. (ask); German & Italian spoken

## ACCOMMODATIONS

**Units:** 4 guest rooms

**All Rooms:** TV/VCR in room or avail. (no reception but great video library), carpet, green plants, fresh flowers, quality toiletries

**Some Rooms:** Balcony, mini-fridge, sound system, dbl. whirlpool tub

**Bed & Bath:** King (3) or double; private baths

**Favorites:** La Italia

**Comfort & Decor:** Quality fixtures and furnishings. Amazing from-a-German-castle bedroom set in little Alt Heidelberg; opulent carved frieze moldings and electronically controlled skylights in La Italia. Europa's Italian-inspired decor mixes modern and antique pieces; Bavaria has a light, airy feel with beautiful hand-painted ceiling panel inserts. Individual heat control.

## RATES, RESERVATIONS, & RESTRICTIONS

**Deposit:** 1st night; 7-day cancellation

**Discounts:** $25 add'l person

**Credit Cards:** V, MC

**Check-in/Out:** 3/11

**Smoking:** No

**Pets:** No

**Kids:** 12 & older welcome; younger by prior arrangement only

**Minimum Stay:** 2 nights on weekends

**Open:** All year

**Hosts:** Sam & Baerbel Morgan
5985 Yachats River Rd.
Yachats, OR 97498
(541) 547-3813
www.ohwy.com/or/s/serenibb.html

# Zone 11
# Greater Portland

Politically quirky, environmentally conscious Portland nestles at a wide river bend where the Willamette River meets the Columbia in northwestern Oregon. The city is full of parks, gardens, and open spaces, including the International Rose Test Garden, from which it earns its nickname, "The City of Roses." It is a city in the traditional sense, with industry and commerce, a vibrant downtown and neighborhoods of character, a symphony orchestra, ballet companies, and major-league sports. But Portland is also a city that takes advantage of its geography, highlighting its riverfront and verdant hills with beautiful parks.

Some of the best bed-and-breakfasts cluster in the Rose Quarter or Historic Irvington District, east of the Willamette and north of Lloyd Center shopping mall. This area includes the Oregon Convention Center, Rose Garden (performing arts/sports) Arena, and the boutique-y Broadway shopping district.

Another popular restaurant and shopping district centers around Burnside and 23rd. Northwest of downtown, this bustling area is home to excellent restaurants and, at the base, some of the city's loveliest hillside neighborhoods (King's Hill, Nob Hill, Hillside, Southwest Hills). You'll also find the Rose Gardens, Washington Park (a zoo), and the Pittock Mansion museum.

South of downtown, the Lair District is a transitional, Bohemian neighborhood with good access to some of the city's medical and higher learning venues.

The downtown area itself is the commerce, business, and mainstream shopping core. Niketown, legendary Powell's Books, and Pioneer Square (courthouse and general civic gathering plaza) are popular destinations. Weekends bring the beloved Saturday Market, a crafts-and-food festival held under Burnside Bridge on Saturdays and Sundays.

Two bed-and-breakfasts profiled are located outside Portland proper. One is in Beaverton, a suburb just to the west of Portland, and the other is in Scappoose, a rural community 25 miles northwest.

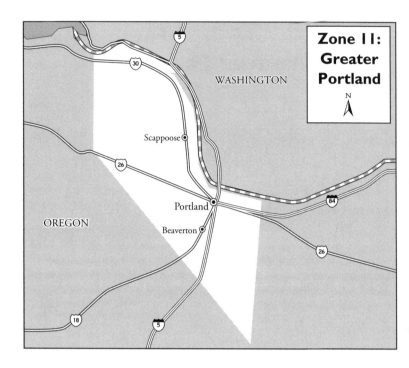

Zone 11:
Greater
Portland

N

WASHINGTON

Scappoose

Portland

Beaverton

OREGON

**Beaverton**
The Yankee Tinker, p. 337

**Portland**
General Hooker's B&B, p. 338
Georgian House B&B, p. 339
Heron Haus, p. 340
The Lion and The Rose, p. 341
MacMaster House, p. 343
Portland's White House, p. 344
Terwilliger Vista House, p. 345

**Scappoose**
Barnstormer B&B, p. 346

## THE YANKEE TINKER, Beaverton

| Overall: ★★★½ | Room Quality: B | Value: A | Price: $65–$75 |
|---|---|---|---|

Tucked into a quiet, middle-class neighborhood, this brick-red single-level home has a well-tended, welcoming feel. Better access to points west (Willamette Valley, wineries, Oregon coast) than Portland, yet still convenient to metro attractions and activities. One little room has only a twin bed and is priced for single occupancy. Given the limitations of the house (a simple, unremarkable ranch) and the neighborhood (typical suburbia), the Wadleighs have created a really pleasant place: immaculate surroundings, experienced hosts, exceptional hospitality.

### SETTING & FACILITIES

**Location:** 10 mi. west of Portland, off 185th Ave. near Farmington
**Near:** Beaverton, Portland, Willamette Valley
**Building:** Single-level private home
**Grounds:** Small, tidy front lawn; pleasant backyard w/ gardens & deck
**Public Space:** Guest sitting room, DR, deck

**Food & Drink:** Self-serve beer, wine, soft drinks, tea, cocoa, cookies; full breakfast
**Recreation:** Public swimming pool & health clubs nearby; wine touring, all Portland attractions
**Amenities & Services:** Piano, TV, VCR, desk, fridge, guest guide, fireplace, games, health club pass

### ACCOMMODATIONS

**Units:** 3 guest rooms
**All Rooms:** Robes, electric blanket, phone, closet
**Some Rooms:** Four-poster, desk
**Bed & Bath:** Queen (2), twin; 1 private bath, 2 share a bath
**Favorites:** Massachusetts

**Comfort & Decor:** Quilts and New England antiques set the tone in each cozy, clean, homey, and attractive room. Walls sport fresh paint and wallpaper borders. Central heat and AC, fans.

### RATES, RESERVATIONS, & RESTRICTIONS

**Deposit:** 1st night; 72-hour cancellation
**Discounts:** Extended stay; $10 add'l person; single-person room w/ twin, $50
**Credit Cards:** V, MC, AE, D, DC
**Check-in/Out:** 4–6 or by arrangement/11
**Smoking:** Outside only
**Pets:** No

**Kids:** Welcome
**Minimum Stay:** None
**Open:** All year
**Hosts:** Jan & Ralph Wadleigh
5480 SW 183rd Ave.
Beaverton, OR 97007
(800) 846-5372 or (503) 649-0932
yankeeb&b@aol.com
www.yankeetinker.com

## GENERAL HOOKER'S B&B, Portland

| Overall: ★★ | Room Quality: D | Value: C | Price: $80–$125 |
|---|---|---|---|

In a gentrifying neighborhood with a Bohemian feel, General Hooker's has the distinction of being the closest profiled bed-and-breakfast to downtown Portland—within walking distance or an easy transit ride. Lori, a fourth-generation Portlander, has offered a business traveler–friendly inn here since 1986. The style is relaxed, "this-is-my-home" innkeeping, with a touch of the artsy (chamber music, objets d'art, classic film library). Hostess is a great source of Portland lore and an active community member. Kitty (named "Happy Hooker") is very sweet and friendly.

### SETTING & FACILITIES

**Location:** Lair Hill district, on Hooker between SW 1st & SW 2nd Ave.
**Near:** Oregon Health Sciences Univ. Med. Center, naturopathic college, Reed College, Lewis & Clark College, Veteran's Medical Center, Shriner's Hospital for Children, parks
**Building:** 1888 Victorian
**Public Space:** LR

**Food & Drink:** Self-serve tea; cold beverages (first one free); cont'l breakfast
**Recreation:** Tennis, health club, all Portland attractions
**Amenities & Services:** Huge classic video library, half-price YMCA passes, guest fridge, iron, travel library, guest guide, safe for valuables, daily newspaper, bus schedules, fireplace

### ACCOMMODATIONS

**Units:** 4 guest rooms
**All Rooms:** TV, VCR, phone, desk
**Some Rooms:** Sink, rooftop patio access, library, fridge
**Bed & Bath:** King, queen, double-and-twin bunk; 2 private baths (1 ensuite), 2 share a bath
**Favorites:** Rose, Daisy

**Comfort & Decor:** Relaxed, casual; art objects allude to world travels. Midquality furnishings mingle with heirloom antiques. Beds aren't great (Iris room has only a futon), and shared bath has dual entrances, necessitating caution and courtesy. Central heat/AC.

### RATES, RESERVATIONS, & RESTRICTIONS

**Deposit:** Credit card; 7-day cancellation
**Discounts:** Single occupancy, off-season
**Credit Cards:** V, MC, AE
**Check-in/Out:** 3–5 or by arrangement/11
**Smoking:** Outside only
**Pets:** No; host kitty
**Kids:** Over 10 welcome

**No-Nos:** Burning candles
**Minimum Stay:** 2 nights preferred
**Open:** All year
**Hosts:** Lori Hall
125 SW Hooker
Portland, OR 97201
(800) 745-4135 or (503) 222-4435
Fax: (503) 295-6410
lori@generalhookers.com
www.generalhookers.com

## GEORGIAN HOUSE B&B, Portland

| Overall: ★★★½ | Room Quality: B | Value: A | Price: $65–$100 |
|---|---|---|---|

A bit farther removed from the bustle of Broadway and Lloyd Center than The Lion and The Rose or Portland's White House, Georgian House is a slightly humbler accommodation offering the best of the quiet, residential aspect of historic Irvington district, with its imminently walkable, tree-lined streets. Gardens are exceptional, hostess is a delight. Site-grown marionberries, blueberries, and raspberries grace the breakfast table in season. The total package is absolutely charming—we loved this place.

### SETTING & FACILITIES

**Location:** Corner of 19th & Siskiyou in historic Irvington District
**Near:** Broadway commercial district, Lloyd Center, Oregon Convention Center, Rose Garden Arena, downtown, transit
**Building:** 1922 Georgian Colonial
**Grounds:** Grassy corner lot; exceptional rear gardens, including rose garden

**Public Space:** LR, TV room, DR, deck
**Food & Drink:** Self-serve tea or cool beverage & cookies; full breakfast
**Recreation:** Antiquing, all Portland attractions
**Amenities & Services:** Portable guest phone, TV/VCR, sound system, fridge, daily newspaper

### ACCOMMODATIONS

**Units:** 3 guest rooms, 1 suite
**All Rooms:** Robes, hairdryer
**Some Rooms:** Private veranda, clawfoot tub, TV, VCR, closet, table & chairs, sound system, fireplace, vanity
**Bed & Bath:** Queen (1 w/ extra queen futon), king/twin conversion; 2 private baths (1 ensuite); 2 share a bath
**Favorites:** Lovejoy Suite

**Comfort & Decor:** Common areas have a Colonial feel. Guest rooms range from the traditional Eastlake (namesake bedroom set, veranda) to Pettygrove (quilt, ducks, plaids) to bright, sunny, roomy Lovejoy Suite. Captain Irving Room (lower level) is spacious and apart from the other rooms. Central heat, individual AC in upstairs rooms; fans.

### RATES, RESERVATIONS, & RESTRICTIONS

**Deposit:** Credit card; 2-week cancellation
**Discounts:** Corporate, extended stay; inquire about add'l persons
**Credit Cards:** V, MC
**Check-in/Out:** Flexible—by arrangement
**Smoking:** Outside only
**Pets:** No

**Kids:** Welcome in Captain Irving Room
**Minimum Stay:** None
**Open:** All year
**Hosts:** Willie Ackley
1828 NE Siskiyou, Portland, OR 97212
(503) 281-3301
Fax: (503) 281-3301
www.moriah.com/georgian

## HERON HAUS, Portland

| Overall: ★★★★½ | Room Quality: A | Value: C | Price: $135–$185 |
|---|---|---|---|

Secluded at the end of a long private drive off Westover, these spacious suites offer excellent downtown and Nob Hill access and plenty of room to spread out. A sense of "mahalo" descends as soon as you cross the threshold. Julie Keppler's remodeled Tudor has a sense of Old World permanence but the wide-open, clean-line decor of today. Common areas are comfortable and graciously appointed, but rooms are big enough you never have to mingle if you'd rather cocoon. With the corporate discount (which catapults the value rating to B), it's an incredible deal for the solo business traveler—why would anyone stay in a downtown hotel?

### SETTING & FACILITIES

**Location:** Just above Nob Hill, NW of downtown
**Near:** Nob Hill/Burnside commercial district, downtown, Pittock Mansion Museum, Rose Test Gardens, parks, zoo
**Building:** 10,000-sq.-ft. 1904 English Tudor
**Grounds:** Thick w/ greenery, flowering shrubs, ivy

**Public Space:** Sunroom, library, study, TV room
**Food & Drink:** In-room mineral water & snack; sit-down cont'l breakfast
**Recreation:** Swimming; all Portland attractions
**Amenities & Services:** Pool, fireplaces, books, games

## ACCOMMODATIONS

**Units:** 6 suites
**All Rooms:** Private-line phone, data port, TV, sitting area, fireplace, desk, library, robes, quality linens
**Some Rooms:** View of Mount St. Helens & Mt. Hood, whirlpool tub
**Bed & Bath:** Queen or king (1 w/ adjacent extra room & double); private ensuite baths

**Favorites:** Mahina, Ko
**Comfort & Decor:** Pale tones, contemporary sensibilities. Track lighting, white-painted woodwork, artwork, and lots of light. Plenty of room to work, including roomy desks. Central heat/AC; individual room-controlled fireplaces.

## RATES, RESERVATIONS, & RESTRICTIONS

**Deposit:** Credit card; 2-week cancellation
**Discounts:** Single corporate; $65 add'l person
**Credit Cards:** V, MC
**Check-in/Out:** 4–6/11
**Smoking:** No
**Pets:** No
**Kids:** 10 & older welcome

**Minimum Stay:** None
**Open:** All year
**Hosts:** Julie Keppeler
2545 NW Westover Rd.
Portland, OR 97210
(503) 274-1846
Fax: (503) 248-4055
www.europa.com/~hhaus/

## THE LION AND THE ROSE, Portland

| Overall: ★★★★★ | Room Quality: A | Value: B | Price: $95–$140 |

Ideally located for urban access, this 15th-and-Schuyler Queen Anne in historic Irvington District is a real head-turner. Turreted and gorgeous, it's trimmed in sky blue, ivory, and plum—you can't miss it. Established in 1993 by Sharon and Kay, the inn has become very popular, and deservedly so. Relax on the elegant, columned porch and watch the world go by, or stroll a block to Broadway and join in. Professionally run, yet hostesses are personable and warm. Partial kitchen access is a great plus. Fabulous decor. A total class act.

## SETTING & FACILITIES

**Location:** Corner 15th & Schuyler in historic Irvington District
**Near:** Broadway commercial district, Lloyd Center, Oregon Convention Center, Rose Garden Arena, downtown, transit
**Building:** 1906 National Historic Register Queen Anne Victorian
**Grounds:** Corner lot w/ elevated lawn (sculptures, fountain) overlooking historic district

**Public Space:** Porch, parlor, LR, DR, butler's pantry
**Food & Drink:** Dessert tea 4–6 p.m.; early coffee; sherry, coffee, tea, soft drinks, or juice; cont'l breakfast, 7:30–8:30; full breakfast, 8:30–9:30
**Recreation:** Antiquing, all Portland attractions
**Amenities & Services:** Piano, TV, daily newspaper, fireplace; fax, copier

## ACCOMMODATIONS

**Units:** 7 guest rooms
**All Rooms:** TV on request, phone, data port, antiques & reproductions, robes, desk
**Some Rooms:** Four-poster or canopy bed, claw-foot tub, whirlpool, fainting couch, window seat, sitting area
**Bed & Bath:** King, queen, double, or twins; 5 private baths, 2 share a bath

**Favorites:** Rose, Lavonna
**Comfort & Decor:** Full-on opulent (but not fussy) Victoriana. Rich-toned wallpapers; mostly tile baths. Extremely clean. Rooms are large and airy (except budget room with double bed). Central heat and AC.

## RATES, RESERVATIONS, & RESTRICTIONS

**Deposit:** Credit card; 96-hour cancellation, $15 fee
**Discounts:** Midweek corporate
**Credit Cards:** V, MC, AE
**Check-in/Out:** 3 or by arrangement ($15 extra after 10)/11
**Smoking:** Outside only
**Pets:** No; host dogs in host quarters
**Kids:** Over 7 welcome
**No-Nos:** Candles in rooms

**Minimum Stay:** 2 days, some holidays & local events
**Open:** All year
**Hosts:** Kay Peffer & Sharon Weil
1810 NE 15th
Portland, OR 97212
(800) 955-1647 or (503) 287-9245
Fax: (503) 287-9247
lionrose@ix.netcom.com
www.lionrose.com

## MACMASTER HOUSE, Portland

| Overall: ★★★★ | Room Quality: B | Value: B | Price: $85–$130 |

Combining two decidedly over-the-top architectural eras, this urban inn is an elegant head-turner (though currently the front exterior is screened by huge rhodie bushes). The interior is no less amazing, boasting an eclectic selection of antiques and fanciful art objects, yet emphasizing comfort. Ideally situated just off the Burnside-and-23rd shopping district, it's an easy walk to fine dining and Washington Park, and a bit longer stroll to downtown. Innovative breakfasts courtesy of chef Patrick. Rooms are fairly spacious for the era. Note that six of the eight rooms share baths, but a staggered breakfast schedule helps eliminate crowding. If you don't mind this aspect, MacMaster House is top-notch in every way.

### SETTING & FACILITIES

**Location:** King's Hill, just above downtown
**Near:** Washington Park (rose garden, zoo, Japanese garden), city center, 23rd Street shopping/dining district, Powell's Bookstore, art museum, Pioneer Square, Pearl District
**Building:** 1886 Historic Register Queen Anne w/ Colonial Revival elements
**Grounds:** Lush & green; ivied patio

**Public Space:** Parlor, foyer, veranda, DR
**Food & Drink:** Bottled water, cold beverages (soda, beer, wine), fresh popcorn; full breakfast (ensuite avail.)
**Recreation:** Shopping, strolling, zoo, museums
**Amenities & Services:** Guest phone, umbrellas, extensive local maps, games, daily newspapers, travel & general library; mailing/fax service

### ACCOMMODATIONS

**Units:** 8 guest rooms
**All Rooms:** Down comforters, quality linens, vanity or desk, TV
**Some Rooms:** Fireplace, soaking/claw-foot tub, antique brass or iron bed, mahogany sleigh bed, four-poster wicker bed, dormer(s), sitting area, view
**Bed & Bath:** Queen or double (some w/ extra twin); 2 private baths, 6 share 2 full and 2 half baths

**Favorites:** McCord Suite, Artist's Suite
**Comfort & Decor:** Soft landscape murals; overall color scheme green-on-white with dark wood accents. Sumptuous and fanciful antiques; brocades, intricate woodwork, eclectic art objects. Third-floor rooms feature dormers and cozy nooks. AC.

## RATES, RESERVATIONS, & RESTRICTIONS

**Deposit:** 1st night; less than 4-day cancellation, $25 fee; less than 24 hours forfeits deposit (varies for longer stays)
**Discounts:** Off-season extended stays, off-season single corporate; $25–30 add'l person; tiny, single-occupancy The Garret, $50
**Credit Cards:** V, MC, AE, D
**Check-in/Out:** 3–7/11:30
**Smoking:** On veranda only
**Pets:** No; host Dalmatian

**Kids:** 14 & older welcome
**Minimum Stay:** 2 nights, June–Oct.; 2 nights, weekends March–Dec.; 3–4 nights, Thanksgiving & Christmastime
**Open:** All year
**Hosts:** Cecelia Murphy, innkeeper, & staff
1401 SW Vista, Portland, OR 97205
(800) 774-9523 or (503) 223-7362
Fax: (503) 224-8808
innkeeper@macmaster.com
www.macmaster.com

## PORTLAND'S WHITE HOUSE, Portland

| Overall: ★★★★½ | Room Quality: A | Value: C | Price: $98–$159 |
|---|---|---|---|

Lounging in the rose-filled courtyard of Portland's White House on a summer day is a grand way to celebrate the Rose City. In fact, everything about this place is grand—from the curved, columnar entry (so reminiscent of its Washington, D.C., namesake) to the richly detailed (and 100% TV-free) interior to the exceptional breakfasts. Lanning and Steve purchased this established bed-and-breakfast in 1997 and brought their exquisite taste in decorating and natural flair for hospitality to an already beautiful building. A few nearby apartment houses detract from the otherwise peaceful and lovely historic district, but it's still a good neighborhood for strolling, with shopping and dining just blocks away and all of Portland easily accessed.

## SETTING & FACILITIES

**Location:** Historic Irvington district, on 22nd at Hancock
**Near:** Broadway shopping district, Lloyd Center, Rose Quarter, Convention Center, public transit, freeway access, downtown, airport
**Building:** 1911 National Historic Register Greek Revival
**Grounds:** Corner lot; 2 courtyard gardens, profuse roses, 2 fountains

**Public Space:** Large foyer, DR, game room, LR, library
**Food & Drink:** Refreshments; full breakfast
**Recreation:** Theater, parks
**Amenities & Services:** Piano, fireplace, puzzles, games, cribs, high chairs; small weddings, receptions, bar mitzvahs, parties, dinners; airport pick-up w/ 48-hour notice

## ACCOMMODATIONS

**Units:** 9 guest rooms
**All Rooms:** Private phone line, data port, high-quality linens, robes, feather beds
**Some Rooms:** Mini-CD player, down comforter, four-poster or canopy bed, whirlpool or claw-foot tub, private deck/balcony
**Bed & Bath:** Queen or king, roll-aways avail.; private ensuite baths
**Favorites:** Chauffeur Quarters

**Comfort & Decor:** Strong sense of period correctness. Elegant common areas feature box-beam ceilings, chandeliers, stained glass, fine art, and an amazing European porcelain collection. Trompe l'oeil garden painting on foyer walls. Guest rooms feature antiques, tile baths, and abundant artificial light. Central heat; individually controlled AC.

## RATES, RESERVATIONS, & RESTRICTIONS

**Deposit:** Credit card or check; 96-hour cancellation, $15 fee
**Discounts:** Midweek corporate, midweek single occupancy (most rooms); $20 add'l person
**Credit Cards:** V, MC, AE, D
**Check-in/Out:** 2–7 (flexible)/11
**Smoking:** Outside only
**Pets:** No; adorable host Scotties on premises
**Kids:** Welcome by arrangement

**Minimum Stay:** None
**Open:** All year
**Hosts:** Lanning Blanks, Steve Holden, JoAnne Young
1914 NE 22nd Ave.
Portland, OR 97212
(800) 272-7131 or (503) 287-7131
Fax: (503) 249-1641
pdxwhi@aol.com
www.portlandswhitehouse.com

## TERWILLIGER VISTA HOUSE, Portland

| Overall: ★★★½ | Room Quality: C | Value: C | Price: $85–$150 |
| --- | --- | --- | --- |

The glamour of the 1940s awaits you in this home built for a prominent Portland family. High ceilings, open, airy spaces, arched doorways, and touches of Art Deco and Hollywood-era glamour (leopard print is a recurring theme). Some signs of fading glory included water damage in a couple of areas at our visit. The home, located in an upscale hillside residential neighborhood, was purchased by the Vaterts in 1994. Backyard, with its moss-covered rock terracing and sumptuous flowering plants, is a great spot for a glass of wine on a summer evening.

## SETTING & FACILITIES

**Location:** Off Terwilliger Blvd. in SW Portland hills
**Near:** Oregon Health Sciences Univ. Med. Center, colleges, Veteran's Med. Center, Shriner's Hospital for Children, many parks
**Building:** 1940 bay-windowed Georgian Colonial
**Grounds:** Half-acre lawn, tiered backyard w/ patio & fountain

**Public Space:** LR, DR, library, patios
**Food & Drink:** Coffee, tea, juices, sodas, sherry; cont'l breakfast, 7:30–8:30; buffet-style full breakfast, 8:30–9:30
**Recreation:** All Portland attractions
**Amenities & Services:** Sound system, fridge, games, data port, phone room/fax/office; special romance package

## ACCOMMODATIONS

**Units:** 5 guest rooms
**All Rooms:** TV, nice linens & bath amenities
**Some Rooms:** Coffeemakers (most), Mt. Hood view, window seat, table & chairs, VCR, private entrance, whirlpool, fireplace, walk-in closet
**Bed & Bath:** Queen (1 w/ twin sofabed) or twin/king (w/ extra room & daybed); private baths (4 ensuite)

**Favorites:** Burgundy Rose, Garden
**Comfort & Decor:** Open, airy spaces with mostly pale tones and wood trim. Blonde Honduran mahogany and Waterford crystal chandeliers on main level, rich knotty pine paneling in library and Garden Retreat room. Hardwood floors, with 1920s area rugs. Amazing original Art Deco touches. Central heat/AC.

## RATES, RESERVATIONS, & RESTRICTIONS

**Deposit:** 1st night; 5-day cancellation, $20 fee
**Discounts:** Jan.–Feb. specials; Canadians inquire; $20 add'l person
**Credit Cards:** V, MC
**Check-in/Out:** 3–6/11
**Smoking:** Outside only
**Pets:** No
**Kids:** Over 10 welcome

**Minimum Stay:** None
**Open:** All year
**Hosts:** Jan & Dick Vatert
515 SW Westwood Dr.
Portland, OR 97201
(888) 244-0602 or (503) 244-0602
Fax: (503) 293-8042
www.terwilligervista.com

## BARNSTORMER B&B, Scappoose

| Overall: ★★★½ | Room Quality: C | Value: B | Price: $55–$110 |
|---|---|---|---|

This freshly restored farmhouse is a treasure for aviation buffs, and a pleasant stay at a value price for anyone looking for a getaway from the hubbub of metro Portland (just 25 miles away). Thoroughly renovated. Restaurant adjacency a plus. Property was historically part of a 40-acre dairy farm. After a long and mixed-use past, it opened as a bed-and-breakfast in 1996. The owners are working to preserve the house, grounds, and outbuildings—including a giant barn—as a slice of local history.

## SETTING & FACILITIES

**Location:** 25 mi. NW of Portland, just west of Scappoose, off Hwy. 30
**Near:** Local airstrip, Columbia River, museums
**Building:** Turn-of-the-20th-century farmhouse
**Grounds:** 4 acres w/ barn, lawns, restaurant, horse pasture, pond, garden
**Public Space:** Guest parlor, summer patio
**Food & Drink:** Self-serve coffee, tea, popcorn; full breakfast (can upgrade to champagne Sunday brunch); restaurant adjacent; limited room service
**Recreation:** Golf, antiquing, bird-watching, river activities, biplane rides, flying lessons
**Amenities & Services:** Hot tub, micro., player piano, VCR rental ($5); meetings, conf.s, retreats; outdoor weddings, picnics, other catered events; special room packages

## ACCOMMODATIONS

**Units:** 6 guest rooms
**All Rooms:** Quilts
**Some Rooms:** TV (5), phone (5), dbl. whirlpool, claw-foot tub, feather bed, four-poster, sitting area, table & chairs, desk, skylight bath
**Bed & Bath:** Queen (2 w/ daybed & trundle); private baths (5 ensuite)
**Favorites:** Pilot's Paradise, Wright Room, Wrong Room
**Comfort & Decor:** Lace, antiques, quilts, and aviation memorabilia combine with modern fixtures, windows, and period reproduction lighting and furnishings. Rooms are good-sized, with fresh, attractive wallpaper and modern baths. Central heat and AC.

## RATES, RESERVATIONS, & RESTRICTIONS

**Deposit:** 1st night; 72-hour cancellation
**Discounts:** Extended stay; $10 add'l person
**Credit Cards:** V, MC, D
**Check-in/Out:** 3–6 or by arrangement/11
**Smoking:** Outside only
**Pets:** By arrangement
**Kids:** Well-behaved children welcome
**Minimum Stay:** 2 nights, some holidays
**Open:** All year
**Hosts:** Christine & Hap Schnase-Cave
53758 West Lane Rd.
Scappoose, OR 97056
(888) 875-1670 or (503) 543-2740
Fax: (503) 543-4704
barnstormer@columbia-center.org
www.barnstormer.com

# Zone 12
# Willamette Valley

Covered bridges, sparkling rivers, trendy wineries, higher education, and bountiful and diverse agriculture are hallmarks of the Willamette Valley. It's rural, relaxed, and scenic as can be, yet it straddles Interstate 5, and is easily accessed from Portland or anywhere in western Oregon. The profiles in this section include an upscale equestrian ranch, a contemporary riverfront retreat, private homes, professionally run inns, historic treasures, and a hazelnut farm that's straight out of a storybook.

Eugene is Oregon's second largest city, with a population of 130,000. It's home to the University of Oregon, and student influence is everywhere—bike paths, hip retailers, ethnic restaurants, liberal attitudes—but so is a sense of safety and community. Attractions include Hult Center (performing arts), 5th Street Market shopping center, Skinner's Butte (historic hill), and Hendricks Park (77 wooded acres with renowned rhododendron garden). Just outside Eugene, Springfield is a sister city built along the McKenzie River, a recreation gateway to the Cascade Mountains.

Corvallis is another college town, but quieter, more introspective, and, perhaps, more conservative than Eugene. Its population is about 50,000, and its Oregon State University's strength is in agricultural and other sciences. Nearby is Albany, a community rife with historic neighborhoods.

Salem, Oregon's capital, is not surprisingly centered around the business of government; other draws include Willamette University and Silver Falls State Park. Nearby Aurora, a town founded as a religious colony, is now an antique buff's paradise. The entire town is a National Historic District, allowing visitors to feel as though they've stepped back in time. Salem, Aurora, and Sublimity (a rural hamlet just outside Salem) offer easy access to the new Oregon Gardens botanical park.

Towns like Wilsonville, Newberg, and McMinnville are little tastes of paradise. Near the Interstate 5 corridor and the metro areas of Portland, Salem, and Eugene, these communities maintain a small-town, even rural, feel and close ties to their agricultural roots. McMinnville celebrates wine and the grape, Newberg is home to hazelnuts and other Oregon signature products, and Wilsonville is an equestrian mecca.

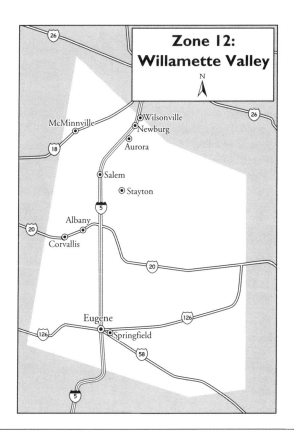

**Zone 12:
Willamette Valley**

N

26

Wilsonville
McMinnville
Newburg

18
Aurora

Salem

Stayton

5

Albany
20
Corvallis

20

Eugene
126
Springfield
126
58

5

26

---

**Albany**
Brier Rose Inn B&B, p. 350

**Aurora**
The Inn at Aurora, p. 351

**Corvallis**
A B&B on the Green, p. 352
Chapman House B&B, p. 353
Harrison House, p. 354

**Eugene**
The Campbell House, p. 355
The Oval Door, p. 357
The Secret Garden, p. 358

**McMinnville**
Mattey House B&B, p. 359
Steiger Haus, p. 360

**Newberg**
Springbrook Hazelnut Farm,
    p. 361

**Salem**
Marquee House, p. 363

**Springfield**
McKenzie View, p. 364

**Stayton**
Our Place in the Country, p. 366

**Wilsonville**
Hunter Creek Farm Bed, Barn &
    Breakfast, p. 367

**349**

## BRIER ROSE INN B&B, Albany

| Overall: ★★½ | Room Quality: D | Value: C | Price: $59–$125 |
|---|---|---|---|

Surrounded by other classic homes, Brier Rose occupies a busy (sometimes noisy) corner lot in a prominent historic district. Listed on the Historic Register as the "Samuel Train house" (one-time Albany postmaster and owner of a local newspaper), this historic building has a perfectly gingerbread exterior painted in mauve and rose tones. Inside, the faded beauty seems only partially restored. In truth, it's a bit musty and worn, but the antiques and original attributes are impressive. Those seeking a casual atmosphere will be pleased; the innkeepers are most accommodating with respect to kids (roll-aways available). Those looking for a white-glove restored Victorian might wish to move along.

### SETTING & FACILITIES

**Location:** Corner of 7th & Ellsworth in Albany's Monteith Historic District
**Near:** Antique stores & other shopping, Amtrak, Bryant Park, Willamette River, Corvallis, covered bridges
**Building:** 1886 Queen Anne Victorian
**Grounds:** Grassy corner lot w/ roses
**Public Space:** Large sitting room, small upstairs TV room

**Food & Drink:** Morning coffee served outside rooms; full breakfast
**Recreation:** Bicycling, historic touring, festivals
**Amenities & Services:** Antique/craft shop, TV/VCR, piano, videos, treadmill, iron, cordless guest phone; tours of property given to public

### ACCOMMODATIONS

**Units:** 4 guest rooms, 1 suite
**All Rooms:** Tub baths
**Some Rooms:** Writing desk, massive armoire, sitting area/room, whirlpool, claw-foot soaker tub
**Bed & Bath:** Queen, 1 king; 3 private baths, 2 share a bath
**Favorites:** Garden Suite (2 rooms), Jacuzzi Room, Parlor Room (best antiques)

**Comfort & Decor:** Original fir woodwork, textured wallpapers, antique lace, leaded glass. Dining room: corbelled ceilings and (amazingly) original, embossed wallpaper. Carpet in guest rooms, and pitched ceilings in many of them. Central AC and heat upstairs; window AC in main-level Parlor Room.

## RATES, RESERVATIONS, & RESTRICTIONS

**Deposit:** 1st night or 50%; 7-day cancellation
**Discounts:** Whole house (overflow rooms avail., sleeps up to 25); $10 add'l person
**Credit Cards:** V, MC
**Check-in/Out:** Afternoon/11 (flexible)
**Smoking:** Outside only
**Pets:** No

**Kids:** Welcome
**Minimum Stay:** 2 nights preferred, weekends & holidays
**Open:** All year
**Hosts:** Dick & Joyce Evans
206 7th Ave. SW, Albany, OR 97321
(541) 926-0345
Fax: (541) 926-6861 (daytime)
brierrose@skipnet.com
www.skipnet.com/~brierrose

## THE INN AT AURORA, Aurora

Overall: ★★★★    Room Quality: B    Value: C    Price: $89–$125

At the end of a sleepy little street in a tiny town of sleepy little streets, The Inn at Aurora is an adult-oriented country respite. Equidistant from Salem and Portland (about 25 miles), Aurora was founded as a Christian communal society in 1856. It became Oregon's first National Historic District, and today is an antiquing mecca. The inn was built in 1995 to resemble the clean-line simplicity of the town's historic buildings, and the Weavers purchased it in 1997. Excellent, caring hosts and airy, comfortable rooms.

### SETTING & FACILITIES

**Location:** 3 mi. east of I-5 between Portland & Salem
**Near:** Aurora airport, parks, Canby, Willamette Valley, Silver Creek Falls, Oregon Gardens
**Building:** 1995 2-story inn & home
**Grounds:** Front lawn, back deck overlooks pasture
**Public Space:** Guest LR, deck

**Food & Drink:** Tea, cocoa, cookies; ensuite comp. beverages (3 of 4 units); early coffee/tea; full breakfast
**Recreation:** Festivals, antiquing, wine touring, golf
**Amenities & Services:** Daily newspaper, fireplace; special getaway packages

### ACCOMMODATIONS

**Units:** 4 guest rooms
**All Rooms:** Handmade Amish quilts, TV, phone, data port, closet
**Some Rooms:** Whirlpool, fireplace, sitting area, fridge, balcony, VCR, robes, dual-sink vanity, futon couch, sleigh bed, desk
**Bed & Bath:** Kings; private baths
**Favorites:** The Suite

**Comfort & Decor:** High ceilings, white walls, pale wood, green plants. Accent tones of plum, forest, blue, burgundy. Shaker-simple, airy, and open. Extremely clean and uncluttered. Original artwork. Seasonal decorations are charming and festive. Central heat and AC.

## RATES, RESERVATIONS, & RESTRICTIONS

**Deposit:** Credit card; 14-day cancellation
**Discounts:** Extended stay, whole house
**Credit Cards:** V, MC, AE
**Check-in/Out:** 3–6 or by arrangement/11
**Smoking:** Outside only
**Pets:** No
**Kids:** No

**Minimum Stay:** None
**Open:** All year (except Christmas Eve & Day)
**Hosts:** Fay & Dave Weaver
15109 Second St. NE
P.O. Box 249
Aurora, OR 97002-0249
(888) 799-1374 or (503) 678-1932
fdweaver@teleport.com
innataurora.aurora.or.us

## A B&B ON THE GREEN, Corvallis

| Overall: ★★★½ | Room Quality: C | Value: B | Price: $80–$87 |
| --- | --- | --- | --- |

This homestay-style bed-and-breakfast is a cut above. While you are doubtless sharing the family's quarters (staying in the rooms of the Sparks' grown children, surrounded by family photos and heirlooms), you are also treated to several deluxe features, including the private phone line, private bath, use of fax (just 25¢/page long distance), and free snacks. The home is Christian, but not overbearingly so. Decor mixes 1980s contemporary with antiques. Breakfast is a formal affair, where both food and presentation is important; Neoma's homemade pie is a frequent feature.

## SETTING & FACILITIES

**Location:** SW of downtown, off Hwy. 34/20, near country club
**Near:** Corvallis Country Club; very short drive to OSU & downtown Corvallis; easy day trips to wineries, Oregon coast, Portland
**Building:** Contemporary 2-level
**Grounds:** Acre of lawn & gardens on a private golf course
**Public Space:** Great room, DR, porch & deck

**Food & Drink:** Candy, cookies, fruit, soft drinks, & ice; morning coffee/tea service; formal breakfast
**Recreation:** Golf, wine touring, historic touring, fishing
**Amenities & Services:** Hot tub, iron, fridge, fireplace, TV/VCR; fax/copier use, moneyback satisfaction guarantee

## ACCOMMODATIONS

**Units:** 4 guest rooms
**All Rooms:** Robes, hairdryer, phone with private line/data port, view, fan, desk
**Some Rooms:** Four-poster
**Bed & Bath:** King (3), 1 queen; private baths (2 ensuite, 2 detached)
**Favorites:** Neoma's; Nancy's & Brian's (also spacious; baths across hall)

**Comfort & Decor:** A clean, homey feel prevails. Common areas: hardwood floors, oriental rugs, Victorian-era furnishings. Guest rooms: mid-to-upper-quality furnishings, fixtures, and linens. Most rooms are carpeted; hall & Neoma's have hardwoods with area rugs.

## RATES, RESERVATIONS, & RESTRICTIONS

**Deposit:** Credit card; cancel up till 4 on arrival date
**Discounts:** Single occupancy, extended stay, frequent guest
**Credit Cards:** V, MC, AE, D, DC
**Check-in/Out:** 4/11 or by arrangement
**Smoking:** Outdoors only
**Pets:** No

**Kids:** Older children only
**Minimum Stay:** None
**Open:** All year
**Hosts:** Neoma & Herb Sparks
2515 SW 45th St., Corvallis, OR 97333
(888) 757-7321 or (541) 757-7321
Fax: (541) 753-4332
neoma@bandbonthegreen.com
www.bandbonthegreen.com

## CHAPMAN HOUSE B&B, Corvallis

| Overall: ★★★ | Room Quality: C | Value: B | Price: $69–$99 |
|---|---|---|---|

This home's pastoral hilltop perch affords tranquility and views of the Cascades, yet is still just minutes from downtown Corvallis and OSU. Great access to the coast. Operated since 1988, Chapman House is a stress-free, "kick-off-your-shoes" kind of place. Large living room has fireplace and 10-foot beamed ceilings. Feels more like a homestay atmosphere than a formal bed-and-breakfast. Some will find it too casual, others will love the way the hosts extend themselves with commonsense extras and uncommon kindness.

## SETTING & FACILITIES

**Location:** West of Corvallis off Hwy. 20/34
**Near:** Outside of town, but still near OSU & Corvallis attractions; wildlife refuges; easy day trips to wineries, Oregon coast, Portland
**Building:** 4,200-sq.-ft. quasi-Tudor 1950s home
**Grounds:** 23 acres overlooking working farm & pastures; mountain views
**Public Space:** Huge living room,

covered patio
**Food & Drink:** Beverages & snacks; healthy & hearty family-style full breakfast
**Recreation:** Bird-watching, bicycling, fishing, golf
**Amenities & Services:** A/V equipment, built-in projection screen; celebration extras; meetings, weddings, receptions, conferences, catered dinners; horse/llama pasture

## ACCOMMODATIONS

**Units:** In flux—please call
**All Rooms:** Carpet, tile bath, TV, phone, data port, desk on request
**Some Rooms:** Four-poster, couch, sitting area, kitchenette (micro., fridge)
**Bed & Bath:** Queen (1 w/ Murphy) or king; private baths w/ tub & shower
**Favorites:** Back corner w/ queen, Murphy, kitchenette

**Comfort & Decor:** Acres of loom-woven Scottish wool carpet in a Jacobian floral pattern adorn both common areas and guest rooms. Lots of quirky, fun, and high-quality decor (tile, wallpapers) and fixtures (lighting, bath). The 1950s vintage accents will seem dated to some, fascinatingly retro to others

### RATES, RESERVATIONS, & RESTRICTIONS

**Deposit:** 50%; 72-hour cancellation
**Discounts:** Corporate, gov't, weekly, senior; $10–15 add'l person
**Credit Cards:** V, MC, AE
**Check-in/Out:** 4/11 or by arrangement
**Smoking:** Outside only
**Pets:** No (horse/llama pasture avail.)
**Kids:** By arrangement

**Minimum Stay:** None
**Open:** All year
**Hosts:** Ruth & Carl Ohlen
6120 SW Country Club Dr.
Corvallis, OR 97333
(541) 929-3059
Fax: (541) 929-4857
bbhouse@peak.org
www.peak.org/~bbhouse

## HARRISON HOUSE, Corvallis

| Overall: ★★★★ | Room Quality: B | Value: A | Price: $70–$80 |
|---|---|---|---|

Just 3 blocks from the OSU campus and walking distance to restaurants and shopping, Harrison House is ideally located. Articulate, well-read hosts are a pleasure. Enthusiastic and gracious, they anticipate guests' needs (excellent local and regional travel info, extensive amenities basket, special attention to dietary needs and preferences) without ever being intrusive. Refrigerator, beverages, and snacks make you feel at ease; sunroom is a nice place to relax and browse the library. Harrison House is our top pick for the Corvallis area.

### SETTING & FACILITIES

**Location:** 3 blocks from OSU campus, .5 mi. from downtown; corner of 23rd & Harrison
**Near:** Albany, Eugene; easy day trips to wineries, Oregon coast, Portland
**Building:** 1939 Dutch Colonial
**Grounds:** 60-year-old rhododendrons, corner lot; side garden
**Public Space:** LR, sunroom, DR

**Food & Drink:** Snacks & cold beverages; afternoon refreshments; full gourmet breakfast
**Recreation:** Golf, fishing, wine tours, historic touring
**Amenities & Services:** Piano, fireplace, fridge, bicycles, maps, books, umbrellas; small weddings, business meetings, etc.

## ACCOMMODATIONS

**Units:** 4 guest rooms
**All Rooms:** Phone, data port, robes, closet, cable TV avail.
**Some Rooms:** Desk(s), private entrance
**Bed & Bath:** Queen (3) or king (1); 2 w/ private bath, 2 (1 w/ half bath) share a full bath

**Favorites:** Allison & Steamship
**Comfort & Decor:** Extremely comfortable yet stylish, contemporary furnishings. Florals, brocades, muted plaids and prints. Overall furnishings theme is Colonial, but rooms offer subthemes of rose/floral, oceanliner, country, and Southwest.

## RATES, RESERVATIONS, & RESTRICTIONS

**Deposit:** Credit card; 72-hour cancellation
**Discounts:** Single occupancy
**Credit Cards:** V, MC, AE, D
**Check-in/Out:** 4 or by arrangement/11
**Smoking:** Outside only
**Pets:** No
**Kids:** Welcome

**Minimum Stay:** None
**Open:** All year
**Hosts:** Maria & Charlie Tomlinson
2310 NW Harrison Blvd.
Corvallis, OR 97330
(800) 233-6248 or (541) 752-6248
Fax: (541) 754-1353
harrisonhouse@proaxis.com
www.proaxis.com/~harrisonhouse

## THE CAMPBELL HOUSE, Eugene

| Overall: ★★★★★ | Room Quality: A | Value: C | Price: $85–$350 |
| --- | --- | --- | --- |

Designed to convey the warmth and personality of a bed-and-breakfast, but with all the amenities of a first-class luxury hotel. With 18 rooms, The Campbell House is by nature a bit less personal than an in-home bed-and-breakfast, but you'll find the staff extremely warm and hospitable. Sumptuous decor and an impressive array of amenities and services anticipate both the needs of business travelers and couples seeking a romantic getaway. The only irritant we experienced was the noise of the passing train. Even this was puckishly anticipated by your hosts, who provide a packet of earplugs (labeled "for the train noise") in the amenities basket. Since Myra and Roger's extravagant remodel of the stately home in 1993, The Campbell House has set the hospitality standard for the Willamette Valley, and we can see why. It's a class act.

## SETTING & FACILITIES

**Location:** Downtown Eugene, Pearl at 3rd, base of Skinner's Butte
**Near:** U of O venues, including 5th Street Market & Hult Center; short drive to coast, wineries, Cascades
**Building:** 1892 lumber/mining heiress' mansion & carriage house
**Grounds:** Hillside yard & gardens; rock work, gazebo; next to wooded public park
**Public Space:** Parlor, library, DR
**Food & Drink:** Coffee/tea/cocoa &

cookies; evening wine & cider; coffee/tea room service from 6:15 a.m.; full breakfast; in-room cont'l option
**Recreation:** Hiking, bicycling, roller-skating, theater
**Amenities & Services:** Gift shop, videos, games, library, umbrellas; full concierge; fitness club passes; secretarial, laundry, interpreter services; fax & copier; weddings, parties, receptions, teas

## ACCOMMODATIONS

**Units:** 18 guest rooms & suites
**All Rooms:** Extensive bath amenities basket, guest guide, desk, phone, data port, iron, honor bar fridge, hairdryer, garden or city view, remote TV/VCR
**Some Rooms:** Claw-foot tub, fireplace, whirlpool tub, wet bar w/ hot beverage service, four-poster, disabled access
**Bed & Bath:** Mostly queens, 1 double, 2 kings; private ensuite baths

**Favorites:** Carriage House #314 & #315; Eva; Campbell Family
**Comfort & Decor:** Sumptuous antique and reproduction furnishings; turn-of-the-20th-century feeling. Rich, mahogany-toned woods predominate; many rooms feature a jewel-tone (especially wine & forest) color scheme accented by gold leaf.

## RATES, RESERVATIONS, & RESTRICTIONS

**Deposit:** 1st night; 48-hour cancellation (7 days for event periods)
**Discounts:** Off-season, midweek, extended stays, Corporate Club
**Credit Cards:** V, MC, AE, D
**Check-in/Out:** 4–11:30/noon
**Smoking:** Outside only
**Pets:** No
**Kids:** Welcome

**Minimum Stay:** 2–3 nights, holidays & special events
**Open:** All year
**Hosts:** Myra & Roger Plant
252 Pearl St., Eugene, OR 97401
(888) 264-2519 or (541) 343-1119
Fax: (541) 343-2258
campbellhouse@campbellhouse.com
www.campbellhouse.com

## THE OVAL DOOR, Eugene

| Overall: ★★★½ | Room Quality: C | Value: B | Price: $80–$115 |
|---|---|---|---|

Relax to the sounds of classical music in the drawing room or library of this casually comfortable downtown bed-and-breakfast. Despite its turn-of-the-20th-century charm, The Oval Door was built as a bed-and-breakfast in 1990. Current owners Nicole Wegerland and Melissa Coray purchased the inn in 1998. Each is a culinary academy graduate, so you know you'll appreciate the food! Extra bed options enable room sharing and children can be accommodated. Excellent location is convenient to all Eugene activities.

### SETTING & FACILITIES

**Location:** Downtown Eugene, Lawrence at 10th
**Near:** Downtown Eugene, convention center, performing arts center, U of O, fairgrounds
**Building:** Early-20th-century-farmhouse–style home, built 1990
**Grounds:** Minimal; corner lot w/ plantings & mature trees
**Public Space:** LR, DR, library, wraparound porch
**Food & Drink:** Tea & cold drinks; full breakfast (early option; in-room option)
**Recreation:** Rollerskating, theater, wine & scenic touring
**Amenities & Services:** Guest phone & fax, fireplace, whirlpool bathtub room; massage by appt., eco-sensitive linens policy

### ACCOMMODATIONS

**Units:** 4 guest rooms
**All Rooms:** Data port, writing table, TV/VCR, hairdryer, robes
**Some Rooms:** Sofa-sleeper, feather bed, sitting area
**Bed & Bath:** Queens (1 w/ extra daybed, 1 w/ sofa-sleeper), 1 w/ twins; private baths
**Favorites:** Queen Anne's Lace
**Comfort & Decor:** Traditional decor; brocades, warm woods, florals. Old-fashioned, attractive, and sweet. Immaculate. Carpet warms the toes. Ceiling fans; individual room heat controls.

### RATES, RESERVATIONS, & RESTRICTIONS

**Deposit:** 1st night; 48-hour cancellation for refund; $25 charged if less than 48 hours' notice given, unless rebooked; full charge for no-show
**Discounts:** Single occupancy, off-season; $15 add'l person
**Credit Cards:** V, MC, AE
**Check-in/Out:** 4–6 or by arrangement/11
**Smoking:** Porch only
**Pets:** No
**Kids:** Welcome by prior arrangement
**Minimum Stay:** 2 nights, special event weekends
**Open:** All year
**Hosts:** Nicole Wergeland & Melissa Coray
988 Lawrence St.
Eugene, OR 97401-2827
(800) 882-3160 or (541) 683-3160
Fax: (541) 485-5339
ovaldoor@ovaldoor.com
www.ovaldoor.com

## THE SECRET GARDEN, Eugene

| Overall: ★★★★½ | Room Quality: A | Value: C | Price: $115–$235 |
|---|---|---|---|

The Secret Garden's prime location (super-convenient to the University of Oregon) would be enough to recommend it, but the inn is truly an exceptional property as well. Well-traveled Becky Drobac's collection of museum-quality antiques is stunning, and her hospitality and warmth are genuine. Photos of her and her husband's prominent families line the stairwell leading to the upstairs. The sprawling inn sits on a corner lot along birch-lined sidewalks amidst the happy chaos of frat houses, remodeled heritage homes, and other near-campus structures. Delicious breakfasts are also a priority (all dietary restrictions and preferences are cheerfully accommodated). Opened in 1997.

### SETTING & FACILITIES

**Location:** 1.5 blocks from U of O campus
**Near:** U of O, downtown Eugene, Hendricks Park
**Building:** 1918 3-story farmhouse w/ many remodels & additions
**Grounds:** Elaborate gardens (including "Secret Garden"), 175 fruit trees
**Public Space:** Great room, DR/sunroom, sitting room, library, deck
**Food & Drink:** Tea & coffee 24 hours; beverage service outside rooms around 7 a.m.; full breakfast; early cont'l option
**Recreation:** Hiking, bicycling, roller-skating, theater, wine & scenic touring
**Amenities & Services:** Fireplace, piano, maps, newspaper, library, fax/modem port, gift shop, extensive guest guide, umbrellas; limited computer & fax avail.; celebration extras

### ACCOMMODATIONS

**Units:** 8 guest rooms, 2 suites
**All Rooms:** Fridge, phone w/ private line, TV/VCR, artwork, robes, bed-warmers
**Some Rooms:** Sitting room, fireplace, soaking tub, ADA disabled access, view, desk, data port
**Bed & Bath:** King, queen, or extra-long twins (sofabed or extra twin/trundle in some, roll-aways avail.); private baths
**Favorites:** Apiary
**Comfort & Decor:** Queen Anne meets international eclectic: European, Far East, and Pan-Pacific. Decorator fabrics, original artwork, and amazing antiques, many with unique histories. Designer linens. Vinyls and all finish work updated and fresh.

## RATES, RESERVATIONS, & RESTRICTIONS

**Deposit:** Credit card; 72-hour cancellation
**Discounts:** Off-season, extended corporate stay; $15 add'l person
**Credit Cards:** V, MC, D
**Check-in/Out:** 3/11:30
**Smoking:** Outside only
**Pets:** No; host terrier
**Kids:** "OK w/ well-behaved parents"
**No-Nos:** Shoes in house

**Minimum Stay:** None
**Open:** All year
**Hosts:** Becky Drobac
1910 University St.
Eugene, OR 97403
(888) 484-6755 or (541) 484-6755
Fax: (541) 431-1699
gardenbb@efn.org
www.secretgardenbbinn.com

## MATTEY HOUSE B&B, McMinnville

| Overall: ★★★ | Room Quality: C | Value: C | Price: $90–$110 |
|---|---|---|---|

Tucked behind a vineyard, this picturesque, lace-white historic Victorian was built by an English dairyman. It went through a period as a strawberry farm, then became a bed-and-breakfast in the late 1980s. In 1993, its British heritage came full circle when it was purchased by the delightfully English Jack and Denise Seed. The decor is simple, the atmosphere is TV-free, and the house has a "hanging-out-with-the-family" feel we found exceptionally relaxing. Hosts are warm and gregarious, premises are homey and welcoming.

## SETTING & FACILITIES

**Location:** Just outside Lafayette, 5 mi. east of McMinnville off 99W
**Near:** Wineries, Linfield College, Newberg, Carlton Lake State Game Refuge, Yamhill County Fairgrounds, commuter airport
**Building:** 1892 Victorian
**Grounds:** 3.5 acres w/ large lawn, arbors, mature trees, vineyards
**Public Space:** LR, parlor, DR, front porch, upstairs balcony

**Food & Drink:** Afternoon refreshments; family-style full breakfast (early cont'l option)
**Recreation:** Historic touring, balloon rides, glider rides, bird-watching, antiquing
**Amenities & Services:** Games, fireplace; weddings

## ACCOMMODATIONS

**Units:** 4 guest rooms
**All Rooms:** Period furnishings, quilts, lace
**Some Rooms:** Claw-foot tub, table & chairs
**Bed & Bath:** Queen (3) or double (roll-away avail.); private baths (3 ensuite)
**Favorites:** Pinot, Blanc de Blanc

**Comfort & Decor:** Brightened-up country Victorian, but softened with pale paints and wallpapers and more comfortable (if sometimes down-at-the-heels) furnishings. Comfy living room; white wicker parlor. Guest rooms: hardwood floors, quilts, wall stenciling. Central heat; some baths have individual thermostats; fans.

## RATES, RESERVATIONS, & RESTRICTIONS

**Deposit:** 1st night; 72-hour cancellation, $15 fee
**Discounts:** Extended stay; $25 add'l person
**Credit Cards:** V, MC
**Check-in/Out:** 4–7 or by arrangement/11
**Smoking:** No
**Pets:** No; host dog may be in residence
**Kids:** 10 & older welcome

**Minimum Stay:** 2 or 3 days, local festivals & events, some holidays
**Open:** All year
**Hosts:** Denise & Jack Seed
10221 NE Mattey Ln.
McMinnville, OR 97128
(503) 434-5058
Fax: (503) 434-6667
seed@matteyhouse.com
www.matteyhouse.com or
www.bbchannel.com/bbc/p214716.asp

---

## STEIGER HAUS, McMinnville

| Overall: ★★★½ | Room Quality: C | Value: C | Price: $70–$130 |
|---|---|---|---|

This casual Northwest contemporary home has a bit of a lodge feel. It has operated as McMinnville's in-town bed-and-breakfast (very convenient to all downtown shops and services) since 1988, with current owners taking over in 1996. The two upstairs rooms (Treetop and twin-bedded Rooftop) make a nice family combo, with a TV sitting room between them; little Dorset, with its desk, is a good value choice for the single business traveler. Morningsun is a 2-room suite with kitchen, but Fireside—just as roomy—was our favorite. Very pleasant backyard.

## SETTING & FACILITIES

**Location:** Wilson at Davis, a block south of downtown
**Near:** Wineries, Linfield College, McMinnville, Newberg, Carlton Lake State Game Refuge, Yamhill County Fairgrounds, commuter airport
**Building:** Pacific Northwest contemporary home
**Grounds:** Secluded back lawn; huge native oaks & flowers

**Public Space:** LR, upstairs sitting room, deck
**Food & Drink:** Refreshments on arrival; full breakfast
**Recreation:** Historic touring, balloon rides, glider rides, bicycling, bird-watching, antiquing
**Amenities & Services:** TVs, fireplace, sound system, VCR

## ACCOMMODATIONS

**Units:** 3 guest rooms, 2 suites
**All Rooms:** Closets, contemporary decor
**Some Rooms:** Bay window, soaking tub, sitting room or area, deck access, bath salts, sofabed, fireplace, TV, VCR, jetted tub, table & chairs, desk, kitchenette (fridge, micro, rangetop, wet bar)
**Bed & Bath:** Queen (4) or twins; private ensuite baths
**Favorites:** Fireside Suite, Morningsun Suite, Treetop Room
**Comfort & Decor:** Blend of country, Northwest, and Native American. Skylights, pitched ceilings, pale walls, wood trim. Some rooms have deep, autumn-tone wallpapers and brick trim. Original art. Mid- to higher-quality contemporary furnishings.

## RATES, RESERVATIONS, & RESTRICTIONS

**Deposit:** 1st night; 1-week cancellation
**Discounts:** Midweek & off-season corporate; $20 add'l person
**Credit Cards:** V, MC, D
**Check-in/Out:** 3–6 or by arrangement/11
**Smoking:** No
**Pets:** No; host kitty outside & host quarters
**Kids:** 10 & older welcome
**Minimum Stay:** 2 days, some local festivals & holidays
**Open:** All year
**Hosts:** Susan & Dale Durette
360 Wilson St., McMinnville, OR 97128
(503) 472-0821 or 472-0238
Fax: (503) 472-0100
stay@steigerhaus.com
www.steigerhaus.com

## SPRINGBROOK HAZELNUT FARM, Newberg

| Overall: ★★★★★ | Room Quality: A | Value: C | Price: $95–$175 |
| --- | --- | --- | --- |

Like Sea Quest on the Oregon Coast, this five-star inn is so rated not so much for its "luxury" in terms of posh amenities, but for an overall exceptional bed-and-breakfast experience. An effortless Year-in-Provence sense of ease settles over you as you wander the acreage, paddle the pond, relax in the artistic common areas, or chat with your gracious hosts. The farm hearkens back to a simpler time, and the accommodations are classic. Rose Cottage is a gem—exquisite craftsmanship, attention to detail, Mission-simple furnishings. Main house rooms are simple and comfortable; common rooms are works of art.

## SETTING & FACILITIES

**Location:** Off Hwy. 99W at mi. marker 21
**Near:** Champoeg S.P., wineries, museums
**Building:** 1912 Craftsman farmhouse & outbuildings, all on National Historic Register
**Grounds:** 10-acre lawn & garden; pond, gazebo; surrounded by 60-acre hazelnut orchard
**Public Space:** Entry hall, LR, DR, sun porch, upstairs sitting room

**Food & Drink:** In-room hazelnuts & baked treat; Main House guests receive full breakfast; Cottage/Carriage House guests have self-serve full breakfast in their kitchens
**Recreation:** Historic touring, bird-watching, balloon flights, antiquing, canoeing, tennis
**Amenities & Services:** Piano, fireplace, pool, tennis court, canoe, books

## ACCOMMODATIONS

**Units:** 4 guest rooms, 2 self-contained cottages
**All Rooms:** Hairdryer, robes
**Some Rooms:** Sofa-sleeper, kitchen, claw-foot tub, laundry facil., iron
**Bed & Bath:** Mostly queens; 4 private baths, 2 have private half baths & share a full bath
**Favorites:** Rose Cottage, "Red Room w/ $5 Bed"

**Comfort & Decor:** Farmhouse-simple, but upscale, combining the best of tradition (tile, Arts and Crafts light fixtures, beamed ceilings, hardwood floors, Turkish rugs, heirloom antiques, period woodwork) with fresh contemporary sensibilities. Foyer is bright yellow with vibrant blue, green, and orange wallpapers. Wonderful art collection.

## RATES, RESERVATIONS, & RESTRICTIONS

**Deposit:** 1st night; 1-week cancellation
**Discounts:** $25 add'l person in Carriage House
**Credit Cards:** Not accepted
**Check-in/Out:** 4–6 or by arrangement/noon
**Smoking:** Outside only
**Pets:** No; host dogs on site
**Kids:** Infants only, by arrangement
**Minimum Stay:** 2 nights, high-season weekends in Rose Cottage & Carriage House

**Open:** Main House May 1–Nov. 1; Carriage House & Rose Cottage all year
**Hosts:** Ellen & Charles McClure
30295 N Hwy. 99W
Newberg, OR 97132
(800) 793-8528 or (503) 538-4606
Fax: (503) 537-4004
ellen@nutfarm.com
www.nutfarm.com

## MARQUEE HOUSE, Salem

| Overall: ★★★½ | Room Quality: C | Value: A | Price: $55–$90 |

On a super-quiet cul-de-sac on a narrow little street, this Colonial is tucked away from the main road and is quieter than most in-city properties. The attractive creekside setting gives it a country feel—a little slice of Washington's Mt. Vernon in the Northwest. The vintage movie theme is fun: living room is homage to *Harvey*, with lots of rabbitry; *Auntie Mame* room has a hunting theme and a brocade fainting couch that folds into a spare bed. Other room themes include *Topper*, *Christmas in Connecticut*, *Pillow Talk*, and *Blazing Saddles*. Rickie is a delightful hostess, and her breakfasts are varied and memorable.

### SETTING & FACILITIES

**Location:** 6 blocks from Capitol in historic Salem neighborhood
**Near:** Willamette University; easy drive to wineries, Silver Falls S.P., Portland
**Building:** 1938 Mt. Vernon Colonial
**Grounds:** Over half an acre; large back lawn slopes to Mill Creek
**Public Space:** LR, DR, veranda
**Food & Drink:** Candy bowl, tea & chilled beverages; comp. popcorn with movies; full breakfast
**Recreation:** Historic touring, movies, college & community events
**Amenities & Services:** Games, fireplace, sound system, TV/VCR w/ classic video library, guest fridge, library; extensive "butler's basket" incl. hairdryer, OTC medicines, sundries; transportation assistance, murder mystery weekends

### ACCOMMODATIONS

**Units:** 5 guest rooms
**All Rooms:** Robes, whimsical movie-theme decor
**Some Rooms:** View, fireplace, fainting couch, data port, desk
**Bed & Bath:** Queen (1 w/ extra twin, 1 w/ sofa-sleeper); 3 private baths, 2 share a bath
**Favorites:** Auntie Mame
**Comfort & Decor:** Antiques and whimsical vintage clothing and artifacts leveraged into an old-time movie theme. Wonderful lamps, fun heirlooms, clever built-ins. Some original wallpapers and fixtures (a bit of a dated look in some areas, but overall charming). Wine red carpet in most guest rooms. Central oil heat; most units have auxiliary heaters and window AC units.

## RATES, RESERVATIONS, & RESTRICTIONS

**Deposit:** 1st night; 48-hour
cancellation
**Discounts:** Single occupancy, gov't;
$15 add'l person
**Credit Cards:** V, MC, D
**Check-in/Out:** 4–6 or by arrange-
ment/11
**Smoking:** Outdoors only
**Pets:** No

**Kids:** Welcome
**Minimum Stay:** University events &
holidays only
**Open:** All year
**Hosts:** Rickie Hart
333 Wyatt Ct. NE, Salem, OR 97301
(800) 949-0837 or (503) 391-0837
rickiemh@open.org
www.marqueehouse.com

## MCKENZIE VIEW, Springfield

Overall: ★★★★½      Room Quality: A      Value: C      Price: $85–$215

The focus is on the river at this serene, upscale, adult-oriented bed-and-breakfast. You're just 15 minutes from town, but worlds apart from the urban bustle. Entire first floor of this home, which Scott and Roberta purchased and opened as a bed-and-breakfast in 1996, is guest space. You'll find plenty of sitting areas for relaxation and privacy inside and outside of the house. Breakfasts are exciting and creative, featuring seasonal items; sample fall trio: pumpkin pancakes, pear clafauti, chicken-apple sausage. Attractive landscaping, fabulous setting, super-accommodating hosts.

## SETTING & FACILITIES

**Location:** Just north of Springfield (NE of Eugene) on banks of McKenzie River
**Near:** Tiny community of Coburg, Springfield, Eugene
**Building:** 1990 riverfront contemporary home
**Grounds:** 6 wooded, riverside acres; garden, gazebo, ferns
**Public Space:** LR, DR, TV room, fireside sitting area

**Food & Drink:** Juice, soft drinks, ice, tea, & cookies; p.m. refreshments; full breakfast
**Recreation:** Rafting, fishing, antiquing, wine touring, Eugene cultural venues
**Amenities & Services:** Guest fridge, TV/VCR, fireplaces, books, iron, cordless guest phone, health club nearby, neighbor tennis court, do-it-yourself cutting garden, phone jack, gift area; fax, email, copier

## ACCOMMODATIONS

**Units:** 2 guest rooms, 2 suites
**All Rooms:** Carpet, robes, desk or table
**Some Rooms:** Fireplace, river view, private porch, soaking tub, window seat, sitting area, skylight bath
**Bed & Bath:** Queens (1 w/ extra daybed), 1 twin/king conversion; private ensuite baths

**Favorites:** Woodland Suite, Moonlight Suite
**Comfort & Decor:** Airy, attractive, with exceptional views. Antique and classy modern furnishings, with mingled Asian and European motifs. Thick carpet, bold accent colors over pale backgrounds. Clean, uncluttered. Heat pump plus auxiliary room heaters; AC.

## RATES, RESERVATIONS, & RESTRICTIONS

**Deposit:** 1st night; 7-day cancellation
**Discounts:** Extended stay, off-season; $25 add'l person
**Credit Cards:** V, MC
**Check-in/Out:** 3/11 (flexible)
**Smoking:** Outside only
**Pets:** No
**Kids:** By arrangement only; not suitable for smaller children
**Minimum Stay:** 3 nights, U of O

graduation; 2 nights, holidays
**Open:** All year
**Hosts:** Roberta & Scott Bolling
34922 McKenzie View Dr.
Springfield, OR 97478
(888) MCK-VIEW
Fax: (541) 726-6968
mckenzieview@worldnet.att.net
www.design-web.com/mckenzieview/

## OUR PLACE IN THE COUNTRY, Stayton

| Overall: ★★★★ | Room Quality: B | Value: B | Price: $75–$115 |
|---|---|---|---|

When a retired interior designer and a semi-retired general contractor decide to renovate a classic turn-of-the-20th-century farmhouse, it's a good omen. Dave and Lynn took over what had become a ramshackle family home in 1993, and turned it into a gracious, adult-oriented bed-and-breakfast that imparts a sense of peace and pampering. A short, pastoral drive from Salem (toward the beckoning Cascades), this inn is close to the restaurants and shopping of metro Salem, but the extra amenities like on-site laundry facilities and a barbecue make it tempting to stick around and make this Your Place in the Country.

### SETTING & FACILITIES

**Location:** 15 mi. east of Salem off Hwy. 22 (N. Santiam Hwy.)
**Near:** Silver Falls S.P., Sublimity, Salem, Oregon Gardens, Cascade Mountains
**Building:** 1911 farmhouse
**Grounds:** 10 acres on low hill; English garden, gazebo, hedges, massive trees
**Public Space:** Great room (2 sitting rooms), front porch, DR

**Food & Drink:** Afternoon tea & snacks; juice & coffee (7:30 a.m.); full breakfast
**Recreation:** Croquet & horseshoes; golf, fishing, boating, wine touring, antiquing, festivals
**Amenities & Services:** BBQ, laundry facil., TV/VCR, videos, books, fireplace, sound system, cordless phone; reservations, outdoor weddings

## ACCOMMODATIONS

**Units:** 4 guest rooms
**All Rooms:** View, robes, designer fabrics
**Some Rooms:** Balcony, writing desk, double-headed oversized shower, four-poster iron bed, claw-foot tub
**Bed & Bath:** King, queen, or twins; private baths
**Favorites:** Rose Room; Tapestry &

Captain's Rooms (nice balconies)
**Comfort & Decor:** Gracious turn-of-the-20th-century "country formal" motif. Plush emerald carpet; designer fabrics in florals and soft prints, pastoral artwork. Tile and upscale vinyls in baths. Spacious eat-in kitchen with views. Electric air filter; central heat/AC.

## RATES, RESERVATIONS, & RESTRICTIONS

**Deposit:** 1st night; 5-day cancellation
**Discounts:** Corporate (Sun.–Thurs.), extended stays, off-season, senior
**Credit Cards:** V, MC
**Check-in/Out:** 3/11
**Smoking:** Outside only
**Pets:** No; host kitty
**Kids:** By arrangement (call)
**No-Nos:** More than 2 per room

**Minimum Stay:** None
**Open:** All year
**Hosts:** Dave & Lynn Sweetland
9297 Boedigheimer Rd.
Stayton, OR 97383
(888) 678-2580
Fax: (503) 769-4556
ourplace@wvi.com
www.wvi.com/~ourplace

## HUNTER CREEK FARM BED, BARN & BREAKFAST, Wilsonville

| Overall: ★★★★½ | Room Quality: A | Value: C | Price: $125–$150 |
|---|---|---|---|

This brand-new inn (opened for business fall 1998) is part of an elaborate equestrian complex still under construction at our visit. While Sallie Cutler and her staff may be new to innkeeping, their instincts look good. Rooms are spacious and elegantly appointed, common areas are sumptuous ("Polo Lounge," "Club Room"), and the equestrian theme is fun whether you're a member of the horsey set or not. Keep an eye on this one—it could become a five-star property. Policies, pricing, and specifics may still be evolving, but we'd rate this tops for weekend-in-the-country group gathering, an elegant base for touring the Willamette Valley, or quiet, spacious digs within striking distance of metro Portland.

## SETTING & FACILITIES

**Location:** 20 min. south of Portland, 3.5 mi. off of I-5
**Near:** Willamette River, Whip N' Spur equestrian training facility, Willamette wine valley
**Building:** 1991-built 6,000-sq.-ft. estate home
**Grounds:** 120-acre equestrian park on the Willamette River; trails, barns, outbuildings
**Public Space:** LRs, office, DRs, decks
**Food & Drink:** Evening fireside refreshments; in-room wine, coffee/tea service; cold beverages & snacks; full breakfast
**Recreation:** River activities; easy access to Portland recreation & cultural venues
**Amenities & Services:** Pool & pavilion, riverside dock, boat ramp, fridge, guest phone, piano, guest guide, sound system, fireplaces, games; computer, copier, fax avail.; horse boarding ($15 night); weddings, parties, meetings; hunt field rental; catering

## ACCOMMODATIONS

**Units:** 5 guest rooms
**All Rooms:** Exceptional theme decor, TV, VCR, hairdryer, robes, coffee service, large closets
**Some Rooms:** Whirlpool tub, sitting area, river view
**Bed & Bath:** King (mostly), or twins (roll-away, crib avail.); 3 private baths (2 ensuite), 2 share a bath
**Favorites:** The Champions
**Comfort & Decor:** Upscale equestrian elegance is the theme throughout. Top-quality appointments, English country furnishings. Custom wall treatments. Trainers and Pony share a bath; tall folk may prefer Tally Ho's detached full-sized bath over Kentucky Derby's ensuite but slant-ceiling bath. Central climate control.

## RATES, RESERVATIONS, & RESTRICTIONS

**Deposit:** Credit card; 7-day cancellation
**Discounts:** Midweek, whole-house booking
**Credit Cards:** V, MC
**Check-in/Out:** After 3:30 (by arrangement)/noon
**Smoking:** Outside only
**Pets:** Not in house; dog kennels & overnight horse stabling avail.
**Kids:** Welcome
**No-Nos:** Shoes in house
**Minimum Stay:** None
**Open:** All year
**Hosts:** Sallie Cutler
14441 SW Wilsonville Rd.
Wilsonville, OR 97070
(503) 625-3424
Fax: (503) 636-3643
info@huntercreekfarm.com
www.huntercreekfarm.com

# Zone 13
# Southern Oregon

Southern Oregon, for our purposes, is the southern Interstate 5 corridor and its offshoots. In the bed-and-breakfast world, and in this book, southern Oregon is dominated by Ashland. A gem of a town, Ashland would make nice place to visit just because of its climate (warm and sunny, yet crisp and mountain-ringed), its charming Victorian neighborhoods, the sprawling Lithia Park, and its proximity to exceptional outdoor recreation (whitewater rafting, fly fishing, skiing, snowmobiling, hiking, boating). However, that's not the reason people come to Ashland. They come for the world-renowned, Tony-award-winning Oregon Shakespeare Festival, established in 1935. Ashland boasts over 70 bed-and-breakfasts; those we profile represent a variety of styles and a range of prices. We skipped those that have been "done to death" in other guidebooks (several of which have slipped in recent years anyway) in favor of some of the newer, fresh approaches, and included a few of the more established inns run by proprietors who really put together a class act and stay current with remodeling, decor, and service.

Nearby Grant's Pass is best known as the gateway to world-class whitewater rafting on the Rogue River. It's also a good jumping-off point for much of southern Oregon's best attractions, like Crater Lake and Oregon Caves National Monument. It's even within day-trip distance to the northern California redwoods. Inns can also be found in Medford, Roseburg, and Jacksonville.

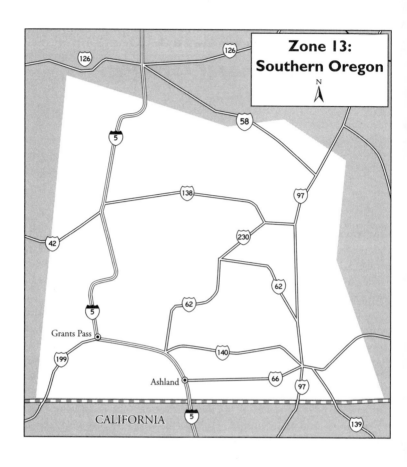

**Ashland**
Antique Rose Inn, p. 371
Arden Forest Inn, p. 372
Country Willows B&B Inn,
  p. 373
Cowslip's Belle B&B, p. 374
GrapeVine Inn, p. 375
The Iris Inn, p. 376
Lithia Springs Inn, p. 377

Mt. Ashland Inn, p. 378
Oak Street Station B&B, p. 380
Shrew's House B&B, p. 381
Winchester Country Inn, p. 382
The Woods House, p. 383

**Grants Pass**
Home Farm B&B, p. 385
Pine Meadow Inn B&B, p. 386

## ANTIQUE ROSE INN, Ashland

| Overall: ★★★★ | Room Quality: B | Value: C | Price: $117–$159 |
|---|---|---|---|

Smashingly beautiful (lavender-gray with plum and white trim) National Historic Register home preserves the elegance of the age. Kathy's delicious, formal breakfasts are sure to leave you feeling pampered. Served at an elegant table in the beautifully restored dining room, the fruit course is followed by more than one entree, such as crab bake with eggs and dill, lemon pancakes with blueberries, plus cinnamon rolls, or tortilla roll-ups with egg and mushrooms, lemon-ricotta blintzes, plus homemade muffins. An early continental can be prepared by arrangement—but what a pity that would be!

### SETTING & FACILITIES

**Location:** Just south of Main on Gresham; 3 blocks from theaters
**Near:** Oregon Shakespeare Festival, Lithia Park; ski area, Crater Lake N.P., Rogue River, lakes
**Building:** 1888 catalogue Queen Anne–style Victorian
**Grounds:** Beautiful, sprawling; mature trees, ivy, reminiscent of European gardens

**Public Space:** Two spacious parlors, porch
**Food & Drink:** Wine, sherry, coffee, tea, & soft drinks; afternoon snacks; full breakfast; early cont'l option
**Recreation:** Theater! (Shakespearean and otherwise), Britt Music Festival; rafting, fishing, wine tasting, golf
**Amenities & Services:** Umbrellas, guest phone, games

### ACCOMMODATIONS

**Units:** 3 guest rooms, 1 cottage
**All Rooms:** Fresh flowers, robes, down comforters
**Some Rooms:** Claw-foot tub, dbl. whirlpool, kitchen, sauna, sitting area, balcony, library
**Bed & Bath:** King or queen; private baths

**Favorites:** Rose Room, Rose Cottage
**Comfort & Decor:** A showcase of Victoriana—ya gotta like lace and roses. High ceilings, antiques, abundant woodwork. Dining room: incredible oak hutch original to house. Mahogany Room: rich paneling, embossed tin ceiling. Many original fixtures.

### RATES, RESERVATIONS, & RESTRICTIONS

**Deposit:** 1st night; 21-day cancellation, $10 fee
**Discounts:** Single occupancy, off-season, shoulder season, no breakfast; $35 add'l person in cottage
**Credit Cards:** V, MC
**Check-in/Out:** 3–5 or by arrangement/11
**Smoking:** Outside only
**Pets:** No; host kitties on premises

**Kids:** Over 10 welcome
**Minimum Stay:** 2 nights, weekends & holidays
**Open:** Cottage, all year; main house, Feb.–Oct.
**Hosts:** Kathy Buffington
91 Gresham, Ashland, OR 97520
(888) 282-6285 or (541) 482-6285
antiquebnb@aol.com
www.wvi.com/~dhull/antiquebnb

## ARDEN FOREST INN, Ashland

| Overall: ★★★★ | Room Quality: B | Value: C | Price: $100–$130 |
|---|---|---|---|

Blending the old with the new, even (dare we say it?) the New Age, Arden Forest is a refreshing combination of contemporary sensibility and old-fashioned comfort. Good food, good conversation, artistic surroundings. The convivial, family-style breakfast can be the best part of your stay. While the inn has been around for years, the current owners took over in 1995 and modernized extensively. Their knowledge of the theater is extensive and enthusiastically shared. A beautiful property.

### SETTING & FACILITIES

**Location:** NE of Main off Laurel
**Near:** Oregon Shakespeare Festival & Lithia Park; Mt. Ashland ski area, Crater Lake N.P., Rogue River, and Emigrant, Howard Prairie, and Hyatt Lakes
**Building:** 1890 historic farmhouse w/ extensive modification
**Grounds:** Commodious backyard, deck, gazebo, waterfall, more to come
**Public Space:** LR, DR, library, deck, guest kitchenette

**Food & Drink:** Iced beverages, sherry; full breakfast
**Recreation:** Theater! (Shakespearean and otherwise), Britt Music Festival; rafting, fishing, wine tasting, golf
**Amenities & Services:** Guest kitchenette w/ fridge & micro.; great source of theater info: Bill & Corbet publish their own extensive annual theater guide which, by some accounts, provides more info. than the Festival's

### ACCOMMODATIONS

**Units:** 4 guest rooms, 1 2-BR suite
**All Rooms:** Phone w/ private line
**Some Rooms:** Private deck access, private patios
**Bed & Bath:** King, queen, or twin; private baths
**Favorites:** Upstairs suite
**Comfort & Decor:** Native American

and spiritual motifs mix comfortably with 1930s retro, surrealism, and modern sensibilities. Contemporary furnishings, fixtures, and art (much of it original). Colors and patterns are bold: wine, forest, eggplant. Hardwood floors with rugs. Windows vent; central heat/AC.

### RATES, RESERVATIONS, & RESTRICTIONS

**Deposit:** 1st night; 14-day cancellation, $15 fee
**Discounts:** Off-season, shoulder season, single occupancy; $30 add'l person
**Credit Cards:** V, MC
**Check-in/Out:** 3–6/11 or by arrangement
**Smoking:** No
**Pets:** No
**Kids:** 10 & older welcome

**Minimum Stay:** $10 single night surcharge on weekends
**Open:** All year
**Hosts:** William Faiia & Corbet Unmack
261 West Hersey St.
Ashland, OR 97520
(800) 460-3912 or (541) 488-1496
aforest@jeffnet.org

## COUNTRY WILLOWS B&B INN, Ashland

Overall: ★★★★½     Room Quality: A     Value: C     Price: $95–$195

If you've stayed at Country Willows in the past—take another look. The inn was popular and comfortable before, but when the current owners took over in 1993, they renovated from the ground up. Decorating and food is fabulous; you feel pampered. Relaxing on the second-floor deck, with its custom bent-willow furniture and peaceful lawn and garden view, is like a slice of heaven after a busy day of touring. Breakfasts, served at individual tables in a cafelike atmosphere, are true "celebration meals."

### SETTING & FACILITIES

**Location:** At the end of Clay St., on the SE end of town
**Near:** The Phoenix (spa & day retreat), Oregon Shakespeare Festival, Lithia Park; ski area, Crater Lake N.P., Rogue River, lakes
**Building:** 1896 farmhouse, fully renovated; 1899 barn, remodeled into luxury quarters
**Grounds:** Large front lawn, pond w/ geese, pool
**Public Space:** Front porch, library, LR, DR, multilevel pool deck, upper porch

**Food & Drink:** Port, sherry, hot beverages, & snacks; morning coffee, tea, & granola; full gourmet breakfast
**Recreation:** Croquet, bikes provided, trails nearby; rafting, fishing, wine tasting, golf; Britt Music Festival, theater!
**Amenities & Services:** Library has fireplace, sound system, games, & TV; guidebooks, info & full text of Shakespeare plays, fridge, ice machine, gift shop; pool (seasonal) & spa (All year); discount ski packages

### ACCOMMODATIONS

**Units:** 5 guest rooms, 4 suites
**All Rooms:** Robes, phone, flashlight, iron, hairdryer, fruit basket, highest-quality linens
**Some Rooms:** Fridge, patio, sitting area, kitchenette (wet bar, micro., coffee service), private entrance, walk-in closet, ADA disabled access
**Bed & Bath:** King or queen, some w/ add'l bed or sofabed; private baths

**Favorites:** Pine Ridge, Sunrise, Hayloft Suites
**Comfort & Decor:** "Upscale contemporary country" best describes the mix of designer fabrics, custom colors, and carefully crafted ease. Original artwork, fresh flowers, top-of-the-line linens. Individual heat and AC controls.

## RATES, RESERVATIONS, & RESTRICTIONS

**Deposit:** Credit card or check; 15-day cancellation, $20 fee
**Discounts:** Single occupancy, off-season
**Credit Cards:** V, MC, D
**Check-in/Out:** 3–5 or by arrangement/11
**Smoking:** Outside only
**Pets:** No

**Kids:** Over 12 welcome
**Minimum Stay:** None
**Open:** All year
**Hosts:** Dan Durant & David Newton
1313 Clay St., Ashland, OR 97520
(800) WILLOWS or (541) 488-1590
Fax: (541) 488-1611
willows@willowsinn.com
www.willowsinn.com

## COWSLIP'S BELLE B&B, Ashland

| Overall: ★★★★ | Room Quality: B | Value: C | Price: $105–$140 |
|---|---|---|---|

When Jon and Carmen opened Cowslip's Belle in 1984, the town had only a third as many bed-and-breakfasts as today. Many guests return year after year for the special brand of relaxed, convivial, down-to-earth hospitality they find here. Breakfasts are wonderful, and the location is great. Recent updates included extensive re-landscaping of the backyard, deck, and garden. No whirlpool tubs or other flashy amenities, but we found that a lodging experience at Cowslip's Belle adds up to a whole that is more than the sum of the parts. The place has heart.

### SETTING & FACILITIES

**Location:** On Main between Bush & Laurel, a few blocks from the theaters
**Near:** Oregon Shakespeare Festival & Lithia Park; Mt. Ashland ski area, Crater Lake N.P., Rogue River, lakes
**Building:** 1913 Craftsman bungalow & carriage house
**Grounds:** Attractive mini-park; spacious new back deck, koi pond, waterfall; back gardens
**Public Space:** LR, DR, porch

**Food & Drink:** Gourmet cookies, hot beverages, sherry; to-die-for chocolate truffles on your pillow; full breakfast
**Recreation:** Britt Music Festival; fishing, wine tasting, golf
**Amenities & Services:** Theater schedules, play synopses; games, books, cordless phone; free use of full-service fitness club; tour planning, raft trip booking, bike rental arranging, turndown

### ACCOMMODATIONS

**Units:** 3 guest rooms, 1 suite
**All Rooms:** Teddy bears, down comforter, toiletries
**Some Rooms:** Separate entrance, deck, stained glass
**Bed & Bath:** Queens (3 also have 1 or 2 twins); private ensuite baths
**Favorites:** Rosebud Suite, Cuckoo-bud

**Comfort & Decor:** Romantic, with floral motifs, wallpaper combinations, antiques, upholstery fabrics. Room-darkening drapes dampen noise from road (more a problem in front-of-the-house Gillyvor room than others). Rooms have carpet and AC, room thermostats; windows open.

## RATES, RESERVATIONS, & RESTRICTIONS

**Deposit:** 1st night; 30-day cancellation
**Discounts:** Off-season, shoulder season; $35 add'l person
**Credit Cards:** Not accepted
**Check-in/Out:** After 3 or by arrangement/11
**Smoking:** No
**Pets:** No
**Kids:** Welcome

**Minimum Stay:** None
**Open:** All year
**Hosts:** Jon & Carmen Reinhardt
159 N. Main
Ashland, OR 97520
(800) 888-6819 or (541) 488-2901
Fax: (541) 482-6138
stay@cowslip.com
www.cowslip.com/cowslip

## GRAPEVINE INN, Ashland

| Overall: ★★★½ | Room Quality: B | Value: C | Price: $95–$125 |
|---|---|---|---|

The great "curb appeal" of this 1909 Dutch Colonial snagged us, with its glorious flowers, rounded porch, and distinctive lines. Once inside, the casually elegant surroundings made us glad we stopped. Rooms and common areas are unfussy, with clean, contemporary lines and comfortable, modern furnishings. Shirley opened the inn in 1992. Ideal location for walking to anything downtown. While GrapeVine Inn fronts on busy Siskyou Boulevard, the backyard garden is a peaceful oasis.

## SETTING & FACILITIES

**Location:** Four blocks from theaters, right on Siskiyou (Hwy. 99) just south of downtown
**Near:** Oregon Shakespeare Festival, Lithia Park; Mt. Ashland ski area, Crater Lake N.P., Rogue River, lakes
**Building:** 1909 Dutch Colonial
**Grounds:** Deck/arbor, small fish pond; inviting front lawn & flowers

**Public Space:** Front porch, sitting room, DR
**Food & Drink:** Refreshments; beverages; full breakfast
**Recreation:** Britt Music Festival; rafting, fishing, wine tasting, golf
**Amenities & Services:** Fireplace, umbrellas; reservations; tour planning

## ACCOMMODATIONS

**Units:** 3 guest rooms
**All Rooms:** Phone, mini-fridge, tile bath
**Some Rooms:** Private patio, canopy bed, mini-library, gas fireplace, dual sinks, kitchen
**Bed & Bath:** Queens (twin roll-away avail. for 1 room); private ensuite baths
**Favorites:** The Grape Ivy

**Comfort & Decor:** Spare and contemporary, almost Shaker. Rich color palettes of the guest rooms: golden in The Chardonnay, dark accents in The Cabernet, and greens in The Grape Ivy. Bedrooms have carpet; common areas have hardwood floors.

## RATES, RESERVATIONS, & RESTRICTIONS

**Deposit:** 1st night; 20-day cancellation or forfeit unless rebooked, $15 fee; 30-day notice for holidays/multiple rooms; unless rebooked, guests are responsible for payment of all reservation dates
**Discounts:** Single occupancy; $25 add'l person
**Credit Cards:** Not accepted
**Check-in/Out:** 4–6 or by arrangement/11
**Smoking:** Outside only

**Pets:** No
**Kids:** 12 & older welcome
**Minimum Stay:** 2 nights, weekends & holidays
**Open:** May–Oct.
**Hosts:** Shirley Grega
486 Siskiyou Blvd.
Ashland, OR 97520
(800) 500-VINE or (541) 482-7944
Fax: (541) 482-7944
grapemail@aol.com
www.mind.net/grapevineinn

## THE IRIS INN, Ashland

| Overall: ★★★ | Room Quality: C | Value: C | Price: $80–$110 |
|---|---|---|---|

Just off Main, on a sleepy side street close to the Plaza and theaters, The Iris Inn is ideally located for both quiet and activity access. A relaxed, experienced innkeeper, Vicki has had the inn since 1982. Her pleasant, friendly manner makes guests feel at home. Comfortably renovated Victorian mixes modern amenities and antiques. Quiet location, roomy back deck with attractive gardens.

### SETTING & FACILITIES

**Location:** A block off Main St., just a few blocks' stroll to theaters
**Near:** Oregon Shakespeare Festival, Lithia Park; Mt. Ashland ski area, Crater Lake N.P., Rogue River, lakes
**Building:** 1905 Victorian
**Grounds:** Trim little front yard; larger backyard w/ deck, rose garden

**Public Space:** Front porch, LR, DR
**Food & Drink:** Afternoon refreshments; 24-hour beverages; full breakfast
**Recreation:** Britt Music Festival; rafting, fishing, wine tasting, golf
**Amenities & Services:** Iron, phone in hall, fridge; reservations, turndown

### ACCOMMODATIONS

**Units:** 5 guest rooms
**All Rooms:** Attractive decor, custom robes
**Some Rooms:** Walk-in closet, daybed, claw-foot tub, sitting alcove
**Bed & Bath:** Queens (some queen twin); private baths
**Favorites:** Blue Room, Jade Room

**Comfort & Decor:** Quiet, cute, and neat, the decor includes iris images. Some original stained glass. Photos of previous and original owners enliven the stairwell. Nine-foot ceilings, attractive fabrics, newer paint and carpets. Central heat and AC, windows open.

## RATES, RESERVATIONS, & RESTRICTIONS

**Deposit:** Credit card or check; 20-day cancellation, $10 fee
**Discounts:** Off-season, Oregon Shakespeare Festival members, single occupancy; CDN $25 add'l person
**Credit Cards:** V, MC
**Check-in/Out:** 2–7 or by arrangement/11
**Smoking:** Outside only
**Pets:** No; host kitties (outside) on premises

**Kids:** By prior arrangement only
**Minimum Stay:** None
**Open:** All year
**Hosts:** Vicki Capp (formerly Vicki Lamb)
59 Manzanita St.
Ashland, OR 97520
(800) 460-7650 or (541) 488-2286
Fax: (541) 488-3709
irisinnbb@aol.com
www.irisinnbb.com

## LITHIA SPRINGS INN, Ashland

| Overall: ★★★ | Room Quality: C | Value: D | Price: $85–$195 |
|---|---|---|---|

Although open since 1992, Lithia Springs Inn has a sense of being in its formative years. Policies and amenities seemed a bit fluid at the time of our visit. We recommend the cottage units outside of the main house, which are newer and seemed the most consistent. Themed suites Emperor and Parisian are the most interesting, the former with impressive antiques and the latter with evocative murals. Outside of Ashland proper, so you'll be driving to restaurants and theaters, but location is nice and quiet.

## SETTING & FACILITIES

**Location:** Near I-5 Exit 19 at the far NW edge of Ashland
**Near:** Oregon Shakespeare Festival & Lithia Park; Mt. Ashland ski area, Crater Lake N.P., Rogue River, lakes
**Building:** 1992 main building; new & modern duplex cottages
**Grounds:** 7 acres (incl. vegetable farm); arbor patio, flower garden
**Public Space:** DR, library, LR, gardens
**Food & Drink:** Cold beverages, bottled water, & cookies; morning coffee

& cont'l fare by 7:15 a.m.; full buffet breakfast served 9–10
**Recreation:** Theater, Britt Music Festival; wine tasting, golf
**Amenities & Services:** Games, videos, CDs & sound system, TV/VCR, guest phone, baby grand piano; host's computer avail. to check e-mail & such, massage avail.

## ACCOMMODATIONS

**Units:** 14 guest rooms/suites
**All Rooms:** AC, bath amenities
**Some Rooms:** Mineral springs–fed soaking tub (most rooms), mini-fridge, sound system, skylights, mini-library, desk, wall murals, sofabed, wet bar, sitting area, table & chairs
**Bed & Bath:** Queen or king (some w/ extra twin or sofabed);

private ensuite baths
**Favorites:** Emperor's Suite, Parisian Suite
**Comfort & Decor:** Snug but attractively appointed living room. Mostly midquality decor and appointments in guest rooms, with a few surprising touches. Best feature is the whirlpool spas. Individual heat and AC.

## RATES, RESERVATIONS, & RESTRICTIONS

**Deposit:** Call for details
**Discounts:** 3-for-2 package & other extended stay packages; $20 add'l person
**Credit Cards:** V, MC, AE, D
**Check-in/Out:** 3–6/11 or by arrangement
**Smoking:** Outside only
**Pets:** No

**Kids:** Welcome
**Minimum Stay:** 2 nights, summer & holidays
**Open:** All year
**Hosts:** Duane Smith
2165 West Jackson Rd., Ashland OR
(800) 482-7128 or (541) 482-7128
lithia@mind.net
www.ashlandinn.com

## MT. ASHLAND INN, Ashland

| Overall: ★★★★½ | Room Quality: B | Value: C | Price: $99–$190 |
| --- | --- | --- | --- |

Rustic elegance and abundant amenities await you at this incredible mountain inn. The upscale-rustic retreat was hand-built and opened in 1987. The current owners, who shared the original proprietors' vision, took over in 1995 and added the third-floor suite and the hot tub/sauna area with its awesome Mt. McLoughlin view. Future plans include possible "fairy-tale cabins" in the surrounding woods. The two well-behaved Golden Retrievers are not allowed in indoor guest areas, and make charming trail companions.

## SETTING & FACILITIES

**Location:** 15 mi. from Ashland, about 5 mi. up Mt. Ashland Ski Rd. from I-5
**Near:** Mt. Ashland ski area, Oregon Shakespeare Festival, Crater Lake N.P., Rogue River valley
**Building:** Hand-peeled log beam home
**Grounds:** 40 acres of woodland right on Pacific Crest Trail
**Public Space:** Game room, LR, DR, hot tub/sauna area

**Food & Drink:** Hot & cold beverages; micro. & snack cabinet w/ soups, popcorn, etc.; full breakfast
**Recreation:** Ashland theaters; rafting, fishing, wine tasting, golf
**Amenities & Services:** Bikes, snowshoes, X-C skis provided free; guest phone, sauna, hot tub, small gift shop, games, books, sound system, guest guides, iron; reservations, small weddings & conferences

## ACCOMMODATIONS

**Units:** 2 guest rooms, 3 suites
**All Rooms:** Custom robes, flashlight, hairdryer, foam & down pillows, quilts, antique dresser &/or armoire, carpet, books, comfy chairs
**Some Rooms:** Mt. Shasta view, sitting room, CD player, beverage-stocked mini-fridge, micro., skylit bath, whirlpool
**Bed & Bath:** Queen or king (one w/ extra twin); private baths (all but 1 ensuite)
**Favorites:** Sky Lakes Suite, McLoughlin Suite (unusual configuration; queen

bed in BR, daybed in sitting room; add'l private bath can be "annexed" for a 2-bed, 2-bath unit)
**Comfort & Decor:** Impressive craftsmanship. Log-walled common area: hardwood floors, area rugs, rock fireplace. Stained glass, handmade furnishings. Guest room decor combines wallpaper and log walls with rich tones and fabrics; Berber-style carpet. Heated by main fireplace; rooms also have individual thermostats and windows that open.

## RATES, RESERVATIONS, & RESTRICTIONS

**Deposit:** 1st night; 15-day cancellation, $20 fee
**Discounts:** Single occupancy, winter weekday special; $30 add'l person
**Credit Cards:** V, MC, D
**Check-in/Out:** 3–5/11 or by arrangement
**Smoking:** Not allowed anywhere on property
**Pets:** No; host dogs on property

**Kids:** 10 & older only (unless renting entire house)
**Minimum Stay:** 2 nights, summer weekends & holidays
**Open:** All year
**Hosts:** Chuck & Laurel Biegert
550 Mt. Ashland Ski Rd.
Ashland, OR 97520
(800) 830-8707 or (541) 482-8707
Fax: (541) 482-8707
www.mtashlandinn.com

## OAK STREET STATION B&B, Ashland

| Overall: ★★★ | Room Quality: C | Value: C | Price: $99–$109 |
|---|---|---|---|

Casual, comfortable bed-and-breakfast with gracious hosts, thoughtful touches, exceptional breakfasts. One of the closest bed-and-breakfasts to the theaters. Oak Street Station has been a bed-and-breakfast for years. When John and Sue decided to open their own place, they chose the first bed-and-breakfast they had ever stayed at together—Oak Street Station. They remodeled the old home, brightened it up with hard work and good taste, and developed a reputation for casual ease and fabulous food. (When several other local bed-and-breakfast hosts tell you about a competitor's "great food," you know it's something special!)

### SETTING & FACILITIES

**Location:** 2 blocks north of theater plaza on Oak St.
**Near:** Oregon Shakespeare Festival, Lithia Park; Mt. Ashland ski area, Crater Lake N.P., Rogue River, lakes
**Building:** 1880s home, fully restored
**Grounds:** Long, narrow backyard: rambling, inviting

**Public Space:** Front porch, parlor, DR
**Food & Drink:** Afternoon refreshments; full breakfast
**Recreation:** Theater!, Britt Music Festival; rafting, fishing, wine tasting, golf
**Amenities & Services:** Piano, guest fridge, cordless guest phone in hall

### ACCOMMODATIONS

**Units:** 3 guest rooms (plus an "overflow" room w/ double bed & no bath)
**All Rooms:** Light & airy, fresh flowers, refreshments, windows on 2 sides
**Some Rooms:** Ceiling fans, windows that open
**Bed & Bath:** Queens (one w/ extra twin); private baths

**Favorites:** Christina, Elaine
**Comfort & Decor:** High-ceilinged parlor with Victorian period furnishings. Bright, fresh colors and a comfortable, unpretentious atmosphere. Central heat and AC.

### RATES, RESERVATIONS, & RESTRICTIONS

**Deposit:** 1st night; 3-week cancellation
**Discounts:** Single occupancy; $20 add'l person
**Credit Cards:** Not accepted
**Check-in/Out:** 2–5 or by arrangement/11
**Smoking:** Outside & porch only

**Pets:** No
**Kids:** Welcome
**Minimum Stay:** None
**Open:** All year
**Hosts:** Sue & John Blaize
239 Oak St
Ashland, OR 97520
(800) 482-1726

## SHREW'S HOUSE B&B, Ashland

| Overall: ★★★ | Room Quality: C | Value: C | Price: $110 |
| --- | --- | --- | --- |

This "bed-and-breakfast alternative," very unlike a traditional in-home bed-and-breakfast, offers rooms with private entrances, private patios, wet bar, and individual phone lines. Good for privacy, but a bit cold compared to other Ashland inns. But if you want to play the recluse, this is the place—you can even have breakfast brought to your room. It's also one of the few good bed-and-breakfasts in town that give you a TV of your own (some of the others make you feel a bit tawdry even asking for one . . .). New owner Barbara Simard took over the property in late 1998, and specific policies may be evolving.

### SETTING & FACILITIES

**Location:** Siskiyou Blvd. (Hwy. 99) several blocks SE of downtown
**Near:** Oregon Shakespeare Festival, Lithia Park; ski area, Crater Lake N.P., Rogue River, lakes
**Building:** 1920s Craftsman bungalow, 1890s Victorian cottage; extensively remodeled
**Grounds:** Corner lot w/ in-ground swimming pool & private decks by each room

**Public Space:** Guests generally stay in their spacious, private rooms; host LR & DR can be shared
**Food & Drink:** Full breakfast in DR or ensuite
**Recreation:** Theater!, Britt Music Festival; rafting, fishing, wine tasting, golf
**Amenities & Services:** Pool (in season); (Evolving)

### ACCOMMODATIONS

**Units:** 4 guest rooms
**All Rooms:** Private entrances & patios, guest guides, cable, phone w/ private line, wet bar, mini-fridge, toaster oven
**Some Rooms:** Whirlpool bath, fireplace
**Bed & Bath:** Queen or king (some w/ extra bed); private ensuite baths

**Favorites:** The Baroque
**Comfort & Decor:** Each room is spacious; attractive (though not expensive) decor. Modest finish work and amenities, but the overall value is good. A few antiques, fireplaces; king beds (in 3 of the 4 rooms). Central heat and AC; no individual room control.

## RATES, RESERVATIONS, & RESTRICTIONS

**Deposit:** 1st night; 2-week cancellation
**Discounts:** Off-season, single occupancy, extended stay, whole-house, no breakfast; $15 add'l person
**Credit Cards:** V, MC
**Check-in/Out:** 3–6/11
**Smoking:** No
**Pets:** No
**Kids:** 12 & older welcome; under 12 w/ prior approval

**No-Nos:** Leaving windows open (central AC)
**Minimum Stay:** 2 nights, some weekends & holidays
**Open:** All year
**Hosts:** Barbara Simard
570 Siskiyou Blvd.
Ashland, OR 97520
(800) 482-9214 or (541) 482-9214
shrews@mind.net
www.shrews.com

## WINCHESTER COUNTRY INN, Ashland

| Overall: ★★★½ | Room Quality: B | Value: D | Price: $140–$200 |
|---|---|---|---|

Winchester Country Inn began with the main house (seven rooms) and a restaurant in 1983. Today, the complex, just a block uphill from Main Street, offers a total of 18 rooms. Because of its size and multibuilding layout, Winchester is more of a hotel than a bed-and-breakfast; a bit impersonal. The clean, predictable atmosphere will appeal to some, as will the restaurant-style breakfast with entree choices. Air-conditioning may be a useful feature in the heat of late summer.

## SETTING & FACILITIES

**Location:** Just uphill from the "action" of downtown & the theaters
**Near:** Oregon Shakespeare Festival, Lithia Park; ski area, Crater Lake N.P., Rogue River, lakes
**Building:** Four-building complex: main house w/ restaurant, cottage, carriage house, renovated Victorian
**Grounds:** In-city lot on quiet side street; gazebo, brick paths
**Public Space:** Sitting room in main building & Heritage House

**Food & Drink:** In-room sherry & treats; early coffee; full breakfast
**Recreation:** Britt Music Festival; rafting, fishing, wine tasting, golf
**Amenities & Services:** Games, gift shop, TV/VCR & videos avail., morning newspaper, hairdryers, irons; restaurant, meetings, conferences, banquets, weddings

## ACCOMMODATIONS

**Units:** 18 guest rooms

**All Rooms:** Sitting area, fresh flowers, antiques & reproduction furnishings, phones

**Some Rooms:** Claw-foot tub, bay window seat, private deck, honor bar, tile bath, disabled access, whirlpool

**Bed & Bath:** Queen or king (some w/ extra bed or sofabed; roll-aways avail.); private baths

**Favorites:** Barbara Howard, Eleanor Rose

**Comfort & Decor:** Pastels predominate, with accents of burgundy, green, and/or blue in some rooms. Mid- to high-quality appointments. Open spaces. Individual room thermostats for heat and AC. Windows open in most rooms.

## RATES, RESERVATIONS, & RESTRICTIONS

**Deposit:** Final night; 30-day cancellation, 10% fee

**Discounts:** Off-season, shoulder season, dinner packages; $30 add'l person

**Credit Cards:** V, MC, AE, D

**Check-in/Out:** After 3/11

**Smoking:** No

**Pets:** No

**Kids:** Welcome

**Minimum Stay:** None

**Open:** All Year

**Hosts:** Laurie & Michael Gibbs
35 S. Second St.
Ashland, OR 97520
(800) 972-4991 or (541) 488-1113
Fax: (541) 488-4604
AshlandInn@aol.com
www.winchesterinn.com

## THE WOODS HOUSE, Ashland

| Overall: ★★★ | Room Quality: C | Value: C | Price: $110–$120 |
|---|---|---|---|

Located in Ashland's historic district, The Woods House has been an inn since 1984. Current owners Françoise and Lester bought it in 1991. Although it's right on Main, the property is set back and quiet, especially in the back garden. The resident Newfoundland (outside) dog, Jasmine, is an absolute doll. The inn is conveniently located less than five blocks from the downtown plaza—close enough for most to walk.

## SETTING & FACILITIES

**Location:** About 6 blocks from the theaters on Main between Wimer & Manzanita
**Near:** Oregon Shakespeare Festival, Lithia Park; Mt. Ashland ski area, Crater Lake N.P., Rogue River, & Emigrant, Howard Prairie, & Hyatt Lakes
**Building:** 1908 Craftsman, remodeled 1984
**Grounds:** Front lawn w/ huge, mature trees; spacious, tiered backyard; side patio
**Public Space:** Front porch, parlor, DR, 2nd-floor back porch

**Food & Drink:** Cookies, sherry, & hot beverages; full breakfast; early cont'l ensuite option
**Recreation:** Britt Music Festival; wine tasting, golf; walking Jasmine (resident dog)
**Amenities & Services:** Sound system & library; fridge w/ ice, beverages, & space for personal items; book exchange library, games, morning newspaper, two guest phones & phone lines, in-room phones avail.; laundry & ironing facil., turndown

## ACCOMMODATIONS

**Units:** 6 guest rooms
**All Rooms:** Robes, custom soaps, bath crystals
**Some Rooms:** Private entrance, desk, tile bath, walk-in closet, tub bath
**Bed & Bath:** Queen or king (several w/ extra twin); private ensuite bath

**Favorites:** Cupid's Chamber, Victoria's
**Comfort & Decor:** Fresh flowers, carefully chosen wall treatments, wood floors with area rugs create a fresh-but-not-fussy atmosphere in which you can relax and feel comfortable.

## RATES, RESERVATIONS, & RESTRICTIONS

**Deposit:** 1st night; 21-day cancellation
**Discounts:** Off-season, shoulder season, single occupancy; $35 add'l person
**Credit Cards:** V, MC (checks preferred)
**Check-in/Out:** 2–5 or by arrangement/11
**Smoking:** Outside only
**Pets:** No; large host dog (outside) on premises
**Kids:** By prior approval only

**No-Nos:** Smoking inside, pets, children w/o prior approval
**Minimum Stay:** 2 nights, summer weekends (single nights by chance)
**Open:** All year
**Hosts:** Françoise & Lester Roddy
333 N. Main St., Ashland, OR 97520
(800) 435-8260 or (541) 488-1598
Fax: (541) 482-8027
woodshse@mind.net
www.mind.net/woodshouse/

## HOME FARM B&B, Grants Pass

| Overall: ★★½ | Room Quality: C | Value: B | Price: $65–$80 |
|---|---|---|---|

Utterly charming, unpretentious, spic-and-span hobby farm offers a restful stay near the banks of the Rogue River. The casual, relaxed country ambiance makes you feel like you're at Grandma's house—providing you liked Grandma. A short stroll to the river. Enjoy the Murrays' pets as you wander the grounds. A sweet slice of the country life.

### SETTING & FACILITIES

**Location:** About 3 mi. from I-5's Exit 48 at Rogue River, between Grants Pass & Ashland
**Near:** Medford, Crater Lake, Oregon Caves, California redwoods
**Building:** Two 1944 farmhouses, fully remodeled in 1992
**Grounds:** 4.5 acres w/ fruit trees, "checker stump," raspberries, huge lawn, trails

**Public Space:** Parlor, DR, sun porch, deck
**Food & Drink:** Coffee & tea out at 6 a.m.; full breakfast
**Recreation:** White-water rafting, fly-fishing, mountain biking, theater (40 min. to Ashland's Shakespeare Festival), antiquing, wine tasting
**Amenities & Services:** Projection TV/VCR, sound system; weddings, family reunions

### ACCOMMODATIONS

**Units:** 4 guest rooms
**All Rooms:** Books, comfortable furnishings
**Some Rooms:** Private entrance, disabled access, sitting area
**Bed & Bath:** Queen or king; private baths
**Favorites:** Each is comparable; bunkhouse rooms are larger

**Comfort & Decor:** Bright and cheerful country decor includes quilts and homey touches. Main house rooms have central heat with individually controlled vents; bunkhouse rooms have individual heat control. All have window AC units and windows that open.

### RATES, RESERVATIONS, & RESTRICTIONS

**Deposit:** 1st night; 7-day cancellation, $10 fee
**Discounts:** Extended stay, single occupancy; $10 add'l person
**Credit Cards:** Not accepted
**Check-in/Out:** 3–6 or by arrangement/11
**Smoking:** Outside only
**Pets:** No; plenty of host pets on site!
**Kids:** 10 & older welcome; younger by prior arrangement only

**Minimum Stay:** None
**Open:** All year
**Hosts:** Cheri & Bill Murray
157 Savage Creek Rd.
Grants Pass, OR 97527
(800) 522-7967 or (541) 582-0980
Fax: Same as local phone; call first
homefarm@chatlink.com
www.chatlink.com/~homefarm

## PINE MEADOW INN B&B, Grants Pass

| Overall: ★★★★ | Room Quality: B | Value: B | Price: $80–$110 |
|---|---|---|---|

Thoroughly modern farmhouse-style home nestled on magical, wooded grounds offers a casually elegant retreat and healthy gourmet breakfasts. Nancy and Maloy did their homework before opening this dream bed-and-breakfast in the Rogue River Valley. They understand all the little extras that make a stay memorable, and their enthusiasm—the quiet, abiding kind—is undiminished after several years of offering their home as a bed-and-breakfast. Their dream is intact, and their joy in providing a peaceful, elegant respite for their guests is contagious. Pine Meadow Inn B&B is a gem.

### SETTING & FACILITIES

**Location:** About 6 mi. off I-5 at Grants Pass, outside the tiny hamlet of Merlin

**Near:** Ashland, Medford, Rogue River, Crater Lake, Oregon Caves, California redwoods

**Building:** Midwest-style farmhouse (built 1991)

**Grounds:** 9-acre wooded parcel; paths, English cutting garden, gardens, fruit trees, koi pond, & waterfall

**Public Space:** LR, DR, porch, deck

**Food & Drink:** Cookie & candy in rooms; full breakfast

**Recreation:** White-water rafting, fly-fishing, mountain biking, hiking, theater (40 min. to Ashland's Shakespeare Festival), antiquing, wine tasting

**Amenities & Services:** Games, puzzles, enormous 24-hour hot tub, amenities basket, extensive library; turndown

## ACCOMMODATIONS

**Units:** 4 guest rooms
**All Rooms:** Iron, phone, hairdryer, toiletries, binoculars, ceiling fan, luxury mattress, carpet, fresh flowers, room-darkening shades
**Some Rooms:** Dual sinks, sitting area
**Bed & Bath:** Queen (1 w/ queen plus twin sofabed); private ensuite baths
**Favorites:** Willow

**Comfort & Decor:** Roomy, fresh, and comfortable, melding modern quality with antique charm. Quality wallpapers, window treatments, bedding. Original artwork. Exceptional craftsmanship, with rounded corners and painted woodwork. Central heat and AC; windows open.

## RATES, RESERVATIONS, & RESTRICTIONS

**Deposit:** 1st night; 15-day cancellation, $15 fee
**Discounts:** Single occupancy, extended stays, off-season, corporate, whole house
**Credit Cards:** V, MC, AE, D
**Check-in/Out:** 4–6 or by arrangement/11
**Smoking:** No
**Pets:** No

**Kids:** 10 & older welcome
**Minimum Stay:** None
**Open:** All year
**Hosts:** Nancy & Maloy Murdock
1000 Crow Rd.
Merlin, OR 97532
(800) 554-0806 or (541) 471-6277
Fax: (541) 471-6277
pmi@pinemeadowinn.com
www.pinemeadowinn.com

# Zone 14
# Mt. Hood and Columbia Gorge

Portland's playground, Mount Hood and the Columbia Gorge are just an hour east of Oregon's metropolitan center and offer some of the finest, best-developed, and easily accessible outdoor recreation in the Pacific Northwest. Along Interstate 84, the highway that follows the Columbia River and Oregon's border with Washington, the Columbia River Gorge National Scenic Area includes dozens of waterfalls, hiking trails, historic museums (this was a major route for westward expansion), Bonneville Dam, and some of the nation's best windsurfing. "The Gorge" is the canyon cut by the mighty Columbia as it flows to the Pacific Ocean. Where the Gorge cuts through the Cascade Mountains, and the cool, moist air of the west meets the warmer, dry air of the east, conflicting air currents create the prime motion sought by windsurfers. Central Gorge tourists are served by the Oregon communities of Hood River and Mosier and the Washington towns of White Salmon and Bingen, just across the river.

South of the Gorge, the main route from Portland to Mount Hood is Highway 26. This is the route of the historic Barlow Trail, a major path of westward pioneer travel. Today, it moves skiers from Portland to the year-round slopes on Mount Hood's southern side. The towns of Sandy, Welches, Brightwood, Zigzag, Rhododendron, and Government Camp offer services along the way. Rivers including the Sandy and the Salmon run through the area, lakes such as Mirror and Trillium offer scenic beauty, and wilderness areas such as Salmon-Huckleberry and Mount Hood provide hundreds of miles of hiking trails.

East of the mountain, Highway 35 connects Highway 26 and Interstate 84 via the Hood River Valley, an orchard-filled scenic byway. The communities of Parkdale and Mount Hood offer lodgings along this idyllic corridor, providing access to both the attractions of Mount Hood and those of Hood River and the Gorge.

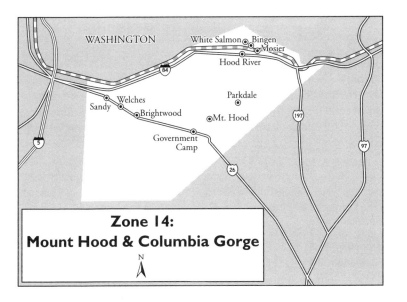

**WASHINGTON**

White Salmon • Bingen
• Mosier
Hood River

Parkdale
◉

Welches
Sandy • • Brightwood
◉ Mt. Hood

Government
Camp

## Zone 14:
## Mount Hood & Columbia Gorge

N
∧

---

**Bingen**
The Bingen Haus, p. 390

**Brightwood**
Brightwood Guest House, p. 391

**Government Camp**
Falcon's Crest Inn, p. 392

**Hood River**
The Beryl House, p. 393
Columbia Gorge Hotel, p. 394
Hood River Hotel, p. 395
Lakecliff Estate, p. 396

**Mosier**
The Mosier House, p. 397

**Mt. Hood**
Mt. Hood Hamlet B&B, p. 398

**Parkdale**
Mt. Hood B&B, p. 399

**Sandy**
Brookside B&B, p. 400

**Welches**
Doublegate Inn B&B, p. 401
Old Welches Inn, p. 402

**White Salmon**
The Inn of the White Salmon,
p. 403

## THE BINGEN HAUS, Bingen

| Overall: ★★½ | Room Quality: D | Value: C | Price: $65–$90 |
|---|---|---|---|

Bingen is a tiny little burg straddling Washington's Highway 14 just across the river from bustling Hood River and Oregon's Interstate 84. It's just down the hill from White Salmon. Bingen Haus is a huge, historic home with plenty of common area and a faded, funky charm. A longtime bed-and-breakfast, it was purchased by Diana and Eric in late 1998, so many changes were underway at this writing. The new owners are pleasant, laid-back, and service-oriented; we felt confident they will offer a quality lodging experience. While the premises and furnishings show their age, gradual refurbishing was in progress. It will remain a value lodging, with the benefit of welcoming children and providing an easy-access highway location.

### SETTING & FACILITIES

**Location:** 0.8 mi. east of Hood River bridge on north side of Hwy. 14
**Near:** White Salmon (town & river), Columbia Gorge Nat'l Scenic Area, Hood River (town & river), Columbia River, Mt. Adams recreation areas
**Building:** 1860–1900 Victorian hybrid
**Grounds:** Roses, border planting, picnic area
**Public Space:** Parlor/game room, DR, back parlor, entertainment room, fireplace lounge, balcony
**Food & Drink:** Self-serve hot beverages; espresso; buffet-style full or extended cont'l breakfast
**Recreation:** Windsurfing, golf, skiing, scenic driving, antiquing, galleries
**Amenities & Services:** Library, games, big-screen TV, hot tub, guest fridge; recreational & celebration packages

### ACCOMMODATIONS

**Units:** 7 guest rooms
**All Rooms:** Carpet
**Some Rooms:** Bay window, sitting area, closets (6), ceiling fans (6)
**Bed & Bath:** Double (4), king, queen, twin; 3 shared baths
**Favorites:** 1 & 2
**Comfort & Decor:** Hodgepodge furnishings include antique and wicker pieces. Wide variety of wallpapers and window treatments. Wood paneling or trim in some rooms. Central heat some rooms, electric baseboard in others.

### RATES, RESERVATIONS, & RESTRICTIONS

**Deposit:** Last night; 24-hour cancellation
**Discounts:** Extended stay; $15 add'l adult
**Credit Cards:** V, MC, D
**Check-in/Out:** 4–7 or by arrangement/11
**Smoking:** Outside only
**Pets:** No; host dog & cat
**Kids:** Welcome
**No-Nos:** Noise after 10
**Minimum Stay:** None
**Open:** All year
**Hosts:** Diana Lee-Greene & Eric Greene
Hwy. 14, P.O. Box 818
Bingen, WA 98605
(509) 493-4888
bingenhaus@gorge.net

## BRIGHTWOOD GUEST HOUSE, Brightwood

| Overall: ★★★★★ | Room Quality: A | Value: B | Price: $125 |
|---|---|---|---|

One of the few single-unit properties in the book, this one is such a
favorite spot for romance or solo contemplation, we had to include it.
The artistic, peaceful one-room guest house offers every amenity you'd
need for a weekend away—bring a toothbrush and the clothes on your
back, and you're set. Breakfasts are adventuresome and fabulous—a celebration of tastes and textures, delivered to your private, detached guest
house (hostess lives right next door) for you to enjoy at your table or
outside on the bamboo-surrounded deck next to the koi pond. Jan is a
gracious spirit with a natural gift as a hostess. Not your run-of-the-mill
lodging or dining experience.

### SETTING & FACILITIES

**Location:** Brightwood is 12 mi. east
of Sandy; guest house is another 1.5
mi. off Hwy. 26
**Near:** Welches, Zigzag, Rhododendron, Mt. Hood, Mt. Hood Wilderness,
Salmon-Huckleberry Wilderness,
Salmon River
**Building:** Private guest cottage w/ loft
**Grounds:** 2 wooded acres on the historic Barlow Trail; stream, Japanese
water garden
**Public Space:** Entire cabin is yours,
as the only guest

**Food & Drink:** Self-serve tea &
coffee; sumptuous full ensuite breafast
**Recreation:** Hiking, skiing, Oregon
Trail historic touring, fishing, golf,
rafting
**Amenities & Services:** Extensive
kitchenette, abundant bath & kitchen
amenities, kimonos, slippers, TV/VCR,
classic & foreign films, books, games,
puzzles, art supplies, iron & board, daily
newspaper, bicycles, washer & dryer,
menus; exceptional service in every
respect

### ACCOMMODATIONS

**Units:** 1 self-contained cabin w/ loft
**All Rooms:** See "Amenities &
Services"
**Bed & Bath:** Feather bed in loft,
futon in LR; private ensuite bath
**Comfort & Decor:** Aromatic cedar
paneling surrounds a decor style that
artistically and effortlessly mixes various Asian motifs. Clean lines. While the
two beds could sleep four, this is really
a retreat best suited for two. The on-
the-floor loft feather bed (accessible
by ladder) or the living room futon
may not suit everyone, nor will the
intimate (but well-laid out) scale.

## RATES, RESERVATIONS, & RESTRICTIONS

**Deposit:** 1st night; 72-hour cancellation
**Discounts:** Rate decreases to $112.50 for 2–4 nights, $106.25 for 5–6; $100 for 7; $15 add'l person/night
**Credit Cards:** Not accepted
**Check-in/Out:** After 3/11 (flexible)
**Smoking:** Outside only
**Pets:** No
**Kids:** Over 13 only
**Minimum Stay:** 2 nights, some week-ends & holidays
**Open:** All year
**Hosts:** Jan Estep
64725 E. Barlow Trail, P.O. Box 189, Brightwood, OR 97011
(888) 503-5783 or (503) 622-5783
Fax: (503) 622-5783 (call)
www.moriah.com/brightwood/ or www.holidayjunction.com/usa/or/cor0 002.html

## FALCON'S CREST INN, Government Camp

| Overall: ★★★★½ | Room Quality: B | Value: C | Price: $95–$179 |
|---|---|---|---|

You won't forget BJ and Melody. If ever a couple was born to run an over-the-top bed-and-breakfast, it's these two. BJ (a Santa Claus look-alike) is the gruff, exacting, behind-the-scenes force, the chef who makes the fabulous food happen. Melody is the ebullient hostess, whose stories light up the room; her narration and presentation are an integral part of a Falcon's Crest experience. Rooms are comfortable and just a bit whimsical; common areas are expansive and glorious, with lots of glass and mountainside views. Treat yourself to one of the six-course extravaganza dinners, an indulgence starting at $37.95.

### SETTING & FACILITIES

**Location:** Just off Hwy. 26, at the east end of Government Camp
**Near:** Mt. Hood Skibowl, Mt. Hood Meadows, Trillium Lake, Welches, Timberline Lodge
**Building:** 6,500 sq.-ft. chalet-style home
**Public Space:** Sitting areas in open style, balconies
**Food & Drink:** Cocktails, wine, & beer avail.; in-room truffle; morning coffee/tea service; full breakfast
**Recreation:** All year alpine skiing, X-C skiing, Oregon Trail historic touring
**Amenities & Services:** TV, sound system; full-service restaurant offers cocktails & fixed-price dinners by reservation, starting at $37.95; evening turndown; high teas, parties, gatherings

### ACCOMMODATIONS

**Units:** 3 guest rooms, 2 suites
**All Rooms:** Theme decor, deluxe appointments, phone
**Some Rooms:** Four-poster, exercise room, private deck, private hot tub, dbl. whirlpool, view
**Bed & Bath:** Queen (3), king, twins; private baths
**Favorites:** Each is special
**Comfort & Decor:** Theme decor includes rattan and toy animals in Safari Room, 1920s heirlooms in Sophia Room, Old West artifacts in Cat Ballou Room, Southwest flair in Mexicali Suite, and French country style in Master Suite.

## RATES, RESERVATIONS, & RESTRICTIONS

**Deposit:** Credit card (reservations required); 7-day cancellation
**Discounts:** Extended stay
**Credit Cards:** V, MC, AE, D
**Check-in/Out:** 4/noon
**Smoking:** Outside balconies only
**Pets:** No
**Kids:** Older children welcome
**No-Nos:** More than 2 per room

**Minimum Stay:** None
**Open:** All year
**Hosts:** Melody & Bob ("BJ") Johnson
87287 Government Camp Loop
Government Camp, OR 97028
(800) 624-7384 or (503) 272-3403
Fax: (503) 272-3454
falconscrest@earthlink.net
www.falconscrest.com

## THE BERYL HOUSE, Hood River

| Overall: ★★★ | Room Quality: C | Value: A | Price: $70 |
|---|---|---|---|

Just above the nouveau chic windsurfing hubbub of Hood River, amidst the quiet of long-standing orchards, on a plateau with views north to Mt. Adams and south to Mt. Hood, stands this classic turn-of-the-20th-century farmhouse hand-renovated by Kim Pfautz and John Lovell into The Beryl House B&B. These veteran travelers know what you need: comfortable rooms, a quiet location, and an abundant, fresh, gourmet breakfast (aptly described by one guest as "Alice Waters meets Paul Bunyan") served when you want it.

## SETTING & FACILITIES

**Location:** 4 mi. from downtown & I-84 on Barrett Dr. off Country Club Rd.
**Near:** Columbia River, Columbia Gorge Nat'l Scenic Area, Hood River, Mt. Hood
**Building:** Classic 1906 American farmhouse
**Grounds:** Lawn surrounded by orchards

**Public Space:** Dual parlors, spacious deck, DR
**Food & Drink:** Early coffee; family-style full breakfast
**Recreation:** Windsurfing, rafting, golf, mountain biking, skiing, antiquing, galleries
**Amenities & Services:** Piano, hammock, woodstove; discount ski tickets

## ACCOMMODATIONS

**Units:** 4 guest rooms
**All Rooms:** Simple, clean, comfortable
**Some Rooms:** Extra bed
**Bed & Bath:** Queen, queen & single, double four-poster, or king/twin conversion; share two 3/4-baths (private detached bath option may be avail. by arrangement)

**Favorites:** Equally pleasant
**Comfort & Decor:** Spacious, sunny rooms in pastel colors, with natural or painted wood floors. Homey and casual, clean and comfortable. African and other international objets d'art from Kim's travel work.

## RATES, RESERVATIONS, & RESTRICTIONS

**Deposit:** Credit card or 50%; 7-day cancellation
**Discounts:** Off-season, extended stay, single occupancy, groups
**Credit Cards:** V, MC (add 2% to cash price)
**Check-in/Out:** 4–7 or call/11
**Smoking:** Outside only
**Pets:** Small, quiet, well-behaved dogs welcome

**Kids:** Small, quiet, well-behaved children welcome
**Minimum Stay:** None
**Open:** All year
**Hosts:** John Lovell & Kim Pfautz
4079 Barrett Dr.
Hood River, OR 97031
(541) 386-5567
berylhouse@aol.com
www.moriah.com/beryl

## COLUMBIA GORGE HOTEL, Hood River

| Overall: ★★★★½ | Room Quality: A | Value: D | Price: $150–$270 |
|---|---|---|---|

Perhaps this is "pushing" the definition of "small inn/B&B," but we include the magnificent pale-yellow-stucco and red-tile-roofed edifice for several reasons. For one, the breakfast—which other guidebooks have called "insultingly large"—is an extraordinary celebration meal. Also, the hotel allows pets of all sizes and shapes, as long as they are well behaved and under owner supervision. While rooms are smallish, common areas are lavish and comfortable, and the grounds make for delightful strolling. Veteran hospitality industry professionals, Boyd and Halla Graves and their staff work hard to make your stay memorable.

### SETTING & FACILITIES

**Location:** Just west of Hood River, off I-84 Exit 62
**Near:** Hood River, Columbia Gorge Nat'l Scenic Area, Bonneville Dam
**Building:** 1904 hotel w/ Mediterranean embellishments
**Grounds:** Beautiful gardens; stream & waterfall
**Public Space:** Lobby, lounges
**Food & Drink:** Afternoon champagne & caviar; in-room chocolates; morning coffee service; five-course breakfast
**Recreation:** Windsurfing, golf, mountain biking, skiing, antiquing, galleries
**Amenities & Services:** Morning newspaper, restaurant & lounge on premises (room service avail.), meeting room, gift shop; evening turndown, 24-hour front desk, fax service, safe deposit boxes, laundry service, valet parking, weddings/celebrations, massage by appt.

### ACCOMMODATIONS

**Units:** 40 guest rooms (some suites)
**All Rooms:** TV, phone, robes
**Some Rooms:** Disabled access
**Bed & Bath:** King, queen, or double, some w/ add'l bed(s); private baths
**Favorites:** Fireplace Room, Waterfall Room, Riverside King

**Comfort & Decor:** Rooms (except family suites & some specialty rooms) are not large, but are sumptuously appointed in a gilt-edged, French Renaissance manner. Fine fabrics, European soaps. Bellhop service. Individually controlled heat/AC.

## RATES, RESERVATIONS, & RESTRICTIONS

**Deposit:** 1st night; 14-day cancellation, $25 fee
**Discounts:** $30 add'l person
**Credit Cards:** V, MC, AE, D
**Check-in/Out:** After 4/noon
**Smoking:** Valentino Lounge only
**Pets:** Well-behaved pets welcome; $25 fee; must be on leash when outside your room
**Kids:** Babies in arms & well-supervised

children over 12 welcome
**Minimum Stay:** None
**Open:** All year
**Hosts:** Boyd & Halla Graves
4000 Westcliff Dr.
Hood River, OR 97031-9970
(800) 345-1921 or (541) 386-5566
Fax: (541) 387-5414
cghotel@gorge.net
www.columbiagorgehotel.com

## HOOD RIVER HOTEL, Hood River

| Overall: ★★★★ | Room Quality: B | Value: B | Price: $69–$145 |
|---|---|---|---|

As with its showy sister to the west, Columbia Gorge Hotel, the Hood River Hotel is more a small hotel than a bed-and-breakfast. But its rooms and common areas have historic character and charm, and the breakfast option is a good one (free continental at time of your choice in the restaurant, or credit toward the price of a full breakfast from their extensive menu). Plus, they allow kids and pets. A hip, classy, European-style small hotel in the middle of the "action" of Hood River; easy walking distance to shops, galleries, entertainment.

## SETTING & FACILITIES

**Location:** Downtown Hood River
**Near:** Everything in Hood River, Columbia Gorge Nat'l Scenic Area, Hood River Valley, Mt. Hood
**Building:** 1913 Historic Register hotel
**Public Space:** Lobby/guest lounge, exercise/sauna/spa area

**Food & Drink:** Restaurant/deli; cont'l or upgrade to full breakfast
**Recreation:** Windsurfing, rafting, golf, mountain biking, skiing, antiquing
**Amenities & Services:** Hot tub, exercise room, sauna, gift shop; discount ski tickets, live music on Fridays

## ACCOMMODATIONS

**Units:** 32 guest rooms, 9 suites
**All Rooms:** Antique/reproduction furnishings, quality beds & linens
**Some Rooms:** Disabled access, kitchen, canopy/four-poster/sleigh beds, extra bed, desk/vanity, sitting area
**Bed & Bath:** Various (mostly queen or 2 doubles), roll-aways & cribs avail.; private baths
**Favorites:** Riverview rooms & suites

**Comfort & Decor:** Lace, floral prints, rich woodwork. Remodeled lobby has soaring ceiling; rooms retain the size of an older hotel but are retrofitted with private baths. Local artisan finish work (tile, slate, marble, brick); some older-building quirks remain (slightly slanted floors, steam heat). Some units have AC, some ceiling fans.

## RATES, RESERVATIONS, & RESTRICTIONS

**Deposit:** Varies; call
**Discounts:** Off-season, single occupancy, special packages; $10 add'l person; under 10 free
**Credit Cards:** V, MC, AE, D
**Check-in/Out:** After 4/noon
**Smoking:** Some smoking rooms avail.
**Pets:** Welcome by arrangement; $15 fee
**Kids:** Welcome

**Minimum Stay:** None
**Open:** All year
**Hosts:** Jacquie Brown-Barone & Pasquale Barone
102 Oak Ave.
Hood River, OR 97031
(800) 386-1859 or (541) 386-1900
Fax: (541) 386-6090
hrhotel@gorge.net
www.hoodriverhotel.com

## LAKECLIFF ESTATE, Hood River

| Overall: ★★★★ | Room Quality: B | Value: B | Price: $90–$110 |
|---|---|---|---|

You'll want to make your reservation in advance for this popular Hood River bed-and-breakfast. A decade in business, Bruce and Judy Thesenga have developed quite a following. Their architect-designed home has a secluded, wooded location perched upon a cliff, offering exceptional views (no immediate river access). Comfortable home, lively hosts, lots of common area for relaxing after an active day in the Columbia Gorge.

## SETTING & FACILITIES

**Location:** Just west of Hood River, off I-84's Exit 62, overlooking Columbia River
**Near:** Columbia Gorge Hotel, Columbia Gorge Nat'l Scenic Area
**Building:** 1908 Historic Register summer home
**Grounds:** Wooded lot, lawn on 175-foot cliff

**Public Space:** LR, sunroom/DR, rumpus room, deck
**Food & Drink:** Morning coffee service to your room; full breakfast
**Recreation:** Windsurfing, golf, mountain biking, skiing, antiquing, galleries
**Amenities & Services:** Big-screen TV, VCR, videos, games

## ACCOMMODATIONS

**Units:** 4 guest rooms
**All Rooms:** Attractive furnishings
**Some Rooms:** River view, garden view, washbasin, stone fireplace
**Bed & Bath:** Queen or twin/king conversion (roll-away avail.); 2 private baths, 2 share a bath
**Favorites:** Garden Room, Lynn's Room

**Comfort & Decor:** Classic Pacific Northwest, relaxed and comfortable. Guest rooms: homey, not overlarge. Common areas: guests have plenty of room to stretch out. Immaculate. Wooded location and solid construction make this home cool on even the hottest summer day.

## RATES, RESERVATIONS, & RESTRICTIONS

**Deposit:** 50%; 14-day cancellation, $15 fee
**Discounts:** $15 add'l person
**Credit Cards:** Not accepted
**Check-in/Out:** 4–7/11
**Smoking:** No
**Pets:** No
**Kids:** Over 12 welcome

**Minimum Stay:** None
**Open:** Memorial Day through Labor Day
**Hosts:** Bruce & Judy Thesenga
3820 Westcliff Dr., P.O. Box 1220
Hood River, OR 97031
(541) 386-7000
lakecliff@linkport.com

## THE MOSIER HOUSE, Mosier

Overall: ★★★½    Room Quality: C    Value: B    Price: $85–$100

Woodworker and art historian Matthew Koerner fell in love with this dilapidated but formerly grand Queen Anne in the 1980s. With the help of his brother, Michael, and sister, Martha, he purchased it and began a restoration process that would take a decade. The siblings, with the help of an on-site innkeeper, began offering the painstakingly restored home as a bed-and-breakfast in 1997. When we visited, the labor of love was continuing with ambitious and lovely landscaping in progress. Mosier, a sleepy little hamlet of just over 250 people, is right off Interstate 84 between Hood River and The Dalles. The town and the house are named for area pioneer Jefferson Newton Mosier.

### SETTING & FACILITIES

**Location:** Off I-84 Exit 69, 5 mi. east of Hood River
**Near:** Columbia Gorge Nat'l Scenic Area
**Building:** 1904 Queen Anne Victorian
**Grounds:** Gardens, stream, pond
**Public Space:** Porch, parlors, DR, reading nook

**Food & Drink:** Afternoon/evening beverage & hors d'oeuvres; full breakfast
**Recreation:** Horseshoes; windsurfing, rafting, golf, skiing, antiquing, galleries
**Amenities & Services:** Guest fridge, handmade soaps; special events

### ACCOMMODATIONS

**Units:** 5 guest rooms
**All Rooms:** Claw-foot tub or access, robes
**Some Rooms:** Columbia River Gorge view, extra bed, private entrance, porch
**Bed & Bath:** Queen (3), twins, double & twin
**Favorites:** Master Guest Room, North Room

**Comfort & Decor:** Rooms are not overlarge; simply furnished and very clean. Abundant woodwork (both natural and painted) shows exceptional craftsmanship. Reading lamps, vent fans, tile baths. Hardwood floors with area rugs; comfortable furnishings.

## RATES, RESERVATIONS, & RESTRICTIONS

**Deposit:** 1st night
**Discounts:** Single occupancy, extended stays, midweek, whole house, off-season; $10 add'l person
**Credit Cards:** V, MC
**Check-in/Out:** 4–7 or by arrangement/11
**Smoking:** Outside only
**Pets:** No
**Kids:** Welcome
**No-Nos:** Quiet hours 10 p.m.–8 a.m.

**Minimum Stay:** 2 nights holidays
**Open:** All year
**Hosts:** Matthew, Michael, & Martha Koerner, owners;
Cindy Hunter, innkeeper
704 3rd Ave., P.O. Box 476
Mosier, OR 97040
(541) 478-3640
Fax: (541) 478-3640
innkeeper@mosierhouse.com
www.mosierhouse.com

## MT. HOOD HAMLET B&B, Mt. Hood

| Overall: ★★★★½ | Room Quality: B | Value: B | Price: $95–$125 |
|---|---|---|---|

Elegant, inviting home is the perfect combination of Colonial charm and modern comfort. While the handmade quilts and gleaming hardwood floors hearken to another era, the built-in comforts are totally 21st century. Paul and Diane are former schoolteachers, with great stories and good advice on local happenings, restaurants, etc. Close enough to Hood River for fine dining, yet halfway to the ski resorts and awesome hiking trails of southern Mt. Hood.

## SETTING & FACILITIES

**Location:** Just south of Mt. Hood Corner (jct. Hwy. 35 & road to Parkdale) on Hwy. 35
**Near:** Mt. Hood, Mt. Adams, Columbia River Gorge, Hood River, Parkdale, Timberline Lodge, Lost Lake, ski areas
**Building:** 1990s-built New England Colonial–style home
**Grounds:** Lawn & gardens on 9-acres

**Public Space:** GR, library, 2nd-floor sitting/phone area, patio
**Food & Drink:** Beverages; family-style full breakfast
**Recreation:** Antiquing, festivals, golf, mountain biking, hunting, fishing, kayaking
**Amenities & Services:** Hot tub, fireplace, fridge, laundry by arrangement

## ACCOMMODATIONS

**Units:** 3 guest rooms plus overflow
**All Rooms:** TV, VCR, Mt. Adams or
Mt. Hood view, top-quality fixtures
**Some Rooms:** Whirlpool, fireplace,
sitting area
**Bed & Bath:** Queen or king; private
ensuite baths

**Favorites:** Vista Ridge or Cloud Cap
**Comfort & Decor:** Country-
Colonial furnishings. Airy, open, well-lit
spaces, fine finish work. Great room is
glass-walled, with garden and Mt. Hood
views. Library is cozy. AC.

## RATES, RESERVATIONS, & RESTRICTIONS

**Deposit:** 1st night; 3-day cancellation
**Discounts:** Multiple rooms/nights, sin-
gle occupancy; $10 add'l person
**Credit Cards:** V, MC, AE, D
**Check-in/Out:** 4–7 or by arrange-
ment/11
**Smoking:** Outside only
**Pets:** By arrangement
**Kids:** Over 12 welcome; younger if
taking multiple rooms

**Minimum Stay:** 2 nights, 3-day weekends & New Year's
**Open:** All year (may close Thanksgiving week)
**Hosts:** Paul & Diane Romans
6741 Hwy. 35, Mt. Hood, OR 98041
(800) 407-0570 or (541) 352-3574
Fax: (541) 352-7685
hoodhamlet@gorge.net
www.mthoodhamlet.com

## MT. HOOD B&B, Parkdale

| Overall: ★★★½ | Room Quality: B | Value: C | Price: $85–$145 |
|---|---|---|---|

We absolutely adore this place, and so will you if you like fabulous food
(and plenty of it), animals, and the quiet charms of the country. Beautifully situated where the lush orchards of the Hood River Valley meet the
wooded foothills of Mt. Hood, Mike and Jackie's property is beautiful,
and their hospitality unsurpassed. Breakfast and snacks are homemade,
creative, and delicious, and Jackie is mindful of dietary requests and
restrictions.

## SETTING & FACILITIES

**Location:** 18 mi. south of Hood River
& 18 mi. NE of Mt. Hood Meadows ski
area, in the Hood River Valley
**Near:** Mt. Hood, Mt. Adams, Columbia
River Gorge, Parkdale, Timberline
Lodge, Lost Lake, ski areas
**Building:** Classic farmhouse,
outbuildings
**Grounds:** 42 acres; beautiful gardens,
barn, pastures, pond, waterfall, gazebo
**Public Space:** LR, DR, deck

**Food & Drink:** Afternoon refreshments; exceptional & bountiful full
breakfast
**Recreation:** Farm animal communing,
horseshoes, croquet; antiquing, festivals, hunting, kayaking
**Amenities & Services:** Videos,
indoor tennis/basketball court, pool
table, sauna, hot tub; weddings,
gatherings

## ACCOMMODATIONS

**Units:** 3 guest rooms, 1 suite
**All Rooms:** Country decor, TV, VCR
**Some Rooms:** Four-poster, spa tub, woodstove, kitchenette, feather beds
**Bed & Bath:** Queen (3), king & 3 twins; 2 private baths, 2 share a bath
**Favorites:** The Homestead, Mt. Hood Room

**Comfort & Decor:** Country farm-house decor. Three inside guest rooms are old-fashioned and cozy; detached Homestead cottage is a rustic, fort-like hideaway with the comforts of a private apt Very welcoming. Wood heat plus auxiliary central heat.

## RATES, RESERVATIONS, & RESTRICTIONS

**Deposit:** 1st night; 7-day cancellation
**Discounts:** Ski specials; $15 add'l person
**Credit Cards:** V, MC
**Check-in/Out:** After 3/11
**Smoking:** Outside only
**Pets:** No
**Kids:** Welcome
**Minimum Stay:** None

**Open:** All year
**Hosts:** Jackie & Mike Rice
8885 Cooper Spur Rd.
Parkdale, OR 97041
(800) 557-8885 or (541) 352-6885
Fax: (541) 352-6885 (call ahead)
mthoodbnb@gorge.net
www.mthoodbnb.com

## BROOKSIDE B&B, Sandy

| Overall: ★★ | Room Quality: D | Value: B | Price: $50–$65 |
|---|---|---|---|

The world needs bed-and-breakfasts like Brookside. This unpretentious home is a bed-and-breakfast in the European tradition—the Brooks simply share their home with you and make sure no one leaves the breakfast table hungry. Family-friendly, pet-tolerant, even smoker-accommodating (while most areas of the house are smoke-free, the breezeway smoking room is pleasant). The grounds are lots of fun, from the clownish critters to the deeply peaceful cedar-lined banks of the brook.

## SETTING & FACILITIES

**Location:** 3.5 mi. east of Sandy, just off Hwy. 26
**Near:** Midway between Portland metro & Mt. Hood
**Building:** 1948 2-level family home
**Grounds:** Hobby farm w/ gardens, critters (llamas, peacocks, pygmy goats, & more), cedar grove, brook
**Public Space:** Upstairs sitting area, kitchenette, breezeway/smoking area,

other TV/sitting areas, deck
**Food & Drink:** Kitchenette access makes beverage chilling & preparation easy; full breakfast
**Recreation:** All year alpine skiing at Mt. Hood, X-C skiing, Oregon Trail, rafting, Portland metro attractions
**Amenities & Services:** Hot tub, farm animals; excellent hiking advice

## ACCOMMODATIONS

**Units:** 5 guest rooms
**All Rooms:** Unpretentious, homey decor
**Some Rooms:** Sitting area
**Bed & Bath:** Double, queen, single, or king & daybed; I private bath, 4 share 2 baths
**Favorites:** Queen w/ private bath &

teddy bears; king w/ sitting area
**Comfort & Decor:** Simple and casual, rooms and common areas are decorated with well-worn but not shabby furnishings and family artifacts. Modest but comfortable; kitchenette and hosts' attitude encourage you to feel at home.

## RATES, RESERVATIONS, & RESTRICTIONS

**Deposit:** Ist night; 72-hour cancellation
**Discounts:** Extended stay, multiple rooms; $35 single room avail.; $5 add'l ages 12 & older
**Credit Cards:** Not accepted
**Check-in/Out:** Flexible/generally 11
**Smoking:** Breezeway room & outside only

**Pets:** Welcome
**Kids:** Welcome
**Minimum Stay:** None
**Open:** All year
**Hosts:** Barbara & Jack Brooks
45232 SE Paha Loop
Sandy, OR 97055
(503) 668-4766
www.ideal-web.com/brookside

## DOUBLEGATE INN B&B, Welches

| Overall: ★★★★ | Room Quality: B | Value: B | Price: $95–$125 |
|---|---|---|---|

We were instantly comfortable in this warm, welcoming home. Abundant common areas include the great room with its dual sitting areas and piano, and the cozy upstairs lounge with its games and leather furnishings. Guest rooms sport quality craftsmanship and themes artistically executed, never cloying. Thoughtful "extras" about—a bowl of pistachios, a literature rack, in-room romantic cassettes, bath salts. Commodious deck is a great place to listen to the sound of the river.

## SETTING & FACILITIES

**Location:** 1.5 mi. off Hwy. 26 from its stoplight intersection w/ Welches Rd.
**Near:** Salmon River, Zigzag, Rhododendron, Barlow Trail, Mt. Hood, Mt. Hood Wilderness, Salmon-Huckleberry Wilderness, Brightwood
**Building:** 1920s farmhouse, expanded/remodeled
**Grounds:** Front lawn w/ pond; side patio w/ flowers; backyard garden;

surrounded by cedars
**Public Space:** GR, DR, guest lounge, deck
**Food & Drink:** Snacks, popcorn, cold sodas, hot beverages; full breakfast
**Recreation:** Skiing, Oregon Trail, fishing, golf, rafting, bicycling
**Amenities & Services:** TV/VCR, fridge & micro., library, guitar & piano, games, iron, phone, sound system

## ACCOMMODATIONS

**Units:** 3 guest rooms
**All Rooms:** Jetted/soaking tub, quilts, robes
**Some Rooms:** Sitting area, canopy bed, dbl. tub, deck access, desk, daybed
**Bed & Bath:** Queen (1 w/ extra daybed); private baths
**Favorites:** Each is special

**Comfort & Decor:** Charming, cozy theme rooms. Bit O' Country: quilts, deck access. Victorian Suite: romantic, roses and lace. English Cottage Suite: largest, with pale tones, light florals, wood, leather, AC. Common areas are an artful mix of Northwest contemporary and relaxed country.

## RATES, RESERVATIONS, & RESTRICTIONS

**Deposit:** 50%; 7-day cancellation
**Discounts:** $15 add'l person
**Credit Cards:** V, MC, AE, D
**Check-in/Out:** 4–6/11
**Smoking:** Outside only
**Pets:** No
**Kids:** Over 14 welcome
**Minimum Stay:** 2 nights, weekends; 3 nights, holiday weekends

**Open:** All year
**Hosts:** Gary & Charlene Poston
26711 E. Welches Rd.
Welches, OR 97067
(503) 622-4859
Fax: (503) 622-4859
doublegate@mthoodlodging.com
www.mthoodlodging.com

## OLD WELCHES INN, Welches

| Overall: ★★★½ | Room Quality: B | Value: B | Price: $75–$110 |
|---|---|---|---|

Delicious gourmet breakfast served at an elegant table is a hallmark of Old Welches Inn. The breakfast room is bright and sunny, or enjoy patio dining when the weather permits. Guest rooms are smallish, but common areas, food, and amenities make up for it. Judi and Ted divide their time between Welches and Florida, so their Southern hospitality comes naturally.

## SETTING & FACILITIES

**Location:** 1 mi. off Hwy. 26 from its stoplight intersection w/ Welches Rd.
**Near:** Zigzag, Rhododendron, Barlow Trail, Mt. Hood, Mt. Hood Wilderness, Salmon-Huckleberry Wilderness, Brightwood
**Building:** 1890 historic home
**Grounds:** Large w/ patio seating & slope to banks of Salmon River

**Public Space:** LR, sunroom, patio, breakfast area
**Food & Drink:** Afternoon/evening refreshments, tea; full breakfast
**Recreation:** Hiking, skiing, Oregon Trail, fishing, golf, rafting, bicycling
**Amenities & Services:** TV/VCR, video library, books

## ACCOMMODATIONS

**Units:** 4 guest rooms (also ask about adjacent cottage)
**All Rooms:** Theme decor, period furnishings
**Some Rooms:** River view
**Bed & Bath:** Queen (2), double, or double & twin; 1 private bath, 3 share 2 baths
**Favorites:** Trillium, Forget-Me-Not

**Comfort & Decor:** Gracious decor. Elegant wallpapers, attractive ceiling treatments and moldings. Comfortable, not fussy. Trillium: "horse & hound" motif. Columbine: antique duck decoys and Salmon River view (distinctly Northwest). Sweet Briar: iron double bed, rose arbor theme.

## RATES, RESERVATIONS, & RESTRICTIONS

**Deposit:** Credit card; 7-day cancellation (24 days, holiday weekends)
**Discounts:** Extended stay
**Credit Cards:** V, MC, AE, D
**Check-in/Out:** 3–6/11
**Smoking:** Outside only
**Pets:** No; host dog on premises
**Kids:** 12 & over welcome
**Minimum Stay:** 2 nights, peak season & holiday weekends

**Open:** All year
**Hosts:** Judith & Ted Mondun
26401 E Welches Rd.
Welches, OR 97067
(503) 622-3754
Fax: (503) 622-5370
oldwelchesinn@bbdirectory.com
www.bbdirectory.com/inn/oldwelch-esinn/

## THE INN OF THE WHITE SALMON, White Salmon

Overall: ★★★★          Room Quality: B          Value: C          Price: $99–$129

An inn since 1937, this brick-faced European-style lodging has been a haven for Columbia Gorge, White Salmon River, and Mt. Adams-area vacationers for over six decades. The Holens, a well-connected couple with great information about the area, have run the inn since 1990. Their professional innkeeping staff are friendly and helpful. Breakfasts are bountiful and delicious, with abundant fruit, breads, and pastries, plus your choice of custom-made hot entree (nonguests may join you for $12.95). We've always been comfortable at this inn.

## SETTING & FACILITIES

**Location:** 1.5 mi. off Hwy. 14, across the Columbia River from Hood River, OR
**Near:** White Salmon (town & river), Bingen, Columbia Gorge Nat'l Scenic Area, Hood River (town & river), Columbia River
**Building:** 1937 brick-faced hotel
**Grounds:** Rear patio, wildflower gardens

**Public Space:** Foyer, LR, patio
**Food & Drink:** Beer & wine for purchase; lavish breakfast
**Recreation:** Windsurfing, golf, skiing, antiquing, galleries
**Amenities & Services:** Hot tub, books, games, sound system; discount ski lift tickets in season

## ACCOMMODATIONS

**Units:** 16 guest rooms (some suites)
**All Rooms:** Phone, TV
**Some Rooms:** Two rooms
**Bed & Bath:** Various; private baths
**Favorites:** Suites
**Comfort & Decor:** Common areas are richly evocative of days gone by: brocades, lace, gilt-framed photos. Guest rooms are comfortable and clean, though somewhat dark and on the small side (suites are roomier, and worth the extra tariff). Tasteful antiques. Individual heat/AC control.

## RATES, RESERVATIONS, & RESTRICTIONS

**Deposit:** Credit card; 72-hour cancellation
**Discounts:** Single occupancy, off-eason specials; $20 add'l person over 12; 1–12 years, $1 per year of age
**Credit Cards:** V, MC, AE, D
**Check-in/Out:** After 3/noon
**Smoking:** Outside only
**Pets:** Welcome
**Kids:** Welcome

**Minimum Stay:** None
**Open:** All year
**Hosts:** Roger & Janet Holen
172 W. Jewett, P. O. Box 1549
White Salmon, WA 98672
(800) 972-5226 (reservations only) or (509) 493-2335
innkeeper@gorge.net
www.gorge.net/lodging/iws

# Zone 15
# Central Oregon

If a Portlander *really* wants to relax, she leaves the Interstate 5 corridor entirely, passes the throngs at Mount Hood and the Columbia Gorge, and heads east to the area we're calling Central Oregon. Along the central and eastern slopes of Oregon's Cascade Mountains, the recreation-seeker finds skiing at Mount Bachelor; world-class rock climbing at Smith Rock; hiking at Mount Jefferson, Mount Washington, Three-Fingered Jack, and the Three Sisters; fly fishing in the Metolius River; white-water rafting on the Deschutes; challenging mountain biking, extensive golf courses, and just enough tourism infrastructure to ensure a good meal and a comfortable night's sleep.

The more developed areas of Bend and Sisters contain this zone's most sophisticated lodgings. Bend is the closest town to Mount Bachelor ski area, and is a retail hub for the center Highway 97 corridor. Nearby Sunriver is a vacation home development. Sisters has been developed with a Western theme. This smaller town is a bit more upscale, with galleries and boutique shopping. Both Sisters and Bend offer excellent access to and support for outdoor recreation, including hiking, mountain biking, rock climbing, fishing, and skiing.

A "bump in the road" south of Bend, La Pine offers access to the same recreation opportunities as Bend and Sisters, and it's adjacent to Newberry Crater National Volcanic Monument.

There's just one thing you need to know about Maupin—*river access.* On the Deschutes River, it's a prime location for fly-fishing and white-water rafting, as well as access to hunting.

The tiny, desert-bordered burg of Prineville sits where the mountains meet the desert. Near the towns of Redmond and Madras, it provides access to the Crooked River Gorge scenic area and the Ochoco Mountains recreation area.

Shaniko is another desert-meets-mountains town. Situated squarely on Highway 97, its claim to fame is a ghost town theme.

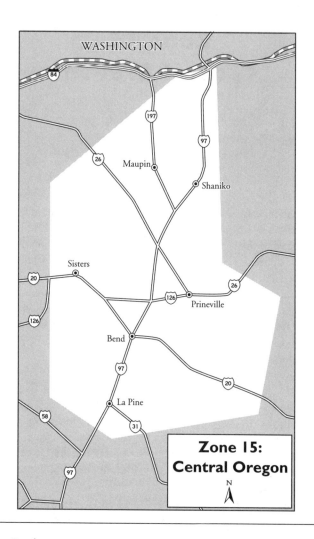

WASHINGTON

Zone 15:
Central Oregon

N

**Bend**
Juniper Acres, p. 407
Lara House, p. 408
Mill Inn, p. 409
The Sather House, p. 410

**LaPine**
DiamondStone Guest Lodge,
p. 411

**Maupin**
C&J Lodge, p. 412

**Prineville**
The Elliott House, p. 413

**Shaniko**
Shaniko Historic Hotel, p. 414

**Sisters**
Blue Spruce B&B, p. 415
Conklin's Guest House, p. 416
Rags to Walkers Guest Ranch,
p. 417
Squaw Creek B&B Inn, p. 419

## JUNIPER ACRES, Bend

| Overall: ★★★½ | Room Quality: B | Value: A | Price: $75 |
|---|---|---|---|

Fine built-as-a-B&B log home on an open juniper-forest parcel character-istic of eastern Oregon's high desert as it transitions to Cascade-Mountain foothills. Vern's craft as a builder shows in this handsome home. Glass-fronted A-frame design gives a vacation-home feel and affords nice views. Easy drive to either Sisters or Bend, and all the area activities of either community.

### SETTING & FACILITIES

**Location:** About 6 mi. NW of Bend, just off Hwy. 20
**Near:** Bend, Sisters, Cascade Mountains
**Building:** Contemporary log home
**Grounds:** 10 acres of open juniper forest in Cascade foothills
**Public Space:** Great room, DR, decks
**Food & Drink:** Beverages, fruit, & cookies; afternoon snacks; full breakfast
**Recreation:** Snowmobiling, golf, museums, fishing, rafting, rock climbing, antiquing, galleries, festivals
**Amenities & Services:** Woodstove, BBQ, guest phone (3 lines), guest fridge; massage by appt.

### ACCOMMODATIONS

**Units:** 2 guest rooms
**All Rooms:** TV, comfy furnishings, closet, fan
**Some Rooms:** Love seat
**Bed & Bath:** Queens; private baths
**Favorites:** Same
**Comfort & Decor:** Upscale contem-porary country—one is florals and country wreaths, the other is more masculine. Pine four-poster beds, plush carpet, excellent sound insulation. Fine log home craftsmanship. Central and woodstove heat; rooms have auxiliary units. Central AC.

### RATES, RESERVATIONS, & RESTRICTIONS

**Deposit:** 1st night
**Discounts:** Single occupancy; tax included; $10 add'l person
**Credit Cards:** Not accepted
**Check-in/Out:** Flexible
**Smoking:** Outside only
**Pets:** No
**Kids:** Welcome by arrangement
**Minimum Stay:** 2 nights, summer weekends & holidays
**Open:** All year
**Hosts:** Della & Vern Bjork
65220 Smokey Ridge Rd.
Bend, OR 97701
(541) 389-2193
Fax: same as phone
VERNDELLA@prodigy.com
www.moriah.com/juniper/

## LARA HOUSE, Bend

| Overall: ★★★★ | Room Quality: B | Value: B | Price: $75–$125 |
|---|---|---|---|

Bend's oldest bed-and-breakfast is still one of Bend's best. Ideally located across from Drake Park, it's within walking distance to everything. An immense home, its rooms are airier and more spacious than the nearby Sather House, with a more contemporary but less opulent feel. Period furnishings coexist with modern fabrics and motifs, resulting in a casual, open, clean-line look as compared to most properties of this vintage. The Summit suite is great fun, with its angled ceilings and dormered nooks.

### SETTING & FACILITIES

**Location:** Right across from Drake Park in Historic Walk district, on corner of Congress & Louisiana
**Near:** Deschutes River, downtown, Mt. Bachelor
**Building:** 5,000-sq.-ft. 1910 Craftsman
**Grounds:** Corner lot w/ deck, sitting areas
**Public Space:** Porch, LR, solarium, DR, deck

**Food & Drink:** Afternoon snack & beverages; full breakfast
**Recreation:** Skiing, golf, museums, rock climbing, antiquing, galleries, local festivals & cultural events
**Amenities & Services:** Fireplace, TV/VCR, videos, hot tub, games; celebration extras

### ACCOMMODATIONS

**Units:** 6 guest rooms
**All Rooms:** Sitting area
**Some Rooms:** Fridge, micro., view, claw-foot or whirlpool tub, writing desk, TV, private entrance
**Bed & Bath:** Queen or king, some w/ extra futon or fold-out single; private (5 of 6 ensuite) baths
**Favorites:** The Summit

**Comfort & Decor:** Charming and comfortable living room has hardwood floors, large brick fireplace, and Craftsman box-beamed ceilings. Guest rooms are spacious and carpeted, mixing period furnishings with modern window treatments; palette leans toward rose, green, burgundy, and white, but rooms vary.

### RATES, RESERVATIONS, & RESTRICTIONS

**Deposit:** Credit card; 14-day cancellation, $25 fee
**Discounts:** Single occupancy, extended stay, corporate, whole house; $15 add'l person
**Credit Cards:** V, MC, D
**Check-in/Out:** 4–6 or by arrangement/11
**Smoking:** Outside only
**Pets:** No; host pets on premises

**Kids:** Call
**Minimum Stay:** Some holidays
**Open:** All year
**Hosts:** Doug & Bobbye Boger, owners; on-premises innkeeper
640 NW Congress
Bend, OR 97701
(800) 766-4064 or (541) 388-4064
Fax: (541) 388-4064
www.moriah.com/larahouse

## MILL INN, Bend

| Overall: ★★½ | Room Quality: D | Value: A | Price: $40–$70 |
|---|---|---|---|

This simple, historic building began its life as a millworker boarding house, and had been a number of things before Ev and Carol bought and refurbished it as a bed-and-breakfast in 1990. Spic-and-span and family friendly, plus great for outdoor-oriented folks. For a real bargain, the Locker Room is a four-bunk shared room that provides a bunk and full breakfast for just $15! Some rooms adjoin and can be configured into a two-room suite with semiprivate bath. An excellent value.

### SETTING & FACILITIES

**Location:** Corner of Colorado & Bond
**Near:** Downtown Bend, Mt. Bachelor
**Building:** 1800s millworkers' boarding house
**Grounds:** Enclosed deck area; none per se
**Public Space:** LR, DR, basement storage area
**Food & Drink:** Coffee, teas, cocoa; full breakfast

**Recreation:** Snowmobiling, golf, museums, fishing, rafting, rock climbing, antiquing, galleries, local festivals & cultural events
**Amenities & Services:** TV/VCR, videos, outdoor spa, games, washer/dryer, fridge, ski wax area, ski/bike storage, woodstove, guest phone, gas log fireplace, data port

### ACCOMMODATIONS

**Units:** 10 guest rooms
**All Rooms:** Carpet
**Some Rooms:** Closet, theme decor
**Bed & Bath:** Various (twin, double, queen, king); 5 w/ private or semi-private baths, maximum of 5 rooms sharing 2 sex-segregated baths

**Favorites:** Silver Thaw best, Timber or Cascade next
**Comfort & Decor:** Fresh, clean vinyls and newer, midquality linens and low carpet. Very, very clean; nicely updated. Smallish rooms. Motel-meets-homestyle comfort. Lots of bright white Formica.

### RATES, RESERVATIONS, & RESTRICTIONS

**Deposit:** Credit card; 24-hour cancellation, 2 weeks for holidays
**Discounts:** Single occupancy, groups; $5 add'l person
**Credit Cards:** V, MC
**Check-in/Out:** Flexible/noon
**Smoking:** Outside only
**Pets:** No

**Kids:** Welcome (crib avail.)
**Minimum Stay:** None
**Open:** All year
**Hosts:** Ev & Carol Stiles, owners; on-premises innkeeper
642 NW Colorado
Bend, OR 97701
(541) 389-9198

## THE SATHER HOUSE, Bend

| Overall: ★★★★ | Room Quality: B | Value: B | Price: $80–$115 |
|---|---|---|---|

Some people are natural-born hostesses. Robbie Giamboi's flair is evident in every aspect of this lovely home—from the beautiful decor in every room (elegant without being cluttered or fussy) to the creative and delicious breakfasts. Room themes include Victorian (pink and blue, with quilt and romantic claw-foot tub), English (masculine with faux marble wall treatment, paisley bedding, and tones of forest, dark blue, and burgundy), Country (a delight in sea green and slate blue, with cozy quilt), and Garden (larger, with green iron king bed, mint carpet, green and ivory decor with floral accents). Super-convenient location means a bit of traffic noise, but walking-distance access to all Bend has to offer.

### SETTING & FACILITIES

**Location:** Corner Broadway & Tumalo in the Heritage Walk district
**Near:** Deschutes River, Drake Park, downtown, Mt. Bachelor
**Building:** 1911 Craftsman
**Grounds:** Corner lot in historic neighborhood; flowered berm, border plantings
**Public Space:** LR, parlor, 2nd-floor sitting area, porch

**Food & Drink:** Afternoon tea; early coffee; full breakfast (early extended cont'l option)
**Recreation:** Skiing, golf, museums, rock climbing, festivals & cultural events
**Amenities & Services:** TV/VCR, games, library, fireplace, phone, data port, fridge; formal teas for 8–20; catering

### ACCOMMODATIONS

**Units:** 4 guest rooms
**All Rooms:** Bathtubs, closet or armoire
**Some Rooms:** Claw-foot tub, TV, sofa, desk or table, robes
**Bed & Bath:** Queen, king, or twin/king conversion (roll-away avail.); private baths
**Favorites:** Garden

**Comfort & Decor:** Elegant wallpapers, fine furnishings, lace window treatments, distinctive light fixtures. While overall common area style is Victorian, original touches make every space special. Guest rooms feature beautifully executed themes (see above). Quality bedding and appointments.

### RATES, RESERVATIONS, & RESTRICTIONS

**Deposit:** Credit card; 1-week cancellation (2 weeks, holidays)
**Discounts:** Single occupancy, winter specials, corporate, extended corporate stay; $10 add'l person
**Credit Cards:** V, MC, D
**Check-in/Out:** 4–6 or by arrangement/11
**Smoking:** No

**Pets:** No
**Kids:** 12 & older welcome
**Minimum Stay:** Holidays only
**Open:** All year
**Hosts:** Robbie Giamboi
7 NW Tumalo Ave., Bend, OR 97701
(888) 388-1065 or (541) 388-1065
Fax: (541) 330-0591
www.moriah.com/sather/

## DIAMONDSTONE GUEST LODGE, LaPine

| Overall: ★★★★½ | Room Quality: B | Value: B | Price: $80–$120 |

Upscale lodge and Western art gallery has unique high-desert flair. Very private and intimate, ideally suited for whole-house rental by one party. When one party has entire property, guests have full kitchen use; otherwise, microwave, refrigerator, and other "kitchenette" style facilities are shared. Upstairs is a king suite. Downstairs are two queen bedrooms with a bath between—these rent for $80 separately (as a single room with private bath), or $135 as a 2-room, semi-private-bath suite. With overflow areas (ask about new cabin), property sleeps up to 11.

### SETTING & FACILITIES

**Location:** 25 mi. south of Bend, 8 mi. north of LaPine; about 2 mi. off Hwy. 97
**Near:** Quail Run Golf Course, Little Deschutes River, LaPine S.P., LaPine, Sunriver, Bend, Mt. Bachelor, Newberry Crater Nat'l Volcanic Monument, lakes
**Building:** Custom western lodge-style home
**Grounds:** 5 acres high desert at Cascade foothills, w/ paths, swimming pond, sitting areas, lots of privacy

**Public Space:** LR, DR, decks, kitchen/kitchenette
**Food & Drink:** Beverages; snacks; full breakfast
**Recreation:** Golf, hiking, skiing, snowmobiling
**Amenities & Services:** Hot tub, sauna, sound system, woodstove, videos, books, kitchen access (full or limited), gift shop, art gallery, bicycles (on-site use); small weddings, gatherings, BBQs & catered meals

### ACCOMMODATIONS

**Units:** 2 suites w/ overflow potential
**All Rooms:** TV/VCR, cable & premium channels, phone, custom furnishings
**Some Rooms:** Coffee/tea service, private sitting area, table & chairs, bay window
**Bed & Bath:** King (plus sofabed) or queen, roll-away avail.; private baths

**Favorites:** Upstairs king suite (actually best to rent whole house)
**Comfort & Decor:** Upscale, contemporary Western. Native American prints, clean lines. Pale tones with wood, sage- and slate-colored accents. Quality original artwork on display and for sale.

## RATES, RESERVATIONS, & RESTRICTIONS

**Deposit:** $50 nonrefundable deposit for 1 night; 1 night's nonrefundable deposit for multinight; 2 nights' nonrefundable deposit for stays of a week or more
**Discounts:** Single occupancy, extended stay, off-season; $15 add'l person
**Credit Cards:** V, MC, AE, D
**Check-in/Out:** 4/11 or by arrangement
**Smoking:** Outside only

**Pets:** Welcome (including horses), $20 fee; host pets on site outside
**Kids:** Welcome
**Minimum Stay:** 2 nights, some holidays
**Open:** All year
**Hosts:** Doug & Gloria Watt
16693 Sprague Loop
LaPine, OR 97739
(800) 600-6232 or (541) 536-6232
Fax: (541) 536-9711
dougwmul@aol.com
www.diamondstone.com

## C&J LODGE, Maupin

| Overall: ★★★ | Room Quality: C | Value: C | Price: $65–$115 |
|---|---|---|---|

Great hosts and the premiere white-water rafting location make this a unique choice. Rooms are charming and comfortable at this well-loved work-in-progress, open since 1989. Note the quilts in each room, custom made by local quilting guild for Carrol and Judy's room themes. Breakfasts are simple and healthy, with an emphasis on scratch cooking and organic, locally grown items. Summertime dinners are a special treat, and the rafting trips are some of the Northwest's best.

## SETTING & FACILITIES

**Location:** On the banks of the Deschutes River, just south of Hwy. 197 bridge
**Near:** Maupin, Shaniko, The Dalles, Mt. Hood area
**Building:** Motel-like space constructed by joining and heavily remodeling a house, beauty shop, and garage
**Grounds:** 250 feet of Deschutes River frontage w/ large lawn, picnic areas, patio
**Public Space:** Spacious "Juniper Room" dining & common area

**Food & Drink:** Coffee & tea; full breakfast, early cont'l option; lunch buffet for river rafters; dinners avail. March–Nov. (7 days peak season, weekends shoulder season)
**Recreation:** White-water rafting, fly-fishing, hunting, rockhounding, horseback riding, croquet
**Amenities & Services:** TV/VCR, games, sound system, phone; late-check-out shower/freshen-up facil.; flip chart, overhead projector; guided rafting service; meetings, retreats, weddings, banquets, parties

## ACCOMMODATIONS

**Units:** 11 guest rooms
**All Rooms:** Theme decor/artifacts, local history book, bathtub, private entrance
**Some Rooms:** Jetted tub, river view
**Bed & Bath:** Queens & kings, plus 1 w/ extra twin beds; private baths
**Favorites:** Shearars (bridal suite), Duck; great themes: Railroad, Fishing

**Comfort & Decor:** Common area has peeled-log beams, local artwork, lots of tables, all in contemporary blonde wood. Rooms sport down-home comfort and theme decor. Comfortable, clean, and carefully (though not lavishly) updated. Individual heaters and AC units.

## RATES, RESERVATIONS, & RESTRICTIONS

**Deposit:** 1st night; 3-day cancellation
**Discounts:** Single occupancy, winter specials; $15 add'l teen/adult, $5 ages 6–12, free 5 & under; family rates
**Credit Cards:** V, MC, AE
**Check-in/Out:** After 2/11
**Smoking:** Outside only
**Pets:** No
**Kids:** Welcome
**No-Nos:** TV during dinner, noise after 10, fishing cleats on stairs

**Minimum Stay:** 2 nights holidays
**Open:** All year
**Hosts:** Judy & Carrol White
304 Bakeoven Rd., P.O. Box 130
Maupin, OR 97037
(800) 395-3903 or (541) 395-2404
Fax: (541) 395-2494
cnjlodge@ptinet.net
www.deschutesriver.com

## THE ELLIOTT HOUSE, Prineville

| Overall: ★★★ | Room Quality: D | Value: B | Price: $70 |
| --- | --- | --- | --- |

Relaxed, cordial hosts obviously have a lot of fun with this place. It's not spit-and-polish, but rather lovingly thick with period artifacts, including a 1916 Wurlitzer player piano and a 1906 Edison phonograph (one or the other often provides background music for the china-and-candlelight, made-from-scratch breakfasts). The historic home is purported to be central Oregon's only Queen Anne Victorian. Great flexibility for small group get-togethers—overflow sleeping areas available.

## SETTING & FACILITIES

**Location:** Corner of Claypool & W First
**Near:** Meadow Lakes Golf Course, Crooked River Gorge, Ochoco Mountains, Redmond, Madras
**Building:** 1908 National Historic Register Queen Anne Victorian
**Grounds:** Corner lot w/ hedge, fence, grass
**Public Space:** LR, parlor, DR, porch, "attic hideaway" TV room
**Food & Drink:** Afternoon refreshments; full breakfast
**Recreation:** Golf, rockhounding, waterskiing, swimming, rock climbing, antiquing
**Amenities & Services:** Claw-foot tub, TV, VCR, guest fridge, bicycles, golf clubs; special events & small group gatherings

## ACCOMMODATIONS

**Units:** 2 guest rooms (1 party at a
time)
**All Rooms:** Antiques
**Some Rooms:** Closet
**Bed & Bath:** King or double; private
baths (or semiprivate if both rooms
rented by same party; bath never
shared by 2 parties)
**Favorites:** Cabbage Rose for

antiques, Crab Apple for king bed
**Comfort & Decor:** Rooms are small.
Cabbage Rose (on cooler side of
house) has tall, iron double bed. Crab
Apple (on warmer side) is a bit more
contemporary. Home is chockablock
with very special antiques. Floral and
patterned wallpapers; rich woodwork.
Genteel worn-and-comfy.

## RATES, RESERVATIONS, & RESTRICTIONS

**Deposit:** Call
**Discounts:** None
**Credit Cards:** Not accepted
**Check-in/Out:** Flexible
**Smoking:** Kitchen or outside only
**Pets:** No; sweet dogs & kitties on
premises
**Kids:** 12 & older welcome

**Minimum Stay:** None
**Open:** All year
**Hosts:** Andy & Betty Wiechert
305 W First St.
Prineville, OR 97754
(541) 416-0423
Andybet@ibm.net
www.empnet.com/elliotthouse

## SHANIKO HISTORIC HOTEL, Shaniko

| Overall: ★★½ | Room Quality: D | Value: B | Price: $66–$96 |
| --- | --- | --- | --- |

The ghost town of Shaniko has long been a Highway 97 roadside curios-
ity. The historic hotel and a few buildings (ice cream shop, museum,
wedding chapel, curio and antique shops) have been restored for
tourists, making the place a fun stop, especially late spring to early fall,
when more things are open. The hotel and nearby RV park (same owners) are up for sale but will likely remain available. Rooms are a super
value, especially for families—all but the Bridal Suite are $66 double
occupancy.

## SETTING & FACILITIES

**Location:** Smack dab in the middle of
Shaniko on Hwy. 97
**Near:** Shaniko "ghost town" attrac-
tions, John Day Fossil Beds
**Building:** Circa 1900 2-story brick
hotel
**Grounds:** None per se—boardwalk
porch
**Public Space:** Parlor/lobby, mezza-
nine sitting area

**Food & Drink:** Cafe on premises,
ice cream parlor next door; room
includes choice of simple breakfast
at cafe
**Recreation:** Historic touring,
museum, bicycling, rockhounding,
rock climbing
**Amenities & Services:** TV/VCR in
lobby, gift shop, in-room area activities
guide; reunions, groups

## ACCOMMODATIONS

**Units:** 18 guest rooms
**All Rooms:** Carpet, bathtub (all but 1), fan
**Some Rooms:** Dbl. whirlpool spa, senior-accessible main floor
**Bed & Bath:** 13 queens (1 w/ extra twin), 5 doubles; private ensuite baths
**Favorites:** Bridal Suite

**Comfort & Decor:** Lobby is spacious and welcoming. Rooms are small and very clean. Midquality, mixed furnishings. Individually controlled baseboard heat. One ground-level room (just one step) works well for mobility-impaired guests (other 17 are upstairs).

## RATES, RESERVATIONS, & RESTRICTIONS

**Deposit:** Credit card; 3-day cancellation
**Discounts:** Single occupancy, groups; $10 add'l person; kids free in sleeping bags; 12 & under get free breakfast
**Credit Cards:** V, MC, D
**Check-in/Out:** After 2/11 (flexible)
**Smoking:** Outside only
**Pets:** No

**Kids:** Welcome most rooms
**Minimum Stay:** None
**Open:** All year
**Hosts:** Jean & Dorothy Farrell, owners; Cherry Brown, manager
Shaniko, OR 97057
(800) 483-3441 or (541) 489-3441
Fax: (541) 489-3441 (call first)

## BLUE SPRUCE B&B, Sisters

| Overall: ★★★★½ | Room Quality: A | Value: B | Price: $125 |

While venerable Conklin's is a well-honed work of art, with seasoned hosts and outstanding view, and Rags to Walkers is in a class by itself, with its genteel ranch setting, you can't beat the size and comfort of the spacious, well-equipped rooms at the brand-new Blue Spruce. Its access to town is best of any Sisters bed-and-breakfast, and Vaunell and Bob, while new hosts, have done their homework on classy amenities. Add quality craftsmanship and ample privacy, and even first-time bed-and-breakfast-goers will be comfortable here. Great food, too. Scores high in every respect.

## SETTING & FACILITIES

**Location:** 4 blocks south of Cascade (main street) at east end of town
**Near:** Downtown Sisters (closest B&B to town), Bend, Redmond, Cascade Mountains
**Building:** New contemporary Northwest B&B
**Grounds:** Front yard & parklike backyard
**Public Space:** Great room, front porch

**Food & Drink:** Arrival & evening treats; in-room chilled water & sodas, candy; full breakfast
**Recreation:** Museums, fishing, rafting, rock climbing, antiquing, galleries, festivals
**Amenities & Services:** Fireplace, entertainment center, game table, player piano, bicycles, backpacks, picnic baskets

## ACCOMMODATIONS

**Units:** 4 guest rooms
**All Rooms:** Gas fireplace, sitting area, TV/VCR, mini-fridge, spa tub, robes, towel heater, custom quilts
**Some Rooms:** Futon couch; custom lodgepole, juniper, or iron bed
**Bed & Bath:** Kings (2 w/ futon couches); private baths
**Favorites:** Equal, differing in decor only

**Comfort & Decor:** Extra-large guest rooms, each with an upscale "rustic" theme. Artfully chosen antiques, custom wood- and metal-crafted items— cross-cut saw and genuine tree in forest/logger room; antique trophies in hunting room; creels and custom artwork in fishing room; horseshoe bed and stagecoach artifacts in Western room. Central heat/AC.

## RATES, RESERVATIONS, & RESTRICTIONS

**Deposit:** 1st night; 30-day cancellation
**Discounts:** Off-season
**Credit Cards:** V, MC, D
**Check-in/Out:** 4/11
**Smoking:** Outside only
**Pets:** No; boarding nearby
**Kids:** By arrangement (official occupancy 2 per room max.)

**Minimum Stay:** None
**Open:** All year
**Hosts:** Vaunell & Bob Temple
444 S. Spruce St., Sisters, OR 97759
(541) 549-9644
Fax: (541) 549-4440
vbtemple@outlawnet.com
www.bluespruceband.com

## CONKLIN'S GUEST HOUSE, Sisters

| Overall: ★★★★½ | Room Quality: B | Value: B | Price: $90–$140 |
|---|---|---|---|

This gracious home in a sublime location is everything a bed-and-breakfast experience should be. It has a bit of history; rooms are deluxe and comfortable, most with private sitting areas (they're mini-suites, really); common areas are upscale and attractive; grounds are extraordinarily beautiful (that view!); hosts are friendly but never intrusive. Having a queen plus at least one single bed in each room provides nice flexibility.

## SETTING & FACILITIES

**Location:** Half a mile off Hwy. 20 at the east end of Sisters
**Near:** Sisters airport, Redmond, Bend, Cascade Mountains
**Building:** Turn-of-the-20th-century schoolhouse, extensively remodeled & expanded to farmhouse
**Grounds:** Fenced lawns, wildflower berm, trout ponds, pool, gazebo, view of Three Sisters mountains
**Public Space:** LR, dining/sun room
**Food & Drink:** Afternoon refreshments; coffee/tea/beverages; full breakfast
**Recreation:** On-site catch-and-release trout fishing, museums, rafting, rock climbing, antiquing, galleries, festivals
**Amenities & Services:** Coffee/tea bar, baby grand piano, fireplace, sound system, heated pool; groups, reunions, parties, weddings; limousine service; massage therapy by appt.

## ACCOMMODATIONS

**Units:** 5 guest rooms
**All Rooms:** 2 or more beds, designer decor
**Some Rooms:** Claw-foot tub (plus shower), disabled access, sitting area, skylight, view, fireplace, deck
**Bed & Bath:** Queen plus single, queen plus 2 singles (1); private ensuite baths

**Favorites:** Morning Glory
**Comfort & Decor:** Living room is elegantly appointed in deep, rich tones. Sunroom is a delightful breakfast or reading spot. Guest rooms are cheerfully decorated in designer fabrics, floral motifs, and decorator palettes. Well-appointed baths with quality fixtures.

## RATES, RESERVATIONS, & RESTRICTIONS

**Deposit:** Only for special events; 36-hour cancellation
**Discounts:** Single occupancy, extended winter stays; $20 add'l person
**Credit Cards:** Not accepted
**Check-in/Out:** After 2/noon
**Smoking:** Outside only
**Pets:** Permitted outside on leash
**Kids:** Over 12 welcome

**Minimum Stay:** Local festival weekends only
**Open:** All year
**Hosts:** Frank & Marie Conklin
69013 Camp Polk Rd.
Sisters, OR 97759
(800) 549-4262 or (541) 549-0123
Fax: (541) 549-0123
www.conklinsguesthouse.com

## RAGS TO WALKERS GUEST RANCH, Sisters

| Overall: ★★★★½ | Room Quality: B | Value: B | Price: $95–$150 |
| --- | --- | --- | --- |

Bonnie and Neal have been sharing their gracious home with guests since 1996. From a background in the clothing trade to their Tennessee Walker ranch comes the name, Rags to Walkers. Whether you ride or not (and they have many programs for beginning to experienced riders), this property won't fail to impress. The grounds alone make you feel like you've stepped onto the set of *Dallas*. Your hosts are warm, relaxed, and alternative-lifestyle friendly. The property is a winner—beautiful inside and out, with spacious rooms and common areas.

## SETTING & FACILITIES

**Location:** Just off Cloverdale, a road connecting Hwy. 20 & Hwy. 126 3.5 mi. east of Sisters

**Near:** Aspen Lakes Golf Course, Sisters, Bend, Redmond, Cascade Mountains

**Building:** Contemporary open-plan farmhouse w/ Arts & Crafts aspects

**Grounds:** 100-acre Tennessee Walker ranch; ponds, waterfalls, 2.5 mi. of paved paths amongst white-fenced pastures surrounded by Ponderosa pine

**Public Space:** LR, DR, game room, decks, porch

**Food & Drink:** In-room cookies; early coffee; full breakfast

**Recreation:** On-site in-line skating, fly-fishing; nearby skiing, golf, rafting, rock climbing, festivals

**Amenities & Services:** Videos, exercise equipment, pool table, piano, hot tub, river rock fireplace, bicycles, golf carts, trout pond, wet bar; full equestrian center (trail rides, lessons, weekly horse leases), horse boarding; catered meals, corporate retreats, weddings

## ACCOMMODATIONS

**Units:** 4 suites (also luxury 7-BR, 7-bath vacation rental home)

**All Rooms:** TV/VCR, robes, feather bed mattress topper, closet, quality linens & furnishings

**Some Rooms:** Gas fireplace, clawfoot or dbl. soaker tub, window seat, playroom/kid BR, private deck, view

**Bed & Bath:** King or queen; private baths

**Favorites:** #1, #5 (#2–3 is great value for 4 persons)

**Comfort & Decor:** Traditional styling, contemporary colors, and upscale country comfort. Pillowy Native American–print sofas face an ebony baby grand and a river-rock fireplace under a soaring 2.5-story ceiling in the great room. Guest rooms are decorated with soft hues and bold accents. Tile baths, pale carpet, fine finish work, good mattresses.

## RATES, RESERVATIONS, & RESTRICTIONS

**Deposit:** 25% nonrefundable (can apply to future booking); 30-day cancellation

**Discounts:** Winter specials, 7th night free

**Credit Cards:** V, MC

**Check-in/Out:** 3/noon

**Smoking:** Outside only

**Pets:** No (state-of-the-art dog & cat kennel nearby); host dog & cat outside

**Kids:** Welcome

**Minimum Stay:** Local festivals

**Open:** All year

**Hosts:** Bonnie & Neal Halousek
17045 Farthing Ln.
Sisters, OR 97759
(800) 422-5622 or (541) 548-7000
Fax: (541) 923-5107
rags@bendnet.com
www.bendnet.com/rags

## SQUAW CREEK B&B INN, Sisters

| Overall: ★★★ | Room Quality: C | Value: B | Price: $80–$90 |
| --- | --- | --- | --- |

Welcoming and unpretentious, this bed-and-breakfast makes you feel like family. The property is typical eastern Cascade slope: Ponderosa pine and aspen with an open understory. Squaw Creek runs through it, and deer frequent the feeders. Spacious deck, relaxed but hardworking hostess, and super flexibility for your special group or event.

### SETTING & FACILITIES

**Location:** 1.5 mi. east of Sisters, just off Hwy. 126
**Near:** Sisters, Redmond, Bend, Cascade Mountains
**Building:** 2-level contemporary home
**Grounds:** 8.5 natural wooded acres
**Public Space:** LR, DR, deck
**Food & Drink:** In-room coffee service; full breakfast
**Recreation:** Skiing, golf, museums, rafting, rock climbing, antiquing, festivals
**Amenities & Services:** Hot tub, fireplace, pole barn for snowmobile, etc., storage; flexible for groups, including RV hook-ups; BBQ dinners and other services by arrangement

### ACCOMMODATIONS

**Units:** 4 guest rooms
**All Rooms:** Private entrance, satellite TV, VCR, coffee service, robes
**Some Rooms:** Fireplace
**Bed & Bath:** King (plus queen futon), queen, or twins (roll-away avail.); private baths
**Favorites:** Fit for a King, Fireside
**Comfort & Decor:** Sun-dried sheets and casual, contemporary country decor. Living room has a big lava rock fireplace. Furnishings are modest, comfortable, fairly new. Room theme decor includes seashore (Grandma's Beach House), rustic barnwood (The Twins), or simple country (Fit for a King, Fireside).

### RATES, RESERVATIONS, & RESTRICTIONS

**Deposit:** 25%; 72-hour cancellation
**Discounts:** Various (call); $10 add'l person
**Credit Cards:** V, MC
**Check-in/Out:** Call
**Smoking:** Outside only
**Pets:** Welcome w/ preapproval & deposit
**Kids:** Welcome
**Minimum Stay:** 2 nights, local festivals & holidays
**Open:** All year
**Hosts:** Susie & Keith Johnson
P.O. Box 1993, 68733 Junapine Ln.
Sisters, OR 97759
(800) 930-0055 or (541) 549-4312
Fax: same as phone
squawcreek@sisterslodging.com or
squawcreek@moriah.com
www.sisterslodging.com

# Zone 16
# Eastern Oregon

The Wild West is alive and well in eastern Oregon. This region is home to vast, wide-open spaces, cattle and bison ranches, nature preserves on a colossal scale, and roads that stretch for 100 miles between towns. Here, you'll find fossil beds, forests, sagebrush plains, wild rivers, and Oregon Trail history.

In the northeast corner of the state, the Wallowa-Whitman National Forest, Eagle Cap Wilderness, and Hells Canyon Recreation Area offer superb hiking and other outdoor recreation. Lodgings are profiled in Joseph and Halfway; services are also available in Enterprise and Wallowa. The region's only major highway, Interstate 84, passes through Pendleton, La Grande, Baker City, and Vale on its way between Portland and Boise, Idaho. Pendleton is home of the world-famous Pendleton Round-Up rodeo, held each September, as well as the Pendleton Woolen Mills and a preserved underground city (tours available).

Eastern Oregon University is located in La Grande, giving this little town the flavor of a college community amidst its frontier surroundings. Just down the Interstate, Baker City is a history buff's paradise. Home of the excellent Oregon Trail Interpretive Center and the Oregon Trail Regional Museum, the town is chockful of historic buildings and markers. Scenic driving into nearby hills leads to mining and ghost towns.

Toward the east edge of the state is Vale (also known as Vale-on-the-Trail), just before I-84 passes into Idaho. Its downtown is adorned with murals commemorating its Oregon Trail heritage, and historic Trail sites are nearby (complete with authentic, preserved wagon wheel ruts). Water recreation is found at Bully Creek Reservoir and Lake Owyhee, and a short drive takes you to Nyssa, "Thunderegg Capital of the World." For the uninitiated, a thunderegg is a geode: a plain-looking, egg-shaped rock with sparkling crystals inside.

John Day occupies the crossroads of Highways 26 and 395, along the John Day River in Malheur National Forest. Nearby Prairie City is a quiet, outdoor recreation–oriented community at the edge of Strawberry Mountain Wilderness. Both towns are near the John Day Fossil Beds National Monument, a fascinating series of in-situ fossil-viewing sites and interpretive centers.

Smack-dab in the middle of the wide-open expanses of eastern Oregon, the town of Burns is another crossroads, an oasis among thousands of acres of cattle country. Here, Highways 20, 395, 78, and 205 meet, and weary travelers can find rest and a meal.

South of Burns, the Frenchglen and Diamond areas are the most remote and isolated in this guide. Visitors can bird-watch at the Malheur Wildlife Refuge, enjoy scenic driving through the Steens Mountain Wilderness, explore Diamond Craters Outstanding Natural Area, or commune with wildlife at Hart Mountain National Antelope Refuge.

Lodgings in eastern Oregon tend to be a little rough around the edges (notable exceptions being the polished Parker House in Pendleton and Sage Country Inn in Burns), but the hospitality is genuine. Don't underestimate the distances, and make sure there's plenty of gas in the tank when you head into this frontier.

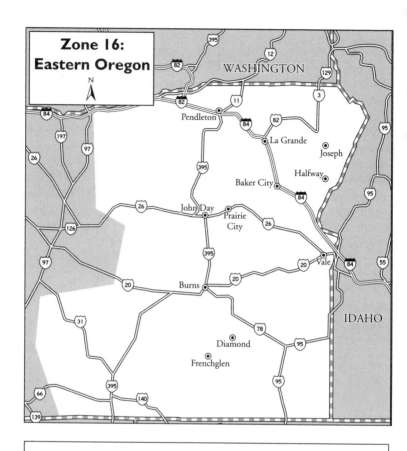

## Zone 16: Eastern Oregon

N

WASHINGTON

Pendleton

La Grande

Joseph

Halfway

Baker City

John Day

Prairie City

Burns

Vale

IDAHO

Diamond

Frenchglen

**Baker City**
Baer House B&B, p. 423
Grant House, p. 424

**Burns**
Sage Country Inn, p. 425

**Diamond**
Hotel Diamond, p. 426

**Frenchglen**
Frenchglen Hotel, p. 427
Steens Mountain Inn, p. 428

**Halfway**
Clear Creek Farm B&B, p. 429

**John Day**
Sonshine B&B, p. 430

**Joseph**
Chandler's Bed, Bread, & Trail
  Inn, p. 431

**La Grande**
Stang Manor Inn, p. 432

**Pendleton**
The Parker House B&B, p. 434

**Prairie City**
Riverside School House, p. 435
Strawberry Mountain Inn, p. 436

**Vale**
1900 Sears & Roebuck Home,
  p. 437

## BAER HOUSE B&B, Baker City

| Overall: ★★★½ | Room Quality: C | Value: A | Price: $65–$80 |
|---|---|---|---|

The Greears completely restored (read: gutted!) this historic home as a labor of love and testament to their Christian faith over a 2.5-year period, finishing in 1998. The dual-turreted, powder-blue-and-white home pops majestically out on historic Main Street just south of Campbell. Rooms are welcoming, cheerful, and relaxing, with just a bit of traffic noise (c'mon, how busy can Baker's Main Street be?). It's easy to feel at home with these gracious hosts. Soaring 12-foot ceilings, original woodwork, and tea rose carpet maintain the historic ambiance, while all wiring, plumbing, and finish work is new.

### SETTING & FACILITIES

**Location:** Corner Madison & Main on north edge of historic downtown
**Near:** Oregon Trail Interpretive Center & Regional Museum, mining & ghost towns, Hells Canyon, Snake River, Anthony Lakes ski resort, Blue Mountains, Wallowa-Whitman Nat'l Forest, Eagle Cap Wilderness
**Building:** 1882 National Historic Register Italianate Victorian
**Grounds:** Grassy corner lot in Historic District
**Public Space:** Parlor, kitchenette, DR

**Food & Drink:** Self-serve beverages; full breakfast
**Recreation:** Museums, antiquing, skiing, hiking, fishing, golf, local festivals, scenic driving
**Amenities & Services:** Antique heirloom piano, kitchenette (fridge, micro., coffeemaker, sink), laundry facil., guest phone, TV, library, games; small conferences, reunions, & gatherings; breakfast for nonguests $7.50 by arrangement

### ACCOMMODATIONS

**Units:** 3 guest rooms (1 can expand to 2-BR suite)
**All Rooms:** Data port, guest guide, robes, "I forgot it" basket, claw-foot tub (private or shared)
**Some Rooms:** Bay window, four-poster, carpet, decorative fireplace
**Bed & Bath:** Queens (suite's 2nd room is double); 1 private detached bath, 2 share a bath

**Favorites:** Anthony
**Comfort & Decor:** Rooms named for nearby historic towns. Pondosa, with its southern exposure, is a good winter, spring, or fall room. Flagstaff is cooler and more masculine. Anthony is the most spacious, bright, and sunny room, overlooking Main. Baths freshly remodeled, large and super-clean. Central heat, window fans, hall ceiling fan.

## RATES, RESERVATIONS, & RESTRICTIONS

**Deposit:** $35; 48-hour cancellation
**Discounts:** Single occupancy, corporate, government, extended stay, group; 2-BR suite, $120
**Credit Cards:** V, MC, AE, D
**Check-in/Out:** 4–10/11
**Smoking:** Outside only
**Pets:** No

**Kids:** 12 & older welcome (unless taking whole house)
**Minimum Stay:** None
**Open:** All year
**Hosts:** Nick & Judy Greear
2333 Main St., Baker City, OR 97814
(541) 524-1812
baerhouse@triax.com
www.triax.com/baerhouse

## GRANT HOUSE, Baker City

| Overall: ★★★ | Room Quality: C | Value: A | Price: $62–$75 |
|---|---|---|---|

This quiet home has a sense of tradition enhanced by period fixtures and custom quilts, then updated with contemporary Northwest art and subtle Russian artifacts. (Hostess has an active interest in Russia and in Baker's Russian sister city, Zeya.) Hostess lives on-site and shares living quarters; house has a very relaxed, comfortable feel. Music-making occasionally inspired by two pianos and other instruments in living room. Charming guest rooms named for local mines. Short walk to downtown from this attractive, quiet side street.

### SETTING & FACILITIES

**Location:** 3 blocks west of Main off Campbell
**Near:** Oregon Trail Interpretive Center & Regional Museum, mining & ghost towns, Hells Canyon, Snake River, Anthony Lakes ski resort, Blue Mountains, Wallowa-Whitman Nat'l Forest, Eagle Cap Wilderness
**Building:** English Tudor Revival, oldest parts built in 1881
**Grounds:** Front & back lawns, mature trees, small back deck

**Public Space:** Upstairs sitting room, living/dining room
**Food & Drink:** Self-serve tea; full vegetarian breakfast
**Recreation:** Museums, antiquing, skiing, fishing, golf, festivals, scenic driving
**Amenities & Services:** Musical instruments, historic reference library, cordless guest phone, hot tub; receptions, gatherings, music events hosted

### ACCOMMODATIONS

**Units:** 3 guest rooms (w/ overflow possibilities)
**All Rooms:** Robes, quilt, phone jack
**Some Rooms:** Library, window seat,
**Bed & Bath:** Queen (2) or double; shared bath
**Favorites:** Rosebud
**Comfort & Decor:** Overall Arts and Crafts sensibility. Rich original woodwork, leather and upholstered furnishings. Fresh and pale, figured wallpapers. Original artwork, including Oregon artists. Comfortably roomy guest rooms, modern-style; humble, but spacious shared bath. Central heat, fans. While sunny Rosebud is lovely, choose cooler Maiden's Dream in summer.

## RATES, RESERVATIONS, & RESTRICTIONS

**Deposit:** 50%; 24-hour cancellation
**Discounts:** Single occupancy, no breakfast, groups & extended stays negotiable; $15 add'l person
**Credit Cards:** V, MC
**Check-in/Out:** 4–8 or by arrangement/11
**Smoking:** Outside only
**Pets:** Clean, well-behaved guest dogs welcome by arrangement ($10 fee)

**Kids:** Well-behaved children welcome
**Minimum Stay:** None
**Open:** All year
**Hosts:** Diane Pearson
2525 Third St., Baker City, OR 97814
(800) 606-7468 or (541) 523-6685
granthouse@triax.com or
granthbb@triax.com
www.neoregon.com/granthouse.html

## SAGE COUNTRY INN, Burns

| Overall: ★★★½ | Room Quality: B | Value: A | Price: $60–$75 |
|---|---|---|---|

Surprising oasis in mid-eastern Oregon, this beautifully restored Georgian Colonial is a class act. Opened in 1996, the inn is operated by three friends who take turns staying in the house and acting as hostess. Conveniently located just half a block off Highway 20, within walking distance to stores, restaurants, and services. Food is elegant and creative, rooms are clean and attractive, and common areas are impressively decorated yet comfortable. Merits more than a one-night stopover.

### SETTING & FACILITIES

**Location:** .5 block south of Hwy. 20/395, between Diamond & Court Ave.
**Near:** Steens Mountain, Malheur Wildlife Refuge, Strawberry Mountain Wilderness; major highway crossroads; dining, shopping, movie theater, laundromat
**Building:** 1907 Georgian Colonial
**Grounds:** Large lawn w/ mature trees (enjoyed by local deer & quail), rose garden, little cabin outbuilding; parklike landscaping

**Public Space:** Parlor, DR
**Food & Drink:** Afternoon/evening refreshments; morning coffee/tea; full breakfast; early cont'l option
**Recreation:** Swinging on the adult-size swing set; strolling around Burns; hunting, fishing, boating, X-C skiing
**Amenities & Services:** TV/VCR, sound system, guest mini-fridge, phone jacks (ensuite phone avail.); dinner parties (groups 10–30), weddings (including grand scale), meetings, retreats, luncheons, pet boarding

### ACCOMMODATIONS

**Units:** 4 guest rooms
**All Rooms:** Fresh flowers, armoires, quality linens
**Some Rooms:** AC, dormered ceilings
**Bed & Bath:** Queen, twins, double; 3 w/ private baths, 1 w/ shared
**Favorites:** Kathreen's, Cattle Baron's

**Comfort & Decor:** Period furnishings. Lots of striking bird's-eye pine paneling. AC in two warmest rooms (Court Street and Dormer), fans in others; windows open. Individually controlled heat. Home is nicely insulated for noise transfer; very quiet.

## RATES, RESERVATIONS, & RESTRICTIONS

**Deposit:** Credit card or check, 72-hour cancellation preferred
**Discounts:** Senior citizen, extended stays
**Credit Cards:** V, MC
**Check-in/Out:** After 3/11 or by arrangement
**Smoking:** Outside only
**Pets:** Not allowed inside inn
**Kids:** 10 & older welcome; younger by arrangement

**Minimum Stay:** None
**Open:** March–Dec.
**Hosts:** Carole Temple, Georgia Marshall, Susan Pielstick
P.O. Box 227, 351-1/2 W. Monroe
Burns, OR 97720
(541) 573-SAGE (7243)
pstick@ptinet.net
www.ptinet.net/~pstick

## HOTEL DIAMOND, Diamond

| Overall: ★★★★ | Room Quality: C | Value: B | Price: $55–$90 |
|---|---|---|---|

Pleasant, comfortable rooms in restored 1898 hotel near outstanding natural resources. Owner-operators Jerry and Judy Santille are veteran innkeepers, having operated the Oregon-State-Parks-owned Frenchglen Hotel for several years before purchasing (and while remodeling) the Hotel Diamond. Their experience with guests and with the unique local area is a valuable resource. Their restoration, completed carefully over four years' time, is classy and complete, resulting in a comfortable, modern accommodation in a very out-of-the-way setting (literally, "the end of the pavement!").

## SETTING & FACILITIES

**Location:** SE edge of Malheur Wildlife Refuge, about an hour SE of Burns
**Near:** Diamond Craters Outstanding Natural Area, Steens Mountain, Malheur Nat'l Wildlife Refuge (including Harney & Malheur Lakes & Krumbo Reservoir), Hart Mountain Nat'l Antelope Refuge
**Building:** Attractively restored historic hotel
**Grounds:** Grassy yard surrounded by towering poplars attracts abundant wildlife
**Public Space:** Lobby/DR; small upstairs reading room; huge screened porch

**Food & Drink:** Complimentary cont'l breakfast; fruit, beverages, & munchies; larger breakfasts prepared to order and dietary specifications may be purchased; family-style dinner avail. (6 or more people, 24 hours' notice)
**Recreation:** Wildlife watching & photography, geologic & historic backcountry driving, fishing, horseback packing trips
**Amenities & Services:** On-site restaurant & small store/gift shop (both for hotel guests only), sound system, croquet, mountain bikes; gas avail. to hotel guests at owner's cost

## ACCOMMODATIONS

**Units:** 6 guest rooms
**All Rooms:** Robes, armoires, quilts, artwork
**Some Rooms:** TV, bay window, AC (most rooms)
**Bed & Bath:** Queen; private bath (3 rooms); double bed (2 rooms) or double & twin (1 room), which share a bath
**Favorites:** A, B, 7

**Comfort & Decor:** Fresh, clean, and modern; rich wood wainscoting and simple, attractive, western homestead decor. Upstairs sitting area features head mounts of many local wildlife species (and the requisite Jackalope). Only Room 7, which is housed in a naturally insulated stone portion of the building, lacks AC; all rooms are comfortable, but the upstairs (shared bath) units are small.

## RATES, RESERVATIONS, & RESTRICTIONS

**Deposit:** 50%; if cancelled, deposit is refunded less $5 fee if room is rerented
**Discounts:** None
**Credit Cards:** V, MC
**Check-in/Out:** After 2/11
**Smoking:** Outside only
**Pets:** No
**Kids:** No

**Minimum Stay:** None
**Open:** March 15–Nov. 15
**Hosts:** Jerry & Judy Santille
Address not published at hosts' request
(541) 493-1898
www.central-oregon.com/hotel diamond/

## FRENCHGLEN HOTEL, Frenchglen

| Overall: ★★★ | Room Quality: D | Value: C | Price: $53–$56 |
|---|---|---|---|

Location, location, location! You'll find pure relaxation and laid-back isolation in this simple, baths-down-the-hall historic hotel. Owned by the Oregon State Parks system, the hotel is a historic landmark built in 1916 and remodeled by the Civilian Conservation Corps (the "CCC's") in 1938. Operator John Ross provides upkeep and meal service and is a knowledgeable, congenial host. Meals are simple and quite good. No TV or phones; this is self-propelled relaxation.

## SETTING & FACILITIES

**Location:** About an hour south of Burns on Hwy. 205

**Near:** Steens Mountain, Malheur Nat'l Wildlife Refuge (including Harney & Malheur Lakes & Krumbo Reservoir), Diamond Craters Outstanding Natural Area, Hart Mountain Nat'l Antelope Refuge

**Building:** 1916 Historic Register hotel

**Grounds:** Adjacent to grassy, shady little Frenchglen Hotel State Wayside (park)

**Public Space:** Screened front porch, DR/lobby

**Food & Drink:** Breakfast, lunch, & dinner avail. for purchase in restaurant; dinner by reservation only

**Recreation:** Wildlife watching & photography, geologic & historic back-country driving, fishing, hunting, horseback packing trips

**Amenities & Services:** View of Steens Mountain, on-site restaurant, another restaurant & store nearby; horseback packing tour outfitters nearby; tour planning

## ACCOMMODATIONS

**Units:** 8 guest rooms

**All Rooms:** Carpet, peg hooks, window fans

**Some Rooms:** Closets

**Bed & Bath:** Double (1 w/ extra twin); rooms share 2 sex-segregated baths

**Favorites:** 2

**Comfort & Decor:** Shaker-simple (quilt, small table, bed), the hotel is rustic without being creepy-crawly. Quiet location, but noise travels within hotel. Window fans provide sufficient airflow on all but hottest August days. Floors are carpeted, walls are lathe or paneling. Vintage and more recent wildlife photos adorn hall walls.

## RATES, RESERVATIONS, & RESTRICTIONS

**Deposit:** 72-hour cancellation requested; full refund if rerented (or if calamity strikes)

**Discounts:** None

**Credit Cards:** V, MC, D

**Check-in/Out:** As early as noon/10

**Smoking:** Outside only

**Pets:** No

**Kids:** Welcome

**Minimum Stay:** None

**Open:** March 15–Nov. 15

**Hosts:** John Ross
Frenchglen, OR 97736
(541) 493-2825
fghotel@ptinet.net
www.ohwy.com/or/f/frenchhs.htm

## STEENS MOUNTAIN INN, Frenchglen

| Overall: ★★ | Room Quality: D | Value: C | Price: $75 |
|---|---|---|---|

Rooms are a bit more modern and spacious than at adjacent Frenchglen Hotel, and bathrooms, while less-than-conveniently located downstairs, are private. Hosts live downstairs and operate the Frenchglen Mercantile store, gas station, and (excellent!) restaurant/bar next door. New rooms and amenities may be added to this work-in-progress.

## SETTING & FACILITIES

**Location:** About an hour south of Burns on Hwy. 205 in Frenchglen
**Near:** Steens Mountain, Malheur Nat'l Wildlife Refuge (including Harney & Malheur Lakes & Krumbo Reservoir), Diamond Craters Outstanding Natural Area, Hart Mountain Nat'l Antelope Refuge
**Building:** Shake-exterior private home
**Grounds:** Shady & parklike

**Public Space:** Shady 2nd-story deck
**Food & Drink:** Acclaimed restaurant adjacent; meals not included in price
**Recreation:** Wildlife watching & photography, geologic & historic back-country driving, fishing, hunting, hiking, horseback packing trips
**Amenities & Services:** View of Steens Mountain, adjacent restaurant & store; horseback packing tour outfitters nearby

## ACCOMMODATIONS

**Units:** 2 rooms
**All Rooms:** High ceilings, fresh white paint & wood trim
**Bed & Bath:** Queens; private baths separate & downstairs

**Comfort & Decor:** Spare and fresh, the rooms have hardwood floors, quilts, and minimal decor. Downstairs baths are tiled, roomy, and no-frills.

## RATES, RESERVATIONS, & RESTRICTIONS

**Deposit:** 1st night; 72-hour cancellation requested; full refund if rerented
**Discounts:** Midweek, off-season, extended stays
**Credit Cards:** V, MC, D, AE
**Check-in/Out:** 2/noon (flexible; luggage drop-off avail.)
**Smoking:** Outside only

**Pets:** May be accommodated by arrangement
**Kids:** Welcome
**Minimum Stay:** None
**Open:** Call for winter closure times
**Hosts:** Lance & Missy Litchy
Highway 205, Frenchglen, OR 97736
(541) 493-2738
Fax: (541) 493-2835

## CLEAR CREEK FARM B&B, Halfway

Overall: ★★★½     Room Quality: C     Value: A     Price: $60–$89

The grounds, hospitality, and sense of "right livelihood" at Clear Creek Farms is beyond relaxing—it's inspirational. This ever-evolving experiment in ecologically sensitive bison ranching and back-to-the-land self-sufficiency is a thing of beauty. The food is excellent, and the gardens, orchards, and grounds a balm for the soul. Avoid the outbuilding rooms.

## SETTING & FACILITIES

**Location:** Just outside the hamlet of
Halfway, off Hwy. 86, at the southern
edge of the Wallowa-Whitman Nat'l
Forest
**Near:** Hells Canyon recreation area,
Baker City (historic Oregon Trail area)
**Building:** Circa 1900 farmhouse w/
1998 addition, converted outbuildings
**Grounds:** 160-acre working ranch
includes orchards, gardens, ponds
**Public Space:** DR, parlor, library,
porch, study
**Food & Drink:** Cookies; full break-
fast; box lunches & full dinners usually
avail. by arrangement

**Recreation:** Horse & llama trekking,
wildlife & bird-watching, bison tours,
catch-and-release fishing
**Amenities & Services:** Gift shop,
bicycles (free w/ "Guest of the Ranch"
package or by arrangement); pick-your-
own fruit & berries; horse boarding;
ask about current status of such
diverse programs as "Work-Study-
Play" (room & board in exchange for
learning to be a ranch hand & paying
small tuition) & "Guest of the Ranch"
(3 meals a day & "make the rounds w/
the bison boss," extra $25/day)

## ACCOMMODATIONS

**Units:** 8 guest rooms
**All Rooms:** Each is quite different
**Some Rooms:** Add'l beds, claw-foot
tub in one unit
**Bed & Bath:** Queens, some doubles;
2 private ensuite baths, 2 private
detached baths, 4 share 2 baths
**Favorites:** Garden Room (new in
1998), Rose Room
**Comfort & Decor:** "Genteel-turn-
of-the-century-farmhouse meets

rustic-working-bison-ranch." Clean,
bright, and updated; 1998 addition
areas are quite upscale, with painted
woodwork, heat pump and AC. The
outbuilding rooms are very rustic, to
the point of being unfinished, including
exposed wiring, rail-less "balconies,"
and six- and eight-legged creatures are
everywhere.

## RATES, RESERVATIONS, & RESTRICTIONS

**Deposit:** 1st night; 7-day cancellation
**Discounts:** Longer stays, single occu-
pancy, multiple rooms, special pack-
ages; $10–18 add'l person
**Credit Cards:** V, MC
**Check-in/Out:** As early as noon/10
**Smoking:** Outside only
**Pets:** Well-behaved pets welcome
**Kids:** Welcome

**Minimum Stay:** None
**Open:** All year
**Hosts:** Barbara Phillips
48212 Clear Creek Rd.
Halfway, OR 97834
(800) 742-4992 or (541) 742-2238
Fax: (541) 742-5175
baphillips@igc.org
www.neoregon.com/ccgg

## SONSHINE B&B, John Day

| Overall: ★★½ | Room Quality: C | Value: A | Price: $60 |

Down-home (but not rustic) hospitality in this homestay-style lodging.
Pleasant, knowledgeable hosts are long-time locals who have offered

lodging since 1990. Carolyn works part-time, but her hours enable her to be available for all hostess duties: check-in, check-out, and (most importantly!) breakfast. Delightful food is made from scratch; game meat is a specialty (e.g., elk steak and eggs). Yard and porch are small but especially attractive. Make yourself at home!

## SETTING & FACILITIES

**Location:** Two blocks north of main street (Hwy. 26), adjacent to city park & Kam Wah Chung Museum
**Near:** City park & pool (summer only); shopping, restaurants, museums, & churches of John Day; John Day Fossil Beds Nat'l Monument; Strawberry Mountain Wilderness; Magone Lake & John Day River
**Building:** Private home, built 1940, remodeled 1985
**Grounds:** Neat, attractively landscaped, shady little yard; small koi pond

**Public Space:** Shared LR, DR, kitchen, front porch
**Food & Drink:** Full breakfast
**Recreation:** Bicycling, hunting, fishing, wildlife watching, historical/museum touring
**Amenities & Services:** Porch swing, deck/BBQ area, mountain bikes; hosts have local roots & will gladly tell you all the "secrets" of good places to visit; dinners by arrangement

## ACCOMMODATIONS

**Units:** 2 guest rooms
**All Rooms:** Comfortable, modern
**Some Rooms:** Desk & mini-library, private sink
**Bed & Bath:** Queens; shared bath

**Favorites:** Equal, 1 w/ private sink area, 1 w/ desk
**Comfort & Decor:** While food is more important here than decor, the home is middle-class contemporary, clean, and comfortable.

## RATES, RESERVATIONS, & RESTRICTIONS

**Deposit:** Half in advance
**Discounts:** Commercial, single occupancy, repeat, off-season, extended stays
**Credit Cards:** Not accepted
**Check-in/Out:** By arrangement
**Smoking:** Outside only
**Pets:** Welcome; host cat on site

**Kids:** Welcome
**Minimum Stay:** None
**Open:** All year
**Hosts:** Carolyn & Carl Stout
210 NW Canton
John Day, OR 97845
(541) 575-1827 or (541) 575-1153
cstout@orednet.org

## CHANDLER'S BED, BREAD, & TRAIL INN, Joseph

| Overall: ★★½ | Room Quality: D | Value: B | Price: $60–$80 |
| --- | --- | --- | --- |

This well-established in-home bed-and-breakfast has been owned and operated by Ethel and Jim Chandler since 1985. The result is a property that is casual, comfortable, and homey, if a bit dated decor-wise. Your hosts, aided by long-time assistant Sanchez, anticipate your needs with thoughtful extras such as abundant extra towels, dual pillows, and reading lamps for each bed, and plenty of tried-and-true information about recreation at nearby Wallowa Lake, Eagle Cap Wilderness, and Hells Canyon. Multiple sitting areas, including the outdoor deck, provide ample opportunities for solitude outside your room.

## SETTING & FACILITIES

**Location:** South end of Joseph on Main St.
**Near:** Hells Canyon recreation area, Joseph, Enterprise, Wallowa Lake, Eagle Cap Wilderness
**Building:** 2-story private home w/ shake exterior
**Grounds:** Compact corner lot screened from street by trees & fencing; abundant decking & gazebo
**Public Space:** Sunroom, DR, LR; upstairs "nooks & crannies," including TV & game area

**Food & Drink:** Fresh cookies & hot beverages upon arrival; full breakfast
**Recreation:** Near fishing, snowmobiling, llama & horse packing, rafting, antiquing, galleries
**Amenities & Services:** Games, 2 guest phones, TV, hot tub (w/ plenty of towels) over gazebo, guest fridge, micro., wet bar; flexible room & bed configurations to accommodate groups; they work w/ local guide services including fishing, llama packing, & backcountry skiing

## ACCOMMODATIONS

**Units:** 5 guest rooms
**All Rooms:** Extra pillows, robes
**Some Rooms:** View
**Bed & Bath:** Various; 3 private baths, 2 share 1.5 baths
**Favorites:** 2

**Comfort & Decor:** "Family vacation home" feel—casual and unpretentious, if a bit dated. High, beamed ceilings compensate somewhat for overall dim illumination. Rooms have ceiling fans. Vintage regional memorabilia.

## RATES, RESERVATIONS, & RESTRICTIONS

**Deposit:** Credit card; 7-day cancellation
**Discounts:** Off-season, single occupancy, 2 rooms as suite (as avail.); $10 add'l person
**Credit Cards:** V, MC
**Check-in/Out:** After 2/11
**Smoking:** Outside only
**Pets:** No
**Kids:** Over 12 welcome

**Minimum Stay:** None
**Open:** All year
**Hosts:** Ethel & Jim Chandler, owner/operators;
Crystal Sanchez, innkeeper
700 NW Main St.
Joseph, OR 97846
(800) 452-3781 or (541) 432-9765
chanbbti@eoni.com
www.eoni.com/~chanbbti

## STANG MANOR INN, La Grande

| Overall: ★★★★ | Room Quality: B | Value: B | Price: $80–95 |

This opulent, white-columned, "wedding cake" of a house is a real head-turner. Inside and out, it hearkens back to a glamorous era, when its owner entertained celebrities, raised his family, and presided over La Grande's largest lumber mill. Whether you choose the intimate Guest Room (as Stang houseguest Bing Crosby did!) or the three-room Suite, with its two  bedrooms and fireplace sitting area, you'll find plenty of elbow room. Property was up for sale at our visit, so inquire about change in ownership and policies. Ideally suited for a bed-and-breakfast (the four ensuite baths are original to the house), it likely will remain one.

## SETTING & FACILITIES

**Location:** Corner of Spring & Walnut Streets
**Near:** I-84, Eastern Oregon Univ., Baker City, Pendleton, Oregon Trail Interpretive Center, Lewis & Clark Trail, Oregon Trail, Hells Canyon, Blue Mountains, Wallowa-Whitman Nat'l Forest
**Building:** 1925 Georgian Colonial

**Grounds:** Large lawn w/ plantings, rose garden, on quiet corner lot
**Public Space:** LR, sunroom, DR
**Food & Drink:** Full breakfast
**Recreation:** Historic touring, cultural (theater/art/college-related) activities, skiing
**Amenities & Services:** Daily newspaper, books, games, videos, puzzles, fireplace; meeting space, special events

## ACCOMMODATIONS

**Units:** 3 guest rooms, 1 suite
**All Rooms:** Phone, aromatic-cedar-lined closet, hairdryer, soaking tub
**Some Rooms:** TV, desk, four-poster, walk-in closet, canopy bed, fireplace
**Bed & Bath:** Queens (1 w/ extra room & twin, 1 w/ extra room & 2 twins, 1 w/ extra room & double); private ensuite baths
**Favorites:** The Suite

**Comfort & Decor:** Common areas gracefully appointed, whereas guest rooms, while regal and clean, could tolerate a bit of updating. Original hardwood floors; most guest rooms carpeted. Original tile, moldings, and plasterwork. Dining room is a statement, in pink and lace, with tea-rose carpet.

## RATES, RESERVATIONS, & RESTRICTIONS

**Deposit:** 1st night; 24-hour cancellation
**Discounts:** Single occupancy (most rooms), corporate, gov't, whole-house; $15 add'l person
**Credit Cards:** V, MC
**Check-in/Out:** By arrangement/11 (flexible)
**Smoking:** Outside only
**Pets:** No; host kitty Elsie

**Kids:** 10 & older welcome (unless whole-house rental or arranged)
**Minimum Stay:** None
**Open:** All year
**Hosts:** Margie & Pat McClure
1612 Walnut St., La Grande, OR 97850
(888) 286-9463 or (541) 963-2400
Fax: (541) 963-2400 (call ahead)
www.stangmanor.com
www.eoni.com/stang

## THE PARKER HOUSE B&B, Pendleton

| Overall: ★★★★ | Room Quality: B | Value: A | Price: $65–$85 |
|---|---|---|---|

Peach stuccoed with white Ionic columns and white wicker porch furnishings, Parker House commands a perch on a slight hill overlooking downtown Pendleton. This beautifully preserved home stayed with the original family for over 70 years, resulting in a richly evocative historic experience. Your full-time hostess (whose hospitality background is evident in the attention to amenities and details) lives on-site. "At-your-convenience" breakfast takes time pressure off shared bath situation. Excellent location, elegant surroundings, exceptional hostess.

### SETTING & FACILITIES

**Location:** 1 mi. off I-84, a block from downtown, on Main between NW Ellis & NW Despain
**Near:** Pendleton Underground, Pendleton Woolen Mills, Pendleton Round-Up site & museum, Lewis & Clark Trail, Oregon Trail, Hells Canyon, Blue Mountains, Wallowa-Whitman Nat'l Forest
**Building:** 1917 Neoclassical/Italianate hybrid
**Grounds:** Tidy, rose-bordered front lawn; backyard w/ herb & cutting gardens

**Public Space:** Front porch, LR, sun room, DR
**Food & Drink:** In-room bottled water, cookies, chocolates; self-serve hot beverages; early morning coffee; full breakfast
**Recreation:** Antiquing, historic touring, hunting, fishing, golf, casino gaming
**Amenities & Services:** Cordless guest phone, guest desk, sound system, fireplace, elevator; small weddings, receptions, parties

### ACCOMMODATIONS

**Units:** 4 guest rooms, 1 2-room suite
**All Rooms:** Robes, closet or armoire, fresh flowers (seasonal)
**Some Rooms:** Balcony access, fireplace, chandelier, desk
**Bed & Bath:** Queen (3), king, double; 1 huge shared bath, plus suite has half-bath & main floor half-bath
**Favorites:** Gwendolyn, Attic (cooler months)

**Comfort & Decor:** Decorative plasterwork, antique furnishings and fixtures; original decor touches. Guest rooms include down pillows, excellent mattresses, iron or Mission-style or Eastlake-style beds, and wicker and/or period furnishings. Shared all-tile bath has huge soaker tub, original fixtures, and a wrap-around European shower.

## RATES, RESERVATIONS, & RESTRICTIONS

**Deposit:** 1st night; 72-hour cancellation
**Discounts:** Midweek corporate
**Credit Cards:** V, MC, AE
**Check-in/Out:** After 4/11
**Smoking:** No
**Pets:** No; host pets in host quarters

**Kids:** 10 & older welcome
**Minimum Stay:** None
**Open:** All year
**Hosts:** Sandy Parker
311 N. Main St., Pendleton, OR 97801
(800) 700-8581 or (541) 276-8581
www.moriah.com/parkerhouse

## RIVERSIDE SCHOOL HOUSE, Prairie City

| Overall: ★★ | Room Quality: D | Value: C | Price: $75 |
|---|---|---|---|

Now this is rural! Simple and spacious, this solo unit in converted schoolhouse is perfect for two close-knit couples or a family with one or two children. Enjoy absolute privacy and a great view of Strawberry Mountain, with the constant, subtle background music of the burbling John Day River. Drag a rocker out to your deck and watch the livestock from the shade of the apple tree. Bring your own evening entertainment; the table and chairs invites a card or board game, while the rockers and woodstove suggest a good book. Five hours from Portland.

## SETTING & FACILITIES

**Location:** Just outside Prairie City, which is on Hwy. 26, 13 mi. east of John Day, or about 70 mi. SW of Baker City via Hwy. 7
**Near:** Adjacent to headwaters of John Day River; easy drive to Prairie City, Strawberry Mountain Wilderness
**Building:** Circa 1900 schoolhouse
**Grounds:** Lush green lawn surrounded by horse & cattle pastures
**Public Space:** Self-contained private unit

**Food & Drink:** Coffee, cocoa, & filtered drinking water; full or cont'l breakfast prepared to guests' tastes
**Recreation:** Fishing, wildlife (& farm animal) watching; hunting, X-C skiing, snowmobiling, historic touring
**Amenities & Services:** Absolute peace & quiet; kitchenette includes sink, full-sized fridge, micro., toaster, coffeemaker; TV avail.; no phone; ensuite breakfast, horse boarding

## ACCOMMODATIONS

**Units:** 1 large unit
**All Rooms:** 2 beds, rocking chairs, table & chairs, woodstove, kitchenette, bathrooms, front deck
**Bed & Bath:** 2 queens; private bath: separate shower & toilet rooms
**Comfort & Decor:** Country simplicity: clean, bright, open, and airy, the
room is decorated with quilts and pale paint. Ceiling fans, guest-controlled heat. Woodstove on brick hearth. Entry is knotty-pine flooring; main room has indoor/outdoor-type carpet. Dim in the evening; could be drafty in winter.

## RATES, RESERVATIONS, & RESTRICTIONS

**Deposit:** 1st night by check
**Discounts:** Longer stays, no breakfast, single occupancy; $10 add'l person
**Credit Cards:** Not accepted
**Check-in/Out:** By arrangement
**Smoking:** Outside only
**Pets:** Inquire

**Kids:** Welcome
**Minimum Stay:** None
**Open:** All year
**Hosts:** Judy Jacobs
Rt. 2, Box 700
Prairie City, OR 97869
(541) 820-4731

## STRAWBERRY MOUNTAIN INN, Prairie City

| Overall: ★★★ | Room Quality: C | Value: B | Price: $65–$95 |

This beautiful manor house has a lot going for it, especially its bucolic setting in the peaceful John Day Valley, its view of Strawberry Mountain, and its recreation access. Located right on the highway (a quiet highway), it's easy to find. Guest sitting room is pleasant, with its bay window and large sectional couch, but could get a bit crowded if all five rooms were occupied; front porch and side deck are great options. We found it a little annoying that hosts leave beauty product literature around.

### SETTING & FACILITIES

**Location:** Just east of Prairie City on Hwy. 26
**Near:** Communities of Prairie City & John Day; shopping, restaurants, museums; John Day Fossil Beds Nat'l Monument; Strawberry Mountain Wilderness; Magone Lake & John Day River
**Building:** 1911 late Victorian manor
**Grounds:** Large backyard (illuminated at night) w/ fruit trees, chickens, deck, swing; "hobby farm" feel; views of cow pastures & Strawberry Mountain

**Public Space:** Guest-only sitting room, patio, porch, detached game room
**Food & Drink:** Full breakfast
**Recreation:** Billiards/ping-pong, historical/museum touring; hunting, fishing, wildlife watching
**Amenities & Services:** Hot tub, TV/VCR, videos, piano, billiards, sound system, puzzles, outdoor play area; small group retreats, weddings & parties catered, fax avail.

### ACCOMMODATIONS

**Units:** 5 guest rooms
**All Rooms:** Robes, in-room phones
**Some Rooms:** View, antique bed, writing desk
**Bed & Bath:** 1 king 2 twin trundles & private bath; a queen & a king room share 1 spacious bath; 2 double bed rooms share 1 small bath
**Favorites:** Blue Room

**Comfort & Decor:** All guest rooms and guest sitting room have plush, sound-muffling carpet. Decor is fresh, new, and cheerfully but not expensively done. Rooms are very clean and accent pieces are well chosen; midquality mattresses, linens, and towels

## RATES, RESERVATIONS, & RESTRICTIONS

**Deposit:** 1st night; 10-day cancellation
**Discounts:** Extended stays, off-season, gov't (on per diem), entire house
**Credit Cards:** V, MC, AE, D, DC, O, Novus
**Check-in/Out:** 3–7/noon
**Smoking:** Outside only
**Pets:** Not allowed inside (outside accommodations avail.); host pets on site

**Kids:** Welcome
**Minimum Stay:** None
**Open:** All year (reservations required Nov. 1–March 1)
**Hosts:** Linda & Bill Harrington
HCR 77 Box 940
Prairie City, OR 97869
(800) 545-6913 or (541) 820-4522
strawberry@moriah.com
www.moriah.com/strawberry

## 1900 SEARS & ROEBUCK HOME, Vale

Overall: ★★★     Room Quality: C     Value: A     Price: $50–$75

Sears & Roebuck Company once provided the materials and plans for homes ranging from humble cottages to glorious estates. Judy Gallant's bed-and-breakfast is a beauty, complete with turret, dormered roofline, and wide front porch. Her renovation combines the best of the past (beveled French glass, wide crown molding, wainscoting) with the best of today (central air, big-screen TV). Located in the town sometimes known as "Vale-on-the-Trail," the bed-and-breakfast is close to a rich variety of heritage sites and within walking distance of the town's impressive murals depicting Oregon Trail events.

## SETTING & FACILITIES

**Location:** NE side of town
**Near:** Vale murals & historic homes walking tour, Oregon Trail historic sites, Bully Creek Reservoir, Lake Owyhee, Four Rivers Cultural Center, Nyssa ("Thunderegg Capital of the World") & Ontario
**Building:** Impressive, turreted, 2-story home
**Grounds:** Front lawn w/ flowers; pleasant backyard
**Public Space:** LR, den/sitting room, kitchen, DR, porches, grape arbor patio

**Food & Drink:** Gourmet cont'l breakfast; hot entrees by arrangement
**Recreation:** Historic touring (on foot, by car, or w/ local horse-drawn buggy tour), fishing, hunting, rock-hounding
**Amenities & Services:** Big-screen cable TV, VCR, sound system, full kitchen, gas BBQ, phones & fax, laundry facil., heated game- & fish-cleaning room w/ stainless steel sinks; garden parties & weddings; horse boarding facil.; dog kennels on site

## ACCOMMODATIONS

**Units:** 6 guest rooms (counting den sofabed; 5 rooms upstairs)

**All Rooms:** Attractive wallpaper, period decor, quality linens

**Some Rooms:** Carpet, armoires, large closets, antique beds

**Bed & Bath:** Mostly queens; 5 rooms share 1 spacious full bath (3/4 bath also avail. on main floor, adjacent to den/sofabed room; shower & toilet room in outbuilding w/ laundry & game-cleaning facil.)

**Favorites:** Tonya's Room, Lisa's Room

**Comfort & Decor:** Varied floral patterns (wallpaper, carpet, upholstery, tablecloths) blend effortlessly in Victorian fashion. Well-chosen antiques. Central air, but most rooms have individual window AC units to supplement. Five rooms sharing one bath is a bit much; creative timing and/or use of downstairs or outbuilding facilities may be necessary.

## RATES, RESERVATIONS, & RESTRICTIONS

**Deposit:** 1st night; 48-hour cancellation

**Discounts:** Single occupancy, entire house, state employees (& others on per diem), extended stays (weekly rates)

**Credit Cards:** Not accepted

**Check-in/Out:** 4/11 (very flexible)

**Smoking:** Outside only

**Pets:** Not inside (quality on-site kennels)

**Kids:** Welcome

**Minimum Stay:** None

**Open:** All year

**Hosts:** Judith A. Gallant
484 N. 10th St., Vale, OR 97918
(541) 473-9636
twobarj@micron.net
www.moriah.com/sears

# Additional Bed-and-Breakfasts and Small Inns

While our 300 profiles give you a fine range of bed-and-breakfasts and small inns, some may be fully booked when you want to visit, or you may want to stay in areas where we have not included a property. So we have included this listing of 300 additional bed-and-breakfasts and small inns, spread geographically throughout the Northwest. All properties meet our basic criteria for this guide: They usually have about 3–25 guest rooms, a distinct personality and individually decorated guest rooms, are open regularly, and include breakfast in the price (with a few exceptions). Prices are a range from low to high season. Unlike the previous 300 profiles, we have not visited all of these properties so we cannot recommend them across the board. We suggest you get a brochure, look on the Internet, or call and ask about some of the categories that are on the profile format to find out more. While some of these supplementals are famed and excellent, others may not be up to the level of the profiled properties.

## BRITISH COLUMBIA

### Zone 1: Victoria

**In-town**

Battery Street Guest
  House
CDN $65–$95
(250) 385-4632

Carberry Gardens Bed &
  Breakfast   CDN $125
(250) 595-8906

The Edwardian Inn
CDN $75–$105
(888) 388-0334 or
  (250) 380-2411

Heritage House B&B
CDN $125
(250) 479-0892

Humboldt House
CDN $245–$285
(888) 383-0327 or
  (250) 383-0152

Marketas Bed & Breakfast
CDN $65–$90
(250) 384-9844

Medana Grove Bed &
  Breakfast
CDN $110–$125
(800) 269-1188 or
  (250) 389-0437

Mulberry Manor Bed &
  Breakfast
CDN $175–$218
(877) 370-1918 or
  (250) 370-1918

Postern Gate Inn
CDN $140–$195
(250) 744-8787

The Sea Rose Bed &
  Breakfast
CDN $115–$170
(888) 335-ROSE or
  (250) 381-7932

**North of Town**

Abbey Rose Bed &
    Breakfast    CDN $110
(800) 307-7561 or
    (250) 479-7155

Cedar Shade Bed &
    Breakfast
CDN $70–$80
(250) 652-2994

Cobble House Bed &
    Breakfast
CDN $74–$84
(250) 743-2672

Eagle's Nest Bed &
    Breakfast    CDN $125
(250) 658-2002

Iris Garden Country
    Manor B&B
CDN $95–$150
(877) 744-2253 or
    (250) 744-2253

LaBine Manor
CDN $75–$130
(250) 652-7810

**West of Town**

Florence Lake Bed &
    Breakfast
CDN $85–$150
(800) 663-6000 or
    (250) 474-5398

M'Chosin Haven
CDN $85
(250) 478-0558

An Ocean View Bed &
    Breakfast
CDN $105–$140
(800) 342-9986 or
    (250) 386-7330

A Snug Harbour Inn
CDN $180–$280
(888) 936-5222 or
    (250) 726-2685

# Zone 2: Vancouver

**Downtown & Vancouver Proper**

Apricot Cat Guest House
CDN $70–$95
(604) 215-9898

La Villa Antoine Bed &
    Breakfast
CDN $80–$100
(604) 266-8285

Manor Guest House
CDN $85–$170
(604) 876-8494

Nelson House B&B
CDN $98–$168
(604) 684-9793

The Shamrock's Nook
    Bed & Breakfast
CDN $75–$110
(604) 329-9535

Three Gables Bed &
    Breakfast
CDN $95–$200
(604) 874-3566

**North Vancouver**

Capilano Canyon Guest
    House
CDN $150–$175
(888) 387-8588

Kings on Kings
CDN $90–$125
(604) 987-7886 or
    (604) 313-2419

Queen Anne Manor
CDN $95–$175
(604) 929-3239

**South of Downtown**

Camilla House Bed &
    Breakfast
CDN $95–$145
(604) 737-2687

Chelsea Cottage B&B
CDN $95–$120
(604) 266-2681

Deep Cove B&B
CDN $95
(604) 929-2932

Diana's Luxury Bed &
    Breakfast
CDN $99–$145
(877) 321-3411 or
    (604) 321-2855

Douglas Guest House
CDN $120
(888) 872-3060 or
    (604) 872-3060

English Country Garden
CDN $105–$130
(604) 737-2526

White Swan B&B
CDN $95–$105
(604) 261-7709

Windsor House
CDN $120
(888) 872-3060 or
    (604) 872-3060

**South of Vancouver**

Cedar Inn of Tsawwassen
CDN $75–$125
(604) 948-8069

SouthLands House by the
    Sea    CDN $125–$165
(604) 943-1846

**West Vancouver**

Cedar Cottage B&B
CDN $100–$115
(604) 926-0950

Chickadee Tree
CDN $135
(604) 925-1989

The Chirp & Whistle
CDN $80–$100
(604) 922-5992

Crow's Nest B&B
CDN $110+
(604) 921-8015

Lighthouse Retreat B&B
CDN $135
(604) 926-5959

The Palms Guest House
CDN $150–$250
(800) 691-4455 or
    (604) 926-1159

# WASHINGTON

## Zone 3: Washington Coast & Olympic Peninsula

**Aberdeen**
Aberdeen Mansion Inn
$95–$125
(888) 533-7079

A Harbor View    $65–$95
(360) 533-7996

**Forks**
Brightwater House B&B
$75–$85
(360) 374-5453

Eagle Point Inn    $85
(360) 327-3236

Fisherman's Widow
$60–$65
(360) 374-5693

Misty Valley Inn    $65+
(360) 374-9389

**Long Beach Peninsula**
Caswell's on the Bay
$95–$150
(888) 553-2319

Kola House B&B
$65–$75
(360) 642-2819

The Lion's Paw $80–$100
(800) 972-1046

Our House in Nahcotta
$95    (360) 665-6667

Scandinavian Gardens Inn
$105–$145
(800) 988-9277

Whalebone House
$95–$105
(888) 298-3330 or
    (541) 665-5371

**Ocean Shores**
Silver Waves Inn B&B
$49–$125
(888) 257-0894 or
    (360) 289-2490

**Pacific Beach**
Beach Avenue Bed &
    Breakfast    $85–$105
(360) 276-4727

**Port Angeles**
Angeles Inn Bed &
    Breakfast    $60–$80
(888) 552-4263

Bayton's on the Bluff
$60–$65
(888) 400-5569

Colette's Bed & Breakfast
$155–$175
(360) 457-9197

Elwha Ranch    $90–$120
(360) 457-6540

The Haven Bed &
    Breakfast    $95
(800) 794-8913 or
    (360) 452-0906

Lake Sutherland Lodge
$65–$90
(888) 231-1444

Tudor Inn    $85–$125
(360) 452-3138

**Port Townsend Area**
Baker House    $75–$85
(360) 385-6673

Diamond Point Inn
$75–$125    (Gardiner)
(888) 797-0393 or
    (360) 797-7720

English Inn    $85–$105
(360) 385-5302

F.W. Hastings House
(see Old Consulate Inn)

Old Consulate Inn
$96–$195
(800) 300-6753

**Sequim**
Dungeness Panorama
$85–$110
(360) 683-4503

Glenna's Guthrie Cottage
    Bed & Breakfast
$50–$110
(800) 930-4349

Margie's Inn on the Bay
$75–$142
(800) 730-7011 or
    (360) 683-7011

**South Bend**
Maring's Courthouse
    B&B    $55–$65
(800) 875-6519 or
    (360) 875-6519

The Russell House
$60–$65
(360) 875-5608

## Zone 4: Northwest Washington

**Anacortes**
Burrows Bay Bed &
    Breakfast    $110–$135
(360) 533-7996

Old Brook Inn    $80–$90
(800) 503-4768 or
    (360) 293-4768

**Arlington**
Mt. Higgins House
$95–$115
(888) 296-3777 or
    (360) 435-8703

**Bellingham**
Slater Heritage House
    B&B    $65–$95
(888) 785-0706 or
    (360) 384-4273

**Blaine**
Water's Edge Bed &
    Breakfast    $80–$130
(360) 371-2043

**Camano Island**
Camano Island Inn
$120–$160
(888) 718-0783 or
    (360) 387-0783

Inn at Barnum Point
$99–$185
(800) 910-2256 or
    (360) 387-2256

**La Conner**
Rainbow Inn    $80–$115
(888) 266-887 or
    (360) 466-4578

Skagit Bay Hideaway
$195
(888) 466-2262 or
    (360) 466-2262

**Mount Vernon**
The Parsonage on Pleasant
    Ridge    $95–$125
(360) 466-1754

Storyville Bed & Breakfast
$90–$125
(888) 373-3207 or
    (360) 466-3207

**Point Roberts**
Cedar House Inn
$36–$49
(360) 945-0284

**San Juan Islands**
**Lopez Island**
Aleck Bay Inn
$129–$179
(360) 468-3535

**Orcas Island**
Anchorage Inn    $165
(360) 376-8282

Old Trout Inn
$125–$175
(360) 376-8282

Windsong Bed &
    Breakfast Inn
$120–$150
(800) 669-3948 or
    (360) 376-2500

**San Juan Island**
Argyle House    $90–$135
(800) 624-3459 or
    (360) 378-4084

Halvorsen House B&B
$99–$150
(888) 238-4187

Highland Inn    $250
(888) 400-9850 or
    (360) 378-9450

Hillside House
$85–$175
(800) 232-4730 or
    (360) 378-4730

Moon & Sixpence
$90–$165
(360) 378-4138

San Juan Inn    $82–$180
(800) 742-8210 or
    (360) 378-2070

States Inn    $85–$125
(360) 378-6240

The Tower House Bed &
    Breakfast    $95–$120
(800) 858-4276 or
    (360) 378-5464

**Snohomish**
Snohomish Grand Valley
    Inn    $70–$95
(360) 568-8854

**Whidbey Island**
Country Cottage of
    Langley    $120–$179
(800) 713-3860 or
    (360) 221-8709

Inn at Langley
$189–$285
(360) 221-3033

Spink's Ocean View
$125+    (888) 799-5979
    or (360) 579-2494

Twickenham House Inn
$120    (360) 221-2334

The Whidbey Inn
$110–$160
(888) 313-2070 or
    (360) 221-7115

# Zone 5: Greater Seattle/Tacoma
**Bainbridge Island**
Monarch Manor
$125–$250
(206) 780-0112

**Everett**
Gaylord House
$85–$175
(888) 507-7177 or
    (425) 339-9153

Harbor Hill Inn
$75–$105
(888) 572-3925 or
    (425) 259-3925

Inn at Port Gardner
$89–$210
(888) 252-6779 or
    (425) 252-6779

**Federal Way**
Killarney Cove    $90–$95
(253) 838-4595

Palisades at Dash Point
$195    (888) 838-4376 or
    (253) 030-4376

**Kitsap Peninsula**
**Fox Island**
Island Escape    $125
(253) 549-2044

**Gig Harbor**
Nestled In    $110
(253) 851-6052

Peacock Hill Guest House
$85–$115
(800) 863-2318 or
    (253) 858-3322

**Manchester**
Laurel Inn Bed &
 Breakfast  $58–$88
(888) 888-9661 or
 (360) 769-9544

**Olalla**
Childs' House Bed &
 Breakfast  $65–$95
(800) 250-4954 or
 (253) 857-4252

**Poulsbo**
The Manor Farm Inn
$120–$170
(360) 779-4628

**Puyallup**
Tayberry Victorian
 Cottage  $ 75–$95
(253) 848-4594

**Seattle**
Bed & Breakfast on
 Broadway  $95–$125
(888) 329-8933 or
 (206) 329-8933

Bed & Breakfast on
 Capitol Hill  $55–$96
(206) 325-0320

The Guest House Bed &
 Breakfast  $115+
(206) 439-7576

Hill House Bed &
 Breakfast  $90–$155
(800) 720-7161 or
 (206) 720-7161

Prince of Wales
$99–$125
(800) 327-9692 or
 (206) 325-9692

Shafer-Baillie Mansion
$89–$145
(800) 922-4654 or
 (206) 322-4654

Three Tree Point  $135
(888) 369-7696 or
 (206) 669-7644

Wall Street Inn
$95–$130
(206) 448-0125 or
 (206) 624-1117

**Silverdale**
Heaven's Edge Bed &
 Breakfast  $115–$150
(800) 413-5680 or
 (360) 613-1111

**Tacoma**
Plum Duff House
$80–$100
(253) 627-6916

The Villa  $95–$160
(888) 572-1157

**Vashon Island**
Back Bay Inn  $118
(206) 463-5355

Van Gelder's Retreat
$75–100
(206) 463-3684

## Zone 6: Washington's I-5 South
**Centralia**
Candalite Mansion
$50–$65 (360) 736-4749

**Longview/Kelso**
Misty Mountain Llamas
 B&B  $85–$90
(360) 577-4772

**Olympia**
Forest Haven B&B
$60–$125
(360) 956-7800

**Salkum**
Shepherd's Inn  $65–$80
(800) 985-2434 or
 (360) 985-2434

**Silver Lake**
Silver Lake Bed &
 Breakfast  $75–85
(360) 274-7866

**Yelm**
Blue Berry Hill Farm
$25 per person
(360) 458-4726

## Zone 7: Cascades
**Eatonville**
Mill Town Manor
$85–$115
(360) 832-6506

Mountain View Cedar
 Lodge B&B
$95–$135
(888) VIEW-2NW or
 (360) 832-8080

**Enumclaw**
The White Rose Inn
$85–$95
(800) 404-7194 or
 (360) 825-7194

**Highway 20 West
Marblemount**
Salmonberry Way Bed &
 Breakfast  $49–$59
(360) 873-4016

**Ross Lake**
Ross Lake Resort
$56–$84
(206) 386-4437

**Leavenworth**
Bosch Gärten  $98–$105
(800) 535-0069 or
 (509) 548-6900

Mountain Home Lodge
$100–$330
(800) 414-2378

Tamarack Timbers  $95
(877) 615-8175 or
 (509) 548-4049

**Mazama (see also
Winthrop)**
Freestone Inn
$165–$220
(800) 639-3809

Mazama Country Inn
$80–$95 (summer, no
meals)    $160–$185 (win-
ter, all meals)
(888) 843-7951 or
    (509) 996-2681

North Cascades Basecamp
$70–$80 (spring, summer
fall B&B)    $125–$125
(winter, all meals)
(509) 996-2334

**Mt. Baker/Highway 543**
Mt. Baker's Cabin
    Country Bed &
    Breakfast    $75
(360) 599-2903

**Packwood**
Hotel Packwood
$25–$38
(360) 494-5431

Tatoosh Meadows Resort
$125–$175
(800) 294-2311

**Roslyn**
Harry's Inn    $75
(509) 649-2551

The Roslyn Inn
$48–$290
(509) 649-2936

**Skykomish**
Skykomish Hotel
$35–$49
(360) 677-2477

**Snoqualmie Summit**
Wardholm West    $50
(425) 434-6540

**Trout Lake**
Trout Lake Country Inn
$50–$85
(509) 395-2894

**Winthrop (see also
Mazama)**
Duck Brand Hotel &
    Cantina    $55–$65
(509) 996-2192

Fly Rod Ranch    $75–$90
(509) 996-2784

River Run Inn    $88+
(800) 757-2709 or
    (509) 996-2173

# Zone 8: Northeast Washington
**Chelan/Manson**
Apple Country Bed &
    Breakfast    $70
(509) 687-3982

Brick House    $68–$87
(800) 799-2332 or
    (509) 682-2233

Captain's Quarters
$115–$135
(888) 877-1748 or
    (509) 682-5886

Inn Above the Lake
$75–$115
(509) 682-3184

**Kettle Falls**
My Parent's Estate    $65+
(509) 738-6220

**Omak**
Hidden Hills Resort
$75–$105
(800) 468-1890 or
    (509) 486-1895

**Pateros**
Amy's Manor Bed &
    Breakfast    $80
(888) 923-2334 or
    (509) 923-2334

**Republic**
K-Diamond-K Guest
    Ranch    $65–$105
(509) 775-3536

Pine Point Resort    $87+
(509) 775-3643

**Tonasket**
Hidden Hills Resort
$75–$105
(509) 486-1895

# Zone 9: Southeast Washington
**Cashmere**
Grandview Orchard Inn
$60–$70
(509) 782-2340

**Clarkston**
The Cliff House    $75
(509) 758-1267

Highland House
$50–$85
(509) 758-3126

Swallowhaven    $65–$100
(800) 441-8357 or
    (509) 758-8357

**Ellensburg**
Campus View Inn
$65–$79
(800) 428-7270 or
    (509) 933-2345

Inn at Goose Creek    $109
(800) 533-0822 or
    (509) 962-8030

The Inn on Eighth
    Avenue    $60–$69
(800) 320-5282 or
    (509) 925-5282

**Goldendale**
Victorian House
$40–$60
(888) 426-7281 or
    (509) 773-5338

**Naches**
Whistlin' Jack Lodge
$90–$230
(800) 827-2299

**Odessa**
Derr House    $50–$60
(800) 469-0076

**Pullman
(see also Uniontown)**
Country Bed & Breakfast
$50–$75
(509) 334-4453

**Uniontown**
The Churchyard Inn
$55–$135
(509) 229-3200

Premier Alpaca Ranch
$70–$85
(509) 229-3700

**Yakima & Yakima Valley**
Von Hellstrum Inn
$50–$70
(800) 222-8658 or
      (509) 839-2505

# OREGON

## Zone 10: Oregon Coast
**Astoria**
Astoria Inn B&B
$70–$90
(800) 718-8153 or
      (503) 325-8153

Benjamin Young Inn
$75–$135
(800) 201-1286 or
      (503) 325-6172

**Cannon Beach Area**
Stephanie Inn
$159–$319
(503) 436-2221

**Coos Bay**
Blackberry Inn    $35–$60
(541) 267-6951

Talavar Inn    $93–$115
(541) 888-5280

This Olde House B&B
$85–$145
(541) 267-5224

**Florence**
Betty's Barn Home
$55–$65
(541) 997-2764

The Blue Heron Inn
$65–$100
(800) 997-7780 or
      (541) 997-4091

Oak Street Bed &
      Breakfast    $65–$85
(800) 853-4005 or
      (541) 997-4000

**Lincoln City**
Brey House Bed &
      Breakfast    $80–$145
(541) 994-7123

Chandler House B&B
$118–$165
(541) 994-5010

Lake House Bed &
      Breakfast    $95–$115
(541) 996-8938

Young's Bed & Breakfast
$65–$70
(541) 994-6575

**Manzanita**
Arbors Bed & Breakfast
$100–$110
(503) 368-7566

**Newport**
Ocean House B&B
$90–$165
(800) 562-2632 or
      (541) 265-6158

Sea Cliff Bed & Breakfast
$95–$105
(888) 858-6660 or
      (541) 265-6664

Solace by the Sea Bed &
      Breakfast    $135–$175
(541) 867-3566 or
      (888) 4SOLACE

Tyee Lodge Oceanfront
      Bed & Breakfast
$100–$120
(888) 553-TYEE or
      (541) 265-8953

**Seaside**
Country River Inn
$59–$110
(800) 605-3337 or
      (503) 738-8049

Guest House Bed &
      Breakfast    $75–$95
(800) 340-8150 or
      (503) 717-0495

Riverside Inn    $55–$99
(800) 826-6151 or
      (503) 738-8254

Sand Dollar Bed &
      Breakfast    $65–$125
(800) 738-3491 or
      (503) 738-3491

Summer House
$69–$109
(800) 745-BEST or
      (503) 738-5740

Tenth Avenue Inn B&B
$55–$75
(800) 569-1114 or
      (503) 738-0643

**Southern Coast**
**Bandon**
Beach Street Bed &
      Breakfast    $100–$175
(888) 335-1076 or
      (541) 347-5124

Dunshee House
$75–$100
(541) 347-5030

Sea Star Guesthouse
$50–$85
(541) 347-9632

**Brookings**
Chetco River Inn Bed &
      Breakfast    $115–$135
(541) 670-1645

Holmes Sea Cove
$80–$85
(888) 290-0312 or
      (541) 469-3025

Lowden's Beachfront
      B&B    $95
(800) 453-4768 or
      (541) 469-7045

Oceancrest House    $96
(541) 469-9200

Sea Dreamer Inn
$60–$80
(800) 408-4367 or
   (541) 469-6629

South Coast Inn
$84–$94
(800) 525-9273 or
   (541) 469-5557

**Sixes**
Sixes Hotel   $85
(800) 828-5161 or
   (541) 332-3900

**Three Capes Scenic Loop**
Hudson House   $80–$95
(888) 835-3533 or
   (503) 392-3533

**Tillamook**
Blue Haven Inn
$70–$85
(503) 842-2265

**Yachats**
Heceta Light Station Bed
   & Breakfast
$125–$150
(541) 547-3696

Kittiwake Bed &
   Breakfast   $125
(541) 547-4470 or
   (541) 547-4415

## Zone 11: Greater Portland
**Portland**
Century Garden
$69–$120
(503) 235-6846

The Clinkerbrick House
$50–$70
(503) 281-2533

Kennedy School Bed &
   Breakfast   $99–$109
(503) 249-3983

Knott Street Inn B&B
$85–$100
(503) 249-1855

Macmaster House
$85–$130
(800) 774-9523 or
   (503) 223-7362

Pittock Acres Bed &
   Breakfast   $75–$95
(800) 769-9774 or
   (503) 226-1163

Portland Guest House
$65–$95
(503) 282-1402

Tudor House Bed &
   Breakfast   $75–$110
(800) 786-9476 or
   (503) 287-9476

Westlund's River's Edge
$75   (503) 621-9856

**Tigard**
Woven Glass Inn
$65–$75
(800) 484-2192 or
   (503) 590-6040

**West Linn**
River Bend House
$85–$100
(503) 557-1662

Swift Shore Chalet   $80
(503) 650-3853

## Zone 12: Willamette Valley
**Corvallis**
The Ashwood   $60–$70
(541) 757-9772

Courtyard Inn   $69–$95
(800) 647-7136

**Cottage Grove**
Apple Inn Bed &
   Breakfast   $75–$95
(800) 942-2393 or
   (541) 942-2393

Tuckaway Farm Inn
$75–$85
(541) 849-3144

**Eugene**
Excelsior Inn   $69–$180
(541) 342-6963

Hanson Country Inn
$85   (541) 752-2919

Kjaer's House in the
   Woods   $70–$80
(800) 437-4501 or
   (541) 343-3234

McGarry House Bed &
   Breakfast   $80–$85
(800) 953-9921 or
   (541) 485-0037

Moloney's Inn   $65–$75
(541) 746-1745

**McKenzie Bridge/
Blue River**
Osprey Inn   $110–$135
(541) 822-8186

River's Edge Inn
$85–$125
(800) 250-1812 or
   (541) 822-3258

**McMinnville**
Williams House Bed &
   Breakfast   $45–$95
(503) 434-9016

Youngberg Hill Vineyard
   & Inn   $130–$150
(888) 657-8668 or
   (503) 472-2727

**Mill City**
Ivy Creek B&B
$65–$110
(503) 897-2001

**Monmouth**
Howell House
$59–$110
(800) 368-2085 or
   (503) 538-2050

**Newberg**
Avellan Inn   $85–$115
(503) 537-9161

Partridge Farm
$80–$100
(503) 538-2050

Smith House Bed &
   Breakfast   $65–$70
(503) 538-1995

**Salem**
Bookmark Bed &
   Breakfast   $50–$70
(503) 399-2013

Cottonwood Cottage
$55–$60
(800) 349-3979 or
   (503) 362-3979

State House   $50–$70
(800) 800-6712 or
   (503) 588-1340

The Stone Lion Inn
$50–$60
(888) 673-3465 or
   (503) 463-6374

**Sheridan**
Brightridge Farm Bed &
   Breakfast   $90
(503) 843-5230

Middle Creek Run B&B
$85–$125
(503) 843-7606

# Zone 13: Southern Oregon
**Applegate**
Applegate River Lodge
$125–$145
(541) 846-6690

**Ashland**
Anne Hathaway's Cottage
$90–$160
(800) 643-4434 or
   (541) 488-1050

Ashberry Inn   $90–$105
(800) 460-8076 or
   (541) 488-8000

Ashland's English Country
   Cottage   $79–$109
(800) 760-4428 or
   (541) 488-4428

Bayberry Inn   $105
(800) 795-1252 or
   (541) 488-1252

Chanticleer Inn
$75–$350
(800) 898-1950 or
   (541) 482-1919

Colonel Silsby's Bed &
   Breakfast Inn
$90–$125
(800) 927-2070 or
   (541) 488-3070

A Dome Studio Bed &
   Breakfast   $110
(541) 482-1755

Green Springs Inn
$59–$109
(541) 482-0614

Hersey House and
   Bungalow   $115–$150
(888) 343-7739 or
   (541) 482-4563

McCall House Bed &
   Breakfast   $90–$190
(800) 808-9749 or
   (541) 482-9296

Morical House
$110–$160
(800) 208-0960 or
   (541) 482-2254

Mousetrap Inn
$98–$103
(800) 460-5453 or
   (541) 482-9228

Neil Creek House
$85–$100
(800) 460-7860 or
   (541) 482-6443

NightinGail's Inn   $115
(800) 460-8037 or
   (541) 482-7373

Oak Hill Bed & Breakfast
$105   (800) 888-7434 or
   (541) 482-1554

Pedigrift House Bed and
   Breakfast   $85–$125
(800) 262-4073 or
   (541) 482-1888

Peerless Hotel   $65–$188
(800) 460-8758 or
   (541) 488-1082

The Queen Anne Bed &
   Breakfast   $115–$150
(800) 460-6818 or
   (541) 482-0220

Romeo Inn   $95–$180
(800) 915-8899 or
   (541) 488-0884

Wolfe Manor Inn
$109–$139
(800) 801-3676 or
   (541) 488-3676

**Glide**
Steelhead Run Bed &
   Breakfast   $65–$105
(888) 348-0563 or
   (541) 496-0563

**Gold Hill**
Rogue River Guest House
$60–$120
(541) 855-4485

Willowbrook Inn
$60–$80
(541) 582-0075

**Grant's Pass**
Flery Manor   $75–$125
(541) 476-3591 or
   (541) 471-2303

Weasku Inn   $195–$295
(800) 493-2758 or
   (541) 471-8000

**Jacksonville**
Jacksonville Inn
$150–$245
(800) 321-9344 or
   (541) 899-1900

The McCully House Inn
$105   (800) 367-1942 or
   (541) 899-1942

Orth House Bed &
  Breakfast   $100–$175
(541) 899-8665

Touvelle House
$115–$135
(541) 899-8938

**Kerby**
Kerbyville Inn   $59–$89
(541) 592-4689

**Klamath Falls**
The Boarding House Inn
$53–$70
(541) 883-8584

**Medford**
Under the Greenwood
  Tree   $95–$125
(541) 776-0000

Waverly Cottage & Suites
$40–$100
(541) 779-4716

**Oakland**
Beckley House Bed &
  Breakfast   $90
(541) 459-9320

**Prospect**
Prospect Historical Hotel
$60–$85
(800) 944-6490 or
  (541) 560-3664

**Roseburg**
House of Hunter
$65–$85
(800) 540-7704 or
  (541) 672-2335

**Steamboat**
Steamboat Inn
$130–$245
(800) 840-8825

# Zone 14: Mt. Hood and Columbia Gorge
**Bridal Veil**
Bridal Veil Lodge
$70–$75
(503) 695-2333

**Government Camp**
Huckleberry Inn   $78
(503) 272-3325

**Hood River**
Avalon Bed & Breakfast
$65   (888) 386-3941 or
  (541) 386-2560

Brown's B&B   $45–$65
(541) 386-1545

Gorge View Bed &
  Breakfast   $75
(541) 386-5770

Inn at the Gorge B&B
$78   (541) 386-4429

Panorama Lodge B&B
$85   (541) 387-2687

**Hood River Valley/
Parkdale**
Old Parkdale Inn
$95–$135
(541) 352-5551

**Sandy**
Fernwood at Alder Creek
$85–$125
(503) 622-3570

**The Dalles**
The Columbia House
$60–$85
(800) 807-2668 or
  (541) 298-4686

Windrider Inn   $50
(541) 296-2607

# Zone 15: Central Oregon
**Bend**
Villa Genovese
$70–$110
(541) 318-3557 or
  (541) 388-4232

**Detroit**
Repose & Repast
$60–$80
(503) 854-3204

**Redmond**
Llast Camp Llamas   $65
(541) 548-6828

# Zone 16: Eastern Oregon
**Baker City**
A Demain B&B
$60–$75
(541) 523-2509

Powder River Tackle
  Company, Bed &
  Breakfast, & Guide
  Service   $50–$60
(541) 523-7143

**Pendleton**
Dorie's Inn   $75–$85
(541) 276-1519

Working Girls Vintage
  Hotel   $50–$70
(800) 276-6398 or
  (541) 276-0730

**Summer Lake**
Summer Lake Inn
$60–$100
(800) 261-2778 or
  (541) 943-3983

**Sumpter**
Sumpter Bed & Breakfast
$60   (800) 640-3184 or
  (541) 894-0048

**Wallowas/Hells Canyon**
Botz Country Inn (Elgin)
$50–$65
(541) 437-8982 or
  (541) 437-5404

Tamarack Inn (Weston)
$60–$95
(800) 662-9348 or
  (541) 566-9348

Tickled Trout Bed &
  Breakfast (Enterprise)
$65–$85
(888) TROUT30 or
  (541) 426-6039

# Index

Abigail's Hotel, Victoria, 40–41
Alexander's Inn, Ashford, 224–225
All Season's River Inn, Leavenworth, 237–238
amenities & services profiles, 13
Anderson's Boarding House, Seaside, 328–329
Angelica's B&B, Spokane, 266–267
Angels of the Sea B&B, Vashon, 207–208
Ann Starrett Mansion, Port Townsend, 99–100
Antique Rose Inn, Ashland, 371
architectural design profiles, 12
Arden Forest Inn, Ashland, 372
Artist's Studio Loft B&B, Vashon, 208–209
author contact information, 2
autonomy of accommodations, 9
Autumn Pond, Leavenworth, 238–239

A B&B on the Green, Corvallis, 352–353
Bacon Mansion, Seattle, 185–186
Baer House B&B, Baker City, 423–424
Bandon Beach House, Bandon, 308–309
Barnstormer B&B, Scappoose, 346–347
bathroom selection, 8–9
Bayview B&B, West Vancouver, 74–75
Beachside B&B, West Vancouver, 75–76
Beaconsfield Inn, Victoria, 41–42
bed-and-breakfasts (B&Bs)
    groups traveling to, 5, 27–28
    guests of, 3–5
    hosts of, 6
    making the most of your stay, 15–16

in the Northwest, 16
    gathering information on, 16–17
    on the Internet, 18
planning your visit to
    choosing/booking reservations, 6–7
    considerations while, 8–9
    negotiating rates, 7–8
    Web sites on, 7
profiles information on, 11–15
ratings of
    overall, 10
    room quality, 10–11
    value and price, 11
special need guests of, 5
what makes it a, 2–3
See also Northwest bed-and-breakfasts (B&Bs); small inns
Benson Farmstead, Bow, 125–126
The Beryl House, Hood River, 393–394
Big Trees B&B, Bellingham, 117–118
The Bingen Haus, Bingen, 390
Birchfield Manor, Yakima, 293–294
Birds of a Feather B&B, Victoria, 42–43
BJ's Garden Gate, Port Angeles, 94–95
Blackbird Lodge, Leavenworth, 240
Blair House, Friday Harbor, 130–131
Blue Heron Inn, Castle Rock, 212–213
Blue Spruce B&B, Sisters, 415–416
The Blue Willow B&B, Seattle, 186–187
booking reservations, 6–7
Boreas B&B Inn, Long Beach (WA), 91–92
Bradley House, Cathlamet, 213–214
Braemar Manor, North Vancouver, 59–60
Brier Rose Inn B&B, Albany, 350–351

Brigadoon B&B, Sequim, 106–107
Brightwood Guest House, Brightwood, 391–392
British Columbia
  bed & breakfasts (B&Bs) of
    budget accommodations in, 23
    dinner served in, 24
    family-oriented, 25
    farm or rural setting of, 26
    group/conference/wedding
      accommodations in, 27
    historic, 28
    island setting of, 29
    mountain setting of, 30
    on-line sources on, 17
    romantic oriented in, 31
    smoking allowed in, 33
    solo-oriented, 32
  in Vancouver (Zone 2), 58–76
  in Victoria (Zone 1), 40–54
    waterside setting of, 33
  general information on, 35–36
  small inns of, 439–440
  Vancouver (Zone 2) of
    general information on, 55–56
    listing of B&Bs in, 58–76
    listing of small inns in, 440
    map of, 57
  Victoria (Zone 1) of
    general information on, 37–38
    listing of B&Bs in, 40–54
    listing of small inns in, 439–440
    map of, 39
Brookhaven Lodge, Rockport, 251
Brookside B&B, Sandy, 400–401
The Buchanan Inn, Bainbridge Island, 168–169
Buck Bay Farm, Orcas Island, 149–150
Bush House Country Inn, Index, 235–236
business travelers, 4–5

C&J Lodge, Maupin, 412–413
Cady Lake Manor, Belfair, 171–172
The Campbell House, Eugene, 355–356
Canadian currency, 36
Cannon Beach Hotel, Cannon Beach, 310–311
Capitol Hill Inn, Seattle, 187–188

Carriage House B&B, Moses Lake, 283–284
Casablanca, Kennewick, 282–283
Cascade Mountain Inn, Concrete, 230–231
Cascades (Zone 7)
  general information on, 221–223
  listing of, 224–257
  map of, 222
  small inns of, 443–444
Central Oregon (Zone 15)
  general information on, 405
  listing of B&Bs in, 407–419
  map of, 406
  small inns of, 448
Chambered Nautilus, Seattle, 188–189
Chandler's Bed, Bread, & Trail Inn, Joseph, 431–432
Channel House, Anacortes, 114–115
Channel House, Depoe Bay, 314–315
Chapman House B&B, Corvallis, 353–354
check-in/out information, 14
Chelsea Station, Seattle, 190
Chestnut Hill B&B, Orcas Island, 150–151
Chick-ADee Inn, Ilwaco, 88–89
China Beach B&B Retreat, Ilwaco, 89–90
Chinaberry Hill, Tacoma, 200–201
Chuckanut Manor B&B, Bow, 126–127
Claddagh House, Victoria, 44
Clear Creek Farm B&B, Halfway, 429–430
Clementine's B&B, Astoria, 303–304
Cliff House B&B, Waldport, 330–331
closed/open season information, 15
Cobblestone B&B Inn, Spokane, 267–268
The Colonial Manor, Mount Vernon, 147–148
Columbia Gorge Hotel, Hood River, 394–395
Commencement Bay B&B, Tacoma, 202–203
conference accommodations, 27–28
Conklin's Guest House, Sisters, 416–417
Cooney Mansion B&B Inn, Aberdeen, 82–83

Coos Bay Manor, Coos Bay, 313–314
A Cottage Creek Inn, Redmond, 183–184
Country Hill B&B, Maple Falls, 246–247
Country Willows B&B Inn, Ashland, 373–374
The Courtyard, Cannon Beach, 311–312
Cowslip's Belle B&B, Ashland, 374–375
Cozy Rose Inn, Grandview, 281–282
Craigmyle Guest House, Victoria, 45
credit card information, 13–14
currency exchange rates, 36

Dashwood Manor, Victoria, 46
Denonno's B&B, Skykomish, 253
deposit requirements, 13
Devoe Mansion, Tacoma, 203–204
Diamondstone Guest Lodge, LaPine, 411–412
dinner service available, 24–25
discount information, 13
Domaine Madeleine, Port Angeles, 95–96
Doublegate Inn B&B, Welches, 401–402
Dove House, Chauntecleer House, & Potting Shed, Langley, 141–142
The Doveshire B&B, Ocean Park, 92–93
Duffy House, Friday Harbor, 131–132

Eagle's Nest Inn, Whidbey Island, 161–162
Eagle's View B&B, Pacific City, 325–326
Eastern Oregon (Zone 16)
  general information on, 420–421
  listing of B&Bs on, 423–438
  map of, 422
  small inns of, 448
Edenwild Inn, Lopez Island, 144
The Edwin K B&B, Florence, 316–317
The Elliott House, Prineville, 413–414
English Bay Inn, Vancouver, 64–65

Falcon's Crest Inn, Government Camp, 392–393
family accommodations, 3–4
The Farm, A B&B, Trout Lake, 256
Floras Lake House B&B, Langlois, 320
Flying L Ranch, Glenwood, 234–235

food & drink profiles, 12–13
Fotheringham House B&B, Spokane, 268–269
Four Winds Guest House, Coulee Dam, 263–264
Foxbridge B&B, Poulsbo, 181–182
Franklin Street Station, Astoria, 304–305
Frenchglen Hotel, Frenchglen, 427–428

Gaslight Inn, Seattle, 191–192
General Hooker's B&B, Portland, 338
Georgian House B&B, Portland, 339
Gilbert Inn, Seaside, 329–330
Glacier Guest Suite, Glacier, 232–233
The Gold House Inn, Grand Coulee, 264–265
Gracie's Landing, Depoe Bay, 315–316
Grandma's House B&B, Woodland, 220
Grandview B&B, Astoria, 306
Grant House, Baker City, 424–425
Grapevine Inn, Ashland, 375–376
Greater Portland (Zone 11)
  general information on, 335
  listing of B&Bs in, 337–347
  map of, 336
  small inns of, 445–446
Greater Seattle/Tacoma (Zone 5)
  general information on, 165–166
  listing of B&Bs in, 168–209
  map of, 167
  small inns of, 442–443
The Green Cape Cod B&B, Tacoma, 204–205
The Green Gables Guesthouse, Seattle, 192–194
Green Gables Inn, Walla Walla, 288–289
Greywolf Inn, Sequim, 107–108
group accommodations
  information on, 5
  Northwest B&Bs with, 27–28
Growly Bear B&B, Ashford, 225–226
Guest House Cottages, Whidbey Island, 162–163

Harbinger Inn, Olympia, 215–216
Harbor House B&B, Blaine, 124–125
Harrison House, Corvallis, 354–355
Hasty Pudding House, Anacortes, 115–116
The Haterleigh B&B, Victoria, 47–48

Haus Lorelei, Leavenworth, 241–242

Haus Rohrbach, Leavenworth, 242–243

Hearthstone Inn, Cannon Beach, 312–313

Heorn Haus, Portland, 340–341

historic B&Bs, 28–29

Home by the Sea B&B, Port Orford, 326–327

Home Farm B&B, Grants Pass, 385

homestay B&Bs, 6

Hood River Hotel, Hood River, 395–396

hosts, 6

Hotel Diamond, Diamond, 426–427

The Hotel Usk, Usk, 274–275

Huckleberry Lodge, Forks, 83–84

The Hummingbird Inn, Roslyn, 252

Hunter Creek Farm Bed, Barn & Breakfast, Wilsonville, 367–368

Illahee Manor, Bremerton, 173–175

The Inn at Aurora, Aurora, 351–352

Inn at Nesika Beach, Gold Beach, 319

The Inn at Penn Cove, Coupeville, 129–130

Inn at Swifts Bay, Lopez Island, 145–146

The Inn of the White Salmon, White Salmon, 403–404

Internet

booking reservations using the, 7

information on Northwest on the, 17

Northwest B&Bs on the, 18

The Iris Inn, Ashland, 376–377

Iron Horse Inn, South Cle Elum, 253–254

island setting B&Bs, 29–30

Island Tyme, Whidbey Island, 163–164

The James House, Port Townsend, 101–102

Jasmer's at Mt. Rainier, Ashford, 226–227

Joan Brown's B&B, Victoria, 48–49

Johnson Heritage House, Vancouver, 65–66

The Johnson House, Florence, 318

Juniper Acres, Bend, 407

Kangaroo House, Orcas Island, 152

Katy's Inn, La Conner, 138–139

Kingston Hotel, Vancouver, 66–67

Laburnum Cottage, North Vancouver, 60–61

La Cachette B&B, Seabeck, 184–185

Lakecliff Estate, Hood River, 396–397

The Langtry, Vancouver, 67–68

Lara House, Bend, 408

Lighthouse B&B, Bandon, 309–310

The Lion and the Rose, Portland, 341–342

Lithia Springs Inn, Ashland, 377–378

Lizzie's, Port Townsend, 102–103

Llama Ranch B&B, Trout Lake, 257

Log Castle B&B, Langley, 142–143

The Log House, Inchelium, 265–266

Love's Victorian B&B, Spokane, 270–271

Lytle House, Hoquiam, 87–88

Mackay Harbor Inn, Lopez Island, 146–147

McKenzie View, Springfield, 364–365

Macmaster House, Portland, 343–344

Manitou Lodge, Forks, 84–85

Maple Meadows B&B, Point Roberts, 157–158

Maple Rose Inn, Port Angeles, 97–98

maps

of B&B in Washington & British Columbia, x–xi

of Greater Portland (Zone 11), 336

of Greater Seattle/Tacoma (Zone 5), 167

of Mt. Hood/Columbia Gorge (Zone 14), 389

of Northeast Washington (Zone 8) of, 259

of Northwest Washington (Zone 4), 112

of Oregon Coast (Zone 10), 300–301

of Oregon Willamette Valley (Zone 12),349

of Southeast Washington (Zone 9), 277

of Southern Oregon (Zone 13), 370

of Vancouver (Zone 2), British Columbia, 57

of Victoria (Zone 1), British
Columbia, 39
of Washington Coast and Olympic
Peninsula (Zone 3), 80
of Washington I-5 South (Zone 6),
211
Marianna Stoltz House, Spokane,
271–272
Marquee House, Salem, 363–364
Marsh Haven Farm B&B, Langlois, 321
Mary Kay's Romantic Whaley Mansion
Inn, Chelan, 260
Mattey House B&B, McMinnville,
359–360
Mildred's B&B, Seattle, 194–195
Miller Tree Inn, Forks, 85–86
Mill Inn, Bend, 409
Morning Star, Yachats, 331–332
The Mosier House, Mosier, 397–398
Mountain Meadows Inn, Ashford,
227–228
mountain setting B&Bs, 30
Mountainside Manor B&B, North Van-
couver, 61–62
Mt. Ashland Inn, Ashland, 378–379
Mt. Baker B&B, Glacier, 233–234
Mt. Hood B&B, Parkdale, 399–400
Mt. Hood/Columbia Gorge (Zone 14)
general information on, 388
listing of B&Bs in, 390–404
map of, 389
small inns of, 447
Mt. Hood Hamlet B&B, Mt. Hood,
398–399
Murphy House, Poulsbo, 182–183

Nantucket Inn, Anacortes, 116–117
Newport Belle B&B, Newport, 321–322
1900 Sears & Roebuck Home, Vale,
437–438
Northeast Washington (Zone 8)
general information on, 258
listing of B&Bs in, 260–275
map of, 259
small inns of, 444
North Garden Inn, Bellingham,
118–119
Northwest
favorite properties in the, 20

special dishes of the, 21
special moments while visiting the,
21–22
ten reasons to visit the, 18–20
Web sites
on B&Bs in the, 18
for booking reservations, 7
on the, 17
*See also* British Columbia; Oregon;
Washington
Northwest bed & breakfasts (B&Bs)
budget accommodations, 23–24
dinner served in, 24–25
family-oriented, 25–26
farm or rural settings of, 26–27
group, conferences, wedding
accommodations, 27–28
historic, 28–29
in island setting, 29–30
in mountain setting, 30
pet-friendly and small inns, 30–31
romantic oriented, 31–32
with rustic setting, 32
smoking allowed in, 33
solo-oriented, 32–33
top 30 by room quality, 22–23
top 30 overall, 22
top values listed, 23
waterside setting of, 33–34
*See also* bed & breakfasts (B&Bs);
small inns
Northwest Washington (Zone 4)
general information on, 111–112
listing of B&Bs in, 114–164
map of, 112
small inns of, 441–442

Oak Street Station B&B, Ashland, 380
Oar House B&B, Newport, 323
O Canada House, Vancouver, 68–69
The Olde Glencove Hotel, Gig Harbor,
175–176
Old Welches Inn, Welches, 402–403
Olympic Lights, Friday Harbor,
132–133
open/closed season information, 15
Oregon
bed & breakfasts (B&Bs) of
budget accommodations in, 24

Oregon
  bed & breakfasts (B&Bs) of
    (continued)
    dinner served in, 25
    family-oriented, 25–26
    farm or rural setting of, 27
    group, conference, wedding
      accommodations in, 28
    historic, 29
    listing of Central Oregon (Zone
      15), 407–419
    listing of Coast (Zone 10),
      302–334
    listing of Eastern Oregon (Zone
      16), 423–438
    listing of Greater Portland (Zone
      11), 337–347
    listing of Mt. Hood/Columbia
      Gorge (Zone 14), 390–404
    listing of Willamette Valley (Zone
      12), 350–368
    mountain setting of, 30
    on-line sources on, 17
    romantic oriented in, 32
    with rustic setting, 32
    smoking allowed in, 33
    solo-oriented, 33
    in Southern Oregon (Zone 13),
      371–387
    waterside setting of, 34
  Central Oregon (Zone 15) of
    general information on, 405
    listing of B&Bs in, 407–419
    map of, 406
    small inns of, 444–445
  Coast (Zone 10) of
    general information on, 298–299
    listing of B&Bs in, 302–334
    map of, 300–301
    small inns of, 444–445
  Eastern Oregon (Zone 16) of
    general information on, 420–421
    listing of B&Bs in, 423–438
    map of, 422
    small inns of, 448
  general information on, 297
  Greater Portland (Zone 11) of
    general information on, 335
    listing of B&Bs in, 337–347
    map of, 336
    small inns of, 445–446
  Mt. Hood/Columbia Gorge (Zone
    14) of
    general information on, 388
    listing of B&Bs in, 390–404
    map of, 389
    small inns of, 447
  small inns of, 444–448
  Southern Oregon (Zone 13) of
    general information on, 369
    listing of B&Bs in, 371–387
    map of, 370
    small inns of, 446–447
  Willamette Valley (Zone 12) of
    general information on, 348
    listing of B&Bs in, 350–368
    map of, 349
    small inns of, 446
Oregon Coast (Zone 10)
  general information on, 298–299
  listing of B&Bs in, 302–334
  map of, 300–301
  small inns of, 444–445
Oslo's B&B, Spokane, 272–273
Otters Pond B&B, Orcas Island,
  153–154
Our Place in the Country, Stayton,
  366–367
Outlook Inn, Outlook, 285
The Oval Door, Eugene, 357
Ovenell's Heritage Inn, Concrete,
  231–232
overall rating
  described, 10
  top 30, 22

Palmer Farm B&B, Benton City, 278
Panacea, Friday Harbor, 133–134
The Parker House B&B, Pendleton,
  434–435
Pendrell Suites, Vancouver, 69–70
Penny Farthing Inn, Vancouver, 70–71
pet-friendly B&Bs, 14–15, 30–31
Pine Meadow Inn B&B, Grants Pass,
  386–387
Pine River Ranch, Leavenworth,
  244–245
The Portico Victorian B&B, Ritzville,
  286
Portland. See Greater Portland (Zone 11)

Portland's White House, Portland, 344–345
price rating, 11
Prior House B&B Inn, Victoria, 49–50
privacy issues, 9
The Purple House, Dayton, 279

A Quail's Roost Inn, Chelan, 261

Rags to Walkers Guest Ranch, Sisters, 417–418
Ravenscroft Inn, Port Townsend, 103–104
reader letters/comments, 2
recreation profiles, 13
Redmond House B&B, Snohomish, 158–159
Reflections, Port Orchard, 179–180
reservations
    booking your, 6–7
    considerations while making, 8–9
    negotiating rates for, 7–8
Ridgeway Farm B&B, La Conner, 139–140
Rimrock Inn, Wenatchee, 290–291
River Run Cottages, Ladner, 58–59
Riverside School House, Prairie City, 435–436
Roaring River B&B, North Bend, 250
Roberta's B&B, Seattle, 195–196
Rockaway Beach Guest House, Bainbridge Island, 169–170
room quality ratings
    described, 10–11
    top 30 overall, 22–23
room selection, 8
Rosebriar Hotel, Astoria, 307–308
Run of the River, Leavenworth, 245–246
rustic setting B&Bs, 32
Rutherglen Mansion, Longview, 214–215
Ryan's B&B, Victoria, 50–51

Sage Country Inn, Burns, 425–426
St. Bernards, Arch Cape, 302–303
St. Helen's Manorhouse, Morton, 249
Salisbury House, Seattle, 197–198
Samish Point by the Bay, Bow, 127–129
Sandlake Country Inn, Sandlake, 327–328

The Sather House, Bend, 410
Schnauzer Crossing, Bellingham, 119–120
Sea Quest B&B, Yachats, 332–333
The Seasun's B&B, Port Angeles, 98–99
Seattle. *See* Greater Seattle/Tacoma (Zone 5)
The Secret Garden, Eugene, 358–359
security issues, 9
Selah Inn, Belfair, 172–173
Serenity B&B, Yachats, 333–334
7C's Guest Ranch, Rainier, 218
Shaniko Historic Hotel, Shaniko, 414–415
The Shelburne Country Inn, Seaview, 105–106
Shrew's House B&B, Ashland, 381–382
Shumway Mansion, Kirkland, 177–178
Simone's Groveland Cottage B&B Inn, Sequim, 108–109
small inns
    of Cascades (Zone 7), 443–444
    of Central Oregon (Zone 15), 448
    of Eastern Oregon (Zone 16), 448
    of Greater Portland (Zone 11), 445–446
    of Greater Seattle/Tacoma (Zone 5), 442–443
    list of pet-friendly, 30–31
    of Mt. Hood/Columbia Gorge (Zone 14), 447
    of Northeast (Zone 8), 444
    of Northwest (Zone 4), 441–442
    of Oregon Coast (Zone 10), 444–445
    of Southeast Washington (Zone 9), 444
    of Southern Oregon (Zone 13), 446–447
    of Vancouver (Zone 2), 440
    of Victoria (Zone 1), 439–440
    of Washington Coast/Olympic Peninsula (Zone 3), 440–441
    of Washington I-5 South (Zone 6), 443
    of Willamette Valley (Zone 12), 446
    *See also* bed-and-breakfasts (B&Bs); Northwest bed & breakfasts (B&Bs)
smoking allowed B&Bs, 14, 33
solo-oriented B&Bs, 32–33
Sonshine B&B, John Day, 430–431

South Bay B&B, Bellingham, 121–122
Southeast Washington (Zone 9)
  general information on, 276
  listing B&Bs of, 278–295
  map of, 277
  small inns of, 444
Southern Oregon (Zone 13)
  general information on, 369
  listing of B&Bs in, 371–387
  map of, 370
  small inns of, 446–447
  special needs guests, 5
Spinnakers Brewbup & Guest House,
  Victoria, 52–53
Spring Bay Inn, Orcas Island, 154–155
Springbrook Hazelnut Farm, Newberg,
  361–362
Squaw Creek B&B Inn, Sisters, 419
Stang Manor Inn, La Grande, 432–433
Steens Mountain Inn, Frenchglen,
  428–429
Stehekin Valley Ranch, Stehekin,
  254–255
Steiger Haus, McMinnville, 360–361
Stone Creek Inn, Walla Walla, 289–290
A Stone's Throw B&B, Index, 236–237
Stratford Manor, Bellingham, 122–123
Strawberry Mountain Inn, Prairie City,
  436–437
Sunnyside Inn B&B, Sunnyside,
  287–288
Susan's Surrey House, Snohomish, 160
Swantown Inn, Olympia, 216–217
Sylvia Beach Hotel, Newport, 324–325

Tacoma. *See* Greater Seattle/Tacoma
  (Zone 5)
Terwilliger Vista House, Portland,
  345–346
Thistledown House, North Vancouver,
  63–64
Thornewood Castle, Tacoma, 206–207
Toad Hall, Sequim, 110
A Touch of Europe B&B Inn, Yakima,
  294–295
The Tree House B&B, Mercer Island,
  178–179
A Treehouse B&B, Vancouver, 71–72
Trumpeter Inn, Friday Harbor, 135–136

Tugboat Challenger, Seattle, 198–199
Turtleback Farm Inn, Orcas Island,
  156–157

*The Unofficial Guides to Bed &
  Breakfasts*, 1
U.S. citizen identification, 36

value rating
  described, 11
  top B&Bs listed, 23
Vancouver (Zone 2), British Columbia
  B&Bs listed, 58–76
  general information on, 55–56
  map of, 57
  small inns of, 439–440
Victorian Gardens 1888 B&B, Kent,
  176–177
Victoria (Zone 1), British Columbia
  general information on, 39
  list of B&Bs in, 40–54
  map of, 39
  small inns of, 439–440
Villa Heidelberg, Seattle, 199–200
Vintage Inn, Vancouver, 219

Warm Springs Inn, Wenatchee, 291–292
Washington
  bed & breakfasts (B&Bs) of
    budget accommodations in, 23–24
    dinner served in, 25
    family-oriented, 25
    farm or rural setting of, 26
    group, conference, wedding
      accommodations in, 27–28
    historic, 28–29
    island setting of, 29–30
    listing of Coast/Olympic Peninsula
      (Zone 3), 82–110
    listing of Greater Seattle/Tacoma
      (Zone 5), 168–209
    listing of I-5 South (Zone 6),
      212–220
    listing of Northwest (Zone 4),
      114–164
    mountain setting of, 30
    on-line sources on, 17
    romantic oriented in, 31–32
    with rustic setting, 32

smoking allowed in, 33
solo-oriented, 32–33
waterside setting of, 33–34
Cascades (Zone 7) of
general information on, 221–223
listing of B&Bs in, 224–257
map of, 222
small inns of, 443–444
Coast/Olympic Peninsula (Zone 3) of
general information on, 78–79
listing of B&Bs in, 82–110
map of, 80
small inns of, 440–441
general information on, 77
Greater Seattle/Tacoma (Zone 5)
general information on, 165–166
listing of B&Bs in, 168–209
map of, 167
small inns of, 442–443
I-5 South (Zone 6) of
general information on, 210
listing of B&Bs in, 212–220
map of, 211
small inns of, 443
Northeast (Zone 8) of
general information on, 258
listing of B&Bs in, 260–275
map of, 259
small inns of, 444
Northwest (Zone 4) of
general information on, 111–112
listing of B&Bs in, 114–164
map of, 112
small inns of, 441–442
small inns of, 440–444
Southeast (Zone 9) of
general information on, 276
listing of B&Bs in, 278–295
map of, 277
small inns of, 444
Washington Coast/Olympic Peninsula
(Zone 3)

general information on, 78–79
listing of B&Bs in, 82–110
map of, 80
small inns of, 440–441
Washington I-5 South (Zone 6)
general information on, 210
listing of B&Bs in, 212–220
map of, 211
small inns of, 443
waterside setting B&Bs, 33–34
Waverly Place B&B, Spokane, 273–274
Wayward Navigator, Victoria, 53–54
Web sites
for booking reservations, 7
on the Northwest, 17
on Northwest B&Bs, 18
wedding accommodations
information on, 5
Northwest B&Bs with, 27–28
Weinhard Hotel, Dayton, 280–281
Wellspring, Ashford, 228–229
West End Guest House, Vancouver,
73–74
Wharfside B&B, Friday Harbor,
136–137
The White Swan Guest House, Mount
Vernon, 148–149
The Whitetail Inn, Colville, 262–263
The Wild Iris, La Conner, 140–141
Wildwood Manor, Friday Harbor,
137–138
Willamette Valley (Zone 12)
general information on, 348
listing of B&Bs in, 350–368
map of, 349
small inns of, 446
Winchester Country Inn, Ashland,
382–383
The Woods House, Ashland, 383–384

The Yankee Tinker, Beaverton, 337
Yodeler Inn B&B, Maple Falls, 248